Down

HISTORY & SOCIETY

Interdisciplinary Essays on the
History of an Irish County

Editor:
LINDSAY PROUDFOOT

Series Editor:
WILLIAM NOLAN

 GEOGRAPHY PUBLICATIONS

The editor and publisher are grateful to the
following for their generous subventions towards
the costs of publication:
Academic Publications Committee, University
College Dublin;
The National University of Ireland;
Publications Fund, The Queen's University of
Belfast;
Ulster Local History Trust.

Published in Ireland by
Geography Publications,
Kennington Road,
Templeogue, Dublin 6W

ISBN 0 906602 80 7

Design and typesetting by Phototype-Set, Lee Road, Dublin Industrial Estate, Dublin 11.
Printed by Betaprint, Dublin

Contents

List of Figures

List of Plates

PLATES BETWEEN PAGES 230 AND 231

Contributors and Editors

Anthony Buckley
Curator of Anthropology, Ulster Folk and Transport Museum, Cultra, County Down

Tim Campbell
Part-time lecturer, Department of Geography, Stranmillis College, Belfast

Leslie Clarkson
Professor, Department of Economic and Social History, Queen's University, Belfast

Marilyn Cohen
Upper Mont Claire, New Jersey

Nancy Curtin
Professor, Department of History, Fordham University, New York

Ciarán Devine (Ciarán Ó Duibhinn)
Institute of Irish Studies, Queen's University, Belfast

David Dumville
Professor of Paleography and Cultural Studies, University of Cambridge

Raymond Gillespie
Lecturer, Department of History, St Patrick's College, Maynooth

Jim Grant
Downpatrick, County Down

Anne Hamlin
Director of the Built Heritage, Environment and Heritage Service, Belfast

Fred Hamond
Industrial Historian, Belfast

Barrie Hartwell
Senior Research Officer, Department of Archaeology, Queen's University, Belfast

Myrtle Hill
Director of the Centre for Women's Studies, Queen's University, Belfast

Henry Jefferies
Historian, Thornhill College, Derry

Jim Mallory
Reader, Department of Archaeology, Queen's University, Belfast

Finbar McCormick
Lecturer, Department of Archaeology, Queen's University, Belfast

Tom McNeill
Senior Lecturer, Department of Archaeology, Queen's University, Belfast

Harold O'Sullivan
Local Historian, Dundalk, County Louth

Vivienne Pollock
Department of History, Ulster Museum, Belfast

Lindsay Proudfoot
Reader, Department of Geography, Queen's University, Belfast

Father Oliver Rafferty SJ
Christ Church, Oxford

Stephen Royle
Lecturer, Department of Geography, Queen's University, Belfast

Ingrid Sperber
Department of Philology, Uppsala University

Roy Tomlinson
Senior Lecturer, Department of Geography, Queen's University, Belfast

Brian Walker
Director, Institute of Irish Studies, Queen's University, Belfast

Caroline Windrum
Institute of Irish Studies, Queen's University, Belfast

Acknowledgements

The editor, contributors and publisher wish to acknowledge the following people and institutions for their help in the production of this book. The Ulster Folk and Transport Museum kindly granted permission to use photographs from the Green collection; the Ulster Museum similarly granted permission to use items from the Welch collection; the Director, Cambridge University Collection of Air Photographs facilitated the publication of air photographs and the Belfast Harbour Commissioners kindly gave permission to use a painting in their collection by J.H. Connop. Acknowledgement is also due to Lawrence Kirk of Vista Photographic for supplying the photograph of this painting.

Caroline Windrum wishes to acknowledge the Down County Museum for funding her one year prison history research fellowship at the Institute of Irish Studies, Queen's University, Belfast and also Ms Carrie Wilson, for previous data collection on the same project.

Few of the chapters would have been completed successfully had it not been for the generous help and advice given by the staff of various archives and libraries in Belfast, Dublin and elsewhere. We are particularly pleased to acknowledge, therefore, the co-operation offered by the staff of the Linen Hall Library (Belfast), the National Archives (Dublin), the National Library of Ireland, Trinity College Library (Dublin), the Public Record Office of Northern Ireland, the Ulster Museum and the Ulster Folk and Transport Museum.

Finally, particular thanks are due to Mrs Gill Alexander of the School of Geosciences, Queen's University, for her patient decipherment of numerous frequently illegible maps and diagrams. The clarity and elegance of the finished product is entirely her own.

List of Abbreviations

A.D.D.C.	Archives of the diocese of Down and Connor.
A.F.M.	*Annala rioghachta Eireann: Annals of the kingdom of Ireland by the Four Masters from the earliest period to the year 1616,* ed. John O'Donovan, 7 vols (Dublin, 1848-51).
Anal. Hib.	*Analecta Hibernica,* including the reports of the Irish Manuscripts Commission (Dublin, 1930-).
Archaeology of Ulster	J.P. Mallory and T.E. McNeill, *The Archaeology of Ulster. From colonisation to plantation* (Belfast, 1991).
Archiv. Hib.	*Archivium Hibernicum: or Irish historical records* (Maynooth, 1912-).
A.S.C.D.	E. Jope (ed.), *Archaeological survey of county Down* (Belfast, 1966).
A.U.	Annala Uladh, *The Annals of Ulster (to AD 1131),* Part 1, ed. S. Mac Airt and G. Mac Niocaill (Dublin, 1983).
B.A.R.	British Archaeological Reports.
Bealoideas	*The Journal of the Folklore of Ireland Society* (Dublin, 1927-).
B.G.	Board of guardians.
B.L.	British Library.
B.M.	British Museum.
Cal. Carew MSS	*Calendar of Carew manuscripts preserved in the archiepiscopal library at Lambeth. 1515-74* (etc.) 6 vols (London, 1867-73).
Cal. Doc. Ire.	*Calendar of documents relating to Ireland* ed. H.S. Sweetman and G.F. Handcock 5 vols (London, 1875-86).
Cal. justic. rolls Ire.	*Calendar of the justiciar rolls of Ireland,* ed. James Mills et al 3 vols (Dublin, 1905-).
Cal. papal letters	*Calendar of entries in the papal registers relating to Great Britain and Ireland: papal letters, 1198-1304 (etc)* (London, 1893-).
Cal. pat. rolls Ire.	*Calendar of patent and close rolls of chancery in Ireland, Charles 1, years 1 to 8,* ed. James Morrin (Dublin, 1864).
Cal. pat. rolls Ire.,	*Calendar of patent and close rolls of chancery*

Hen. VII-Eliz.	*in Ireland, Henry VII to 18th Elizabeth,* ed. James Morrin (Dublin, 1861).
Cal. pat. rolls Ire., Jas 1	*Irish patent rolls of James 1: facsimile of the Irish record commissioners' calendar prepared prior to 1830,* with foreword by M.C. Griffith (Dublin, 1966).
Cal. S.P. Ire.	*Calendar of the state papers relating to Ireland 1509-73* (etc.) 24 vols (London, 1860-1911).
Cal. S.P. Dom.	*Calendar of state papers, domestic series, 1547-80 (etc.)* (London, 1856-).
C.B.É.	*Cnuasach Bhealoideas Éireann,* Roinn Bhealoideas Éireann, Coláiste na hOllscoile, Baile Átha Cliath.
Celtica	*Celtica* (Dublin, 1950-).
Census Ire., 1659	*A census of Ireland circa 1659, with supplementary material from the poll money ordinances (1600-1661)* ed. S. Pender (Irish Manuscripts Commission, Dublin, 1939).
Census Ire., 1841	*Report of the commissioners appointed to take the census of Ireland for the year 1841 [504],* H.C. 1843, xxiv.
Census Ire., 1851, I, I [etc.]	*The census of Ireland for the year 1851: part I showing the area, population and number of houses by townlands and electoral divisions,* vol. iv, province of Ulster, H.C. 1852-3, xci.
Commons Jn. Ire.	*House of Commons Journal (Ireland).*
Commrs Public Works	Commissioners of public works.
C.R.O.	County Record Office.
D.A.N.I.	Department of Agriculture of Northern Ireland.
D.D.A.	Dublin Diocesan Archives.
Down	Harris, Walter, *The ancient and present state of the county of Down* (Dublin, 1744).
Ecclesiastical antiquities	Reeves, Rev. W., *Ecclesiastical antiquities of Down, Connor and Dromore* (Dublin, 1847).
Econ. Hist. Rev.	*Economic History Review* (London, 1927-).
Éigse: A journal of Irish studies	(Dublin, 1939-).
Gilbert, *Contemp. hist. 1641-52*	J. T. Gilbert (ed.), *A contemporary history of affairs in Ireland, from A.D. 1641 to 1652* (Irish Archaeological Society, 3 vols, Dublin, 1879).
Gilbert, *Irish confed.*	J.T. Gilbert (ed.), *History of the Irish*

	confederacy and the war in Ireland, 1641-3 (7 vols, Dublin, 1882-91).
H.C.	House of Commons.
H.M.C.	Historical Manuscripts Commission.
H.M.S.O.	Her Majesty's Stationery Office.
I.A.C.D.	E.R.R. Green, *The industrial archaeology of county Down* (Belfast, 1963).
I.A.N.I.	W.A. McCutcheon, *The industrial archaeology of Northern Ireland* (Belfast, 1980).
I.C.R.	Irish College, Rome.
I.F.C.	Irish Folklore Commission.
I.H.S.	*Irish Historical Studies.*
I.M.C.	Irish Manuscripts Commission.
Inq. Ult.	*Inquisitionum in officio rotulorum cancellariae hiberniae ... repertorium* (2 vols, Dublin, 1826-9), ii.
Ir. Geog.	*Irish Geography (Bulletin of the Geographical Society of Ireland)* (vols i-iv, Dublin, 1944-63); continued as *The Geographical Society of Ireland, Irish Geography* (vol v -, Dublin, 1964-).
M.P.	Member of Parliament.
MS; MSS	manuscript; manuscripts.
N.A.I.	National Archives of Ireland.
N.A.I., 620	Rebellion Papers, National Archives of Ireland.
N.H.I.	*A New History of Ireland,* under the auspices of the Royal Irish Academy (Oxford, 1968-).
N.L.I.	National Library of Ireland.
N.M.I.	National Museum of Ireland.
no.; nos	number; numbers.
N.P.	not published.
O.P.W.	Office of Public Works.
O.S.	Ordnance Survey of Ireland.
O.S.M.	Ordnance Survey memoirs.
P.P.	Parliamentary Papers.
pers. comm.	personal communication.
Private coll.	private collection.
P.R.O.	Public Record Office (London).
P.R.O.I.	Public Record Office of Ireland.
P.R.O.N.I.	Public Record Office of Northern Ireland.
Q.U.B.	The Queen's University, Belfast.
R.C.P.	Relief Commission Papers.

R.D.	Registry of Deeds, Dublin.
R.D.S. Scient. Proc.	*Royal Dublin Society Scientific Proceedings.*
R.G.S.U.	Records of the General Synod of Ulster.
R.I.A.; A.R.É.	Royal Irish Academy; Acadámh Ríoga na hÉireann.
R.I.A. Proc.	*Proceedings of the Royal Irish Academy.*
R.I.A. Trans.	*Transactions of the Royal Irish Academy.*
R.N.I.F.B.	Report on the sea and inland fisheries of Northern Ireland.
R.S.A.I. Jn.	*Journal of the Royal Society of Antiquaries of Ireland.*
S.P. Henry viii	*State Papers, Henry viii* (11 vols, London, 1830-52).
Statistical survey Down	Rev. J. Dubourdieu, *Statistical survey of the county of Down* (Dublin, 1802).
T.C.D.	Library of Trinity College Dublin.
U.J.A.	*Ulster Journal of Archaeology.*
vol.; vols	volume; volumes.

Introduction

COUNTY DOWN – HISTORY AND PLACE

LINDSAY PROUDFOOT

The geographical identity of a place, that elusive and unique sense of difference which distinguishes each locality from its neighbours, is notoriously hard to define and even harder to uncover. What is it that gives a townland or village, a city or a region, its character and sense of identity? And how, whether as historians, archaeologists or geographers but almost always as outsiders, are we to recapture these identities and render them intelligible to others? How, in short, are we to distinguish between one place and another in terms which do justice to the complex human relationships and experiences which – past and present – manifestly form an important part of each one of them?

Clearly, some things are likely to be particularly important in determining this elusive 'sense of place'. Every locality and community, however defined, is spatially as well as historically constructed. Each is the unique product of the varying interaction over time between the physical factors of its immediate natural environment, its soil, climate, drainage, relief, resources and location, and the ability of successive generations of its inhabitants to exploit these. In turn, their ability to do so reflected the fundamental changes which periodically took place in the nature and organisation of society, its technological and economic base and resource relationship with the natural world. But in each case the *local* impact of these *structural* changes depended on the circumstances pertaining to the immediate locality – the presence (or absence) of a particular resource endowment, the social organisation of the local community, the pattern of property ownership and so on. Factors such as these might accelerate or hinder the pace of change, but in either case, being in combination place-specific, they acted to reinforce the local 'sense of place'.

When we turn to Ireland in general and to county Down in particular, we find that this perspective provides us with a powerful insight into the history of the county as 'place' and into the history and identity of the 'places' within it. Save for some minor adjustments in 1605, when the woodlands of Killultagh (in the lower Lagan valley) were transferred to county Antrim, county Down was more or less created in its modern form *ca* 1570, as part of Sir Thomas Smith's settlement of the area.[1] As in other parts of sixteenth-century Ireland, therefore, the county represented an alien restructuring of the existing cultural landscape, an administrative unit imposed from outside designed to serve the purposes of the country's newly-resurgent English administration. Paradoxically, however, by incorporating existing and much older territorial divisions such as those between the local Gaelic clans,[2] the new county was based on a series of much older territorial identities, which both ensured their survival – and provided a powerful link with the past. Thus county Down's southern boundary more or less follows the border between the twelfth-century kingdoms of the *Ui Echach Coba* in the Mournes and the *Ind Airthir* to the west (in what is now county Armagh), which ran along the Newry corridor. This survived throughout the middle ages as one of the most stable local political divisions, and is recognisable as bounding the Magennis and O'Hanlon countries in the fifteenth century, and the lordships of Iveagh and Newry and Mourne (to the east) and The Fews (to the west) in the sixteenth century. To the north, the modern county boundary follows the border between the sixteenth-century lordships of Kilwarlin and south Clandeboye (in Down) and Killultagh and north Clandeboye (in Antrim), much of which followed the course of the Lagan river. This boundary too carried resonances of an earlier past. Along part of its length, in the upper Lagan valley, it had demarcated between the fifteenth-century MacCartan lordship of Kinelarty in what is now mid-Down, and the southern reaches of the then much more extensive lordship of Clandeboye, which at that time extended from north Down into what is now south Antrim.

While it would be wrong to envisage these early boundaries as having the same precise cartographic definition as those of the modern county – the mapping of Ireland and the acquisition of cartographic knowledge was, after all, part of the modernising process – they nevertheless approximated to some of the more important local physiographic divisions. Thus from the start, county Down also inherited a strong physical identity, and this sense of physical 'place' has been important in the subsequent evolution of the various territorial identities within it. Clearly, Down's position as one of Ireland's littoral counties has been important in this. Bounded on the north and east by Belfast Lough and the Irish Sea, the modern county incorporates an area where the historic links have been as much with Scotland as with the rest of Ireland. On a clear day, Galloway, the Isle of Man and even the mountains of Wales are visible from various parts of the county Down coast. At a time when travel by sea was far easier than journeys made by land, these not-so-distant horizons would have appeared beguilingly accessible.[3] Not surprisingly, therefore, the archaeological record provides plenty of evidence that county Down formed part of a 'North Irish Sea cultural region', which enjoyed numerous and extensive cultural contacts across the North Channel, long before the first planter set foot in Ireland.[4]

Most prominent among Down's physical features are the Mourne Mountains, a complex of five Tertiary granitic intrusions which rise to over 2,500 feet in the extreme south of the county (fig. 0.1).[5] The Mournes dominate the horizon from virtually every part of Down, and as Estyn Evans recognised over forty-five years ago, they provide a distinctive combination of relatively harsh maritime and upland environments which, historically, have given rise to a series of unique cultural landscapes.[6] The ancient territorial divisions incorporated within the modern county boundary have already been shown to reflect this, and the 'Kingdom of Mourne' resonates to the present day as one of the most powerful and evocative images of place in Down. Historically, too, the Mournes have acted as a barrier to north-south movement, funnelling the major impulses of trade and communications through the Newry corridor to the west, thus reinforcing south Down's relative isolation.

To the north of the Mournes, beyond the small eighteenth-century 'landlord' town of Castlewellan, the Slieve Croob Hills rise to around 1,600 feet, and are formed of the remains of the metamorphic aureole of another ancient granitic intrusion. Geologically speaking, the Mournes and the Slieve Croob Hills are relatively recent, and both intrude through much more ancient Silurian grits, shales and slates. These form a low erosional plateau at around 400-500 feet, and this extends northwards across mid-Down to the more heavily-eroded Triassic New Red sandstones of the lower Lagan Valley and the Dundonald Gap. The latter forms a lowland corridor running east-west from Belfast to Newtownards, and is dominated at its eastern end by Scrabo Hill (538 feet), a knob of Bunter sandstone which has been preserved by a dolerite sill cap. Scrabo has been extensively quarried for building stone, and in a *vignette* which epitomises much of the historical construction of the local sense of place, is crowned by a Gothic tower, reputedly built in the 1860s as a memorial to the 3rd marquis of Londonderry by his grateful tenantry. To the north of the Dundonald Gap, the relatively resistant Ordovician and Silurian rocks reappear to form the Holywood Hills, a line of low bluffs which rise to around 600 feet and overlook Belfast Lough. On either side of the central plateau, the land slopes down, to the Lagan valley and the Lough Neagh Basin to the west, and to the Lecale and Ards peninsulas and the shores of Strangford Lough to the east.

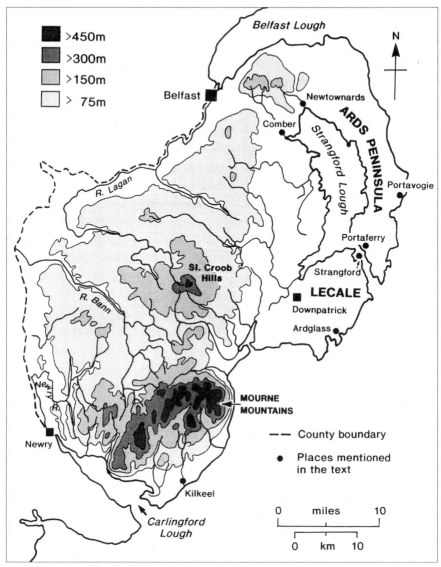

Fig. 0.1   County Down: topography and places mentioned in the text.

Over much of the county, however, the geology exerts very little structural control over the local relief. Instead, this is largely determined by the depositional features, particularly drumlins but also kames, left by the last – Midlandian – glaciation, which ended around 13,000-10,000 years ago.[7] From the northern half of the Ards peninsula, south-west across Strangford Lough, where they form numerous small islets on its sheltered western shore, and on across mid-Down, drumlins dominate the countryside. They constitute the northern end of the Irish

Midland drumlin belt, which stretches south-west across the historic Ulster-Leinster borderlands as far as Leitrim, Sligo and Roscommon. The conventional analogy of this landscape to a 'basket of eggs' is not inapt, and evokes the closely-textured and enclosed local worlds of past farming communities in these districts. Typically dispersed, the traditional farmsteads usually favour the higher (and drier) ground on the drumlins, and avoid the marshy lands of the poorly-drained inter-drumlin hollows. Travel in such conditions was never easy, and the drumlin belt long acted as a major barrier between Ulster and the rest of Ireland.

Elsewhere, other parts of county Down offer different physical identities. On the southern tip of the Ards peninsula, for example, the drumlin landscape gives way to an ice-scoured plateau which extends across the Strangford Narrows to the Lecale peninsula beyond. Here, the lush heavily-hedged fieldscapes of the drumlin belt give way to a more open landscape, frequently enclosed by stone walls. Open but not barren, the presence of relatively fertile kame-based soils ensured that these districts shared in the local cereal-based prosperity of the eighteenth and early nineteenth centuries. Around the county Down coast, life responded to different rhythms. The commercial potential of Strangford Lough was limited by the tidal race at its mouth and the extent of its tidal range, which exposes vast mud flats at the head of the lough at low tide. Accordingly, harbour development came late (in the seventeenth and eighteenth centuries) and was limited to those communities around its southern shores which enjoyed better access to its deep water channels. Notably, Newtownards and Comber both developed as important centres on its northern shores without ever having the benefit of harbour facilities. To the east, on the rocky and exposed Irish Sea coastline, harbours which could be safely entered at every state of the tide were relatively rare, and prior to 1700, Ardglass and Strangford were about the only ports of any note between Carlingford and Carrickfergus.

The newly-created county thus encompassed a variety of physical environments which had been exploited since prehistory, and accordingly, the county framed cultural landscapes of great antiquity. As time went on, and the processes of social and economic modernisation gathered pace, the county system increasingly came to play an ever more vital role in mediating 'the structures of everyday life' for its people. Clearly, some aspects of life remained resolutely outside the county orbit. Both the Roman Catholic and Anglican Churches, for example, retained identical and identically-named dioceses which were medieval in origin and which effectively divided county Down into two. Under both jurisdictions, much of the western half of the county formed the separate diocese of Dromore, though in the Anglican Church this was united with its northern neighbour, Down and Connor, in 1842. In both Churches, the latter diocese included all of north and east Down as well as county Antrim, though again, in the Anglican jurisdiction, Connor separated from Down in 1945. Nor did the pattern of magnate landownership in the county conform neatly to its boundaries: virtually all of county Down's leading landed families had extensive property interests elsewhere in Britain or Ireland. On the other hand, the bulk of the county's numerous lesser landowners were more exclusively local in their property ownership.

But in other respects, the idea of the county – the county as 'place' as it were – came to play an increasingly meaningful role in the daily life of their inhabitants. Thus at various times over the last 400 years, county Down provided the basis for the cess or tax its population paid; the infrastructural improvements carried out in their name; the appointment of the judiciary who regulated their behaviour; the militias who fought for (or against) them, and the constituencies in which increasing numbers of them were able to vote. In short, as Ireland modernised and the state took over and centralised administrative and juristicial roles which had once been exercised on a devolved basis by local communities, so each county, as agents of this modernisation, came to acquire an ever more vital functional identity.

The essays which make up this interdisciplinary account of county Down, its people and their history, offer various perspectives on these processes of social and historical construction. The book does not purport to be a compendium of local history. Rather, the authors, chosen for their expertise in their field, have been asked to explore those aspects of county Down's past which – from a late twentieth-century perspective at least – appear to resonate most powerfully in the present. In many respects, the approaches adopted by the essayists mirror the gradual emergence of the modern county as a recognisable entity. Thus the chapters dealing with the earlier periods are, by virtue of their material, the least focussed on the modern county. Mallory and Hartwell, for example, use the seminal *Archaeological survey of county Down* as a point of departure to measure recent progress in archaeological research in the county, but the issues they raise are far wider, and challenge our understanding of prehistoric societies in Ireland as a whole.

The same is also true of the essays by Dumvill and Sperber, Hamlin, McCormick and McNeill. These deal with various aspects of political, social and religious change within the area covered by the modern county during the early Christian and medieval periods. Not all the territorial identities which were ultimately to be incorporated within present-day Down had fully crystalised at this time. Consequently, the discussion in these chapters is framed by developments and personalities which, though they contribute to the 'meaning' of Down, also transcend it. Dumville and Sperber provide two views of the sixth-century county Down saint, St. Finnian of Movilla, while Hamlin analyses the evidence for the earliest monasteries in the county within the wider context of the life of St. Patrick and the pre-twelfth century religious contacts between Ireland and the Continent. McNeill also takes the *Archaeological survey of county Down* as his starting point, and offers an evaluation of medieval settlement in the county which is informed by a lively appreciation of the implications of feudalism for twelfth-century Ireland as a whole. McCormick offers a different perspective, and provides a detailed exposition of the changing environmental basis of medieval farming in Lecale, an area which retains a profound sense of place to this day.

Subsequent chapters deal with later issues and periods, and consequently focus on the modern county as a functional unit. Even so, Gillespie reminds us that the creation of the new county did not bound all the life experiences of its inhabitants. Some at least among the seventeenth-century colonists who took up land in Down, inhabited mental and social worlds which manifestly transcended its borders. O'Sullivan is concerned with the ways in which the volatile politics of the seventeenth century impacted on the Magennis lordship of Iveagh. This detailed case study is about how the losers accommodated themselves to a new world. Gillespie's theme recurs in Proudfoot's chapter on landownership and improvement during the eighteenth and early nineteenth centuries, but in both cases the people concerned were an elite, relatively wealthy and highly mobile. How far other less affluent social groups enjoyed similarly broad horizons at this period is not at all clear, but the point is well made insofar as it reminds us that the material world inhabited by the men (and women) of Down was paralleled, indeed arguably driven, by their 'inner' world of perception, faith and belief.

Various authors explore these ideas, and consider their consequences for the material and non-material worlds within county Down and beyond. The diversity of religious experience in both the pre- and post-Reformation period is examined by Jefferies, Rafferty and Hill, while Buckley and Devine engage with those other means of cultural transmission: language and folk belief. Predictably, the picture which emerges is one of cultural diversity and, occasionally, tension, as deeply-rooted communities sought to preserve their identity and traditions within a rapidly changing world which was frequently perceived as hostile. Sometimes the objects of hostility were surprisingly familiar. Both Rafferty and Hill uncover evidence of increasing 'official' concern in the nineteenth century by both the Roman Catholic and Anglican hierarchies over the survival or, in the case of the Church of Ireland, revival of populist practices of worship. In each case these were seen as undesirable, and were either suppressed or died out. They nevertheless provide a fascinating insight into one local interface between official religion and popular belief, other aspects of which are discussed by Buckley.

More usually, however, communal suspicions were externalised, and two chapters examine the political expression of the county's conflicting identities at different periods. Curtin surveys the events which occurred in Down before and during the United Irishmen's rebellion of 1798, while Walker explores the changing patterns of political affiliation in the county during the nineteenth century, and sets these within the context of Irish politics at large. The broad dimensions of the 1798 conflict are well known, but Curtin provides us with an evocative account of the social tensions, disruption and unlikely alliances which prevailed in county Down during that time. By contrast, Walker deals with a period when the means of political expression were altogether more formalised, but the underlying tensions remained real enough. Windrum, by contrast, explores the related theme of the social construction of the county's provision for custodial sentencing when these tensions gave rise to disruptive or violent behaviour.

The remaining chapters deal with various material expressions of recent historical change in the county. In two analyses which are made possible by the rapid improvement in the volume and quality of demographic data during the nineteenth century, Clarkson and Grant examine different aspects of Down's population history during and after the Potato Famine of 1845-49. Grant demonstrates that although county Down as a whole was not nearly as badly affected by the potato blight as other districts in the west of Ireland, there were nevertheless significant local pockets of famine-induced immiseration, which required considerable efforts at alleviation by government and community alike. Clarkson uses recently-compiled historical statistics to explore both the long-term consequences of the Famine and the more general changes which subsequently occurred in the pattern of demographic behaviour in the county, and which only partly mirrored experience elsewhere in Ireland.

A recurrent theme in Clarkson's analysis is the growing importance of Belfast in attracting rural migrants, and Campbell and Royle provide a detailed account of the city's eastward suburbanization and its socio-economic and spatial impacts. The dynamics prompting the city's growth are clear enough: industrialization and wealth creation, certainly, but also the desire on the part of the city's wealthier social groups to escape the more negative consequences of this growth, and create aspirational lifestyles on the city's rural fringe. The landed aristocracy and gentry provided them with a perfect role model, and both Tomlinson and Proudfoot discuss various aspects of the landscape aesthetic which the Belfast bourgeosie sought to emulate. Tomlinson stresses the importance of the role of eighteenth and nineteenth-century landowners and farmers in planting woodlands in a county which, even by Irish standards, was by then largely denuded of trees.

Belfast's growth did not occur in isolation, and nor was industrialization confined to the city alone. An important factor in the city's growth was the constant improvement in its communications, both across the Irish Sea with England and Scotland and more locally with its own hinterland. As part of this, Hamond traces the progressive improvement in the number and quality of roads and railways in county Down during the eighteenth and nineteenth centuries, and also charts the development of the county's ports. These varied considerably in terms of their role and importance. Although none came near to rivalling Belfast in terms of their trade, Newry was significantly more important in this respect than the remainder. Nevertheless, as Pollock demonstrates, Ardglass, Kilkeel and Portavogie were already significant in the early nineteenth century as fishing ports, and continued to provide seasonally-important employment opportunities for both men and women from throughout the region and beyond until the 1930s. Gendered employment such as the use of women to salt and pack herring was not the exclusive preserve of this industry. Cohen demonstrates that the continuing reliance by the county's major linen manufacturers on female labour during the nineteenth century had far-reaching consequences both for the local linen industry and the family alike.

As this brief introductory *resumé* shows, the subject matter and the perspectives brought together in this book are very varied. That is entirely appropriate, for in this variation we begin to sense something of the diversity of place and people, aspiration and belief, which – past and present – have grown together to form a place, indeed a whole series of places, that we call county Down.

References

1.   R. Gillespie, *Colonial Ulster. The settlement of east Ulster 1600-1641* (Cork, 1985), p. 18.

2.   Ibid., pp 18-21.

3.   E. Estyn Evans, *The personality of Ireland. Habitat, heritage and history* (Cambridge, 1973).

4.   *Archaeology of Ulster*. D. Moore (ed.), *The Irish sea province in archaeology and history* (Cardiff, 1970).

5.   The geological material in the following section is drawn from J. B. Whittow, *Geology and scenery in Ireland* (2nd ed., London, 1978).

6.   E. Estyn Evans, *Mourne country: landscape and life in south Down* (Dundalk, 1951).

7.   F. Mitchell, *Shell guide to reading the Irish landscape* (Dublin, 1986).

Chapter 1

DOWN IN PREHISTORY

J. P. MALLORY AND B. N. HARTWELL

Introduction

County Down is archaeologically unique in Northern Ireland insofar as
it is the only county to have seen full publication of its prehistoric
monuments (and almost all but one major class of its medieval
monuments). So thorough was the scope of *An archaeological survey
of county Down* that some have attributed the delay in any other
county survey in the north to the fact that the Down survey provided
an act that was too hard to follow. Moreover, the publication of the
survey, which was preceded by an intense period of research
excavation by Dudley Waterman and Pat Collins, seems to have
resulted in a situation in which subsequent excavation in the county
has been largely rescue-oriented, with the pace of archaeological
discovery slackening accordingly. Perhaps the single major exception
to this has been the recent excavations of a newly discovered ritual
complex at Ballynahatty, just outside the well-known Giant's Ring. This
notwithstanding, and in full admission that the praises of the *A.S.C.D.*
are justifiably numerous, it must be recognised that archaeology has
moved on over the past thirty years. Consequently, in this chapter we
will attempt to initiate a dialogue with the *A.S.C.D.* and reflect on how
the models of a previous generation have been vindicated or
challenged by more recent research and theory. Such an exercise
should also stimulate some questions on where future research in the
region might be directed.

The Mesolithic

There is probably no period in Irish prehistory where our perceptions
have altered more than the Mesolithic. In the *A.S.C.D.*, an image was
presented of a single Mesolithic period which began *ca.* 6000 B.C. and
was largely confined to the coastal regions of counties Antrim and
Down. Indeed, it was thought that the forests and swamps would have
so hindered mobility that 'the coastal strips were alone available to
primitive man' and that the economy would have been primarily
confined to 'gathering along the shore, and a little hunting'.[2] The old

model of Irish strandloopers, for here 'gathering' was intended to indicate the collection of shellfish, was difficult to dispel and could hardly be challenged when the distribution of diagnostic Mesolithic flint tools was confined almost entirely to the coastal regions, particularly around Belfast Lough and along the southern shores of Strangford Lough.

The pioneering work of Peter Woodman[3] did much to change the earlier paradigm. Today, the Mesolithic has not only been extended back in time to at least *ca.* 7000 B.C., but it has been divided into two main and quite distinctive periods, only the latter of which was portrayed in the *A.S.C.D.* The Early Mesolithic with its distinctive microlithic industry flourished for the first thousand years of human settlement in Ireland, and traces of such occupation were known from county Down, where microliths or face-trimmed axes were recovered from the plough-soil at Rough Island, Castle Espie, Ardmillan, and several other coastal sites. These were all old finds and were obscured by a predominantly Later Mesolithic background of heavy-bladed material. The viability of the earlier economic model was increasingly challenged following the excavation of Mount Sandel[4] on the Lower Bann, and the recording of a number of other Early Mesolithic sites along the Bann. The economic model shifted, placing new emphasis on riverine occupation with a predominantly fishing and pig hunting economy, while the coastal settlements took on an increasingly seasonal appearance, whose function, in some cases, was probably more to do with the collection and processing of flint tools than subsistence. One might have predicted inland riverine sites also to have occurred in county Down and one has been discovered at Ballymaglaff, near Dundonald, along the River Enler.[5]

The current model of the Early Mesolithic economy and settlement envisages seasonal movements of families and bands from coastal sites in the spring to inland waterways for the summer and early autumn runs of salmon and eels, with the proviso that there could be longer term settlement in particularly favourable areas such as Mount Sandel. This is still only a model with a minimum of archaeological support and it will require further substantiation.[6] For example, the balance between meat, fish and plants as elements in the nutritional basis of Ireland's Mesolithic communities is still vague and there has been a tendency to presume that the gathering of plants was very much a secondary activity. This can be challenged theoretically, however, by the fact that Ireland possesses over 120 edible native plants, and although recovery of plant remains tends to be limited to hazel nut shells and several assorted other plants, such as water lily seeds, much of the subsistence basis may still elude us.[7] We need a more exhaustive assessment of the likely productivity of Ireland's Mesolithic landscape in terms of its plants and animals. County Down possesses a wide variety of environments – the coastal sand-dunes of the Dundrum area, the islands of Strangford Lough, the Mourne Mountains, and various inland waterways for example. These could provide fresh-water fish and land mammals as well as salt-water fish, shell fish, sea mammals and an incredible abundance of economically exploitable birdlife such as geese.[8] Arguably, future archaeological models should attempt environmental reconstructions of the region which take account of this diversity.

The transition to the Later Mesolithic, where our primary evidence for the economy is provided by coastal shell-middens, is also very problematic. Much of the evidence for Mesolithic settlement in Down is confined to sites along the western and southern shores of Strangford Lough and some of its islands. Both Rough Island and Ringneill Quay produced molluscs while the latter also yielded the remains of wild birds.[9] The remains of red deer, found at a number of other coastal shell-middens, are not known from the Down sites. None of the sites were excavated according to modern standards and the need for both a well-preserved and well-excavated Mesolithic site in the Strangford region has long been a high priority.

A major problem of the transition from the Early to the Later Mesolithic is posed by what appear to have been relatively abrupt changes in technology and, possibly, subsistence strategy. The first saw the replacement of a microlithic technology involving composite tools – variously interpreted as harpoons or spears for hunting and fishing – by a broad blade industry whose type fossil is the butt-trimmed or Bann flake. This is well represented along the coasts of Strangford Lough and is generally interpreted as a knife rather than a projectile head. As there is no external source for this particular change, which runs very much counter to contemporaneous developments in Britain, an indigenous explanation is sought but remains elusive. It is suggested that a change in subsistence strategy (rather than subsistence base) led to 'a highly mobile low density economy'.[10] The Later Mesolithic sites of county Down appear to follow the main pattern of short-term seasonal and/or specialist sites: island locations such as Rough Island are dismissed as too small to have held long-term settlement. The only possible structure from this period in county Down is represented by some postholes from Glendhu, which underlay a shell-midden attributed to the Later Mesolithic, and this may have served either as a shelter or possibly for fish-drying.[11] Woodman's suggestion of a shift from a partially stable Early Mesolithic settlement to a more mobile settlement structure in the Later Mesolithic has been challenged by Cooney and Grogan.[12] They call attention to trends observed elsewhere in north-west Europe which suggest increasingly sedentary, Later Mesolithic populations. Much of this rests on evidence for Scandinavian coastal populations, who were able to exploit a wide range of seasonally available food sources in the same area. It has always been recognised that coastal dwelling hunter-gatherers and especially fishing populations could achieve remarkably complex societies, for example, the Kwakiutl of the Pacific Northwest or the Chumash of southern California. Theoretically, one might wonder whether the same was true of county Down, where the range of fish and sea mammal resources in Strangford Lough might render the area comparable with some of the other highly productive hunter-fisher regions of the world.[13] Nevertheless, the evidence so far seems to fit Woodman's model – which was consciously juxtaposed against other regions of north-west Europe – much better than that extended to Ireland by Cooney and Grogan. This again reflects the absence of good bio-botanical models for the relevant period. Moreover, if such models were to bear out the assumptions made by Cooney and Grogan, then archaeologists would need to explain why the coastal region of county Down was being exploited so far below its economic potential (or discover sites that better fit their model).

The technological transition from microliths to a heavy-bladed industry remains unexplained.[14] If its causation was primarily social rather than economic, the reasons may never be discovered. Given the current trend (fashion might be more appropriate) to seek explanations for cultural change in social rather than economic terms, we may conjecture that the Early Mesolithic microlithic tool-kits reflected the male gendering of activites such as the manufacture of weapons and the subsistence pursuit itself. Thus, males flaked the flint, fitted the barbs to the harpoons, were solely responsible for spearing fish, and enjoyed any attendant prestige. The technological shift in the Later Mesolithic seems to indicate an abandonment of the flint-barbed harpoons and projectiles and, presumably, their replacement by organic weapons fashioned from wood, bone or antler using the multi-purpose butt-trimmed (Bann) flake. Also, there seems to be a presumption that traps, fish-weirs and other devices might have replaced harpoon-fishing. Arguably, the fashioning of weirs, working of nets and cords could all be regarded as more appropriately female activities or pursuits that would normally be undertaken without respect to gender. The technological change might then be interpreted as the collapse of a primarily male activity and its replacement by a more effective strategy of fishing that was no longer male-specific but also involved women. One of the additional advantages of the new system would be that the use of traps would permit greater mobility between base camp and subsistence area. Thus the women, whose activities were invariably constrained in hunter-gatherer societies by the need to care for the young, could more easily schedule their tasks. Conceivably, these alternative fish-procuring strategies might lead to a rapid dissolution of the existing male-gendered technological and subsistence complex, as there would no longer be any compulsion for males to invest their energy in the production of microlith-armatured harpoons. Such a change could have been remarkably swift and help account for the fact that we find no transitional sites between Early and Later Mesolithic technologies. Unfortunately, such an explanation while possible is also exceedingly difficult to corroborate.

The Neolithic

The *A.S.C.D.* was written at the beginning of radiocarbon dating in Ireland and hence it could only allude to a few dates which suggested that the earliest appearance of farming populations in Ireland dated to the end of the fourth millennium B.C.[15] Today, we have sufficient dates to suggest that one might have to extend this chronology backwards by another thousand years. Of greater interest is the model proposed: sea-borne colonisation, with coastal Down as one of the earliest landfalls for the first Neolithic colonists. The defleshed burials interred in Millin Bay could even be interpreted as the 'ancestors' of the earliest immigrants, the bones of which were carried across the sea to be buried in their new home. A similar interpretation was proposed for the remains in the Audleystown court tomb. A possible source for these Neolithic colonists was sought from the Continent, where 'western French elements are perhaps detectable in the pottery' as well as in tomb design, although similarities with the Severn-Cotswold region were also remarked upon. Essentially, the *A.S.C.D.* suggested (and rather novelly) that the earliest penetration of the Neolithic economy into the British Isles may have involved almost simultaneous movement into southern Britain and northern Ireland; subsequent developments, for example, the Grimston Ware of Yorkshire, may have owed more to the initial Irish colonisation than the reverse.

The model of Neolithic colonisation has altered little in the intervening years, although the radiocarbon chronology would now set the initial appearance of farming settlements at about 4000 B.C., if not a few centuries earlier. Arguments in favour of an indigenous adoption of agriculture by Later Mesolithic natives have been proposed on a number of occasions, but the model presented in the *A.S.C.D.* is still viable and is supported by the similarities between Ireland and Britain or the Continent in domestic architecture, stone tools and pottery.[16] Moreover, the earliest domestic cereals had to be imported into Ireland from somewhere, as had domestic cattle, sheep and goats. The colonisation model is thus still the preferred option.[17] This is not to deny contacts between Neolithic farmers and Mesolithic hunter-gatherers, but these contacts would appear to have been internal to Ireland, (between farmer colonists and native hunter-gatherers), rather than across the Irish Sea (as Irish hunter-gatherers obtained their Neolithic 'way of life' from Britain or the Continent).

The nature of the contacts between the native population and intrusive farmers is still far from certain, although it has long been clear that there must have been a chronological overlap between the two communities.[18] The presumption would generally be in favour of local hunter-gatherer communities coming into contact with farmers and acquiring from them the new livestock (by trade or theft). This is occasionally reflected on shell-midden sites which have yielded evidence for both Mesolithic occupation and some exotic (Neolithic) species, such as cattle or sheep, but the evidence for such contacts in county Down is minimal.[19] There is no clear Neolithic presence in the shell midden at Rough Island, and the remains of sheep and cattle recovered from Ringneill can only be said to date from after the Mesolithic. Evidence for a continuity in lithic technologies has not been argued for county Down with regard to other items which have occasionally been proposed as diagnostic of a 'Mesolithic survival' elsewhere. For example, the so-called Sandhills Ware pottery has not been found in association with Later Mesolithic material. It is perhaps well to emphasise all of these points, not for their conclusions but in view of their bearing on the models presented above. Farmer colonists from Britain might well be expected to settle along the eastern coast of Ireland, including areas such as county Down, and here we might expect a fairly large Later Mesolithic population. If there was one area where we might expect to find intense interaction, perhaps over a protracted time, it would certainly be here, although those portions of Down with the greatest quantity of Later Mesolithic material may well have been the least inviting to early farmers (see below). But even if this were the case, we might then expect to find a still greater temporal overlap between the native populations and the farming populations which were spreading through the island.

The material culture of the first farmers was briefly surveyed in the *A.S.C.D.*, where the various pottery types were traced to both distant and local sources. The flint resources of county Down, unlike those of county Antrim, were limited largely to glacial drift and raised beaches which produced generally poorer quality flint. In areas especially poor in flint, such as the Dundrum sandhills, beach pebbles were also employed. The implement types figured in the *A.S.C.D.* are still

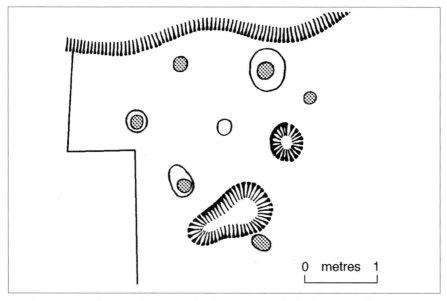

Fig. 1.1   Neolithic settlement in the Dundrum sandhills (Source: Collins, *U.J.A.*, xxi (1958), fig. 4).

considered valid today: leaf and lozenge-shaped arrowheads, javelin heads, end scrapers, the still functionally-obscure hollow scraper, and the plano-convex knife. Axes were fashioned from greenstone, dolerite and porcellanite, this last being a ubiquitous material for polished stone tools in the north-east of Ireland, with outcrops at Tievebulliagh and Rathlin Island. The only local source observed was Mourne granite, which was used to fashion some axes. The most distant foreign source recorded was for an axe from Drumgooland in the Upper Bann, which derived from the Great Langdale axe factory in the Lake District. Perforated stone axes or hammers were also noted.

The evidence for Neolithic settlement in the *A.S.C.D.* was sparse and other than some stake-holes from the Dundrum sandhills, no Neolithic architectural remains were known (fig. 1.1). The distribution of the megalithic tombs, however, seemed to confirm a predicted settlement pattern: the light, easily-moved soils of the uplands were exploited, while there was a marked absence of tombs in the drumlin area of Strangford Lough and in the upper parts of the Mournes. The evidence for settlement in the coastal sandhills, where fishing may have been important, was seen as a reflection of the wide range of economic activities possibly practised by Neolithic farmers. Thus the *A.S.C.D.* concluded that the attribution of these coastal territories as 'a refuge of a preceding Mesolithic stock had perhaps been exaggerated', although continuity of occupation of these regions was demonstrable.

The authors of the *A.S.C.D.* were clearly aware that a 'normalist' view which sought to typify Neolithic settlement and economy for the entire county would suffer from the conflicting nature of the evidence. Recently, Julian Thomas has challenged the entire 'normalist' picture of Neolithic Britain, concluding that 'the population of Neolithic Britain did not live in major timber-framed buildings, quite probably did not reside in the same place year-round, did not go out to labour in great walled fields of waving corn, were not smitten by over-population or soil decline, and much of their day-to-day food may have been provided by wild crops'.[20] His view, largely based on the absence of evidence for the traditional model, was restricted to British rather than Irish sources, yet one could well imagine how conveniently the paucity of evidence for substantial Neolithic settlement in county Down might also accommodate his revised model. Or does it?

Since the publication of the *A.S.C.D.*, the lack of architectural evidence for Neolithic settlement has in no way been relieved. On an all-Ireland basis, however, the few Neolithic farmsteads known to its authors have been augmented by the discovery of substantial Neolithic houses at Ballyglass,[21] county Mayo, two from Tankardstown, county Limerick, one from Newtown, county Meath, one from Ballynagilly, county Tyrone,[22] and two recently discovered at Ballygalley, county Antrim. In general, all of these structures are about 6 metres wide and range from about 7 to 15 metres in length, sometimes employing an apsidal end. Constructed of split oak planks, the labour estimates for the construction of one of the smaller houses (at Ballynagilly) was *ca.* 550 hours. Seemingly, we are gradually uncovering a pattern of dispersed Neolithic farmsteads comprising one or two houses (perhaps more at Ballygalley?), which architecturally would not have been out of place in Continental Europe, although there they would commonly be found clustered in small hamlets or larger villages. The revisionist model of Neolithic architecture suggested by Thomas, whatever its merits for Britain, is 'hard to sell' so far as the Irish evidence is concerned, if it implies that there were no stable farmsteads. By implication, the notion that most settlement was 'seasonal', i.e. that the economy was still essentially mobile rather than sedentary, might also be challenged in that such farmsteads hardly accord with the 'flimsy structures' predicated for the British Neolithic.

The evidence of field systems, in particular their archaeological expression in terms of field walls, is another area where the Irish evidence may reflect a different picture. The extensive later Neolithic co-axial systems in county Mayo (the Céide Fields) are now of European repute.[23] They pose the question to all Irish archaeologists of whether they were an essentially local phenomenon or typical of most of this island. The grounds for proposing a local phenomenon are the particular nature of the region in which they are found – a rising upland territory fronted by sea cliffs, suggesting an image of hard-pressed farmers forced to parcel out land in an organised system in a region where there was nowhere else to go. On the other hand, there are hints of earlier field systems in north-east Ireland, such as the traces of a field wall of possible later Neolithic date on the Galboly Plateau, county Antrim.[24] The construction of Neolithic stone walls by county Down populations is also indicated by the dry stone wall that underlay the Neolithic cairn at Millin Bay. Set on windblown sand, its situation precluded its interpretation as an agricultural wall in the *A.S.C.D.*, but without knowledge of the pre-cairn surface, such a use cannot be entirely dismissed.

Clearly, an organised sedentary agricultural component seems to have existed in the Irish Neolithic, but did this extend throughout the entire island? This is where Julian Thomas' views may have some merit, since the patterns of Neolithic occupation frequently uncovered in county Down are not immediately explicable as part of a mixed agricultural system. Neolithic ceramics in the Dundrum sandhills, for example, suggest a different economic pursuit to settled farming and we should be wary of imagining that the entire Irish landscape was 'domesticated' during the Neolithic. The advantage of Thomas' approach is that it challenges the conventional perception of the Irish Neolithic as little more than a version of 'traditional' nineteenth-century Ireland without the horses, wheeled vehicles and metal tools, and with different crops.

The *A.S.C.D.*'s discussion of Neolithic pottery concentrated on illustrating the basic types, dividing them between those with a foreign affiliation and – presumably – ultimate origin, such as the earliest Western Neolithic wares of the Lyles Hill style and the later, indigenous Sandhills Ware. The differences were thus rooted in generic developments and the *A.S.C.D.* notes that in general the same type of pottery encountered in settlement sites is to be found in burial contexts.

Ceramic studies have moved on since the publication of the *A.S.C.D.* Sheridan has undertaken petrological analysis of Neolithic pottery from a number of sites and has shown that they tend to suggest small local production centres rather than the extensive trade systems occasionally encountered in southern Britain.[25] The *A.S.C.D.*'s interest in the find context of the pottery has continued in more recent studies, but the types of questions posed by some recent British studies have seldom been broached in Irish contexts.[26] Issues raised by the variation in ceramics run from the clearly functional – the capacity of the vessels, their use for storage, cooking or serving food – to their possible use as ethnic markers or as expressions of female or ritual social roles. Thomas suggests that the different styles of Neolithic ceramics found in Britain may have served different functions.[27] The undecorated Neolithic wares (seen in the Irish Lyles Hill series) tend to be ubiquitous and may therefore not have been 'closely identified with a particular social group', and this would permit them to circulate through a variety of social contexts. The critical variable here may be the vessels' form, which studies reveal might be differentially distributed according to the nature of the site. Unfortunately, these ideas cannot really be tested for the county Down material because of the paucity of find contexts and the small number of vessels known from the earlier ceramic series. As for the rather later decorated wares, we might look for patterning in form, decoration and contexts within or across different regions in Ireland. Such a specific study has not yet been carried out on the thirteen county Down sites listed by Michael Herity as containing decorated pottery.[28] In some cases there seems to be a uniformity of types within a single context, for example the court tomb at Ballyedmond yielded remains of three different Broad-rimmed vessels, but in other instances, for example Ballyalton court tomb, we find a mixture of ceramic types. But this is only a cursory inspection and it points again to the need for further research into regional variations in Irish prehistory.

One of the areas where the authors of the *A.S.C.D.* undertook significant research prior to writing the survey was in their examination of the county's megalithic tombs. Court and portal tombs constituted the basic types, and each was excavated in some numbers. Passage tombs, so impressive in the Boyne Valley and other cemeteries, are conspicuously few in county Down and with some exceptions are either mentioned only in very early reports (and are now destroyed) or else are stylistic anomalies, for example, the remarkable mortuary structure at Millin Bay (see below).[29] The *A.S.C.D.* noted the distribution of court tombs, particularly in the Carlingford/south Down region and also northern Lecale, and argued that this was probably their point of origin in Ireland. This was very much in opposition to de Valera's theory, which derived the court tombs from the west and suggested that the tombs there might have been built by the earliest farmer colonists.[30]

At the time of the *A.S.C.D.*, megalith studies focussed on the observation of architectural patterns (which could support discussions of genetic or contact links between regional styles) and general distributions, including probable areas of Neolithic settlement. The more socially-oriented approach to archaeology encountered in recent

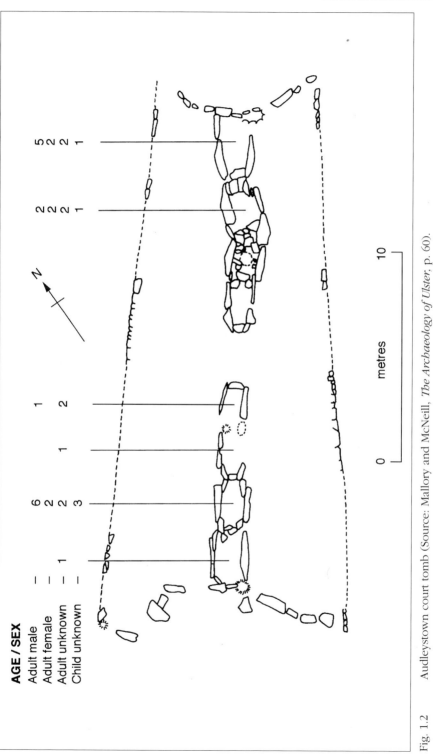

Fig. 1.2   Audleystown court tomb (Source: Mallory and McNeill, *The Archaeology of Ulster*, p. 60).

literature attempts to recover the symbolic meaning of architectural form and is also interested in the full range of patterns that might accompany the burial ritual itself, for example the distribution of burials (or parts of burials) within tombs according to age and sex, or the arrangement of features within the 'ritual landscape'.[31] County Down offers at least two suitable sites for such analysis, Audleystown and Millin Bay. The inhumed burials from the Audleystown court tomb, which provided the most abundant human remains from this tomb type in Ireland, clearly argued for defleshing prior to their deposition (fig. 1.2). More recent studies of this phenomenon have emphasised ethnographic parallels where it has been observed that dead flesh may be regarded as a pollutant that interferes with the rite of passage to the next world and that the deceased must be translated into a pure osseous form before burial.[32]

Possibly associated with this is the prior firing of some of the chambers at Audleystown. Some commentators have seen the pattern of burials as evidence for the selective treatment of different anatomical parts of the deceased after deposition. Previous observations of Audleystown merely emphasised a rough correlation between the number of the deceased and the number of grave goods per chamber.[33] While segregation by age or sex according to compartment has been observed in British tombs,[34] similar patterns are not so clear at Audleystown where males, females, adults and children were all found together in the six chambers offering evidence of burial.[35] Cooney suggests that the 'mingling of bones together may have idealised the concept of community',[36] but the social 'meaning' of these tombs is still far from clear. Although the preservation of human remains is likely to be erratic, there is still a case for assuming that, as at Audleystown, some court tomb chambers did not include any burials, while in other cases we often find objects interpreted as grave goods without any graves.[37] The number of chambers varied from two to five, and it is difficult to imagine that this variation was totally random. The number of chambers may have been impelled by the cosmic or social ordering of their builders' universe. The disposition of some of the court tombs of the Mourne-Carlingford region represent another aspect of this 'ritual landscape'. Here, a number of tombs occur in pairs (or threes). One is reminded of the tendency towards paired clusters of Neolithic temples on Malta,[38] while the bifurcation of societies into two moieties or halves is too well known to require much comment. Although some of the county Down examples have been excavated, for example Ballyedmond and Mourne Park, no complete 'pair' has seen excavation that might reflect on the contemporaneity of the tombs or the variability between them.

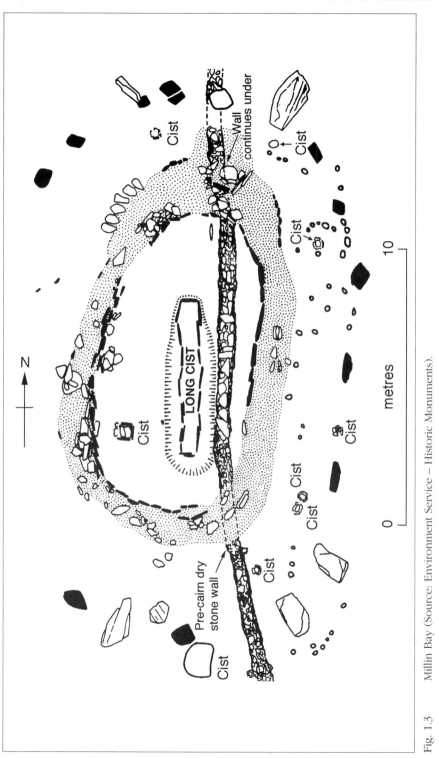

Fig. 1.3   Millin Bay (Source: Environment Service – Historic Monuments).

The other major ritual site is Millin Bay, where the remains of skulls were grouped together with long bones (fig. 1.3).[39] The fifteen burials inhumed in the long cist included adults, adolescents and children and both males and females were identified. The remains included nine skulls, thirteen right femurs and eleven left humeri. The skulls comprised three adult males, one unsexed adolescent and four children, while the cremated remains of an adult male skull made up the ninth. The sample is small and only three females were identified in the report. None of these were represented by their skulls which might suggest selective disposal (or removal) of particular elements of the anatomy according to sex. Generally, it is difficult to perceive specific gender patterns in Irish megalithic tombs (other than the Linkardstown cists which are absent from the north of Ireland). While the number of males known in court tombs well exceeds known females, there are so many unsexed adult skeletons that it is difficult to confirm this pattern overall.[40]

A further monument type that demands at least summary comment is the stone circle at Ballynoe (fig. 1.4). The authors of the *A.S.C.D.* lacked detailed information from the excavations of 1937/38, and their survey of this complicated monument could only relate it to their own work at Millin Bay.[41] The subsequent publication of the field notes from the 1937-38 excavations has remedied this,[42] while in an inspired move by the editors, interpretations of the site were also solicited from two leading authorities on Irish megaliths. That these latter offered such diametrically opposed chronological and architectural schemes is not only a tribute to the complexity of the site but also a stimulus to further examination of what has been regarded as one of the earliest stone circles in Ireland.[43]

One final monument investigated prior to the publication of the *AS.C.D.* was the 'Giant's Ring' at Ballynahatty (plate 1.1). Since the area of this site has been the recent focus of a major research project, it is one of the few areas of prehistoric research where our advances since the *A.S.C.D.* have been empirical as well as theoretical, and we therefore provide a brief survey of the initial results from this major ritual complex.

The Ballynahatty complex

The townland of Ballynahatty is situated in a loop of the River Lagan which flows into the sea at Belfast 8 kilometres away. It forms a discrete topographical unit, 40 metres high and is bounded on three sides by steep slopes. There are now three surviving sites on this plateau, the Giant's Ring itself, a passage tomb and a standing stone.

The Giant's Ring is the largest and best preserved of the hengiform

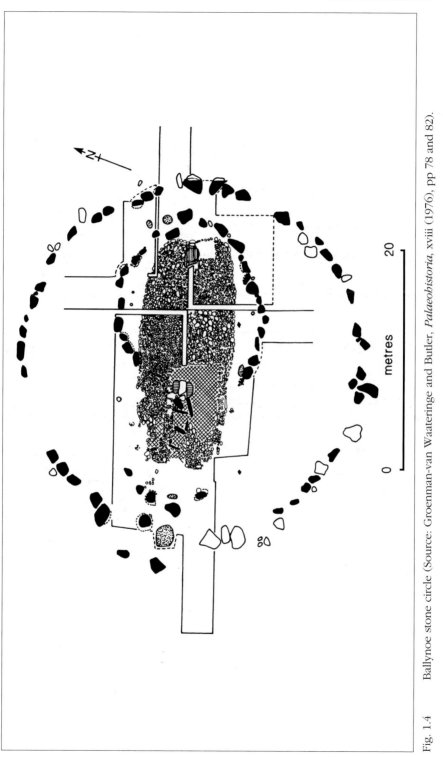

Fig. 1.4   Ballynoe stone circle (Source: Groenman-van Waateringe and Butler, *Palaeohistoria*, xviii (1976), pp 78 and 82).

Plate 1.1   Giant's Ring, Ballynahatty td., from the north.

enclosures in Ireland and the most distinctive prehistoric field monument in county Down. It consists of a bank surviving to a height of 4 metres, encompassing an area 200 metres across, near the centre of which are the remains of the passage grave. Of the three recorded excavations of the site, Henry Lawlor's campaign was the most extensive but revealed little of the structure and function of the Ring.[44] He trenched 540 metres of the interior, dug a section three quarters of the way through the bank and put a circular trench around the megalith. He finally dug four feet down under the capstone and found a porter and a lemonade bottle from a previously unrecorded 'excavation'. Some fragments of burnt bone from the fill and an adjacent area of burning suggested that the funeral rite had involved cremation. The excavation took one week and this, together with the intractable nature of the glacial sand and gravel subsoil, produced inconclusive results and misinterpretation.

In 1954, A. E. P. Collins undertook the first scientific excavation of the bank and an area around the megalith during fieldwork for the *A.S.C.D.*[45] He showed that the bank material had been dug from a shallow internal trough giving the interior the appearance of an upturned saucer. This was in contrast to Lawlor's notion that the stones of the bank were '... carried by the hands of a large number of workers from the country round ...'.[46] This arrangement of a shallow, internal, flat-bottomed quarry ditch providing the material for an outer bank is similar to a number of other enclosures in Ireland, such as Dowth Hall in the Boyne Valley, county Meath[47] and 'Rath Maeve', one kilometre south of the Hill of Tara.[48] Although Collins resolved some of the structural problems of the Ring, its date and function remained elusive. The bank itself and its relationship to the megalith may provide some clues. Collins not only found that originally there was a small outer marker or retaining bank, but also that the inner face may have been consolidated by a facade of stones. If the angle of the stone facade is projected upwards and the eroded bank material reinstated (the outer slope being limited by the retainer bank), the original bank profile has to be reconstructed with a broad, flattened top. If this was the case, rather than the bank enabling complete exclusivity of activities taking place within the enclosure, it may have provided a platform for spectators to observe events but with the inner wall preventing them from actually taking part. MacAlister saw the presence of the megalith as signifying a funeral function with the enclosure acting as a zone of exclusion.[49] This assumes that the two sites are of contemporary construction and use. It can only be demonstrated, however, that the enclosure bank is later than the passage grave.[50]

The nature of the ceremonies supported by this structure remains elusive, although the physical focus of activity appears to have been the passage grave around which the Ring was laid out.[51] Evidence provided by the minimal lithic finds suggested a late Neolithic date. For further evidence of extensive ritual and funerary activity we must turn to documentary evidence and the results of air photography.

During the eighteenth and nineteenth centuries the area to the immediate north and west of the Ring was cleared for agricultural use, and large quantities of human bones were turned up by the plough. A circular stone chamber was found and reported as a radially segmented, stone lined chamber, with a corbelled roof.[52] The top of the structure was 45 centimetres below ground level and may have been covered with small stones to form a cairn. Although the roof had been partially dismantled on discovery, the original entrance was on the east side of the structure, blocked by a removable stone, at a floor depth of 1.4 metres. Moving clockwise from the entrance, the first two compartments of the interior each contained two Carrowkeel Ware bowls with cremations. The next compartment was vacant but the one opposite the entrance contained two complete human skulls and three more jaws in a bed of sand sitting on some burnt bone. Also present were human ribs and a humerus and some animal bone. The remaining two compartments each contained parcels of burnt human bone. The cremated bones contained skull fragments and were therefore not connected to the unburnt bone. At least nine cremated individuals were represented here, possibly many more. The division of the chamber into compartments, the vacant compartment itself, the careful placement of cremations in pots or packages and the order-liness of the deposits suggest that, as with Audleystown, occupancy may have been predetermined. This tomb seems not to have been for the deposition of nameless ancestors but for the interment over time of known individuals, perhaps a family group. The Carrowkeel Ware bowls emphasise that this is a burial in the passage grave tradition though of an anomalous type. The unburnt bone neatly placed on the burnt bone in a bed of sand opposite the entrance seems to be later and intrusive in nature. It is the product of a different type of burial rite, involving the exposure of cadavers and defleshing – the process of excarnation. The animal bones were presumably food offerings or the deliberate wasting of food, and seem to be associated with the unburnt head and jaws. There is therefore evidence of two alternative mortuary traditions within the same tomb. This is not an uncommon practice and may represent an attempt to promote legitimacy of occupation by associating the burials of one social group with the ancestral remains of another.[53] Although buried, the tomb must have been identifiable and the chamber accessible over a period of time.

The published report of this discovery records the destruction in the previous century of other sites contained within one or two fields on the north-west side of the Giant's Ring. They included two flat cemeteries from which vast quantities of human bones were removed; a cemetery mound containing several cremations in stone cists; at least five cists containing urns and either cremations or unburnt bone, some with flint grave goods; a megalithic tomb containing an urn and some bones; and a standing stone and a deep pit filled with burnt stone and charcoal. Similar cists, including one of the compartmented type, were found in at least three adjacent fields.[54] The range and quantity of burials is extensive and again represents a number of mortuary traditions. The area around the Giant's Ring therefore acted as a magnet for possibly hundreds of burials through the Late Neolithic and Early Bronze Age. Many inhumations were apparently placed in simple, shallow graves without any recognisable marker. The extent of the cemetery may only have been limited by the steep sides of the plateau.

In recent years air photography has provided evidence of further sites, some of which have been excavated. A circular crop mark, 60 metres north-west of the Giant's Ring produced the base of a stony bank.[55] The central area had been removed by quarrying to a depth of 3 metres and backfilled within the last 200 years. This can probably be related to an eighteenth century reference:

> Contiguous with this Rath (i.e. the Giant's Ring), there was a small mount that some of the neighbours dug through, in order to get stones for building; and in the centre thereof a great quantity of bones was found.[56]

Air photography has revealed a line of three small round barrows, presumably Early Bronze Age, only 75 metres south west of the Ring and extensive disturbance of the soil which may relate to the flat cemeteries or cist burials. The dominant feature, however, is Ballynahatty 5 (BNH5), a large oval double palisaded enclosure, 70 x 90 metres in extent, with a similar but much smaller enclosure within its eastern end (BNH6) (fig. 1.5). These have both been the subject of extensive excavation.[57] BNH5 consists of radially paired, ramped post holes, averaging 1.8 metres in depth that may have held free-standing posts approximately 6 metres high and 30 centimetres in diameter. The earth-fast lower section had rotted *in situ* but scatters of charcoal suggest that the posts had probably been burnt. This gave a date of between 3018 and 2788 cal. B.C. At least 250 mature trees, probably oak, were felled and hauled to the site and each post pit would have taken about twenty-six hours of digging with antler picks. The whole

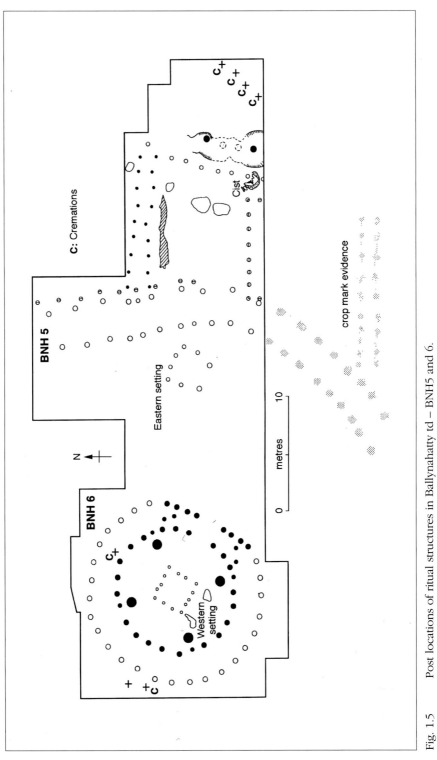

Fig. 1.5   Post locations of ritual structures in Ballynahatty td – BNH5 and 6.

enterprise could have taken at least 15,000 hours to complete. If the posts were carved in any way, or if there was a linking superstructure, it would have taken considerably longer. There appears to be no formal entrance although part of the perimeter is masked in the air photograph.

The eastern end of BNH5 had been distorted slightly in order to enclose the 'eastern setting', a small rectangle of eight postholes, 0.8 metres deep, measuring 2 by 3 metres. It is characterised by two larger postholes flanking the open side which gives a south-south-west orientation.

A similar arrangement of thirteen posts (the 'western setting'), was found within the inner enclosure, BNH6, on exactly the same orientation. In addition, on the same axis but at the rear of the setting was found the cremated remains of a woman of thirty to forty years, in a hole lined with split stones. The absence of any domestic artifacts, the position of the settings within a ceremonial landscape and the associated burial strongly suggest a mortuary function, and they may possibly be regarded as mortuary enclosures. The larger postholes may represent gate posts to allow access to the interior where bodies could have been exposed for defleshing. Without necessarily changing the function, the western setting then seems to have been reoriented towards the east-south-east and the open side infilled to form a closed timber square (2.8 x 2.8 metres), probably supporting a platform. Beyond each corner, four massive posts were erected in flat-bottomed ramped holes up to 2.4 metres deep and 1.6 metres wide. Encircling these were two concentric rings of posts set in postholes 1.8-2 metres deep of similar construction and with a maximum diameter of 16 metres. The entrance on the east-south-east side in line with the western setting was more elaborate and consisted of three infilled panels of planking on either side of the outer ring and probably two panels on either side of the inner ring. The evidence for planked construction associated with Neolithic domestic architecture has already been outlined. If the two concentric rings of posts were contemporary and free-standing, BNH6 would have appeared as an enormously impressive stand of sixty-six posts, 6 metres high, in a 16 metres diameter area. To create some visual order into what was a meticulously planned and constructed building, the individual posts of the concentric rings may have been connected by lintels as has been demonstrated at the Sarn-y-Bryn-Caled complex in Wales.[58]

The end of the structure must have been equally spectacular. The western setting was probably dismantled and the remaining structure then deliberately burnt to the ground. The earthfast parts of the outer ring rotted *in situ* but those of the inner ring were dug out of the ground and all of the burnt material scraped from the surrounding soil and packed down into the open holes. The pits on either side of the entrance also contained several flint end scrapers, flint debitage produced as waste from tool making, fire shattered flint and a stone ball. Only four low stone cairns were left to mark the position of the four great central posts.

A further complex of over forty postholes and trenches seems to have been attached to the eastern end of BNH5. Although these structures were lower, reflected in a post hole depth of 1.2 metres, many of the postholes show evidence of a similar cycle of activity to BNH6. One of the post pits cuts through the edge of a small cist burial containing two pots with cremations. Sub-rectangular in shape and smaller, it shares some characteristics with the compartmented cist discussed above, including a distinct entrance and Carrowkeel Ware pottery. Both of these sites have the appearance of small sunken passage graves.

Looking further afield, two sites in the valley of the River Boyne provide close parallels to the timber circles. At Knowth, a single ring timber circle, with many characteristics similar to BNH6, was constructed in front of the eastern entrance to the passage tomb.[59] It was associated with Grooved Ware pottery which has also been found at Ballynahatty. At Newgrange, a large pit enclosure was excavated by Sweetman,[60] and this provides a more complex model for the larger enclosure of BNH5 and was again built close to a passage tomb.

Ballynahatty should therefore be seen as a focus of community ceremony and death rituals in the Late Neolithic and Early Bronze Age Lagan Valley. A place close to, but set apart from, the rich lowlands that probably supported a substantial Neolithic population. It was obviously a society which had social cohesion, with some imposed or inherited authority that was able to motivate the population. The apparent ritual function that underpins these monuments strongly suggests some form of spiritual leadership. The crucial importance of death rituals in a traditional agrarian society has been discussed by Thomas.[61] The death of each individual can be seen as ultimately affecting the survival of society as a whole. Mortuary rituals promote links between the changing present and what must have been perceived as society's immutable past. Over time, however, the past becomes subject to reinterpretation and power becomes concentrated in the hands of those who are able to intercede between the living and their ancestors. This authority must have been sufficient to motivate society to produce the extraordinary earth and timber structures of the later Neolithic. The traditions of cremation, inhumation and excarnation should be viewed as strategies for the transformation and purification of bone which provided this tangible link with the past.

The Early Bronze Age

The *A.S.C.D.* could do little to elucidate settlement in the Early Bronze Age,[62] held then to begin *ca.* 1800 B.C. but now thought of as starting *ca.* 2500-2300 B.C. The economy was presumed to have been increasingly pastoral, although the harvesting of grain could not be denied due to the discovery of grain impressions on pottery. Most of the discussion of Early Bronze Age remains was taken up with the descriptions (verbal and illustrative) of bronzes, particularly flat axes, gold work and funerary ceramics. Ireland was seen as a major metallurgical centre, supplying not only itself but also neighbouring Britain with bronze and gold artifacts. The origins of metal-working in Ireland were sought on the continent, particularly in Iberia. The various ceramic types generally recovered from cremation burials, for example bowls, vases and urns, were summarised along with their possible foreign relationships and origins. The absence of clear settlement sites and hence solid evidence for domestic ware, coupled with the occasional discovery of presumed funerary wares on sand dunes and other sites, suggested that with the exception of the so-called pygmy cups, many of the types of pottery found in burials may also have served in settlements.[63]

In terms of settlement evidence, there is very little to add to the *A.S.C.D.,* as clear architectural evidence for domestic habitation still remains elusive. The main exception has been the discovery of two circular dwellings (approximately 4 and 7 metres diameter) on the Meadowlands Housing Estate in Downpatrick[64] which broadly conform with other sites of the same period.[65] A Bronze Age date for the site was secured by the considerable remains of Cordoned Urn ware. It is frequently suggested that patterns of settlement shifted from the Neolithic to the Bronze Age,[66] and this is borne out if one accepts the distribution of bronze axes and burials as proxy evidence for settlement location.[67] The relatively dense area of Neolithic settlement suggested by the court tombs of the Mourne-Carlingford uplands, tends to shift to the east Belfast-Comber region during the Early Bronze Age.

The evidence for mortuary practices and their associated ceramics has also remained relatively static, except for the discovery of a major cemetery at Cloughskelt. Here a rescue excavation uncovered twenty-three graves accompanied by bowls and Encrusted Urns, making this one of the largest Bronze Age cemeteries known in Ireland.[68] A single Early Bronze Age burial was excavated near Downpatrick, and this yielded a stone cist that contained the burnt remains of an individual accompanied by a bowl, a bronze knife or dagger, a bronze awl and two flint scrapers.[69]

The structure of Early Bronze Age society as seen through its mortuary evidence was not a topic for discussion in the *A.S.C.D.*, whereas today there have been a number of attempts to make some 'social' sense out of the burials. These have still not progressed very far since the main variables such as disposal types (inhumation, cremation), grave structures (pit, cist), and ceramic types (bowls, vases, urns) not only vary chronologically and regionally but also overlap. That Ulster seems to have preferred bowls over vases compared to Leinster may be valid,[70] but both provinces clearly employed both types of vessels and little can be made of such observations as they are presently constructed. Indeed it is clear from distribution maps that there was an exceptional preference for bipartite vases in north Down, for it is here that the highest single concentration of such vessels in Ireland is found.[71] Although attempts at social reconstruction have been made at some of the larger cemeteries in southern Ireland,[72] the sole county Down cemetery of comparable size has seen only minimal publication.[73]

Identifying Early Bronze Age settlements on the basis of material culture (as opposed to radiocarbon dates) generally depends on the recovery of Early Bronze Age ceramics from a settlement site, for example the Cordoned Urns from the Meadowlands Estate in Downpatrick cited above, or the Irish bowls from the sandhill sites at Ballykinlar and Dundrum.[74] The latter are generally interpreted as indicating seasonal camp sites. The lack of Early Bronze Age settlement sites has already been noted, and it is difficult to resist the conclusion that we are dealing with small scale communities, sometimes equipped with one or two houses, and, possibly, a small enclosure.[75] The problem, nevertheless, is the ceramic residue, since we find ourselves identifying such sites on the basis of what is often presumed to be their mortuary rather than 'table' ware. There is evidence for so-called course flat-rimmed ware on Early Bronze Age settlements, for example at Bayfarm III at Carnlough, county Antrim, but even here some of the ceramics would not be out of place in a grave. And with far more burials than settlements, archaeologists are hardly going to prefer reinterpreting all their structural remains as ritual sites. So what do the various mortuary wares 'mean' on otherwise secular sites?

Alison Sheridan's recent technological analysis of the Irish bowls and vases provides a good starting point for the discussion.[76] Evidence from their manufacture and the petrological analysis of inclusions and clay types suggests that these pots were made locally. The techniques involved and the standard of the vessels suggests that they were produced by specialist or semi-specialist potters. Generally there is very little indication of prior use, at least amongst those found in a funerary context, and hence they 'were probably made specifically as a grave gift'.[77] The most likely secular function would have been as a serving container for food or drink; their size does not suggest storage, while both their manufacture and the absence of diagnostic evidence for burning suggests that they were not employed for cooking.

The question thus arises of what function these so-called funerary wares served on settlement sites. There are several possibilities each with their own attendant problems. If the bowls and vases were solely fine serving ware that was regarded as appropriate also for burial, then the main problem is determining what was employed for cooking. In theory, the large urns may have served this purpose, but given their friability and high levels of decoration this seems unlikely. Moreover, if the bowls and vases were the normal 'table ware', we would certainly expect to find it better represented on the settlement sites than by the occasional sherds which are all that have been discovered. In short, there are very real problems in presuming that such vessels were 'extracted' from the deceased's fine ware for deposition. If, on the other hand, they were made 'for the occasion', then we are left with the incongruous picture of the deceased's relatives casting around for a mortuary vessel potter or vendor to supply them with the necessary vessels on demand. The absence of technological standardisation, according to Sheridan, suggests that the vessels were not produced in bulk, but it is difficult to imagine a potter preparing only single vessels for firing throughout the year.

Another problem is the frequency of fine decoration on the bowls and vases. This suggests that they were prestige ware which, if manufactured solely for the purposes of accompanying or storing the remains of the deceased, could hardly have been given much public exposure. Conceivably, the vessels may have been acquired by their owners or their families prior to their demise and were then prominently displayed in their own dwellings but without other use. Vulnerable to accidental breakage, such vessels would find their way into the settlement record only in small amounts. They would never have occurred in large quantities since their ultimate purpose, as suitable vessels to accompany the deceased, hardly required a surplus.

The Late Bronze Age

In its treatment of the Late Bronze Age (ca. 1200-300 B.C.),[78] the A.S.C.D. devoted most attention to reviewing the technology and typology of bronze artifacts, largely single finds but also occasional hoards, and some of the gold finds. While the authors thought that the presence of the large cauldrons suggested an aristocratic element, 'the picture does not seem to reflect a 'heroic age'. Evidence for settlement was almost entirely confined to an open settlement on top of Cathedral

Hill in Downpatrick around which was a tenuously dated Iron Age enclosure. Burials certainly attributable to the Late Bronze Age were absent.

There have been few Late Bronze Age finds in county Down since the publication of the *A.S.C.D.* Evidence for settlement architecture has not materially increased beyond the possible huts on Cathedral Hill, while a single Late Bronze Age burial from the Ballybeen Housing Estate can now be added to similar cremations elsewhere surrounded by a ring ditch or covered by a barrow.[79] The purely typological discussion engaged in by the authors of the *A.S.C.D.* has been augmented by more theoretical discussions of the meaning of the Bronze Age depositions.[80] The absence of grave goods (along with the graves) occasioned the *A.S.C.D.* to warn that 'this does not necessarily imply a society poorer than that which buried treasure with its dead; it may merely mean a changed outlook'.[81] More recent work has attempted to understand what that 'changed outlook' was. Finds of weapons, for example, have been explained as 'graveless grave goods', reflecting changes in the pattern of deposition whereby items were no longer deposited with a corpse but were expended according to a different ritual pattern. Similarly, the burial of ornaments, especially those of gold, might have been 'gendered' female, reflecting a complimentary pattern of offering.[82] The recent pre-occupation over whether single objects or hoards were deposited on dry land or in bodies of water – the latter regarded as the appropriate venue for ritual offerings – is absent from the *A.S.C.D.*

Ideas over what constituted a 'heroic society' have also changed since the publication of the *A.S.C.D.* The exclusion of county Down from such a society seems to have been a product of the prevailing assumption that a heroic society required hill-fort settlements and abundant evidence of horse gear. The first element was commonly ascribed to the Iron Age (hence the presumption that the Cathedral Hill site served as an Iron Age hill-fort) while the second was well evidenced by the finds of horse-bits, all from the Iron Age. Today, we know that the construction of hill-forts began in the Late Bronze Age, from at least *ca.* 1100 B.C., while the proliferation of weapons, particularly swords, coupled with the quantity of hoards has led others to name this period 'the age of depositions',[83] arguing that it was the archetypical Celtic 'heroic' society.

The Iron Age

The *A.S.C.D.* recognised two periods in the Early Iron Age, an earlier La Tène phase during which the north-east of Ireland adopted art styles and some metal working from continental Europe, and a later Roman

Iron Age beginning after the first century A.D. when Ireland was in contact with and influenced by developments in Roman Britain.[84] To the former period were ascribed the horse-bits, iron swords, and some other items as well as the hill-fort on Cathedral Hill in Downpatrick. This consisted of two phases: a bank and ditch enclosure presumably dating to the Early Iron Age, and a later timber-laced rampart which, because of its parallels with pre-Roman Conquest Britain, was believed to date to this same pre-Roman period. The Roman period was evidenced by a handful of finds, the most prominent being the old discovery at 'Loughey'. This was interpreted as the burial goods of a (Romano-) British woman, although more recent chemical analysis of the goods suggests both native Irish and Continental material.[85]

One of the key problems of settlement archaeology anywhere in Ireland is the lack of evidence for domestic settlement. A survey of Iron Age sites dated by radiocarbon[86] found only three sites in county Down, of which two – Gransha[87] and Tullylish[88] – are more likely to be from the Early Mediaeval period. The third date (180 cal. B.C. – 340 cal. A.D.) derives from the wall slot in one of the hut circles on top of Scrabo Hill (fig. 1.6). This unique site with its series of enclosures and

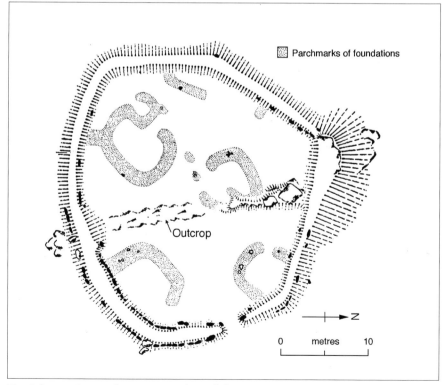

Fig. 1.6   Hut enclosure on Scrabo Hill (Source: *A.S.C.D.*, p. 179).

circular house foundations was attributed to the Early Mediaeval period in the *A.S.C.D.,* and publication of the excavations in the early 1970s has been limited to two brief reports.[89] The site has seen long-term attrition from the neighbouring golf-course, but hinted at a full Iron Age community with few parallels elsewhere in Ireland. The remains of at least one floor-plan of an Iron Age hut were retrieved, and this is one of the very few sites to challenge the impression that the Irish abandoned the manufacture of pottery in the Iron Age. The publication of what has been discovered on this significant site and further attempts to retrieve more information from it are of the first importance in deepening our understanding of Iron Age Ireland.

A second possible settlement was believed to have stood on Cathedral Hill in Downpatrick. The *A.S.C.D.* attributed the earthen ramparts that surround the hill to the Iron Age, as these also included timber revetments. More recent excavations of Cathedral Hill, however, not only failed to find any evidence for the type of (British) Iron Age defences depicted in the *A.S.C.D.*[90] but also argued that the supposed prehistoric defences were in fact the result of Mediaeval landscaping.[91] The chronology of these defences, like so many other aspects of Down's prehistory, is still a matter of dispute.

Conclusion

This chapter has attempted to survey some of the developments that have overtaken the publication of the *Archaeological survey of county Down.* It has ignored, for reasons of space, a large quantity of more recent publications[92] on both the periods and material culture of Irish prehistory in order to concentrate on a few selected aspects. If there is any message to be gained from this survey, it is that no county can ever be regarded as 'completed' either in terms of archaeological survey or of the data required to discuss an ever increasing agenda of archaeological issues. Some of the questions that have been considered apply to any county in Ireland with almost equal validity; others are located more particularly in county Down's geographical situation and physical variability. This is especially true of the Mesolithic and Neolithic issues, and these invite the attention of a new generation of archaeologists.

References
1. *A.S.C.D.*
2. Ibid., p. 2.
3. P. Woodman, *The Mesolithic in Ireland,* B.A.R., lviii (Oxford, 1978).
4. P. Woodman, *Excavations at Mount Sandel 1973-77* (Belfast, 1985).

5. P. Carr, 'An early Mesolithic site near Dundonald, county Down' in *U.J.A.*, xxxxviii (1985), pp 122-3.

6. *Archaeology of Ulster*, pp 12-17.

7. R. McLean, 'An examination of the diet in Ireland during the Mesolithic' (unpublished ms., Dept. of Archaeology, Q.U.B., 1991).

8. R. Brown, *Strangford Lough: the wildlife of an Irish Sea lough* (Belfast, 1990).

9. L.H. Van Wijngaarden-Bakker, 'Faunal remains and the Irish Mesolithic' in C. Bonsall (ed.), *The Mesolithic in Europe* (Edinburgh, 1989), pp 125-133.

10. P.C. Woodman, 'Problems in the colonisation of Ireland' in *U.J.A.*, xxxxix (1986), pp 7-17.

11. P.C. Woodman, 'Excavations at Glendhu, county Down' in *U.J.A.*, xxxxviii(1985), pp 31-40.

12. G. Cooney and E. Grogan, *Irish Prehistory: a social perspective* (Dublin, 1994), pp 21-2.

13. Brown, *Strangford Lough*.

14. *Archaeology of Ulster*, pp 27-8.

15. *A.S.C.D.*, pp 6-21.

16. M. Zvebilil and P. Rowley-Conwy, 'Foragers and farmers in Atlantic Europe', in M. Zvelibil (ed.), *Hunters in transition* (Cambridge, 1986), pp 67-96; M. J. O'Kelly, 'The megalithic tombs of Ireland' in C. Renfrew (ed.), *The Megalithic monuments of Western Europe* (London, 1983), pp 113-126.

17. G. Cooney, 'Irish Neolithic settlement and its European context' in *The Journal of Irish Archaeology*, iv (1987-88), pp 7-11; *Archaeology of Ulster*, pp 30-1; Cooney and Grogan, *Irish Prehistory*, pp 26-33.

18. P.C. Woodman, 'The Irish Mesolithic/Neolithic transition' in S.J. de Laet (ed.), *Acculturation and continuity in Atlantic Europe* (Bruges, 1976), pp 296-309.

19. P.C. Woodman, *pers. comm.*

20. J. Thomas, *Rethinking the Neolithic* (Cambridge, 1991), p. 28.

21. S. Ó Nualláin, 'A neolithic house at Ballyglass near Ballycastle, county Mayo' in *R.S.A.I. Jn.*, cii (1972), pp 49-57.

22. E. Grogan, 'Neolithic settlements' in M. Ryan (ed.), *Irish Archaeology illustrated* (Dublin, 1991), pp 59-63.

23. S. Caulfield, *Céide fields and Belderrig guide* (Killala, 1988).

24. *Archaeology of Ulster*, p. 43.

25. A. Sheridan, 'Pottery production in Neolithic Ireland: a petrological and chemical study' in J. Henderson (ed.), *Scientific analysis in archaeology and its interpretation* (Oxford, 1989), pp 112-135.

26. For example, M. Herity, 'Irish decorated Neolithic pottery' in *R. I.A. Proc.*, lxxxii (1982), pp 247-404.

27. Thomas, *Rethinking*, p. 87.

28. Herity, 'Irish decorated Neolithic pottery'.

29. M. Herity, *Irish Passage Graves* (Dublin, 1974), pp 226-231.

30. R. de Valera, 'The court cairns of Ireland' in *R.I.A. Proc.*, lx (1960), pp 9-140.

31. G. Cooney, 'Body politics and grave messages' in N. Sharples and A. Sheridan (ed.), *Vessels for the ancestors* (Edinburgh, 1992), pp 128-142.

32. Thomas, *Rethinking*, p. 112.

33. M. Herity, 'Finds from Irish court tombs' in *R.I.A. Proc.*, lxxxvii (1987), pp 103-281.

34. Thomas, *Rethinking*, p. 120.

35. *Archaeology of Ulster*, pp 60-1.

36. Cooney, 'Body politics', p. 141.

37. R. McConkey, 'A study of the chambers in the court tombs of Ireland' (unpublished ms., Dept. of Archaeology, Q.U.B., n.d.).

38. C. Renfrew, *Before civilisation* (London, 1973).

39. A. E. P. Collins and D. M. Waterman, *Millin Bay: a late Neolithic cairn in county Down* (Belfast, 1955).

40. Cooney and Grogan, *Irish Prehistory*, pp 69-70.

41. *A.S.C.D.*, pp 87-9.

42. W. Groenman-van Waateringe and J. J. Butler, 'The Ballynoe stone circle: excavations by A. E. van Giffen 1937-1938' in *Palaeohistoria*, xviii (1976), pp 73-110.

43. A. Burl, *The stone circles of the British Isles* (New Haven and London, 1976).

44. H. Lawlor, 'The Giant's Ring' in *Proc. Belfast Natural History and Philosoph. Soc.* (1917-18), pp 13-28.

45. A. E. P. Collins, 'Excavations at the Giant's Ring, Ballynahatty' in *U.J.A.*, xx (1957), pp 44-60.

46. Lawlor, 'The Giant's Ring', p. 21.

47. R. Hicks, 'Some henges and hengiform earthworks in Ireland; form, distribution, astronomical correlations and associated mythology', unpub. Ph.D. thesis, University of Pennsylvania, 1975, p. 70.

48. G. Stout, 'Embanked enclosures of the Boyne region' in *R.I.A. Proc.*, xci, C, (1991), p. 257.

49. Lawlor, 'The Giant's Ring', p. 26.

50. B. Hartwell, 'Ballynahatty – a prehistoric ceremonial centre' in *Archaeology Ireland*, xviii (1991), pp 14-17.

51. Ibid., p. 14.

52. R. McAdam and E. Getty, 'Discovery of an ancient sepulchral chamber' in *U.J.A. (first series)*, iii (1885), p. 358.

53. Thomas, *Rethinking*, p. 40.

54. McAdam and Getty, 'Discovery', p. 364.

55. *Archaeology of Ulster*, p. 76.

56. *Down*, p. 218.

57. B. Hartwell, 'Neolithic ceremonies' in *Archaeology Ireland*, viii, no. 4 (1994), pp 10-13.

58. A. Gibson, 'Excavations at the Sarn-y-Bryn-Caled cursus complex, Welshpool, Powys and the timber circles of Great Britain and Ireland' in *Proc. Prehistoric Society*, lx (1994), pp 143-223.

59. G. Eogan and H. Roche,' A Grooved Ware wooden structure at Knowth, Boyne Valley, Ireland' in *Antiquity*, lxviii (1994), pp 322-30.

60. P. D. Sweetman, 'A late Neolithic/Early Bronze Age pit circle at Newgrange, county Meath' in *R.I.A. Proc.*, lxxxv, C. (1985), pp 195-221.

61. Thomas, *Rethinking*, p. 105.

62. *A.S.C.D.*, pp 24-42.

63. J. Waddell, *The Bronze Age burials of Ireland* (Galway, 1990), p. 5.

64. A. J. Pollock and D. M. Waterman, 'A Bronze Age habitation site at Downpatrick in *U.J.A.*, xxxii (1964), pp 31-58.

65. Cooney and Grogan, *Irish Prehistory*, pp 98-9.

66. *Archaeology of Ulster*, pp 95-6.

67. Cooney and Grogan, *Irish Prehistory*, pp 100-101.

68. L. N. W. Flanagan, 'The composition of Irish Bronze Age cemeteries' in *Irish Archaeological Research Forum*, iii, 2 (1976), pp 7-20.

69. A. E. P. Collins and E. E. Evans, 'A cist burial at Carrickanab, county Down' in *U.J.A.*, xxxi (1968), pp 16-24.

70. Cooney and Grogan, *Irish Prehistory*, pp 113-4.

71. B. Ó Ríordáin and J. Waddell, *The funerary bowls and vases of the Irish Bronze Age* (Galway, 1994), p. 32, fig. 11.

72. C. Mount and P. Hartnett, 'Early Bronze Age cemetery at Edmonstown, county Dublin' in *R.I.A. Proc.*, xciii, C (1993), pp 21-79.

73. Flanagan, 'Composition'.

74. Ó Ríordáin and Waddell, *Funerary Bowls*, pp 101-5.

75. Cooney and Grogan, *Irish Prehistory*, p. 99.

76. A. Sheridan, 'The manufacture, production and use of Irish bowls and vases' in Ó Ríordáin and Waddell, *Funerary Bowls*, pp 45-75.

77. Sheridan, 'Manufacture', p. 71.

78. *A.S.C.D.*, pp 42-52.

79. J. P. Mallory, 'The Long Stone, Ballybeen, Dundonald, county Down' in *U.J.A.*, xlvii (1984), pp 1-4.

80. R. Bradley, *The passage of arms* (Cambridge, 1990).

81. *A.S.C.D.*, p. 51.

82. Cooney and Grogan, *Irish Prehistory*, pp 158-167.

83. J. T. Koch, 'Eriu, Alba and Letha: when was a language ancestral to Gaelic first spoken in Ireland?' in *Emania*, ix (1991), pp 17-37; *Archaeology of Ulster*, pp 115-142.

84. *A.S.C.D.*, pp 53-8.

85. J. Henderson, 'The Iron Age of 'Loughey' and Meare: some inferences from the glass analysis' in *The Antiquaries Journal*, lxvii (1987), pp 29-42.

86. R. B. Warner, J. P. Mallory and M. G. L. Baillie, 'Irish Early Iron Age sites: a provisional map of absolute dated sites' in *Emania*, vii (1990), pp 46-50.

87. C. J. Lynn, 'Excavations on a mound at Gransha, county Down' in *U.J.A.*, xlviii (1985), pp 81-90.

88. R. Ivens, 'The Early Christian monastic enclosure at Tullylish, county Down' in *U.J.A.*, l (1987), pp 55-121.

89. H. Owens, 'Scrabo' in *Exacavations (1970)* p. 9; H. Owens, 'Scrabo' in *Excavations (1971)*, p. 11; see also M. Kemp, 'Scrabo Hill: The Iron Age Hill-fort and Site Catchment Analysis', unpub. B.A. thesis, Dept. of Archaeology, Q.U.B., 1987.

90. *A.S.C.D.*, p. 99.

91. N. Brannon, 'Life and Death at an early monastery' in A. Hamlin and C. J. Lynn (ed.), *Pieces of the past* (Belfast, 1988), pp 61-4.

92. For example, the Iron Age which is represented synthetically in B. Raftery, *Pagan Celtic Ireland* (London, 1994) and in a series of major catalogues by the same author; or, for the Bronze Age, G. Eogan, *Hoards of the Irish Late Bronze Age* (Dublin, 1983). For general artifactual studies, see J. P. Mallory, 'Artifact studies in Northern Ireland' in *Archeomaterials*, vii (1993), pp 57-82.

Plate 1.2   Audleystown court cairn.

Plate 1.3   Ballynoe stone circle.

Chapter 2

FARMING AND FOOD IN MEDIEVAL LECALE

FINBAR McCORMICK

Ireland, generally, is more suitable for livestock rearing than arable farming. Aalen[1] estimated that in modern times only 11 per cent of the farmable land is used for tillage and fruit growing while the remainder is accounted for in pasturage (69 per cent) and hay (20 per cent). In earlier periods farming landscapes dominated by livestock must have been even more significant. The earliest reliable quantification dates to the seventeenth century where William Petty estimated that only about 6.5 per cent of the farmable land was used for tillage.[2] These overall figures, however, disguise local variations and there must have been considerable temporal change in some areas. We know, for instance, that during the thirteenth century extensive areas of land within the Pale and especially in the south east of Ireland were brought into cultivation in the newly established Anglo-Norman estates.[3] Documentary records showing the importance of arable farming during the medieval period are especially good for some areas, such as county Carlow,[4] but we have no detailed records for county Down. It is intended in this essay to consider a district of county Down that may have been dominated by an arable farming economy during the Early Christian and medieval periods. Ironically, animal bones provide much of the evidence for this hypothesis.

Lecale is a geographically distinct peninsula in eastern county Down. It is bordered on the south and east by the Irish sea and to the north by Strangford Lough. Its western landward boundary, between Downpatrick and Dundrum, is partially formed by the now drained, but formerly extensive, Quoile marshlands and the Blackstaff river. Beyond that are the highlands of the Mournes and Slieve Croob. Lecale's ancient name is *Mag Inis* which essentially means 'the island plain', thus again emphasising its geographical distinctiveness. The soils for the most part consist of light-medium loams[5] which are eminently suited for the production of grain, and it presently forms one of the most extensively cultivated areas of Ulster.

This was also the case in the past. The Ordnance Survey memoirs for the area, which date from 1833 to 1837, state that in some parishes, such as Dunsfort and Ballee, there was virtually no grazing and that the land was used almost exclusively for cultivation.[6] The low density of livestock could sometimes lead to a dearth of manure,[7] but in the nineteenth century this was compensated for by the use of marl and lime; limestone for the latter having to be imported from Antrim, the Isle of Man[8] and Carlingford.[9] Arthur Young observed that Lecale was almost completely under grain cultivation during the late eighteenth century.[10] The principal crop was barley with very little flax or potatoes being grown, and Young noted that south Lecale was more fertile than the north. Young's only observation regarding livestock referred to a few sheep being grazed in a way that clearly demonstrated the incidental nature of livestock rearing. The sheep were fastened, by means of a sliding tether, to a rope that was secured at two points along a ditch, thus confining them to grazing along its length.[11]

It is difficult to ascertain whether the medieval economy was predominantly agricultural and, if so, whether it was mainly arable. The area has not been subjected to detailed palynological study, since there is only limited potential for this type of work because of a general absence of suitable sites for taking pollen cores. The Ordnance Survey memoirs for the area indicate that most of the bogs had been cut away by the beginning of the nineteenth century.[12] Certain features, however, tend to imply that there was a great concentration of wealth here during the later medieval period, wealth which probably had its basis in arable agriculture. Lecale contains the largest concentration of tower houses in the north of Ireland. While this could be a reflection of insecurity it could be as easily argued that the lords' ability to afford their construction reflected local political stability and their own assured social status and wealth. Such a suggestion is supported by the physical evidence for medieval trade. The port of Ardglass, as well as containing the remains of four tower houses, also contains what is probably the most extensive complex of merchants' warehouses[13] surviving in Ireland (Plate 2.1). The warehouses were built on the quay and were presumably hired out to visiting traders, as was normally the case in European ports at this time.[14] These buildings may have formed one focus for the important grain export trade which existed in Ireland during the fourteenth and fifteenth centuries.[15]

Settlement
During the early Anglo-Norman period much of Lecale consisted of churchlands,[16] and there is a likelihood that these lands already enjoyed this status during the Early Christian period. The Early Christian landscape of Lecale is characterised by a large number of church sites[17]

Plate 2.1   Newark castle, Ardglass, county Down (Source: F. Grose, *The antiquities of Ireland*, ii (London, 1791), plate 13).

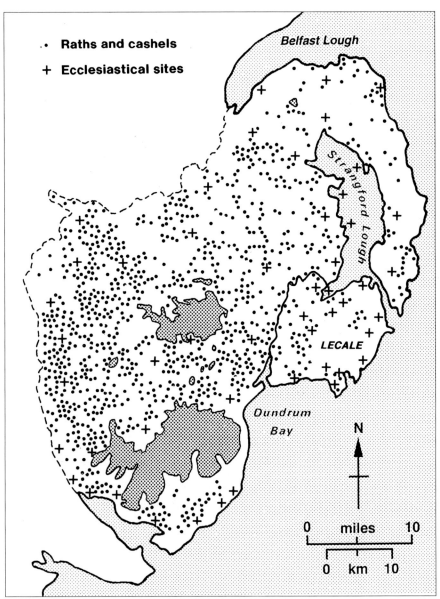

Fig. 2.1   Distribution of ringforts in county Down.

and a relatively small number of ringforts, i.e the scattered farmsteads of the period (fig. 2.1). With the exception of mountainous areas such as the Mournes and Slieve Croob, and large urban areas such as Belfast, the only zone of low ringfort density in the county is in the north east between Strangford and Belfast Loughs, an area which included the major early monasteries of Movilla and Bangor. While the low incidence of ringforts in Lecale might be attributed to destruction owing to intense tillage, it is unlikely that this would account for their low density in the Bangor and Movilla area. It could be the case that in areas where the Church was an extensive land owner, secular ownership was more limited, a situation reflected by a low ringfort density. One could also speculate that monastic settlement and land ownership might have been attracted to Lecale because of the area's potential. In the early Irish Saints' Lives, for instance, farming economies tend to be more arable than livestock based,[18] an observation that tends to support this hypothesis.

A striking feature of the medieval settlement pattern in Lecale was its continuity between the periods before and after the Anglo-Norman colonisation of the late twelfth century. McNeill[19] argues that many of the units of land ownership in the area remained stable during this transition. Continuity of settlement can also be demonstrated from the archaeological record. Ringforts at Castlescreen, Rathmullen and Lismahon were converted into mottes. At Castlescreen, occupation appeared to be continuous between the two periods, with souterrain ware[20] and medieval glazed pottery appearing together in the Phase 3 levels[21] which date to the early thirteenth century. At Rathmullen, too, the excavator could find no clear evidence for abandonment between the Early Christian and Anglo-Norman periods.[22] At Lismahon the question of continuity between the two periods was not considered, but the excavator suggests that the motte phase at the site may represent native rather than Anglo-Norman occupation, and that this was simply imitating 'an English model'.[23] The ringfort at Ballynarry was also heightened at the beginning of the Anglo-Norman period but not into what could be formally described as a motte. Again occupation continued without interruption between the Early Christian and Anglo-Norman periods, with both souterrain ware and glazed pottery being found together during the thirteenth century (Phase 5) levels on the site.[24]

Crannogs, too, seem to display continuity between the two periods.[25] The upper levels of the Lough Faughan crannog, with its stone-wall revetting, also produced a mixture of souterrain ware and twelfth/thirteenth century pottery.[26] The excavator suggested that there was a break in settlement between the earlier and later phases of the site, but the only evidence forwarded for this is unconvincing. Collins argues that the erection of a stone wall indicated ignorance of the crannogs substructural peat-brushwood-timber construction, thus implying 'a prolonged break in occupation'.[27] The drawn sections of the site, however, do not provide any evidence for discontinuity of occupation. The excavated settlement sites in Lecale, therefore, tend to show a strong degree of continuity between the Early Christian and the early Anglo-Norman period. Unlike ringforts in other parts of Ireland, where secondary, medieval archaeological material tends to represent limited activity rather than large scale occupation, the evidence from Lecale settlement sites indicates continued, or intensified, levels of activity during the Anglo-Norman period.[28] In the same way, the main Irish midland crannogs at Ballinderry, Lagore and Moynagh have produced little or no evidence for settlement after the end of the Early Christian period, while significant occupation, including the building of stone structures, continues at Lough Faughan into the Anglo-Norman period.

Agriculture

Our knowledge of early agriculture in the area is dependent on archaeological evidence. Several medieval sites in Lecale have been excavated and a small number of these have produced information concerning its agricultural economy especially through the pioneering faunal work of Margaret Jope. In fact, Lecale contains one of the greatest concentrations of excavated non-urban medieval sites in Ireland, many of which were examined as part of the *Archaeological survey of county Down*. The most important sites to have produced environmental material are Lough Faughan crannog,[29] Rathmullen rath and motte[30] and the motte and bailey at Clough.[31] In addition, nearby sites such as Ballyfounder rath[32] at the southern end of the Ards peninsula, and Greencastle Castle[33] on the north-eastern shores of Carlingford Lough, have also provided much useful environmental data. Other Lecale sites, such as Castlescreen rath and motte, Lismahon motte and Dundrum castle[34] have produced artifactual evidence for agricultural activity.

Most of these sites show evidence for both animal husbandry and arable farming. In the case of husbandry, direct evidence is provided by the presence of animal bones. The evidence for tillage is usually, although not always, less direct. Lough Faughan produced the charred remains of oats and barley,[35] predominantly oats, but at other sites tillage is only indirectly attested by the presence of quernstones,[36] millstones[37] or ploughshares.[38]

It is impossible to ascertain the relative importance of livestock and arable farming on the basis of the material retrieved from archaeological excavations. It is not feasible to quantify the relative importance of animal bone and charred cereal remains. Certain aspects of the animal bone assemblages, however, suggest that cereal production was much more important in Lecale than in other areas. The distribution of the minimum number of individuals[39] of the main meat producing animals from a series of sites in Lecale and its vicinity is shown in table 2.1. The data is shown diagrammatically in fig. 2.2:a-c.

TABLE 2.1

Minimum number of individuals (MNI) distribution of main species from different sites

Site	Phase	Approx date	Cattle	Sheep[40]	Pigs	MNI total
Lecale			%	%	%	
Rathmullen	1	6-8th C	36	48	16	25
	2	Pre 9th C	31	17	52	65
	3/4	9-12th C	29	15	56	28
	5	Early 13th C	27	27	46	26
Lough Faughan		Early Christian	70	9	21	76
		13th C	66	7	27	74
Clough Castle	1	Early 13th C	27	12	61	92
Non-Lecale						
Ballyfounder	Primary	Early Christian	60	12	28	25
Greencastle	1	13th C	56	21	23	57
	2	14-15th C	43	36	21	107

The most comprehensive recent excavations in the area have been at Rathmullen, a raised rath located in the rich southern part of Lecale. During the thirteenth century the rath was converted to a motte, which in turn was replaced by a towerhouse, some 45 m. north of the motte known as Russell's castle. The distribution of the species on the site during the Early Christian period is exceptional for a rural site. During phases 2-4 pigs account for 52-56 per cent of the main three species present. The highest incidence of pigs on any other rural Early Christian period site is at Moynagh crannog, county Meath, where they accounted for 37 per cent of MNI of the same species.[41]

A high incidence of pigs in an assemblage can sometimes be attributed to extensive forest which can provide mast. Oak mast played a very important role in the diet of pigs, so much so that the *Annals of the Four Masters* notes that it was sold as a cash crop in Armagh in 1031 and 1097. High numbers of pigs, for example, are a feature of early Neolithic Britain when forests were much more widespread than during later periods.[42] In the context of Rathmullen, however, the uniquely high incidence of pigs is most likely to be the result of ample grain resources and the limited availability of grazing land. Pigs, unlike sheep or cattle, do not thrive on grassland, but being omnivorous prefer the food consumed by humans, especially grain.[43] It is extremely unlikely that Lecale was more wooded than other areas of Ireland at this time, so a surfeit of mast is unlikely to account for the high pig values. Pig numbers, however, can be adequately explained within the context of an area producing a large grain surplus with limited

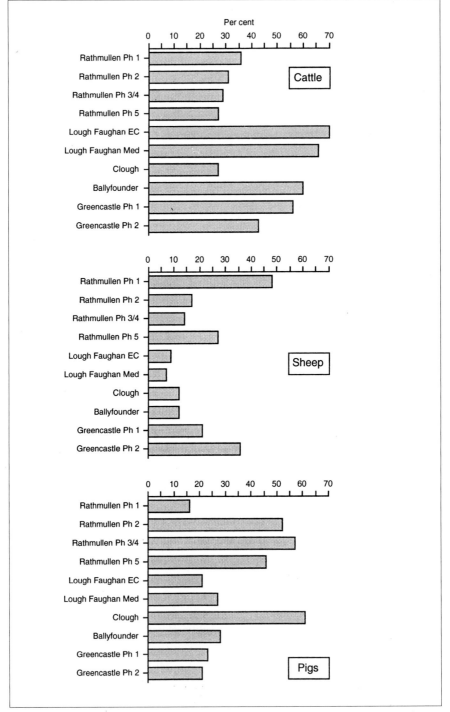

Fig. 2.2a-c   Percentage distribution of minimum number of individuals (MNI) of main
meat-producing animals on archaeological sites in Lecale and vicinity.

availability of land for livestock grazing.[44] This dominance continues at Rathmullen into the Norman period, albeit at a slightly reduced rate, whereas at Clough castle the incidence of pigs remained as high as 61 per cent during the early thirteenth century.[45]

The importance of cereals in medieval Lecale is also suggested by other aspects of the archaeological record. The thirteenth-century levels at Rathmullen produced two large worn millstones apparently from a vertically wheeled mill,[46] thus implying the large-scale processing of grain. Millstones of this size are not known from any other Irish sites. Unique too is the presence in thirteenth-century levels at Ballynarry ringfort of what is probably the only known stone-lined grain storage pit in Ireland.[47] The pit is roughly circular in shape and 2.4 m deep and was dug into the deposits of a raised rath without penetrating the natural horizons. Thus dryness was ensured by keeping the bottom of the pit above the local watertable.

Not all the archaeological sites in Lecale provide an animal bone assemblage that reflects a landscape dominated by arable farming. The extremely high incidence of cattle (71 per cent) in the Early Christian levels at Lough Faughan crannog is only matched by one of the phases at Lagore crannog, which has a value of 71 per cent.[48] Is it possible that the crannog at Lough Faughan was a royal site, and that the high incidence of cattle represents the traditional expression of wealth and status in terms of cattle ownership, or else tribute, in the form of cattle, being brought to the site?

The high incidence of sheep during Phase 1 (sixth-eighth century) at Rathmullen is also enigmatic. On some sites such as Moynagh crannog and Knowth, both in county Meath, the evidence suggests an increase in sheep rearing towards the later phases of the Early Christian settlement. This might imply growth in wool production, perhaps stimulated by Scandinavian trade, but at Rathmullen the early date of Phase 1 precludes such an explanation. Again, it may simply be that the high incidence of sheep is yet another facet of the importance of cereal growing in the area. There has long been a direct association between sheep rearing and cereal cultivation because the dung of sheep is more fertile than that of the other main domesticates. It is, for instance, richer in nitrogen, potassium and phosphorus than cattle dung.[49] Thus when there has been an expansion of arable farming, there is often a corresponding increase in sheep rearing as, for instance, in the case of Iron Age England.[50] In Ireland, an example of the direct association between sheep rearing and cereal production can be seen on the duke of Norfolk's estates in the south of the country during the late-thirteenth century. In that instance the tenants were obliged to fold their sheep on the stubble of demesne land thus depriving their own land of enrichment from sheep manure,[51] a situation that gave rise to much dispute.

Dietary change

The animal bones from Lecale and other county Down excavations show a marked change in meat diet between the native Early Christian inhabitants and the Anglo-Normans. The Irish of the Early Christian period were extremely conservative eaters. At Lough Faughan they were almost exclusively dependent on the flesh of cattle, sheep and pig, the only variety in the diet was provided by the very occasional consumption of venison, domestic chicken and seafish, probably cod.[52] The faunal remains from the site suggest that its inhabitants' diet underwent no development or change during the thirteenth century. A similarly unadventurous diet was represented in the Early Christian levels at Ballyfounder rath, although in that instance it was supplemented by marine molluscs such as limpets, winkles and dog whelks.[53]

In contrast, the meat diet of the Anglo-Normans residing at Clough castle indicated a much more varied approach to culinary matters.[54] Hundreds of fish bones were present; they were mostly of cod but other species have been tentatively identified as perch,[55] wrasse and haddock. In addition to this, salmon were noted in the Anglo-Norman levels at Rathmullen, while angler fish (monkfish) were noted at Greencastle castle.[56] A greater variety of mammals in the Anglo-Norman diet was made possible by the introduction of rabbits,[57] which are recorded along with hare, at both Rathmullen and Clough. It is in respect of fowl, however, that the greatest change is seen. In Early Christian contexts on Lecale sites, the only fowl represented are domesticated chicken and, at Rathmullen, goose. As well as these species the Anglo-Norman levels at Rathmullen produced pigeon, crow, gull and duck. At Clough the presence of some 219 bird bones indicated their increased importance in the Anglo-Norman diet. The majority were of domesticated chicken and goose but also included were grey lag, pink footed, white fronted, barnacle and the now rare bean goose. All these could have been captured in the nearby inner Dundrum Bay. In addition to this, the remains of duck, pigeon, crane, blackbird, white-tailed eagle and buzzard were also found. The last two were probably killed as vermin rather than as a source of food.

Conclusion

Lecale is a geographically separate area in east Down bordered on three sides by the sea. It is characterised by light fertile soils which makes it one of the most favoured areas for arable farming in Ulster.

Indirect evidence also suggests that arable farming, as opposed to livestock rearing, dominated the rural economy during the medieval period. The Early Christian settlement pattern is striking because of the large number of church sites and relatively few ringforts, and in the early Anglo-Norman period we know that much of the area consisted of churchlands. It can be suggested that the Church deliberately acquired and maintained land in the area in order to exploit its particular arable qualities.

By the fifteenth century most of the land had passed from ecclesiastical to secular ownership, and the large concentration of tower-houses, unparalleled elsewhere in Ulster, may be related to the formation of new lordships based on the agrarian resources of the area. In the eighteenth century, grain was exported from Lecale to many parts of Britain and Ireland, and the extensive towerhouses and warehouses in the port of Ardglass may indicate similar trade patterns during the medieval period.

Examination of faunal remains from Early Christian and Anglo-Norman sites in the area contrast strongly with those noted elsewhere in Ireland, and it seems likely that these suggest, albeit indirectly, an arable basis to the local agricultural economy. Unique archaeological discoveries, such as early vertical millwheels and large stone lined storage pits, again emphasise the local importance of grain production in Lecale. Its isolated location and specialised agriculture have clearly affected past settlement patterns. Finally, the animal bones from excavated sites have shown that in Lecale, the Anglo-Normans enjoyed a much more varied meat diet than the native population of the Early Christian period.

References

1   F.H.A. Aalen, *Man and the landscape in Ireland* (London, 1978), p. 210.

2   C.H. Hull (ed.) *The economic writings of Sir William Petty together with observations upon the bills of morality, more probably by Captain John Graunt*, 2 vols. (Cambridge, 1899) i, pp 179-89.

3   K. Down, 'Colonial society and economy in the high middle ages' in A. Cosgrove (ed.), *A new history of Ireland, ii, medieval Ireland 1169-1534* (Oxford, 1987), pp 459-03.

4   Ibid.

5.   R. H. Buchanan, The barony of Lecale, Unpub. Ph.D. thesis, Q.U.B. (1958).

6.   A. Day and P. McWilliams (ed.), *Ordnance survey memoirs of Ireland: parishes of Down, iv* (Belfast, 1992), pp 19, 70.

7.   Ibid., p. 22.

8.   Ibid., p. 18.

9.   Arthur Young, *A Tour in Ireland 1776-1779* (Dublin, 1780), p. 198.

10.   Ibid., pp 196-201.

11. Ibid., p. 201.

12. Day and McWilliams, *Parishes of Down, iv*, pp 15, 25, 38, 67, 97.

13. *A.S.C.D.*, pp 220-2.

14. *Archaeology of Ulster*, p. 287.

15. T. O'Neill, *Merchants and mariners in Ireland* (Dublin, 1987), p. 21.

16. T. E. McNeill, *Anglo-Norman Ulster* (Edinburgh, 1987), pp 89-90.

17. Ann Hamlin notes the following Early Christian sites in Lecale based on historical and/or archaeological evidence: Ardtole, Ballyorgan, Bright, Down(patrick), Kilclief, Knockavalley, Raholf, Saul, St. John's Point, Templecormac and Tyrella, while Maghera and Seaforde(?) lie near its western boundary. A. Hamlin, The archaeology of early Christianity in the north of Ireland, Unpub. Ph.D. thesis, Q.U.B. (1976), pp 597-692. See also chapter 3 in this volume.

18. M. Stout, Early Christian Ireland: settlement and environment (forthcoming).

19. McNeill, *Ulster*, p. 89.

20. A coarse unglazed native ware dating from the eighth century onwards.

21. C. W. Dickinson and D. M. Waterman, 'Excavation of a rath and motte at Castlescreen, county Down' in *U. J. A.*, xxii, third series (1959), pp 67-82.

22. C. J. Lynn, 'The excavation of Rathmullen, a raised rath and motte in county Down' in *U. J. A.*, xliv and xlv, third series (1981-82), pp 95-6.

23. D. M. Waterman, 'Excavations at Lismahon, county Down' in *Medieval archaeology*, iii (1959), pp 166-68.

24. B. K. Davison, 'Excavations at Ballynarry rath, county Down' in *U. J. A.*, xxiv and xxv, third series (1961-62), pp 39-87.

25. A crannog is an artificial, or semi-artificial island settlement site. Its origins date back to the Bronze Age but most are of Early Christian date.

26. A. E. P. Collins, 'Excavations in Lough Faughan crannog, county Down' in *U. J. A.*, xviii, third series (1955), pp 45-82.

27. Ibid., p. 55.

28. At Lough Faughan, for instance, the quantity of animal bones from the upper habitation levels that contained medieval material is nearly as great as that from the Early Christian habitation levels. Ibid., pp 77-81.

29. M. Jope, 'The animal remains' in Collins, 'Lough Faughan Crannog', pp 77-81.

30. C. Collins, 'Report on the osteological material from the excavations at Rathmullen, county Down' in Lynn, 'Rathmullen', pp 156-63.

31. M. Jope, 'Animal remains from Clough Castle' in D. M. Waterman, 'Excavations at Clough Castle, county Down' in *U. J. A.*, xxi, third series (1954), pp 150-6.

32. M. Jope, 'Animal remains from Ballyfounder rath' in D. M. Waterman, 'Excavations at Ballyfounder rath' in *U. J. A.*, xxi, third series (1958), pp 52-4.

33. M. Jope, 'Report on animal bones from Greencastle, county Down' in D. M. Waterman and A. E. P. Collins, 'Excavations at Greencastle, county Down 1951' in *U. J. A.*, xv, third series (1952), pp 101-2.

34. D. M. Waterman, 'Excavations at Dundrum castle 1950' in *U. J. A.*, xiv, third series (1951), pp 15-20.

35. M. E. S. Morrison, 'Carbonised grain from Lough Faughan crannog' in Collins, 'Lough Faughan crannog', pp 75-6.

36. Lough Faughan, Castlescreen, Rathmullen, Ballyfounder, Lismahon and Clough.

37. Rathmullen.

38. Ballyfounder and Dundrum.

39. The minimum number of individuals (MNI) is a method of quantifying animal bones from archaeological sites. It strives to estimate the minimum number of animals of each species that was killed in order to account for the distribution of

bones on a given site. The methods of estimating this value range from the simple (based on counting the left and right bones of each skeletal part) to the complicated (the same but fine tuning the estimation by taking into account the age, size of the animals and location of the bone). At its most extreme one could argue that each bone of each species comes from a different individual so that the total fragments value for each species equals the MNI value. Different – unspecified – methods have been used in the evaluation of the data in table 2.1, but as the aim of all the bone specialists involved was the same (i.e. calculating the MNI) the data from the individual sites should be broadly comparable.

40. Sheep and goat bones are difficult to distinguish and while it is known that goat were present in small numbers on some of the sites it is assumed that the great majority of the caprovine remains in the present instances are of sheep.

41. F. McCormick, 'The effect of the Anglo-Norman settlement on Ireland's wild and domesticated fauna' in P. J. Crabtree and K. Ryan (ed.), *Animal use and cultural change, MASCA research papers in Science and archaeology*, supplement to viii (1991), pp 40-52. Note: the values for pig and sheep for Clough in table 3 of that article were inadvertently transposed.

42. C. Grigson in I. Simmons and M. Tooley (ed.), *The environment in British prehistory* (London, 1981), p. 198.

43. The only other Irish medieval site to have produced a high incidence of pigs (55 per cent of MNI) is in an urban context in the Scandinavian levels at Dublin (McCormick, 'Effect', p. 43). In that instance they were probably being bred within the town and reared on table waste and other forms of slops and refuse. Evidence for urban pig rearing was provided by the presence of a pig pen in a tenth/eleventh century context at Fishamble Street.

44. The importance of pigs in the Lecale agricultural economy is evidenced by the unique corbelled pig houses of the area. R. H. Buchanan, 'Corbelled structures in Lecale, county Down' in *U. J. A.*, xix, third series (1956), pp 92-112.

45. Elsewhere (McCormick, 'Effects', p. 48), it is suggested that the high incidence of pigs at Clough represented garrison food, but as the site was essentially the equivalent of a manor farm rather than a garrisoned castle the present interpretation is more likely. That pork was an important garrison food is indisputable. The Pipe Roll of John for 1211-12 (*U. J. A.*, 1941) indicates that 160 pigs compared with only 15 cows, were sent to the garrison at Dundrum near Clough.

46. Lynn, 'Rathmullen', pp 115, 136-7. The smaller quern stones found on Early Christian and Anglo-Norman sites are all of Mourne granite but the Rathmullen millstones were probably of Scrabo sandstone quarried some 35 km north of the site. Medieval quarries at Scrabo also produced grave slabs several of which were found in Lecale. See McNeill, *Ulster*, pp 44-45 and chapter 5 in this volume.

47. Davison, 'Ballynarry', pp 48-9.

48. McCormick, 'Effects', p. 43.

49. D. K. White, *Roman farming* (London, 1970), pp 127-8.

50. B. Cunliffe, *Iron Age communities in Britain* (London, 1978), p. 184.

51. Down, 'Colonial society', p. 473.

52. Jope in Collins, 'Lough Faughan crannog', pp 79-81. The 'cod' was represented by a single bone.

53. Marine molluscs were consumed on most Lecale sites that were located near the shore. The shells from Rathmullen indicated no change in their role in the diet between the Early Christian and Anglo-Norman periods. Other sites in Ireland, however, have shown that it was only during the latter period that marine shells

and marine fish began to be transported to inland parts of Ireland. See McCormick, 'Effects', p. 50.

54.   Jope, 'Animal remains' in Waterman, 'Clough Castle', pp 150-6.

55.   If this perch *(Percha fluviatilis)* is correct it is the earliest recorded incidence of this freshwater species in Ireland and suggests that it was introduced during the early years of the Norman settlement.

56.   Jope, 'Animal bones' in Waterman and Collins, 'Greencastle', pp 101-126.

57.   The placename 'Coney Island' near Ardglass attests to the former presence of rabbit warrens in the area, while a 'pillow mound', i.e. an artificial mound built to facilitate rabbit breeding, has recently been identified on a small island in southern Strangford Lough.

Chapter 3

THE EARLY CHURCH IN COUNTY DOWN TO THE TWELFTH CENTURY

ANN HAMLIN

This chapter aims to trace the development of the Church in county Down from its origins in the fifth century, if not earlier, to the eve of the important changes of the twelfth century. It examines the complementary contributions of written sources and archaeology in building up this picture. The first section looks at the obscure early period of conversion and first missionary activity before the great plague of 549. A study of the development of the Church in the county from the mid-sixth to the early ninth century looks in detail at Movilla and Bangor and reviews the written and archaeological evidence for activity at other church sites in this period. The sometimes spectacular but limited impact of the Vikings on county Down churches is traced and the increasing amount of archaeological evidence for the Church after about 800 is outlined. Finally the state of the Church in the county on the eve of the twelfth-century reforms is examined, as well as the prospects for progress in this study in the future.

The beginnings to the plague of 549

Nothing is known with any certainty about how Christianity first came to county Down; indeed Richard Sharpe has claimed that 'how Ireland was converted to christianity is wholly obscure'.[1] The strongest traditions of pre-Patrician Christianity are in Leinster, with hints in north Connacht, but for north-east Ulster we can recall the late Roman Church in the Carlisle area and the evidence for early Christianity in Galloway, especially at Whithorn and Kirkmadrine.[2] The opportunities for contact between Ireland and Roman Britain were many and varied. They included trade, the taking of slaves, piracy, mercenary service, seeking refuge, marriage and gift-giving.[3] There were therefore many routes by which the people of north-east Ulster could have come into contact with Christians in nearby northern Britain, both before and after the time of St. Patrick's mission in the fifth century.

St. Patrick mentions only one place-name in his own writings: *Silva Focluti,* the wood of Foclut, not certainly identified but perhaps in county Mayo. The first attempt to place his work in a topographical setting is by his two hagiographers. Tírechán and Muirchú, two hundred years later, in the second half of the seventh century. In Tírechán's account, Patrick is active mainly in Connacht, but county Down features in Muirchú's work. Patrick arrived by boat at *Inber Slane,* went inland and preached to Díchu, a pagan, who 'lived in the place where there is now the barn named after Patrick' (Saul).[4] Later Muirchú emphasises that Patrick 'favoured and loved the district' [*Mag Inis:* Lecale], and the faith began to spread there.[5] Muirchú's account of Patrick's last days clearly reflects rivalry between the Downpatrick area and Armagh. When he felt death approaching, Patrick set out for Armagh, 'the place he loved more than any other', but he was stopped by the angel Victor and directed back 'to the place from which you come (that is, to Saul)', and he received the last sacrament from the hands of Bishop Tassach,[6] whose church was at Raholp, close to Saul. Muirchú claims that Patrick was buried at *Dún Lethglaisse* (Downpatrick), but the additions to Tírechán's text give Saul as his burial place ('*Sabul Patricii,* in the church near the sea') at one point, and elsewhere admit 'nobody knows where his bones rest'.[7]

These hagiographical texts tell us a great deal about the seventh century but little or nothing about the fifth century. It is clear that in the seventh century there were strong traditions of a missionary saint – Patrick – in Lecale, and especially in the Downpatrick area, two centuries earlier. So strong were these traditions that even powerful Armagh was never able to claim St. Patrick's burial.

The earliest conversion period is very obscure, mainly because there are very few reliable written sources. Entries in the annal collections are not considered to be reliable, although recent work on 'computistics' is leading to some reassessment of their accuracy.[8] It does seem clear that the plague which affected Ireland in 549 – the 'great mortality' of the Annals of Ulster – served to interrupt oral tradition seriously, at a time when the passing on of information by word of mouth must still have been very important. This break in tradition would go a long way towards explaining how little we know from written sources about the earliest missionaries.

It is worth considering briefly, in the light of recent historical research, how the earliest conversions may have been carried out. The initial effort must have been very localised, with a strong emphasis on pastoral missionary work. Royal patronage was important, and several of the earliest bishops' churches were close to important royal centres. The clearest example in county Down is Downpatrick: the death of a bishop of *Druim Lethglaise* is recorded in the Annals of Ulster in 584. The saint associated with Nendrum, Mochaoi, may have been a fifth-century missionary, engaged in pastoral work in the Strangford Lough area. The story of his 150-year sleep[9] suggests a break in tradition between the later fifth century (Mochaoi's death is reported in the 490s) and the seventh century, when the church at Nendrum emerges in written sources. What the nature of his base was, and whether it was on the later site, will be difficult to establish, but an early (sixth-century) radiocarbon date was secured from a small excavation in the outer cashel in 1979.[10]

Deirdre Flanagan suggested that place-names with the element *domnach* – church – related 'to the first phase of Christianity in Ireland and [the element] appears to have fallen into disuse by the seventh century'.[11] Donaghmore, near Newry, is of particular interest because it can be argued that this site, and others of the same name (meaning the big or great church), were early missionary bases, 'mother-churches', centres for evangelising an area.[12] Donaghmore, was the 'great church' of *Mágh Cobha,* the plain which gave its name to the Uí Echach Cobo, one of the three ruling dynasties of the Ulaid. Its patron Erc is styled 'bishop' in the Martyrology of Tallaght, and the 'Litany of Irish Saints' remembers 'seven holy bishops of *Domnach Mór Maigi Coba'*.[13] Although Dromore emerged later in the Early Christian period as the chief church of the Uí Echach Cobo, Donaghmore probably retained its high status as the main early missionary centre in the area. *Domnach Combair* of the (possibly) tenth-century Tripartite Life of Patrick can reasonably be associated with Comber in county Down, although in a later source it is called *Cell Chomair.* Perhaps Comber was also an early missionary base. In the cases of Donaghadee and Donaghcloney the position is far less clear because both appear first as parish churches in the early fourteenth-century papal taxation. We are left with Deirdre Flanagan's conclusion that 'it follows that O.S. *donagh*-names, whether or not they have early documentation, can be dated to [the first phase of Christianity in Ireland]'.[14]

Developments from 550 to the ninth century

After the hiatus caused by the plague of 549 we can have more confidence in the evidence of written sources, whose number increases markedly from the mid-seventh century onwards. The second half of the sixth century saw the emergence of two of county Down's most important ecclesiastical sites, at Movilla and Bangor.

Movilla's name *(Mag-bile)* suggests that it may occupy the site of a sacred tree, perhaps the focus of a pre-Christian tree cult.[15] The church's founder, Finnian, was traditionally a member of the royal family of the Dál Fiatach, one of the three groups from which the kings of the Ulaid were chosen. He died in 579 and is styled 'bishop' in the annals and calendars. It is likely that the church originated as the seat of a bishop for the Dál Fiatach in the sixth century. The name Finnian (Vinnian) is common and it is not always clear which saint is intended in written sources, but Columba may have studied with Finnian of Movilla. Finnian may have brought the Vulgate text of the Bible into Ireland, and he may have written the earliest Irish penitential, the Penitential of Vinnian.[16] There are other indications that Movilla was a centre of scholarship. Crónán of Movilla, who died in 650, was probably one of the Irish churchmen to whom pope-elect John wrote about the observance of Easter in 640.[17] A hymn invoking St. Michael, described by Kenney as 'a fine example of Hiberno-Latin versification', was probably written by Colmán mac Murchon, abbot of Movilla, who died in 736.[18] So, although no Movilla scribe is mentioned in the annals, it clearly was a centre of scholarly activity in this period.

What was the nature of the establishment at Movilla in the period before 800? Many Movilla clergy are listed in the annals and calendars, including six bishops after Finnian, three of them in the seventh century and three undated. After 731 only abbots appear. The writer of the Latin Life of Comgall of Bangor used the Latin word *civitas* in referring to Movilla, and this is used of major ecclesiastical settlements.[19] It is likely that Movilla was a large, complex establishment, embracing several different functions. It had high status as chief church of the Dál Fiatach and of the Ulaid, and was the base for a bishop. There may have been domestic accommodation for the Dál Fiatach kings on their travels as well as for their bishop, and perhaps a graveyard for the royal kindred. There was clearly also a community of monks under an abbot, and in this milieu scholarship flourished. A late calendar lists Cú Bretan, anchorite of Movilla, on 17 October,[20] so there may at times have been somewhere on the site set aside for those wishing to pursue a particularly strict regime. Excavation in 1980 and 1981 produced evidence of craft activity – work in iron, bronze and glass – although it could not be dated closely within the Early Christian period. There were indications that this craft area was towards the edge of the settlement.[21]

With the exception of Armagh, Bangor is the best documented early church in Ulster. It was founded in the decade after the plague of 549, in 555 or 559, by St. Comgall who died in 601 or 602. Comgall was of the south Antrim Dál nAraidi group, traditionally from the Magheramorne area. Bangor was the chief church of the Dál nAraidi, just as Movilla was of the Dál Fiatach, until the political changes of the later ninth century. Bangor looked north and had close links with the church at Antrim and the monastery at Camus on the River Bann, south of Coleraine, known as *Cammas Comgaill*.[22]

The written sources for the early history of Bangor are remarkably good, at a time when the Irish written record is still generally thin, so that it is possible to suggest with some confidence what the nature of the establishment was in the sixth and seventh centuries. Clearly from its foundation Bangor was a monastery, a community of monks living according to a rule, under an abbot. It is also certain that a wide and scholarly literary culture flourished in the monastery.

The Antiphonary of Bangor, a manuscript compiled by several different scribes round about 700, survives in the Biblioteca Ambrosiana, Milan. It has been described as 'a liturgical commonplace book for the Office',[23] and it contains canticles and hymns, collects for the Office, and prayers, collects and antiphons. One hymn praises the rule of Bangor, *'Benchuir bona regula'*, and refers to the monastic 'family' *(muintir)* of Bangor. Another hymn commemorates the first fifteen abbots, from Comgall to Crónán, who died in 691. Other material in the Antiphonary demonstrates acquaintance with an impressive range of sources, an interest in metrical composition, and stylistic virtuosity.[24] Three scribes of Bangor are recorded in eighth-century annals, more than for any other Irish house,[25] and Robin Flower suggested that Bangor was an early centre of historical studies (including perhaps annal-writing) and vernacular literatures.[26] Bangor was clearly interested in the computus, the way of working out the date of Easter. The fourth abbot of Bangor, Sillán, 'was the first of the Irish who learned the *computus* by heart from a certain Greek' about 600,[27] and one of the northern churchmen to whom Pope-elect John wrote about Easter in 640 may have been Báeithín, abbot of Bangor.[28]

Bangor's situation, close to the sea, was important in encouraging contacts with areas outside Ireland. Comgall was one of the 'four holy founders of monasteries' who crossed from Ireland to visit Columba on Iona, according to Adomnán Life of Columba.[29] Columbanus, a monk of Bangor, left about 590 to become a missionary exile, travelling first to France and later to northern Italy. Although he claimed to be *micrologus,* one of little eloquence, he was a prolific writer, argumentative, stubborn and eloquent. His 'Rule of the Monks' was probably based on the strict Rule of Bangor, adapted for his Continental foundations, and his Penitential lays down penalties for infringements of the Rule and other sins. These sources point to a strict regime, regulated down to the smallest details.[30] The Easter question is one of the subjects of Columbanus's letters, and he is a staunch supporter of 'the tradition of my native land....for the celebration of Easter', against the practices he found on the Continent.[31] A later traveller by sea from Bangor was Mael Ruba who founded the church at Applecross in western Scotland in 673.[32] It is tempting to imagine that the Old Irish poem, probably of the ninth century, about a blackbird singing across Belfast Lough was written at Bangor, by a monk looking out to sea.[33]

No archaeological remains are known from this early period at Bangor, but there are a few pointers in the annals.[34] There was a fire in 616, a reminder that all the buildings in the early monastery would have been made of timber or other perishable materials. A strange entry in 753 records the washing up of a whale on the county Down coast. It was found to have three gold teeth, each weighing fifty ounces, and one was placed on the altar at Bangor. Bangor was burned again in 756, on St. Patrick's Day. Despite such setbacks, there is every reason to imagine Bangor as a large monastery by 800, with a high reputation for austere observance and accomplished scholarship, and with daughter-houses and widespread possessions. A ninth-century litany of Irish saints lists 'four thousand monks with the grace of God under the yoke of Comgall of Bangor'.[35] This total probably includes linked foundations but it points to a sizable monastic settlement at Bangor. There is a record of a grant of land in Leinster to Bangor[36] and the Life of St Find-chú of Brí-Gobann suggests a link with Munster,[37] so the monastery's interests extended not only to south Antrim but also far beyond.

The *Triads of Ireland,* written in the ninth century, bestow the following epithets on churches:

> The Head of Ireland – Armagh
> The Seniority of Ireland – Bangor
> The Charity of Ireland – Downpatrick
> The Stability of Ireland – Movilla.[38]

Fiacc's *Hymn* of the eighth century acknowledges the importance of Armagh but also notes the importance of Down: 'In Armagh there is the kingdom: it long ago deserted Emain; a great church is *Dún Leth-glasse:* that Tara is a waste is not pleasant to me'.[39]

Downpatrick (*Dún dá Lethglass* or *Dún Lethglaisi*) is thought to have been the secular headquarters of the ruling dynasty of the Ulaid, the Dál Fiatach.[40] The earliest reference to a cleric in connection with Downpatrick is in 584, when Fergus, bishop of Druim Lethglaise, died. It is unlikely to be a coincidence that a bishop appears in the annals just after the reign of Báetán mac Cairill (572-581) of Dál Fiatach, whom Byrne calls 'one of the most notable of Ulster kings'.[41] For the seventh century we have only the tradition that Patrick was buried in Downpatrick which indicates a cult centre of some kind.

Downpatrick comes into prominence in the annals in the middle of the eighth century, when the deaths of abbots and other clergy begin to be recorded. Byrne suggests that a monastery was founded in the eighth century, 'mainly for dynastic reasons', during the reign of Fiachnae mac Áedo Róin (759-789) or his father. As the centre of Dál Fiatach political power moved north, away from Downpatrick to Duneight by the ninth century, the royal family maintained its control over the prestigious ancient site by providing abbots for the monastery.[42] Recent archaeological excavations on Cathedral Hill in Downpatrick have been very rewarding, revealing a deep enclosing ditch, an Early Christian cemetery, and prolific finds.[43] As work on publication progresses, it will be interesting to see whether the eighth century will emerge as a start-date, or whether any features or finds can be dated to an earlier period.

The development of the early Church in Ireland was intimately bound up with secular history and dynastic fortunes.[44] When written sources are available the links can be traced with some confidence, as for Downpatrick, but in some cases there are indications that early history has been suppressed,[45] and in others we can only suggest possibilities. A minor branch of the Dál Fiatach, the Uí Echach Arda, ruled the Ards peninsula.[46] Where was their power-base? The map of raths and cashels in *An archaeological survey of county Down*, figure 72.1, shows that raths are not particularly common in the Ards peninsula. There is, however, a small concentration in the south, with one prominent, hilltop outlier, Tara Fort, which overlooks Millin Bay.[47] Tara is mentioned in *Mesca Ulad*, one of the tales of the Ulster Cycle, and it is tempting to see it as an early royal site. Tara Fort has not been excavated, but the finding of a sherd of imported pottery (E-ware) at nearby Ballyfounder Rath suggests activity there by about 700.[48]

If Tara *was* the chief seat of the Uí Echach Arda, it is not clear which was their chief church. Local names seem to preserve the name of a saint, Cú Mhaighe (Templecowey Point and St. Cooey's Wells), but he cannot be identified in early sources.[49] Excavation at Derry churches, north of Portaferry, indicated activity there in the pre-800 period. The earliest datable find was a buckle decorated with enamel and millefiori glass of the seventh to eighth century.[50] A female saint, Cumman, is listed in the two early ninth-century calendars at 29 May, but only located to Derry in the Ards in later glosses (additions to the text).[51] Genealogies claim that Cumman was a descendant of Echu Gunnat, from whom the Uí Echach Arda sprang.[52] Although of great interest, Derry is unlikely to have been the chief church of the area. The Uí Echach Arda drop from prominence in the ninth century, perhaps as a result of Viking pressure,[53] and this could have caused the early history of the group to be forgotten or suppressed.

Only one other county Down site has substantial written coverage before 800, and it also has impressive archaeological material. This is Nendrum on Mahee Island in Strangford Lough. The church emerges from legend into history in the seventh century, with a record of six clergy in the Annals of Ulster from 639 to 755, including three bishops and two abbots.[54] Crónán, a bishop, who died in 643, was one of the recipients of Pope-elect John's letter about Easter observance in 640 (compare also Movilla and Bangor).[55] A ninth-century litany recalls 'nine times fifty monks under the yoke of Mochoe of Noendruim'.[56] Even if the number is impressionistic and includes 'daughter-houses' as well as Nendrum, it nevertheless suggests a sizable establishment. Like Movilla, it may have been a complex settlement, the seat of a bishop as well as housing a community of monks ruled by an abbot.

Although the three concentric enclosure walls at Nendrum cannot be dated closely, they certainly define a large area (about six acres). Most, if not all, of the visible stone buildings must date from after 800: the early buildings would all have been of timber. H. C. Lawlor's excavations in the 1920s did, however, produce some finds which could be as early as the seventh to eighth century.[57] A modern study of the Nendrum finds is badly needed, although some of the material is lost or in a poor condition. Uaininn O'Meadhra has carried out a detailed study of the material from the 'school', especially the motif- (or trial-) pieces. Her conclusion is that the likely date-range for these pieces is the seventh to ninth centuries.[58] None of the cross-carved stones at Nendrum is inscribed and again they are difficult to date closely, but some of the slabs with unringed crosses with distinctive hollowed 'armpits' may be as early as the eighth century.[59] Both the written and the archaeological evidence point to a well-established, complex community by 800, with a tradition of scholarship and craft activity.

Figure 3.1 shows the four important sites already discussed. Two other groups are indicated on the map: places documented in written sources of the ninth century or earlier, with some archaeological material, certainly or possibly of this period, and sites known only from early written sources. These written sources include the annals and the two calendars of saints, the *Martyrology of Tallaght* and the *Martyrology of Oengus,* which date from the first half of the ninth century.[60]

The three documented churches shown in the west of the county, Tullylish, *Tamlacht* and Donaghmore, all lie in the area of the Uí Echach Cobo, on or near the line of the great Early Christian period road, the *Slige Midlúachra,* which ran north from Tara to Dunseverick on the north Antrim coast.[61] An event recorded in the Annals of Ulster

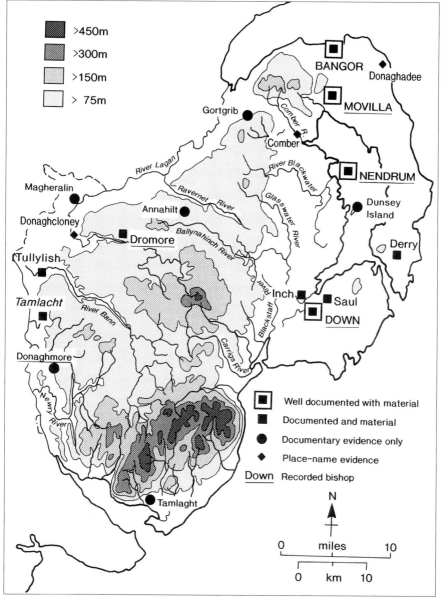

Fig. 3.1   Documentary and place-name evidence for religious sites of the ninth century or earlier.

in 809 may relate to Tullylish in county Down: 'The killing of Dúnchú, superior [princeps] of *Tulach Léis*, beside the shrine of Patrick in the abbot's house [i tigh abad] at *Tulach Léis*'. This is important as an unusually detailed reference to ecclesiastical topography in the annals at this early date. An excavation carried out in 1983 on the slope below the hilltop graveyard at Tullylish produced very interesting results but left open several questions. It was not clear whether the massive, clearly defensive, outer ditch belonged to a secular, pre-Christian fort, or whether it marked the beginning of the ecclesiastical occupation. A later, also massive, ditch can be confidently attributed to a church settlement but it may date from the Viking period or later. The radiocarbon dates do not allow close chronological refinement.[62] A church site in Drumsallagh townland in Aghaderg parish, with ruined foundations and three early cross-carved stones, can probably be identified with 'Tamlachta Umail at Loch Bricrenn' associated with 'three saints of Britain' in the *Martyrology of Tallaght,* Nassan, Beóán and Mellán.[63] Donaghmore has already been discussed as a likely early 'mother-church'. The mention of 'seven holy bishops of *Domnach Mór Maigi Coba'* in a ninth-century litany of Irish saints tends to reinforce the case for this as a centre of pastoral care and the seat of a bishop at an early period.[64] There is no certainly pre-ninth-century material at Donaghmore (the souterrain is undated).

Dromore, on the river Lagan, has a place in figure 3.1 because its saint, Colmán, is located here in the Martyrology of Tallaght, and it possibly has an early cross-carved stone,[65] but the annals indicate greater activity here in the Early Christian period, as the political centre of gravity in the county moved northwards. In the east of the county there is at least one cross-carved stone from Saul which dates from the eighth century,[66] and excavated evidence at Inch may take the occupation in the large enclosure there back to this early period.[67]

The other sites shown in figure 3.1 are documented in sources of the early ninth century or earlier but have no certainly early archaeological material. Reports of burials on Dunsey Island and at Magheralin are not considered sufficient grounds to move these two sites into the category 'with material'.

Before examining Viking activity in county Down it may be useful to reflect on the nature of activity at the sites depicted in figure 3.1. Recent work has helped to clarify the firm distinction between monastic and non-monastic churches.[68] Although the written sources tend to emphasise monastic officials, it is nevertheless clear that the Irish Church was truly hybrid, with elements of monastic and secular organisation closely combined from an early period. Pastoral jurisdiction rested with bishops throughout the Early Christian period. Bishops were responsible for sacramental functions, like consecrating churches and ordaining priests, and for organising the administration of local churches and the pastoral ministry. Bishops were based at major churches. Sometimes, like Movilla and Nendrum, these had a monastic element, but others, like Donaghmore, probably did not. Monasteries and their lands and tenants were ruled by abbots. Monks pursued a religious life under a rule, but at a large establishment like Nendrum may only have formed a small group in a large, predominantly lay population. When a monastery had extensive property, in lands and tenants, the abbot's role became increasingly administrative and his power as lord of men and property could be considerable. Many monastic founders were members of local royal families; so, from the start, monasteries were part of society and their interests were often closely interlinked with the fortunes of the local ruling family. It is not, therefore, surprising to find in the eighth and ninth centuries non-celibate abbots (as at Downpatrick) and signs that some abbots were laymen occupying powerful hereditary positions controlling substantial monastic estates, as well as evidence of the involvement of monasteries in warfare. It is important to accept that these were characteristics of a Church which was intimately bound up with secular society, that they were well established before the Viking period, and that they persisted long after it.

The Church from the coming of the Vikings to the twelfth century

The first recorded Viking raid on Ireland was in 795, probably on Lambay Island, and for about forty years there were hit-and-run raids on island and coastal sites. Three of county Down's important coastal sites were plundered in the 820s. Most dramatic is the account of the raid on Bangor in 824 when 'the heathens plundered *Bennchor*...and destroyed the wooden church, and shook the relics of Comgall from their shrine'. A poem adds a prophecy that the bones would be taken safely to Antrim. In 825 Down was plundered and Movilla 'with its wooden churches' was burned by the heathen. Other northern churches suffered at this time, including Maghera (Derry), Connor (Antrim), and Armagh, which was plundered three times in 832. While the psychological effect must have been enormous, these hit-and-run raids were not necessarily disastrous in physical terms. Hidden treasures could be retrieved, wooden buildings could be rebuilt, and routines could be re-established. Kathleen Hughes may have overstated the Viking impact on Bangor in her study of Irish *scriptoria*.[69] Other factors were at work to influence the position of Bangor at this time. Comgall's relics may have been taken to Antrim in Dál nAraidi, but Byrne points out that the northward move of the Dál Fiatach brought Bangor's traditional northward orientation to an end. In the late ninth or early tenth century the ruling Dál Fiatach group transferred its patronage from Down to Bangor and Dál Fiatach names begin to appear in the Bangor succession list.[70]

The second main wave of Viking raids began in the early tenth century, but it seems that county Down churches were only sporadically affected. Again it was the sites accessible by sea which suffered. Down was plundered twice by the 'foreigners': in 942 (when God and Patrick took revenge) and in 989 when it was also burned. According to the *Annals of the Four Masters,* in 935 'Kilclief was plundered by the son of Barith, and the stone church *[doimbliacc]* was burned, and a great prey was carried out of it'.[71] This suggests that the 'hurdle church' which gave the place its name had been replaced by a stone building by the early tenth century. In 958 the coarb of Bangor was killed by the foreigners.[72] Most intriguing is the unattributed burning of the 'superior' *(airchinnech)* of Nendrum 'in his own house' in 976. It is tempting to imagine a Viking attack, and there was certainly a Viking fleet on Strangford Lough *(Loch Cuan)* sometime in the tenth century, but one of the features of the rich finds from the 1924-6 excavation at Nendrum is the paucity of distinctively Viking material. It seems to be confined to one iron axe, one strap-end, one trial-piece with a Viking-type design, and a fragmentary runic-inscribed stone, probably of the eleventh century.[73]

The last recorded Viking raids on county Down churches appear to be Sitric's on Kilclief and Inch in 1001: 'he plundered *Cill-cleithe* and *Inis-Cumhscraigh,* and carried off many prisoners from both'.[74] Although it is unclear what the nature of these establishments was in the early eleventh century, these events do suggest that there were concentrations of population worth carrying off into slavery.

A reference to the killing of the superior *(princeps)* of Down in 882 by the Ulaid is a reminder that churches suffered from the Irish as well as the Vikings. The annals also point to continuing scholarly activity at some sites which were vulnerable to or were victims of Viking raids. 'Mael Gaimrid, an excellent scribe and anchorite, abbot of Bangor' died in 839, and Colman, bishop, scribe and abbot of Nendrum, died in 873. Among the many Down clergy mentioned in ninth- and tenth-century annal entries are an anchorite and bishop in 823 *(Annals of the Four Masters),* 'Gaíthéne the learned *[suí],* bishop' in 956, and a lector *(fear leighind)* in 992 (Four Masters).

The eleventh century was an important time, at the juncture between old and new orders, yet, as Byrne has pointed out, 'the years from 1014 to 1169 have been sadly neglected by Irish historians. They were neither a period of sorry decline from a golden age of sanctity and learning, nor a mere anarchic prelude to the Anglo-Norman invasion'.[75] Máire Herbert has called the eleventh century 'pivotal...in many areas of Irish life, between the end of the Vikings and the coming of the Normans',[76] yet it is still very poorly understood.

The battle of *Craeb Tulcha* in 994, between the Cenél Eógain and the Ulaid, resulted in a period of great political uncertainty in county Down. The battle ranged as far as Duneight, the Dál Fiatach political capital, and Drumbo, an ecclesiastical site with a surviving round tower. After the slaughter of so many royal sons the Dál Fiatach succession was confused and bitterly contested.[77] The annals suggest that the church at Down was going through a particularly troubled period in the eleventh century. The son of the king of Ulaid was killed in 1007 'in Brigit's church in the middle of *Dún dá Lethglas,* while in 1010 the superior *(princeps)* of Down was outraged, abducted and blinded. In 1016 '*Dún Lethglaise* was totally burned', and it was again burned, 'and many other churches', in 1040.

There are also indications of troubles elsewhere. In 1007 the successor *(comarba)* of Finnén of Movilla was involved in warfare. He had been taken as a pledge for the Ulaid into Cenél Eógain and was rescued by Brian Boru. Comber *(Cell Chomair)* was burned 1031 with its wooden church *(dairtigh),* four clerics were killed and thirty captives were taken away. In 1065 the king of Ulaid was killed in Bangor by his own people and according to the *Annals of the Four Masters* this took place in a stone church *(daimhlaig).* On the other hand, there is also evidence of continuing scholarly activity in the eleventh century, for example at Movilla. Marinus Scottus was exiled from Movilla in 1056 for some misdemeanour; he went first to Cologne, then to Fulda, and later to Mainz. He was walled up in solitude *(inclusus),* yet he wrote a chronicle with wide-ranging contents embracing Ireland and the Continent.[78]

Three instances are recorded of joint abbacies in county Down in the tenth and eleventh centuries. The death of the successor (comarba) of Comgall and Mo-Cholmóc is noted in 953, indicating a link between Bangor and Dromore. This would be consistent with Bangor's reorientation, away from south Antrim to Down. In 1019 Dromore is linked with Movilla, and it is worth recalling that Dromore was a poor diocese in the Middle Ages,[79] so perhaps it was also under pressure at an earlier period (although the death of a bishop of Dromore is reported in 1191). In 1025 the *Annals of Ulster* record a link which would have been most unlikely at an earlier period, between Movilla and Bangor: 'Mael Brigte ua Críchidéin, successor *[comarba]* of Finnén and Comgall' died. Kathleen Hughes saw this practice of holding abbacies in plurality as another sign of the disturbed times resulting from Viking pressure.[80] It is clear, however, that joint abbacies were recorded as early as the mid-eighth century and it is likely that they resulted from political and dynastic pressures, as well as the changing balance of wealth and power between different churches.[81]

Archaeological evidence

After *ca.* 800 it becomes easier to point to archaeological evidence of ecclesiastical activity. It is likely that the uncertainties of the Viking invasion period encouraged the use of stone for building, in addition to, but not superseding, the tradition of construction in wood. It is also certain that travelling Irish churchmen came into contact with impressive stone buildings on the Continent which could have influenced practices in Ireland.[82]

Four stone churches in county Down date from the Early Christian period, probably the tenth or eleventh centuries, at St. John's Point, Raholp, Nendrum and Derry (south church) in the Ards. Incomplete round towers at Drumbo, Nendrum and Maghera must date from the same period, although they are difficult to date closely.[83] The dating of stone crosses is also problematic, but most of the county Down examples probably date from the ninth and tenth centuries. The earliest may be the unringed cross at Kilbroney for which a date around 880 has been suggested.[84] The figure-carved crosses at Donaghmore and Downpatrick probably date from the tenth century, while the fragmentary cross at Downpatrick, the large reconstructed cross at Dromore, and the cross-shaft at Bangor may belong to the ninth- to tenth-century period.[85] Sundials survive at Bangor and Nendrum and a third is recorded from Saul. There are four ecclesiastical hand-bells from county Down, one of iron from the Nendrum excavations and three cast bronze bells, from Bangor, Drumgath and Kilbroney. A date-range from 700 to 900 has been suggested by Cormac Bourke, with the iron bells having an earlier origin than the bronze group.[86] A bell, together with a crozier, was the symbol of an abbot's or bishop's authority, and it is interesting to note the example from Drumgath, for which there is no other evidence from the pre-Norman period. Bells were also used for indicating the hours in the monastic day.[87]

Figure 3.2 brings together the evidence so far considered for churches in the pre-Norman period, to the early twelfth century. Building on the map for the period before the early ninth century (figure 3.1), it distinguishes between sites for which there is both *documentary* and archaeological evidence and sites for which there is only *documentary* evidence. The written sources for this period include the *Tripartite Life of Patrick,* possibly but not certainly of the early tenth century, the annals, the twelfth-century *Martyrology of Gorman,* and glosses to the two earlier martyrologies.[88] As in the earlier map, a site name is underlined when there is a record of a bishop associated with the church. The material evidence ranges in quality and visibility, from a church, cross-base, cross-carved stones and excavated evidence at

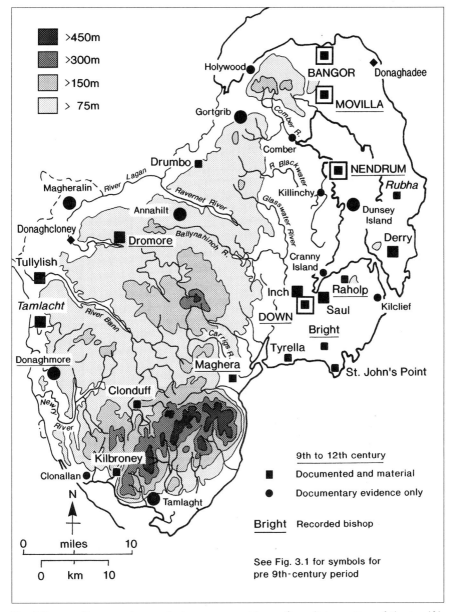

Fig. 3.2   Documentary and place-name evidence for religious sites of the twelfth century or earlier.

Raholp, to reported but destroyed remains at Bright and a souterrain and reported burials at Tyrella.[89]

What can archaeological evidence add to the map of early ecclesiastical sites so far built up in figures 3.1 and 3.2? Ten sites which do not appear in early written sources have material which can reasonably be dated to the Early Christian period and which points to ecclesiastical activity of some kind. Four other sites have material which is less closely datable to this period, like very simple cross-carved stones or crosses, and these are indicated as 'possible' sites on the map (figure 3.3).

A distinctive early cross-carved slab survives from Ardtole, near Ardglass, and a souterrain close to the late medieval ruined church points to Early Christian activity on the hilltop.[90] Chapel Island, off Greyabbey in Strangford Lough, has the low foundations of a small church in an enclosure with other earthworks nearby.[91] One of the two granite crosses in Clonlea graveyard near Newry has a nineteenth-century inscription, but at least one cross and one cross-base are of the Early Christian period.[92] The cross formerly built into Drumadonnell school-house points to Early Christian activity in the vicinity, but there is some doubt about whether it was moved from nearby Drumgooland graveyard.[93] The ecclesiastical bell from Drumgath has already been mentioned. Stone-built graves were reported near the Church of Ireland church in Annalong in 1932, and these, together with the *cill* element in the name, Kilhorn or Kilhoran, suggest an early church here.[94] Two cross-carved stones at Killyleagh may be early, although a Romanesque decorated fragment shows that there was a stone church on the site in the twelfth century.[95] There are traditions of burials having been found near a certainly early cross-carved pillar-stone in Legananny,[96] and a small, apparently recent, graveyard at Ouley is surrounded by a large circular earthwork enclosure, with the site of a holy well on or near its perimeter.[97] Stone-built graves and a fragment of imported E-ware were found during salvage excavations by Dudley Waterman in a part of Saul townland known as Slievegrane Lower, so this can be added to the list of sites of undocumented early ecclesiastical activity.[98]

The picture built up in figures 3.1, 3.2 and 3.3 is still far from complete. The Northern Ireland sites and monuments record has about 185 ecclesiastical sites in its county Down archive, yet only forty-seven sites are shown on the maps in this chapter. The published volumes of the *Place-names of Northern Ireland* point to many possible early church sites on the basis of place-name evidence, especially the element *cill*.[99] Continuing research, on written sources, place-names and local traditions, field survey and excavation, will gradually help to build up a fuller picture than it is possible to offer now.

The Church on the eve of the twelfth-century reforms
What was the state of the church in county Down on the eve of the reforms of the twelfth century? This is a surprisingly difficult question to answer because the written sources do not allow a clear view to be

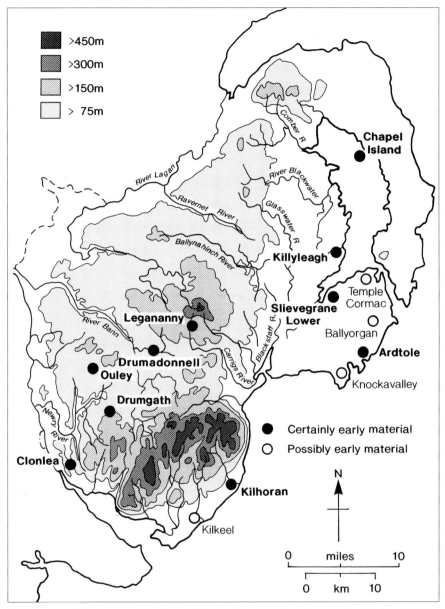

Fig. 3.3   Undocumented sites with archaeological evidence for Early Christian religious activity.

developed. An outside observer, Bernard of Clairvaux, had no first-hand knowledge of Ireland when writing his Life of Malachy. Bernard's aim was to praise his friend, so he had good reason to paint a black picture of the Irish Church in the first half of the twelfth century in order to throw Malachy's reforming work into high relief.[100] The annals are much concerned with warfare and dynastic struggles and largely confine their notice of ecclesiastical matters to the deaths of prominent churchmen and occasional fires and other disasters.

It is far from clear to what extent the churches provided a pastoral ministry for the people and what the state of the old-established monasteries and other ecclesiastical settlements was in the eleventh and twelfth centuries. The terms used for churchmen in the annals and other written sources may provide some information. In the case of Bangor, for example, the annals refer to the successor *(comarba)* of Comgall in the eleventh and early twelfth centuries and the *comarba* of Finnén (Movilla) and of Mo Cholmóc (Dromore) are also mentioned. On the other hand, the official most commonly referred to at Down is the erenagh *(airchinnech)*, though a *princeps* appears in 1010 and a bishop *(espoc)* in 1117. The death of the erenagh of Inch is recorded in 1061, and almost a century later the erenagh of Inch was one of the witnesses to a charter of Murchertach Mac Lochlainn in favour of the recently-founded Cistercian abbey at Newry (1156-7). It is clear from the order of the witness list that the erenaghs were classed as laymen, not clerics.[101] They appear to have been responsible for the administration of church lands, a role which persisted in some areas to the early seventeenth century. Whether these lay erenagh families provided the service of a priest, the sacraments and burial, is not at all certain.

'Lightning burned *Dún da Lethglas,* both ráith and trian' in 1111, so at Down there was clearly a distinction, as at Armagh, between an ecclesiastical enclosure (the *ráith*) and a secular settlement (the *trian*), and there may have been more than one functioning church. The death of an erenagh of Down who was 'eminent in law and history' is recorded in 1082, indicating continuing scholarly activity. It is doubtful whether the monastery at Bangor was as deserted in the early twelfth century as St. Bernard suggested,[102] and it is likely that there was still some activity at Movilla, Nendrum and elsewhere on the eve of the reform period. The stone churches already noted as probably dating from the tenth and eleventh centuries point to the need for churches and some kind of patronage at this time. Two events recorded in the chronicle known as 'Mac Cartaigh's Book' in the twelfth century indicate that two ecclesiastical sites of which little is known from earlier written sources were then worth plundering. Drumbo was plundered in 1130-31, including the round tower, wooden church *(duirrtheac)* and books, and John de Courcy raided Magheralin in 1178: 'Lann Rónáin Fhinn, chief sanctuary of all Ulaidh, was plundered and ... its erenach was beheaded'. The crozier *(bacall)* of Rónán Fionn is also mentioned in 1178 during a period of conflict between John de Courcy and the Ulaid.[103] The indications, therefore, seem to be of some level of continuing activity, particularly in the ancient, prestigious centres; Bangor, Down and Movilla. Some church sites may have been deserted by the early twelfth century, their early origins marked by a continuing unit of land-holding controlled by an erenagh family. Other churches, like Magheralin, may have become prominent only at this time because of changing patterns of patronage and political power.

Conclusion

The twelfth century brought fundamental changes to the Church in Ireland, with the definition of territorial dioceses, the gradual definition of parishes, and the introduction of new religious orders, especially the Augustinian Canons Regular and the Cistercians.[104] This is too complex a subject to deal with adequately here, but we can note that many of the sites shown in figures 3.1 and 3.2 did continue to play a part in the new order from the twelfth century onwards. Some of the major Early Christian foundations provided a basis for new religious houses, including the Augustinian Canons at Bangor, Movilla and Saul, the Cistercians at Comber and Inch, and the Benedictines at Downpatrick and Nendrum.[105] Other early churches clearly provided a nucleus – whether this was a church and graveyard or a unit of ecclesiastical land – for medieval parish churches, which appear in the papal taxation roll of 1302-6.[106] In a few, rare, cases an Early Christian period church building continued in use in the Middle Ages, as at Derry, Raholp and (for the Benedictines) Nendrum.[107] Although some early church sites must have been abandoned or had even disappeared by the twelfth century, others continued in ecclesiastical use to the seventeenth century, with its substantial changes in population and settlement patterns, while others again are used to the present day, including Down, perhaps Bangor, and one of the earliest of all, Donaghmore.

An attempt has been made in this chapter to trace the history and archaeology of the Church in county Down through the seven centuries from the time of St. Patrick to the changes of the twelfth century. It is a complex and dynamic picture, at present glimpsed only imperfectly because of the unevenness of the available evidence. Advances are likely to come from both historical and archaeological research. One subject that would warrant more investigation than has been possible in this chapter is the interaction between ecclesiastical and secular history in this period.[108] Continuing research on place-names, and the advance of archaeological enquiry across all its fronts – field survey, air photography, environmental study, excavation and geophysical prospecting – will also help to fill out the picture and bring fuller understanding of the early Church in county Down.

References

1. Richard Sharpe, 'Some problems concerning the organization of the church in early medieval Ireland' in *Peritia*, iii (1984), p. 239.
2. Charles Thomas, *Christianity in Roman Britain to AD 500* (London, 1981), pp 275-94.
3. R. B. Warner, 'Some observations on the context and importation of exotic material in Ireland, from the first century B.C. to the second century A.D.' in *R.I.A. Proc.*, lxxvi, C (1976), pp 276-83.
4. Ludwig Bieler (ed. and transl.), *The Patrician texts in the Book of Armagh* (Dublin, 1979), pp 78-9.
5. Ibid., pp 81-2.
6. Ibid., pp 116-19.
7. Ibid., pp 164-5; for an important collection of essays on St. Patrick see David Dumville and others, *Saint Patrick A.D. 493-1993* (Woodbridge, 1993).
8. Daniel McCarthy and Dáibhí Ó Cróinín, 'The "lost" Irish 84-year Easter table rediscovered' in *Peritia*, vi-vii (1987-8), pp 227-42.
9. Whitley Stokes (ed. and transl.), *The martyrology of Oengus the Culdee* (London, 1905), pp 158-9.
10. Information from my colleague, Nick Brannon: reference number UB-2365.
11. Deirdre Flanagan, 'The Christian impact on early Ireland: place-names evidence' in Próinséas Ní Chatháin and Michael Richter (ed.), *Ireland and Europe: the early church* (Stuttgart, 1984), p. 31.
12. Sharpe, 'Some problems', p. 256.
13. R. I. Best and H. J. Lawlor (ed.), *The martyrology of Tallaght* (London, 1931); Charles Plummer (ed. and transl.), *Irish litanies* (London, 1925), p. 69.
14. Flanagan, 'Place-names evidence', p. 31, but see also Sharpe, 'Some problems', p. 256, for a different view. Note, however, that Donaghaguy, a townland in Clonallan parish, is not a *domnach* name: Gregory Toner and Mícheál B. Ó Mainnín, *Place-names of Northern Ireland, county Down, i, Newry and south-west Down* (Belfast, 1992), pp 75-7.
15. A. T. Lucas, 'The sacred trees of Ireland' in *Cork Arch. Hist. Soc. Jn.*, lxviii (1963), pp 16-54.
16. James F. Kenney, *The sources for the early history of Ireland: ecclesiastical* (New York, 1929) pp 240-41 and 390-91; Ludwig Bieler (ed.), *The Irish penitentials* (Dublin, 1963), pp 3-4 and 74-95. See also D. N. Dumville, 'Gildas and Uinniau' in M. Lapidge and D. Dumville (ed.), *Gildas: new approaches* (Woodbridge, 1984), pp 51-9, for a case that Finnian (Uinniau) was a Briton. See chapter 4 in this volume.
17. Alfred Holder (ed.), The Venerable Bede, *Baedae historia ecclesiastica gentis Anglorum* (Freiburg, 1883), ii.19.
18. Kenney, *Sources*, p. 269.
19. Charles Plummer, *Vitae sanctorum Hiberniae* (2 vols., Oxford, 1911), ii, p. 13: 'sanctus Fyndbarrus episcopus, qui iacet in miraculis multis in sua ciuitate *Magh Bile*'.
20. James Henthorn Todd and William Reeves (ed. and transl.), *The martyrology of Donegal* (Dublin, 1864), pp 278-9.
21. M. J. Yates, 'Preliminary excavations at Movilla Abbey, County Down, 1980' in *U.J.A.*, xlvi (1983), pp 53-66; Richard Ivens, 'Movilla Abbey, Newtownards, County Down: excavations 1981' in *U.J.A.*, xlvii (1984), pp 71-108; Ann Hamlin and Chris Lynn (ed.), *Pieces of the past* (Belfast, 1988), pp 50-52.
22. Kenney, *Sources*, pp 395-7; Ann Hamlin, 'The archaeology of early Christianity in

the North of Ireland', unpub. Ph.D. thesis, Q.U.B. (1976), ii, p. 556.

23. Michael Lapidge, 'Columbanus and the "Antiphonary of Bangor"' in *Peritia*, iv (1985), p. 105; Kenney, *Sources*, pp 265-6; M. Curran, *The Antiphonary of Bangor* (Dublin, 1984).

24. Lapidge, *op. cit.*; Jane Stevenson, 'Bangor and the *Hisperica Famina*' in *Peritia*, vi-vii (1987-8), pp 202-16.

25. Kathleen Hughes, 'The distribution of Irish scriptoria and centres of learning from 730 to 1111' in N.K. Chadwick (ed.), *Studies in the early British church* (Cambridge, 1958), especially pp 259-61, reprinted in her *Church and society in Ireland A.D. 400 to 1200* (London, 1987), Chapter xi.

26. Robin Flower, *The Irish tradition* (Oxford, 1947), pp 13-23.

27. Dáibhí Ó Cróinín, 'Mo-Sinnu moccu Min and the computus of Bangor' in *Peritia*, i (1982), pp 281-95.

28. Bede, *Historia ecclesiastica*, ii, 19.

29. Alan Orr Anderson and Marjorie Ogilvie Anderson (ed. and transl.), *Adomnan's life of Columba* (Edinburgh, 1961), p. 501.

30. G. S. M. Walker (ed. and transl.), *Sancti Columbani opera* (Dublin, 1957), *passim*.

31. Walker *op.cit.*, pp 18-19.

32. Kathleen Hughes, *The church in early Irish society* (London, 1966), pp 81-2; the Annals of Ulster do not locate Mael Ruba, but he is called 'abbot of Bangor' in the *Annals of the Four Masters*.

33. Gerard Murphy (ed. and transl.), *Early Irish lyrics* (Oxford, 1956), pp 6-7.

34. Here and elsewhere dates are derived from the *Annals of Ulster*. If a different chronicle is referred to this is made clear.

35. Plummer, *Irish litanies*, p. 61.

36. Flower, *Irish tradition*, p. 22; Charles Doherty, 'Some aspects of hagiography as a source for Irish economic history' in *Peritia*, i (1982), p. 307.

37. Kenney, *Sources*, pp 457-8; Whitley Stokes (ed), *Lives of saints from the Book of Lismore* (Oxford, 1890), pp 85-6 and 232-3.

38. Kuno Meyer (ed. and transl.), *The triads of Ireland*, R.I.A. Todd Lecture Series 13 (Dublin, 1906), pp 2-5.

39. Whitley Stokes (ed. and transl.), *The tripartite life of Patrick* (2 vols. London, 1887), ii, pp 408-9.

40. Francis John Byrne, *Irish kings and high-kings* (London, 1973), p. 108.

41. Ibid., p. 109.

42. Ibid., pp 119, 124.

43. Hamlin and Lynn (ed.), *Pieces of the past*, pp 61-4.

44. Donnchadh Ó Corráin, 'The early Irish churches: some aspects of organisation' in Donnchadh Ó Corráin (ed.), *Irish antiquity* (Cork, 1981), pp 327-41.

45. Francis John Byrne, 'A note on Trim and Sletty' in *Peritia*, iii (1984), pp 316-19.

46. Byrne, *Irish kings*, p. 108 and map on pp 120-21; A.J. Hughes and R. J. Hannan, *Place-names of Northern Ireland, county Down, ii, the Ards* (Belfast, 1992), p. 3.

47. *A.S.C.D.*, p. 173, fig. 108.

48. D. M. Waterman, 'Excavations at Ballyfounder Rath, county Down' in *U.J.A.*, xxi (1958), pp 39-52.

49. Hughes and Hannan, *The Ards*, pp 128 and 139-40.

50. D. M. Waterman, 'The early Christian churches and cemetery at Derry, Co. Down' in *U.J.A.*, xxx (1967), pp 63-4; Susan Youngs (ed.), '*The work of angels': masterpieces of Celtic metalwork, 6th-9th centuries AD* (London, 1989), p. 203.

51. Best and Lawlor, *Tallaght*, and Stokes, *Oengus*.

52. Hughes and Hannan, *The Ards*, pp 47-8; Pádraig Ó Riain (ed.), *Corpus genealogiarum sanctorum Hiberniae* (Dublin, 1985), p. 33.
53. Byrne, *Irish kings*, p. 108.
54. Care has to be taken over distinguishing Nendrum from Antrim in the annals as the Irish forms of the names can be similar.
55. Bede, *Historia Ecclesiastica*, II.19.
56. Plummer, *Irish litanies*, p. 67; Kathleen Hughes, 'On an Irish litany of pilgrim saints' in *Analecta Bollandiana*, lxxvii (1959), pp 326-7.
57. H. C. Lawlor, *The monastery of Saint Mochaoi of Nendrum* (Belfast, 1925); *A.S.C.D.*, pp 292-5 and fig. 191. The bell may be early in the date-range suggested by Cormac Bourke for early ecclesiastical bells (see note 86).
58. Uaininn Ó Meadhra, *Early Christian, Viking and Romanesque art motif-pieces from Ireland*, ii (Stockholm, 1987), p. 72.
59. *A.S.C.D.*, pls. 77-8; Ann Hamlin, 'The archaeology of the Irish church in the eighth century' in *Peritia*, iv (1985), pp 293-4.
60. Long believed to have been written about 800, the two early martyrologies, of Tallaght and Oengus, are now thought to have been composed between 828 and 833: Pádraig Ó Riain, 'The Tallaght martyrologies, redated' in *Cambridge Medieval Celtic Studies*, xx (1990), pp 21-38.
61. Colm Ó Lochlainn, 'Roadways in early Ireland' in J. Ryan (ed.), *Féil-Sgríbhinn Eóin Mhic Néill* (Dublin, 1940), pp 465-74.
62. R. J. Ivens, 'The early Christian monastic enclosure at Tullylish, county Down' in *U.J.A.*, l (1987), pp 55-120, especially pp 112-18.
63. *A.S.C.D.*, p. 302 and pl. 76; Hamlin, 'Archaeology of early Christianity', pp 631-3 and fig. 57. The notes to the Martyrology of Oengus call the place *Tamlachta Maccu-cuill* on *Loch Bricrenn:* Stokes, *Oengus*, pp 226-7.
64. Plummer, *Irish litanies*, p. 69.
65 E.D. Atkinson, *Dromore: an Ulster diocese* (Dundalk, 1925), plate following p. 95.
66. *A.S.C.D.*, pl. 75 slab c, now used as the symbol of Down District Council.
67. Ann Hamlin, 'A recently discovered enclosure at Inch Abbey, county Down' in *U.J.A.*, xl (1977), pp 85-8 and pl. 7. Excavations in the parish graveyard are not yet published.
68. Sharpe, 'Some problems'; Ó Corráin, 'Early Irish churches'.
69. Hughes, 'Irish scriptoria', pp 259-60.
70. Byrne, *Irish kings*, p. 119.
71. John O'Donovan (ed. and transl.), *Annals of the kingdom of Ireland by the Four Masters* (Dublin, 1848-51), ii, pp 632-3.
72. The coarb was the successor of the founding saint.
73. Ó Meadhra, *Motif-pieces*, p. 72, fig. 50; *A.S.C.D.*, pl. 81, bottom right shows the runic inscription.
74. *Annals of the Four Masters.*
75. Byrne, *Irish kings*, p. 269.
76. Máire Herbert, 'The preface of *Amra Coluim Cille'* in Donnchadh Ó Corráin, Liam Breatnach and Kim McCone (ed.), *Sages, saints and storytellers* (Maynooth, 1989), p. 67.
77. Byrne, *Irish kings*, pp 127-8.
78. Kenney, *Sources*, pp 614-16.
79. Reeves, *Ecclesiastical antiquities*, pp 103-4; T. E. McNeill, *Anglo-Norman Ulster* (Edinburgh, 1980), pp 12, 33-6, especially fig. 10. But the three death-notices in the Annals of Ulster (993, 1019, 1043) of a 'coarb of Finnén and Mo-Cholmóc' have alternatively been interpreted as records of abbots of Clonard: P. Byrne,

'The Community of Clonard, sixth to twelfth Centuries', *Peritia* iv (1985) pp 157-73, 160, 165-66.

80. Hughes, *The church in early Irish society*, pp 213-14.

81. Ó Corráin, 'Early Irish churches', p. 330 refers to 'grand pluralism in the eighth century'.

82. Kenney, *Sources,* pp 530-621; Hughes. *The church in early Irish society,* pp 253-6.

83. *A.S.C.D.* for all these buildings and for the dating of round towers see Michael Haire and Ann Hamlin, 'The study of early church architecture in Ireland: an Anglo-Saxon viewpoint' in L. A. S. Butler and R. K. Morris (ed.), *The Anglo-Saxon church: papers on history, architecture and archaeology in honour of Dr. H. M. Taylor* (London, 1986), pp 131-45, especially pp 139-43.

84. Dorothy Kelly, 'The heart of the matter: models for Irish high crosses' in *R.S.A.I. Jn.*, cxxi (1991), pp 108-11 and 142-3.

85. *A.S.C.D.* and P. Harbison, *The high crosses of Ireland: an iconographical and photographic survey,* i-ii (Bonn, 1992), for descriptions and illustrations.

86. Cormac Bourke, 'Early Irish hand-bells' in *J.R.S.A.I. Jn*, cx (1980), pp 52-66.

87. Ann Hamlin, 'Some northern sundials and time-keeping in the early Irish church' in Etienne Rynne (ed.), *Figures from the past : studies on figurative art in honour of Helen M. Roe* (Dún Laoghaire, 1987), pp 36-7.

88. See Dumville, *Saint Patrick,* pp 255-8 for the dating of the Tripartite life. Stokes, *Tripartite life*; Whitley Stokes (ed. and transl.), *The martyrology of Gorman* (London, 1895); Best and Lawlor, *Tallaght*; Stokes, *Oengus.*

89. Francis Joseph Bigger, 'Some notes on the churches of Saint Tassach of Raholp and Saint Nicholas of Ardtole' in *R.S.A.I. Jn.,* xlvi (1916), pp 121-30; James O'Laverty, 'The Little City of Bright, County Down' in *U.J.A.,* v (1899), pp 81-3; James O'Laverty, *An historical account of the diocese of Down and Connor, ancient and modern,* i (Dublin, 1878), pp 129-30.

90. *A.S.C.D.*, p. 298 and pl. 75; Francis Joseph Bigger and William J. Fennell, 'Ardtole southerrain, county Down' in *U.J.A.,* v (1899), pp 146-7.

91. *A.S.C.D.*, p. 296. Recent survey has revealed complex earthworks.

92. Kelly, 'Models for Irish high crosses', pp 109-11 and fig. 33d; Harbison, *High crosses of Ireland,* i, pp 47-8 and ii, figs. 130-131.

93. W. C. Kerr, *Ulster Archaeological Society newsletter*, May 1972, pp 7-10; Harbison, *High crosses of Ireland,* i, pp 75-6 and ii, figs. 233-6.

94. R. J. Berry and M. J. Nolan, 'Report on the ancient graveyard at Annalong, county Down' in *R.S.A.I. Jn.,* lxii (1932), pp 219-23; Micheal B. Ó Mainnín, *Place-names of Northern Ireland, county Down, iii, The Mournes* (Belfast, 1993), p. 60.

95. R. S. J. Clarkem, 'Four cross slabs in county Down graveyards' in *U.J.A.,* xxxii (1971), pp 108-9 and pl. 21d; D. M. Waterman, 'Romanesque stone-carving from Killyleagh, county Down', ibid., p. 110 and pl. 23; unpublished slab in Hamlin, 'Archaeology of early Christianity', pp 641-2, pl. 69, and fig. 57.

96. Hamlin, *loc. cit.* p. 644 and *A.S.C.D.*, pl. 106.

97. Northern Ireland sites and monument record, Down 41:33.

98. Waterman, 'Early Christian churches at Derry', p. 69, note 11.

99. Many examples in Toner and Ó Mainnín (i), Hughes and Hannan (ii) and Ó Mainnín (iii).

100. H. J. Lawlor (transl.), *S. Bernard of Clairvaux's life of St. Malachy of Armagh* (London, 1920), for example pp 16-18.

101. Kenney, *Sources*, p. 769 gives references to editions of the charter. I am grateful to Dr. Marie Therese Flanagan for pointing out the interest of this witness list to me.

102. Lawlor (transl.), *Life of St. Malachy*, pp 30-31, 'long ago destroyed by pirates'.
103. Séamus Ó hInnse, *Miscellaneous Irish Annals (A.D. 1114-1437)* (Dublin, 1947), pp 18-19 and 64-7.
104. Hughes, *The church in early Irish society*, chap. 24; J. A. Watt, *The church and the two nations in medieval Ireland* (Cambridge, 1970), chaps 1-2.
105. Aubrey Gwynn and R. Neville Hadcock, *Medieval religious houses: Ireland* (London, 1970), for details of these and other foundations.
106. Reeves, *Ecclesiastical antiquities,* provides the text and a translation of the taxation roll, with extensive discussion.
107. Structural evidence for medieval alterations and (at Nendrum) additions is set out in the *A.S.C.D.*
108. A most impressive and illuminating example of this approach is Máire Herbert, *Iona, Kells and Derry: the history and hagiography of the monastic familia of Columba* (Oxford, 1988).

Chapter 4

ST FINNIAN OF MOVILLA — TWO STUDIES

1. ST FINNIAN OF MOVILLA: BRITON, GAEL, GHOST?

DAVID N. DUMVILLE

While our ignorance of the earliest phases of Irish ecclesiastical history is profound, enough hints about persons and places of the 'Age of the Saints' survive in mediaeval and early modern source-material to tantalise the historian. The period from 431 (the year of the appointment of Palladius by Pope Celestine I to be the first bishop for Irish christians) to 549 (when the 'Justinianic Plague' which had crossed Europe finally struck Ireland) is at best protohistoric;[1] that from 549 to 664, or even the 680s, the century between the two devastating plague-cycles of early mediaeval Irish history, does offer some source-material but is nevertheless in many ways a desperately obscure era.[2] The plagues themselves, by being responsible for institutional discontinuity in many places, no doubt prevented the effective transmission of ecclesiastical record at local level. The founding age of Gaelic christianity extends over a quarter-millennium, 431-684. By the end of that time-span, christianity was securely established from one end of the Gaelic world to the other, although it is far from clear that overt paganism had yet been extirpated everywhere.[3] As the founding era, it was by definition a period of origins. When, from the late seventh century onwards, information about the preceding quarter-millennium was either non-existent or not available in detail sufficient for any particular purpose, recourse was had to invention – to wishful thinking or to unrestrained creativity.[4]

Any attempt to recover a history for Finnian, the patron-saint of Movilla (Moville), county Down,[5] runs immediately into such difficulties and, indeed, into the realisation that there may be neither history nor reality to discover. For St Finnian is a figure viewed as founder of an important church and as belonging to that obscure age of Irish history when contemporary witnesses are at a premium. The only potentially early source to speak of him is Ireland's chronicle-record. We know that by 911 the now lost but partially reconstructable 'Chronicle of Ireland' contained a notice of him.[6] In the version preserved in the 'Annals of Ulster' it reads (as the first entry for the year 579):[7]

> Quies Uinniani episcopi, m. nepotis Fiatach
> The peaceful death of Bishop Uinnianus, son of the grandson of
> Fiatach.

It is unlikely that this is precisely what was originally written. The
bilingual formula *mac nepotis* (otherwise Latin *filius nepotis* or Old Irish
mac uî) is rarely used as a means of stating a man's relationship to his
great-grandfather. Rather, it is usually a replacement for an archaic Old
Irish word which ceased to be productive after about A.D. 700 and
which over time ceased to be understood. That word, variously spelt as
maccu, macu, moccu, mocu, indicated the population-group to which
a person belonged.[8] There are numerous examples of this formula
being misunderstood by later copyists of Irish chronicles. Our first
improvement of the text should therefore be as follows:

> Quies Uinniani episcopi macu Fiatach
> The peaceful death of Bishop Uinnianus of Dál Fiatach.

In the translation I have made a further adjustment. The word
macu/moccu seems to have been interchangeable with *corcu, dál,* and
some other elements indicating population-groups.[9] The one with
which Bishop Finnian *(Uinnianus)* is here associated is usually known
as Dál Fiatach, and I have altered the translation accordingly. It is clear
that Movilla (Old Irish *Mag Bili*) was a principal church of this leading
population-group in the province of the Ulaid in the early middle ages.
That this equation of the text's *mac nepotis Fiatach* with Dál Fiatach is
correct is suggested by two other witnesses: the corresponding
evidence of the 'Martyrology of Tallaght' (in its present form a text of
the first half of the tenth century, preserved in a manuscript of the
second half of the twelfth, but which seems to go back to an original
kept at the culdee-house of Tallaght, county Dublin, about A.D. 800) at
10 September reads *Finnio mac huí Fiatach*;[10] and *Comainmnigud
Naem nÉrenn,* a Middle-Irish list of homonymous saints, has the
additionally corrupted entry, *Findbarr mac hua Fiatan,* for which one
should understand *Findbarr mac(c)u Fiatach.*[11] It is clear that
mediaeval readers of chronicle and martyrology alike understood this
saint to be the patron of Movilla: Oengus mac Oengobann, the
culdee-author of *Félire Oengusso* whose principal source was the
'Martyrology of Tallaght', in his quatrain for 10 September referred to
Findbarr Maige Bili;[12] and in the 'Annals of Inisfallen' the saint's
death-notice reads *Quies Finniae Moige Bile.*[13]

To proceed with our investigation of the annal-entry in the 'Chronicle
of Ireland' for 579 it is necessary first to consider some aspects of the

way in which that chronicle was constructed. Scholars are not agreed about the point at which the first signs of contemporaneous record are found. Since the earliest manuscript-witnesses to Irish chronicling belong to the second half of the eleventh century and since the earliest stage of textual development which can be recaptured by traditional text-historical methods belongs to the year 911, there is still a substantial gap between the founding quarter-millennium of Gaelic christianity and the date of recoverable record. Various techniques have been experimented with in an attempt to identify the point at which contemporaneous record began: some scholars adhere to a date around A.D. 550, others to 600, and others still to the 680s.[14] On the most generous interpretation, an entry for 579 might be contemporary; if record began around 600, an event of 579 would have been within living memory; on the least generous reading, a notice of that year would be wholly constructed. This is not the place to attempt to adjudicate between these rival interpretations: suffice it to say that a possibility exists that the death-notice of Finnian of Movilla is contemporary with such an historical event, but that that is the most favourable judgment which can be made at present.

If we allow that the annal-entry originally read *mac(c)u Fiatach* we should suppose that it was probably written no later than about 700.[15] Such a conclusion immediately calls into question the bishop's name-form as given in the 'Annals of Ulster', the Latin genitive *Uinniani*. This is a form clearly related to late Old Irish Finnian but in fact an unnatural spelling. In the history of the Irish language initial *U-* (the sound /w/-, that is) gave way to *F-* about 600 or early in the seventh century.[16] On the face of it, here is a spelling which could be contemporary with a figure who lived in the mid- and later sixth century. However, two further spellings introduce complications. Medial *-nn-* for an original *-nd-* is the result of a sound-change which took place in the ninth century.[17] Lastly, the spelling *-ian-* has not been adequately explained, for it seems to be attested first in Latin contexts where in the venacular one would expect the Old-Irish hypocoristic termination *-én(e)*.[18] A possible interpretation of the latinised spelling *Uinnianus* is therefore that it is purely graphic, representing an untidy (because incomplete) response over a long period of time to changes in the sound-system of the Irish language. Given that the chronicles which contain this spelling survive first in manuscripts of the fourteenth and fifteenth centuries, this is not an unreasonable deduction. The original spelling of a hypothetically contemporary death-notice of 579 would on this argument have been **Uindén(e)* (perhaps spelt **Uindeen, *Uindeene*) or (with Latin genitival inflexion) **Uindén(e)i*.

There is, however, a substantial difficulty inhibiting acceptance of this theory. We have seen that three name-forms are associated in mediaeval sources with Finnian of Movilla: *Uinnian* (implying Old Irish *Findén, *Findéne*), *Finnio* (and the later *Finnia*), and the dithematic, non-hypocoristic form *Findbarr*. *Findén* and its immediate relatives can be explained as normal Irish hypocorism derivative of Old Irish *Findbarr* (late Old Irish *Finnbarr*). But *Finnio* presents problems of an altogether different order.

It has been pointed out that in the Irish hagiological record only two names are found with *-io*: Finnio and Ninnio.[19] There is little doubt that this suffix is derivative of British Celtic where it took the form *-iawos,* Neo-Brittonic *-iaw,* and occurred quite routinely.[20] Its highly restricted occurrence in Irish contrasts with that of *-óc* terminations, also borrowed from British Celtic (Neo-Brittonic *-awc*), which were extensively used in Irish clerical names.[21] That the examples of *-iau>-io>-ia* constitute merely 'another example of a more general Brittonic influence on the formation of Irish hypocoristics' is scarcely to be credited:[22] we must find a different explanation.

The notice of St Finnian (Findbarr) of Movilla in *Félire Oengusso* for 10 September extends over a whole quatrain.[23]

Clí dergóir co nglaini,	A kingpost of red gold with purity,
co rrecht tar sál sidi	over the swelling(?) sea with law
suí diand Ériu inmall,	a sage for whom Ireland is sad,
Findbarr Maige Bili.	Findbarr of Mag Bili.

By the beginning of the ninth century he was therefore regarded as a saint with external experience or of external origin; the late Old-Irish story *Imacallam Tuáin fri Finnia* states this quite clearly; and there are further stories of the Middle-Irish period which offer the same message.[24] Such testimony can hardly tell us anything of the sixth century, but it does serve to provoke consideration of an external dimension to this saint's activities or cult if more satisfactory evidence warrants it.

We can be certain that the name-form *Finnio* existed at least as early as the opening years of the eighth century, for in the copy of Adomnán's Life of St Columba written by Dorbbéne of Iona (who died in 713) we find it used alongside *Findbarr* for one of Columba's teachers.[25] Both the *-io* termination and the medial *-nn-* point to the name-form's British origin.[26] In this earliest manuscript of Adomnán's work we also find the form *Uinniau* used for the same person.[27] Here we have what lies naturally behind *Finnio,* with the initial *U-* which developed to *F-* not later than the first half of the seventh century and with the original diphthong of the Neo-Brittonic hypocoristic termination -*iau*. Here, then, is a name-form which can be held to be British in origin and appropriate to the sixth century.

When we look around in Irish hagiological texts and in other early Insular ecclesiastical literature, we find the name Uinniau quite well attested. In particular, it is employed in relation to the founding saint of Clonard (county Meath), subsequently also known as Finnian:[28] but in his case only hypocoristic forms seem ever to be used in the literature;[29] his conventional death-date is 549,[30] placing him a generation earlier than his namesake of Movilla. Also attributable to the sixth century are a correspondent of the British author and eventually abbot, Gildas, a correspondence referred to by Columbanus of Bangor, and the author of a Penitential whose work was fundamental to one composed by Columbanus in the same genre.[31]

For a variety of reasons, the tendency of modern scholarship has been to view all these manifestations of *Uinniau/Finniau/Finnio/Findio/Finnia/Findia* or *Findén/*Findéne/Finnian* or (in Latin contexts) *Uinniau(u)s/Uennianus/Uinnianus* as referring to a single sixth-century historical figure. There has been less agreement about who he was, where he worked, and how he came to be culted as a patron-saint at different churches. The principal difficulties have resided in the question of his nationality and in making a convincing connexion between the sixth-century evidence and that of later hagiological sources.

I take the latter issue first. The earliest testimony is provided by Adomnán of Iona in his Tripartite Life of St Columba, written about 700. In referring to one of St Columba's teachers, an elderly bishop, by the three name-forms *Findbarr, Uinniau,* and *Finnio* (assuming for the purposes of this discussion that all these are authorial), Adomnán showed that the onomastic situation was complex. This was not the only one of Columba's tutors referred to by Adomnán: his foster-father was a priest called Cruithnechán,[32] of unknown location; when Columba was a young deacon he had two teachers named by Adomnán, the elderly bishop who is our concern here whose location is only stated as being in Ireland,[33] and another *senex,* Gemmán, who lived in Leinster.[34] The possibility exists, therefore, that Adomnán thought that at that stage of Columba's career all his studies were undertaken in Leinster.[35] It has been pointed out that Clonard lay within Leinster's early sixth-century boundaries and that Columba might accordingly have studied there in the later 540s.[36] This view faces two obstacles, however. First, Adomnán attributed only Columba's tutelage by Gemmán to Leinster. Secondly, in spite of Adomnán's excellent connexions and use of earlier written source-materials, it is clear that Columba was already a figure of legend by his day; both that fact and the genre in which Adomnán worked remind us that his account of the saint is not necessarily historical.[37]

By about 800 at the very latest there were two saints known as *Uinniau/Finnio,* the founders of Clonard and Movilla.[38] There were also two called *Findbarr,* the patrons of Cork and Movilla.[39] As we have seen, there is a case that the patron of Movilla was known and culted in that area at least a century earlier, because of his identification as *maccu Fiatach,* using a formula which ceased to be productive about A.D. 700.[40] The same applies to St Finnian of Clonard, who is attested as *maccu Telduib,* the name of a local population-group which supplied also an abbot and bishop, Colmán, who died in 654 and who came to be culted as another saint of Clonard.[41] The cults of Uinniau of Clonard and Movilla cannot be documented earlier than this period, however. In other words, we have arrived at the lifetime of Adomnán of Iona, who published his hagiography of Columba in 697 x 704, the closing years of his life.[42]

There has been general agreement among the scholars who have discussed this matter that it is difficult to credit the historical existence of more than one person who would have left these unusual linguistic results.[43] If that conclusion is correct, it is a task of scholarship to explain how the multiple cults, and the distortions of sixth-century history which they would therefore represent, came into existence. Pádraig Ó Riain, who first saw a possible solution, has argued that we have a number of localisations of an original single cult, what in German has been called a *Wanderkult.*[44] It is a well attested hagiological phenomenon. The problem resides, however, in determining which local manifestation represents the site of the church of the historical Uinniau.

Four arguments have been advanced on this point. That which has been pressed most insistently concerns the saint's name. At Cork and at Movilla we meet an Old-Irish dithematic name, Findbarr, from which the hypocoristic forms found at Clonard and Movilla can be explained: Findén and its derivatives are straightforwardly Irish, but Uinniau is British with Finnio (later Finnia) as an Irish development. Ó Riain has argued that, since a hypocoristic is by definition derivative of a full name-form and since early Gaelic names were generally dithematic, Findbarr must have been the saintly bishop's original name.[45] This has also allowed him to argue that Clonard can be ruled out as the original cult-centre, since the full name-form was apparently unknown there.[46] Unfortunately, these arguments are insufficiently logical. It cannot be shown beyond reasonable doubt that Findbarr was the saint's full given name. If only a hypocoristic (or two) were known, the desire to recover a full form might have proved powerful: the name Findbarr would have been a credible candidate. Ó Riain has insisted that no such procedure was possible.[47] However, to assert this is to ignore the character of the record, which is strongly self-interrogatory. It is impossible to credit that where saints were customarily known by pet-forms, as they were in innumerable cases, full root-forms were invariably available; likewise, given the scholarly nature of the written tradition of Gaelic hagiology, one cannot credit that there would be no desire to retrieve full names; indeed, as Ó Riain himself has pointed out, we can observe precisely this happening in the case of St Finnian of Clonard.[48] Furthermore, if the bishop's own name were the Gaelic Findbarr, it would be necessary to explain why he had the Neo-Brittonic hypocoristic Uinniau. There are two other possibilities: that Uinniau was in his case the pet-form of a British radical which is unrecorded; or that Findbarr is a Gaelic translation of that British root-form. These options need to be considered.

Information about Uinniau is preserved in sources associable with the north of the Gaelic world, and this forms the second argument for locating him in Ulster. Gildas's correspondent is known to us from a letter of Columbanus of Bangor.[49] What are very likely fragments of that letter are preserved in the canon-law text *Collectio canonum hibernensis* of which one author has been supposed to be Cú Chuimne of Iona.[50] Furthermore, the Penitential of Uinniau is first known to us from its use by Columbanus.[51] We may therefore suppose that both these works were in the library of Bangor Abbey before 590 (when Columbanus left for exile on the Continent). However, to suppose that they were exclusively available in Ulster and its Dalriadic extension in North Britain would be to argue very unwisely from silence.

If Uinniau was one of Columba's tutors, then reason for an interest in him at Iona would be easily deduced. However, Adomnán's remarks about him in the Life of Columba are frustratingly limited. That he lived in Ireland is the full extent of the geographical information provided.[52] Adomnán's failure to name Bishop Uinniau's church or the kingdom or province in which it was situated has been called 'an oversight which may best be explained by assuming that he knew of only one saint so called'.[53] That Adomnán had not heard of Clonard or its saint might be thought unlikely, particularly since an abbot of that house was a guarantor of *Cáin Adomnáin* in 697.[54] It is more likely that he assumed that his readers would know who Bishop Uinniau/Finnio/Finnbarr was. That Adomnán self-evidently referred to the saint of Movilla has been an unsatisfactory third argument for that church as Uinniau's Irish location.

A larger problem is presented by chronology. Columba's tutor was 'an old man' and 'a venerable bishop' at the time when Columba was 'a young deacon', perhaps therefore in the later 540s.[55] If the bishop did indeed die in 579, thirty years further on, as the obit of Uinnianus macu Fiatach in the 'Annals of Ulster' would require,[56] that is surprisingly late for one who was already advanced in years in Columba's youth. If Adomnán's evidence is to be given weight, the chronology of Finnian of Clonard, dying in the plague of 549, looks like a more plausible point of reference.[57] Therefore, if the association of Movilla with Uinniau is primary, the case for cult-diffusion must be separated from received chronology. In principle, that would present no problem, for it is quite probable that much of the detailed chronology of the 'Age of the Saints' is a later construct: however, the very real possibility that the annal-entries for 549 and 579 belonged to a chronicle kept at Iona in Adomnán's day,[58] and in which Adomnán himself may even have had a hand,[59] give some grounds for serious concern about pursuing such an argument.

The final argument for seeing Movilla as Uinniau's location and that of the original cult is based on geography or distribution – that is, the full spread of the cult of St Finnian-Finnio-Finnbarr in the Gaelic world is most easily explained by positing Ulster as the starting point.[60] Unfortunately, the spread is so great that it is not easy to see why on this testimony Clonard (or even Cork) could not provide the origin.

On the evidence so far presented it does not seem to me to be possible now, any more than it was when I last discussed the question in 1984,[61] to locate Uinniau at a particular point in the Gaelic world. Indeed, it is only the extensive evidence of the *Wanderkult* which causes us to place him there at all. For all the other testimony which bears on him could be explained by reference to the christian Brittonic-speaking world (comprising at that date parts of northern Britain, all western Britain, the Isle of Man, and as much of Brittany as had yet been conquered by emigrating Britons).

This brings us naturally to the question of Uinniau's nationality. Ó Riain asked, 'does it really matter whether the saint was ... British or Irish in origin?'[62] The implication was that it does not – as long, that is, as one admits the saint to be Irish! To achieve this, however, one has to go to great lengths to avoid the natural inference from the evidence. The earliest witnesses to the name all give us a Brittonic hypocoristic:[63] Uinniau as a name was borrowed into Irish and subsequently updated to Finnio, then Finnia;[64] one of the testimonies to the spread and diversification of his cult in the Gaelic world is precisely the continuing use of Uinniau and its Irish derivatives Finnio and Finnia; the very isolation of these forms within their Old Irish linguistic context highlights their continuing usage.[65]

If we are to seek an original full form, the place to start is in

Neo-Brittonic. There will be different views as to whether the evidence of the names Findbarr and Bairrfhind also given to St Finnian of Movilla (and indeed to the patron-saint of Cork) are admissible as evidence in the search.[66] I repeat that Old Irish 'Findbarr could ... have been created by conjecture from the hypocoristic'.[67] If, however, we admit either of the Irish forms as evidence for this British ecclesiastic's name, supposing one of them to be a translation of a full British form, we find at once that this is not at all a difficult proposition. At Llandawke in southwestern Wales (in the old Carmarthenshire) is a pillar which seems to have been prepared in the fifth century to bear an ogam-inscription, now incomplete, reading DUMELEDONAS MAQI M....[68] It appears to have been subsequently reused, perhaps about 500, for an unrelated Latin inscription reading BARRIVENDI FILIVS VENDVBARI HIC IACIT.[69] The Latin-letter forms – which could be Irish (ancestors of Old Irish Bairrfhind and Findbarr) but are more naturally taken from their linguistic, formulaic, and geographical contexts to be British – offer the ancestors of Old Welsh *Barrguinn, later *Berrguinn, and *Guinnbar, Modern Welsh Berwyn and Gwynfor. Given the relative closeness of the British and Irish forms until about A.D. 600, it would not be difficult to see how an individual's name would pass easily back and forth between the two languages. If our British saint were *Uindubarros, post-mortem differences would have been occasioned not by apocope or by syncope of composition-vowels, but by the development of British -nd- to -nn- in the second half of the sixth century and of Irish U- to F- around 600 or a little later,[70] giving Early Old Welsh *Uinnbarr and Early Old Irish Findbarr. Certainly one would expect Brittonic and Gaelic speakers to have recognised the cognate name-form until the latter change was complete. In sum, if Old Irish Findbarr does represent accurately the full form of Uinniau's name – and it is far from certain that it is not simply conjectural supply of seventh-century date[71] – the linguistic context may be seen to have existed in the sixth century in which transference of that information from Brittonic would have been quite possible.

If Uinniau's floruit were in the first half of the sixth century, it would be possible to think that his hypocoristic name-form was then *Uindiauos. If, on the other hand, he died after the British loss of final syllables and after the change -nd->-nn- had been effected, he would by then have been Uinniau in his native tongue. That form was borrowed into Irish, but was and remained a linguistic oddity there.[72]

A final point remains. It has recently been asserted that it is a 'fact that the distribution of dedications in Irish churches was already more or less complete by about 650'[73] and the same has been implied with reference to Celtic western Britain.[74] This is a very large claim which has not been demonstrated and cannot therefore be regarded as a 'fact'. It is also hard to see how it might be established with conviction. The evidence would have to be drawn from hagiotoponymy, not directly from evidence of dedications.[75] We should have to rely very largely on seventh-century hagiography whose coverage of the Gaelic world is exceedingly patchy. And of course this assertion ignores the very great impact which the ascetic movement of the late eighth and ninth centuries appears to have had on Gaelic toponymy.[76]

This issue intersects with the question of the localisations of Uinniau's cult to the extent that, if we suppose 650 to be an approximate end-date for the spread of cult, the various particular manifestations should be in place by then. As I have indicated, I do not think that it is necessary to accept such a chronological restriction. It seems in principle implausible to attach any end-date to the continuing spread of Gaelic saints' cults and it is far from clear that 650 would suit the history deduced for St Uinniau/Findbarr by Ó Riain.[77] However, there is no obvious difficulty in admitting that the cult of St Uinniau had been localised at Clonard and Movilla by the mid-seventh century. Their assignment to local population-groups by use of the archaic formula *maccu* would almost by itself establish the point.[78] Depending on when St Uinniau lived and died, there would be more or less time in which to see secondary localisation of cult taking place. Whether Uinniau died at Clonard in 549 or at Movilla in 579, there is also ample time before the mid-seventh century for Uinniau's assimilation to local population-groups to have taken place.

It must be admitted, I think, that such evidence as we have speaks, if weakly, for Clonard as an earlier site of cult and assimilation to local identity. Adomnán's testimony points to Uinniau being old already in the 540s:[79] a death-date in 549 (that attributed to St Finnian of Clonard) would be quite suitable. The assimilation of Uinniau to maccu Telduib, one of whose members, Colmán, ruled Clonard until 654, perhaps from as early as 615,[80] is hard to explain if the Uí Luascáin family – a Leinster, not a Meath, kindred – had not had an early interest in the foundation. On the other hand, various reasons could be plausibly hypothesised for the community of Movilla presenting Uinniau as a member of Dál Fiatach, the local population-group.

All this is uncertain territory, however. Neither of the death-dates need be accepted, for the record is uncertainly contemporary. Uinniau may have been associated with both Clonard and Movilla. Equally, he may have belonged initially to neither, Cork or one of the lesser cult-sites being his hypothetically historical home in Ireland. What it illustrates is that much of the history of the 'Age of the Saints' is irrecoverable, for the reasons which I stated at the outset. Whether or not 'St Finnian' had an original connexion with Movilla, what is clear, I think, is that the primary evidence gives him the Brittonic pet-name Uinniau. It is perverse to suppose that he was other than a Briton. We do not know whether he ever worked in Ireland.[81] Adomnán's Life of St Columba is the earliest evidence, and it is far from contemporary with Uinniau. But, if he did work there, we have no difficulty in recognising a credible context, for the founding era of Irish christianity was one in which British influence was strong.[82]

References

1. On this period see most recently David N. Dumville et al., Saint Patrick, A.D. 493-1993 (Woodbridge, 1993), and Dáibhí Ó Cróinín, Early Medieval Ireland, 400-1200 (London, 1995), chapters 1-2, 6-7.

2. Gearóid Mac Niocaill, Ireland before the vikings (Dublin, 1972), chapter 4.

3. For discussion of militant paganism, see R. Sharpe, 'Hiberno-Latin laicus, Irish láech and the devil's men', Ériu, xxx (1979), pp 75-92; K. R. McCone, 'Werewolves, cyclopes, díberga, and fianna: juvenile delinquency in early Ireland', Cambridge Medieval Celtic Studies, xii (1986), pp 1-22.

4. For one example of this in the closing years of the seventh century, see A. O'Leary, 'An Irish apocryphal apostle: Muirchú's portrayal of Saint Patrick', Harvard Theological Review, lxxxix (1996), pp 287-301.

5. On Movilla, see A. Hamlin, 'The early Church in county Down to the twelfth century', above, chapter 3, and A. J. Hughes & R. J. Hannan, Place-names of Northern Ireland, ii, County Down, ii, The Ards (Belfast, 1992), pp 233-5.

6. On the 'Chronicle of Ireland' see Kathleen Hughes, Early Christian Ireland: introduction to the sources (London, 1972), pp 99-107, and Kathryn Grabowski & David Dumville, Chronicles and annals of mediaeval Ireland and Wales: the Clonmacnoise-group texts (Woodbridge, 1984), pp 53-5, 111-12.

7. The Annals of Ulster (to A.D. 1131), ed. and transl. Seán Mac Airt & Gearóid Mac Niocaill (Dublin, 1983), pp 90-1. Cf. The Annals of Tigernach, ed. and transl. Whitley Stokes (2nd ed., 2 vols, Felinfach, 1993), i, p. 153: Quies Uianni episcopi nepotis Fiatach.

8. For that formula see E. MacNeill, 'Mocu, maccu', Ériu, iii (1907), pp 42-9; cf. Damian McManus, A guide to ogam (Maynooth, 1991), pp 51-2, 56-7, 110-11, 119-20, and T. M. Charles-Edwards, Early Irish and Welsh kinship (Oxford, 1993), pp 123, 141-60.

9. J. MacNeill, 'Early Irish population-groups: their nomenclature, classification, and chronology', R.I.A. Proc., xxix, C (1911-12), pp 59-114.

10. The Martyrology of Tallaght, ed. R. I. Best & H. J. Lawlor (London, 1931), p. 70. This is the first Irish entry. The third begins with what appears to be a doublet: Findbair Maigi.... For the date see ibid., pp x, xx-xxi; Acta sanctorum Hiberniae, ed. John Colgan (Leuven, 1645; reprinted Dublin, 1948), p. 4 (§ 25); Ireland's Desert-Fathers, ed. and transl. Edward J. Gwynn et al. (Chichester, 1996), pp xv-xvi.

11. P. Ó Riain, 'St. Finnbarr: a study in a cult', Journal of the Cork Historical and Archaeological Society, lxxxii (1977), pp 63-82 (at p. 78), but with Fiatach in Corpus genealogiarum sanctorum Hiberniae, ed. Pádraig Ó Riain (Dublin, 1985), p. 145 (§ 707.384).

12. *Félire Óengusso Céli Dé – The Martyrology of Oengus the Culdee*, ed. and transl. Whitley Stokes (London, 1905), p. 193.

13. *The Annals of Inisfallen*, ed. and transl. Seán Mac Airt (Dublin, 1951), pp 76-7.

14. For the most recent discussion, see Máire Herbert, *Iona, Kells, and Derry* (Oxford, 1988), chapters 1 and 12.

15. See above, n. 8.

16. Rudolf Thurneysen, *A grammar of Old Irish* (2nd ed., Dublin, 1975), p. 123 (§ 202). Cf. K. H. Jackson, 'Primitive Irish *u* and *b*', *Études celtiques*, v (1949-51), pp 105-15; W. Cowgill, 'On the fate of **w* in Old Irish', *Language*, xliii (1967), pp 129-38; Dumville, 'Gildas and Uinniau', p. 209 and n. 24.

17. Thurneysen, *A grammar*, p. 93 (§ 151); cf. Dumville, 'Gildas and Uinniau' (n. 20, below), p. 209 and n. 22.

18. Thurneysen, *A grammar*, pp 174, 175 (§§ 272, 274.5). I am indebted to Proinsias Mac Cana for helpful discussion on this point. For the range of possible forms in a parallel case, that of Cumméne, Cummianus, see *Acta*, ed. Colgan, pp 58-9, 408-11, 844; his documentation about Finnian (ibid., pp 393-407) is less rich in this respect.

19. P. Ó Riain, 'Finnio and Winniau: a question of priority', in *Indogermanica et Caucasica. Festschrift für Karl Horst Schmidt zum 65. Geburtstag*, ed. Roland Bielmeier & Reinhard Stempel (Berlin, 1994), pp 407-14, at p. 408. In that article, four bibliographical references remain unexplained. 'Bowen 1956' is Emrys G. Bowen, *The settlements of the Celtic saints in Wales* (2nd ed., Cardiff, 1956). 'Loth 1910' is Joseph Loth, *Les noms des saints bretons* (Paris, 1910). 'Thurneysen 1931-33' is R. Thurneysen, 'Colmán mac Lénéni und Senchán Torpéist', *Zeitschrift für celtische Philologie*, xix (1931-3), pp 193-207; 'Wright 1984' is N. Wright, 'Gildas's geographical perspective: some problems', in *Gildas: new approaches*, ed. Michael Lapidge & David Dumville (Woodbridge, 1984), pp 85-105.

20. Thurneysen, *A grammar*, p. 175 (§ 275). Cf. D. N. Dumville, 'Gildas and Uinniau', in *Gildas: new approaches*, ed. Lapidge & Dumville, pp 207-14, at 209-10.

21. Thurneysen, *A grammar*, pp. 173-4 (§ 271); cf. D. N. Dumville, 'Some British aspects of the earliest Irish christianity', in *Ireland and Europe: the early Church*, ed. Próinséas Ní Catháin & Michael Richter (Stuttgart, 1984), pp 16-24, at 19-20.

22. Ó Riain, 'Finnio and Winniau', p. 408.

23. See above, n. 12.

24. Ó Riain, 'Finnio and Winniau', p. 411; J. Carey, 'Scél Tuáin meic Chairill', *Ériu*, xxxv (1984), pp 93-111, at 101 and 105. On the church, Tamlachta Bairchi, associated with Tuán, see Mícheál B. Ó Mainnín, *Place-names of Northern Ireland*, iii, *County Down*, iii, *The Mournes* (Belfast, 1993), pp 64-5.

25. *Adomnán's Life of Columba*, ed. and transl. A. O. Anderson & M. O. Anderson (2nd ed., Oxford, 1991), pp 186-7 (III.4). For *Findbarr* see ibid., pp. 12-13 (I.1) and 94-5 (II.1). On the manuscript see J.-M. Picard, 'The Schaffhausen Adomnán – a unique witness to Hiberno-Latin', *Peritia*, i (1982), pp 216-49, and A. Harvey, 'Retrieving the pronunciation of early Insular Celtic scribes: the case of Dorbbéne', *Celtica*, xxii (1991), pp 48-63.

26. On British *nn*, see below, n. 70.

27. *Adomnán's Life*, ed. and transl. Anderson & Anderson, p. 94 (misrendered as 'Findbarr' on p. 95). Adomnán's apparent use of three forms makes one wonder whether his sources are reflected thus, and in particular whether *Finnio* was a form which he himself used.

28. For details, see Dumville, 'Gildas and Uinniau', and P. Byrne, 'The community of Clonard, sixth to twelfth centuries', *Peritia*, iv (1985), pp 157-73, at 158-60, 167.

29. For an exception, see below, n. 48. We also find the form *Finniau(i)* twice in *The Martyrology of Tallaght*, ed. Best & Lawlor, pp 20 (2 March) and 74 (27 September).

30. *The Annals of Ulster*, ed. and transl. Mac Airt & Mac Niocaill, pp 76-7.

31. For all these, see Dumville, 'Gildas and Uinniau'.

32. *Adomnán's Life*, ed. and transl. Anderson & Anderson, pp 184-5 (III.2).

33. Ibid., pp 12-13, 94-5 (I.1, II.1), for Ireland. For all the references, cf. nn 25 and 27, above.

34. Ibid., pp 130-1 (II.25).

35. P. Byrne, 'The community', p. 167.

36. Ibid. However, the decisive year for Leinster was 516 when much territory was lost to Uí Néill: it is very uncertain whether Clonard could still have been in Leinster in the 540s. Cf. F. J. Byrne, *Irish kings and high kings* (London, 1973), pp 142,147; and Alfred P. Smyth, *Celtic Leinster* (Blackrock, 1982), pp 8-9, 17.

37. For discussion of Adomnán and Columba, see Herbert, *Iona*, chapters 1-3 and 12.

38. For an assemblage of all the evidence, see Dumville, 'Gildas and Uinniau'.

39. Ó Riain, 'St. Finnbarr'.

40. See above, nn 8-11.

41. On Finnian and Colmán maccu Telduib, see P. Byrne, 'The community', pp 158-60, 167. For maccu Telduib see ibid., pp 159, 160. According to Byrne, Colmán's 'designation *moccu Thellduib* indicates that he belonged to Finnian's branch of Uí Luascán', 'a Leinster people who fell into obscurity in the seventh to eighth centuries'.

42. For the date see *Adomnán's Life*, ed. and transl. Anderson & Anderson, p. xlii. Cf. P. Ó Riain, 'Adamnán's age at death: fact or symbol?', *Studia Celtica Japonica*, new series, v (1992), pp 7-17.

43. Dumville, 'Gildas and Uinniau', p. 212; Ó Riain, 'Finnio and Winniau', p. 409.

44. Ó Riain, 'St. Finnbarr'.

45. 'Finnio and Winniau', pp 410-11.

46. 'St. Finnbarr', pp 74-6.

47. 'Finnio and Winniau', p. 411.

48. 'St. Finnbarr', p. 75, n. 82. He has described this process as 'guesswork', a view with which I am happy to concur.

49. *Sancti Columbani opera*, ed. and transl. G. S. M. Walker (Dublin, 1957), pp 8-9 (Letter 1, § 7).

50. For doubts about the authorship see D. N. Dumville, 'Ireland, Brittany, and England: transmission and use of *Collectio canonum hibernensis*', in *Irlande et Bretagne. Vingt siècles d'histoire*, ed. Catherine Laurent & Helen Davis (Rennes, 1994), pp 84-95. For the letter-fragments, see R. Sharpe, 'Gildas as a Father of the Church', in *Gildas: new approaches*, ed. Lapidge & Dumville, pp 193-205.

51. *The Irish penitentials*, ed. and transl. Ludwig Bieler & D. A. Binchy (Dublin, 1963), p. 5; *Le Pénitentiel de Saint Colomban*, ed. Jean Laporte (Tournai, 1958), pp 23-46.

52. See above, n. 33.

53. Ó Riain, 'St. Finnbarr', p. 65, meaning that Finnian of Movilla must have been intended.

54. M. Ní Dhonnchadha, 'The guarantor list of *Cáin Adomnáin*, 697', *Peritia*, i (1982), pp 178-215, at p. 192 (no. 24). No representative of Cork or Movilla seems to have been involved.

55. For the date, cf. Dumville, 'Gildas and Uinniau', pp 208-9, 213.

56. See above, n. 7.
57. See above, n. 30.
58. A. P. Smyth, 'The earliest Irish annals: their first contemporary entries, and the earliest centres of recording', *Proceedings of the Royal Irish Academy*, lxxii C (1972), pp 1-48.
59. Hughes, *Early Christian Ireland*, p. 118.
60. Ó Riain, 'St. Finnbarr', pp 72-8. Cf. E. G. Bowen, 'The cult of St. Brigit', *Studia Celtica*, viii-ix (1973-4), pp 33-47, at 35-9, and P. Ó Riain, 'The Irish element in Welsh hagiographical tradition', in *Irish antiquity. Essays and studies presented to Professor M. J. O'Kelly*, ed. Donnchadh Ó Corráin (Cork, 1981), pp 291-303.
61. Dumville, 'Gildas and Uinniau', p. 214.
62. 'Finnio and Winniau', p. 412.
63. Old Breton and Old Welsh derivatives are extant: cf. Dumville, 'Gildas and Uinniau', p. 210, n. 29.
64. The forms *Findio* and *Findia* are Middle Irish (or later) scribal archaising hypercorrections.
65. See above, n. 19.
66. To Ó Riain's example of St Finnian of Movilla as Barrén as well as Finnén ('St. Finnbarr', pp 64-5), I can add a full reverse-form, *Barrfhinn Bile*, from a verse secondary addition in the 'Annals of Ulster' (878.3): ed. and transl. Mac Airt & Mac Niocaill, pp 332-3.
67. Dumville, 'Gildas and Uinniau', p. 214. It is unlikely that *Bairrfhind* was created thus: it is, rather, either a secondary development from *Findbarr* or a reflexion of the saint's original Brittonic name.
68. *Corpus inscriptionum insularum celticarum*, ed. R. A. S. Macalister (2 vols, Dublin, 1945-9), i, pp 351-2 (no. 368); V. E. Nash-Williams, *The early christian monuments of Wales* (Cardiff, 1950), p. 113 (no. 150). Cf. McManus, *A guide*, p. 121 (cf. p. 118), for a hint as to dating.
69. Cf. Ó Riain, 'St. Finnbarr', p. 64 and n. 12; Dumville, 'Gildas and Uinniau', p. 210.
70. For British *nd* > *nn* by the second half of the sixth century, see Kenneth Jackson, *Language and history in early Britain* (Edinburgh, 1953), pp 511-13, 695-6; on composition-vowels, see pp 643-51; on Irish syncope, see p. 143.
71. The date is controlled by that of Adomnán's Life of St Columba, written in 697 x 704, in which *Findbarr* and *Uinniau* refer to one and the same person: see above, nn. 25, 27, 33.
72. See above, n. 19.
73. Ó Riain, 'Finnio and Winniau', p. 410.
74. Ibid., pp 411-13, with further reference to Ó Riain, 'The Irish element'.
75. On this problem see O. Chadwick, 'The evidence of dedications in the early history of the Welsh Church', in *Studies in early British history*, ed. Nora K. Chadwick (Cambridge, 1954; rev. imp. 1959), pp 173-88.
76. See my remarks in *Ireland's Desert-Fathers*, ed. and transl. Gwynn et al., pp lxiii-lxiv, with especial reference to D. Flanagan, 'The christian impact on early Ireland: place-names evidence', in *Ireland and Europe*, ed. Ní Chatháin & Richter, pp 25-51, especially 34-6 and 48.
77. 'St. Finnbarr'.
78. See above, n. 8.
79. See above, n. 55.
80. See above, n. 41.
81. If he did not, we must simply hypothesise the spread of his cult from Britain.
82. See Dumville et al., *Saint Patrick*, pp 133-45; cf. Dumville, 'Some British aspects'.

2. LIVES OF ST FINNIAN OF MOVILLA: BRITISH EVIDENCE

INGRID SPERBER

Finnian of Movilla is usually reckoned to have been one of Ireland's important mediaeval saints. Certainly he appears to have been the principal saint of Ulster's Dál Fiatach in the early middle ages: his church of Movilla was the major ecclesiastical centre in that kingdom.[1] It has therefore seemed paradoxical that no Irish hagiography of Finnian moccu Fiatach has survived among the voluminous Hiberno-Latin and vernacular literature in that genre.[2]

The hagiological tradition does not lack references to him or his church: he and other saints of Movilla appear in Irish martyrologies and kalendars,[3] and pedigrees of him reassure us that he was indeed claimed as a member of Dál Fiatach.[4] The full pedigree reads as follows: 'Finnian Maige Bile mac Coirpre maic Ailella maic Thríchim maic Fhéicc maic Fhindchada maic Bresail maic Shírchada maic Fhiatach Fhind a quo Dál Fiatach';[5] in other words, St Finnian was the great-great-great-great-great-great-grandson of the eponym of Dál Fiatach. Another genealogical statement named seven sons of his 'great-grandfather' Tríchem: the second of these was *Ailill i mMaig Bile,* thus purporting to establish that the family had a right to Movilla already in the generation of Finnian's grandfather, Ailill.[6] These pedigrees are of course fantasy, especially if the historical Finnian was a Briton called Uinniau and perhaps one having no connexion with Movilla; but they were fantasy created with the purpose of anchoring St Finnian firmly within Dál Fiatach, a fiction which had no doubt been believed since the seventh century.[7]

The church of Movilla is reasonably well, but by no means exhaustively, recorded in Irish chronicles. Apart from the notice of the death of Uinnianus moccu Fiatach at 579, which is unlikely in its original form to have mentioned Movilla,[8] members of the church are named on nine occasions from 603 to 825,[9] and in the latter year there is an Irish-language entry to the effect that Movilla was burned by vikings.[10] In 831 we read of the drowning of Airmedach, *princeps* (erenagh, that is) of Movilla. Although a gap of almost sixty years follows before another record is available, local continuity is assured by the information that the erenagh whose death is noticed at 890 was also called Airmedach.[11]

The tenth- and eleventh-century record is difficult to interpret. What is certain is that the institution continued in existence. We meet another erenagh, Oengus mac Con Loingsi, who died in 955.[12] A link with the church of St Comgall of Bangor, newly drawn out of the political orbit of Dál Araide and into that of Dál Fiatach, is established by records of the deaths of joint coarbs in 975 and 1025:[13] this link was no doubt facilitated by Bangor's changing political affiliation.[14] It is possible that a joint-coarbship arrangement also existed intermittently with the church of St Mo-Cholmóc of Druim Mór (Dromore), for in 993, 1019, and 1043 we read of the deaths of *comarba Finné(i)n ocus Mo-Cholmóc:* but this may alternatively be interpreted as referring to the patron-saints of Clonard (county Meath).[15] The only other certain notice of Movilla in this period belongs to 1007 and sheds a different kind of light on its affairs:[16] in that year Brian Bórama, overking of Munster and by then *imperator Scottorum,*[17] conducted a military expedition against Cenél Eogain; the recorded result was that he seized from them the abbot of Movilla, Ua Críchidén, who had been given as an Ulster hostage to Cenél Eogain; one Mael Brigte Ua Críchidén, abbot of Movilla and Bangor, perhaps the same person but certainly a member of the same family, died peacefully in 1025.[18]

Undoubtable references to Movilla are thereafter lacking until the 1160s and 1170s, although if an indulgent attitude were taken towards the chronicle-evidence we could see the abbey still under hereditary rule in the second half of the eleventh century.[19] In 1167 an act of secular violence was committed in the middle of Movilla (no explicit mention being made of the church).[20] Violence, albeit of a different sort, again figures in the last two pre-Conquest notices of Movilla. In 1170, in the 'Annals of Loch Cé' and the 'Annals of Ulster', a lengthy and emotional entry tells that *Gním mór ainfial do dénum,* 'A scandalous great deed was done':[21] the principal villains of the piece were Amlaím, monk and son of the coarb of Finnian of Movilla, and Magnus Mac Duinn Shléibe, king of the Ulaid, as well as many other Ulstermen. Amlaím had been deposed, after due process, as abbot of Saul, a new house of Arroasian Canons established presumably in the 1140s by Archbishop Malachy,[22] and he now expelled all the members of the community (presumably thus severing for the time being the house's affiliation with the Arroasian order). Amlaím died in 1175 as abbot of Saul and bishop of the Ulaid.[23] Thereafter, both Movilla and Saul pass out of native record although both seem to have been Augustinian houses until the Dissolution.[24]

Given the importance of the church of Movilla to Dál Fiatach, and its wider renown as indicated by the evidence of the Gaelic martyrologies and chronicles, the absence of hagiography of Finnian moccu Fiatach has proved difficult to interpret.[25] However, a range of non-Irish texts offers testimony that such hagiography did once exist. There are three relevant items. One is not considered here, for it deserves full, separate, and technical treatment. This is the hagiographical corpus concerning St Frigdianus (Frediano) of Lucca in Italy.[26] It has long been known that some of the Lives of this sixth-century saint claim an Irish origin for him: on closer inspection they have proved to be partly derivative of hagiography of St Finnian of Movilla.[27] The other two items have a Scottish dimension.

The first is found in *Noua Legenda Anglie*, literally 'New Legends of England' but rather a 'New English Legendary', a massive corpus of abbreviated Lives of saints, first put together by John of Tynemouth in the mid-fourteenth century at St Albans Abbey (Hertfordshire) under the heading *Sanctilogium Angliae, Walliae, Scotiae, et Hiberniae*, subsequently revised, and at length issued in printed form with new material in 1516. A critical edition by Carl Horstman was published in 1901,[28] but the work as a whole has never been translated into English. The Life of St Finnian which it contains is translated here for the first time.[29] This Life, however, was not derived from Movilla but rather attests to the existence of his cult in Scotland. We are told at the outset that Bishop Finnian was known also by the Welsh name Winninus *(qui et wallico nomine Winninus appellatur)*. At the end of the Life the cult-site is identified as Kilwinning in the district of Cunningham in Ayrshire *(in loco qui ab eius wallico nomine Kilwinnin appellatur)*. Apart from these two references to his Welsh name and one to Scotland, the content of the Life is wholly Irish, save in as much as Finnian is represented as having received training both in Britain and at Rome. The saint's feast-day is 10 September, the same as that of Finnian of Movilla.

Nevertheless, the references to the Welsh name and the Scottish cult-site are of importance. *Win(n)in,* if one removes the Latin termination, seems likely to be a derivative of the Brittonic form *Uinniau.* Did the author of the Life know and understand the significance of that form? Does such a comment indeed enhance the possibility that the connexions of Finnian of Movilla with the British world were in the first instance historical in kind? Or is its presence related to the location of the cult? – Kilwinning is situated in Cunningham, the northern district of Ayrshire, in the heart of what was once the kingdom of Strathclyde, inhabited by a people of British (that is, by another formulation, Welsh) speech.[30] A partial answer to these questions is perhaps proffered by the content of this Life, to which we shall turn shortly.

The second Scottish item comes directly from a Scottish source. This is the 'Breviary of Aberdeen', *Breuiarium Aberdonense,* a printed liturgical book published in two parts at Aberdeen in 1509/10 and now surviving only in a handful of copies.[31] A facsimile reprint was issued by the Bannatyne Club in 1854 but neither a critical edition nor a translation has ever been published. In the volume covering 29 November to 18 June and described as the Breviary's *Pars Hyemalis* ('Winter Part') we meet St Uynninus, undoubtedly the patron of Kilwinning, first at 21 January in the kalendar and then among the *legenda* of the saints for January.[32] This is a liturgical text and has therefore a wholly different character from the Life in *Noua Legenda Anglie.* But there are also several striking differences of content.

Although the saint's Irish background is acknowledged, his Irish name is nowhere given, the feast-day in question is not that of Finnian of Movilla (10 September), and the author brings him to Scotland at his coming of age. The events of his life are concentrated in Ayrshire and Dumfriesshire and a reported *post-mortem* miracle seems to have occurred at Kilwinning itself. Nevertheless, there are points of comparison between the narrative and that of the other hagiography. In other words, while no attempt has been made to reject the saint's Irish origins, in all other respects he has been assimilated to a southwestern Scottish context of a cult centred on Kilwinning and (farther south and east) Holywood. His feast-day, 21 January, does not appear to be shared with any other manifestation of the cult of St Finnian.

How is this distribution of evidence to be explained? A comprehensive solution cannot be offered here, for its achievement would depend on thorough investigation of the hagiography of Frediano of Lucca.[33] However, two lines of enquiry can be pursued, concerning St Finnian in his Irish (and particularly Ulster) context and St Winninus of Kilwinning in Strathclyde.

The Life in *Noua Legenda Anglie* makes St Finnian (the name is given wrongly as Finanus, as though he were St Fínán) a member of Dál nAraide (*Aradei* in the Latin text),[34] one of the leading population-groups of early mediaeval Ulster. His parents are named as they are in Irish genealogical and hagiological sources (albeit with the spelling mistake *Capreus* for *Carpreus* in naming his father).[35] In all Irish sources, however, Finnian is made a member of a rival and usually dominant group, Dál Fiatach. If the attribution to Dál nAraide is a slip of the pen, it is extraordinary because of its political implications; it is also one which is likely to have been made only by a Gaelic writer.[36]

Although no serious attempt has been made in this text to attach Finnian to Kilwinning, equally there is a remarkable absence of reference to Movilla. Instead, we find a much broader concern with northern Ireland. St Patrick is said to have foretold Finnian's holy fame. Finnian was educated first by a Bishop Colmán who has usually been taken to be the patron of Dromore (commonly known as St Mo-Cholmóc), although this does not seem to be irrefutably demonstrable. Coelán, abbot of Nendrum *(Coelanum Noendrumensem)*, usually known as St Mo-Choe, declined to accept him as a pupil, recognising his greater virtue. Here, then, the saint is shown as superior to the patrons of two other important churches in what is now county Down. To complete his education he studied first in Britain with Bishop Nennius (sometimes, but uncertainly, identified with St Ninian of Whithorn in Galloway)[37] and then at Rome. On returning to Ireland he performed a miracle at the nunnery of Killevy (county Armagh),[38] resuscitated a Bishop Nath Í (not certainly identified),[39] and then had a series of adventures with royalty.

He clashed with a son of King Daimíne, ruler of Airgialla, who through his sons is particularly associated with Clogher, county Tyrone *(Clochar mac nDaimíne).*[40] He brought round an arrogant King Diarmait who is certainly Diarmait mac Cerbaill, Uí Néill king of Tara (544-65), a figure almost universally treated as a villain in Irish hagiography.[41] And King Tuathal, described as Diarmait's predecessor and therefore certainly identifiable as Tuathal Maelgarb, Uí Néill king of Tara (536-44), died in arrogance, as Finnian predicted. The only sense in which these rulers, who belonged to quite different branches of Uí Néill, were successive kings was as kings of Tara and therefore claimants to overkingship of the northern half of Ireland.

It is striking that no king of the province of the Ulaid is to be found in this account, nor any mention of Dál Fiatach or of Movilla. The context for the origin of this text may need to be sought at a time when the cult of St Finnian was expanding among the Cruithin, Airgialla, and Uí Néill.

The Scottish liturgical text, on the other hand, acknowledges the Irish royal origin of St Winninus but gives no details. In all other respects the focus is on Scotland. The principal cult-site, Kilwinning, is Gaelic in its first element, but the second seems to represent a popular assimilation of Winnin to the shape of English name-forms, perhaps by hypercorrection.[42] The name Winnin itself presents problems and one can suppose that, like Ninnian from an original Ninniau, it represents a corruption from Uinniau, a Brittonic name-form otherwise associable with St Finnian.[43] What is interesting and unexplained is how in the middle ages the equation of Finnian and Winnin(us) came to be made. There seem to be three possibilities: (1) it was inherited from the (now lost) hagiography of St Finnian of Movilla; (2) it arose from the assimilation of a local Strathclyde cult to a more widespread Gaelic one after Strathclyde began to be absorbed into the Gaelic kingdom of Alba in the eleventh century, an assimilation which provided a context for borrowing from the hagiography of St Finnian; (3) the equation is original and historical, in as much as St Finnian – if we accept him as a sixth-century figure – seems to have had British associations. The last of these is the least likely but cannot be wholly excluded. What is perhaps most interesting in all this is the evidence for the assimilation of British and Gaelic cults in the territory of the kingdom of Strathclyde.

I conclude by presenting a hypothesis to explain the relationship of our texts to this process. At some point, perhaps in the absence of hagiography of the original saint of Kilwinning, but perhaps in order to suppress it, that of St Finnian of Movilla was substituted, along with his feast-day. The local patron's original feast-day eventually proved too entrenched to be rejected and reasserted itself. Meanwhile, the hagiography of St Finnian was adapted in order to root it thoroughly in its local south-west Scottish context. The precise chronology of this process remains to be determined.[44]

There follows a translation of the Life of St Finnian/Winnin from Carl Horstman's edition of *Noua Legenda Anglie*,[45] succeeded by a parallel-text edition and translation of the liturgy of St Winnin from the 'Breviary of Aberdeen'.[46]

LIFE OF ST FINNIAN FROM *NOVA LEGENDA ANGLIE*

On God's Servant Finnian, Bishop and Confessor

The most reverend Bishop Finnian *(Finanus)*, who is also known by the Welsh name Winninus, was son of Cairpre *(Capreus)* and Lasair *(Lassara)* and was descended from Dál nAraide *(Aradei)* and the nobility of Ulster.

The blessed Patrick, bishop of the Irish, foretold that Finnian would be a venerable and famous bishop. Once, at a great feast, when his parents had been abundantly entertaining their entire family for three nights, there was no wine left. However, the boy's parents were confident of his sanctity according to the prophecy of Saint Patrick. With the infant's hand, they made the sign of the cross over three vessels filled with weak ale, which assumed the colour and flavour of excellent wine.

Later, when Bishop Colmán *(Colmannus)* arrived, the docile boy was entrusted to him, and, for a few years, he was taught by him, in obedience and humility. Once, when the holy boy was reading, and the blessed bishop for some reason was raising his hand to whip him, an angel of the Lord held the hand back, suspended in the air. When this happened, Finnian, who had thrown himself down on the ground, said: "My father, why do you not strike me?" He answered: "My son, that is my wish, but I am hindered by divine power. Thus, if you wish to be whipped, you should go to another teacher. Until then, I shall not hurt you."

And the bishop sent him to the venerable old man Coelán *(Coelanus)*, abbot of Nendrum [Mahee Island in Strangford Lough], earnestly entrusting him with the care of the boy's body and soul. But when the abbot saw the boy's face, at once he said: "This boy will never be my disciple, for he far excels me in honour and merit in heaven and on earth. For he will be a bishop, bright in wisdom and illustrious in religion and holiness." On hearing this, Finnian, inspired by the spirit of prophecy, said: "Soon you will see coming here the one whom I shall follow, and by whom I shall be taught: he will come to my help in any need." And lo, some ships from Britain, carrying a most holy bishop by the name of Nennius, reached the island's port, in front of the monastery. When they had been received with joy and honour, the said fathers carefully entrusted the young Finnian to the venerable bishop. Finnian accompanied the bishop on his return to his country, and for a few years, as a worthy monk, he studied the rules and institutions of the monastic life in the bishop's see, which is known as *Magnum Monasterium.* Poring over the pages of the holy scriptures, he made great progress, and he wrought many miracles by the invocation of the name of God.

A Greek, who had been suffering for many years for his gruesome crimes, and who was harassed by a legion of demons as he travelled around the world, seeking health, was liberated by Finnian's prayer from all his diseases of body and soul. The daughter of the king of Britain felt a strong and sinful desire for him, and one day she shamelessly lured him into the forbidden act. By God's just decision she died shortly afterwards, in the presence of her father and the people. Finnian, moved by the laments of her parents and the other people present, revived her to a life in chastity and holiness.

Trusting in the Lord, Finnian drank a cup of water, poisoned by a certain envious person, and felt absolutely no harm afterwards.

Although he was well instructed in monastic rules and in the holy scriptures, Finnian decided to travel to the apostolic see, for there he could fully drink in what he might lack of holy knowledge. He remained there for seven years, a studious investigator <of the Scriptures>, and was ordained priest. But once, in church, as he was preaching the word of God to the people of Rome, some clerics, out of envy, let organs, trumpets, and other musical instruments sound all at once, so that his voice should not be heard by the people. However, by divine virtue, his voice was heard over the extraordinarily loud noise, and God was glorified in his saint.

Later, by preaching and by miracles, he converted two numerous peoples of idol-worshippers, who lived near Italy, to the faith of Christ. When they attacked him, he made their feet stick to the ground: and, when their king had given orders that a wooden cross should be fixed into the ground on which to crucify the holy man, one of the king's hands became stuck to the cross and the other to his side. But when they had repented and been converted to the christian faith, he immediately released them. Furthermore, followed by two lions from a nearby forest and carrying their cubs in his arms as if they were calves, he walked through the town before the people, for they had promised to believe in God if he did so. Moreover, he revived a man who had been slain by them.

After accomplishing these things, the servant of God hastened to his native land, bringing with him relics of the saints, a marble altar, and three round stones given to him by angels, which he, throughout his life, used by night as lamps when reading, writing, and praying. It is not known to anyone how many brilliant miracles he brought about in Ireland after having been ordained bishop. In a church which is called Killevy *(Cella Montis),* he revived a nun from death; he brought back to life a bishop's servant who had drowned; he called back from the dead a bishop by the name of Nath Í *(Nathus),* who rested in peace after receiving the last communion from Finnian's hands; he revived and baptised a widow's son, who had been dead for three days.

He excommunicated a son of iniquity who had wounded one of his disciples with a spear, saying: "The birds of the air will eat your flesh, and the earth will not receive your bones, which will be dispersed, and your unfortunate soul will descend to endless hell". Shortly after this, a wind from the south blew this enemy of God into a deep valley by the sea, where he died, dangling on a wooden stake which had pierced through him.

The son of King Daimíne *(Damenus)* was disturbing the servant of God when he was consecrating the Host and irreverently prevented him from doing the holy work. But the saint prayed profusely, with his hands stretched out towards the Lord, and a huge hammer fell from the sky on the head of the king's son and killed him, as he deserved.

With his prayers, Finnian made two barren noblewomen conceive and bear children.

He went to King Diarmait *(Diarmecius),* to address him humbly on behalf of a friend. The king ordered that the gates to the town should be bolted, but they were immediately opened by divine power. On learning this, the king climbed into a chariot in order to avoid the saint, but the chariot broke and he fell. Stricken with blindness, he ordered that the saint should be brought to him. The holy man refused, saying: "If he grants my petitions, he will obtain what he wants from God". Then the messenger said to the king: "Truly, he has left to your judgment the issue concerning which you had sent me". When the king had agreed, the man of God ordered that some holy water, with which he should be sprinkled, and his own belt, with which he was to be girded, should be brought to the king. When the king had been sprinkled with the holy water and girded with the belt, he recovered his health.

What is more, Tuathal *(Tuatalus),* the said king's predecessor, when asked for alms, refused to give butter to a man who needed that for his lamps, since he was a studious reader of the holy scriptures both by day and by night. Then Finnian, knowing the future, uttered a word of prophecy in his mother-tongue, predicting that Tuathal would die shortly. When he heard this, it made him repent, and on his knees he asked for pardon, saying: "Master, tell me how I shall die". The saint answered: "One of your servants will kill you". The other man, however, considering himself wise and swelling with excessive pride, even dared to ask God's servant ironically: "How long is the distance between us and the kingdom of God?" The saint answered: "Not too long, for those who dwell there hear the humble man's voice". Then the other man, persisting in his arrogance, said: "Where is hell, in heaven or on earth or under the earth? How wide and how deep is it?

Is it far between us and hell?" The distinguished teacher, somewhat excited by godly zeal, answered him: "I have not measured hell, but you will measure it with your feet. For the road which leads thither, which is wide and short, will have been measured before the end of this day, because you will be there." This prophecy was fulfilled before evening by the king's unexpected death.

I have resolved to select these few from among the very many miracles of this great and very holy bishop, to edify readers. He observed the commandments of Almighty God. He was often visited by angels coming to comfort and advise him; and he received very many other divine revelations. At the end of his life, he lay on his sickbed for a full year, afflicted by infirmity. When the hour of death had come, he received the sacrament of the body and blood of Christ, and he committed his soul into the hands of his Creator, on the tenth day of September. His body was buried in Scotland, in Cunningham *(Cunigham),* at the place which from his Welsh name is called Kilwinning *(Kilwinin).*

BREVIARY OF ABERDEEN: TEXT

Sancti Wynnini episcopi et confessoris ad uesperas oracio.

Sancti Wynnini presulis tui et confessoris incliti solennia agentes, te, Domine, suppliciter deprecamur, ut, dum tui nominis in honore ipsius gesta recolimus et eodem pro nobis benigne intercedente, patrocinia senciamus eterna. *Per Dominum nostrum Iesum.*

Ad matutinas .ix. lectiones fiant. Lectio .i.

Wynninus, scotica prouincia ortus ex illius illustri regum stirpe, et nobili educatus familia et nutritus, suorum parentum cura non parua et solicitudine alitus, et ingenuis eruditus disciplinis binisque in eodem reuolutis lustris mundanis abiectis rebus diuino se mancipauit officio, et eidem deuote deseruire studuit; et sic in perfectam etatem indesinenter perseuerauit, atque exteras sepius postulabat regiones et solitariam a parentum cura ducere uitam. *Tu autem, Domine, miserere nostri.*

Lectio .ii.

Onerosum certe fuit suorum parentum et amicorum iugis frequencia et uicinorum uisitacio assidua, ob id quod suam in Deum contemplacionem continuam uariis impediebant curis. Ea cupiens studiose

BREVIARY OF ABERDEEN: TRANSLATION

Prayer of Saint Finnian (Wynninus), bishop and confessor, for vespers.

As we celebrate the solemnity of St Finnian, Thy bishop and confessor, we pray to Thee, o Lord, that, while we consider what he has wrought in honour of Thy name, and while he benevolently intercedes on our behalf, we may be aware of Thy protection everlasting. *Per Dominum nostrum Iesum.*

There are nine lections for matins. The first lection.

Finnian was born in the kingdom of Ireland, a scion of an illustrious race of her kings. He was brought up in a noble family and was nourished by his parents with great attentiveness and care. He was instructed in the noble arts, but at the age of ten he rejected worldly matters and gave himself over to divine service, to which he attended with zeal and diligence. He continued thus steadfastly until he came of age, often travelling to foreign regions and seeking to lead a solitary life removed from his parents' concerns. *Tu autem, Domine, miserere nostri.*

The second lection.

The constant attendance of his parents and friends, and his neighbours' frequent visits, were truly a burden to him, since they interrupted with various troubles his continuous contemplation of

deuitare, ab eorum aspectibus longius abesse, oportunum <tempus> elegit: paratis nonnullis clam classibus, et que nauigandi usui erant (per)emptis necessariis, atque comilitonibus electis quibusdam sue professioni congruis, prospero uento et felici in Scociam minorem delatus est et ad locum, que Cunnighame dicitur, premitus terram cum suis applicuit.

Lectio tertia. Qui, mox terram illam ingressus, non habentes unde uiuerent, piscandi gracia ad fluuium uocabulo Garnok applicuit. Cumque itinere fatigatus paululum super illius ripas consedisset, cuidam puero imperauit ut hamum in eodem fluuio emitteret, ut inde pisciculos aliquos prenderet. Qui, iussu beati Wynini uicibus iteratis in eodem immittens, nichil prendidit. Contristatusque beatus Wyninus fluuium maledixit, "Ita", inquiens, "in te nullatenus per secula piscis capietur". Qui quidem fluuius, paululum desiliens, proprium reliquit alueum et in aliam partem cursum suum contra naturam derigere fecit usque in hodiernum diem.

Lectio .iiii. Discedens itaque uir Dei de eodem loco, ad alium se transtulit locum, qui nunc Sacrum Nemus a uulgo appellatur, ubi cum discipulis suis uiris uite approbatissimis permanendi locum eligerunt. Non habentes aquam ibidem unde biberent, celitus emissa oracione fons

God. Eagerly desiring to avoid these cares, and to be far away from those people's sight, he chose an appropriate time. He secretly prepared some ships, purchased the necessities which they would use on the journey, and chose some companions fit for his rule of life. Favourable winds brought him to Scotland, and they first made land at the place which is called Cunningham [a district of Ayrshire].

The third lection. He went ashore without delay. As there was nothing to sustain them, he went to a river called Garnock to fish. When he had sat down on its bank for a little while, tired from his journey, he told a boy to put a fish-hook in the river, to catch some fish. At the blessed Finnian's command, the boy did so repeatedly but caught nothing. The blessed Finnian was saddened, and he cursed the river, saying: "Never shall fish be found in you". The river, shifting a little, left its bed, and, against nature, changed its course to the opposite direction; and it remains thus to this day.

The fourth lection. The man of God left this place and went to another, which the people now call the Sacred Grove [Holywood, Dumfriesshire], where he and his disciples – men of the holiest standards of life – chose a place for their permanent abode. There was no water for them to drink

lucidissimus ebuliuit. Ex quo bibentes uarii, ex infirmitatibus, usque in presens, sanati su<nt>.[47] Eaque nocte apparuit beato Wynnino angelus Domini, dicens: "Wynnine, uiriliter age et confortetur cor tuum in Domino. Hunc enim locum ad incolendum preparauit Deus ipse altissimus." *Tu autem.*

Lectio .v. Quibus dictis angelica disparuit uisio. Beatus uero Wyninus, tali confortatus oraculo, Deo uero et omnipotenti gracias humiliter exhibuit, ibique mansionem suam cum ceteris suis discipulis construxerunt, in quo uarios sua predicacione ad Christi fidem persuaserunt. Tandem, in bona senectute et sancta, ab illius patrie clericis et populo in epyscopum consecratur suffultusque quam plurimis miraculis obdormiuit in Domino. Et apud Kilwynne honorifice traditur sepulture, ubi nunc monachorum uiget claritas et illorum uirorum sanctitas perpetua. *Tu.*

Lectio sexta. Quidam dehinc in uilla beati Uynnini qui graui laborabat infirmitate imminere et incurabili morbo adeo[48] ut eius uita omnino desperetur. Perducentes autem illum parentes eius ad basilicam beati Wynnini, ut inde sanaretur. Qui Deo et beato Wynnino preces cum

there, but a very clear spring, granted to them from heaven, burst forth at their prayers. Even to this day, many who drink from this spring are cured of their ailments. That same night, an angel of the Lord appeared to the blessed Finnian, saying: "Finnian, act with courage, and your heart will be strengthened in the Lord, for God the Most High has intended this place to be inhabited". *Tu autem.*

The fifth lection. After these words, the angelic vision disappeared. The blessed Finnian, comforted by this prophecy, humbly thanked the true and almighty God. Together with his disciples he built a house at that place, in which by their preaching they converted many people to the christian faith. At last, in good and holy old age he was consecrated bishop by the clergy and people of that country, and, resplendent with very many miracles, he fell asleep in the Lord. He was buried with honour at Kilwinning [in Cunningham, Ayrshire] where now the renown of the monks and the everlasting holiness of those men are thriving. *Tu.*

The sixth lection. Not much later, there was a certain person who lived on the blessed Finnian's estate, who was suffering from such serious disease and incurable sickness that hope of his life was altogether lost. In order that he might be healed, his parents

lacrimis fundebant humilimas. Extabat autem ante basilicam crux lapidea miro artificio constructa, quam sanctus ipse Wynninus in uita sua propriis manibus in honore beate Brigide uirginis erexerat. Ad quam iuuenem languidum affligebant et nomen sa<n>cti uiri sepius inuocabant. Orantes igitur paululum sacerdotum consilio basilicam ingrediuntur. Languido coram eo deposito et paulisper requie data statim resipiscebat. Domumque denuo ferentes, prestine sanitati restitutus est.

Tres ultime lectiones de exposicione euangelii unius confessoris et pontificis cum oracione ut supra.

brought him to the blessed Finnian's church, pouring forth most humble prayers to God and the blessed Finnian together with their tears. In front of the church was a cross of stone, made with wonderful skill, which St Finnian, when he was alive, had erected with his own hands in honour of the blessed virgin Brigit. They put the sick young man down by the cross, continuously invoking the name of the holy man. Advised by the priests, they entered the church a little, praying. They put the ailing man down in his presence, and after a short repose he suddenly recovered. As they were taking him home, he was restored to his original health.

The three last lections are to be taken from the interpretation of the gospel for a single confessor and bishop, with a prayer as above.

References

1. See Ann Hamlin, 'The early Church in county Down to the twelfth century', above, chapter 3.

2. For the observation that 'the record of Finnian of Movilla ... failed to develop along the usual lines. His later coarbs in Movilla must never have felt their monastery to be sufficiently important to justify the composition of a Life of their patron', see P. Ó Riain, 'St. Finnbarr: a study in a cult', *Journal of the Cork Historical and Archaeological Society*, lxxxii (1977), pp 63-82, at p. 73. However, the evidence considered in this chapter suggests that such hagiography did indeed exist but that it has simply not survived. For discussion of the circumstances of (non-) production of hagiography, see J. M. H. Smith, 'Oral and written: saints, miracles, and relics in Brittany, c. 850-1250', *Speculum*, lxv (1990), pp 309-43. That a vernacular Life of St Finnian of Movilla survives in a seventeenth-century manuscript – Bruxelles, Bibliothèque royale, MS. 2324-2340 (3410) – seems to be an error: S.H. Bindon, 'Catalogue', *R.I.A. Proc.*, iii (1845-7), pp 477-502, at 479-81, which shows *S. Finnianus Maighbile* in a table of contents but with no accompanying folio-number. For a fuller description of the manuscript see J. van den Gheyn, *Catalogue des manuscrits de la Bibliothèque royale de Belgique*, v (Bruxelles, 1905), pp 384-9.

3. See, for example, *The Martyrology of Tallaght*, ed. R. I. Best and H. J. Lawlor (London, 1931), pp 4 (January 2: *Lochait abb Maige Bili*), 14 (February 3: *Cuana, .i. Glinni, ab' Maigi Bile*), 16 (February 11: *Finniani episcopi Maighe Bile uel Finnian Cluana Iraird*), 37 (April 29: *Breccani abbatis Maigi Bili*), 39 (May 3: *Carpre episcopus Maige Bile*), 58 (July 27: *Beogain ab' Maigi Bile*), 61 (August 7: *Cronain Maige Bile*), 66 (August 25: *Sillain meic Findchain episcopi et abbatis Maig<e> Bile*), 69 (September 9: *Aithgen ep. Maige Bile*), 70 (September 10: *Finnio m. h. Fiatach ... Findbair Maigi et sancti Segeni abbatis Bennchair)*, 76 (October 1: *Sinell sac. Maigi Bile*), 82 (October 21: *Mc. h. Gairb ab' Maigi Bili*). Later martyrologies offer also May 31 (*Eogan episcopus et sapiens Maighe Bile*) and December 12 (*Finnia Maigi Bile*): for details see ibid., pp 47, 247.

4. *Corpus genealogiarum Hiberniae*, ed. M.A. O'Brien (2nd ed., Dublin, 1976), p. 643 (on p. 646 O'Brien's equation of Finnia moccu Tellaig – in a genealogical statement on pp 44 and 411 – with Finnian of Movilla is a mistake; the saint of Clonard was intended by the genealogist); *Corpus genealogiarum sanctorum Hiberniae*, ed. Pádraig Ó Riain (Dublin, 1985), pp 23 (§136.1-2: *Recensio maior*), 64 (§423: *Recensio minor*), 96 (§662.140-1: *Recensio metrica*), 132 (§703.18), 145 (§707.373-384), 160 (§712.5), 174 (§722.40), 185 (729.1c-d); '*Genealogiae regum et sanctorum Hiberniae*' by the Four Masters, ed. Paul Walsh (Maynooth, 1918), p. 83 (§11).

5. I have drawn this from *Corpus*, ed. Ó Riain, p. 23 (§136.1), with minor modifications. Variant readings for Finnian are *Findia* and *Findbarr*, as well as *Findén*.

6. Ibid. (§136.2).

7. For discussion of this see D. N. Dumville, 'St Finnian of Movilla: Briton, Gael, ghost?', above.

8. The entries in the 'Annals of Roscrea', 'Annals of Tigernach', and 'Annals of Ulster' do not mention Movilla. That in the 'Annals of Inisfallen' does: indeed it has only its headword, *Quies*, in common with the other texts. See *The Annals of Inisfallen*, ed. and transl. Seán Mac Airt (Dublin, 1951), pp 76-7: *Quies Finniae Moige Bile*.

9. *The Annals of Ulster (to A.D. 1131)*, ed. and transl. Seán Mac Airt & G. Mac

Niocaill (Dublin, 1983): 603:4, 619.2, 650.4, 694.7, 736.4*b*, 743.10, 747.3, 749.6*c*, 825.3*b*.

10. Ibid.: 825.10 (*Loscuth Maighi Bile cona derthigib o ghentibh*). This entry is also found in *Chronicum Scotorum*. Comparable information is in *Cocad Gaedel re Gallaib* and the 'Annals of Inisfallen'.

11. *The Annals of Ulster,* ed. and transl. Mac Airt & Mac Niocaill, 831.3 and 890.6. The conclusion derives from the coincidence of occurrence of this rare name. Only with evidence that, by some textual dislocation, the two entries were one could this deduction be subverted.

12. Ibid.: 955.1*a*; cf. *The Annals of Clonmacnoise,* ed. Denis Murphy (Dublin, 1896), p. 156 (950.1: *Enos mc Conloingsie arch-Deane of Moyvile*).

13. *Chronicum Scotorum,* ed. and transl. William M. Hennessy (London, 1866), pp 222-3 (973, *recte* 975.2); *The Annals of Ulster,* ed. and transl. Mac Airt & Mac Niocaill, 1025.1*e*.

14. See above, n. 1.

15. Ibid.: 933.1*a*, 1019.3, 1043.4*a*. These have been claimed as coarbs of St Finnian of Clonard, and in view of the patronym in the obit at 1019 (Domhnall m. Maíl Shechlainn) this is hard to deny, at least in this instance: see P. Byrne, 'The community of Clonard, sixth to twelfth centuries', *Peritia,* iv (1985), pp 157-73. For a reasonably certain alliance of Bangor and Dromore, see *The Annals of Ulster,* ed. and transl. Mac Airt & Mac Niocaill, 953.2: *Mael Cothaid, comarba Comgaill ocus Mo-Colmóc.* There are other 'coarbs of Finnian' recorded, who have all been claimed for Clonard, but they await further investigation: ibid., 944.5, 956.4a (*ocus fer léighinn Aird Macha*), 973.4.

16. Ibid.: 1007.7.

17. The formula is drawn from his chaplain's record entered in the 'Book of Armagh' in 1005: *Book of Armagh. The Patrician documents,* facs. ed. Edward Gwynn (Dublin, 1937), fol. 16vb.

18. *The Annals of Ulster,* ed. and transl. Mac Airt & Mac Niocaill, 1025.1*e*.

19. Ibid., 1061.1*d* ('... Tigernach Bairccech, comarba Finnén ocus ardanmchara Érenn ..., in penitentia quieuerunt') and 1098.7 ('Flaithbertach m. Tigernaigh Bairccidh, comarba Finnian, in perigrinatione quieuit'). From the assumption that Tigernach's epithet refers to the Mournes of county Down – see Mícheál B. Ó Mainnín, *Place-names of Northern Ireland,* iii, *County Down,* iii, *The Mournes* (Belfast, 1993), pp 1-3, 119-25 – these two coarbs, father and son, have been assigned, not especially logically, to Movilla. Tigernach was the abbot who exiled from Ireland Marianus Scotus, the chronicler, who has on that account been placed at Movilla from 1052 to 1056: B. MacCarthy, *The Codex Palatino-Vaticanus, No. 830* (Dublin, 1892), pp 31-2 (items B-D); cf. p. 4.

20. *Annala Uladh. Annals of Ulster,* ed. and transl. William M. Hennessy & Bartholomew MacCarthy (4 vols., London, 1887-1901), ii, 1167.1.

21. Ibid., 1170.5; cf. *The Annals of Loch Cé,* ed. and transl. William M. Hennessy (2 vols., London, 1871), i, pp 140-3 (1170.4).

22. Aubrey Gwynn & R.N. Hadcock, *Medieval religious houses: Ireland* (London, 1970), p. 194. For continuing troubles see J.A. Watt, *The Church and the two nations in medieval Ireland* (Cambridge, 1970), p. 69.

23. *Annala Uladh. Annals of Ulster,* ed. and transl. Hennessy & MacCarthy, ii, 1175.3.

24. Gwynn & Hadcock, *Medieval religious houses,* pp 188, 194. See also T. E. McNeill, *Anglo-Norman Ulster* (Edinburgh, 1980), p. 101.

25. See above, n. 2.

26. Socii Bollandiani, *Bibliotheca hagiographica latina antiquae et mediae aetatis* (2

vols., Bruxelles, 1898-1901), i, p. 476 (nos 3173-7); Henri Fros, *Bibliotheca hagiographica latina antiquae et mediae aetatis. Novum supplementum* (Bruxelles, 1986), pp 362-3.

27. *Acta sanctorum Hiberniae,* ed. John Colgan (Leuven, 1645; reprinted Dublin, 1948), pp 633-51; James F. Kenney, *The sources for the early history of Ireland: ecclesiastical* (New York, 1929; rev. imp., 1966), pp 184-5 (no. 40); J. Hennig, 'A note on the traditions of St. Frediano and St. Silao of Lucca', *Mediaeval Studies,* xiii (1951), pp 234-42.

28. *Nova legenda Anglie: as collected by John of Tynemouth, John Capgrave, and others, and first printed, with new Lives, by Wynkyn de Worde a.d. mdxui,* ed. Carl Horstman (2 vols., Oxford, 1901).

29. Ibid., i, pp 444-7. For a partial version see James O'Laverty, *An historical account of the diocese of Down and Connor, ancient and modern* (3 vols., Dublin, 1878-84), i, pp 354-5; this was reused by H. C. Lawlor, *The monastery of St Mochaoi of Nendrum* (Belfast, 1925), pp 61-2.

30. Little enough has been written about the place-name Kilwinning (cf. below, n. 42): for St Finnian in Scottish toponymy, see William J. Watson, *The history of the Celtic place-names of Scotland* (Edinburgh, 1926), pp 165, 187, 189, 193, 429. On Kilwinning itself, W.F.H. Nicolaisen, *Scottish place-names, their study and significance* (London, 1976; rev. imp., 1979), pp 132-3, has rather naïvely speculated that it and its like were the 'work of Irish missionaries ... amongst Cumbric speakers initially', seeing it therefore as a sixth-century formation. A Tironensian (subsequently Cistercian) abbey was established at Kilwinning in the second half of the twelfth century and survived until the Reformation: I. B. Cowan & D.E. Easson, *Medieval religious houses: Scotland* (2nd ed., London, 1976), p. 69. The district-name Cunningham is English as it stands, but of unknown date: see the very sensible treatment by Nicolaisen, *Scottish place-names,* pp 69-71, 79-80; cf. Watson, *The history,* pp 186, 191. On Strathclyde and its language (conventionally called 'Old Cumbric'), see Kenneth Jackson, *Language and history in early Britain* (Edinburgh, 1953), pp 6, 9-10 (cf. 707), 218-19; 'The Britons in southern Scotland', *Antiquity,* xxix (1955), pp 77-88; 'Angles and Britons in Northumbria and Cumbria', in *Angles and Britons – O'Donnell Lectures,* ed. Henry Lewis (Cardiff, 1963), pp 60-84.

31. Kenney, *The sources,* p. 484; *Kalendars of Scottish Saints,* ed. A. P. Forbes (Edinburgh, 1872), p. xxxi.

32. Ibid., p. 111 (following St Agnes): *Uynnini episcopi et confessoris .ix. lectiones.* The text on St Uynninus occupies folios xxxviii ra31 – xxxix ra17.

33. See above, nn. 26-7.

34. We meet *Aradei* also as the people of St Colmán of Dromore (county Down) in §1 of his Life in *Codex Salmanticensis: Vitae sanctorum Hiberniae ex codice olim Salmanticensi nunc Bruxellensi,* ed. W. W. Heist (Bruxelles, 1965), p. 357. They are *Aradenses* in the Life of St Comgall of Bangor (§1: ibid., p. 332) and in that of St Mac Nisse of Connor (§3, in a prophecy of St Patrick: ibid., p. 405). Heist's index (ibid., p. 415) is misleading on this point, confusing Dál nAraide with the Araid of Munster. For *Aradenses* in texts in another collection, see *Vitae sanctorum Hiberniae partim hactenus ineditae,* ed. Charles Plummer (2 vols., Oxford, 1910), i. p. 200, n. 2, and ii, p. 3, n. 3 (with reference to R, otherwise *Collectio Oxoniensis).*

35. See above, n. 4. His mother is named specifically in the tract on Irish saints' mothers: *Corpus,* ed. Ó Riain, p. 174 (§722.40), *Lassar máthair Fhinneáin epscoip.*

36. On the politics of Ulster from the fifth century to the twelfth, see F.J. Byrne, *Irish kings and high kings* (London, 1973), pp 106-29.

37. Cf. Lawlor, *The monastery*, p. 62, n. e.

38. Cf. Kenney, *The sources*, pp. 366-71.

39. In the hagiography of St Finnian of Clonard there is a priest Nath Í associated with Achad Chonairi: *Vitae*, ed. Heist, p. 104 (§28).

40. On Daimíne mac Cairpri Daim Argait, see *Corpus*, ed. O'Brien, p. 580. His father died in 514, and he himself in 565, according to the 'Annals of Ulster'. On Clogher see R. B. Warner, 'Irish place-names and archaeology. III. A case study: Clochar macc nDaimini', *Bulletin of the Ulster Place-name Society*, new series, iv (1982), pp 27-31, and 'The archaeology of early historic Irish kingship', in *Power and politics in early medieval Britain and Ireland*, ed. S. T. Driscoll & M.R. Nieke (Edinburgh, 1988), pp 47-68.

41. Byrne, *Irish kings*, pp 87-105; D. A. Binchy, 'A pre-christian survival in mediaeval Irish hagiography', in *Ireland in early mediaeval Europe. Studies in memory of Kathleen Hughes*, ed. Dorothy Whitelock *et al.* (Cambridge, 1982), pp 165-78.

42. Cf. above, n. 30.

43. See above, n. 7.

44. I am obliged to Professor D. N. Dumville for his help in the preparation of this article.

45. The paragraphing of the translation is mine.

46. I have followed common editorial practices in presenting the Latin text. Punctuation and capitalisation are modern. The original is inconsistent in the use of *u* and *v*: I have *u* throughout. In the name *Wyn(n)inus* I have silently substituted *W-* for *vv-*. In every other respect the orthography is that of the original. All abbreviations have been silently expanded. Angle-brackets < > have been employed to indicate editorial insertions, round brackets ( ) to mark editorial deletion.

47. *sū*, Breviary.

48. *a deo*, Breviary.

Chapter 5

COUNTY DOWN IN THE LATER MIDDLE AGES

T. E. McNEILL

During the last thirty years, much work has been done on Ireland's history and archaeology between the twelfth and the sixteenth centuries. The period attracts attention because it forms a hinge between protohistoric Ireland, which is often seen as a special or unique society, and an Ireland linked to Britain and Europe, politically, economically and culturally. The earldom of Ulster, which included modern county Down, was the first earldom to be formally created in Ireland after the English incursion in 1168-9, yet it always lay at the fringe of English Ireland, in close relationship to the most prominent Irish kingdoms. Some of the best work in the *Archaeological survey of county Down* concerned the rural sites of the twelfth to fifteenth centuries; it still remains the most complete survey of the castles and churches of an Irish county yet published. Other, more recent, surveys of the history and archaeology of medieval Ulster have built on this, and in these county Down has figured largely. Accordingly, this renders another chronological account of medieval Down redundant. Instead, this chapter considers the most problematic aspects of the county's medieval archaeology with three aims in view: first, to demonstrate the selective nature of our knowledge; second, to stimulate discussion of a possible future research agenda; and third, in the hope that such a discussion might help preserve evidence for future examination. The discussion does not purport to provide a considered programme for future research; rather, it attempts to identify some major areas where further work would advance our present understanding of the period.

The English incursion into late-twelfth century Ireland, which led to the inclusion of county Down within the earldom of Ulster, can only be understood against the background of secular and religious changes in Irish society earlier in the century, and these are particularly well exemplified in Down. There were four main secular powers in the county. First, it lay within the over-kingdom of Ulaid, and by the twelfth century this kingship had become the preserve of the lineage of Dál Fiatach, whose family name was Mac Duinn Shléibe (anglicised to

MacDunleavy). Their lands lay in the east of the county, but the western part, the kingdom or lordship of Uí Echach (Iveagh), became increasingly independent during the twelfth century under the leadership of the Magennis family. Further west still – west of the River Bann – lay the Uí Néill of Cenél Eóghain. Traditionally hostile to Ulaid, their kings were from the Mac Lochlainn family, but were later replaced by the Uí Néills. To the south lay the lands of Airgialla, under the Uí Cearbhaill dynasty, who were also pushing eastwards into Louth and Meath. Paralleling these political changes was the twelfth-century reform of the Church under the influence of continental experience and ideas. With its ancient monastery and close dynastic links to Cenél Eóghain, Armagh epitomised the old regime in the north of Ireland. The monastery belonged to no monastic order but claimed instead a supremacy over other religious houses. Nor was this claim based on a territorial diocese, such as a bishop's, but rather on ancient rights peculiar to Ireland.

County Down illustrates two aspects of this situation in particular: first, the interlocking of secular and religious politics; and second, how new ideas affected kingship as well as the Church. The intermeshing of lay and religious politics was reflected in the creation of the new dioceses: Ulaid was divided into the dioceses of Connor and Down, with the latter covering Dál Fiatach and Iveagh. Malachi was the bishop from 1124, and succeeded for a time in uniting both dioceses. He was also made abbot of Bangor, where he restored the abbey buildings and, more importantly, recovered its lands from lay lords. These successes brought him directly into secular political life, and in 1127 he obtained the patronage of Dál Fiatach to found the first of the new monasteries in Ireland, at Erenagh, south of Downpatrick. The new monastery was linked in some way to the earlier one at Inch on the north side of Downpatrick; possibly it simply took over its lands *en bloc*. In the same year, however, the king of Cenél Eóghain forced Malachi to move to Lismore in Munster, illustrating once again the link between the Church and politics. The power of Cenél Eóghain around Armagh rested partly on an alliance with the traditional dynasty who controlled the abbey. In 1129 Malachi returned to Armagh and reasserted his authority there, before moving to Down some eight years later. In 1139 he set off for Rome, returning with renewed enthusiasm for the new monastic orders. In county Louth the king of Airgialla founded the Cistercian monastery of Mellifont. At much the same time, and with the further support of Dál Fiatach, Malachi founded Saul abbey for the Augustinian Canons, and, separately in 1144, a new house for the Benedictines at Newry (in Iveagh).

In 1157, Muirchertach Mac Lochlainn, king of Uí Néill, reversed his predecessor's hostility to the Church reformers in county Down and granted a charter to the new Cistercian abbey of Newry. His motives were mixed. The land he granted came from Iveagh, not from his own resources, although he 'persuaded' the kings of Iveagh and of Dál Fiatach to associate themselves with the gift. He patronised Newry for political reasons. Its site and lands lay across the route from Down into Louth and Meath, and so any Ulaid force which wished to go south would have to cross Church lands. Doing this would provoke the hostility of the Church: thus Muirchetach was placing a 'demilitarised zone' of church land between Ulaid and Louth and Meath to prevent any interference in his expansion schemes there.

In secular politics, Ulaid was further weakened at this time by Muirchetach Mac Lochlainn, who encouraged the Magennises of Iveagh to free themselves from Dál Fiatach lordship. To the south, in 1165, Eochaid Mac Duinn Shléibe of Dál Fiatach granted the mountains of Benna Bairrche to Donnchad Uí Cearbhaill of Airgialla for helping him to make peace with Mac Lochlainn: they were settled by the Mugdorna of present county Monaghan, and so got a new name the Mournes (fig. 5.1). At the same time, Dál Fiatach were building up a central base for their lordship, something new in Irish politics. It can be seen in the early eleventh century, when Cenél Eóghain are recorded as burning the fort and township of Duneight in the north of the county. Excavation of the fort showed that it was both larger and more strongly defended than a traditional rath. Later the Dál Fiatach apparently shifted their base south to Downpatrick, where they built twin secular and religious centres. The secular site must be the massive fort now known as the English Mount, although the insertion of a motte into it shows it to be earlier than the English incursion. Its area and the strength of its earthworks made it unprecedented in Ireland.

Recent excavation and analysis of Downpatrick cathedral has shown that there was an earlier building on the site, unaisled but with choir, transepts and nave. In its plan and scale it looked neither to the traditional Irish church nor even to the small but highly decorated Irish Romanesque buildings of the type started at Cormac's chapel in Cashel. It cannot be a coincidence that the first of the new monasteries founded by Malachi was at Erenagh, some two and a half miles south of the cathedral site. Erenagh was linked with the site of Inch, just over the Quoile marshes from the English Mount.

Secular stronghold, cathedral and new abbey seem to have been deliberately assembled together, linking the reformed church closely to the Dál Fiatach dynasty, physically and politically. This represented something new in Ireland and the conjunction offers a major opportunity for further research. The cathedral remains need to be

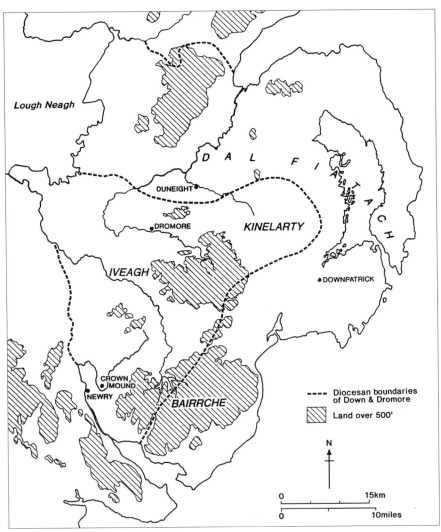

Fig. 5.1   County Down in the late twelfth century: secular and religious divisions, with some key places mentioned in the text.

analysed both for their date and for their affinities. Erenagh now lies beneath farmland, levelled for ploughing since the early-nineteenth century, but possibly with its remains not totally destroyed. English Mount is still there, although the interior is scarred by the remains of cultivation ridges. The physical appearance of these two sites in particular could tell us much about the use of the buildings (especially in the case of English Mount) and the affinities of the design. Where did Malachi look to for the design of his new monastery? Erenagh was founded in 1127, the year which saw the start of Cormac MacCarthy's new chapel at Cashel which itself marked the beginning of the Irish Romanesque style. Did MacDunleavy have a hall in his new fort which gave expression to the new forms of kingship with buildings appropriate to a European feudal lord?

Behind the details of the individual sites may lie more. If there was a township associated with Duneight in the eleventh century, what might have been beside the fort and cathedral of Downpatrick? Was there any evidence of the two key elements of the new feudal lordship already at work elsewhere in Ireland? The first of these was the close association between lordship and 'place', with individual sites acting as the administrative centres for particular blocks of land. The second was the association of these places with permanent centres of population, living from the fruits of power and supplying the material needs of the powerful through trade, itself one of the key roots of European urbanism. The Downpatrick area provides one of the best examples to test how far these ideas may have penetrated Ireland before the invasion of English lords.

In 1166, Eochaid Mac Duinn Shléibe was captured and blinded by Mac Lochlainn. His kingdom passed to his brother Magnus, who was killed by his brother Donn Shléibe in 1172. A third brother, Ruaidrí, killed Donn Shléibe in 1177. Coincidentally, in the same year Aedh Uí Néill replaced Mac Lochlainn as king of Uí Néill. The scene was set for the intervention of new players in the drama. One was a member of King Henry's knightly entourage in Dublin, John de Courcy, who came north to Down at the end of January 1177 and seized the Dál Fiatach kingship of Ulaid. We should stress two aspects of this story. First, it is unlikely that de Courcy would set off on a random conquest at that time of year. He is said to have planned the journey to arrive on the fourth day after he set off. To do this he had to cross the lands of the Irish kings of Airgialla and Uí Echach, and he evidently achieved this without messengers reaching Ruaidrí Mac Duinn Shléibe, since de Courcy is recorded as surprising him at Downpatrick. We can only conclude that John's expedition had the support of a substantial body of Irish lords in Airgialla and Iveagh, if not among Dál Fiatach. The second point relates to the ways in which de Courcy used his new power. He set off on raids to the north and west of Down, and above all into Cenél Eóghain. He asserted himself like an Irish king, carrying the fight to the traditional enemy, Cenél Eóghain, who for the first time in generations were worsted by the men of Ulaid. In thus restoring the balance of power in favour of Ulaid and Airgialla, de Courcy justified his actions. After their initial resistance to him, members of the MacDunleavy family are to be found called 'Kings of the Irish of Ulster' under the English earls.

County Down under the earls of Ulster

Sometime in 1203/05 John de Courcy was replaced by Hugh de Lacy, with the formal title of earl of Ulster. From then on, this was to be the name of the English lordship and its head. While we can emphasise the lordship's Irish origins under John de Courcy, the changes it brought in its train were profound. The English brought a wholly different concept of lordship to Ireland, which rested on new ideas of land organisation and how best to exploit the power and wealth which accrued from its possession. The key difference was that henceforth, the basic unit of land ownership – and power – was the landed estate, each with its own defined core. These estates might consist of a small tract of land or the whole earldom, and they were arranged accordingly in a hierarchy of size and power. To an Irish lord, social and political authority was measured not by landed acres but by the number of supporters whom he could command. The two ideas merged, of course; land without people to work it is worthless, while people without resources are not much better. The difference remained, however, and was linked to the new ideas which emphasised the commercial potential of land when exploited as a resource for monetary profit. The future key to land use and land ownership was the market, and herein lay the real impact of the English earldom.

The English controlled less than half of county Down directly and this secular division was reflected in the organisation of the Church. Prior to 1190, the diocese of Down was divided. A charter of that date was witnessed by the first bishop of Dromore, who was also named as bishop of Iveagh. The boundaries of the diocese, as reconstructed from the list of parishes made in 1306, show it to have covered Iveagh and the MacArtan sub-kingdom of Kinelarty. The diocese of Down was divided into deaneries, and these included Dalboyn, which lay mostly in the south of modern county Antrim but also included Drumbo and Hillsborough, Duneight, and the traditional inauguration place of the Fiataig at Crew Hill, near Glenavy. Dalboyn deanery is listed out of order in the diocese, and its parish values are low, which might indicate – as elsewhere – that this was an Irish area controlled, in this case, by the MacDunleavys. County Down was thus divided between the Irish lands in the centre and the west, and the English earldom which controlled the Mournes (in part), Lecale, the Ards, the western shore of Strangford Lough, and the north. This gives us a particular opportunity for research, because we can compare life on either side of this Anglo-Irish divide. This is particularly so because the division lacks the strong physical basis it has elsewhere in Ireland, where it is possible to contrast the good arable lands occupied by the English with the hilly country retained by the Irish.

Shortly after 1177, John de Courcy selected Carrickfergus as the chief place of his lordship. He had no castle in Downpatrick, unless at the very beginning, and outside north Down and the north Ards he had little land in the county. He compensated for this by building castles at Dundrum and Greencastle. In doing so, the earl expressed his power in terms which would have been understood by his fellow lords in England. It is possible that Greencastle was intended to succeed Dundrum, and that there was only one site in use by the earl at any one time. As well as this, the position of the Church was stronger in Down than in Antrim. The monasteries at Downpatrick, Inch, Greyabbey and Movilla, together with the bishop of Down, all held a fair proportion of the earldom's lands in the modern county.

Towns and trade

The introduction of the concept of the market in the period after 1200 led to the growth of towns as communities, self-consciously and legally separate from the rural settlement hierarchy. In 1260, the mayor of Downpatrick organised the defence of the district against a raid by Brian Ó Néill, King of Cenél Eóghain, and was rewarded by the king of England with grants of land in Lecale. Finds of coins (John de Courcy minted his own) from the early period of the English lordship are evidence of the new economic order. Similarly, the individual masons' marks at Inch abbey, carved by the men who worked on the moulded piers, are evidence of the way in which they were paid by piece-work. There was no tradition of stone castle building in Ireland before the coming of the English. Men had to be brought over to direct the works and to carry out the more specialised tasks. They were skilled professionals who expected to be paid in coin for their work. Men of their training and experience would not be satisfied with payment in food or in kind. Further evidence for marketing is provided by the Scrabo sandstone grave markers which were traded throughout the county.

Following the discovery of a kiln in 1960, we know that pottery was being made professionally (although perhaps not on a full-time basis) at Downpatrick during the thirteenth century. The pots from the kiln site have not yet been examined thoroughly enough to define the product and thus we cannot pick up a piece of pottery and say with confidence whether it came from Downpatrick or not. We can say that the pottery was clearly being marketed, probably as far as Newtownards. Similarly, excavations of sites from the thirteenth century have not yet been analysed sufficiently to establish how much of the pottery which they contain may be traced to the Downpatrick kiln. Nor do we know whether the gentry alone, or the burgesses, or the peasantry, bought the pottery. Working out the pattern of trade from the Downpatrick kiln, in relation to the other kiln at Carrickfergus, and then comparing this pattern with that of the stone grave slabs, has still to be done. At stake is our best chance of understanding the social and geographical contexts of trade in county Down. Water transport dominated the pattern of distribution of the heavy grave slabs, but the pottery might show us a different pattern based more extensively on land communications.

Within the earldom, all economic development hinged on the lords' management of their landed estates, whether directly themselves or through their barons. In terms of the evidence, at least, this was where a second revolution occurred after the earldom's establishment. To the archaeologist, the presence of castles marks both a new type of site and a new source of dated artefacts in a clear social context: most of the pottery finds, for example, come from castle excavations. To the historian, the grants of lands and the surveys of the lords' landed estates represent a source of evidence about settlement which, in Ulster, differs from almost everything before 1177. Nevertheless, both share similar features. Even the lesser castles relate to relatively large holdings of land and to the upper classes of society, and the same holds true of the documentary information. The grants and surveys record the acts of the English king, the earl or his barons, or else their sources of income.

This income was most probably generated by the ability of local farmers to produce grain, preferably wheat. The population of Europe as a whole rose steadily throughout the twelfth and for much of the thirteenth century, without a commensurate increase in agricultural productivity. There was therefore steady pressure to take more land into cultivation, fuelled by the constantly rising price of grain. Eastern parts of Down contain better land for tillage than areas farther west, and whether by luck or by design the earldom benefited from this. There can be little doubt that the new lords of the land would have been keen to produce as much corn from their estates as possible for the small but expanding urban markets of England and Europe.

Agriculture and rural settlement

Elsewhere in Europe, castles, manors and mills were frequently the location for nucleated villages, and this raises a second major research question: to what extent was the creation of the earldom of Ulster and its English lordships accompanied by a change to English (or European) patterns of agricultural settlement and production? There is evidence for both change and continuity, but neither case is convincing. On the one hand, we would expect the lords of the earldom to have set up such structures in Ulster. There are references to local grain production, and contemporary estate surveys certainly list mills at a number of the manors concerned. The most detailed survey of the lands of mediaeval county Down is contained in the Pipe Roll, or official treasury accounts, for the year 1211-1212. At Dundonald, for example, money was spent on a barn, on wages for harvesting the corn and mowing the meadows to produce the hay vital for the beasts used to plough or for traction, and on equipment for three ox-teams for ploughing. In the document, estates are normally described as 'manors', a term which in England carries with it implications of a centralised unit of land holding operating as a single legal unit.

The evidence of animal husbandry also suggests an increased emphasis on commercial farming. In the same Pipe Roll, money is accounted for from the sale of cattle, their hides and from wool, as well as from flour. At the same time we find references to a new animal in the county, the rabbit, reared for its fur rather than for its meat. At Rathmullen motte, for example, there were many rabbit bones, but apparently not from animals which had been eaten. The evidence from Rathmullen and the motte at Clough suggests that the pattern of animal husbandry shifted from cattle to sheep and pigs, while, at the same time, more bird species appear by comparison with earlier periods. Interpretation of the figures for excavated bones requires care, however. One of the most prominent animals of the period, the horse, and particularly the knight's war horse, is notoriously under-represented in excavated samples, presumably because its bones were disposed of differently. Moreover, a site may have a predominance of one species for a particular reason: the relatively large number of pigs from Rathmullen and Clough – large in comparison with those from contemporary towns in the south for example, Dublin and Waterford – might be caused by a difference in the local farming regime. Moreover, we do not know for certain whether we are dealing with bones derived from patterns of production or consumption.

Against this picture, of the anglicisation of farming and estates, may be set other evidence. One of the features of Ireland's earthwork castles, particularly in Ulster, is that while they are almost always marked by a motte, they often differ from those of England and France in having no subsidiary defended courtyard or bailey. At least two of the excavated mottes in county Down, Clough and Lismahon, had houses on the top of the motte, rather than, as we would expect from England, in the bailey below. Had there been farm buildings attached to the mottes, they should have been protected in the bailey. Where no baileys are present, we have to ask whether such farm buildings existed but – in contrast to theoretically more peaceful England – were left exposed, or whether none was present. Without a farmyard, however, how can there be centralised farming?

Various contemporary medieval documents, from Ulster rather than specifically from county Down, provide evidence of a rather more scattered pattern of settlement and farming than we would expect under an 'English' system of collaborative common-field farming. Documents frequently list lands as parcels, with little impression of centralisation. Following the death of the last resident earl of Ulster in 1333, his estates were surveyed for the king, and all his lands in the country of Blathewyc, stretching from the Lagan to the south Ards, were described as being in the single manor of Dundonald. Most of the lands were in units of two carucates (nominally 240 acres) or less, and many were described as being let, presumably on short term leases, for they are not listed among the lands held from the earl through normal feudal tenancies. This survey coincided with a period of stress in the Earldom, when it was recovering from the Bruce War and the disturbances which followed the murder of the earl himself, and it was also a time when the whole economy of Europe was over-burdened and possibly in decline. However, other, earlier, surveys of individual estates are cast in the same form. Indeed, even the 1211-12 Pipe Roll, in which the term 'manor' was used liberally (and therefore seems to be describing centralised estates) can be read in a similar way.

It is not the introduction of a market-based economy and agriculture which is in question here. What is unclear is how far the earls and their chief tenants went in transforming the settlement pattern and the methods of farming to bring these into line with the open-field agriculture practised in England. To do so would probably have meant bringing in peasants, from those parts of England which suffered from over-population, to farm their estates in the English way. Presumably, they would have tended to settle in nucleated villages rather than to adopt the earlier Irish pattern of dispersed settlement. It is usually assumed that this happened in the south-east of Ireland, on better evidence than we can show for Ulster. There are three points at issue here: the commercialisation of agriculture, which need not have meant drastic change in methods or settlement; the creation of new patterns of settlement, particularly nucleated villages; and the introduction of an open-field agricultural system. It remains a possibility, however, if no more, that only the first of these occurred in the county. A market economy could have been introduced while the farming was left to the indigenous population. The English migration may have involved lords, urban merchants and craftsmen and some farmers, but all within the context of an Irish peasantry left in control of the land but working to an agenda set by the new feudal regime.

This question could be examined by means of systematic excavation, similar to that carried out on county Down's castles during the 1950s. Potential sites exist which might be expected to yield evidence of village settlements. Two could be instanced. Ardkeen, on the eastern shore of Strangford Lough, has a probable motte (perhaps set within an earlier enclosure) sited on a hill some two hundred yards north of a mediaeval parish church. It was named as one of the earl's manors in 1225 and again in 1285. The land between the motte and the church would undoubtedly be the site of a village if one had existed. Kilclief is now marked by a later stone tower house and a small and degraded motte, again a few hundred metres away. John de Courcy granted it to the bishop of Down, and in 1305 he had a large estate there with an income partly derived from (urban) burgage rents. Presumably the borough would have been sited between the two castles. The most difficult thing to prove is a negative, but at Ardkeen in particular the land does not look as though it has been deeply ploughed, and traces of a nucleated settlement, had one existed, should have survived. Because the documents would indicate these places as the sites of villages, if they turned out not to be such we might conclude that the case against a change in settlement patterns in Ulster was very much strengthened. For the rest of Ireland, the interest in the problem stems from Ulster's relatively marginal political and economic position within the English Lordship in Ireland. If, therefore, we could demonstrate that changes took place here, then we could be more confident about assuming major changes in the south-east.

The Irish in mediaeval Down

Events within the earldom are likely to have affected the rest of the county, Kinelarty and Iveagh. If the new economy did not in itself require the immigration of a peasantry, but only men with the specific new skills of the market, then it is much easier to conceive of Irish land and lords participating in the new order. The evidence for a new economy in the 'Irish' areas of county Down comes from two sources. A late-sixteenth century plan of Newry shows it as a small town, but a town nonetheless with streets and houses. It could have developed in this way as a result of patronage by the Bagenals, who took over the lands of the abbey after its dissolution, but this is unlikely to have been the whole story, since in Ulster the later sixteenth century was not a great time for economic ventures to succeed. The plan of Newry by John Rocque in 1758, records the town at the start of its eighteenth-century development and depicts Boat Street (the present Castle Street) dividing half way along its length at the 'old market place'. This is a triangular space in front of the Bagenal castle, which may owe its origin and position to the castle site. On the other hand, triangular market places are a hallmark of mediaeval towns, and the castle site may owe its position to a pre-existing market at the end of the ridge away from the abbey. If there was a town there in the middle ages, it might have been built around a market of such a shape, set at the entrance to the precincts of the abbey. A classic parallel is the triangular market of the little town of Battle in Sussex, set at the great gate of the abbey founded over the spot where Harold died in 1066. At Newry, the pattern suggests the existence of a town on a European model – the key to the economic change within the earldom – but in this case on Irish land.

Politically, John de Courcy came in to Down as both the supplanter and successor of the MacDunleavys. To the Magennises and the MacArtans, he offered protection from Cenél Eóghain as much as he represented a threat. Detaching the see of Dromore from the diocese of Down signalled this, as did his battles, within Down and without, against Cenél Eóghain. Elsewhere in Ireland, notably along the northern and western borders of Meath and Louth, the frontiers of English lordships are marked by a massive concentration of mottes, many of them with baileys. In county Antrim, the border of the earldom with Uí Thuirtre is similarly defined at the strategically crucial north-east corner of Lough Neagh. We can see something similar at the entry to Lecale around Dundrum Bay, but it is not very pronounced, and on this evidence the area does not seem to have been one of particular tension.

By contrast, there are mottes at Duneight, Dromore, Ballyroney and at the Crown Mound, near Newry. The first three are recorded as being built and occupied by the earl. These sites were isolated in the lands of Iveagh, a point emphasised, perhaps, in the Pipe Roll of 1211-12, when supplies of food were sent to Ballyroney for the ten men guarding the district, an indication of the lack of lands attached to the castle. The same situation is found between 1252 and 1255. In 1252, the king's justiciar, acting because the earldom was in the king's hands, built the castle of Maycove, or Magh Cobha, only for it to be attacked by Brian Ó Néill the next year. The justiciar persisted, however, and re-established the castle over the following two years. The castle has been identified with reasonable certainty as that of Seafin, near Ballyroney motte, which was itself the earlier castle of Maycove. Seafin consists of a tower attached to a small polygonal walled enclosure of a type associated elsewhere in Ulster and Ireland with borderlands. They were designed not as castles in the sense of lordly residences but as places to accommodate small bodies of troops to counter raids.

The mottes of western Down are described in the *Archaeological survey of county Down* as a western screen for the earldom. Arguably, this is misleading. In the first place, it is difficult to see how they could have acted effectively as a strategic line of castles barring access to the earldom as if they were Hadrian's Wall. Secondly, and more importantly, the *Survey* concludes that the earldom stretched as far west as this line of mottes. In fact, they lay beyond its borders in Iveagh, but nevertheless still gave protection to the earldom, not by barring access but by harassing a raiding party as it retreated. They were a visible symbol of the parallel interests of the earl and Magennis against Cenél Eóghain. Just because their interests were similar, however, did not mean that the relationship between the earldom and Iveagh was uniformly peaceful, any more than the relations between the earl and his barons, or those between different barons, were always peaceful either. The same 1211-12 Pipe Roll which records the mottes in Iveagh, also records payments to one body of men who guarded the town and district of Downpatrick against attacks from Iveagh, and to a second band who went on a raid into Iveagh. In 1260, Magennis and MacArtan were recorded as owing cows for rent to the English king (in the absence of the earl) as indeed did Uí Néill of Cenél Eóghain.

The political and economic power of the earls extended beyond their immediate territory, and Irish county Down was closely involved in both networks. Coins and pottery reached into Irish lands, reflecting their economic links with the earldom. Politically, the MacDunleavys and Magennises occupied a position relative to the earl which was intermediate between that of his closest advisers – his major English barons – and the kings of western Ulster, especially Uí Néill of Cenél Eóghain, who were normally hostile to the earldom. To the county Down Irish, the Earls might appear as much protectors as intruders, and there seems to have been no inherent, automatic hostility between them.

Close to Newry lies the Crown Mound motte and bailey (fig. 4.2). It is an impressive site, with the largest bailey in the county – a well-defined rectangular platform south of the motte. The castle is set high above the Clanrye river on lands apparently granted to Newry abbey by Muirchertach Mac Lochlainn. It is possible that the Crown Mound was built by the Magennises, but this interpretation depends on the significance of its omission from the castles mentioned in 1211-12. Was this accidental, or did it indeed mean that the Crown Mound castle was not held by the English but by the Irish? What we may have here is the same conjunction of sites seen at Downpatrick before 1177: a new monastery, a town and a secular power centre, all the work of Irish kings. The castle-remains in Newry have almost certainly been destroyed by the construction of the dual carriageway and blocks of

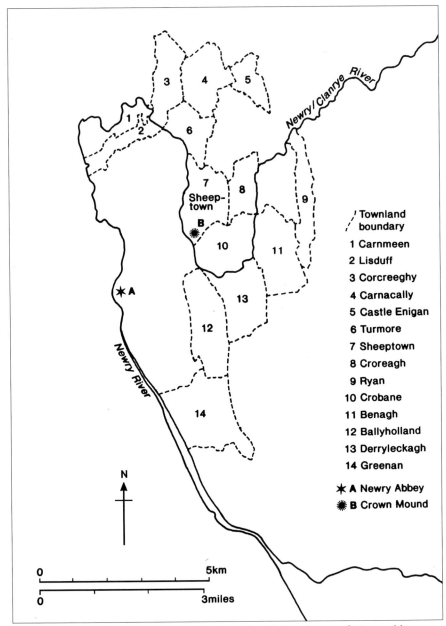

Fig. 5.2   The townlands mentioned in the foundation charter of Newry abbey.

flats along the line of Castle Street, but the Crown Mound and its environs are as intact as modern farming practice permits. Although the coming of English lords presumably acted as a major catalyst for these developments, they may have found in the local Irish a people who were already receptive to such thinking and who wanted to develop along similar 'English' lines. This can only be a hypothesis for Newry and Downpatrick, but it should be tested.

County Down in the fourteenth and fifteenth centuries

These questions lead us to the last problem concerning the county during our period, and that reflects how little we really know. In short, what lay behind the events of the later fourteenth and fifteenth century? The fourteenth century is variously described as a period either of dislocation and cultural reaction or else of chaos and collapse. Politically the earldom ended as a coherently organised entity. It suffered badly at the start of the century during the Bruce War and as a consequence of the murder of the earl in 1333, which ended the sequence of resident earls. Subsequent attempts to administer the earldom in the name of absentee heirs broke down in the face of their neglect and the inability of the royal administration in Dublin to provide support for the local officials. Over the whole of Europe, the fourteenth century saw massive economic change. Following the Black Death of 1348-49 and earlier subsistence crises, the population fell to around half its previous level *circa* 1300 and this had profound effects. In many areas, the market for grain collapsed and regional economies responded by increasing specialisation and greater interchange of goods. In the case of Ireland, this meant concentrating on cattle rearing especially for the export of hides. Culturally, the period has been seen as one of a 'Gaelic Revival', during which many English lords acquired Gaelic habits of dress, language, lifestyle and law. Centralised royal authority disintegrated and English contemporaries linked this to the processes of cultural change, describing both as 'degeneration'.

The political changes involved the rise or intrusion of new lords in the area. Around the end of the fourteenth century, a dissident faction of the Uí Néill of Cenél Eóghain, who had previously advocated good relations with the earls of Ulster, moved into south Antrim at the expense of the Uí Thuirtre and the English family of Savage. These were the descendants of Aedha Buidhe, known as the Clann Aedha Buidhe or Clandeboye. The Uí Néill moved steadily into north Down at the expense of the absent earl and his English tenants. The Savages, with Uí Thuirtre, moved into the Ards and Lecale, where the family of the Whites also emerged as powerful figures. Both presumably seized lands from the Church, which had been the major local lord in the thirteenth century. As a result, Lecale and the Ards were subsequently recognised as forming part of the English polity, at least during the fifteenth century. Prior to this, in the thirteenth century, the de Mandevilles established a major local lordship known as Dufferin along the western shore of Strangford Lough. Subsequently, their lands passed in part to the MacQuillans, and then (when the MacQuillans were forced to concentrate on north Antrim) to the Whites.

It is difficult to date these changes with any precision. Normally we have the information that in a given year the land belonged to one family, followed by a statement in a later year that it belonged to another. What is even less clear is what these changes meant. The problem can be expressed in terms of two extreme interpretations of the period, each based on statements which are in themselves true. On the one side, there is evidence for dislocation, violence and decline and, on the other, clear signs of continuity, normality and some prosperity. In favour of the case for violence and change, we can point to the fact that, according to the chroniclers who recorded them, political changes of ownership occurred and were often accompanied by war. The relatively strong earldom collapsed, leading to a series of successor lordships characterised by the widespread adoption of tower houses. In county Down tower houses are rather plainer than those of the south of Ireland, and generally lack the decorative details, side rooms and elaborate wall-head display of defensive features which occur elsewhere. Their simplicity seems to have resulted from a desire to produce an effective defensive structure with little expenditure on display. These towers are found mainly in the 'English' area of the county, in Lecale and along the shores of Strangford Lough, suggesting that these communities were frequently the subject of attack. There are no traces of the construction of new church buildings in the Irish Late Gothic style, which signal the wealth of patrons elsewhere. Moreover, at Inch abbey the church was in fact reduced in size.

On the other hand, there is a strong suspicion that the changes in lordship were not accompanied by any significant concomitant change in the organisation of society or its economy, both of which continued to prosper. Something of the sort is implied by the expulsion of the MacQuillans and their followers from county Down in 1433 and their return in 1444 after wandering as a deracinated band of aristocratic warriors through Meath, Donegal and elsewhere. Moreover, in Lecale, the port of Ardglass developed with the construction of warehouses and tower houses to serve the commercial and residential needs of resident and visiting merchants. The archbishops of Armagh continued to provide for the administration of church law in both the Irish and English areas of the county alike, without any sign of either a general breakdown or particular local difficulties. In such a scenario, the reduction in size of Inch abbey church may simply reflect the general disappearance of lay brothers in Cistercian abbeys across Europe as the living standards of the peasantry rose. The lack of a new church building simply reinforces the idea of stability and continuity. In the west of Ireland, for example, many of the new friaries commissioned at this time seem to have been associated with changes in land tenure and a breakdown of the parish system, and this clearly did not occur in county Down. That said, the county's churches lack clear evidence of the sort of local patronage visible for example in the churches of the Pale, and this poses difficulties for the 'continuity/normality' model.

The crux of the debate lies in our conclusions concerning the county's castles during this period. County Down's tower houses are undoubtedly more overtly defensive in design than contemporary, unfortified manor houses of the south of England, and must represent a response of some sort to violence. What is not clear is whether the level of violence implied – small-scale raids by neighbours – should be regarded as evidence of a more violent society than in contemporary England of the Hundred Years' War and the Wars of the Roses, where individual battles saw larger armies and higher casualties than occurred over decades in the whole of Ireland. Tower houses represent a society living with an acceptable level of violence: we may stress its relative scarcity or frequency, according to our taste.

One clear piece of evidence is that the Gaelic lords now thought it appropriate to live in castles like their local English counterparts. MacArtan lords are recorded as having a castle at Annadorn, near Loughinisland, while the Uí Néill of Clandeboy had castles in Belfast and, later, Castle Reagh. The Magennises had more: at Loughbrickland, at Newcastle, and at Rathfriland, some ten miles up the Clanrye river from the Crown Mound and Newry. Even more spectacularly, they appear to have taken over the earl's castle of Dundrum. Not only did they occupy it, but they also added its present outer ward, to judge by the date of the outer gate. The very fact of this association with a castle implies a shift in the nature of Gaelic lordship. Castle building implied a clear association between a particular lord and a particular place which, outside Ireland, linked lordship to a specific block of land. In adopting castles, Irish lords such as the Magennises were showing themselves to be increasingly preoccupied with the lands of their lordship. There is a clear contrast between the implications of this and the behaviour of the errant MacQuillan lords, and there seems to be no clear conclusion which we can accordingly draw about Irish lordship in general. Perhaps the difference lies in the fact that the Magennis lordship was already long-established and became more firmly rooted still, while the MacQuillans were newcomers whose position was never stable.

The distribution of tower houses in English county Down suggests either a shift in the pattern of settlement, associated with the movements of lords, including the incursions of the Savages into the English areas, or else a change in economic conditions during the fourteenth century. The latter is reasonably well attested in Tipperary and Galway, but less so, for example, in Meath; so it cannot be assumed. We know of some eighteen towers in the English areas, apart from the urban ones in Strangford and Ardglass. Four lie on what were Church lands before 1350, including the bishop's castle at Kilclief. Another four lie on what were lay holdings at the same time, including the earl's manor of Ardkeen. This leaves the majority, eleven, sited on lands which are not listed as being centres of holdings before 1350. Some may have been at such places which were simply omitted from our surviving documents, but not all: equally, towers on Church lands, as at Saul, may represent a change in the pattern of lordship.

These twin issues of defence and change lead us to a consideration of what went on around the towers, both Irish and English, whether in their immediate vicinity or further afield. Many of the towers are now hemmed in by later buildings, but some are not. Audley's castle has even preserved the trace of a bawn around it, while Castlescreen was set in an earlier rath. Whether they were the focus of other buildings, and, if so, of what sort, are obvious questions for further research. The Irish castles are not well preserved: the outer ward at Dundrum castle is covered by cultivation ridges, while Newcastle, Annadorn and Castle Reagh have been destroyed. Rathfriland is partially preserved in a garden, although the ground has clearly been landscaped, and the other sides of the castle have been destroyed. Even so, it is important to remember that these tower houses still remain as our only specific indication of the location of late mediaeval settlements. Their excavation and the examination of their artefactual record would allow us to trace the lords' wider social and economic links, as well as providing us with a better understanding of the nature and extent of this later settlement.

Conclusion

Arguably, the fifteenth century is the period about which we know least during the historical era. Remove the tower houses and the political narrative of the chronicles, with all their faults of omission, and we are left with very little evidence. It is a period which we see through the filter of the earlier changes and developments of the thirteenth century and the later wars of the sixteenth century. Inevitably, it becomes a sort of half-way house between the two. It suffers extensively from the sort of general problems inherent in studying Ireland before modern times. There is little alignment between the documentary and archaeological record, and as a result we are left with scant information concerning the social structures underpinning both the events irecorded by chronicles and the physical remains. This provides a common theme which runs throughout the period: how do we interpret isolated pieces of evidence in a meaningful and coherent fashion? There are going to be few new documents discovered from the period; however, we are not as badly served as is often stated. If we want new sources of evidence, we must look to archaeology, but an archaeology directed towards fresh sources of information rather than the re-examination of known types of standing monument.

This is where we must leave the *Archaeological survey of county Down* behind and move on in our approach. New research agendas must concentrate on the context of the monuments and on the land between them. This is much more difficult for two obvious reasons. The first is that we simply do not know where to look for remains of settlements if they are not marked by upstanding monuments. This is a challenge which prehistorians have accepted and have started to resolve with the techniques of field-walking and pre-excavation prospecting. It must be admitted that they have one great advantage over the historical archaeologist in that stone tools, especially of flint, have been recognised and collected since the nineteenth century; flint is still easier to find in a field than fragments of pottery. On the other hand, we have the monuments as guides, and it is reasonable to start with their immediate environs. Even so, the rate of destruction of the evidence remains a problem. The most obvious loss here is the remains at Newry, which would have been the single most informative site in the county and a key site in furthering our understanding of mediaeval Ireland. The steady attrition of the past by farming is also obvious. The remains which we seek are always fragile and vulnerable to the spade and plough. Now that farming has the ability to bulldoze and level whole fields, the prospects for acquiring the other sorts of evidence which we need are not good. But if we do not ask the questions we will not look for it, and if we do not look, we will never find it.

Further reading
T. E. McNeill, *Anglo-Norman Ulster* (Edinburgh, 1980).
T. E. McNeill, 'Lordships and invasions, Ulster 1177-1500' in C. Brady, M. O'Dowd and B. Walker (ed.), *Ulster, an illustrated history* (London, 1989).
J. P. Mallory and T. E. McNeill, *The archaeology of Ulster* (Belfast, 1991).

Plate 5.1   Dundrum castle (Ulster Museum, W05/26/5).

Chapter 6

THE DIOCESE OF DROMORE ON THE EVE OF THE TUDOR REFORMATION

HENRY A. JEFFERIES

'It was the medieval (Irish) church which refused Protestantism and remained Catholic at the Reformation. In the long perspective of Irish history, that must surely rank as the most important single contribution of the middle ages to the shaping of modern Ireland'. Thus John Watt declared in the conclusion of his important book on *The church in medieval Ireland*.[1] Yet Watt presented his readers with a conundrum in that the Church which withstood the Reformation was, he claimed, in decline, suffering from shortcomings in its leadership and from serious defects in its administrative structures.[2] Indeed, he observed that the negative reports about the Irish Church on the eve of the Tudor Reformation have 'been seen by historians as indicating an overall degree of disorder in the late medieval Irish Church not far short of the total breakdown in the organised religion in that war-torn country'.[3]

The conventionally negative accounts of the Irish Church at the close of the middle ages are based to quite a remarkable degree on only a handful of documents among the state papers of Henry VIII.[4] Yet those state papers are too few in number, too superficial in their observations, and too intrinsically political in their nature to form a meaningful basis for any study of the Church in late medieval Ireland. For a better understanding of the Irish Church it is necessary to examine the surviving evidence relating to the dioceses and – ideally – the parishes.

The diocese of Dromore makes a particularly interesting case-study in so far as it has been presented as the epitome of the 'decayed' late medieval Irish Church. In his pioneering study, *The medieval province of Armagh*, Aubrey Gwynn describes Dromore as the 'most unfortunate' of all of the dioceses in the northern province towards the close of the middle ages.[5] It was, he concluded, in a 'deplorable state'.[6] More recently, Dromore has again been characterised as the 'cinderella' diocese of the ecclesiastical province of Armagh.[7] Dromore was certainly without a resident bishop for most of the fifteenth and sixteenth centuries,[8] but in his absence the see came under the direct supervision of the archbishop of Armagh, the metropolitan of the church in the northern province and the primate of all Ireland. This chapter explores the ways in which the diocese was supervised by Primate Cromer in the second quarter of the sixteenth century (1521-1543), and shows, *inter alia*, that there is no reason to think that the parish clergy failed in their responsibilities to provide an adequate pastoral ministry for the people of Dromore on the eve of the Reformation. The implication must be that if, in this most 'unfortunate' of dioceses, pastoral care was better than historians previously thought, then perhaps the overall picture of a 'decayed' late medieval Irish Church might require reconsideration.

Parishes and priests

Although the diocese of Dromore dates from the end of the twelfth century, churches in the area by 1500 had been centres of Christian worship and ministry for a thousand years. Despite the dismantling of most of the medieval church buildings and the widespread destruction of Early Christian monuments during the seventeenth century, the antiquity of the church in the diocese is attested by *Domhnach* place-names, as in Donaghmore and Donaghcloney, and *Cluain* place-names

TABLE 6.1

Benefice values in the diocese of Dromore, 1422

Benefice	Value (marks)	Benefice	Value (marks)
Prebend		*Rectory & Vicarage*	
Aghaderg	10	Aghalee	4
Clonallan	9	Magherally	3
Dean's	7	*Vicarage*	
Donaghcloney	7	Aghaderg	4
Dromara	7	Clonallan	4
Magheralin	7	Clonduff	4
Other Cathedral	7	Drumballyroney	4
Union		Drumgooland*	4
Annaclone	6	Donaghcloney*	3
Rectory		Donaghmore	3
Clonduff	6	Dromara	3
Donaghmore	5	Drumgath	3
Drumgooland	5	Garvaghy	3
Magheradrool	4	Magheralin	3
Shankill	3	Tullylish	3
Tullylish	3	Seagoe	2
Annahilt	1	Seapatrick	2

* with chapel   One mark equalled approximately 13s.4d.
Source: Dowdall's register, pp 214-5 (116).

as in Clonallan and Clonduff.[9] There are also ancient stone crosses at Donaghmore, Dromore and Kilbroney.[10] A recent study by Dorothy Kelly has suggested that the Kilbroney high cross, and another at Clonlea six kilometres away, are among the earliest in Ireland and mark the transition from timber to stone crosses during the eighth century.[11] The ancient Bell of St Brónach of Kilbroney, which may date from about the tenth century, is still preserved in the Catholic church in Rostrevor.[12]

According to a fifteenth-century taxation record copied into Primate Dowdall's register in 1546, Dromore diocese then encompassed twenty-three parishes, two of which had a chapel of ease.[13] Figure 6.1 shows that, at this time, the churches were well distributed throughout the diocese, despite the mountainous terrain of the Mournes and Slieve Croob in the south and south west. In Dromore diocese, as in all of those areas in Ulster which were not colonised by Anglo-Normans, there was generally a rector and a vicar in each parish (table 6.1).[14] Normally, the rector received two thirds of the parochial tithes and the vicar one third, which was also the practice in neighbouring diocese of Armagh *inter Hibernicos*.[15]

The vicar was obliged to reside in his parish and exercise the cure of souls,[16] and in return enjoyed possession of the parochial house and glebe (*fearann sagairt*).[17] He retained the small fees charged for such church services as baptisms, weddings and funerals – the latter probably taking the form of a meal after the event.[18] In some of the poorer parishes, like Aghalee or Magherally, the positions of vicar and rector could be held by the same priest in order to ensure that he received a satisfactory income.[19] Rectors who had a separate vicar to serve their cure were largely sinecurists, with limited responsibilities within the parish.[20] Bishop Montgomery's well known statement that 'the parsonages were usually bestowed upon students that intended to take orders' has been shown to be inaccurate.[21] In theory, rectors were also obliged to reside in their parishes in order to perform the Daily Office and celebrate Mass.[22] Failure to carry out these duties – without a special licence – could lead to the delinquent being removed from his benefice.[23] Licences were issued, at least for temporary absences, to the cathedral canons who held a rectory as their prebend.[24] Diocesan administrators, on the other hand, could be sinecurists who drew the rectorial tithes from their parish to supplement their otherwise meagre salaries. For example in 1492, Dnus Dónal Maginn, archdeacon of Dromore, received only 13s 8d by right of his office, but as prebendary of Magheralin received a further £2 13s 4d.[25] Nonetheless, it has to be emphasised that with a resident vicar to minister to the parishioners, the role of the rector was secondary and his absence – licensed or

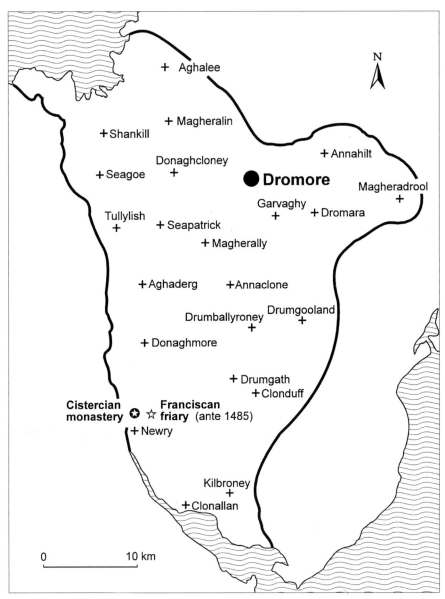

Fig. 6.1 Churches in Dromore diocese, *ca.* 1422.

otherwise – did not unduly affect the pastoral care offered in the parish. This was also the case where the benefice was owned by a monastery as part of its endowment. Where the parish contained a religious house, as for example at Newry – where there were important Cistercian[26] and Franciscan houses – and Aghaderg, where the Franciscans may have had another house at Drumsallagh,[27] pastoral care remained largely the preserve of the parish clergy.

Although we have little direct evidence about clerical incomes in Dromore diocese on the immediate eve of the Reformation, earlier sources help to throw light on the subject. The taxation record made in 1422 under Primate Swayne provides considerable information concerning clerical incomes at that time, and the fact that it was copied into Primate Dowdall's register in 1546 suggests that it may offer some useful indications concerning clerical incomes in the later period.[28] If we compare the income data in Primate Dowdall's register with the occasional references to benefice values in the late medieval papal registers, we find only modest variations between the two.[29] Accordingly, this gives us some confidence in using the Swayne figures as an approximate guide to at least the relative distribution of clerical incomes in the Tudor period. According to Primate Swayne's figures, the seven prebendaries were reckoned to receive an average of £5 2s 10d from their prebends, the rectors without cures £3 3s 4d, and the rectors who served their parish cure, £2 6s 8d. The vicars only received £2 on average. These figures appear remarkably low, yet they are quite consistent with data for clerical incomes in the rural deanery of Tullyhogue in Armagh archdiocese in 1544.[30] Of course, there is a real difficulty in determining what exactly such figures mean. We have no idea of what the 'cost of living' was like in Dromore in the later middle ages. Yet it is clear that the clergy was not wealthy. Indeed, given the responsibilities of the vicars and rectors who exercised the cure of souls and the slenderness of their incomes, the life of the parish priest in Dromore diocese at the end of the middle ages must have been demanding and not one likely to appeal to men for whom worldly wealth was a priority.

In the absence of a diocesan archive, information on the quality of the parish clergy in Dromore in the later middle ages is hard to come by, but some observations may be made. Most of the diocesan priests in Dromore came from a small number of erenagh families which had been closely associated with the church for centuries. These included the Maginns, McBrunes, McGuirins, McKinnevins, O'Makrells, O'Rooneys and O'Shiels.[31] Similar long-standing associations have been observed in Derry diocese.[32] Everywhere, these families had a noble tradition of service to the Church which they maintained throughout the later middle ages, and, sometimes, into the nineteenth century as well.[33] Other priests from Dromore diocese served parishes elsewhere in the archdiocese of Armagh. For example, Dnus Liam O'Makrell was curate of Castletown in 1522; Dnus James McBrune and Dnus Séan McBrune were, successively, vicars of Dunleer in 1518-1519; Dnus Tomás O'Rooney was chaplain at Termonfeckin in 1519; while Dnus Patrick O'Rooney officiated at Berlistown and Drumshallon in the

1530s. Dnus Hugh O'Shiel was the curate of Ballymakenny in 1533, and subsequently vicar of Dromin and rector of Heynestown.[34]

A significant number of Dromore priests were titled *magister*, indicating that they were university graduates.[35] Others are likely to have studied in the *studia particularia*, the substitute for a university in late medieval Ireland,[36] where masters, themselves usually associated with the Church, offered an education in one or more subjects.[37] The *studia* were often run by graduates from universities overseas and were thus not wholly isolated from wider intellectual currents in contemporary Europe.[38] Canon Liam O'Shiel of Dromore declared in 1495 that he had studied canon law for some time, although he was not a graduate, and is likely to have been a product of one of these local Irish schools.[39] Dnus Hugh O'Shiel, prebendary of Clonallan and a long-standing member of the metropolitan court of Armagh during the primacy of Archbishop George Cromer (1521-1543), seems to have been another non-graduate canon lawyer who probably studied in a *studium particular.*[40] Mention ought also to be made of Adam and Gilbert Maginn, who were described as two scholars of Dromore in the early fifteenth century.[41] Finally, there is the interesting case of Mgr. John Maginn, official principal of Dromore and prebendary of Magheralin, who built a stone tower beside the church at Magheralin in 1442 to house his books and other valuables.[42] Clearly, in Dromore diocese, the means and desire for education were not wanting.

There is no evidence to suggest that the late medieval parish priests in Dromore did anything other than serve their parishioners satisfactorily. Whatever the individual priest's sense of responsibility to God, in an 'age of faith' the expectations of even a proportion of his parishioners would have obliged him to meet at least basic standards of pastoral care. If he failed his parishioners he could be reported by them to the archdeacon or the bishop and removed from office. Among the late medieval Armagh registers there is only one record of a priest of Dromore diocese who was expelled in this way. Dnus David McDonegan, vicar of Clonduff, was deprived of his benefice in 1461 for absenteeism and neglect of his parish cure.[43]

The late medieval papal registers tend to confirm the impression that the priests of the diocese generally performed their duties satisfactorily. The Roman curia operated a system of delation whereby a priest who exposed a benefice holder as a grave sinner was awarded his benefice. This system was open to abuse since the accuser was allowed to choose the judges to investigate his charges. Normally the Roman curia mandated three judges to investigate a case, but two judges or even one judge acting alone could conduct the inquiry and pass sentence. The defendant could find the expense of mounting an appeal to Rome prohibitively expensive.[44] Between 1482 and 1513 there are records of only six delations in the published calendars relating to Dromore,[45] although there were three more such cases in 1530.[46] Significantly, none of the delators made accusations of priestly misconduct or pastoral negligence, although such charges would have helped their case against the beneficed clergyman. Instead they resorted to technical allegations which questioned the defendant's *titulus*, a tendency which can be seen more widely in the archdiocese of Armagh and elsewhere in Ireland at the end of the middle ages.[47]

One aspect of the late medieval priesthood in Dromore marks them off from their modern-day Catholic successors: many were married. Several were the sons of priests, and probably the fathers of priests themselves in turn.[48] Previous generations of historians tended to be fascinated or shocked by clerical concubinage in medieval Ireland, but it is less surprising when placed in context. Although canonically unlawful, the practice was widely accepted across much of medieval Europe (and nowhere more so than in Wales) as natural and permissible.[49] Evidently, a great many priests and people decided that the married state (a civil marriage, of course, not *facie ecclesiae*) was irrelevant as far as a priest's ministry was concerned.[50] Thus priestly marriage cannot be taken as evidence that a priest was a poor pastor. Such a view reflects more recent modes of thought which were themselves shaped by the Council of Trent. In one sense, therefore, the Protestant practice of clerical marriage simply represents the regularisation of a long-standing custom once common throughout the medieval Church. That being said, it cannot be assumed that where successive parochial incumbents shared the same surname, the benefices in question were necessarily subject to 'hereditary succession'.[51] The surnames may simply reflect the fact that the benefice holders were normally drawn from local erenagh families.[52]

There is physical evidence to indicate that some of the parishes in the diocese of Dromore were in good order towards the end of the middle ages. The pre-Reformation churches at Kilbroney, Magheradrool and Magheralin all show signs of having been built or substantially modified in the fifteenth or sixteenth century (plate 6.1).[53] Unfortunately, virtually all of the other pre-Reformation churches in the diocese were dismantled or replaced in the seventeenth century or after, but the surviving earlier buildings suggest a considerable degree of vitality in the local Church on the eve of the Reformation.

Administration

In the later middle ages, each bishop of Dromore was entrusted by the pope with direct responsibility for ensuring that the parochial clergy

Plate 6.1   Magheralin Old Church (Source: Green collection, Ulster Folk and Transport Museum).

provided the people with an appropriate level of pastoral care in their parishes. The bishop had several means at his disposal to achieve this. He judged the standards expected of men who sought to be ordained by him to the priesthood. He also enjoyed the power to collate and institute priests into the parochial benefices. The bishop could use annual synods of his clergy to set out an agenda for reform. He was also obliged to visit every parish in the diocese at least once a year to ensure that standards were being maintained. Any priest who was found to be negligent, or who lived scandalously, could be brought before the bishop's consistory court for trial and punishment.

The problem with this ideal scenario was that towards the end of the middle ages, the diocese of Dromore had become too poor to support a resident bishop. About the year 1510, Primate Octavian del Palatio informed Henry VIII that the annual revenues of the bishop of Dromore did not exceed £27 6s 8d.[54] Because the see was so poor, he explained, no one wished to be bishop there, and the diocese had been without a resident bishop for almost twenty years. A major cause of this relative poverty was the small size of the episcopal estates in the see. Generally they were tenanted by erenaghs – the heads of the clans who occupied the lands. It appears that, unlike other northern dioceses such as Clogher, Derry and Raphoe, or Armagh *inter Hibernicos*, the bishop of Dromore did not possess land in every parish.[55] Within the diocese, the erenaghs were concentrated around the episcopal settlement at Dromore and in the far west, in parishes which had been beyond the reach of medieval Anglo-Norman settlement.[56] It seems certain that the Normans had taken possession of the church lands elsewhere, and that the bishop of Dromore failed to recover them when Norman control declined. Some of the former erenagh lands had been transferred by the Normans to monasteries in areas which were more firmly under their control. In 1476 Patrick Maginn, a clerk of Dromore diocese, made a lease with Bro. Nicholas O'Hegarty, abbot of the Augustinian monastery at Bangor, for the churchlands in the parish of Clonduff, and another lease with Bro. Oliver Walls, prior of the Benedictine priory at Downpatrick, for the churchlands in the parish of Drumgooland.[57] Whether for this or other causes, the fact remains that the bishop of Dromore had little land and his tenants, the erenaghs, paid quite modest rents of only about £2 each a year.[58]

Elsewhere, as well as paying rent, the erenaghs also gave the bishop refection, or food and drink for himself and his entourage whenever he visited the parish in person.[59] According to Bishop Montgomery, the Protestant bishop of Clogher, Derry and Raphoe, in 1607 the refections given by the erenaghs of his dioceses were worth thirty or forty times the cash rents.[60] In other words the refections consumed during visitations made up the great bulk of the bishop's income. By Montgomery's time, the erenaghs were widely regarded as clergymen, and he noted that 'anciently they used to have *primam tonsuram*', an indication that they had at least taken minor holy orders.[61] Montgomery found the erenaghs to be generally proficient in Latin, and a number of them received priest's orders.

In Dromore, most of the priests who can be identified in the later middle ages came from erenagh families, and frequently the erenagh of a parish was also either its rector or vicar.[62] Here as elsewhere, erenaghs were the successors of the abbots who controlled local churchlands during the Early Christian era.[63] They inherited the Church's duty to provide hospitality for pilgrims, travellers and the needy. Many of them had hospitals or guest-houses for that purpose. In parts of Ulster they were also responsible, with the rector and vicar, for maintaining the local parish church building.[64]

As well as the revenues derived from the erenaghs, the bishop of Dromore held the prebend of Kilbroney as part of his episcopal *mensa*. Its revenues included not only the rectorial tithes but also the laity's offerings to the Staff of St Brónach,[65] and in 1428 and again in 1526, it was valued altogether at £2 13 8d.[66] The bishop's revenues from Desertmoy (Seapatrick) were worth another £1 6s 4d a year in 1431.[67] Other sources of episcopal revenue included the procurations paid by rectors and vicars whenever the bishop visited their church,[68] and the synodals paid by all beneficed clergy when they attended diocesan synods.[69]

In 1511, Pope Julius II provided Brother Tadhg O'Reilly, OSA, to the see of Dromore, but, due to the financial straits he found himself in, he seems not to have been able to exercise an effective ministry within the diocese. After Bishop O'Reilly died in 1526 the see was left vacant for the next ten years.[70] However, during this and similar periods of vacancy, the diocese came directly under the custodianship of the archbishop of Armagh. Normally, however, he appointed senior clergymen from the diocese as sub-custodians.[71] In 1479, for example, Archdeacon Séan O'Shiel, Canon Peter O'Rooney and Mgr. James Maginn, the official principal of Dromore, were the sub-custodians.[72] Evidence of the archbishops' exercise of their custodianship over the diocese is generally scarce, with only occasional records surviving among the Armagh registers. However, the register of Dr. George Cromer, the reform-minded archbishop of Armagh from 1521 to 1543, is exceptionally informative in this regard. Cromer fully appreciated the value of the annual diocesan synod as an instrument of reform,[73] and in Armagh used long-established synodal traditions to exhort his priests to ever-higher standards and address issues of concern both in the diocese and the province as a whole.[74]

Primate Cromer had his chief residence and the centre of his ecclesiastical administration at Termonfeckin, a few miles north east of Drogheda. Despite the fact that he made regular (probably annual) visits to Armagh city, there is no evidence to show that he ever ventured into the diocese of Dromore.[75] It is possible, nonetheless, that he met the assembled Dromore clergy at Kilbroney, as at least one of his predecessors had done.[76] Throughout his period as *custos* of Dromore he was dependent upon the knowledge and expertise of local clergymen – in particular the archdeacon and the official principal. Such senior clergymen were the archbishop's commissaries and he delegated much of his administrative duties in the diocese to them. They could deal with minor offences committed by the priests or their parishioners, while the official principal also dealt with more serious matters in his capacity as judge of the diocesan church court.[77]

The official principal was thus appointed by the bishop (or the primate acting *in custos*) specifically to investigate allegations of grave sins committed by priests or lay people. If the allegations were proved, the official imposed some appropriate penance. The church court records from Armagh make it clear that for scandalous sins like adultery, fornication, fighting in church or perjury, the penance was often a public one.[78] Some penitents were ordered to dress in white linen and stand at the front of their parish church on a Sunday holding a candle for the duration of the Mass. Priests could lose a year's salary for failing to keep their part of the parish church in good order; for more serious faults, they could be deprived of their benefice altogether.[79] For example, in 1461, Archbishop Bole, custodian of Dromore diocese, executed a mandate for the deprivation of the vicar of Clonduff after the primate's commissaries had found him to be an absentee and negligent.[80]

The church courts did not deal with serious sins only. Private individuals brought suits to the courts about marriage problems, disputes about wills, the use of libellous words, the payment of debts or cases of assault. Any litigant who was dissatisfied with the verdict of the diocesan court could appeal to the metropolitan court of the archbishop of Armagh. Rome was, of course, the final court of appeal in the Catholic Church. Once every third year the archbishop of Armagh had the right to visit Dromore diocese, either in person or through commissaries, to ensure that its clergy were carrying out their responsibilities in a satisfactory manner.[81]

As in other dioceses, the dean of Dromore was responsible for supervising the cathedral clergy, for ensuring that the fabric of the cathedral building was in good order and that cathedral services were appropriate to the mother-church of the diocese. In return, by right of his deanery, the dean received part of the tithes of Clanbrassel in Oneilland and probably a third share of the tithes of Dromore parish.[82] These resources were considerable and reflected his status within the church hierarchy. Unfortunately, at Dromore, few records survive of the activities of the dean and chapter during the early sixteenth century. It is known that in 1539 Dnus Seán Maginn was dean, and he was probably a member of the same clerical clan as Canon Patrick Maginn, prebendary of Dromara, and Dnus Art Maginn, rector of Annahilt (and himself possibly the son of the late Archdeacon Art Maginn).[83] It was not unknown for a father and son to be canons of Dromore cathedral at the same time. In 1504 Dnus Dónal O'Shiel was given a licence by the Roman curia to become a canon of Dromore on condition that he and his father, who was already a canon serving the cathedral, did 'not both at once administer therein'.[84] One other office at Dromore is worthy of note, that of the archpriest. This benefice involved a cure of souls and seems to have been the equivalent of the vicar of a cathedral parish.[85]

On the eve of the Henrician reformation, Dromore was served by Archdeacon Art Maginn,[86] who was a native of the diocese and a Bachelor in Canon Law.[87] He had been appointed archdeacon some time after 1504,[88] and, six years later, Primate Octavian del Palatio highly commended him to Henry VIII, recommending that he be made the bishop of Dromore.[89] For reasons which are now obscure, Archdeacon Maginn was not promoted to the see, but his legal expertise nevertheless remained much in demand. In 1519, he represented Dnus Gelasius McGuinness, prior of St Patrick's cathedral, Downpatrick, before the metropolitan court of Armagh in a tithe dispute against the dean and chapter of Christ Church cathedral, Dublin.[90] In the same year he defended the archdeacon of Armagh and the prioress of Termonfeckin in another suit before the archbishop's court.[91] Seven years later, he was one of the experts called upon by Primate Cromer to investigate a forged papal bull.[92]

Mgr. Maginn was also a canon of Armagh.[93] This office obliged him to swear an oath of obedience to the archbishop, binding him more closely to the primate than was the case when the archbishop acted solely in his capacity as *custos* of Dromore. Under Archbishop Cromer, Maginn conducted visitations in the diocese, and, on receiving the appropriate mandates from the primate, inducted priests into their benefices.[94] As a reward for his endeavours, Archbishop Cromer augmented Maginn's income in 1526 by assigning the rectorial tithes of Tullylish and Magheralin to the corps of the archdeaconry for his lifetime.[95] Three years later, in 1529, Archbishop Cromer took the unusual step of appointing Maginn to the office of diocesan principal while he remained archdeacon.[96] Possession of both offices extended Maginn's authority considerably and signified the primate's confidence in him. The experiment was evidently considered to be a success, as a year later Archbishop Cromer conferred the offices of archdeacon and official principal in the archdiocese of Armagh on Mgr. Cormac Roth.[97]

Nothing reflected the authority of a bishop more than his power to present men to benefices or remove them from office for grave faults. Reference has already been made to Archbishop Bole's removal of the vicar of Clonduff from office in 1461,[98] while in 1504 Liam O'Rooney was deprived of the vicarage of Drumgooland by Archbishop del Palatio because he failed to have himself ordained within the year required by law.[99] O'Rooney eventually recovered the living after appealing to Rome, and died, still in its possession and as prebendary of Dromara, in 1529.[100] Odo O'Shiel was less fortunate. Removed by Cromer from the rectory of Annaclone in 1528 because he too had failed to be ordained within the statutory year, he was immediately replaced by Dnus Eugene McGuinness, prebendary of Aghaderg.[101]

Archbishop Cromer's power to present to the benefices in Dromore was considerable. By comparison, in Armagh *inter Anglicos*, that part of the original Armagh diocese heavily settled by the Anglo-Normans, his right to present was very limited indeed.[102] Perhaps not surprisingly, therefore, Cromer used some of the prebends in Dromore to support key priests in his metropolitan administration. Thus Mgr. Cormac Roth, president of the metropolitan court of Armagh (1521-1539), was made prebendary of Kilkeel,[103] while Mgr. Carroll O'Cahan, another important member of the metropolitan court, was prebendary of Clonallan from 1526 until his death in 1534.[104] The prebendary was subsequently presented to Dnus Hugh O'Shiel, another of the archbishop's court officers.[105]

Archbishop Cromer administered the diocese of Dromore as though it were an extension of his own archdiocese *inter Hibernicos*. He exercised full control over the revenues of the bishopric, leasing the bishop's *mensa* and leasing episcopal lands to erenaghs.[106] He addressed disciplinary matters within the diocese[107] and provided the priests to serve its cathedral and parish cures.[108]

Conclusion

The conventional image of late medieval Dromore as a forsaken diocese was founded upon the fact that it was without a resident bishop. Historians imagined that in this state the diocese would have collapsed or decayed. This chapter has shown, however, that during part of the early sixteenth century at least, the diocese was closely and effectively supervised by the primate, Archbishop Cromer, acting *in custos* but also in partnership with Archdeacon Art Maginn.

On a more general level, there is no evidence that in Dromore the late medieval priesthood neglected its pastoral responsibilities. On the contrary, even in the papal registers where one might have expected to find some delators making allegations of immorality or negligence to advance their suits, no criticisms of the priests' ministries can be found. It appears that the Church authorities were able to weed out those individuals who were unsatisfactory. Moreover, the foundation of a Franciscan friary at Newry, and the archaeological evidence for the renewal of some of the parish churches, suggests that religious life in the late medieval diocese was vibrant enough.[109]

This revisionist interpretation of the state of the Church in Dromore diocese does not stand alone. In the better-documented dioceses of Armagh, Derry and Kildare, there is a great deal of evidence to suggest that the late medieval parish clergy offered a pastoral ministry which satisfied both Church and laity alike.[110] It was from these foundations that here, as elsewhere in Ireland, the Catholic Church drew the inherent strengths which were to stand it in good stead during the following years of war, dispossession and religious persecution.

References

1. J. Watt, *The church in medieval Ireland* (Dublin, 1977), pp 216-7.
2. Ibid., pp 181-3.
3. Ibid., pp 182-3.
4. Watt acknowledges this. Ibid., p 181.
5. A. Gwynn, *The medieval province of Armagh, 1470-1546* (Dundalk, 1946), p. 146.
6. Ibid., p. 144.
7. A. Lynch, 'Religion in late medieval Ireland' in *Archiv. Hib.*, xxxvi (1981), p. 4.
8. Gwynn, *Medieval province*, pp 141-9.
9. R. Sharpe, 'Churches and communities in early Christian Ireland: towards a pastoral model' in J. Blair and R. Sharpe (ed.), *Pastoral care before the parish* (Leicester, 1992), pp 108-9.
10. *A.S.C.D.*, pp 274, 291-2, 303. The crosses at Dromore and Donaghmore were damaged in the seventeenth century but were re-erected towards the end of the nineteenth century.
11. D. Kelly, 'The heart of the matter: models for Irish high crosses' in *R.S.A.I. Jn.*, cxxi (1991), pp 108-11, 142-3.
12. *A.S.C.D.*, p. 442. Similar Early Christian bells are preserved at the Catholic churches of Culdaff and Omagh in Derry diocese.
13. Dowdall's register, pp 214-5 (113), P. R. O. N. I., DIO 4/4/13.
14. For Dromore see Dowdall's register, pp 214-15 (113). For Ulster generally see *Inquisitionum in officio rotulorum cancallariae Hiberniae .... reportorium, II* (Dublin, 1829) [hereafter *Ulster inquisitiones*], app., *passim.*

15. Dowdall's register, pp 214-5 (113); *Ulster inquisitiones*, app., county Tyrone, pp 2-5.

16. This was the situation across Ulster. See *Ulster inquisitiones*, app., *passim.* Clogher, Derry and Raphoe, f. 7., T. C. D., MS 110.383.

17. *Ulster inquisitiones*, app., counties Cavan, Coleraine, Donegal, Fermanagh and Tyrone, *passim.*

18. This was the practice in south-east Ireland in 1537, where lay people could either pay the priest a few pence or provide him with a dinner. See Commoners of Kilkenny, presentment, liv, P. R. O., S. P. 60/5/64; Irishtown presentments, viii, xii, P. R. O., S. P. 60/5/78; Commons of county Waterford, presentments, liv, P. R. O., S. P. 60/5/85. For Ulster see 'The ancient estate of the diocese of Derry, Raphoe and Clogher', Bodleian Library, Oxford, Laud Miscellaneous Ms, Ms 612, f. 8.

19. Dowdall's register, pp 214-5 (113).

20. Clogher, Derry and Raphoe, T. C. D., Ms 10,383.

21. Ancient estate, f. 8. H. A. Jefferies, 'Derry diocese on the eve of the plantation' in G. O'Brien (ed.), *Derry/Londonderry. History and society* (Dublin, 1997, forthcoming).

22. See Visitation of Armagh *inter Hibernicos* 1546, Primate Cromer's register, P. R. O. N. I., Ms DIO 4/4/12.

23. For an example in Derry, see Canon Leslie's typescript of Bishop Reeve's Calendar of Primate Octavian's register, no. 301. For an example in Armagh, see The register of Primate Cromer, II, f. 3v (6), P. R. O. N. I., Ms DIO 4/2/11.

24. In the neighbouring diocese of Armagh there is a sixteenth-century record of a canon's oath obliging him to reside in his prebendary parish. See Dowdall's register, p. 73 (60).

25. A. Fuller (ed.), *Calendars of the papal registers relating to Great Britain and Ireland, 1492-1498*, xvi (Dublin, 1986), no. 863.

26. *A.S.C.D.*, p. 290.

27. For the Franciscan friary at Newry see C. McNeill and J. Otway-Ruthven (ed.), *Dowdall deeds* (Dublin, 1960), no. 106. For a suggestion that there may have been a Franciscan friary at Drumsallagh, see Reeves, *Ecclesiastical antiquities*, p. 113.

28. Dowdall's register, pp 214-15 (113).

29. M. J. Haren (ed.), *The calendar of papal registers relating to Great Britain and Ireland, 1484-1492*, xv (Dublin, 1976), no 863; *Idem, The calendar of papal registers relating to Great Britain and Ireland, 1503-1513*, xviii (Dublin, 1989), nos 243, 332, 374.

30. Dowdall's register, pp 185-6 (106).

31. The priests' names are too numerous to list here, but the same surnames may be found throughout the Armagh registers and the papal letters relating to Dromore. See for example, Octavian's register, no 493; Cromer's register II, f. 23 (54).

32. Jefferies, 'Derry diocese' (forthcoming).

33. K. Simms, 'Frontiers in the Irish church – regional and cultural' in T. B. Barry, R. Frame and K. Simms (ed.), *Colony and frontier in medieval Ireland: essays presented to J. F. Lydon* (London, 1995), pp 196-200.

34. Cromer's register, II, f. 1 (1); Ibid., I, f. 3(9), f. 37 (56); Ibid.,I, ff 49-51 v (67); Ibid., II, f. 68 (167), f. 85 (198); Ibid., II, f. 72v (172); Dowdall's register, p. 42 (36), p. 50 (46).

35. Cromer's register, I, ff. 31-31v (67); Ibid., II, f.23 (54). For the only calendar to identify graduates see H. J. Lawlor, 'Calendar of register of Peter Fleming, 1404-16' in *R.I.A. Proc.*, xxx, C (1912), nos 9, 62, 64, 128, 131, 164.

36. K. Simms, 'Bards and barons: the Anglo-Irish aristocracy and the native culture' in R. Bartlett and A. MacKay (ed.), *Medieval frontier societies* (Oxford, 1989), p. 195.

37. K. Nicholls, *Gaelic and gaelicised Ireland in the later middle ages* (Dublin, 1972), pp 79-83.

38. C. Mooney, *The church in Gaelic Ireland: thirteenth to fifteenth centuries* (Dublin, 1969), p. 23.

39. *Calendar of papal registers,* xvi, no. 336.

40. Cromer's register, I, f. 100 (125); Ibid., II ff. 31-31v (72), f. 47 (121), f. 60v (147), f. 64v (158), f. 72v (172), f. 81 (190), ff. 92v-93 (207); Dowdall's register, p. 41 (35A).

41. Fleming's register, no. 65.

42. Reeves, *Ecclesiastical antiquities,* pp 110-11.

43. A. Lynch, 'A calendar of the re-assembled register of John Bole, archbishop of Armagh, 1457-71' in *Seanchas Ard Mhacha,* xv (1992); Prene's register, no. 37.

44. For examples see M. A. Costello (with Ambrose Coleman) (eds), *De Annatis Hiberniae: a calendar of the first fruits' fees levied on papal appointments to benefices in Ireland, 1400-1535, i* (Dublin, 1912), pp 297-8.

45. *Calendar of papal registers,* xv, no. 863; xvi, nos 330, 336; xviii, nos 243, 332, 374.

46. Costello, *De Annatis Hiberniae,* p. 297.

47. H. A. Jefferies, 'The archdiocese of Armagh, 1518-1560' (forthcoming thesis).

48. *Calendar of papal registers,* xv, no. 863; xviii, nos 243, 332; Costello, *De Annatis Hiberniae,* p. 297.

49. J. Delumeau, *Catholicism between Luther and Voltaire: a new view of the counter-reformation* (London and Philadelphia, 1977), pp 154-5. For Wales, see G. Williams, *Recovery, reorientation and reformation: Wales c. 1415-1642* (Oxford, 1987), pp 339-45.

50. A. Barnes, 'The social transformation of the French parish clergy, 1500-1800' in B. B. Diefendorf and C. Hesse (eds.), *Culture and identity in early modern Europe (1500-1800)* (Michigan, 1993), pp 142-6.

51. Simms, 'Frontiers', pp 177-200.

52. This is amply illustrated in the case of Derry diocese. See Jefferies, 'Derry diocese' (forthcoming).

53. *A.S.C.D.,* pp 303, 307-8.

54. Octavian's register, no. 198.

55. *Ulster inquisitiones,* app., counties Coleraine, Donegal, Derry, Fermanagh and Tyrone, *passim.*

56. Simms, 'Frontiers', p. 179.

57. Costello, *De Annatis Hiberniae,* p. 296.

58. See Cromer's register, II, f. 23 (54); Swayne's register, no. 75, 147, 478. In Derry diocese the erenaghs also collected death duties for the bishop and the bishop's share of marriage dowries. See Clogher, Derry and Raphoe, ff. 1, 8, T. C. D. Ms 10,383; and *Ulster inquisitiones,* app., counties Coleraine, Donegal, Tyrone *passim.*

59. Ibid.

60. Ancient estate, f. 36.

61. Ibid.

62. Swayne's register, nos 355, 478, 479; Octavian's register, no 493; Cromer's register, II, f. 33 (54).

63. Ancient estate, f. 36v.

64. *Ulster inquisitiones*, app., counties Coleraine, Donegal, Tyrone *passim.*
65. Swayne's register, no. 143.
66. Ibid., no. 520; Cromer's register, II, f. 22v (51).
67. Swayne's register, no. 418.
68. This was usual in Derry. See Clogher, Derry and Raphoe, f. 9, T. C. D., Ms 10,383.
69. Ibid., f. 5.
70. Gwynn, *Medieval province*, pp 147-8.
71. Swayne's register, no. 182; Octavian's register, no. 6.
72. Ibid.
73. The only survey into the conduct of diocesan synods in Ireland on the eve of the Reformation is H. A. Jefferies, 'Diocesan synods and convocations in the archdiocese of Armagh before the Tudor reformations' in *Seanchas Ard Mhacha*, xvii (1996).
74. Gwynn, *Medieval province*, p. 20; Swayne's register, no. 60; Octavian's register, nos 612, 622.
75. Dowdall's register, p. 47 (43).
76. Sweteman's register, no. 221.
77. For a study of the operation of Catholic Church courts in Ireland during the sixteenth century see H. A. Jefferies, 'The church courts of Armagh on the eve of the Tudor reformations' in *Seanchas Ard Mhacha*, xvi (1995), pp 120-32.
78. Ibid., pp 13, 18, 20.
79. Ibid., p. 21.
80. Prene's register, nos 181, 373.
81. Sweteman's register, nos 50, 221; Octavian's register, nos 252, 494.
82. *Ulster inquisitiones*, app., county Armagh.
83. Costello, *De Annatis Hiberniae*, pp 297-8.
84. *Calendar of papal registers*, xviii, no. 332.
85. Ibid., xv, no. 550.
86. The only published account of the archdeacons of an Irish diocese before the Tudor reformations is by A. Lynch, 'The archdeacons of Armagh, 1417-71' in *Journal of County Louth Archaeological and Historical Society*, xix (1979).
87. Octavian's register, no. 198.
88. *Calendar of papal registers*, xviii, no. 347.
89. Octavian's register, no. 198.
90. Cromer's register, I, ff. 31-31v (51).
91. Ibid., ff. 49-51v (67).
92. Ibid., II, f. 24 (56).
93. *Calendar of papal registers*, xviii, no. 374; Cromer's register, I, ff. 49-51v (67).
94. Ibid., II, f. 36v (84, f. 43v (107).
95. Ibid., II, ff. 19v-20 (46).
96. Ibid., II, ff. 43 (105).
97. Ibid., II, f. 56 (130).
98. Prene's register, no. 181.
99. *Calendar of papal registers*, xviii, no. 374.
100. Ibid.; Ibid., xvi, no. 1266; Cromer's register, II, f. 43v (107), f. 43v (108).
101. Ibid., f. 39 (91).
102. Jefferies, 'Archdiocese of Armagh', chapter 2 (forthcoming).
103. Cromer's register, II, f. 45v (116). This was formerly a chapel dependent upon the parish church of Kilkeel in county Down. See Fleming's register, nos 63, 67.
104. Cromer's register, II, f. 20 (47; f. 81 (190).
105. Ibid., II, f. 81 (190).

106. Ibid., II, f. 22v (51); f. 23 (54).

107. Ibid., II, f. 24 (56), ff. 26-26v (61); f. 35v (82); f. 39 (91).

108. Ibid., II, ff. 19v-20 (46); f. 22v (52); f.24v (57); f. 35v (82); f. 36v (84); f. 39 (91); f. 43v (107); f. 43v (108); f. 45v (116); f. 82 (192); f. 84 (195).

109. Watt, *Church*, pp 193-202; B. Bradshaw, *The dissolution of the religious orders in Ireland under Henry VIII* (Cambridge, 1974), pp 8-16.

110. Jefferies, 'Archdiocese of Armagh' (forthcoming); *Idem*, 'Church courts'; *Idem*, 'Diocesan synods'; *Idem*, 'Derry diocese'; M. A. Lyons, 'Church and society in Kildare in the early sixteenth century', Unpublished M.A. thesis, Department of History, St. Patrick's College, Maynooth, 1991, pp 84-95, 269-70.

Chapter 7

THE SOCIAL WORLD OF COUNTY DOWN IN THE SEVENTEENTH CENTURY

RAYMOND GILLESPIE

In 1744 two men who might with some justice be seen as the founding fathers of Irish local history, the Dublin antiquarian Walter Harris and the Waterford apothecary Charles Smith, published their *The antient and present state of the county of Down*. The dilemma which they faced in preparing their work has changed little over the last 250 years. How can the historian capture something of the complexity of a lost society, shaped by a complex web of relations between people and their environment and between and within social groups? This essay is an attempt to describe something of one social world which evolved among the best documented group of seventeenth-century county Down: the landed gentry.

The problematic nature of the task of understanding the evolution of a local society can be seen in the apparently contradictory picture which Harris and Smith painted of the social world of county Down. On the one hand the main heroes of the volume, the landlords and gentry who had arrived in the county in the course of the seventeenth century, are seen in a rather traditional mould as embattled colonists living in an alien world, in constant fear of rebellion, such as had occurred in 1641. The description of Newcastle, for instance, was embellished by the relation of 'an instance of great barbarity committed here in the rebellion of 1641' and Tullylish church was also the scene of a massacre in 1641 which was 'attended with such circumstances of cruelty as one could think human nature could scarce be guilty of and what the wildest savages in America would start and shudder to bear a part in'. In one view this was a world where barbarity lurked beneath the surface of civility which had been introduced and was preserved by the colonial elite. In the case of Killyleagh where the rebels had 'pursued their thirst for blood' now 'the scene is happily changed, the Protestant religion flourishes and the linen manufacture accompanies it'.[1] Other evidence confirms this insecurity which Harris and Smith captured. The pious Killyleagh Presbyterian merchant James Trail had in his library, listed in 1732, a copy of Sir John Temple's history of the

1641 rebellion which warned of the dangers of trusting the Catholic Irish.[2] Some tried to quantify this danger. In 1660 the poll money return had divided the population of the county into English and Scots on the one hand and Irish on the other, the latter comprising about 57 per cent of the total. Some landowners would go even further. Sir John Rawdon of Moira who held lands scattered throughout the county made his own private survey of his estates in 1716, the year following a Jacobite scare, to determine how many Catholics and Protestants lived on each townland on the estate.[3]

There is, however, another side to the work of Harris and Smith. The settlers are also depicted in a rather less traditional guise as well settled in the county and both proud of its history and curious about its topography, natural resources and antiquities. Improvements made by the new seventeenth-century arrivals are recorded as sitting beside antiquities of the past as part of a natural succession. At Seaford, the authors recorded not only the modern place-name but also the older Irish name, and noted that a mile away there was the house of Francis Annesley who had recently built 'a well laid out village' beside 'a Danish rath surrounded by a broad deep fosse, and ... on the top of it a plain strong castle of stone, the building of which is ascribed to the Danes'. It seems clear that the new innovations were being seen as part of the long history of Ireland rather than the introductions of a recently arrived elite. Again at Saintfield the recent improvements, including the introduction of the linen industry, were described alongside a disquisition on the meaning of the Irish name of the place, *Tullach na neve*.[4]

This identification by the seventeenth-century settlers with the history and place of county Down did not suddenly materialise with the writing of the first county history in the 1740s. There are unmistakeable signs that this process was well under way by the later part of the seventeenth century. Perhaps some of the clearest indications are to be found in the writing of family histories in the late seventeenth century by two of the most important families in the county, the earls of Mount Alexander and the viscounts Clandeboy, later earls of Clanbrassil. The texts, known respectively as the 'Montgomery manuscripts' and the 'Hamilton manuscripts' tell the story not of colonisation but of the founding of dynasties, which by the end of the seventeenth century were distinct from the families from which they had originated. Thus in writing the Montgomery manuscripts between 1697 and 1704, William Montgomery stressed that the motto of the family was the same as that of the earls of Eglinton in Scotland 'because our Montgomeries were from that family' yet the arms were different, for 'now Sir Hugh's posterity (and none else) may pretend to carry the arms and use the motto of the lords viscount of Ards', and the viscounts were described as 'chief of that nation or tribe in Ireland'.[5] A sense of separation from Scotland and pride in the history of the family in Ireland had developed yet in a curious way links were also retained. It was this sort of development which underpinned the growth from the end of the seventeenth century of that political movement termed 'colonial nationalism', which argued for much greater legislative freedom for Ireland. It is no surprise that the library of James Trail should have contained a copy of William Molyneux's *Case of Ireland...stated*, which became the manifesto of the movement.[6]

I

This brief excursus into the mental world of some of the county Down settlers at the end of the seventeenth century serves to demonstrate just how complex was their view of the world. It was a delicate balance of pride and insecurity constructed as a result of relationships both within their own social group and between themselves and their tenants, both settler and native. However it would be wrong to regard this simply as local paranoia, a result of the seventeenth-century colonisation process. A *modus vivendi* had been somewhat painfully established between native and newcomer in the early years of the seventeenth century, although the fragility of this meant that it broke down under economic, religious and political pressures as in the 1640s and again in the late 1680s. Such breakdowns can be seen as short-term crises, temporarily masking a more general accommodation. As the north Down settler landowner William Waring wrote to Friar Magennis, who protected Waring's property during the Jacobite disturbances of the late 1680s, 'have I been such a bad man among you these thirty years in Clanconnel that you will not allow me to be your neighbour nor to live in my native country'? After the Williamite war another Magennis wrote to Waring apologising for his lack of correspondence during the war 'though truly my wishes were never wanting to embrace any service that would tend to your good for the old kindnesses I have received at your hands'.[7]

Moreover it is difficult to see monolithic groups such as settler or native within the region. Even settler groups when placed under stress, as in the 1680s, would splinter into factions motivated by different interests. The County Down Association, formed in 1689 to protect Protestant interests in the county against Jacobite incursion, split almost as soon as it was formed over the actions of James Hamilton of Tollymore. Some alleged that 'he had been careless of what concerned the public yet he showed much prudence in the preservation of his private fortune'. Further allegations of dictatorial tendencies followed. It was claimed that Hamilton had been selective in those whom he had summoned to the initial meeting of the association, failing to summon those who 'would not readily resign a blind assent to his humour' and in the process created a military junto.[8]

Just as it is difficult to understand the evolution of social relations in county Down in terms of a neat division between two ethnic groups, it is equally impossible to understand the underlying structures of that society in terms of factors attributable to colonial county Down alone. The county was neither a coherent unit nor was it a neat, enclosed community. The county itself was formed only in 1570 as part of Sir Thomas Smith's scheme to settle the area and hence was an innovation in the social organisation of that region. The mental maps of those who lived in county Down were not confined to the county itself. These are easiest to trace through the experiences of the gentry community. Most of those who composed the second and subsequent generation landed community had wide experiences. The sons of the first earl of Clandeboy, for instance, were educated in Glasgow before being sent in 1633 with a tutor to explore continental Europe. They travelled through France and Italy.[9] Later in the century William Montgomery of the other prominent north Down family was educated in Leiden, while in 1687 Samuel Waring from Waringstown was sent to travel in Italy and Germany to complete his education. He committed his experiences to paper in the form of an account of his travels.[10] Such experiences provided different perspectives on the social world: taste and fashion in dress, literature, manners and architecture were certainly moulded by them. In more pressing ways too old problems were put in a new light. The Tridentine Catholicism of Europe which travellers experienced was clearly not that of the tenants of their estates, although it may have created a grudging admiration of some of the continentally-educated priests who served in the county.

Travel was not always so exotic. Members of the county Down gentry were both privy councillors and members of the Irish parliament, and this necessitated extended periods of residence in Dublin. A few, such as the Cromwells of Downpatrick were also members of the London parliament, while the younger son of one of the members of the Trevor family of south Down became speaker of the English House of Commons under James II. More localised were the contacts afforded by religion. The formation of the Synod of Ulster in 1690 provided opportunities for Presbyterian elders from the Presbytery of Down to meet others from throughout the province of Ulster. Thus while allegiance would have been to an individual congregation or Presbytery, that did not mark the boundary of their experience.

By the end of the seventeenth century it was possible to have a view of the world much wider than the limitations imposed by the county boundary without ever leaving home. The spread of the printed word as the book trade developed opened new horizons for many. On the death of Samuel Foley, bishop of Down and Connor, in 1695, he was found to have a library of 574 titles with imprints from such diverse places as Antwerp, Venice, Paris, Cologne and Rome as well as London and Dublin.[11] On a less exalted level the Killyleagh Presbyterian James Trail could muster 116 titles, mainly religious works, in 1732. Most of these seem to have originated in England or Ireland although among them were the recent philosophical works of John Locke and Francis Hutchison.[12] Among the gentry, books were often acquired by special order from Dublin as in 1676 when John Rawdon from Moira paid three shillings for a work entitled *Mensa mistica,* or by gift or inheritance as in 1735 when Trail acquired his brother in law's books.[13] However the task of obtaining books, and so widening the mental maps of the county's inhabitants, was not always that complex. The Dublin almanac maker and astrologer John Whalley had, by 1697, established an agent at Newry for his almanacs. These works ranged widely over European politics, presuming some knowledge of current affairs, and provided predictions for the coming year.[14] Moreover there were also locally published products. The establishment of a printer at Belfast in 1699 ensured that religious works, at least, were available for sale through chapmen in the county.[15]

II

To view the social world of county Down over the entire seventeenth century as only a society of colonists or as an undifferentiated or isolated unit, therefore, would be a mistake. Even among the landed gentry there were delicately balanced views of the world which they inhabited. There were also factional disputes among the gentry and the experiences they brought to bear on their world in an attempt to understand it were vastly wider than the limits of the county. To explore the way in which county Down society worked we need to think not of the county as some form of community but rather as a series of interconnected units, such a estates, groups of estates or wider cultural sub-regions, which fitted within each other in the manner of Chinese boxes.

At the most general level, these 'interconnected units' loosely cohered to form a single cultural region, marked off from surrounding districts by a series of frontiers. The southern boundary of the county, where it met the province of Leinster, for instance, was a well established cultural frontier by the seventeenth century and as late as Harris's time the town of Newry could still be referred to as a 'frontier town'.[16] The county's western boundary was until the seventeenth century mainly a topographical feature, comprising a lowland corridor from Lough Neagh to Newry, until the inclusion of county Armagh in the Ulster Plantation created a real social division. Thereafter to move from Armagh to Down was to move from a world where the seventeenth-century distribution of property, and hence wealth and influence, was controlled by government to another where private enterprise ruled. The terms of the Ulster Plantation scheme ensured that landowners in Armagh were constrained in the size of the estates which they could acquire and the terms on which they might lease land to their tenants, while in Down there were no such constraints. As a result in Armagh there emerged a social world in which no single landowner dominated, while in Down the acquisitions of property by private treaty from native Irishmen by James Hamilton and Hugh Montgomery ensured that they would dominate the county's social world into the eighteenth century. To the east lay the sea, which was itself an important frontier. The ease of communication by sea as opposed to land, ensured that many of the inhabitants of county Down looked north and south rather than west for their natural hinterland. That this was still so during the sixteenth century is clear from the number of families of Anglo-Norman origin living in the Lecale area who also held land in Meath. It was only slowly that communications with west Ulster developed, mainly as a result of the growth of the port of Newry and, in the early eighteenth century, the development of the Newry Navigation.[17]

The northern boundary of the 'cultural county' is rather harder to fix than the others. The northern limits of the Montgomery estate and the Lagan valley provide some guidance but there are other considerations also. The growth of Belfast, on the county Antrim side of the river Lagan, in the course of the seventeenth century had a significant effect on the economic and social life of county Down. By the later seventeenth century freemen of Belfast were drawn not only from within the city itself but also from Bangor, Newtownards and Comber. After the construction of the Long Bridge in 1682 Belfast became more accessible to those from county Down. The movement was not entirely from Down to Belfast for by 1679 Belfast merchants had established agents at Dromore and Hillsborough to buy butter.[18] In addition to the influence of the town of Belfast, the importance of Belfast Lough as a way of linking north Down and south Antrim must also be taken into consideration, especially since Bangor, on the southern shore, and Carrickfergus, on the northern shore, were linked by a ferry.[19] There are thus good reasons for extending the county's geographical boundary of the Lagan valley northwards, perhaps as far north as the boundary of the vast estate of the earl of Antrim which ran due west from Larne, in short reuniting the old lordship of Clandeboy which had been split by the county boundary in 1570.

Despite the fact that seventeenth-century Down can in some sense be seen as a 'particular place', it would be dangerous to assume that contemporaries saw it as some variant of the county communities which English historians have used as a way of understanding the local past. Two factors have been used to identify the presence of county communities in Early Modern England: administrative structures which created a sense of common county interest and the existence of a county society through local intermarriage.[20] Neither of these features seems to have been present in Down during the seventeenth century. Few of the county's great landed families intermarried with each other at the most important level of the eldest son, although intermarriage of the younger children did take place. The two main landed families in north Down, the Hamiltons and Montgomerys, showed no wish to deepen relations further than the 'love and kind deference now among us' which made them 'interwoven neighbours'.[21] The sons of the early Montgomery settlers married into prominent Scottish families. As Scottish lands were sold in the 1630s they saw more attraction in making contacts within Ireland, and the next generation chose wives from Cavan, Dublin, Enniskillen, Roscommon and Howth. The Hamiltons married into families from England, Wales and, more locally, from county Meath. In south Down the Trevor family, originally Welsh, continued the practice of marrying sons into families from Wales well into the seventeenth century but also made some advantageous matches into Pale families.[22]

If county Down families were not held together by marriage networks neither were they bonded by participation in a local government structure for the county. Most of those who settled in county Down in the early years of the seventeenth century came from fairly clearly defined social backgrounds. Their main aim in coming to Ireland was profit and an increase in their status. Some found their scope for advancement in Scotland or England confined by the stagnant land market there, while others saw in Down a way to reverse declining fortunes at home.[23] Their willingness to settle in the county was matched by royal encouragement to do so as part of a desire in London to encourage stability and settlement without incurring the sort of problems which the Plantation scheme in late sixteenth-century Munster had created. This combination of ambition and royal munificence gave rise to estates with considerable rights which most landlords wished to defend rather than pool as part of a local government structure. In 1612, for example, Sir Hugh Montgomery refused to accept a royal warrant for the arrest of a murderer who was one of his tenants, since he claimed the right to discipline these himself.[24] As royal government gradually encroached on these jurisdictions during the early seventeenth century, landlords became less and less happy about participating in a structure which they perceived could only undermine their authority.[25] What finally did this, however, was the war of the 1640s and the policies of the Cromwellian regime during the ensuing decade. The ten rentless years of the 1640s undermined landlord finances which were already perilous before the outbreak of the rebellion. The compounding fines for royalist activities levied in the 1650s brought many to the edge of bankruptcy. Lord Clandeboy, for example, was reported to be 'much straitened in his estate' and he 'had to contract great debts on his estate by which [the] family [was] brought down in style from his father's time'. Others experienced similar problems and much of the land sales which the Montgomery family contracted with the Colvilles in the later seventeenth century can be traced to their experience in the 1650s. Not all suffered severely. Families such as the Warings, Rawdons, Colvilles, Gills and Trevors played a complex political game which ensured their survival. In addition by purchasing debentures from discharged Cromwellian soldiers and buying land from older indebted settlers they built up handsome estates for themselves.[26] The result was that in the latter half of the seventeenth century there emerged a more diversified local society in which the dominance of the two north Down families weakened as some semblance of a 'county society' was created. Nevertheless by 1700 Down was still a long way short of the sort of social cohesion which an English county might display.

One indication of how the county Down gentry constructed their social world in the absence of a wider county model is provided by the late seventeenth-century family histories of the two most successful settler families, the Hamiltons and Montgomerys. While these texts are primarily concerned with their respective families there is also a subtext focused on the estate. Both histories are concerned with the founding of a dynasty but a dynasty whose position is underpinned by landownership, and much of the story is taken up with that subject. A considerable portion of the Hamilton manuscripts, for instance, is spent dealing with the problem of the feared breakup of the estate as a result of a claim to property by the dowager countess Clandeboy in the 1660s. In the case of the Montgomery manuscripts the longest part of the history is taken up not with recent events but with the story of the acquisition of the estate and with the life of Sir Hugh Montgomery, the first viscount Ards. This early world was portrayed in arcadian terms: women spun, men ploughed and each family had its own cabin complete with anachronistic potato patch. 'The golden peaceable age renewed' William Montgomery wrote, 'no strife, contention querulous lawyers...disturbing the tranquillity of those times; and the towns and temples were erected with other great works done'.[27] Clearly the estate and its image was an important element in the shaping of the priorities of those who lived in the county at the end of the seventeenth century.

III

Based on this insight, it is possible to understand the administrative entity that was county Down as being made up of three distinct worlds. First in the north of the county there was a world of large compact estates, dominating virtually all aspects of life. In the south and west of the county, however, the picture was different as the slow breakup of the Magennis lordship gave rise to fragmented estates, scattered among a number of holders. In the east there was yet a third pattern as absentee landowners and those with little influence struggled to maintain control of their properties.

The origin of most landed estates in seventeenth-century Down lay not with government sponsored land confiscation and plantation, but in the private deals struck between native Irish lords and the newcomers from Scotland or England. A generation later a second wave of estates was to be created as a result of sales by debt-ridden settlers to those with cash to spare. In north Down the first transfer of land from native to newcomer took the form of a tripartite agreement in 1605 between the local lord, Conn O'Neill, and two Scots, James Hamilton and Hugh Montgomery. What underlay this transaction was the perilous financial position of O'Neill, who had already been imprisoned in Carrickfergus castle for debt in 1598. Over the early years of the seventeenth century Conn's financial position failed to improve and he was finally forced to sell the third of the lands which he reserved in 1605 to Hamilton and Montgomery.[28] This process was important in that it created two very large consolidated estates in north Down which enabled the two landlords to exert considerable control over their property. There is little doubt that landlords created not only an economic structure on their lands but a social one also and they were clear about their role in that structure. Even the levelling force of a Presbyterian communion service in the 1620s could not persuade Sir James Hamilton to receive communion with his tenants.[29] The first stage in developing this sort of social and economic control over a region, and in making it economically viable, was to introduce settlers, since the population of Down in the late sixteenth century was very low.[30] Here the coastal position of the north Down estates was important since they were the first landing point for settlers from Scotland. By 1610 Sir James Hamilton reported that his coastal lands were much sought after and by 1630 the Hamilton estates could muster 928 settlers and those of Montgomery 1,012, or about two-thirds of the settlers who appeared for the county Down muster in that year.[31] After the early 1630s the flow of migrants was reduced although by 1659 the north Down region was still one of the most densely settled parts of the county, and by this stage much of the new settlement was taking place in the interior of the county.[32]

Landlord control in this world could be effectively exercised through the leasing policy which they chose to adopt on their lands. Variations in landlord strategies gave different social characteristics to each estate. On the Hamilton property, for instance, the first viscount Clandeboy showed a marked reluctance to promote the growth of a substantial tenantry. While he conceded that tenants should be 'men of good substance and means' they should not be allowed to become too powerful and troublesome. He observed 'I had rather let it [land] to such honest men of meaner ranks, who if they do not pay me their rent shall, whether they will or not, permit me to fetch away their distress', although in practice Sir James managed to acquire a number of troublesome tenants.[33] Indeed when it came to selecting agents to run the estate Hamilton preferred to use his brothers rather than employ a professional.[34] On the other hand, Sir Hugh Montgomery was prepared to recruit substantial individuals in Scotland, such as John Shaw of Greenock and William Edmonston from Stirling, to settle his estates.[35] Hamilton's strategy of actively managing his estate himself was reflected in the trouble he took to master the geography and resources of his estate by having it mapped by Thomas Raven in 1625.[36] Montgomery, meanwhile, preferred to parcel the estate into manageable units which could be leased to substantial tenants who were more likely to pay the rent. The document which regulated this relationship was the lease, and this acted as the main bond between landlords and tenant.[37] Each lease was a negotiated contract which laid out not only the obligation of the tenant to hold land for a period of time and to yield a rent to the landlord but also played a part in shaping the landscape to the landlord's specification. There were often conditions in leases requiring tenants to build or to plant. In towns such as Bangor on the Hamilton estate, the building lease was extensively used as part of the process of urban development.[38]

The relationship between landlord and tenant was not only controlled by the lease, itself a rather crude legal instrument. Landlords were dependent on tenants for their income and hence tenants had to be encouraged to develop their lands to ensure that their holdings would be sufficiently profitable to provide a surplus for the rent. In this process they were actively encouraged by the landlord who provided incentives for change in the form of rent-free periods or capital improvements. William Waring of Waringstown noted in 1674 that when he acquired new land 'I must lay out money...to help the tenants to drain, ditch and enclose where the land is capable of it and to help them to build houses'.[39] Moreover while the population of county Down grew rapidly in the early seventeenth century it was still low in relation to available resources. The demand by landlords was for good tenants rather than for land and hence good tenants had to be nurtured and encouraged. Thus rural society took on a rather paternalistic air. In 1618 Sir Hugh Montgomery was even prepared to incur royal displeasure than 'happily wrong such tenants as are come to inhabit with me as I have set rights unto'. When he died in 1636 the tenantry 'loudly lamented their loss of him...because he had been in general careful to protect them all (within his reach) from injuries'. In his 1659 will the second viscount Clandeboy echoed these sentiments, stipulating that his tenants 'be used with all favour that may be as the occasions of time will permit'.[40] Perhaps it is not surprising that at the outbreak of the 1641 rebellion in the county it was the landlords who rose to the occasion, levying their tenants into troops and paying for the newly raised forces themselves.

Moving from the landlord-dominated world of north Down into the south and west of the county, the structure of the social organisation changed. There were still a few large, compact, landed estates which operated in a similar fashion to those of Hamilton and Montgomery in north Down. Around Newry, for instance, the Bagenal family acquired a large and compact estate during the sixteenth century which they developed by introducing settlers from north Wales and building the town of Newry as an estate centre.[41] The vast bulk of mid-Down, however, was not held by settler landlords at the beginning of the seventeenth century but lay under the control of the Magennis family. During the late sixteenth century the Magennises had been singularly successful in persuading both the Dublin government and the earl of Tyrone of their loyalty, so that at the end of the Nine Years War they seemed well placed to survive in the emerging new order. However, to underpin their new-found position they were required to clarify their land titles by seeking royal patents for their lands under the 1606 commission for defective titles. As part of this process the Magennis lordship was broken into a series of freeholds whereby the lord's former followers were granted lands in their own right. Between

December 1610 and February 1611 grants were issued to the new freeholders.[42]

The result of this process was that 85 per cent of the old Magennis lordship was granted to their former native holders, the remainder being church land or land which had previously been alienated. The settlement was to prove a precarious one. By 1641 only 48 per cent of the previous Magennis land still remained in their hands. Unlike the situation in north Down the alienation proceeded piecemeal. There were various groups who were well placed to take advantage of this situation. Soldiers with army pensions, and lawyers, clergy and merchants who often had large cash balances on hand sought investment opportunities in land. A number of new settlers had acquired small fragmented estates scattered over the old lordship. The most important of these purchasers was a former Elizabethan soldier, Sir John Trevor, whose family later intermarried with another beneficiary of the breakup of the lordship, Marmaduke Whitchurch of Loughbrickland.[43] The second major beneficiary of this fracturing of the Magennis lands was a Dublin lawyer, Arthur Hill, who was the second son of the Devon settler, Moses Hill.[44]

The reasons for the breakup of the lordship are complex but the immediate cause was the build-up of debts which the various branches of the Magennis family experienced in the early seventeenth century. They chose to relieve this situation not with one large alienation, as did Con O'Neill in north Down, but by a series of small mortgages and sales, and these helped shape the subsequent character of landed society in south Down. It was difficult to exercise control over this sort of estate in the way Hamilton and Montgomery did over theirs. Leases, including those with improving clauses, might be made but it was not always easy to enforce their terms. In 1615, for instance, the lord deputy, Sir Arthur Chichester, warned both these landlords of the penalties they faced by continuing to allow the native Irish custom of ploughing by tail to be used on their lands.[45] Some evidence of this lack of control can be seen in the way in which the legal processes worked at local level. In north Down the normal way of dealing with problems involving tenants was in the local manorial courts operated by the local landlords under the terms of their royal patent. Indeed, Sir James Hamilton normally included in his leases a clause forbidding tenants from taking their disputes to the royal courts before they had been dealt with at local level. As a result no disputes from north Down appear among the pleadings which survive from the Court of Chancery in Dublin. Most of the disputes coming to chancery originated in the fragmented estates of mid-Down and Lecale where landlord control was weak.[46] It was also there that partible inheritance was allowed, although this was rare in the rest of east Ulster as it was controlled by the supervision of the manor court. Perhaps the best touchstone of the priorities of the Trevors was provided during the crisis of the 1640s. While most of the north Down families chose the Irish theatre of the war of the three kingdoms for their activities, reflecting their concern for their county Down property, the Trevors chose Wales, suggesting that they may have seen their long term future in that country.[47] It was not that the Trevors felt their Irish interest to be unimportant but rather that it was intractable, scattered as it was through south and west Down.

The world of east Down provides an example of yet another type of gentry world. Like north Down this was also a landscape of compact estates. Around Downpatrick Sir Edward Cromwell, a former army officer, purchased an estate from Patrick McCartan which was subsequently confirmed by royal grant in 1605.[48] From the other side of the ethnic divide there was the Anglo-Irish Savage estate in the barony of Upper Ards at the southern end of the Ards peninsula, which was typical of many of the Anglo-Irish who had held land in the Lecale area from the medieval settlement. Both of these estates were characterised by limited landlord intervention even though this was more practical here than on the scattered estates of south and west Down. Thus in the early seventeenth century when the urban world of north Down was rapidly expanding, Portaferry (on the Savage estate) remained 'some fishermen's cabins and an old Irish castle'.[49] In the case of the Savages the cause of the landlord paralysis was twofold. Like many native Irish lords the Savages were heavily encumbered by debt. The will of Patrick Savage, proved in 1643, shows that his debts amounted to £2,077 13s. 0d. or about thirteen times his annual rental income. Part of this situation had arisen from the second factor which limited Savage's room for manoeuvre. The links between these Anglo-Irish lords and the occupiers of land were not those conditioned by commercial considerations and dictated by leases, but were determined rather by bonds of duty. As one deed expressed it, land was held 'by the services due and of right accustomed'. Thus custom severely limited the possibility for improvement.[50] The Savages were saved from the bankruptcy which befell many of the older landholders in county Down by a marriage with one of the daughters of the Montgomery family. The latter not only provided loans to shore up the Savages' estate, but also provided the economic and managerial expertise necessary to transform it into a more commercial undertaking.

The other significant landed family in this part of east Down was the settler family of Cromwell. Here enthusiasm for improvement was also conspicuously lacking, although they did attempt to make some improvements on their lands. By 1630 they had begun to develop the natural resources of their estates by introducing iron works and importing specialists to work them. In 1640 they built a bridge over the River Quoile and carried out limited drainage of bogs.[51] However. neither Sir Edward Cromwell nor his son, Thomas, had much enthusiasm for the life of an improving landlord. Sir Edward had been forced into Ireland, hoping thereby to solve his English debts. In this he failed, since the opportunities of fast gain, short of an outright sale, in the Down settlement were slight. By 1642 his debts stood at £3,550 despite a mortgage of £1,000 raised ten years earlier.[52] Unlike most of the other landed families in the county, the Cromwells came from an already well-established English gentry family. They held an English title which allowed them to attend the London parliament, and they exercised this right. They had little interest in provincial society apart from the profits their lands might offer, and an absence from Dublin or London usually gave rise to the complaint that they were 'far from my lord deputy and all civil administration'. By 1677 Thomas Cromwell, then permanently resident in England, attempted to dispose of the reversion of the estate.[53] In the normal run of affairs this might not have mattered a great deal if the family had employed a satisfactory agent to manage the estate during their long absences. However they were singularly unfortunate in their choice of agents and at least one had to be dismissed in the 1630s for his inefficiency.[54] Thus for a variety of reasons the landlord world of east Down was rather different from that to the south and west, and both differed radically from the large and powerful landed gentry of the northern part of the county. The aspirations of the Savages and Cromwells were constrained by custom on the one hand and lack of commitment on the other.

IV

Describing the social world of county Down in the seventeenth century is not a simple task. It is not merely the story of colonisation which created a provincial gentry whose horizons were bounded by the county boundary. Rather it is a complex process of adoption and adaptation, a shaping of the world to meet the changing needs of a wide range of gentry aspirations and needs. Ideas from a wide variety of sources, available through personal experience or books, were taken and applied to the local situation. Influences from Europe, Britain and Ireland were all at work in shaping the development of local estates which were the main focus of the lives of the landlords. When the county Down gentry wished to construct houses, for example, they relied not only on local tradition but on the latest architectural fashion, demonstrating not only their concern for their estates through the scale of the building, but also their contact with a wider world of culture. Thus when Sir Hugh Montgomery moved into the old Dominican priory at Newtownards he embellished it with a tower in the latest fashion. The Warings of Waringstown continually remodelled their house according to the changing architectural fashions of a wider world.[55] In the seventeenth century, the county Down gentry lived in a series of 'interlocking communities'. The primary focus, the estate, formed part of another world comprised of similar types of estates which, in turn, belonged to a wider cultural unit which very crudely corresponded with the county. However this was in no sense an isolated unit, for the standards of gentry display and behaviour were drawn from Irish, British and even European contexts. The county Down world which we have lost was indeed a complicated one.

References

1. *Down*, pp 76, 81, 106.
2. 'A catalogue of my books taken February 1731', P. R. O. N. I., D.1460/1.
3. Henry E. Huntingdon Library, San Marino, California, Hastings Ms, Box 75.
4. *Down*, pp 71, 78.
5. For a detailed examination of this theme see Raymond Gillespie, 'The making of the Montgomery manuscripts' in *Familia*, ii no. 2 (1986), pp 23-9.
6. 'A catalogue of my books', P. R. O. N. I., D.1460/1; for this being distributed in the county see J. R. R. Adams, *The printed word and the common man* (Belfast, 1987), pp 85-6.
7. P. R. O. N. I., D.695/136, 157.
8. *A faithful history of the north of Ireland from the late King James' accession to the crown to the siege of Londonderry* (London, 1690); *Some reflections on a pamphlet entitled a faithful history of the northern affairs of Ireland* (Dublin, 1691), pp 13, 38.
9. P. R. O. N. I., D.1071B/B/1, pp 33-6.
10. George Hill (ed.), *The Montgomery manuscripts* (Belfast, 1869), pp 397-9; P. R. O. N. I., D.697/225-6.
11. Cambridge University Library, Munby, C3.
12. 'A catalogue of my books', P. R. O. N. I., D.1460/1.
13. 10 Feb. 1676, P. R. O. N. I., T.3765/L/2/11/1; 'List of Capt. Read's books', P. R. O. N. I., D.1460/1.
14. John Whalley, *Advice from the stars or an almanac for the year of Christ 1697* (Dublin,[1697]), sig. A4v.
15. Wesley McCann, 'Patrick Neill and the origins of Belfast printing' in Peter Isaac (ed.), *Six centuries of the provincial book trade in Britain* (Winchester, 1990), pp 125-38; for the output, see Adams, *The printed word*, p. 175.
16. For the detail of this, see Raymond Gillespie and Harold O'Sullivan (ed.), *The borderlands: essays on the history of the Ulster-Leinster border* (Belfast, 1989), esp. pp 75-92.
17. For this point see Raymond Gillespie, *Colonial Ulster: the settlement of east Ulster, 1600-41* (Cork, 1985), pp 21-5.

18. R. M. Young (ed.), *The town book of the corporation of Belfast* (Belfast, 1892), pp 259-80; *Calendar of state papers, domestic 1679-80*, pp 282-3.

19. Gillespie, *Colonial Ulster*, p. 23.

20. The classic formulation of this position is to be found in Alan Everitt, *The community of Kent and the great rebellion, 1640-60* (Leicester, 1966); and *idem, Change in the provinces: the seventeenth century* (Leicester, 1969). The view has not gone unchallenged, see Clive Holmes, 'The county "community" in Stuart historiography' in *Journal of British Studies*, xix (1980), pp 54-73; and *idem, Seventeenth century Lincolnshire* (Lincoln, 1980).

21. Hill (ed.), *Montgomery manuscripts*, pp 81, 183.

22. For Montgomery, see John Lodge, *The peerage of Ireland* (4 vols., Dublin, 1754), i, pp 353-76; for Hamilton, see T. K. Lowry (ed.), *The Hamilton manuscripts* (Belfast, 1867), *passim*; for Trevor, see Harold O'Sullivan, 'The Trevors of Rosetrevor: a British colonial family in seventeenth century Ireland', unpublished M.Litt. thesis, T.C.D., 1985, pp 21-3.

23. The background of the settlers is discussed in Gillespie, *Colonial Ulster*, pp 29-43.

24. *Cal. S. P. Ire., 1611-14*, pp 234, 241.

25. Gillespie, *Colonial Ulster*, pp 84-108.

26. Raymond Gillespie, 'Landed society and the interregnum in Ireland and Scotland' in Rosalind Mitchison and Peter Roebuck (ed.), *Economy and society in Scotland and Ireland, 1500-1939* (Edinburgh, 1988), pp 38-47; P. R. O. N. I., D.695/112-127, 141-2.

27. Hill (ed.), *Montgomery manuscripts*, pp 64-5, 66.

28. The process is traced in D. A. Chart, 'The breakup of the estate of Conn O'Neill' in *R.I.A. Proc.*, xlviii, c (1942-3), pp 119-51; Gillespie, *Colonial Ulster*, p. 142.

29. Thomas McCrie (ed.), *The life of Mr. Robert Blair* (Edinburgh, 1848), p. 61; Raymond Gillespie, 'Funerals and society in early seventeenth century Ireland' in *R.S.A.I. Jn.*, cxv (1985), pp 88-9. Many of the general issues here are dealt with in W. H. Crawford, 'The significance of landed estates in Ulster, 1660-1820' in *Irish Economic and Social History*, xvii (1990), pp 44-57.

30. The early demography of the settlement is considered in Gillespie, *Colonial Ulster*, pp 47-63.

31. T.C.D., Mun/P/24/4; British Library, Additional Ms 4770.

32. Seamus Pender (ed.), *A census of Ireland, c. 1659* (Dublin, 1939).

33. T.C.D., Mun/P/24/4-5; Gillespie, *Colonial Ulster*, pp 135-6.

34. Lowry, *Hamilton manuscripts*, p. 12.

35. Gillespie, *Colonial Ulster*, pp 30, 118.

36. Raymond Gillespie, 'Thomas Raven and the mapping of the Clandeboye estate, c. 1625' in *Bangor Historical Society Journal*, i (1981).

37. M. K. Garner, 'North Down as displayed in the Clanbrassil leasebook' in *Proceedings of the Belfast Natural History and Philosophical Society*, viii (1970); more generally, see Raymond Gillespie, *Settlement and survival on an Ulster estate: the Brownlow leasebook, 1667-1711* (Belfast, 1988).

38. Gillespie, *Colonial Ulster*, p. 172.

39. P. R. O. N. I., D.695/9.

40. P. R. O. SP.63/256/96; Hill (ed.), *Montgomery manuscripts*, p. 144; Scottish Record Office, Edinburgh, GD. 109/2682.

41. For the Bagenal background, P. H. Bagenal, *Vicissitudes of an Anglo-Irish family* (London, 1925); for an unusually clear view of an estate, see Harold O'Sullivan, 'A 1575 rent roll with contemporaneous maps of the Bagenal estates in the

Carlingford district' in *Journal of the Louth Archaeological and Historical Society*, xxi (1984-8), pp 45-50.

42. The result of the freeholding was not enrolled in Chancery until 1617, *Calendar of patent rolls, James I*, pp 394-6.

43. For the detail of the freeholding and the geography of the Trevor lands, see O'Sullivan, 'The Trevors of Rosetrevor', pp 25-59 (esp. map on p. 59).

44. On the death of Arthur's brother, Peter, he acquired the county Antrim lands also, see W. A. Maguire, *The Downshire estates in Ireland* (Oxford, 1972), pp 3-4. The geography of Arthur's holdings may be seen from the map on p. 273.

45. Bodleian Library, Oxford, Clarendon MS ii, no. 106.

46. Gillespie, *Colonial Ulster*, pp 157, 162.

47. O'Sullivan, 'The Trevors of Rosetrevor', pp 92-118.

48. *Cal. patent rolls, James I*, p. 74.

49. Hill (ed.), *Montgomery manuscripts*, p. 304.

50. Gillespie, *Colonial Ulster*, p. 141.

51. British Library, Additional Ms 4770; Gillespie, *Colonial Ulster*, p. 24.

52. Lawrence Stone, *The crisis of the aristocracy* (Oxford, 1965), p. 779; for the family, see R. E. Parkinson, *The city of Downe* (Belfast, 1927), pp 33-41.

53. Historical Manuscripts Commission, *Report on the Salisbury manuscripts*, xviii, pp 97, 155.

54. Strafford Letter Books, 14, no. 251, Sheffield City Library, Wentworth-Wodehouse Ms.

55. *A.S.C.D.*, pp 286, 437-8.

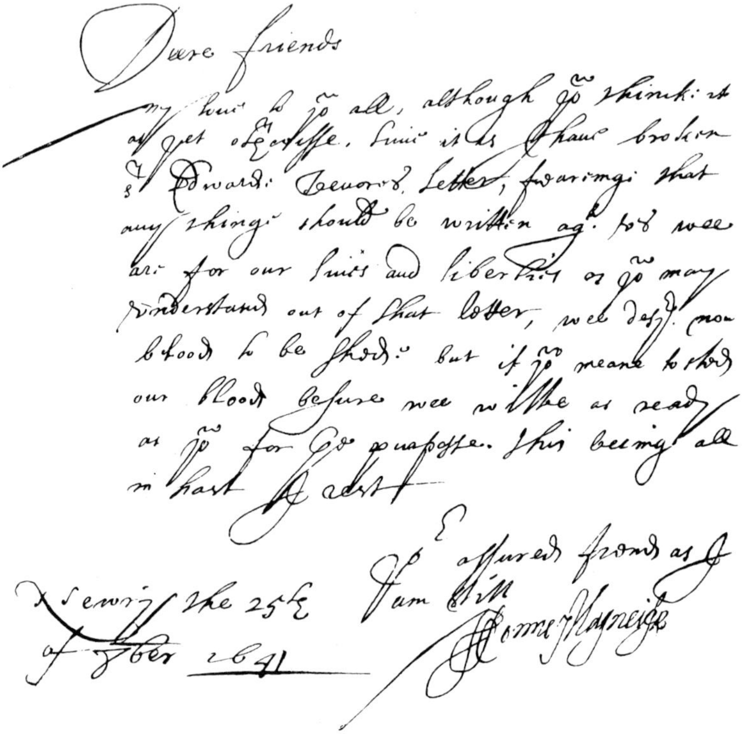

XXVI. CON. MAGENNIS TO COMMANDERS IN COUNTY OF DOWN.

1641.
Oct. 25.
Magennis to Commanders in Down.

Deere friends,

My loue to you all, although you thincke it as yet otherwise, truie it is I haue broken Sir Edwarde Treuores letter, feareinge that any thinge should be written against us, wee are for our liues and liberties as you may understand out of that letter, wee desy[re] noe blood to be shede, but if you meane to shed our blood be sure wee wilbe as ready as you for the purposse. This being all in hast, I rest

Your assured frend as I am still

Newry, the 25th of October, 1641. Conne Magneise.

Endorsed : For my loueinge and worthy friends Captain Veaughan, Marcus Treuor, and all other Comanders of Downe, these be [delivered].

Fig. 7.1   Con Magenis to commanders in county of Down (from Gilbert, *Contemp. his.*, i, illustration iv and p. 364).

Chapter 8

THE MAGENNIS LORDSHIP OF IVEAGH IN THE EARLY MODERN PERIOD, 1534 TO 1691

HAROLD O'SULLIVAN

From Irish lord to loyal vassal

Shortly after his appointment to the lord deputyship of Ireland in February 1605, Sir Arthur Chichester introduced a policy for the division of the old Irish lordships into freeholds to be held by English tenure and usually by knights service This was to be effected by means of a commission appointed in 1606 for the 'division and bounding of the lords' and gentlemens' livings'.[1] While the establishment of such a commission was entirely consistent with the programme introduced at the beginning of his deputyship, that all the Irish were to be regarded as 'free natural and immediate subjects of the king,' no longer owing homage or dependency to their former Irish lords, it was also presented as a means for the lords themselves to secure protection against the activities of crown escheators finding defects in their land titles either on grounds of 'concealment' or 'forfeitures of rebellion'.[2] The English common law regarding land tenure had never been effectively applied in Ulster, but after O'Neill's surrender at Mellifont in 1601 it was inevitable that the crown authorities would take steps to replace the Irish customary law which had heretofore prevailed. In order to effect a smooth transition, a commission of defective titles was established by the king to deal with the troubles 'caused to his subjects on strict points of law' by escheator inquiries into their estates. The new arrangements enabled a landowner to compound for the replacement of a defective or uncertain title by means of a new patent. These policies may be regarded as marking the commencement of a new order in Ireland but essentially they marked the conclusion of a much earlier policy, introduced at the very beginning of the kingdom of Ireland in 1541 when the then lord deputy, St Leger, introduced the policy of surrender and re-grant as a means for regularising land titles in areas outside the scope of the former Irish lordship.[3] Two distinct systems of land tenure had existed in Ireland since the Anglo-Norman settlement of the twelfth century, that under the English common law, which prevailed in the areas under the jurisdiction of the crown lordship, where lands were held in feudal tenure from the king providing for inheritance by primogeniture; and in the areas outside this jurisdiction by customary Irish law, where the lands were held corporately by the kin group or sept, the individual holding only a life interest which upon his death reverted to the sept. The procedure of surrender and regrant which was introduced in 1541 was intended to enable an Irish lord to surrender his lands to the crown and in return to accept a regrant of them by letters patent under English common law. An important feature of the change was the introduction of the principle of primogeniture, that is inheritance by direct descent through seniority of the male line. Such a procedure, however, did not resolve the problems created by the customary law of tanistry, which provided for the succession of a lordship to pass to an heir apparent selected by the sept, nor did it facilitate the sub-infeudation of the lordship to provide adequate land titles for the subordinate families within the sept.[4]

The lordship of the Uí Eachach Cobha (anglicised Iveagh) of the pre-Norman kingdom of the Uladh, passed to the Magennises of the Clann Aodh following the establishment of the earldom of Ulster in the twelfth century.[5] From that time onwards the Magennises became the leading Irish family in the southern part of the earldom and were of sufficient importance to be summoned by Henry III to join with him in 1244 in his planned invasion of Scotland. Again in 1314, Edward II summoned Admilis alias Eachmilidh Magennis as 'chief of the Irish of Iveagh' to participate with him in a similar adventure.[6] The subsequent decline of the earldom had its corollary in the growing strength of the Magennis lordship, whose expansion eastwards to the coast was marked by their capture of De Courcy's stone castle at Dundrum.[7] By the beginning of the Tudor era the Magennises had become one of the most important of the marcher lordships of east Ulster but were divided into several distinct families each striving for the overlordship of the sept. Among the most significant of these were the Rathfriland, Corgary, Kilwarlin and Castlewellan Magennises, the latter holding sway in the eastern parts of the lordship including the area around Dundrum taken in from Lecale.[8] A succession dispute arose in 1539 following the death of Murtagh Magennis of Corgary and lord of Iveagh. He had been captured by the Louthmen at the battle of Bellahoe that year and was 'treacherously' slain 'at the instance of a party of his own tribe who bribed them to put him to death'.[9] The disputants for the succession were Donal Og of Rathfriland and Art McPhelim of Castlewellan. Following a meeting at Maynooth late in

1540 between these and other Ulster lords with the new lord deputy, St Leger, it was agreed that the dispute be submitted to arbitration by Arthur McGlassney Magennis, holder of the bishop's mensal of Kilbroney and son of the celebrated Glassney Magennis, prior of Downpatrick, and Patrick Gernon of Killencoole, county Louth, a lawyer and Geraldine supporter who had fled the Pale and taken refuge with Conn Bacach O'Neill but was subsequently pardoned by St Leger.[10]

Following his defeat at Bellahoe by the county Louthmen under Lord Deputy Grey, O'Neill signed articles of surrender at Dundalk on 28 December 1541 providing for the renunciation of his obedience to the pope and his acceptance of the king as supreme head of the Church. He also gave pledges to live under the laws of 'his most serene lord' and to pay him an annual rent for his lands. These were the preliminary steps in a surrender and regrant process which had progressed sufficiently by September 1542 for O'Neill to travel to London to receive his patent and the title of earl of Tyrone from the king. His companions included Donal Og of Rathfriland and Art McPhelim of Castlewellan both of whom received knighthoods.[11] In their case the outcome of the arbitration, which was concluded in May 1541, provided that while Donal Og should succeed to the lordship, Art McPhelim was to be excluded from his jurisdiction, suggesting that the latter was to receive separate letters patent in respect of his lands at Castlewellan. Sir Donal cemented his good relations with the crown administration by agreeing to cut the 'great pass' called 'Ballogh Enary' or Henry's Pass through the southern slopes of the Mournes north of Kilkeel, thereby facilitating coastal access northwards to Newcastle and Dundrum.[12] In 1553 he engaged in a further process of surrender and regrant and was appointed governor of Iveagh, being described as 'a civil gentleman and useth as good order in his house as any man of his vocation in Ireland'. The anglicisation process begun in 1540 was further advanced by evidence of the sub-infeudation of subordinate Magennises whose names are mentioned in lists of pardons granted in the years between 1552 and 1559:

> 1552 Brian McShane Magennis of Islandmoyle; 1553 Edmond Magennis; 1553 Glassney McArt McPhelim; Magennis of Inch in Lecale; 1554 Hugh McArt Corrocks? Edmond McArt; 1555 Rory Magennis, Kilwarlin? 1556 Donal Magennis, Newry; 1556 Edmond Magennis, Lecale; 1558 Phelim Magennis; 1559 Phelim McShane Magennis.[13]

Sir Donal's claim to the lordship of Iveagh was again challenged by

Sir Art McPhelim Magennis in 1559, when the lord deputy pronounced that as Sir Donal had been elected by the country he should be admitted as the Magennis. In the following year Sir Donal agreed to make contributions to the state for the maintenance of eighty gallowglasses, an undertaking he repeated in 1562 during the period of the Shane O'Neill rebellion.[14]

Following the death of Shane O'Neill in 1567 a policy of plantation was put in place in Ulster using as pretext the Act of Attainder of O'Neill and the claim by the crown to the earldom of Ulster. While the plantation policy had particular reference to the McMahons, the O'Hanlons of Orier and the McCartans of Kinnelarty, one Magennis family was also implicated; a Captain John Sankeye received a demise for twenty-one years in the 'barony of the Legan in the Magennis country' of 'the new castle and cottages at Aghekorke and lands in Aghewynmulragh, Dromore, Little Kerrocks, Great Kerrocks, Ballenemoney, Dromrey and Dromseske', evidently the lands of the Magennises of Corrocks and Aghenemulragh.[15] Following the return of Sydney as deputy in 1575 the plantations in Orier, Kinnelarty and the Magennis country were cancelled and the lands in question returned to the native Irish. In that year also, Hugh Magennis of Rathfriland, successor to his father, Sir Donal, petitioned Sydney to have his estates formally granted to him by the queen, pointing out that 'ever since his revolt from Shane O'Neill' he had shown 'fidelity to her majesty'. The petition was granted and in the following year he was recognised by the crown 'as chief of his nation' and made 'captain of the whole country of Iveagh'.[16] About this time also he received a knighthood. While the objective of Sir Hugh's petition was evidently to remove him from any obligation or liability to the O'Neills, who persisted in claiming the overlordhip of the Magennises, it was not however to be that simple, as the crown was not always in a position to protect a loyal vassal in the turmoils which beset Ulster in the last quarter of the sixteenth century. In August 1580, Tirlogh Luineach, who succeeded Shane as the O'Neill, accused Sir Hugh of being 'half English', and raiding into the Magennis country took a prey of 400 cattle, 60 mares, 200 swine, 300 sheep, killing sixteen of Sir Hugh's men. In response the latter sought and obtained a 'licence of revenge' from the lord deputy.[17]

In March 1584, Sir Hugh Magennis further secured his position by obtaining a grant 'in capite' from the crown of 'the entire country or territory of Iveagh', to be held by him and his heirs for the service of one knight's fee and a rent of 120 fat cows, and for every townland beyond twenty one, a fat cow or thirteen shillings and four pence sterling.[18] Provision was made for the succession to pass to his eldest son, Arthur Roe, and thence to Phelim and Hugh. He agreed to attend hostings, to provide twelve horsemen and twenty-four footmen, supply one labourer one day in each year and provide such beeves as the army might require for one night at twelve shillings each. Furthermore, he was to aid the sheriff in the execution of legal processes. The territories mentioned in the grant were the island of Corgirry (Corgary), Derryloghan (in the civil parish of Annaclone), Clare (in Clanconnell, civil parish of Tullylish), Ballelagh (in the civil parish of Seapatrick), Dirrylowghaghry, Begnive, Dicovead, Ballironey (a district in the civil parish of Drumballyroney), Clanbarde (probably the division of Ballyward in the civil parish of Drumgooland), Insulamreaghe, Castlewellan and Balliwolinge; as well all manors, castles and lands in the said country and islands as in the towns of Rathphrillan (Rathfriland), Narrowwater (Clonallan), Lugbreghen (Loughbrickland, civil parish of Aghaderg) and Ballaghbegalle called Shyleike in the said country. This grant did not however include the territories of Kilwarlin in the north of the lordship which was at this time held by Ever McRory Magennis. In May 1585 the latter was described as 'captain and chief of his name' in a grant of 'the lordship and manor of Kilwarlin and all its rights', which he had previously surrendered to the crown.[19] Kilwarlin consisted of fifty-four townlands in what is now the barony of Lower Iveagh. He too was to hold his estates by the service of a knight's fee and a rent of fifteen shillings sterling; as well as providing footmen for each rising out he was also to maintain in good order and at least forty feet in breadth the way or pass of Kilwarlin. Since these grants would have encroached upon other Magennis interests, it is not surprising that Sir Hugh Magennis 'and others' were in Dublin in 1588 'to end some brawls and to take leave of Perrott', the departing lord deputy. That some agreements were made is suggested by the following pardons issued in respect of the Magennises in 1590:

> Ivor Magennis [Kilwarlin], Brian Og Magennis [Kilwarlin], Mortogh Magennis [Corgary], John Magennis [Corrocks], Brian McDonal McBrian Magennis [Greenan or Clanconnell], Edmond McDonal McBrian Magennis [Clanconnell], Rory McCon Magennis, Murtogh McEdmond Og Magennis, Art McRoss Magennis [Loughbrickland], Hugh McRoss Magennis [Loughbrickland], Glassney Magennis [Clanconnell], Edmond Og McArt Og Magennis.[20]

As the issue of these pardons may have been a prelude to land grants the agreements may have been reached on the basis of fee farm grants, reserving a rent or chiefry to either Sir Hugh Magennis of Rathfriland or Ever McRory Magennis of Kilwarlin, who held them in freehold under the crown.

Sir Hugh attended Perrott's parliament in Dublin in 1586 as one of the knights of the shire for county Down. He was one of the 'disturbers', led by some of the Old English gentry of the Pale, who effectively blocked a number of bills which Perrott had endeavoured to have passed, including one extending English laws against 'Popish recusancy to Ireland'.[21] Nonetheless, he was appointed jointly with the sheriff in 1587 to a commission to execute martial law in county Down and was described by Sir Henry Bagenal, as 'the civilist of all the Irishry' who lived 'very civilly and English-like in his house and every festival day weareth English garments amongst his followers'. Bagenal also claimed that Sir Hugh had been brought by his father Sir Nicholas from the 'bonaght of the O'Neills', and instead was paying an annual rent for his lands which he had taken 'by letters patent to hold after the English manner, to him and his heirs'.[22]

The drift by Hugh O'Neill, earl of Tyrone, into insurrection was sparked off as much by his vendetta with Sir Henry Bagenal, the crown commissioner for Ulster, as by the progressive intrusion by the crown administration into Ulster affairs, a province which had been for centuries an area of special influence for the O'Neills.[23] Yet the immediate cause of the conflict related more to the personal enmity between O'Neill and Bagenal than from any conscious decision by O'Neill to challenge English authority in Ireland. Shortly after the battle of the Erne Fords, Bagenal charged O'Neill with treason and O'Neill countered by alleging that Bagenal had belittled his efforts in the battle and offered to stand trial in Ireland or in England. The trial took place in Dundalk in 1594 where O'Neill was cleared of the charges but cautioned 'not to meddle with compounding controversies in Ulster'. In a balancing act the court warned Fitzwilliam and Bagenal that 'they had used the earl against law and equity' and that the former had not behaved 'indifferent [impartially] to the earl'. Later that year Fitzwilliam was replaced by Sir William Russell who was instructed to inform O'Neill that Bagenal had been forbidden to act against him. This act of mediation was not successful. In May 1595, O'Neill intercepted Bagenal in Monaghan where he defeated him in a battle at Clontibret. The lord deputy with 3,000 men set out for the borders in June and, at the Market Cross of Dundalk, O'Neill was proclaimed traitor. Inevitably the Magennises, however reluctant, were drawn into the approaching conflict. By March 1594 it was reported that Magennis and O'Hanlon had capitulated to O'Neill, 'but not from any love they bear him', while Ever McRory Magennis of Kilwarlin was expelled from his lands, an event in which Sir Hugh's son Art Roe was implicated, having married O'Neill's daughter, Sarah. On the eve of his proclamation at Dundalk, O'Neill took a prey of 1,500 cattle from Sir Hugh Magennis and his neighbour Sir Henry Bagenal, whose mills at Newry he destroyed.[24]

Sir Hugh Magennis' death in January 1596 sparked off the inevitable succession dispute. While Art Roe's right to succeed was clearly recognised in the English patent granted to his father in 1584, his claim was rejected by his cousin Glassney MacAholly [Eachmilidh] Magennis, the head of the Clanconnell branch, whose territories lay between the Bann and Lagan rivers in the parishes of Donacloney and Tullylish. The latter claimed the succession by virtue of his office of tanaiste and on the 16 January 1596 it was reported that he had come to the 'stone whereon the Magennises were wont to receive their ceremony and hath called himself [the] Magennis'.[25] Notwithstanding O'Neill's family relationship with Art Roe, Glassney's actions had his approbation, a stand taken by O'Neill more from his claim to ascendancy in Ulster than from any animus towards his son-in-law. O'Neill's message was clear, only Irish law would prevail in Ulster especially in a lordship over which he claimed suzerainty. Art Roe appealed to Dublin where the lord chancellor set up a commission to examine the matter.[26] In the meantime Art Roe joined in support of O'Neill, who married Art's sister Catherine in August 1597, thus making Art his brother-in-law as well as his son-in-law.[27] In July 1597, Art was in action with O'Neill against the lord deputy, Burgh, when the latter captured Armagh. While his position with O'Neill had been strengthened, the succession dispute had not been resolved by May 1598, when 'great discontent' was reported between himself and Glassney MacAholly as well as with his uncle Edmond. Following Burgh's death in October 1597 he was succeeded as lord lieutenant by Thomas Butler, earl of Ormond, who immediately opened negotiations with O'Neill at Dundalk. Amongst the matters discussed was a request by O'Neill that Art Roe's claim to the succession be settled. In March 1598, Art Roe together with other marcher lords came to Dundalk where they made their submission to Ormond. In the following month articles were concluded with O'Neill on the basis of which he was granted a pardon under the great seal.[28]

As before the peace was only short-lived, broken again by O'Neills' vendetta with Bagenal. In August 1598, the latter set out from Dundalk with a force of 4,000 foot, 320 horse and four artillery pieces to relieve the Blackwater fort north of Armagh city, deep in O'Neill's country. O'Neill deemed the force hostile and attacked it, the outcome of which was the great battle of the Yellow Ford where Bagenal was defeated with upwards of 2,000 of his troops killed or injured. Bagenal himself was killed by a shot in the brain. For the next few years Art Roe was on active service with O'Neill and was important enough to be one of the six witnesses selected by the latter in the fruitless conferences held by him with the Lord Lieutenant Essex in August 1599.[29] With the replacement of Essex by Lord Deputy Mountjoy in January 1600, the desultory campaigns of the past, punctuated by truces, were replaced by a period of total war during which devastation was visited on many parts of Ulster including the Magennis lordship of Iveagh.

Mountjoy, in the first year of his lord deputyship, pursued a policy of containment in Ulster stationing large garrisons in such places as Dundalk, Ardee, Kells, Carlingford and Newry, where a force of 1,000 troops was placed. In May he advanced into the Moiry Pass in south Armagh and after a sharp encounter with O'Neill broke through to Newry. This was a diversionary manoeuvre intended to draw O'Neill into south-east Ulster while a force under Sir Henry Docwra landed in Lough Foyle and began the construction of fortifications at Derry.[30] The manoeuvres were followed by a policy of harassment of the marcher lords. Chichester laid waste the countryside within twenty miles of Carrickfergus while Sir Samuel Bagenal did likewise about Newry. That burning, spoiling and preying were an integral part of Mountjoy's policy can be adduced from Fynes Moryson's comment that 'it did further the greatest end of finishing the wars, no way so likely to be brought to an end as by a general famine'. Terrorised by this turn of events the marcher lords began to capitulate, at first Niall Garbh O'Donnell, Conn O'Neill and Sir Arthur O'Neill of Clandeboy, followed early in 1601 by Turlogh McHenry O'Neill of the Fews in south Armagh, Ever MacCooley McMahon of Farney in Monaghan and Sir Oghie O'Hanlon of Orier in east Armagh.[31] In September 1600 Mountjoy again entered the Moiry Pass, and succeeded in breaking through to Newry though encountering stiff resistance from O'Neill's army. He then began the construction in the pass of a castle which was completed by the following June.[32] In May a general rising out was proclaimed in the five shires of the English Pale together with the Irish 'submittees' of Monaghan and Armagh, with the intent that they would 'attempt something against the arch-traitor O'Neill and to put them in blood against him and his confederates'. Following completion of the castle in the Moiry Pass, a force of six companies of foot and one of horse under Sir Richard Moryson [Fynes Moryson's brother] was dispatched into county Down with the objective of capturing Downpatrick.[33] After leaving their encampment at Carrickbane outside Newry they advanced into Iveagh from whence they marched overnight into Lecale 'less the rebels should have leisure to burn the country and carry away the prey'. They overtook the retreating Irish and taking 'all the prey', captured and looted Downpatrick. On 16 June they advanced 'through high mountains and woods and some dangerous passes' to the Blackstaff river, forcing Phelim Mac Ever Magennis of Castlewellan to surrender Dundrum castle. MacCartan of

Kinelarty also surrendered drawing his creaghts of cattle into Lecale. Ardglass surrendered without a fight, 'one Jordan' – happily surrendered his castle – not having come out of it for three years until 'by his lordship's coming' he was freed.

Mountjoy's foray into Down in 1601 must have brought with it the kind of devastation that similar forays had wreaked elsewhere in Ireland, making surrender the only choice for the hapless native chiefs. Ever McRory Magennis of Kilwarlin had surrendered along with Phelim Mac Ever of Castlewellan, but while Arthur Magennis of Rathfriland and his uncle Edmond Boy made approaches for a surrender, these were rebuffed until the 30 June when Arthur, 'terrified by the plantation of the garrison at Lecale' was given nine days protection to enable him to sue for pardon at Dundalk. A similar pardon was granted to Rory Og Magennis. On 3 July having been conveyed by Sir Francis Stafford the governor of Newry to Dundalk, Arthur, kneeling before the lord deputy and council, made his 'humble petition'; seeking a pardon (which was granted), and confirmation of the lands granted to his father by letters patent. This was promised, save for the lands of Glassney Magennis.[34] He was also enabled, subject to conditions, to accept such tenants as came in from the rebels and to retain and absolutely command all his own tenants until Allhollantide, excepting Glassney Magennis. 'His people' were also freed from all actions of private wrongs in war subject to the payment of a fine of 300 cows by Magennis. Considering Magennis's prominence and his personal relationships with O'Neill, Mountjoy's terms were not ungenerous and were consistent with his policy of drawing the marcher lords away from O'Neill. When O'Neill was to bring pressure to bear on them before his march to Kinsale in November 1601, most held to their compacts with Mountjoy including O'Neill's half-brother Turlogh McHenry of the Fews, O'Hanlon of Orier and Art Roe Magennis of Iveagh. The Annals describe O'Neill's army as consisting of O'Neill with the Kinel-Owen and 'such of the people of Oriel and Iveagh-of-Uladh as adhered to him, were in a strong battalion apart'.[35] While there is no mention of the leader of the detachment from Iveagh, in all likelihood it was Edmond Boy, Art Roe's uncle and brother of O'Neill's wife, Catherine. After the flight of the earls in September 1607, Edmond fled the country to Spain where his sister was instrumental in securing for him an allowance of 30 crowns per month. After Kinsale the war was to drag on until 30 March 1603, when O'Neill made his submission at Mellifont. In all the circumstances O'Neill's settlement was generous: in addition to a pardon he was restored to his earldom and to his estates in Tyrone and Armagh. His ascendancy in Ulster was, however, at an end.

From Irish lordship to English freehold

Soon after Chichester had taken steps to establish the commission of 1606 for the 'division and bounding of the lords' and 'gentlemens' livings', Art Roe Magennis actively sought the application of the commission to the lordship of Iveagh.[36] He hoped to avoid any finding of 'forfeiture of rebellion' (which would have rendered his land titles defective), grounded on his relationships with O'Neill during the period of the Nine Years War, and to secure the grant of the entire territory of Iveagh by new letters patent as his demesne lands, thus reducing all the other Magennis families to the status of leaseholders on his estate. Apart from any objections that would have been raised by the latter, Chichester was determined to reduce 'overmighty lords' such as Magennis to the status of freeholder, holding his immediate estates of the crown, while according a similar status to those who might have previously been regarded as his tenants. It was also Chichester's expectation to recover church and bishop's lands in Iveagh, which he believed had been alienated by the Magennises, with a view to establishing a resident Protestant episcopacy in Dromore. He further hoped to escheat to the crown such church or former monastic lands as might be discovered. These he intended to grant to ex-soldiers and others whose plantation in Iveagh might provide the nucleus for a colonial settlement and serve to accelerate the acculturation process. Apart from the properties of the Cistercian Abbey of Newry, which had been granted to Bagenal, no other medieval monastic establishments had been founded in Iveagh and thus no Church or monastic properties were discovered during the freeholding.

The decision by the lord deputy and council on Magennis's application was promulgated in February 1607.[37] It called for the division of the lordship of Iveagh into freeholds in accordance with a scheme to be drawn up by the solicitor-general, Sir Robert Jacob, assisted by a locally-based commission and the courts of assizes to be held in Newry between the years 1607 to 1610. While Art Roe Magennis put up a stiff resistance to the scheme when it was finally approved by the king in June 1610, it seems, nevertheless, that he managed to acquire a larger proportion of land than Chichester wished. In a letter to the earl of Salisbury on 27 February 1611, Chichester referred to the completion of the work as being 'a matter of great consequence as most I had taken in hand assuring quietness to all the parts and borders adjoining'. He also mentioned the possibility that the scheme might have miscarried as a result of letters 'procured from thence' [London], 'at the instance' and 'upon the false information of Sir Arthur Magennis or the bishop, or both'.[38]

A local official who had an important role in the freeholding of

Iveagh was Captain Edward Trevor from Brynkynallt near Chirk in the marcher country of north Wales and Shropshire, who first came into Ireland in the force led by Sir Samuel Bagenal in the wake of the defeat at the battle of the Yellow Ford in 1598.[39] At the end of the war he settled in Newry which had by this time evolved into a Welsh settlement due to its use as a garrison during the Nine Years War and the Bagenal connections with north Wales. His first wife, Agnes Ball a Dublin woman, died in childbirth in Narrowwater in 1610; he then married Rose Ussher, the daughter of Henry Ussher, archbishop of Armagh. Trevor was typical of his kind. Apart from a small estate in Brynkynallt, which he had inherited from his father, he had little else other that his army service in Ireland and family connections through marriage with the Bagenals of Newry. In May 1607 he was appointed superintendent of the districts of Iveagh, Newry and Mourne. This was one of the new administrative functions associated with the shiring of Ulster, which envisaged the creation of two shires in what is now county Down. The military character of the shiring process is evident from the fact that all the superintendents were either serving or retired army officers. Apart from Trevor, Sir Toby Caulfield, Sir Francis Roe, Sir Fulke Conway and Sir Edward Blaney had been captains under Sir Samuel Bagenal. All succeeded in establishing families and extensive estates in Ulster in the early Stuart period.[40]

As the freeholding of Iveagh proceeded, massive changes were taking place in land ownership and settlement elsewhere in east Ulster, sparked off by the acquisition of the O'Neill estates in Clandeboy and the Ards in the early years of the reign of James 1 by the two Scotsmen, James Hamilton and Hugh Montgomery, Chichester and others.[41] A similar development occurred in Kinelarty and Lecale where Phelim McCartan sold a substantial part of his ancestral lands to another ex-soldier, Sir Edward Cromwell. These transactions coincided with a massive migration of lowland Scots into Ulster.[42] These migrants provided a ready-made pool of tenants for the newly-purchased estates, parts of which had been denuded of population by Chichester in the Nine Years War. A similar development took place in south Down, in the baronies of Kinelarty, Lecale, Newry and Mourne where some English, but even more Welsh migrants, settled on the Bagenal and Cromwell estates. Thus even before the flight of the earls in September 1607 and the subsequent plantation of their escheated lands in mid and west Ulster, much of county Down had begun to be settled by this new migration, peacefully and generally without government intervention. Only in Iveagh did the government actively intervene and then only with the consent of the land-owning families.

The scheme for the freeholding of Iveagh of January 1608 provided for the grant in freehold tenure of certain specified lands to fifteen individuals, including thirteen Magennises among whom were Art Roe Magennis of Rathfriland and Brian Og McRory Magennis of Kilwarlin (appendix A). Save for the latter, whose grant was in common soccage at a yearly rent of £20 payable to the crown, these grants were in military tenure: Art Roe's by knight's service of one whole knight's fee and the remainder by way of knight's service and an annual payment of 20s.0d. per townland. In addition the recovered bishop's lands were granted to the see of Dromore where John Todd had been appointed bishop in 1608. Art Roe was also involved in eleven fee farm grants, five of which were made to members of the Magennis sept. These lands may have been former bishops holdings alienated to the Magennises at an earlier period. The Magennises managed their affairs well in the freeholding of Iveagh, and secured over 75 per cent of the townlands distributed. Art Roe received 31 per cent or 36 per cent if the fee farm lands are included. Eighty-five per cent of the townlands was granted to Irish families and, apart from the freehold assignment obtained by Edward Trevor from Murtagh McManus in Kilmore, the residue was adjudged as bishop's lands.[43] Apart from twenty-nine townlands which were adjudged erenagh lands and set by the bishop in fee farm to named erenagh individuals, no church or monastic lands were discovered.[44]

Substantial sections of the bishop's lands were subsequently alienated by Bishop Todd in fee farm grants to Edward Trevor (fourteen townlands), William Worsley of Nottingham, Todd's brother-in-law (forty-three townlands), and Arthur Bagenal of Newry (seven townlands).[45] This enraged Chichester who had the bishop arrested and legislation introduced into parliament for the recovery of the alienated properties. He was only partially successful; as he put it himself, 'in a general case in a manner throughout the realm for which every man interested will make his own as we may justly conjecture'.[46] While some recoveries were made notably of the lands granted to Worsley, Lord Deputy Wentworth used contemporary legislation to support Bishop Leslie's attempt to recover alienated bishop's lands in his sees of Down, Connor and Dromore. This involved Trevor and Magennis Viscount Iveagh and led to a compromise whereby the solution found was that the fee farm leases were replaced by leases of sixty years with increased rentals.[47]

The real significance of the freeholding of Iveagh was the break-up of the Irish lordship and the abolition of its customary laws. Following the division of the land into estates of freehold tenures under the English common law, the freeholders were no longer tied to their customary lord. Instead they were liable to pay their rents to the king's sheriff and were subject to periodic inquisition by the king's escheators whose duty it was to discover alienations made without consent and to enforce feudal incidents such as the suing out of livery by heirs, escheat or forfeiture, wardship, and marriage, all of which carried financial implications for the estate.

Apart from the inherent problems of adapting to the new system in the aftermath of the Nine Years War, when their economic base was low, the freeholders had to contend with officials such as Trevor, who served as sheriff as well as commissioner at the time of the freeholding, and George Sexton, the crown escheator and clerk of the peace for county Down. Their enforcement of the law would have been tempered by an understandable expectation of a financial return for services rendered. Trevor, for example, was empowered to accept reduced fines in the making of the freeholds, taking one third of the fines 'of those of ability and less from the poorer sort'.[48] They were therefore in a position to apply leverage to those freeholders who might have been unsure as to the precise nature of the proceedings involved or through want of ready money would have had difficulty in paying costs. This provided opportunities for speculative carpet bagging activities, such as taking land in recompense for services rendered (the cost of which could have been inflated), advancing loans under onerous conditions with land as security, and the purchase of lands at favourable prices. The evidence that these activities took place in Iveagh in the early Stuart period, while scattered and fragmentary, is sufficient to implicate newcomers such as Trevor, Sexton and Marmaduke Whitchurch, one of Bagenal's retainers and a commissioner in the freeholding.[49] All of these managed to amass substantial tracts of land in Iveagh in the period preceding 1641, by which time Trevor and his son Mark had between them over 16,000 acres plantation measure scattered throughout Upper and Lower Iveagh including the entire estate of the Magennises of Milltown.[50] Whitchurch, by foreclosure on a debt, secured almost the entire estate of Lough-brickland while Sexton acquired a scattered estate consisting of lands granted in the freeholding to Arthur Magennis of Rathfriland, Hugh McConn McGlassney Magennis of Milltown, Brian Og McRory Magennis of Kilwarlin, Art Og McGlassney Magennis of Leighquirren (Clanconnell), and Art Og McBrien Og McEdmond Magennis of Loughbrickland.[51] Others also obtained substantial acreages either by purchase or foreclosure on mortgages following the freeholding of Iveagh. By 1641, Sir Moses Hill, former lieutenant in Chichester's company, and Arthur, his second son and heir, had acquired the greater part of the Kilwarlin Magennis's lands; Sir William Reeves obtained lands in Kilwarlin; Sir Faithful Fortescue gained lands of Con

Boy McPhelim McHugh Magennis of Dromnevaddy in Glasquirrin (Magherally and Seapatrick parishes), and Edward Trevor, Francis Kinnaston, Edward Brugh and David Boyd acquired the lands of O'Lawry in the sessiaghs of Ballyconnell in Moyragh (Moira), parish of Magherelin.[52] By 1641 the lands held by native Irish proprietors in Iveagh had been reduced from 85 to 48 per cent and much of this was encumbered by debt.

The Magennises as landed gentry

At the beginning of the seventeenth century the lordship of Iveagh appears to have operated as a subsistence economy with much of its land surface consisting of bogs, marsh, woods and forests. In the mountainous areas many of the inhabitants were in creaghts, bands of semi-nomadic herdsmen engaged in the transhumant practice (known in Irish as booleying), of taking their livestock into the upland areas in summer and returning to the lowlands in winter. The townland and mountain of Slievenaboley in the civil parish of Drumgooland is a reminder. The herdsmen and their families lived in primitive cabins or huts or creaghs, evidently so-called because of the temporary nature of their construction.[53] More settled families included those in the arable areas, but even they were only marginally better off and lived in one-roomed thatched cabins of mud walling. The gentry often lived in stone houses or tower houses which probably dated to not much earlier than the sixteenth century. Few of these have survived. The introduction of the 'English' landed gentry system with its emphasis on renting out the landowner's estate for varying terms of years or lives or at will, to tenants paying a fixed rent was a new departure, of which neither the landowner nor tenant had much experience. Its substitution for a system of land tenure which had existed from time immemorial could not be expected to translate itself successfully within a space of a few decades and it is therefore not surprising that many of the new landowners did not survive the initial years.[54] The 'English' system had a constant requirement for money borrowed either for capital development or to meet social needs such as the provision of estates of inheritance for male or marriage portions for female children, respectively. The educational needs of, especially younger, male heirs destined to pursue careers in the law or in the army, also required ready cash, whether to fund their attendances at university or the Inns of Court in London. The considerable legal costs associated with estate management included the periodic payments to the crown of feudal incidents such as suing out of livery upon inheritance or fines for pardons of alienation in the buying and selling of lands. Legal services were expensive and many cash-rich lawyers carried on a money lending business, taking their client's lands as security. Many of the Magennises failed to manage debt which explains the loss of their estates and disappearance as landed gentry, although many of them continued to live on as tenants on their former lands. Neither was debt peculiar to the Magennises. In the 1630s many settlers were also in debt for similar reasons, including a downturn in the economy due to bad harvests. Thus in addition to the earl of Antrim, Sir Hugh Montgomery of the Ards, Cromwell of Lecale and Conway of Killultagh were heavily encumbered, while Mark Trevor was committed to prison in England in the 1650s because of a debt incurred by his father in Ireland in the 1630s.[55]

Despite their initial difficulties the Magennises soon adapted themselves to the usages of English common law and there is ample evidence to show that they were able to acquit themselves in litigation with each other as well as with the settlers. Accustomed as they were to a subsistence economy in which livestock was a commonly accepted currency, the need for ready cash soon led them to borrow, mortgaging land (of which they had plenty) in return for ready cash. The most spectacular failure was the Kilwarlin estate granted to Brian Og McRory. It consisted of some forty-five townlands located in the modern parishes of Blaris, Hillsborough and Annahilt with a further six in Dromore and two in Dromara. It amounted to about 28,000 acres plantation measure, the next largest after Art Roe's estate of Rathfriland. Unlike the latter, Brian Og gave long leases of between twenty-one to one hundred and one years on fixed rents which may have included the payment of large entry fines. Kilwarlin must have suffered severely during the Nine Years War, possibly as a result of the expulsion of Brian's elder brother, Ever McRory, by Art Roe of Rathfriland and the subsequent spoiling attacks by Chichester during Mountjoy's campaign. This may have dispersed the tenants, leaving the lands unoccupied and waste. In such circumstances Brian Og would have had little choice. By the time of his death in October 1631, large sections of Kilwarlin lands had been let on long lease or otherwise alienated, mostly to the native Irish but also to settlers such as Moses Hill and his son Peter, Trogmorton Stotisbury of Glennawe in county Antrim, Sir Edward Trevor, George Sexton and the Old Englishman, John Jennings who was probably a lawyer.[56] In August 1635, Brian Og's son and heir, Rory McBrian, passed the entire Kilwarlin estate to Richard Parsons, Edmond Strafford, William Ussher and John Echlin, who were probably the trustees of Sir Moses Hill's estate.[57] At the same time he leased the towns and lands of Ballyculcavy, Ballykeele, Ballycarnebane, Ballycornerough and one quarter of Aghnebarron to his younger brother Conn for a term of one hundred years.[58] Moses Hill was one of those who with Montgomery, Hamilton and Chichester purchased the O'Neill lands of Clandeboy, and who was reported in 1611 as having constructed a fort and timber framed, brick-walled house at 'Hillsboroughe' in Malone near Shaw's bridge. He appears to have also acquired the Kilwarlin lands of Ballyknock, Ballygowan, Lurganville, Corcreeny, Athnatrisk, Maze and Maghrageery in the civil parish of Crumlin, now Blaris, at this time. A trust may have been established in 1635 in favour of Moses's son, Peter, who was succeeded by Arthur, his younger brother, a Dublin lawyer. By 1641 Arthur possessed the entire Kilwarlin estates which were described in the Down Survey as accounting for one third of the whole barony of Lower Iveagh. A Hill rent roll for the Kilwarlin estate, dated May 1638, reveals that many of the leases entered into by the Magennises, including those of Conn Boy of Culcavy, James Maginn of Drumnetanty, Knoghe McQuonan of Ballykeele, Neil McQuonan of Aghnecloy, Donal Og O'Gownley, of Carrowbane, Murtagh McGormley of Ballykeele and John Jennings of Ballyworphy continued in being, at least to the period of the English Commonwealth, when they were confiscated and acquired by Arthur Hill.[59] They were confirmed to him by a decree of the court of claims in May 1667.

Four other Magennis freeholders lost their estates in the years before 1641. These were; Art Og McBrien Og McEdmond Boy Magennis of Loughbrickland, Hugh McConn McGlassney Magennis of Milltown, Con Boy McPhelim McHugh Magennis of Dromnevaddy and Rory Og McRory McCollo McHugh Magennis of Islandmoyle and Cabragh. The Loughbrickland Magennises lost their estate of more than 1,250 acres profitable in the parish of Aghaderrig to Marmaduke Whitchurch of Carlingford and Killeavy in south Armagh as a result of Art Og's failure to repay a debt incurred in 1611.[60] Whitchurch had been lieutenant of Bagenal's horse company at the battle of the Yellow Ford where he also supplied the oxen for the train of artillery. He was a commissioner in the freeholding of Iveagh and was 'party to the distribution and balloting of the lands given unto the natives upon the said plantation'. Following his death in 1635 his daughter and heir, Rose, married Mark, one of the sons of Edward Trevor. Hugh McConn McGlassney Magennis obtained a freehold grant of an estate of about 3,300 acres profitable in the old Irish sub-division of Milltown, located principally in the parish of Clonallan but with small portions in the nearby parishes of Kilbroney and Drumgath. By 1611 portions of the estate has been acquired by Edward Trevor who seems at the same time to have obtained in concealment a substantial acreage in the parish of Kilbroney, where he established his seat at Rose Trevor.[61] In a chancery case in February 1635, Trevor took an action against Hugh, his son Art and Hugh McRoss Magennis, Art's father-in-law, seeking a declaration that Hugh had by deed dated 23 June 1618 conveyed all his lands of Milltown to Trevor and that the latter had in turn leased the lands to Hugh for the term of his natural life.[62] Trevor evidently won the action as a chancery inquisition, dated 13 April 1635, found Trevor in possession of six of the nine townlands of Milltown. The Dromnevaddy estate allocated to Conn Boy McPhelim Magennis had eight townlands in the old Irish sub-division of Glasquerin, and consisted of at least 1,330 acres spread over the parishes of Seapatrick and Magherally. In 1632 five of the townlands had been disposed of to Sir Faithful Fortesque.[63] In 1619 Conn Boy was reported as having 'divers disputes' with Marmaduke Whitchurch and while the outcome is not known the residue of the Dromnevaddy lands were in Mark Trevor's possession in 1641.[64] The estates of Rory Og McRory McCollo McHugh Magennis of Islandmoyle and Cabragh in the parishes of Clonduff and Kilcoo had also been disposed of before 1641, mainly to Edward Trevor.

Another problem confronting the Magennises was the need to provide estates of inheritance for their children. In the case of the Clanconnell Magennises, Glassney McAholly, the freehold grantee of fourteen townlands which consisted of over 4,000 acres profitable in the old Irish sub-division of Clanconnell in Tullylish and Donacloney parishes, was married four times and had many children, seven of whom can be positively identified.[65] Art Og his eldest son had a freehold grant in his own right of the 'chief four towns in the Lequirin' an old Irish sub-division in the parish of Magheralin. When Glassney died in 1620 he left his estate to Edmond Boy, one of the sons of the third marriage, who subsequently conferred estates of inheritance on three of his half-brothers; Art Og McGlassney obtained four townlands including Ballynagarrick; Hugh Roe received four townlands all of which are subsumed into the modern townland of Banoge in Donacloney parish; and a Brian Roe obtained half of the townlands of Edengreen and Derryhirke.[66] Despite this division, the Clanconnell Magennises managed to retain the estate intact until it was forfeited during the English Commonwealth. The Shankill, Corrocks and Aghnemullragh Magennises also sub-divided their lands and disposed of portions of them to the Trevors. Their lands were forfeited in the period of the English Commonwealth and Brian with his eldest son, Glassney, of the Shankill Magennises were transplanted to Connacht. Brian's brother, Arthur, was a Protestant and had a lease from his father of Ballynefarin and Ballynanny which were also confiscated but Arthur's son, John, succeeded in recovering them during the restoration period. In contrast, the Castlewellan estate, under Ever McPhellimy

Magennis, the freehold grantee, was saved from division. The estate passed to Ever's only son, Phelim, after his death in 1649.[67] The Castlewellan lands were situated in the old Irish, sub-division of Castlewilliam and consisted of eleven townlands located in the parishes of Drumgooland and Kilmegan, amounting to 6,778 profitable acres. Unlike the other Magennis families, the Castlewellan branch escaped indebtedness and prospered prior to 1641. Castlewellan was forfeited during the English Commonwealth and while Phelim is mentioned as a titulado in Castlewellan in 1659 he was also mentioned in King Charles II's Gracious Declaration of 1660 as having served 'under our ensigns beyond the seas'.[68]

Two other Protestant Magennis families emerged in Tollymore and Corgary before 1641. Tollymore had been granted to Brian McHugh McAholly Magennis and consisted of seven and a half townlands situated in the Irish sub-division of Munterreddie in the parishes of Kilcoo and Maghera. It contained at least 2,000 acres.[69] Before his death in 1619, Brian McHugh disposed of Ballyfofanny to Edward Trevor. Brian McHugh was succeeded by Phelim, his only son and heir, who was sixteen years of age at the time of his father's death. Brian McHugh's only daughter, Ellen, married William Hamilton of Monilla in county Armagh. When Phelim died in 1628 he left a son Bernard who was a Protestant.[70] On Bernard's death without issue sometime after 1660, the estate passed to his aunt Ellen and through her to the Hamiltons. It was the only Magennis estate not to have been confiscated during the English Commonwealth. The Corgary Magennises traced their descent from Murtagh, lord of Iveagh, who was killed by the Louthmen in 1529. His son, Arthur, was the bishop of Dromore in the period 1540 to 1577: Arthur's son Murtagh 'McEnaspicke' was the freeholder grantee of Corgary, an estate of ten townlands containing 1,776 acres profitable located in the Irish sub-division of Clanagan in the parishes of Donaghmore and Aghaderrig.[71] By Murtagh's death in 1631 the estate was encumbered by debt with two of the towns already disposed of to the Trevors. Murtagh's son, Agholy, born out of wedlock is given as the proprietor of Carrickrovaddy in 1641. Upon the marriage of his son and heir, Daniel, to Rose O'Hanlon in 1622, Murtagh assigned the greater part of the estate and its encumbrances to him. Daniel pre-deceased his father (in 1626) leaving an infant son, Arthur, who upon the death of his grandfather was taken into wardship by the crown. Anthony Dopping then clerk of the pleas in the court of exchequer was appointed as his ward.[72] This gave Dopping effective control of the estate during Art's minority and he further tightened his grip on it by buying out the encumbrances. Dopping also promoted a scheme for manorial rights to be attached to the estate under the title of the manor of Clanagan, the letters patent for which were issued in April 1642 when Art came of age. Art was reared a Protestant. Notwithstanding his religion and his non-involvement in the insurrection of 1641, his estate was confiscated during the English Commonwealth. The lord of Iveagh's fee-farm tenants fared no better than the freeholders prior to 1641. As with their neighbours in Clanconnell, the three fee-farm tenancies of Clanconnell and Greenan managed to survive to 1641: Brian McDonal's sons, Fergus and Hugh of Greenan, Donal Og McEdmond Boy's sons, Edmond Og and Brian, and Glassney's two sons, Donal and Arthur, were forfeiting proprietors in the confiscations of the English Commonwealth. Donal's son, Murtagh, was the forfeiting proprietor of Beeme and was transplanted to Connacht. Both O'Lowry of Moira and Brian McArt McEver of Loghdegan also disposed of their interests before 1641. With the exception of Clonvaraghan, all of the others had disposed of substantial parts of their respective estates in the same period.

The Magennises of Rathfriland

The political acumen displayed by Art during the Nine Years War was also apparent in the freeholding of Iveagh, when he obtained a freehold grant of one hundred and thirty-four townlands in Upper and Lower Iveagh as well as thirty-seven other townlands let on fee-farm leases, the lessees of which were required to pay a chief rent to him. His freehold estate contained some 27,000 acres profitable together with a further 17,800 acres unprofitable.[74] He also acquired a knighthood and was elevated to the peerage of Ireland as Viscount Iveagh in July 1623.[73] By this date Art was one of the few survivors of the ancient dynastic families of Ulster still in his place, and as son-in-law of the late departed earl of Tyrone was, despite his anglicisation, a respected figure amongst the Irish of the province. This is evident from the bardic poetry of the period which includes a lament on the death of his father Hugh in 1597, another for Art himself in 1629 and a poem addressed to Art's son Hugh, seeking his patronage. The marriage of Hugh's brother, Daniel, to Elisabeth Magennis was marked by a *crossantacht,* a composition of verse and prose. If he was the Viscount Iveagh in Dublin he was still the Lord of Iveagh amongst the natives of Ulster.[75]

Art Roe had five sons: Hugh who succeeded him, Sir Conn of Newcastle; Arthur [Art Roe of Fenis], Daniel of Glascoe and Rory. Sometime after the freeholding of Iveagh he appears to have settled estates upon four younger sons; over 2,800 acres profitable in Maghera and Kilcoo parishes including Newcastle to Conn; 2,363 acres profitable in the parishes of Dromore and Dromara to Arthur; 854 acres profitable in the parishes of Aghaderg and Drumballyronan to Arthur and 1,985 acres profitable in the parishes of Seapatrick and Tullylish to Rory.[76] All four played leading roles during the insurrection of 1641 in county Down and were outlawed in 1642; their estates were confiscated in the period of the English Commonwealth.

In 1613 Hugh, the heir to Rathfriland, was sent to Oxford to be educated 'to do his majesty and his country service..............being a gentleman of more than ordinary note in his country and on whom a fair inheritance is likely to descend'. After three years in Oxford it was reported that 'the time he had spent there has in no way bettered him in those things which we specially desired nor had sorted to that effect as we expected'.[77] Evidently the youth's adherence to his roots and culture was the disappointing feature as he went on to study law in the Middle Temple in London before returning to Ireland.[78] In 1628 he married Mary the daughter of Sir John Bellew of Castletown, Dundalk, an unusual match considering that the Old English of the Pale generally held themselves aloof from intermarriage with the native Irish.[79] Hugh was not in good health during the latter part of his life and at his death in 1639 he left two sons; Arthur, who succeeded him, and Hugh, both of whom were then minors.[80]

The inquisition post-mortem taken after Hugh's death in 1639 revealed that the estate was heavily encumbered by debt, a substantial part of which was held by Hierom Alexander of Dublin. Alexander's interests were later bought out by Arthur Hill who also acquired the interests of Patrick O'Doran of Moneygar, another encumbrancer.[81] In 1637/8 representations were made on Hugh's behalf by the earl of Antrim to the lord deputy Wentworth, urging that 'his elderly and impoverished cousin germain' be admitted to composition by the commission for defective titles 'as other men are' and that 'no part of that which he now possesses be diminished or taken from him'.[82] Apart from the divisions made in respect of his brothers a further third of the estate was tied up by way of a jointure for his mother, the redoubtable Lady Sarah, who was to survive both her husband Arthur and son Hugh, and play her own part in the insurrection of 1641. When Hugh's son, Arthur, succeeded him in 1639 he was still a minor and a ward of court in Dublin. Although his inheritance was then valued at £1,200 per annum it was heavily encumbered by Lady Sarah's jointure and by a debt of £4,500. Due to the insurrection of 1641, Arthur never succeeded to his estates, which, were confiscated by the English Commonwealth and distributed among various adventurers. William Hawkins, William Barker and Joseph Deane received Rathfriland and Narrowwater in

Upper Iveagh, while Captain John Magill and George Rawdon, obtained lands in Lower Iveagh in the parishes of Kilmore, Seagoe and Magherelin.

Although the Irish lordship of the Magennises had in one sense come to an end with the freeholding of Iveagh, their retention of relatively substantial estates and the elevation of its leading family to the peerage conferred a measure of political leverage which enabled them to preserve some elements of their ancient lineage and heritage intact. This was in marked contrast to the situation elsewhere in Ulster, not only in the escheated lordships of O'Neill and O'Donnell but also in the other marcher lordships of O'Hanlon, McCartan and the Clandeboy O'Neills. Political ascendancy had now passed to the new landed magnate class created by the British settlement — families such as the Montgomerys of the Ards, the Hamiltons of Killyleagh, the Cromwells of Lecale, the Hills of Kilwarlin and the Trevors and Bagenals of Upper Iveagh and Newry, respectively. This was amply demonstrated in the 1613 elections when the settlers created sufficient new freeholders to overcome the Magennis candidate.[83] Thereafter the Magennises never contested elections to the house of commons, content perhaps to have one of their own in the lords. The Montgomerys complained that the Magennises tended to support English rather than Scots candidates. While individual members of the Magennises embraced Protestantism, as a class they were regarded as being both Irish and Roman Catholic and their adherence to the latter creed was not without a cost. At this period Protestantism was regarded as the outward badge of loyalty to the state and the basic requirement for the full enjoyment of the rights and privileges accorded to loyal subjects of the crown. The Magennises had therefore to submit to the discrimination then practised by the state against Roman Catholics, including the payment of fines for non-attendance at Protestant services. Bishop Buckworth, the Protestant bishop of Dromore, claimed that these fines made it possible for the cathedral church of Dromore to be 'almost new built, covered, glassed and in part furnished with seats with the recusants' fines'.[84] By the time of the insurrection of 1641, several of the Magennis families had become Protestant, a process which might have continued but for the polarisation introduced by the wars. Equally speculative is the question of how many of the Magennises would have survived as landed gentry into the latter part of the century.

The Magennises in the period of insurrection and civil war

Lacking any degree of political influence, the Magennises were not

major actors in the politics of the 1630s when the growing struggle
between the king, Charles I, and the several parliaments of his
kingdoms began to take shape. Intuitively they would have supported
the king and even his lord deputy, Wentworth, whose faction in the
Irish parliament was opposed on the one hand by the Old English,
who struggled to regain some of the influence lost to the new British
settlers, and on the other by the settlers themselves, who resented the
cutting back of their powers and influence by the over-mighty lord
deputy, whose concern for the maintenance of the king's prerogatives
was paramount.[85] When the flash point came it was furnished by the
king himself through connivance with Randal McDonnell, earl of
Antrim, in the recruitment of an army of native Irish to aid him in his
struggle with the Scots parliament. The conspiracies in which these
three engaged in the years 1638 to 1640 were the remote beginnings of
the insurrection which broke out in Ulster in October 1641.

In pursuit of the scheme for an invasion of Scotland, Antrim
requested Lord Deputy Wentworth in March 1639 to issue a
commission to him under the great seal to raise three regiments each
consisting of sixteen hundred foot and two hundred horse with power
to appoint officers.[86] Among the officers appointed were Hugh
Magennis Viscount Iveagh and his brothers, Sir Conn and Daniel,
Phelim O'Neill of Kinard in county Tyrone, Art Og O'Neill, Turlogh
McHenry O'Neill of the Fews in county Armagh, Connor Lord Maguire
of Fermanagh and Hugh McMahon of Monaghan. All of these, save
Hugh Magennis who died beforehand, played leading roles in the
subsequent insurrection. In May 1639 Wentworth reported on the
matter to the Dublin privy council, a body which was composed in the
main of magnates of the British settlement including such as, Lord
Montgomery of the Ards, Hamilton Viscount Clandeboy and Sir Edward
Trevor of Rosetrevor. In their minds the situation was clear enough; the
king had been negotiating behind their backs to establish an Irish army
in Ulster which was ostensibly intended for use in Scotland. The army
was never raised; neither the king nor Antrim had the resources
necessary for the purpose, but the affair further undermined confidence
amongst the British settlers not only in the native Irish but also in the
king and Lord Deputy Wentworth. On the other hand the native Irish,
especially in Ulster, who had heretofore been excluded from political
affairs, became progressively more politicised and began to look to the
king as a possible defender of their interests against the magnate class
whom they suspected had designs on their landed estates. The failure
of Antrim's scheme did not deter Charles I from turning again to
Ireland for armed support in his troubles with the Scots. In 1640, at the
king's bidding, Wentworth organised an army to be used 'to reduce

those in Scotland to their due obedience'.[87] It was quartered in Carrickfergus under the command of James Butler, earl of Ormond, and Sir William St Leger as sergeant-major general but, after Wentworth's departure from Ireland in April and the political situation which ensued, the force was gradually run down. The officer corps of the army was Protestant in character but the rank and file were mainly Irish and Roman Catholic. Amongst the former were Sir Arthur Tyringham of Newry who commanded a regiment of foot, Sir Edward Trevor's natural son, Patrick, who held a captaincy in Sir Thomas Wharton's regiment, Lord Cromwell of Lecale who had a captaincy of horse and Lord Conway of Killultagh who also held a captaincy of horse. In May 1641 orders were given for the disbandment of the army with detailed instructions to ensure the peaceful return of disbanded troops to their respective homes, the return of arms and munitions to secure stores and arrangements for the recruitment and transportation of those willing to enlist for foreign service. The first two regiments to be disbanded were those of Wharton and Tyringham, whose arms and munitions may have been returned to the stores at Newry Castle which 'belonging to Colonel Arthur Hill, was soe considerable as the Earle of Strafford would onely intrust the ammunition which he intended to serve the north into the said castle in the year 1638 and 1639 which, being there in the year 1641, was surprised by the Irish rebells and soe was the first provision of ammunition they had in Ulster'.[88]

That a conspiracy for an armed insurrection evolved in Ulster in the period 1640/1641 can hardly be doubted, what was and is still an open question was its extent. Contemporary historians of the British settlement had no doubt that it was widespread and involved all the native Irish in the province. There is, however, little evidence to support this view. It seems more likely that a small group, mainly native Ulster Irish, with limited means and almost certainly limited objectives, lit the fuse to what was an already explosive political situation. Matters quickly went out of control, leading in turn to a total breakdown in law and order, first in Ulster and then throughout the whole country. By the time it was brought to an end in September 1643, a similar politically disturbed situation in England had evolved into civil war between the king and his rebel parliament. It was this latter event which ensured the continuance of warfare in Ireland until 1652 by which time the Cromwellian forces of the English Commonwealth held the upper hand.

In the early morning of Saturday, 23 October 1641, a meeting of the leading British colonists of the locality took place in Newry castle. They included the governor, Sir Arthur Tyringham, Sir Edward Trevor of Rose Trevor; Lieutenant Hugh Trevor of Loughbrickland; Sir Charles Pointz and his son; the Protestant vicar, Mr Tudge, and the outgoing member of parliament for Newry, Mr Weston. What the purpose of the meeting was is not known but if security was their concern it was already too late. Earlier that morning, before dawn, Sir Con Magennis of Newcastle and his brother Daniel of Glascoe, Patrick McCartan of Kinelarty and others had taken possession of the town with the connivance of some and the opposition of none of its inhabitants. They seized the castle and made prisoners of all inside except Tyringham who made good his escape to Dromore where he raised the alarm and sent a messenger to his 'cousin' Captain Vaughan at Downpatrick informing him of what had happened and warning him to be ready for an attack. On the previous evening the castles at Dungannon, county Tyrone, Mountjoy and Charlemount in county Armagh had been taken by Sir Phelim O'Neill of Kinard and his followers. The insurrection of 1641 had begun. In the weeks which followed the taking of Newry, the insurgents moved into south Down leaving the settlers holding a line from Dromore eastwards to the Ards peninsula on the coast. South of this, the Irish overran settler estates, seizing cattle and destroying corn.[89] Sir Edward Trevor was reported as having lost his house, stock, plate and household stuff to Daniel Magennis of Glascoe, the uncle of Viscount Iveagh.[90] The town of Downpatrick was burned and the nearby properties of Cromwell of Lecale, the Kynastons of Saul and Margaret Trevor, described as the 'relict' of John Trevor of Lecale, suffered losses of corn, cattle and 'many leases of good value'. Nor were the Protestant Magennises immune. Arthur Magennis of Ballynefarney, one of the Shankill Magennises, claimed in a deposition of 1642 that he had lost goods to the value of £1,658 and that he 'hath been detained in prison or hoult by Sir Conn Magennis in his life time and by means of one Richard Stanihurst Lieut-Colonel there and after their decease by the said Daniel Og Magennis'.[91] It is therefore likely that other Protestant Magennis families and estates, such as those of Corgary and Tollymore, may have been similarly affected.

The failure of the Irish to press their attacks into north Down may have been due to a strategy adopted in the early weeks of the insurrection to avoid attacks on Scottish settlers, who were more numerous here, in the hope that they might stand aside and remain neutral in the developing conflict. It was a fatal error on their part in that it gave the landed magnates of north Down and south Antrim time to rally support, which was readily forthcoming from all sections including the Scots. Colonel Matthews and Captain Crawford achieved some success in repulsing enemy forces lodged along the Bann river at Dromore and in the environs of the town.[92] These successes created a false sense of security among the defenders who then dispersed, some to plunder the locality others to return to their farms, so that by the time Chichester's forces reached the town on 28 October it was found to be almost deserted. Chichester remained only one night and having heard of the approach of Sir Conn Magennis of Newcastle with a force of some 1,500 men he retreated to Lisnegarvey leaving Dromore to its fate. Magennis occupied the town until 1 November after which Chichester returned to find that, apart from a general plunder, no other atrocities had been committed. Later that month Sir Phelim O'Neill and Sir Conn Magennis led a force of Irish, variously estimated at 4,000 to 9,000 men and drawn from the surrounding counties of Down, Armagh, Antrim and Tyrone, to Lisnagarvey (Lisburn). Its garrison, under the command of Sir Arthur Tyringham, was estimated to have been about 500 foot and 80 horse, later reinforced by a troop of horse and a company of foot commanded by a Captain Boyde. The attack on the town ended in the defeat of the Irish with their losses estimated as hundreds of men killed by Rawdon's horse in the streets of the town. Lisnegarvey marked a turning point of the insurrection in county Down.

Although several atrocities had been alleged to have been committed by the Irish on the civilian population before their defeat at Lisnegarvey, the latter event sparked off a frenzy of killings notably in Armagh and Tyrone. There it was reported that 'for days and weeks after, they murdered many hundreds of Protestants whom they had kept prisoners in the counties of Armagh and Tyrone and tormented them with several manners of deaths'.[93] Inevitably these were followed by tit-for-tat killings committed by the British settlers the most notable of which were the massacres of Mr Upton's tenants at Templepatrick in county Antrim and at Island Magee in January 1642.[94] Heretofore, Down in general and Iveagh in particular had been relatively free of atrocities and the prisoners taken at Newry were held in comparative safety. In January 1642 an arrangement was made for the transfer of Mr Tudge, Lieutenant Hugh Trevor and his wife with fourteen others to Newcastle for eventual exchange with Irish prisoners held by Sir James Montgomery in Lecale. This was about the time of the Island Magee and Templepatrick massacres and to further exacerbate the situation it was reported that the Irish exchange prisoners had been killed by Montgomery.[95] Sir Conn Magennis, angered by these reports, galloped after the party as they travelled towards Newcastle and coming upon them he had them brought into a wood where they were all hanged. Sir Conn was said to have suffered such pangs of remorse for the part he played in the massacre that the spirit of Mr Tudge haunted him for the rest of his life, and it was said that on his deathbed he left directions that no more Protestants were to be killed other than in battle.[96] Another killing reported at Newry was that of a Brian O'Rowney who had come from Drogheda with a message for Sir Edward Trevor, urging him to 'be of good courage and march away to Drogheda'.

The immediate reaction of Charles I to the insurrection was to issue commissions to various magnates in Ulster to raise regiments at the expense of the state, but while these were subsequently repudiated by the pro-parliamentarian lords justices in Dublin, several regiments were formed and served through the war. These included the Lagan Force under Sir Robert Stewart in west Ulster and the county Down regiments raised by Lord Montgomery of the Ards, Lord Clandeboye of Killyleagh and Lord Conway of Killultagh, whose agent, George Rawdon, served as his sergeant-major. In addition, troops of horse were subsequently established under Arthur Hill of Hillsborough and Sir James Montgomery, while Mark Trevor of Rose Trevor raised a party of dragoons.[97] The landing of a Scots force under General Munro at Carrickfergus in April 1642 marked a turning point in the insurrection.[98] This force immediately marched southwards through Iveagh accompanied by the locally-raised regiments of Chichester, Conway, Montgomery and Clandeboye, with the objective of capturing Newry and relieving the areas occupied by the Irish.

Arthur Magennis, the third Viscount Iveagh, then a minor and ward of court, was in Dublin when the insurrection broke out. He was one of those expelled from Dublin by the lords justices in November 1641 and afterwards joined Lord Gormanston's forces in county Meath before returning to Iveagh.[99] He was reported as having participated in the burning of Downpatrick in February 1642 and in April/May 1642 he is mentioned as leading a party of 2,500 foot and sixty horse in Kilwarlin Wood to oppose the southern advance of Munro's new Scots army.[100] After a series of skirmishes Munro advanced to Loughbrickland where a party of Irish were encountered dug in on the crannog island in the lake. After a successful assault the island was captured and the 'whole sixty therein' put to the sword. Newry was reached that evening and the townspeople fled the oncoming storm; some took refuge in the castle, the garrison claiming that they could hold out for seven months if necessary. However, on the following day in return for the release of the prisoners, Sir Edward Trevor, Sir Charles Pointz and others, the garrison was allowed to march away unharmed, only the townspeople being detained 'till trial be had' of their complicity in alleged atrocities. On 5 May after an examination of the townspeople, 'if all were papists, and the indifferent separated from the bad whereof sixty with two priests were shot and hanged, the indifferent were banished'.[101] After such an example it is not surprising that the soldiers then took some twelve women, throwing them into the river and there shooting at them until a Lieutenant-Colonel Turner intervened and stopped the slaughter. In fairness to Munro these summary executions were the work of Lord Conway's British forces, wreaking vengeance for the atrocities alleged to have been committed by the insurgents. Having consolidated his position in Newry, Munro turned his forces inland into county Down through Iveagh, Mourne and Kinelarty plundering and looting as they went and reportedly killing many of the population found in their path. The British forces complained that the Scots had made off with most of the plundered cattle so that they were 'reluctant to act jointly with the Scots in the future'. Even the lords justices noted that the Scots and their camp followers 'do export cattle in mighty numbers'.[102]

With the county firmly back in the hands of the settlers, steps were taken to escheat the Irish of their lands. This had become a commonplace procedure in Ireland since the Tudor era and was envisaged by the lords justices as early as December 1641 when, in a comment on the alleged defection of the Old English of the Pale, they advised the absentee lord lieutenant, Lord Lisle, that 'their discovering of themselves now will render advantage to his Majesty and this State....and those great countries of Leinster, Ulster and the Pale now lie the more open to his Majesty's free disposal and to a general settlement of peace and religion by introducing of English'.[103] Such a statement confirmed a suspicion long held by the remnant of the northern Irish that the crown administration in Ireland had a secret agenda for the further confiscation of their lands. Three months later parliament passed into law the Adventurers Act of March 1642 which provided for the allotment of forfeited lands in Ireland to such English as would 'adventure' money for the reduction of the rebellion in Ireland. In county Down the procedure for the issue of indictments for treason and outlawry against those alleged to have been implicated in the insurrection was initiated at Killyleagh in July 1642, where fifty Magennises were proclaimed outlaws.[104]

The outbreak of civil war in England in August 1642 severely reduced the resources available to both crown and parliament in support of their respective 'Irish factions' and with the establishment of the Roman Catholic Confederation at Kilkenny, whose first general assembly was held in October-November of that year, a new medium was provided to the king to pursue negotiations for a cessation of hostilities and secure support in his struggle against his parliamentarian rebels. The Confederation had affirmed its loyalty to the king and asserted that they were acting only in defence against his "Irish" enemies, the new Scots army in Ulster and their parliamentarian fellow-travellers in the Irish administration in Dublin. Against the wishes of the lords justices, negotiations were opened at the instance of the king who appointed the earl of Ormond as his emissary. A cessation was concluded in September 1643 which effectively recognised the *status quo*, the terms of which placed county Down within the 'English Quarters'. In the ensuing years as the resources available to all the warring factions dried up, a stalemate developed which lasted until January 1649, when a peace treaty was concluded between Ormond and the Confederation. During these years, Arthur Magennis Viscount Iveagh participated in the proceedings of the general assembly of the Confederation and was a member of its supreme council in 1644. In November of that year, under the terms of an arrangement made by the council, he commanded a regiment of foot to France for service under the queen regent. He subsequently returned and was a commander of a regiment of foot in Owen Roe's Ulster army during the latter's campaign in Connacht in the summer of 1647.[105]

The ending of the Scots ascendancy in Ulster was accomplished by Owen Roe O'Neill in June 1646 with his defeat of Munro's forces at the battle of Benburb. That defeat might also have changed the balance of power in Ireland in favour of the king and his Irish supporters but for the split in the Confederation brought about by the condemnation by the Papal Nuncio, Rinuccini, of the peace proposals made with Ormond in July 1646. By this time, however, a war weariness had set in and for many the prospect of a negotiated settlement was attractive, especially for those with landed estates who were anxious to avoid confiscation of their properties. While the peace of 1646 collapsed in the face of Rinuccini's denunciations, the will for a settlement remained strong and was made more urgent by Ormond's surrender to the parliamentarians in July 1647 and his replacement by Colonel Michael Jones.

Owen Roe O'Neill was a strong supporter of the papal nuncio and opposed the truce. However there were elements within his army, led by Sir Phelim O'Neill and including Arthur Magennis, Viscount Iveagh, who were in favour of it. Despite his involvement in the early phase of the insurrection, Magennis was a loyal supporter of the king. A contemporary judgement of him was that he was very young and, 'a member rather of the State of Dublin than any way confederate of the Irish' and 'as being in his minority, bred in the Court of Wards' in 1641.[106] Frustrated by O'Neill's obstinacy and the rigidity of his support for the nuncio and the clerical faction within the Confederation, three regimental commanders, Sir Phelim O'Neill, Arthur Magennis and Alexander McDonnell, decided in May 1648 to defect to the supreme council of the Confederation. While Sir Phelim's personal jealousy towards his kinsman probably explained his defection, the others, including Magennis, were motivated by fear of the loss of their landed interests in the event of a breakdown in the peace plan. It was a consideration which motivated many others in the Confederation, notably the Old English.

With the return of Ormond to Ireland as lord lieutenant in September 1648, events proceeded apace. Magennis who attended the general assembly in Kilkenny in October had been stationed with his regiment in the Kerry-Limerick area, but was subsequently moved to Wexford where his command was described in 1648 as an 'Ulster royalist regiment'. In September, on foot of a rumour that Colonel Michael Jones, the parliamentarian commander at Dublin was contemplating entering into a cessation with Owen Roe O'Neill, Magennis with others addressed a letter to Jones protesting against such a course, asserting that 'no true hearted Englishman or any of that extraction will join with such a party against us whose intention never swerved from maintaining and submitting to the English government'.[107] All the other signatories were Old English. In October, Magennis addressed a letter to Ormond assuring him of his loyalty and support. He was mentioned in the articles of peace of 1649, which revoked any outlawries charged against him since 1641 and granted a right of appeal to the king regarding any forfeitures or attainders suffered by him.[108]

With the execution of Charles I in January 1649 many of those who had formerly stayed on the sidelines or who had supported the parliamentarian faction came over to Ormond, This was particularly the case in county Down where, after secret negotiations involving in particular Colonel Mark Trevor of Rose Trevor, Munro's forces and the Ulster British under Lords Montgomery, Clandeboy and Conway all came over to Ormond – only Colonel Arthur Hill and Major George Rawdon stood aside.[109] Thereafter events quickened as the parliamentarian rump led by Colonel Jones in Dublin and Sir Charles Coote in Ulster (with whom Owen Roe O'Neill had entered into a compact) stood alone against royalist ascendancy over the entire country. However in August 1649 the parliamentarians defeated Ormond's forces at Rathmines from where they had been besieging Dublin and in the same month Oliver Cromwell landed at Ringsend. .

Following Cromwell's storming of Drogheda, a force was dispatched northwards under Colonel Venables, to take Dundalk and Carlingford. Dundalk had been deserted by its royalist garrison and after a brief encounter with Venables' Carlingford surrendered under articles allowing the garrison to retreat to Newry. Venables then advanced on Newry where the garrison also surrendered. Meanwhile, Colonel Mark Trevor with a party of about 500 horse had been deployed along the Monaghan-Louth border and advanced northwards into county Down, tracking the progress of Venables' troops as far as Dromore where they encamped for the night. Trevor decided to launch a dawn attack on the encampment which nearly succeeded but a last minute recovery by Venable's men repulsed the attack. Trevor withdrew first to the Bann and then into south Leinster. Venables resumed his progress northwards taking Lisnegarvey on 27 September, where a troop of horse formerly of Lord Conway's regiment under Major Brough joined him. Four days later he was in Belfast where a garrison of 800 men of Lord Montgomery's regiment on refusing to join Venables were disarmed and ejected from the town. Thereafter the war continued in Ulster with the upper hand gradually passing to Venables and his colleague, Sir Charles Coote. After the defeat of the Irish forces by Coote at Scarriffhollis in June 1650 and the surrender of Charlemount fort in August, organised resistance ceased, although Philip O'Reilly held Lough Oughter Castle until he delivered it up under articles to Colonel Theophilus Jones in April 1653.

Viscount Iveagh was not the only Magennis to have fought in the last stages of the war on the side of the king. Others included Conn Magennis of Culcavy and Art Magennis of Corgary while a number of Magennis names occur in the army muster rolls of the period.[110] Iveagh's regiment were part of the garrison defending Wexford when it was stormed by Cromwell's forces in October 1649: most of them escaped the subsequent massacre. The remnants of the regiment were still in south Leinster in March 1650. Although he was included in the articles of surrender of O'Farrell's Leinster army in May 1652, Magennis was one of those excepted from pardon for life or estate in the Act for the Settlement of Ireland of August 1652. Others listed in this Act were Lord Montgomery of the Ards, Sir James Montgomery, Rory McBrian Og Magennis, Donal Og Magennis, Ever Magennis of Castlewellan and Edward Boy Magennis. Lord Iveagh was still in the field in December when he was reported to have been with Lieut-General O'Farrell in county Cavan.[111] On 5 March 1653, Iveagh signed articles of agreement for his surrender at Balsturnoit [probably Belturbet] to commissary-general Reynolds providing him with '100 months asylum to stay in the nation and fifty to draw to getting those formerly under his command and such parties as shall join with him to make up a regiment and to transport into Spain.....'. It is likely that he was among the forces under O'Farrell and O'Reilly who transported themselves via the port of Drogheda to Spain later that year.[112] Sometime after this he enlisted in the duke of Gloucester's regiment of foot in Spanish Flanders where in 1660 he was reported as being the captain-lieutenant of the duke's company, i.e., acting captain in place of the duke who was also the regimental commander. His role was essentially that of a professional soldier. Even before his departure his estates in Iveagh along with other

Magennis properties there had been sequestered, the first step in the process of confiscation in what was to become known as the Cromwellian Settlement of Ireland.

Aftermath

With the exception of the Tollymore Magennises all the other landed Magennises, including those who were Protestants, suffered forfeiture under the English Commonwealth and four can be traced as having been transplanted to Connacht. These were Edmond McShane Magennis of Corrocks in the parish of Clonallan, Murtagh Magennis of Meenan in the parish of Aghaderrig, Brian Magennis of Clanconnell and Glassney Magennis of Shankill.[113] The seizure of the forfeited lands was carried out by a commission of the revenue established at Carrickfergus under the governor, Colonel Arthur Hill of Hillsborough, aided by another collaborator with the new regime, Major George Rawdon, Lord Conway's estate agent.[114] This commission was responsible for the subsequent plantation of the forfeited lands, those of Rathfriland and Castlewellan being divided among the adventurers. William Hawkins received over 21,000 acres plantation measure, Joseph Deane over 2,800 acres and William Barker over 3,800 acres.[115] The remainder of the forfeited lands was distributed amongst the ex-soldiers, principally those who had served with Lord Deputy Fleetwood and Captain John Barrett's troop of horse. Their assignees included George Rawdon, Captain John Magill of Gillhall, William Waring, Major Daniel Munro and Captain Leslie, none of whom had served in the Commonwealth forces. In 1650 Hill received a grant of £5,000 from the English Parliament 'in recompense for his many services in Ireland'. A further payment of £1,000 was made in 1656. In that year also Oliver Cromwell as Lord Protector of the Commonwealth made a grant of 3,000 acres in Kilwarlin in trust for Arthur Hill's younger son, Moyses, and erected the Hill estates in Kilwarlin to the status of the manor of Hillsborough and Growle.[116] It also seems likely that Arthur Hill enjoyed the beneficial interest of the lands comprised in the Rathfriland estate on which he held incumbrances amounting to 2,554 acres in this period. In like manner Anthony Dopping, who held Art Gallagh's wardship before the insurrection, continued to enjoy the beneficial interest of the Corgary estate, probably on the basis of the incumbrances which he held thereon.[117] After his death in 1655 his daughters sold these incumbrances to Captain John Gill for £675 and he sold them on to Captain Hans Hamilton of Hamilton's Bawn, county Armagh. Like Gill and Art Gallagh, Hamilton had served in Ormond's forces in the closing stages of the war but unlike Art, they did not suffer forfeiture.

The poll tax returns of 1659 reveal no Magennis name in Lower Iveagh where English and Scots families amounted to 1,352 compared with 1,381 Irish; in Upper Iveagh the balance was much more in favour of the Irish; 448 English and Scots families were listed compared with 2,149 Irish.[118] The surname Magennis is not given among the list of principal Irish surnames although the existence of such surnames as McBrien, Boy or McIlboy of which there were at least fifty in the two baronies, suggests that the surname Magennis was dropped in favour of the prefix. There were four titulado Magennises: Phillip [or Phelim]at Castlewellan; Bernard and Conn at Tollymore and Edmond McBrien at Donaghmore. A considerable dispersal of the Magennises as a result of the wars and the subsequent land confiscations is suggested by these figures. However, in the post-restoration period ex-soldiers who had served the king in Flanders or Magennises who had taken refuge elsewhere in Ireland came home to Iveagh. Some may have returned from Dublin where a sizeable colony of Magennises had been established.

The restoration of Charles II in 1660 created a diversity of expectations within the landed classes. The planters of the Commonwealth period, including their assignees amongst the earlier settlers or Old Protestants such as George Rawdon, expected the confirmation of the land titles procured by them from the former usurped power of the English Commonwealth. Earlier settlers who had remained loyal to the crown and suffered at the hands of the Commonwealth for so doing, such as Montgomery of the Ards and pretended sufferers, such as Mark Trevor and Hans Hamilton, had expectations of compensatory land grants for the sufferings they endured during the period of the usurped power; Roman Catholics and native Irish, such as Art Viscount Iveagh, Conn Boy of Culcavy and Phelim McEver of Castlewellan, who had served and suffered for the royalist cause, not less loyally than the Protestant settlers, sought the full recovery of their forfeited estates. In the event the Commonwealth Settlement was confirmed in Iveagh, on the basis of the political influences which the various protagonists could deploy in London as well as in Dublin. John Magennis, Protestant, leaseholder of the lands of Ballynefarney and Ballynary in Shankill, was restored but his fellow Protestant, Art Gallagh of Corgary was not.[119] Hans Hamilton, one of the principal trustees of the '49 officers security and hence an insider dealer of that security, taking advantage of a provision in the Acts of Settlement and Explanation which enabled encumbrancers on forfeited lands to purchase the freehold from the trustees, purchased Corgary. Subsequently on foot of a certificate from the court of claims established under the Acts he passed letters patent in respect of the lands in 1667.[120] Art Gallagh did not submit to this filching of his ancestral estate to which, 'as an innocent Protestant, under the same legislation, he was entitled to be restored and commenced legal proceedings in the court of chancery in 1670. He won his action but had to compensate Hamilton, probably for the loss of his encumbrances. Only in the case of Phelim McEver Magennis and his son, Ever of Castlewellan, was a Commonwealth grant overturned in favour of an Irish Roman Catholic. Claiming as an innocent person, Phelim won a decree of innocence under the Act of Settlement and although Hawkins and others bitterly opposed its implementation the issue was finally determined by the king in 1665 when he ordered the attorney-general to stay any further prosecutions in the matter.[121] The king was not as successful in the case of Arthur Magennis the third Viscount Iveagh. Despite every effort made on his behalf, his opponents Rawdon and Hawkins were able to deploy sufficient influence to prevent his restoration. Instead he was awarded a pension of £150, subsequently raised to £500 per annum, but this was irregularly paid and in arrears of £1,600 at the time of his death in 1684. He also received the restoration of his chief rents on the fee farms in Iveagh and a grant of an estate of 1,860 acres in Ballintober, county Roscommon.[122]

Secure at last in the estates acquired by them from the English Commonwealth administration and confirmed by the Restoration Land Settlement, the landed magnates began to lease sections of their estates to leaseholders for varying terms of years, and these in turn sub-leased to tenants whose rentals provided them with an income sufficient to become men of substance in their own right. Included among these leaseholders were many Magennises, Protestant as well as Catholic, who by virtue of their lineage regarded themselves as members of the gentry class. The principal of these were the Cabragh and Lurgancahone Magennises, descendants of the Cabragh and Islandmoyle family, who appear as leaseholders from Trevors of Rose Trevor of the lands of Cabragh and Lurgancahone in the post-restoration period.[123] They were related by marriage to the Hall family, one of whom Francis of Glassdrummond, county Armagh, purchased the lands of Narrow Water from Joseph Deane the Commonwealth/ Restoration grantee of the lands of the Rathfriland Magennises in that area in November 1670. The head of the family in the late seventeenth century was Art, the great-grandson of the original freeholder of Islandmoyle, who served as a captain in the Jacobite regiment of Viscount Iveagh in the Williamite wars and as an articleman under the treaty of Limerick reversed his outlawry and subsequently recovered his property in county Down. He was buried in Clonduff graveyard where his gravestone dated 1737 records him as 'Captain Arthur Magennis' and his wife as 'Catherine alias Hall'. The standing and importance of the Lurgancahone Magennises in the eighteenth century is testified by the fact that they had nominating rights to the Irish College in Paris of Roman Catholic students from the diocese of Dromore.

Another important family was the Emdell [or Imdell in Drumballyroney] and Glaskermore Magennises one of whom, Ross Magennis, obtained a sub-lease of lands in 1672 from Captain John Magill, a sub-leaseholder of William Hawkins of the Imdell and Glaskermore part of the former Rathfriland estates.[124] His request for the sub-lease was based upon his desire 'to live on the said lands as his father before him had done'. As these lands were held before 1641 by Daniel Magennis, who was one of the sons of Arthur Magennis the first Viscount Iveagh, it seems possible that Ross was of the Rathfriland Magennises. Ross subsequently leased the townlands of Lisnacroppan and Ballyooleymore from Sir John Trevor of Rose Trevor for twenty-one years at a rental of £36 rising to £40 after the first ten years. He died in 1701 leaving two sons, Arthur and Conn, and a daughter, Catherine, who married Michael Savage. Another prominent Magennis of this period was Murtagh of Greencastle who was a son of Art Gallagh of Corgary.[125] He was a merchant with extensive leasehold interests in counties Louth and Armagh where he had a lease of the earl of Castlehaven's estate in the barony of Orier. When he married Mary, daughter of Thomas Clarke of Dromantine, the dowry was £200. In return Murtagh demised to Clarke the townland of Ballybleagh which he obtained from his father in consideration of a considerable sum of money laid out by Murtagh 'in a suit of law depending between the latter [his father] and some other person'. He joined the Jacobites during the Williamite wars and was outlawed. Not having been an articleman under the treaty of Limerick, all his estates were subsequently forfeited. His son John is mentioned in the will of Arthur Magennis, the last of the Corgary and Castlewellan Magennises in 1753.

Two Protestant Magennis families in addition to those of Tollymore, Corgary and Shankill emerged in the post-restoration period. These were the Magennises of Backnamullagh in the parish of Dromore, and the Magennises of Dromore and Shanrod in the parish of Garvaghy and Maghermayo in the parish of Drumgooland.[126] The Backnamullagh branch had their origins in a Constantine Magennis who in March 1668 acquired the lands of Levallyvacke and Levallymoylagh in the parish of Dromore from the Reeves family. These had formed part of the Kilwarlin estates alienated to Edward Trevor by Brian Og Magennis shortly after the freeholding of Iveagh, who subsequently sold them to Reeves. Constantine has been identified as belonging to the Clanconnell branch through Art Og MacGlassney Magennis of Ballynagarrick. Before his acquisition of these lands he had been the proprietor of the Star Inn in Coventry in Britain and of the lands of Bushell's Commons in Royington in Warwickshire. He died in 1701 leaving three sons Richard, Charles and John. Charles the second son also had a son, Charles, who inherited the estate after Richard the eldest died in 1727. Charles sold the lands to Wills Hill, Viscount Hillsborough, in 1745 for £1,700. Daniel Magennises 'of Dromore' obtained a lease of Ballydrumman, Shanrod and Kilkinamurry from Mark Trevor, Viscount Dungannon in January 1694. He also held lands in fee farm from the see of Dromore as well as Maghermayo in Kilmegan, which he had obtained by way of a renewable lease from Phelim Magennis in 1693. These lands were still in the hands of Daniel's descendants in the 1750s.

Notwithstanding the general clearance of the Magennises from their ancestral lands in the period of the English Commonwealth, a substantial number survived to take the side of James II in the Williamite period and to figure in the outlawry lists of the time (appendix C).

The brief period of Jacobite ascendancy facilitated a last desperate attempt by the Magennises and others to recover lands lost in the Commonwealth-Restoration settlements; the support of the Corgary and Castlewellan Magennises for James II, however, was unconditional. They like many others, Protestant as well as Catholic, gave their support to James because of a sense of loyalty to the crown. Both Daniel of Corgary and Phelim of Castlewellan recovered their respective estates as articlemen under the treaty of Limerick but as Phelim's only son, Ever, was killed at the battle of Aughrim the Castlewellan estates passed to Daniel of Corgary. By the 1740s these estates were so encumbered by debt that they had to be sold by public auction; Corgary to Joseph Innes, a Belfast merchant, and Castlewellan to William Annesley of Dublin.[127]

It is clear that the brief period of Jacobite ascendancy was one of extensive sufferings and loss by the British settlers most of whom were expelled from their lands and had their properties expropriated. Upon the recovery of their ascendancy in the early eighteenth century they sought their revenge by seeking to cut back on the favourable provisions of the Treaty of Limerick and by means of the Popery Acts to reduce to subjection and impoverishment their erstwhile Roman Catholic opponents.

References

1. For the working of this commission see Terence O Ranger, 'Richard Boyle and the making of an Irish fortune' in *I.H.S.*, x (1957), pp 283-4.

2. For the full text of Chichester's policy see Constantia Maxwell *Irish history from contemporary sources 1509-1610* (London, 1923), pp 208-10.

3. For St Leger's policy of surrender and regrant see Brendan Bradshaw, *The Irish constitutional revolution of the sixteenth century* (Cambridge, 1979), pp 196-200.

4. For Irish land law see Fergus Kelly, *A guide to early Irish law* (Dublin, 1988), especially ch. 4.

5. The Magennises or McGuinnesses trace their descent from MacAonghusa Mor their eponymous ancestor who occurs in the regnal list of the Uí Eachach Cobha for the year 956; Aodh who occurs in the list for 1172 is described in the charter of the Cistercian Abbey of Newry c.1156 as Aodh the Great MacAonghusa, chief of Clann Aodh in Uí Eachach Uladh, B.M., Add. MSS 4792 f 155 r-v; for Magennis genealogies see T.C.D., MS H.4.25, H 4.31; see also M.A. O'Brien, *Corpus genealogiarum Hiberniae* (Dublin, 1962).

6. For the letter from Edward 11 to Admilis McAengus see Rymer, *Foedera, syllabus in English with index,* ed. T.P. Hardy, 3 vols (London, 1869-85), ii, p. 245.

7. T.E. McNeill, *Anglo-Norman Ulster* (Edinburgh, 1980), pp 118-27; Katharine Simms, The gaelic lordship of Ulster in the later middle ages, unpublished Ph.d. thesis, T.C.D. (1976).

8. The genealogies in T.C.D., MS H 4.25 and MS H. 4.31 which date to the seventeenth century indicate the relationships of the various Magennis families. I wish to thank Nollaig Ó Muraile, Q.U.B., for this reference. The Thrift MSS in N.A.I. include abstracts from exchequer, chancery and other official documents now lost concerning the various Magennis families of county Down.

9. Abbe MacGeoghegan, *History of Ireland, ancient and modern,* trans. Patrick O'Kelly (Dublin, 1844), ii, p. 528.

10. Bradshaw, *Constitutional reform,* p. 212.

11. *Cal. S.P. Ire., 1509-73,* p. 65.

12. Ibid., under 1549; the Pass can be identified from Lythe's map of Carlingford Lough, see Harold O'Sullivan, 'A 1575 rent-roll with contemporaneous maps of the Bagenal estates in the Carlingford lough district' in *Louth Arch. Soc. Jn.*, xxi (1984-88).

13. *Cal. S.P. Ire., 1509-73,* p. 120, the grant required Magennis 'to induce the people inhabiting within his rule to leave of their wild and savage rites and manner of living'; MacGeoghegan, *History,* iii, p. 61; *Cal. Carew MSS, 1578-88,* pp 241-2; *P.R.I. rep. D.K.,* 8, pp 127, 153; ibid., 9 Dublin, 18, pp 67-9; ibid., 11, p. 42.

14. *Cal. Carew MSS, 1515-74,* p. 332.

15. *Cal. S.P. Ire., 1574-84,* p. 435.

16. Ibid., 1574-84, pp 82-92; *Cal. Carew MSS, 1578-88,* p. 36.

17. *Cal. S.P. Ire., 1574-84,* pp 181, 185, 204, 246, 248.

18. *P.R.I. rep. D.K., 15,* app. 'Fiants Elizabeth 1583-4', p. 26.

19. Ibid., p. 88.

20. *Cal. S.P. Ire., 1584-6,* p. 523; for pardons see *P.R.I. rep. D.K., 16,* pp 67, 150-1.

21. *Cal. S.P. Ire., 1574-84,* p. 570; see also Victor Treadwell 'Sir John Perrot and the Irish parliament of 1585-6' in *R.I.A. Proc.,* C (1985), pp 259-308; *P.R.I. rep. D.K., 16,* p. 40.

22. *Cal. Carew MSS, 1575-88,* p. 437, Bagenal rather prematurely reported that 'in this place only of Ulster is the rude custom of tanistry put away'.

23. For Tyrone's drift into rebellion see Hiram Morgan, *Tyrone's rebellion* (Dublin,

1993); for the general situation in Ulster in the fifteenth and sixteenth centuries see Harold O'Sullivan, 'The March of south-east Ulster in the fifteenth and sixteenth centuries a period of change' in Raymond Gillespie and Harold O'Sullivan (ed.), *The borderlands* (Belfast, 1989), especially ch. 5.

24. *Cal. S.P. Ire., 1588-92*, p. 499; ibid., *1592-96*, pp 149, 229, 'Ever McRory Magennis murdered by the earl of Tyrone's son-in-law [Art Roe of Rathfriland]', pp 279, 358; *Cal. Carew MSS, 1589-1600*, p. 93. 'Ever McRory Magennis of Kilwarlin a man brought under the law and of good obedience to her majesty is now utterly expulsed out of his country'.

25. *A.F.M.*, 1595, 'Hugh Magennis the son of Hugh son of Donal Og, a man of his patrimony of the greatest name and renown among the English and Irish of Ireland died penitently'; *Cal. Carew MSS, 1589-1600*, 'Glassney McCawley Magennis pretending title by the tanist custom came to the stone whereon the Magennises were wont to receive their ceremony and hath called himself Magennis'; two inauguration sites existed for the Magennises, the first and probably the one mentioned in this reference was at Lis-ne Ree adjacent to Knockiveagh noted in Bartlett's map in G.A. Hayes McCoy, *Ulster and other Irish maps c.1600* (Dublin, 1965), p. 2; the second is the Cusleac Aonguis, the footstone of Aongus, north of Warrenpoint.

26. *Cal. S.P. Ire., 1592-96*, p. 257.

27. *Cal. Carew MSS, 1589-1600*, pp 181, 189; Catherine was O'Neill's fourth wife, for her subsequent career see Micheline Kerney-Walsh, *Destruction by peace, Hugh O'Neill after Kinsale* (Monaghan, 1986).

28. Fynes Moryson, *An history of Ireland, from the year 1599 to 1603: with a short narration of the state of the kingdom from the year 1169: to which is added a description of Ireland*, 2 vols (Dublin, 1735), i; *Cal. S.P. Ire., 1598-99*, p. 168; for Edmond Magennis see Kerney-Walsh, *Destruction by peace*, pp 126, 335-6.

29. For the battle of the Yellow Ford see G.A.Hayes-McCoy, *Irish battles* (London,1969), pp 106-32; *Cal S.P., 1589-99*, p. 318, 'Arthur Magennis with Redmond Burk in Cork'; *Cal. Carew MSS, 1589-1600*, 'Arthur Magennis with the earl of Tyrone and others with the Lord Lieutenant at Bellacluithe'.

30. Cyril Falls, *Mountjoy; Elizabethan general* (London,1955), ch. 10.

31. Moryson, *History*, i, pp 225-7.

32. *Cal. S.P. Ire., 1600*, pp 524-3; Moryson, *History*, i, pp 185-8.

33. Moryson, *History*, i, p. 253.

34. Idem.

35. *A.F.M.*, 1601.

36. His application is in S.P., 63/217/47.

37. *Cal. pat. rolls Jas. I*, p. 195.

38. *Cal. S.P. Ire., 1611-14*, p. 16.

39. For Edward Trevor and his family see Harold O'Sullivan, The Trevors of Rose Trevor a British colonial family in seventeenth century Ireland, unpublished M.Litt. thesis, T.C.D. (1985), especially chs 1-3.

40. *Cal. S.P. Ire., 1608-10*, p. 402, Sir Henry Dillon alleged that the 'many petty governors' were so desirous of enriching themselves that they oppressed the country.

41. For the colonial settlements in county Down see Raymond Gillespie, *Colonial Ulster* (Cork, 1985), and Donald F. Cregan, 'An Irish cavalier: Daniel O'Neill' in *Studia Hib.*, no. 3 (1963), pp 60-74.

42. One such was a James Wadell of Airdrie in Lanark who settled in Dromore in 1598. The family is still in possession of a sun-dial inscribed 'James Wadell

Dromore 1598; His son, Alexander Wadell, leased the lands of Islanderry and Ballykelly from Art Og McGlassney McAugholy Magennis in November 1628 which were confirmed to him in the Court of Claims, 1662.

43. *Cal. pat. rolls Ire., Jas. I*, p. 394. Arising from a dispute between Trevor and John Brownlow who also received lands in Kilmore (which had been incorporated into the Ulster Plantation although in Iveagh), Chicester ruled that the lands were in the barony of Orier in county Armagh and should go to Brownlow, Trevor being reprised with lands elsewhere, see T.W. Moody (ed.), 'Ulster Plantation papers' in *Anal. Hib.*, no. 8, p. 266; *Cal. S.P. Ire., 1608-10*, p. 217.

44. An erenagh was the hereditary steward of church lands who was obliged to maintain the church property to which the erenagh lands were assigned.

45. *Cal. pat. rolls Ire., Jas. I*, pp 190-1, 394-6.

46. *Acts privy council, 1613-14*, p. 540; ibid., 1615-16, pp 78, 549; R.D. Edwards (ed.), 'Letters to archbishop of Canterbury' in *Anal. Hib.*, no. 8, pp 33-4.

47. The other landowners, mainly in Down and Connor, were Lord Montgomery, Hamilton Lord Clandeboy, Arthur Hill, William Fullerton, Archibald Edmonson, Bernard Ward, William Wardlowe, James Hamilton, Robert Meriman and James Moore., P.R.O.N.I., D 671/D8/1/37a.

48. N.A.I., Ferguson MSS, ix, F. 82.

49. For Trevor's involvement in the freeholding of Iveagh see O'Sullivan, Trevors of Rose Trevor, ch. 2; for Sexton see *Cal. pat. rolls Ire., Jas. I*, p. 86 and *Inq. Ult.*, County Down, Car. 1, no. 30.

50. O'Sullivan, Trevors of Rose Trevor, app. ch. 2.

51. For Sexton see *Inq. Ult.*, County Down, Car. 1, no. 30; for Whitchurch see N.A.I., Thrift MSS. no. 26 and *Inq. Ult.*, Car. 1, nos 39 and 62.

52. For Fortescue see N.A.I., Thrift MSS. no.75 and *Inq. Ult.*, County Down, Car. 1, no. 34; For Trevor and others see *Inq. Ult.*, County Down, Car. 1 nos 65, 93 and 96.

53. P.R.O.N.I., Daniel O'Brien's copy of the parish maps of the Down Survey for Lower Iveagh c.1657 – 'there are no considerable buildings in the whole barony, only at Dromore, it being a market town, the inhabitants thereof have repaired two or three stone houses and builded up many thatched houses but little or no other buildings saving Creaghs; the chiefest inhabitants whereof are Scots who by reason of the nearness of their country to these parts are grown very prosperous in this barony.'

54. For the evolution of the system in England in the later middle ages see Maurice Keen, *English society in the later middle ages, 1384-1500* (London, 1990), part 2, pp 160-86.

55. Gillespie, *Colonial Ulster*, pp 137-42; O'Sullivan, Trevors of Rose Trevor, pp 46-8.

56. For a pedigree of the Kilwarlin Magennises see N.A.I., Thrift MSS., pedigree no. 5309; *Inq. Ult.*, County Down, Car. 1, nos 31, 46, 22, 23, 24, 25, 29.

57. Ibid., no. 60.

58. Ibid., nos 59 & 67.

59. P.R.O.N.I., Downshire MSS., Rent Roll, May 1638, D.671/D.8/1/67A; Rent-Roll 1659, D.67/D8/1/87 see also Decree Court of Claims May 1667, D.671/D8/1/97.

60. P.R.O.N.I., DOD 765/6 funeral entry Ulster Office, Dublin Castle; *Cal. S.P. Ire., 1608-10*, pp 241, 244, 249; N.A.I., Thrift MSS, no. 256.

61. In 1611 the Plantation Commissioners reported that Trevor had all the materials ready for the building of a castle at Kilbroney, referred to in the Perambulation of Iveagh as Rosetrevor, P.R.O.N.I., T.811/3, 'Record of the Plantation Commission 1611', transcript from Pinkerton MSS., Lambeth Library, 630 F.144; *Cal. pat. rolls Jas. I*, pp 304-5, 373.

62. N.A.I., Thrift MSS., Chancery proceedings no. 917/116, *Inq. Ult.*, Car. 1, no. 51.
63. *Inq. Ult.*, Car. 1, no. 34.
64. O'Sullivan, Trevors of Rose Trevor, app. ch. 2.
65. See Clanconnell Magennis pedigrees in T.C.D., MS.H.4.25, F/266 no. 145a; N.A.I., Thrift MSS, Pedigree no. 5302; P.R.O.N.I., D.695/134.
66. These identifications are derived from N.A.I., Thrift MSS, no. 6, exchequer bill, 9 Jan., 1687/8.
67. For a pedigree for the Castlewellan Magennises see T.C.D., MS.H.4.25 F.2601 and N.A.I., Thrift MSS, Pedigree no. 5305.
68. Pender, *Census Ire. 1649*, pp 76-7.
69. For a reference to the origins of the Tollymore Magennises as 'Muinntir ghleanna Eideadha' 'Munterreddie' see T.C.D., MS.H.4.25 F 261d; the Aidith or O'Hattys were the ruling family of the Uí Eachach Cobha before the Magennises.
70. Bernard served as a cornet in a royalist horse regiment and was recognised as a '49 Officer in the restoration period, John O'Hart, *The Irish and Anglo-Irish landed gentry* (reprint, Shannon, 1969), p. 396.
71. For a pedigree of the Corgary Magennises see N.A.I., Thrift MSS, Pedigree no. 5305; G. McGahan, Dromantine, a typescript history of Dromantine by the Society of African Missions, copy in P.R.O.N.I., T.1514.
72. *Inq. Ult.*, no. 213, 'premises demised for 99 years to Antony Dopping, Arthur Magennis son and heir six years of age'.
73. For a pedigree of Rathfriland Magennises i.e., Clann Aodha see T.C.D., MS.H.4.25 F.260; see also N.A.I., Thrift MSS., Pedigrees nos., 5303, 5310 and 5311; for a nanuscript history and detailed pedigree see N.L.I., Guinness Papers, also William V. McGuinness Jr., *Our ancestors and relatives. The McGuinness family,* (Privately circulated U.S.A., 1994)
74. Calculated from the survey side of the county Down Books of Survey and Distribution, N.A.I., Quit Rent Office copy.
75. C. Ní Dhomhnaill, *Duanaireacht (Dublin 1975)*, pp 108-10; C. Ó Lochlainn, *Éigse* 2/3 (1940), pp 157-62; O. Bergin in D. Greene and F. Kelly (ed.)., *Irish bardic poetry* (Dublin, 1970), pp 120-23 with translation pp 266-88; A. Harrison, *An chrosantacht* (Dublin, 1979), pp 43-4.
76. These estimations are based upon the information given in the BSD regarding the estates held by each of these individuals in 1641 and then comparing the townland names in each case with the townland names given in the grant under freeholding of Iveagh and the several inquisitions of the Rathfriland estate contained in *Inq. Ult.*, notably Car.1 no.13.
77. *Acts of the privy council, 1613-14*, p. 308 and ibid., 1615-16, pp 157, 181 & 490.
78. H.F. McGegge (ed.), *Register of admissions to the Middle Temple* (London, 1949), p. 490.
79. P.R.O.N.I., T.588.
80. Letter from 'Hugh Iveagh' to Wentworth dated January 1634/5 referring to his 'not perfect health, that I can hardly travel abroad', Sheffield City Libraries, Strafford papers, p. 14 (283).
81. *Inq. Ult.*, Car. 1, no. 85.
82. Jane H. Ohlmeyer, *Civil war and restoration in the three Stuart kingdoms* (Cambridge, 1993), p. 54.
83. *Cal. pat. rolls Ire., Jas. I*, p. 397, see also Gillespie, *Colonial Ulster*, pp 145-6.
84. E.D. Atkinson, *Dromore: an Ulster diocese* (Dundalk, 1925), p. 36.
85. For this period see Gillespie *Colonial Ulster*, chs. 5-7; Ohlmeyer *Civil war*, ch. 3; Hugh Kearney, *Strafford in Ireland, 1633-41: a study in absolutism*

(Manchester,1959), chs. 6, 7, 8; M. Perceval Maxwell *The outbreak of the Irish rebellion of 1641* (Dublin, 1994), ch. 2; ibid., 'Ulster 1641 in the context of political developments in the three kingdoms' in Brian MacCuarta (ed.), *Ulster 1641: aspects of the rising* (Belfast, 1993), ch. 5.

86. George Hill, *An historical account of the MacDonnells of Antrim* (Belfast, 1873, reprint. Ballycastle, 1978), pp 219, 252-8; Ohlmeyer, *Civil war*, ch. 3.

87. N.A.I., Carte transcripts, a list of the army for Ormond, 23 April 1640.

88. *Civil Survey*, x, p. 66.

89. Lord Ernest Hamilton, *The Irish rebellion of 1641* (London, 1920), ch. 7.

90. William Montgomery, *The Montgomery manuscripts*, ed. G. Hill (Belfast, 1869), pp 127-139, 193-195; T.C.D., MS 837, Deposition book county Down, no. 8, Robert Kynaston of Saul dated 9 May 1642.

91. T.C.D., MS 837, Deposition no. 9

92. Hamilton, *Irish rebellion*, pp 161-7, 180-2.

93. Ibid., p. 182; for a recent assessment of the killings in county Armagh see Hilary Simms, 'Violence in county Armagh 1641' in MacCuarta, *Ulster, 1641.*

94. Hamilton, *Irish rebellion*, pp 208-10.

95. T.C.D., MS 837, Deposition no. 86 by Lieutenant Thomas Trevor regarding the murder of his father Hugh Trevor who lived at Lisnegead. He (Hugh) had been brought prisoner to Newry thence carried to Carlingford, thence to Lecale to be exchanged—'hearing that the said prisoners belonging to the Irish party were hanged by the English at Lecale aforesaid, bringing the prisoners back again when they were murdered'.

96. For Conn's remorse see T.C.D., MS 837, Depositions nos 9, 89, and 117; for the hanging of O'Rowney see deposition no. 186.

97. Hamilton, *Irish rebellion*, pp 163-7; *Cal. S.P. Ire., 1633-47*, pp 767, 769.

98. David Stevenson, *Scottish covenanters and Irish confederates* (Belfast, 1981), pp 103-5.

99. Gilbert, *Ir. Confed.*, pp 256-7.

100. T.C.D., MS 837, Deposition no. 8 Robert Kynaston, no. 186b Danile Magennis Glascoe; Stevenson, *Scottish covenanters*, pp 105-6.

101. Newriensis (J. F. Small), *An historical sketch of Newry* (Newry, 1876), pp 135-6; Stevenson, *Scottish covenanters*, p. 106.

102. Stevenson, *Scottish covenanters*, pp 108-9.

103. Dunlop, *Commonwealth* (Manchester, 1919), i, pp cxx-cxxi.

104. See app. B. in this chapter, from list in P.R.O.N.I.; also N.A.I, Thrift MSS, no. 431.

105. Gilbert, *Ir. Confed.*, iii, pp 173, 208, vi, pp 212, 283, v, pp 66, 283; Jerold I. Casway, *Owen Roe O'Neill and the struggle for Catholic Ireland* (Philadelphia, 1984), p. 185.

106. Gilbert, *Contemp. hist., 1641-52*, i, pp 34, 195-6; Thomas L.Coonan, *The Irish Catholic confederacy and the Puritan revolution* (Dublin, 1954), pp 290-1.

107. Gilbert, *Contemp.Hist.*, i, pp 242, 275, ii, pp 752, 759.

108. Gilbert, *Ir. Confed.*, vii, p. 196.

109. See O'Sullivan, Trevor of Rose Trevor, pp 125-43.

110. *Cal. S.P. Ire., 1663-65*, petition of Conn Magennis of Culcavy, 7 Dec. 1663; J. O'Laverty, *A historical account of the diocese of Down and Connor*, 5 vols (1878-1895), ii, p. lxv.

111. Gilbert, *Contemp. hist.*, pp 95, 242, 373.

112. P.R.O.N.I., Genealogical research report dated 1954 by Ms C.V. Wedgewood commissioned by Jeanette M. Magenis, 35-36, Bell Boulevard, Bayside, Long Island, New York.

113. R.C. Simington, *The transplantation to Connacht* (Dublin, 1970), p. 246.

114. For the Commonwealth regime in Ulster see Kevin McKenney, The landed interests, political ideology and military campaigns of the north-west Ulster settlers and their Lagan army in Ireland 1641-85, Unpublished Ph.d. thesis, State University of New York at Stoney Brook (1994), ch. 6; Laverty, *Down and Connor*, ii, p. 243.

115. B S D, County Down.

116. W.A. Maguire, *The Downshire estates in Ireland, 1801-45* (Oxford,1972), pp 4-5; G. Benn, *A history of the town of Belfast* (Belfast, 1877), p. 679.

117. P.R.O.N.I., T.1514 and N.A.I., Thrift MSS, no. 131.

118. Pender, *Census Ire.*, pp 76-7.

119. Armagh Public Library, List of claims of innocence, no. 173, John Magennis.

120. The '49 officers security was a trust established under the Acts of Settlement and Explanation, 1662-65 to provide funds to compensate Protestant army officers, who remained loyal to the king, for their arrears of pay; see Kevin McKenney, 'Charles II's Irish cavaliers. The 1649 officers and the restoration land settlement' in *I.H.S.*, xxviii (1993), pp 409-25.

121. Armagh Public Library, List of claims of innocence, no. 414; *P.R.I. rep. D.K., 19*, p. 262; *Cal. S.P. Ire., addenda 1660-62*, pp 523; ibid., 1663-5, pp 361-2, 714.

122. *Cal. S.P. Ire., 1660-2*, pp 55, 255-6, 677; ibid., 1663-5, p 500, 'On the late peace made with the marquis of Ormond in Ireland, he was by orders put into possession of all his estate in that country'; N.A.I., Carte transcripts, xxxv, p. 139.

123. N.A.I., Thrift MSS, Pedigree nos 42, 67, 69, 149, 155, 5306; Laverty, *Down and Connor*, ii, pp 145, 150.

124. N.A.I., Thrift MSS, nos 145, 150.

125. Ibid., Chancery bill, 9 Aug. 1708 and nos 133, 137; Bagwell, *Stuarts*, iii, pp 160-2; T.C.D., MS 744 F.98, Details of land forfeited in Orior, 4332 acres valued at £541.

126. For Backnamullagh see N.A.I., Thrift MSS, Pedigree nos 61, 63; for Dromore see N.L.I., Guinness papers and N.A.I., Thrift MSS, nos 27, 56, 62.

127. McGahan, Dromantine; N.A.I., Thrift MSS, nos 65, 68.

Appendix A
The freeholding of Iveagh in 1608[1]

(1) Rathfriland lands in Upper and Lower Iveagh.
Sir Arthur Magennis of Rathfriland to have twenty-five [named] townlands in Narrowwater, sixty-three [named] townlands in Rathfriland, four half towns in Kallydromad [containing in all twenty-three named townlands] and the sessiagh of Clonloghan. Tullyomy containing eight towns [consisting of twenty-three named townlands].
Estimated acreage: Profitable ... 27,538.2.20; Unprofitable ... 17,814.2.16

(2) Kilwarlin, Crumlin, Magheralin, Annahilt, Blaris, Dromore and Dromora parishes.
Brian Og McRory Magennis all the country or territory of Kilwarlin except Tullyorney [consisting of fifty-five townlands including Ballyedenwarrow i.e. Edenticarrow].
Profitable ... 25,219; Unprofitable ... 3,220

(3) Castlewellan in Drumgooland and Kilmegan parishes.
Ever McPhelimy Magennis the castle and lands of Castlewilliam; Castlewellan, Ballyneclarchill, Ballynagenaghie, Ballynegreghan, Ballyletrom, Ballymagherienegee,[*2] Ballybacknadroman, Ballybenrae, Ballynabooly and Ballylegananagh.
Profitable ... 6,778.3.32; Unprofitable ... none

(4) Clanconnell in Tullyish and Donacloney parishes.
Glassney McAugholy Magennis, the lordship of Clanconnell, Ballykeile in the Lequirin containing fourteen towns.
Profitable ... 4,008.1.22; Unprofitable ... 1,339.2.05

(5) Magheralin parish.
Art Og McGlassney McAugholy Magennis, to have the chief four towns in the Lequirin; Ballylissneseer, Ballinelurganvickenawly, Ballendromentiogery and Ballinderry.
Profitable ... 807.0.0; Unprofitable ... none

(6) Shankill in Aghaderg, Seapatrick and Annaclone parishes.
Ever McArt McRory Magennis to have Shanchall containing twelve towns; Ballyshanchall, Ballycrevie,* Derudmuke, Ballyneskeagh, Ballynecrosse, Ballinafoy, Ballynefarin, Ballaghanaghtymacart,* Ballydromore,* Killcappie, Ballyclerhie and Ballytullyconnogh.*
Profitable ... 3,676.3.08; Unprofitable ... none

(7) Loughbrickland in Aghaderg parish.
Art Og McBrien Og McBrien McEdmond Boy Magennis to have the castle and town of Brickland and nine towns more; Ballybrickland, Drominaeer, Keskein, Clonchaencharm, Ballyvalee, Tullyerch, Drominbekawly, Ballyndown, Ballylisnerery and Ballyivee.
Profitable ... 1,250.0.0; Unprofitable ... 70.0.0

(8) Corrocks in Drumgath and Clonallan parishes.
John Magennis is to have Corrock and Aghnemvillragh and six towns and a half in Clawnawly; Ballymoneycuggely, Croan, Ballencabragh, Quillin, Lurganconnaght, Ballykeehill and Ballycharmen.
Profitable ... 1,411.0.0; Unprofitable ... 30.0.0

(9) Milltown in Clonallan, Kilbroney and Drumgath parishes.
Hugh McConn McGlassney Magennis to have the town of Milton and eight towns in Clanawly; Milton, Aghenegowan, Ballymoysh, Ballycarriccressan, Ballynbawen, Balleagholee, Edentromley and Ballydowlaine.
Profitable ... 3,290.0.0; Unprofitable ... none

(10) Tollymore in Kilcoo and Maghera parishes.
Brian McHugh McAugholy Magennis to have seven and a half towns in Munterreddie; Ballytullydranegan, Ballederrymyne, Ballohavire, Ballaghacullyn, Ballyneburnareogh, Waffney alias Tofeny and Ballytullymore.
Profitable ... 500.0.0; Unprofitable ... 100.0.0

(11) Corgary in Donaghmore parish.
Murtagh McEnaspicke Magennis to have ten towns in Clanaggan; Corrgirrie, Baleenlalogh, Balleknocknenarie, Ballcarrickrovade, Ballylurrganmore, Ballydromiller, Ballyderrycragh, Ballyblagh, Ballydronintigham and Ballylissraniteirne.
Profitable ... 1,776.3.06; Unprofitable none

(12) Dromnevaddy in Magherally and Seapatrick parishes.
Con Boy McPhellim McHugh Magennis to have eight towns in Ballynecross; Dromenevoddie, Ballyagonygan,* Ballynecrosse, Tawnaghmore, Ballyrallyarnoge, Muneleightgarire, Ballydromengally and Ballykeele.
Profitable ... 1,330.0.0; Unprofitable ... 70.0.0

(13) Islandmoyle and Cabragh in Clonduff and Kilcoo parishes.
Rory Og McRory McCollo McHugh Magennis to have Islandmoyle and five towns thereunto belonging; Ballyislandmoyle, Ballecabragh, Ballyleghtallan, Ballyekewkill and Ballynegappock.
Profitable ... 470.0.0; Unprofitable ... 110.0.0

1. The details of the lands granted in the freeholding are taken from *Cal. pat. rolls Ire., Jas. I,* pp 394-6. The estimated acreages are derived from the county Down volume of the Books of Survey and Distribution in N.A.I. In order to identify townlands and other denominations in 1608 freeholding, use was made of the extant Down Survey barony and parish maps which are in P.R.O.N.I. The acreages arrived at must be regarded as estimates: all of the denominations listed in 1608 have not been identified and as the Protestant unforfeited lands were not mapped by the Down Survey we have to rely on Civil Survey returns incorporated in the Books of Survey and Distribution. These lands are consequently underestimated. Unfortunately the Civil Survey for county Down has not survived.
2. Denominations marked * have not been identified.

Appendix B
Magennises alleged to have been involved in the Insurrection of 1641

Name	Address	Family/Parish
Arthur Magennis	late servant to Val Payne	Dundrum
Sir Conn Magennis	Newcastle	Rathfriland
Con Magennis	Dromaliske	Dromgooland
Hugh son of Conn Magennis		
Arthur Magennis Viscount Iveagh		Rathfriland
Donal Oge Magennis	Glaskermore	Rathfriland
Rory Magennis	Loughan	Rathfriland
Arthur Roe Magennis	Gargary	Rathfriland
Ever Magennis	Castlewellan	Castlewellan
Edmond Magennis	Corrocks	Corrocks
Hugh McRoss Magennis	Aghnemulragh	Corrocks
Donal Magennis	Gragulagh	Clanconnell
Ferdorough McArt Magennis		Clanconnell
Art Oge McBrian Magennis	Keska	
Fergus Magennis	Grenan	Greenan
Con Boy Magennis	Cullycavy	Kilwarlin
Edmond McDonal Oge Magennis		Clanconnell
Donal Magennis	Linan	Clanconnell
Phelim Magennis	Ballybanan Kilmeagan	
Arthur Roe Magennis	Gargary Drumgooland	
Ferdorough Magennis	Clonevaghan	Clonvaraghan
Brian McEver Magennis	Shankill	Shankill
Irriall Magennis	Lisraterny (Lisnatierny?)	Corgary
Connell Magennis	Lisraterny	Corgary
Art McBrian Oge Magennis	Liscan	Kilwarlin
Rory Magennis	Edenticulloe	Kilwarlin
Con Boy Magennis	Culcavy	Kilwarlin
Ferdorough Magennis	Linan	Clanconnell
Murtagh Magennis Yeoman	Ballyculter	Balluculter
EdmondBoy McGlassney Magennis	Ballynegarrick	Clanconnell
Hugh Magennis	Ballynegarrick	Clanconnell
Hugh Magennis	Edengreeny	Clanconnell
Phelim Magennis	Loughan	Rathfriland

Hugh Magennis	Aghanalecke	
Phelim McArt Oge Magennis	Ballynegarrick	Clanconnell
Ferdorough McArt Oge Magennis	Ballynegarrick	Clanconnell
Brian Crossagh McArt Oge Magennis	Ballynegarrick	Clanconnell
Ferdorough McManus Magennis	Linan	Clanconnell
Hugh Magennis	Linan	Clanconnell
Donal Magennis	Clone (Cloghe)	Kilwarlin
Brian McEdmond Boy Magennis	Clare	Clanconnell
Phelim Magennis	Edenordry	Clanconnell
Hugh McDonal Oge Magennis	Gragulagh	Clanconnell
Donal Oge McDonal Oge Boy Magennis	Gragulagh	Clanconnell
Hugh Magennis	Grenan	Greenan
Felim McGlassney Magennis	Clanconnell	Clanconnell
Murtagh McGlassney Magennis	Clanconnell	Clanconnell
Glassney Oge Magennis	Clanconnell	Clanconnell
Con Modder Magennis	Tullycorne	Clanconnell

1. Source: N.A.I., Thrift MSS, no. 431.

Appendix C
Magennises outlawed as Jacobites[1]

Murtogh Magennis, Greencastle, Brian Magennis Viscount Iveagh, Edmond Og Magennis, Ballynagarrick [Clanconnell], Art Roe Magennis, Ballynagarrick [Clanconnell], Edmond Magennis, Tullylish, Conn Battagh Magennis, Tullylish, Brian Magennis, Ballydogan parish of Tullylish, Art Roe Magennis, Brughes, county Armagh, Daniel Magennis, Shean, county Armagh, Patrick Modder Magennis, Iveagh, Brian Roe Magennis, Derrycorrisse, Roger Magennis, Newry, Art McFelim Magennis, Castlewellan, Art McEdmond Og Magennis McArt Gallagh, Corgary, Hugh Magennis, Cabragh, Brian Magennis, Ballygorian, John Magennis, Ballyharry, Ross Magennis, Emdell (a), Art Magennis, Emdell, Brian Magennis, Emdell, John Magennis, Loghlans, parish of Tullylish, Hugh Magennis, Loghlans, parish of Tullylish, Brian Magennis, Clonduff, Augholy Magennis, Gortnery [Clanconnell], Glassney Magennis, Newry, Brian Magennis McFerdoragh, Ballydowbane (Ballydulany) parish of Clonallan, Art Magennis, Ballynarry, Conn Magennis of Carrickrovaddy, parish of Donaghmore outlawed overseas, Bernard Magennis of Lisnafligan, outlawed overseas, Colonel Daniel Magennis of Donaghmore Corgary (a), Captain Phelim Magennis, Castlewellan (a), Captain Art Magennis, Cabragh (a).

(a) These subsequently reversed their outlawries and continued to hold their lands into the eighteenth century.

1. Source: T.C.D., MS 744.

Chapter 9

LAND OWNERSHIP AND IMPROVEMENT
ca. 1700-1845

LINDSAY PROUDFOOT

'History', so the aphorism goes, 'is written by the winners'. If ever a group can be said to have been among 'the losers' in Irish history, it must surely have been the landed aristocracy and gentry. In the space of barely two hundred years, from *ca.* 1700 to *ca.* 1900, they moved from exclusive ownership of virtually all productive land in the country, with all the attendant social and political authority this conferred, to a situation where they were economically disinherited, politically disenfranchised and socially disempowered. The process was complex and regionally uneven, and owed at least as much to the modernisation of Ireland's economy as it did to the democratisation of Irish politics and the rise of sectarian nationalism. Yet the end result, the virtual extirpation of the traditional landed class as a significant driving force in Irish society, has frequently been represented as a triumph for the 'Irish people', conceived in exclusively Catholic and Gaelic terms.[1]

The widespread currency of what may be termed this conventional nationalist view, owes much to the origins of the modern landed aristocracy and gentry in Ireland, and to the ways in which they are perceived to have exercised their undoubted authority there. The sixteenth- and seventeenth-century Plantations and land confiscations recreated the landowning class over much of Ireland. Existing Catholic Gaelic Irish and Old English landed families of medieval or earlier origin, who had been linked to their dependants by complex ties of social obligation, were largely replaced by a class of English and Scots adventurers and entrepreneurs, who were the beneficiaries of the active land market created in Ireland by the English Government's interventionism.[2] Separated by language, religion and ethnicity from the mass of Ireland's population, these new – arguably colonial – landowners appear to have brought with them more commercial, and in the context of the times, socially-disruptive attitudes to property and economic exploitation generally.[3] In place of the earlier frequently kin-based dependencies, new financially-based relationships evolved which linked different economic classes on the basis of their different access to wealth in a new geography of production and consumption.

Central to these new geographies were the patterns of conspicuous consumption indulged in by the landowning elite. And it is here that we find a possible second reason for the traditional hostility accorded to Irish landlords in the popular historical imagination. Just as they are widely perceived to have been alien in their origins and thus 'not Irish' – at least in the narrow sense that underpinned nineteenth-century Irish nationalism, so too their patterns of behaviour have been conceived of as being exploitive, parasitical and detrimental to the interests of the Irish people.[4] This argument has an impressive pedigree, and goes back at least as far as late eighteenth-century comment on the size of the annual rent roll exported from Ireland to England for use by absentee Irish landlords.[5] Indeed, this is an aspect of the argument which is hard to gainsay: significant sums of money – over £700,000 a year by the late 1770s – were remitted to England in the form of rents, and this money was consequently unavailable for productive investment in Ireland. How it would have been used had it remained in circulation in the domestic Irish economy is a matter for speculation. What is clear, is that the patterns of conspicuous consumption indulged in by the Irish aristocracy and gentry – the construction of demesnes and country houses, and the pursuit of lavish lifestyles – were in no sense peculiar to them nor evidence of their uniquely exploitive attitudes. Rather, this was entirely normative behaviour indulged in by similar *ancien regime* landed elites throughout eighteenth-century Europe.[6]

It is hard, therefore, to see these patterns of consumption as evidence of a peculiarly exploitive attitude on the part of the Irish aristocracy and gentry towards their tenantry. Equally, recent research has suggested that many of the charges of rack renting, mass eviction and other attempts at coercion conventionally laid at the door of Irish landlords demand substantial qualification. While individual landlords may have operated in this fashion in particular places at particular times, there is evidence to indicate that many more pursued tenurial policies designed to preserve the tenants' interests in their leaseholds – if only because in this way the landlord's own property rights were best served.[7]

There is thus a growing recognition of the diversity of the landed experience in the eighteenth and nineteenth centuries, and of the considerable variation this expanding and far from homogenous group displayed in their wealth, social station and political beliefs. These issues have been explored at a general level elsewhere.[8] This chapter examines the geography of aristocratic and gentry consumption in county Down during the eighteenth and early nineteenth centuries, and attempts to assess in the light of this the landowner's role in facilitating economic modernisation and improvement in the county. The period, roughly from the end of the Williamite land settlements *ca.* 1700 to the eve of the Great Famine *ca.* 1845, is deliberately chosen to reflect some of the most radical social and economic changes which occurred in east Ulster as part of this modernisation. Pre-eminent among these were the growth of rural and latterly, urban textile industries, as well as urbanisation *per se* and population growth. It was these processes and their interaction with the inherited geography of property, place and environment that constituted the material world within which individual landowners pursued their aspirations and sought to ensure their own economic, social and political reproduction. The discussion begins, however, with a resumé of the evidence for the identity of the county's landowning class as it evolved during the period under consideration here.

Origins and identity

As elsewhere in Ulster, the origins of by far the greater proportion of the landowning families in eighteenth- and nineteenth-century Down lay in the land settlements of the sixteenth and seventeenth centuries. The processes these involved and the social and economic characteristics of the landowning class they produced by the mid-seventeenth century are well known and have been detailed elsewhere.[9] It is nevertheless worth emphasising that their initial impact on county Down was highly localised. Both the muster rolls of *ca.* 1630 and the 'census' of 1659 make it clear that British settlement had been concentrated on the fertile lowland soils of the northern half of the county, in an arc which stretched from the lower Lagan valley in the west to the upper Ards peninsula in the east. In 1659, over 70 per cent of the recorded population in these districts bore British surnames. To the south, the percentage of British surnames fell away from around 50 to 60 per cent in Lecale and the Dundrum Bay area, to less than 10 per cent in Mourne and the Dromara Hills. Within this overall pattern there was further differentiation between English and Scots surnames. The former were concentrated in Lecale and the South Ards – where many were of Old English derivation – and in the Lagan valley, while the latter were located along the western shore of Strangford Lough, on the northern Ards peninsula and along the shores of Belfast Lough.[10]

These patterns are likely to have reflected the differential success of the earliest attempts at estate consolidation, mirrored, for example, in the ability of two Scotsmen from Ayrshire, Hugh Montgomery and James Hamilton, to establish viable plantations in Upper Clandeboye. This had previously been the territory of the Gaelic Irish Clandeboye

O'Neills, and had been partly and temporarily settled under Sir Thomas Smith's unsuccessful colonisation scheme of 1572-1573. The acquisition by Montgomery and Hamilton of much of Upper Clandeboye in the period after James I's accession in 1603 was entirely representative of the strategic, political and economic forces then at work promoting land transfers in east Ulster. The occasion was the detention of Con McNeill O'Neill, lord of Upper Clandeboye, after a *fraças* by some of his followers. Seizing his opportunity, Hugh Montgomery offered to obtain a pardon for O'Neill in return for half of his lands in Upper Clandeboye. Montgomery's designs nearly succeeded, but were frustrated at the last moment by James Hamilton, who used his influence to persuade the king that such a single grant was too large for one man. In consequence, in 1605, a new patent was made out, granting one-third each of the Clandeboye O'Neill lands to Con O'Neill, Montgomery and Hamilton.[11]

Two hundred years later, the echo of this sort of ethnic clustering was still observable in the pattern of land ownership. By the 1830s, and despite the social change and economic modernisation of the inter-vening period, a marked cluster of major agricultural estates was still discernible in the hands of families of Scottish origin in the north-east of the county, where it contrasted with the greater frequency elsewhere of estates held by families of English descent.[12] While these ethnic impacts are interesting for their longevity, their importance by the mid-nineteenth century should not be over-stressed. Of more significance were the variations in the levels of wealth enjoyed by individual families, and the relative importance of their county Down possessions within their overall patrimony. A family whose land was concentrated within the county was more likely to play a locally-significant social role than one whose estates were more widely scattered or lay predominantly elsewhere.

Some insight into these issues is provided by the Primary valuation of tenements, commonly known as the Griffith's valuation. This was completed for the county in 1864, and lists the size, composition and rateable value of every property, together with the identity of the owner and occupying tenant(s). This information can be used to identify the county's landowners, and these, defined as people possessing land held either in fee simple, perpetuity or for more than ninety-nine years, are usefully summarised in the *Return of Landowners in Ireland* of 1876.[13] These sources provide us with a 'snapshot' of the structure of land-ownership in county Down at the end of our period. While it does not inform us about the processes of social and economic change which had been continuously modifying this pattern over the preceding two hundred years, it does give us an idea of their consequences.

TABLE 9.1

Landowners in county Down ca. 1864 by acreage

Acreage	Number of Landowners
< 1 acre	1,460
1 < 100	1,715
101 < 500	263
501 < 1,000	65
1,001 < 2,500	37
2,501 < 5,000	23
5,001 < 7,500	8
7,501 < 10,000	4
10,001 < 12,500	3
> 12,501	7
Total	3,585

Table 9.1 lists the total number of landowners as defined in the *Return*, classified according to the amount of land they held in statute acres. Given the breadth of the definition of landownership in the *Return*, the vast majority of the smaller 'landowners' it lists are more likely to have been tenants rather than fee simple owners in their own right. For this reason, the subsequent discussion concentrates on the 147 owners with properties of over 500 acres, although it also considers those of between one to 500 acres for purposes of comparison. Most of these estates were predominantly or exclusively agricultural, but some, for example the Londonderry and Downshire estates, included important urban property: Newtownards and Comber in the case of the first, and Banbridge, Dromara, Hillsborough, Hilltown and Loughbrickland in the second. Many estates in county Down also contained significant numbers of small-scale industrial enterprises – usually associated with linen or other forms of agrarian production. Not all estates were compact affairs, occupying contiguous blocks of land. Even the largest and best-run were frequently divided up into numerous small blocks of land of townland size or less. These differences reflected both the particular history of acquisition which attached to each estate, and the fact that invariably they were created using much older land divisions – townlands or *ballyboes*. At the heart of most – but not all – estates was what Jones-Hughes has described as the 'estate core', usually comprising the owner's country house and the surrounding demesne. The latter normally consisted of the amenity parkland around the house, together with any farmland retained by the owner for his own use.[14]

As defined by the *Return*, the landowning class amounted to just under 1.2 per cent of county Down's 1861 population of 299,302, a proportion which was virtually identical to that in Ireland as a whole.[15] If we omit those 'landowners' holding less than an acre, the proportion of landlords falls to less than three-quarters of one per cent of the county's population. By any standards, therefore, the landed class, whether in county Down or in Ireland at large, was of little significance numerically, but this of course was not where their historical importance lay. Rather, this arose precisely because of the gross disproportionately between their numbers and the economic, social and political influence they wielded through their near-exclusive ownership of land. Thus in county Down, the owners of the 147 largest estates held just over half a million acres between them, or 83 per cent of the county's 610,000 acres. All of the remainder save for 2,000 acres of common land was held by the remaining 3,438 minor landowners.

This inner elite of barely one hundred and fifty families – the equivalent of a respectably-sized church congregation – effectively 'owned' county Down, and for this reason their wealth and identity warrant close inspection. They represented the apex of what was, self-evidently, a steeply pyramidal pattern of local landownership, and again, this was entirely in line with the situation elsewhere in Ireland. Within this inner elite there were also pronounced differences in wealth and rank. At its head were six families who each owned over 18,000 acres, with a poor law valuation ranging from just over £13,000 to more than £62,000 (table 9.2). By far and away the most locally significant figure in this group was the marquis of Downshire, whose 64,356 acres in county Down represented approximately half his Irish lands, valued *in toto* at over £94,000.[16] Even he, however, was eclipsed by the marquis of Londonderry, who owned Newtownards and Comber, as well as extensive industrial and mining interests in county Durham. The latter raised the value of his entire patrimony to over £100,000, and alone produced a working profit of over £60,000 a year by the 1850s.[17] The other estates in this locally-magnate group shared some of the characteristics of the Downshire and Londonderry properties. The Kilmorey and Annesley estates also formed part of larger patrimonies with extensive holdings elsewhere in Britain and Ireland, but were more predominantly rural and, in county Down, contained much higher proportions of marginal land. This was reflected in their average acreable valuations in the county. These ranged from £0.36 per acre for the Kilmorey estate to £0.80 for the Annesley property, compared to £1.46 for the Londonderry estate. The Forde property at Seaforde was similarly circumstanced, and returned an average acreable valuation of £0.77.

These differences in the compositon of the largest estates were mirrored in properties of the second rank. In 1864, sixteen estates are

TABLE 9.2

Landowners with county Down estates of over 5,000 acres ca. 1864, together with their other property

Name	Domicile	Co. Down area	Co. Down Value £	Total area+	Total Value £+
Marquis of Downshire	Hillsborough	73,802	73,378	120,189	94,000
Kilmorey Estate (Trustees)	Surrey	37,545	13,708	52,412	34,000
Earl of Annesley	Castlewellan	23,567	18,886	51,060	29,539
Marquis of Londonderry	Mount Stewart	23,554	34,484	50,323	100,118
Col. W.B. Forde	Seaforde	19,882	15,404	–*	–
Earl of Dufferin	Bangor	18,238	21,043	–	–
Hon. R. Meade (Trustees)	Dromore	13,492	13,719	–	–
Robt.N. Batt	Purdysburn	12,010	6,535	–	–
Lord A.E. Trevor	Denbighshire	10,940	9,142	23,694	17,700
David S. Ker	Montalto	10,688	9,555	–	–
Viscount Bangor	Castleward	9,861	13,156	9,864	13,243
Alfred S. Ker	Ballynahinch	9,856	12,641	–	–
Earl of Roden	Tollymore	8,903	3,264	14,596	13,077
Robt. Perceval-Maxwell	Finnebrogue	8,347	8,801	12,428	12,132
J. Price	Saintfield	6,807	7,641	–	–
J. Mulholland	Ballywalter	6,769	10,668	–	–
Sir Thos. Bateson	Belvoir	6,348	9,330	–	–
John Sharman-Crawford	Crawfordsburn	5,748	5,943	5,749	5,990
Robt. E. Ward	Bangor Castle	5,735	8,517	–	–
Church Temp. Comms.**	Dublin	5,354	6501		
John Blakiston Houston	Belfast	5,233	6,562	7,224	8,509
Alex. Stewart	Donegal	5,002	6,520	44,308	15,655

+ Includes Co. Down acreages and values;
* denotes no land held elsewhere;
** Church Temporalities Commissioners.

recorded as being between 5,000 and 13,000 acres, and of these, eight were wholly located in the county, while two more, the Sharman-Crawford and Viscount Bangor properties, had only negligible land elsewhere. Once again, therefore, we see the same contrast between locally-situated landed interests, such as those of David Ker at Montalto (just outside Ballynahinch), or John Mulholland at Ballywalter on the Ards peninsula, and others which, being regionally diverse, offered their owners the additional security of access to a wider range of economies. Thus the Perceval-Maxwell estate, centred in county Down at Groomsport, also included 3,000 acres in counties Cork and Tipperary, while the earl of Roden enjoyed, in addition to his local lands, 4,000 acres in county Louth and 1,500 in Hertfordshire and Essex. This was perhaps particularly fortunate for the earl. His county

Down estate, located around Tollymore to the west of the Mourne Mountains, included some of the least productive land in the county, and was valued – on average – at less than £0.37 an acre.

Most of the 147 estates in the over 500 acres category were nowhere near as large or as highly rated as the leading properties described here. Nearly half (44 per cent) were less than 1,000 acres, while precisely two-thirds were less than 2,000 acres, with correspondingly lower poor law valuations. These ranged from £2,633 for William Wallace's 1,600 acres at Ballydavy, and £2,173 for Mrs Catherine Hamilton's 1,000 acres at Killyleagh, to a remarkably low £86 for the 670 acres held by Major James Baillie at Ringdufferin. Despite anomalies like these, there is evidence to suggest that the underlying relationship between estate size and value – itself derived from the continuing agrarian nature of the county's economy – remained intact across the entire range of estates throughout our period. A series of statistical tests was used to determine the strength of the relationship between estate acreage and poor law valuation, and these produced correlation coefficients of between +0.73 and +0.89. These were all well within the range of statistical significance at the 99 per cent confidence level, and indicate that in county Down, the poor law valuation rose in line with the increase in estate acreage.[18] It seems reasonable to conclude that in the end, the urbanisation and industrial growth which had been encouraged by many county Down landlords throughout the eighteenth and early nineteenth centuries proved insufficient to distort the inherited patterns of relative landed agrarian wealth. A tentative conclusion might be that, rather, they acted to reinforce them.

The diversity in the size and wealth of these 147 'elite' estates was mirrored by similar variation in the ethnic origins and social characteristics of their owners. Overall, these reflected the overwhelmingly colonial origins of Early Modern landownership in the county, but even so approximately one-quarter of the estates were in the hands of families of Gaelic Irish or Old English descent by *ca.* 1864. These properties were on average less than half the size of the estates owned by descendants of the Anglo-Scots planters, albeit with less variation in size around their respective mean (table 9.3). Thus, only two of the twenty-two estates of over 5,000 acres were in 'Gaelic Irish' ownership, and neither of these – the Mulholland and Meade properties – were among the very largest. These differentials are intriguing but we must caution against inferring too much from them. We cannot, for example, immediately assume that they indicate a continuous thread of Catholic land ownership throughout the Plantation period and the Penal years that followed. In the first place, some of the families concerned may have converted to Anglicanism –

at least three of these landowners' names occur in the *Convert rolls* for the 1760s.[19] Secondly, even if some of them were Catholic in the 1860s, they may simply have re-entered the land market in the early nineteenth century as a result of the then-current processes of economic modernisation and social and political democratisation. What we may infer is that in the mid-nineteenth century, the larger landed properties in the county tended to be owned by families of English or Scottish descent, irrespective of whether they saw themselves as Anglo-Irish, Irish or British.

TABLE 9.3

The ethnic origins and social status of county Down landowners with estates of over 500 acres ca. 1864

	Ethnic origins	
	Total	Percentage of 147
Gaelic Irish/ Old English	34	23.8%
English/Scots	113	76.8%
	Mean estate size (acres)	Standard deviation
Gaelic Irish/ Old English	1,739	2,390
English/Scots	3,846	7,828
	Social status	
	Total	Percentage of 147
Aristocrats/ Baronets	25	17.0%
	Mean estate size (acres)	Standard deviation
Aristocrats/ Baronets	12,511	15,559
Gentry	2,015	2,600

The evidence for the variation in the social rank of the county's landowners is more straightforward. The number of titled landowners in the county was relatively small: only twenty-five, or just 17 per cent of the inner elite were aristocrats or baronets. But what they lacked in numbers, they made up for in terms of the extent of their landed acres. Eighteen of the twenty-five owned estates of more than 500 acres, and these included five of the six largest properties in the county (table 9.2). Between them, these titled owners held over 238,000 acres, or just under 40 per cent of the county. Accordingly, their estates were of considerably larger average size than those held by the remainder of the 'inner elite' (table 9.3).

The geography of landlord consumption

Given the wide range of wealth available even within the upper echelons of landed society in county Down, it was inevitable that the importance of individual landowners as agents of social, economic and environmental change was going to be equally varied. Moreover, the mere possession of wealth did not in itself guarantee that a landlord would interest himself in any of these things. Unencumbered wealth simply provided the opportunity to engage in these sorts of activity. Whether the landlord actually did so depended on his own perceptual world – his values and beliefs, and how these influenced his own role in the material world around him. So-called 'improving landlords' have been characterised by historians as being particularly willing to invest in economically productive agricultural, urban or industrial developments, either on their own or in co-operation with their tenants. The evidence for this in county Down is explored below, but it should be noted that there is considerable debate over the extent to which Irish landlords as a whole engaged in such improvement.[20] Arguably, a more characteristic reflection of their attitudes may have been the construction of the numerous demesnes and country houses already alluded to, which are still closely associated with Irish landlordism in the popular imagination.

In contrast to the various forms of productive improvement, however, this demesne and country house construction can at best be said to have had only limited economic benefits or, at least, no particular economic *disbenefits*. The first edition of the six inch Ordnance survey map of Ireland identifies over 10,000 individually named country houses, but many of these were no more than large farmhouses or rectories, lacking the appurtenances of true landed status.[21] A more accurate picture of the real extent of large-scale country house construction may be provided by Bence-Jones' estimate that between 1660 and 1900, some 2,000 major country houses were built in Ireland.[22] This certainly accords well with the 2,500 or so country houses identified from the Ordnance survey maps as standing in demesnes of at least 50 acres (20 hectares [ha.]).

Demesnes

Figure 9.1 shows the distribution of the 134 demesnes identified in county Down on basis of the first edition of the six inch Ordnance survey map, surveyed for the county in 1833. These identify the

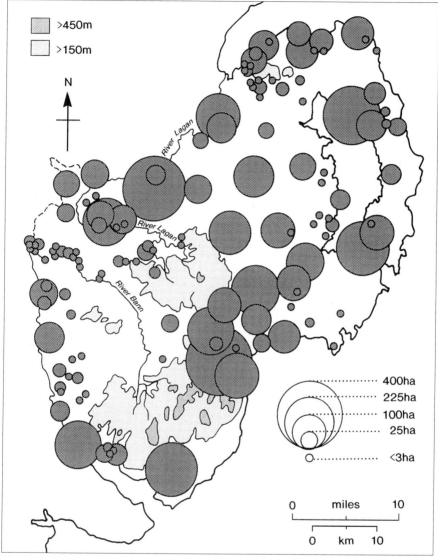

Fig. 9.1   Distribution of demesnes depicted in the first edition six inch Ordnance survey map, *ca.* 1833.

location of the 'estate cores' of the majority of the 'elite' properties of more than 500 acres. The varied size of these demesnes reflected the pyramidal size distribution of the parent estates.[23] They ranged from 0.8 acres (0.33 ha.) at Ballywhite House near Portaferry, to 975 acres (395 ha.) at the earl of Clanbrassil's park at Tollymore on the northern edge of the Mournes, with the largest demesnes clustering around the edge of the Mournes and on the shores of Strangford Lough. While these demesnes obviously involved the alienation of land for the private – predominantly non-commercial – use of the landlord, this represented a less significant form of resource depletion than might be supposed. The total amount of land devoted to the 134 demesnes identified here was approximately 14,800 acres (6,000 ha.), roughly 0.4 per cent of the total area of the county. This was a negligible loss, particularly given the agriculturally marginal nature of the land absorbed by some of the larger demesnes around the Mourne Mountains, such as Tollymore and Mourne Park, and the existence of subsidiary agricultural and forestry enterprises on others.[24]

Mention of these secondary economic functions raises the question of the purpose of these demesnes, and here we have to consider the social and symbolic meanings which attached not only to their design, but also to that of the country houses built upon them. Both underwent pronounced changes during the course of the eighteenth and nineteenth centuries, and it is easy, but probably misleading, to dismiss these simply as a response to the vagaries of fashion. By the 1830s, and in common with most demesnes in the rest of Ireland, virtually all of the parkland in county Down had been laid out according to the aesthetic principles of the late eighteenth-century 'Romantic' movement. This landscape aesthetic had its origins in seventeenth-century French and Italian schools of landscape painting, and particularly in the work of Nicholas Poussin (1594-1665) and Salvator Rosa (1615-1673). In essence, it sought to create 'picturesque' land-scapes, which in their combination of wood, hill and water, embel-lished with 'decayed' artificial ruins and follies, gave expression to human feelings of awe at the sublimity of nature.

This form of landscape design became particularly popular in eighteenth-century England, where it was associated with 'Capability' Brown and Humphrey Repton. Although neither of these designers is thought to have worked in Ireland, their influence certainly extended there. In both countries, these naturalistic designs relied on the same repertoire of features: sinuous shelter belts of trees around the park boundary, copse planting, and man-made lakes, 'rivers' and hills. As in other parts of Ireland, considerable use was made of the natural variety in county Down's topography to achieve the desired effects with minimal effort. Thus at Castleward, the late eighteenth-century parkland incorporates a vista of Strangford Lough and its islands, suitably embellished with the remains of an earlier tower house and a purpose-built neo-Classical summer house (plate 9.1). At Tollymore, the foothills of the Mourne Mountains provide a suitable background for the vistas from the earl of Clanbrassil (later earl of Roden's) demesne, itself massively planted between 1777 and 1789 with over 300,000 trees.[25] At

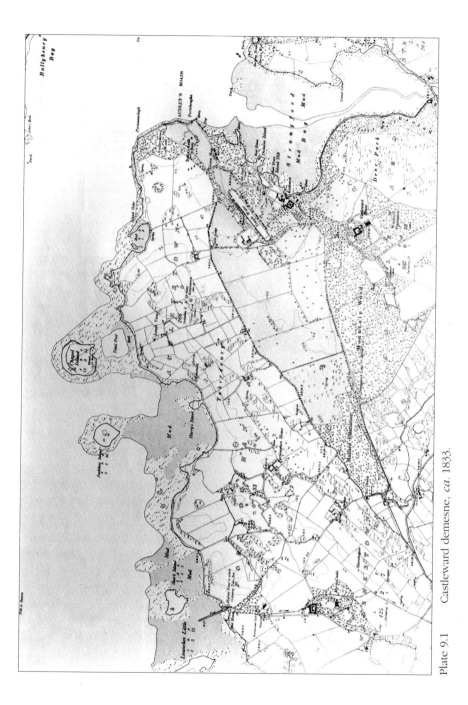

Plate 9.1   Castleward demesne, *ca.* 1833.

Castlewellan, the Annesley's original eighteenth-century 'cottage' (now demolished) fronted onto the existing lake and was sheltered by the wooded Slievenalat Mountain behind.

At Hillsborough, on the other hand, similar effects were created by more extensive manipulation of the landscape. Between 1742 and 1800, the Hill family spent over £34,000 on urban and rural improvements, including £4,830 on improving the gardens and park. Although representing less than one per cent of the family's total expenditure of £493,092 during this period, thé money funded a major transformation of the demesne. This included the construction of the wall around the enlarged park between 1770 and 1780 (£1,285), and the extension of the lake between 1787 and 1792 (£250). Recurrent minor expenses included the cost of carriage of seeds and trees from Dublin and Scotland, and the Head Gardener's wages. At £26 a year these were larger than the bailiff's salaries on the subsidiary estates.[26]

But as in England, so too in Ireland these later eighteenth-century picturesque designs replaced – and in many cases obliterated – an earlier tradition of more formal Baroque landscape planning which had reputedly originated in seventeenth-century France in the work of André Le Nôtre at Versailles. Such was the appeal of the later naturalism that hardly any complete examples of the earlier formal style survive in Ireland. One rare exception is Kilruddery, county Wicklow, where the parterres, radial beech walks and formal canals provide some insight into the type of parklands which were once more widespread in the early eighteenth century. In county Down, a few traces of this early formalism remain, half submerged beneath the flowing vistas and plantings of the later eighteenth century. At Castleward, the Temple Water – a formal canal – is all that remains of the earlier design (plate 9.2), while at Moira Castle and Gill Hall, avenues of typically geometric Baroque design survived among more naturalistic – and presumably later – planting until at least the 1830s.

Country houses

These demesne parks were thus evolutionary features in the county Down landscape, and it is in the symbolism inherent in their changing form that we must seek their deepest social and cultural meaning. The same is also true of the country houses, but in their case, the diversity of styles was greater and the age of the buildings much younger than was the case with the demesnes. Thus relatively few seventeenth-century country houses survive in Ireland, perhaps predictably enough, given the violence and uncertainty of that century and the growing wealth of the landed class in the one that followed. In county Down, the only important seventeenth-century houses to survive to the

Plate 9.2   Temple water, Castleward demesne. An early 'formal' canal incorporated within the later 'naturalistic' parkland.

present day are Finnebrogue, Downpatrick, built for the Maxwell family; Gill Hall, Dromore, recently ruined but built *ca.* 1670-80 and enlarged to designs of Richard Cassels fifty years later; and Waringstown House, built *ca.* 1667 for William Waring.

During the eighteenth century, Irish country house design was transformed as landowners used their growing wealth to build or reconstruct their houses using styles adapted from ancient Greek and Roman architecture. This revival of interest in Classical antiquity was itself part of the eighteenth-century 'Enlightenment', that period in European, and particularly English, French and Scottish thought, characterised by its humanism, intellectual enquiry and sense of civic responsibility.[27] Earlier eighteenth-century Irish houses, particularly of the grander sort, tended to be built in a rather subdued version of the so-called 'Palladian' style, named after the sixteenth-century Italian architect, Andrea Palladio (1508-80), but first brought to prominence in seventeenth-century England by Inigo Jones (1573-1652). The introduction of Palladianism into Ireland is conventionally dated to the 1720s and the Dublin architect, Sir Edward Lovet Pearce (1699-1733) and his disciple, the German architect Richard Cassels (1690-1751). Their work, however, tended to eschew some of the characteristic features of English Palladianism, for example giant porticoes and

217

Plate 9.3   Castleward, Neo-Classical west façade, built 1760-3 by Bernard Ward.

pilastered pediments, in favour of more subtle combinations of minor elements – Venetian windows, pedimented doors and so forth – and above all, the 'winged' ground plan. In this, the main house was attached to minor service blocks by straight or curving colonnaded wings, as at Russborough, county Wicklow, or Castletown, county Kilkenny.[28]

No major Palladian mansions survive in county Down, and few even display evidence of Palladian influence. Two which do are Castleward, built in 1760-3 by Bernard Ward (afterwards 1st Viscount Bangor), and Florida Manor, Ballygowan, originally home to the Crawford family. Castleward is renowned for its combination of styles: Classicism on the west front and Strawberry Hill Gothick on the east, reputedly the result of a stylistic argument between Bernard Ward and his heiress wife. The west façade (plate 9.3) has a pedimented breakfront, which rises to the full height of the house, supported on the upper two storeys by four giant engaged Ionic columns, and is one of relatively few Irish examples of this typically English Palladian feature. Although heavily restored, Florida Manor retains evidence of the typically Irish Palladian plan of a central block attached, in this case, by curving pilastered sweeps to lower wings.

The majority of eighteenth-century houses in county Down were less grandiose than Castleward, and were originally built in the plainer neo-Classical style of the later part of the century. Many, however, were subsequently altered during the nineteenth century, as the wealth generated by Belfast's growth permeated rural society and created a new class of rural-based urban capitalists. Examples of unaltered late eighteenth-century houses are thus relatively few, and include the now ruinous Bishop's Palace at Dromore, built *ca.* 1781 for the Hon. William Beresford, then Anglican Bishop of Dromore, and Strangford House, built *ca.* 1789 for the Norris family. In contrast, nineteenth-century building styles were much more varied, and included late-Georgian houses such as the marquis of Londonderry's Mount Stewart (1823-5) and the Forde family's Seaforde (1816-20), Italianate *palazzios* such as the Mulholland's Ballywalter (1846), Tudor-Revival houses such as Bangor Castle (1847) and the Gordon's Delamont, and Scots-Baronial mansions such as the 4th earl of Annesley's Castlewellan (1856-8). Many of these houses either incorporated or replaced existing eighteenth-century structures. Ballywhite House, Downpatrick, for example, was embellished in the Italianate manner *ca.* 1870 for a local solicitor, but had originally been a plain mid-eighteenth century Georgian block. Similarly, Burrenwood, Castlewellan, an elaborate *cottage orneé,* was built *ca.* 1820 by General Robert Meade, but incorporated an earlier cottage built by his mother, Theodosia Hawkins-Magill, countess of Clanwilliam.[29]

Symbolism and social meaning

The question remains, however, of what social and cultural meaning attached to this 'country house mania' in county Down and elsewhere. One conventional view is that these houses are best interpreted as a form of status-assertion by the landed elite, designed to demonstrate their social authority and economic power within Irish society. Thus the high demesne walls and imposing ornamental gates and lodges which demarcated demesnes such as Seaforde, Hillsborough or Clandeboye from the less exalted and distinctly less comfortable worlds of the peasant and tenant farmer beyond, have been represented as symbolising the social distance and apparent conflicts of interest which are assumed to have separated these different social groups. On one side of the demesne wall, carefully contrived rides and plantations and fantasy grottoes provided a sequestered idyll for the favoured elite; on the other, the vast majority of Ireland's population sought to secure their existence in face of the harsh realities imposed by a peasant agriculture struggling to feed a rapidly expanding population.

Although the polarities between landlord and tenant interests have been argued to have been less complete than this view might propose, it is hard to ignore the fact that these demesnes and country houses constituted an exclusive social arena for an elite whose wealth was derived from the productive efforts of a massively more numerous dependent tenant class.[30]

Recently, however, Foster has argued that these houses and their demesnes represented an attempt by the landed elite to create for itself a specifically *Irish* identity, which would legitimise their presence in Ireland in the eyes of the majority of its people. The argument asserts that the colonial origins of the landed elite, together with the continuing external and internal political and sectarian threats they faced, created an atavistic sense of insecurity among them, which they needed to assuage in a material form which would encode the permanency of their position in Ireland. Thus their actions were informed throughout by 'a subconscious recognition of the political and social insecurity of their position ...... (they) built in order to convince themselves not only that they had arrived, but that they would remain'.[31]

The key to this analysis lies in the importance of the country houses and demesnes as symbols of the landowners' ability to modify social, economic, cultural and physical space and to alter the social relationships which operated within these. As items of conspicuous expenditure, country houses symbolised the landowners' ability, as a class of consumers, to determine their patterns of consumption according to their own interests. As newly built features in the landscape, these houses and demesnes bore witness to the landlords' ability to reconstruct Ireland's geography – even if only on a local scale – in accordance with their own – perhaps idiosyncratic – values and aspirations.[32] Finally, as centres of local employment and consumption, these estate cores might be expected to have reinforced existing ties of dependency and clientship which linked landlords to subordinate groups.[33]

For all these reasons, it is reasonable to argue that the widespread country house and park building in county Down and elsewhere should have underscored the centrality of the landowners' role, and thus legitimised it, if only on the grounds of pragmatism, in the eyes of their social and economic dependants. Arguably, however, as an attempt to legitimise the elite's position in Ireland, this 'building mania' failed. Its social meaning and architectural expression were both so completely internalised within the landed elite's own cultural milieu in Ireland, and so thoroughly referenced in the Enlightenment generally, that they failed to engage other communal identities to any significant extent. For the vast majority of Ireland's population, the language of Palladianism or Neo-Classicism, or of the various nineteenth-century Baronial, Tudor or Elizabethan styles signified little. Thus even relatively modest Georgian houses such as Ballydugan at Portaferry or Rademon near Crossgar, let alone mansions such as Castleward or Castlewellan, demanded a familiarity with cultural repertoires which were socially exclusive and the preserve of the leisured classes. As text, they would have been instantly recognised by the county Down landowners' peers elsewhere in Britain and Europe; the cottiers and tenants beyond their park gates are likely to have viewed them with incomprehension.

The context for consumption: landlords and economic improvement

Yet it was this tenantry who created much of the wealth used to build these houses and demesnes. And in county Down as elsewhere, the efficiency of this wealth creation depended in part on the landlords' attitudes towards their property and the extent to which they were prepared to invest in economic improvements or encourage their tenants to do so. Once again, this was a question of both landlord intent and opportunity. By no means all the county's landlords were avid improvers, and those that were faced varying opportunities for improvement which reflected their own and their tenants' circumstances within the county at large. Thus county Down's colonial history, the nature and extent of its natural resources, its proximity to Belfast and the growing industries of the Lagan valley, and the consequences of its rapid population growth in the decades before the Great Famine, all bore on the pattern and extent of landlord involvement in productive improvement.

The county's landlords were involved in three main areas of economic activity: agriculture, linen production, and the creation and enhancement of urban markets. The chronology and extent of their involvement in each varied. Generally speaking, it is fair to assert that whereas the survival of lengthy leases and zealously guarded customary tenant rights limited landlord participation in agricultural improvement until at least the late eighteenth century, 'improving' landlords by contrast played a significant role in promoting linen production in county Down from at least the 1740s. Paradoxically, of course, in so doing they helped create the conditions in which a rising class of proto-industrial capitalists – the linen drapers – could flourish and ultimately usurp the landowners' role as the main promoters of change in the industry.[34] Similarly, much of the landlord's involvement in urban and village improvement dated from the mid-eighteenth century and was designed, among other things, to facilitate the marketing of linen.[35]

Agriculture

As in other Irish regions during the period under review, much of the onus for agricultural improvement in county Down lay with the tenant rather than the landlord. A primary cause of this appears to have been the nature of the tenurial bargains struck during the seventeenth-century land settlements. The uncertain economic and political conditions of that time encouraged landlords to offer long leases at low rents in order to attract adequate tenants onto their estates.[36] The *quid pro quo* was that the tenants were responsible for all forms of capital improvement on their farms – including enclosure. Typically, leasehold agreements might require the tenant to reclaim a specified area of land each year, build a farmhouse and out-offices to a specified standard and fence the entire farm.[37] Arguably, this created a tradition of relative tenurial independence, in which tenant farmers came to see themselves as having established their own distinct property rights in their farms by virtue of their own or their forebears' efforts in creating these.[38] In this moral economy we may conceivably see the origins of the nineteenth-century 'Ulster Custom' or 'tenant right', which gave a departing tenant the right to charge his successor a sum for his 'interest' in the farm he was vacating. The precise nature of this interest was unclear, even to contemporaries. It was generally held to include the unexpired value of any capital improvements the tenant had previously made, plus any difference between the rent he had been charged and the property's current market value. Whatever the political agendas which were attached to these 'three fs' – fair rent, fixity of tenure and free sale – in the later nineteenth century, and whatever their real effect in promoting tenant improvement in Ulster or elsewhere, they reflected a tenurial tradition in which the landlords' involvement in agricultural wealth creation had been minimal.[39]

Thus for much of the eighteenth and early nineteenth centuries, the limits of most landlords' involvement in agricultural improvement lay in their own demesnes and home farms. Here, particularly as the fashion for agrarian modernisation spread among more enlightened landowners during the later eighteenth century,[40] new breeds of cattle and sheep were introduced, new crops sown and new systems of husbandry and land management tried out. At Hillsborough, for example, the earl of Hillsborough (later 1st marquis of Downshire), spent over £656 between 1780 and 1793 on the purchase of new cattle for 'grazing the demesne', together with a further £243 on draining and ditching and over £52 for seed.[41] Other examples of similar expenditure included the new farm buildings built on the Annesley demesne at Castlewellan in the 1760s and on the Forde demesne at Seaforde after 1807, and the new breeds of sheep introduced at Castlewellan and onto the Nugent estate at Portaferry in 1826.[42] The latter reflected the growing contemporary enthusiasm among local gentry for this type of improvement, leading Lewis to conclude in 1837 that:

the anxiety of the principle resident landowners to improve every branch of agriculture having led them to select their stock of cattle at great expense, the most celebrated English breeds are imported and the advantages are already widely diffusing themselves.[43]

As the nineteenth century progressed, these endeavours increasingly came to be supplemented by the intervention of growing numbers of landlords in the structure and organisation of their tenants' farms, in response to what Bardon summarises as the seemingly endless conflict between population pressure and productivity.[44] The growth in demand for land from domestic linen weavers in the later eighteenth century and the increasing profitability of arable agriculture prior to the agricultural price collapse of 1815, encouraged landlords to shorten leases, raise rents and divide existing farms.[45] This further encouraged the growth of population which was already facilitated by the increasing demand for labour from the expanding arable sector and the ready availability of a cost-effective means of supporting this in the form of a potato and milk diet.

In marginal areas such as the Mourne Mountains and the Dromara Hills, the result was the expansion of cultivation onto progressively less fertile upland soils and, under the influence of local traditions of partible inheritance, the spread of partnership or rundale farming and nucleated clachan settlement. The origins of this form of farming are obscure, but it is reasonably clear that in the immediate pre-Famine period in areas such as county Down, it had evolved into an infield-outfield form of commonfield agriculture. Within this, groups of frequently kin-related tenants were jointly responsible for the tenancy of a farm and worked this on a co-operative basis. The land held in partnership was divided into individual holdings and it was these, particularly on the permanently cultivated arable, which became subject to excessive subdivision as population pressure grew.[46]

By the second quarter of the nineteenth century, the problems posed by such extreme subdivision were becoming increasingly apparent. According to one witness to the Devon Commission, it lessened the value of the ground and the security of the rent to the landlord and increased the numbers of impoverished people in the countryside, particularly when the linen trade was in recession.[47] Landlord reaction was generally tempered by the exigencies of existing tenurial relations and particularly by the prevalence of tenant right. Their most frequent response, largely determined by the growing profitability of pastoral farming after 1815, was to try to consolidate and enlarge existing small farms where these fell out of lease, irrespective of whether they were held in partnership or in severalty. Various strategies were used. The landlord might require the departing tenants to offer their neighbour first refusal of their interest in the farm, or he might ban the sale of this interest altogether and offer the outgoing farmers (generally smaller) compensation for any improvements they had made. Neither policy was popular with tenants, and by 1844 tenant improvement was reported to be at a standstill in parts of the county in consequence.[48] Nevertheless, the advantages to the landlord of controlling or eradicating tenant right were considerable. By the 1840s, intense competition, particularly for smaller farms, and high prices in general meant that tenant right was generally 'selling beyond its value' at between £10 and £40 an acre for land worth between 20 and 35 shillings in rent. The sums paid were largely irrespective of the length of the lease or of the existence of any improvements, and were widely acknowledged to be detrimental to the incoming tenant's ability to invest in further capital improvements.[49]

Landlord attempts to control tenant right and consolidate their tenants' farms are well exemplified in the baronies of Kinelarty and Iveagh Upper prior to 1845. These baronies covered much of mid- and south Down from Ballynahinch in the north to Carlingford Lough in the south, and thus included most of the Mourne Mountains. They were characterised by sustained population growth until at least the mid 1830s, and by locally extensive areas of clachan settlement and partnership farming in the more marginal districts. It was the gradual disappearance of these which represented the most profound landscape change associated with the landlords' attempts at farm consolidation. The change was not always straightforward. The continuing importance of domestic linen production and population growth alike ensured the persistence of partnership farming in some districts. Nevertheless, on the Banbridge and Hilltown estates of the marquis of Downshire in Iveagh Upper, for example, the proportion of land held under partnership fell from 14 per cent in 1813 to 11 per cent in 1857 and 8 per cent by 1880. In the same period the proportion on the Annesley's Castlewellan estate (also in Iveagh Upper) fell from 33 to 7 per cent. In Kinelarty, over 30 per cent of the land on the Ker estate at Ballynahinch was held in partnership in 1802, but this too subsequently fell.[50]

These sorts of changes clearly had implications for the whole structure of tenant agriculture. As the number of farms fell so their average size increased. On the Downshire's Hilltown estate, the proportion of holdings of less than 15 acres fell from over 87 per cent in 1813 to 58 per cent in 1857. On their Banbridge estate, similarly-sized holdings fell from 78 to 55 per cent over the same period, while on the Annesley's Castlewellan estate, the decline was from 88 to 65 per cent.[51] In rundale districts, this consolidation and enlargement was nearly always accompanied by the reorganisation of the existing highly fragmented fieldscapes into a more regularly ordered – and commercially viable – pattern of individually larger fields, in a process known as 'squaring' or 'striping'. Figure 9.2 depicts the results of this in

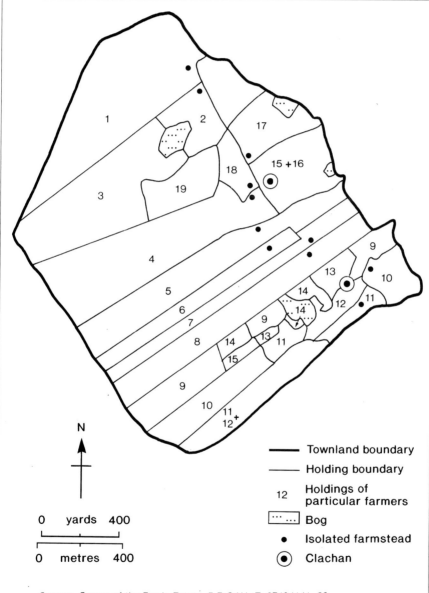

N

0   yards   400

0   metres   400

——— Townland boundary

——— Holding boundary

12   Holdings of particular farmers

[···...] Bog

•   Isolated farmstead

⊙   Clachan

Source: Survey of the Forde Estate, P.R.O.N.I. T. 2749/1/1–80

Fig. 9.2   Farm consolidation on the Forde estate in Kinelarty townland, Slieve Croob, *ca.* 1833.

one townland on the Forde estate in Kinelarty in 1833. Laid out on the slopes of Slieve Croob, the parallel elongated 'ladder farms' (holdings 5-12) were entirely typical creations of the process of striping, while the larger consolidated farms to the north were more typical of squaring. Only two of the earlier clachans survived, the rest having been abandoned in favour of the newly built dispersed farmsteads located on the new holdings. Hand in hand with these alterations went improvements to drainage – particularly the draining of bogs. This was regarded as one of the most profitable forms of improvement a proprietor could invest in and was consequently popular, particularly after the Board of Works was set up in 1831 and empowered to make loans to landlords to fund it.[52] In many areas, drainage improvements hastened the decline of rundale still further by destroying areas of marginal common grazing. These had formed an essential element in the finely tuned balance between arable and pastoral resources which characterised the rundale system.

Linen marketing and urban improvement

The importance of the landlords' role in encouraging the spread of the rural domestic linen industry by facilitating farm subdivision has already been alluded to, but this did not represent the limit of their involvement in the industry. Throughout the eighteenth century, landlords sought to promote linen production by offering premiums to their tenants for producing high-quality webs, purchasing surplus stock in times of recession and subsidising – through the linen board – their purchase of spinning and weaving equipment.[53] More importantly, Ulster landlords, including some from county Down, were particularly active in the affairs of the board. This had been established by the Government in 1711 to oversee the industry and to extend its expertise throughout Ireland. The northern landowners' involvement was to prove crucial in establishing the independence of the Ulster linen drapers from further regulation by the board after its attempted implementation of the 1782 Linen Act. This act was the latest in a series designed to prevent fraud by drapers licensed as sealmasters to 'seal' or approve unbleached (brown) or bleached (white) linen. It was regarded as particularly discriminatory by the Ulster sealmasters because it required them not only to provide a bond of £200 and sureties for their future conduct, but also to perfect a warrant of attorney confessing judgement on that bond, thus in effect admitting in advance their liability to pay any future fine levied on them by the board. Faced with what they conceived to be a threat to their livelihood, the Ulster drapers at first refused to trade until they received an assurance from the board that they would not be liable to the new oath or sureties. Failing to receive adequate assurances, they subsequently exploited a loophole in the Act which allowed them to continue sealing linen under the authority of five (sympathetic) Ulster trustees, Sir Richard Johnston, John O'Neill of Shane's Castle, and Lords Brownlow, Hillsborough and Moira.[54]

County Down landlords thus played a vital role in furthering the interests of Ulster linen manufacture at an important juncture in its history, and in a real sense were instrumental in securing the province's growing domination of the industry at a national level. In physical terms, however, their involvement had a longer-lasting legacy in the towns and villages they founded, refounded or modernised as part of their promotion of linen marketing. These activities formed part of a larger programme of landlord involvement in urban and village improvement, which by the 1830s had affected virtually all of the county's towns and villages to some extent. In common with other parts of Ireland, it was prompted by a variety of aesthetic, social and political as well as economic motivations, and involved complex trade-offs between landlord and tenant interests. Recent research has demon-strated that the conventional view of landlords wielding extensive arbitrary power to re-order their tenants' environments almost at will, is a gross over-simplification. Much more frequently, these so-called 'estate' towns and villages – itself probably a misnomer – evolved over time in line, perhaps, with some proprietorial vision, but governed as to pace and detail by the willingness and ability of tenants to invest their own capital in the building stock.[55]

Table 9.4 summarises the evidence for such improvement in the county's towns and villages as it existed by the mid-nineteenth century. Various points are worth noting. It is clear, perhaps predictably enough, that the network of towns and villages in the county was largely a product of the informal colonisation processes of the seventeenth century, even although Down did not form part of the area officially escheated or 'planted' by the government. Nineteen of the twenty-seven surviving market charters granted in the county date from the seventeenth century and of these, fourteen were granted in the heyday of the Ulster Plantation prior to the 1641 rebellion. While these charters cannot be assumed to be synonymous with an immediate flowering of urban life, they nevertheless signal the widespread perception among seventeenth-century landlords that this was both possible and desirable. Eventually, of course, their expectations were fulfilled, but it is clear that this seventeenth-century 'urban revolution' was itself built upon an earlier but relatively limited medieval urban legacy, of which Ardglass, Downpatrick and Dromore formed the most prominent part.

Thus the number of entirely 'new' towns and villages known to have

TABLE 9.4

Urban and village property ownership and improvement
ca. 1864

Town-village	Griffiths' valuation (£) in 1864	Main proprietor in 1864	% owned by main proprietor	Formal plan (c. 1840)	Earliest recorded market charter	Special functions
Ardglass	1096	de Vere Beauclerk	62	–	pre 1471	Sea-bathing, Port
Ballynahinch	2376	Ker	29	–	1694	Brown Linen
Ballywalter	459	Mulholland	–	–	–	
Banbridge	6800	Marquis of Downshire	20	Yes	1767	Brown Linen
Bangor	3737	Viscount Bangor	23	Yes	1612	
Bryansford	255	Earl of Roden	83	–	–	
Castlewellan	1648	Earl of Annesley	69	Yes	1754	Brown Linen
Clough	341	Ker	56	–	–	
Comber	2737	Marquis of Londonderry	47	–	1626	
Crossgar	535	Cleland	66	–	nd	
Donaghadee	2637	Delachrois	49	Yes	1626	Ferry port
Downpatrick	8925	McAuley	0.2	–	1617	
Dromara	309	Marquis of Downshire	28	–	nd	Brown Linen
Dromore	2871	nd	–	–	1610	Brown Linen
Dundrum	615	Marquis of Downshire	58	–	1629	Sea-bathing, Port
Gilford	3319	Dunbar McMaster & Co.		–	1692	Industrial village (Linen)
Greyabbey	563	Montgomery	35	–	1626	
Groomsport	313	Maxwell	90		1626	
Hillsborough	1680	Marquis of Downshire	50	Yes	1674	Brown Linen
Hilltown	1000	Marquis of Downshire	79	Yes	Post 1767	
Kilkeel	953	Earl of Kilmorey	23	Yes	1767	Port, Brown Linen
Killough	883	Viscount Bangor	47	Yes	1683	Salt, Port
Killyleagh	1598	Lord Dufferin & Clandeboye	19	–	1612	Port
Kircubbin	609	Ward	30	–	1769	Brown Linen
Loughbrickland	319	Whyte	25	–	1638	
Moira	705	Sir Thos. Bateson	49	Yes	1681	Brown Linen

TABLE 9.4 *(contd).*

Urban and village property ownership and improvement
ca. 1864

Town-village	Griffiths' valuation (£) in 1864	Main proprietor in 1864	% owned by main proprietor	Formal plan (c. 1840)	Earliest recorded market charter	Special functions
Newcastle	1747	Earl of Annesley	89	–	–	Sea Bathing, Port
Newry	20076	Earl of Kilmorey	6	Yes	1613	Port, Brown Linen
Newtownards	9304	Marquis of Londonderry	31	Yes	1626	
Portaferry	2251	Nugent	47	–	1627	Ferry, Brown Linen
Rathfriland	2724	Meade	22	Yes	1608	Brown Linen
Rostrevor	1456	Ross	30	Yes	1769	Sea-bathing
Saintfield	1351	Price	38	Yes	1700	
Scarvagh	259	Reilly	62	–	–	
Seaforde	299	Forde	56	Yes	1721	
Strangford	620	Lord de Ros	51		1632	Ferry
Waringstown	250	Waring	70		nd	Brown Linen
Warrenpoint	4722	Hall	27	Yes	1776	Sea-bathing

been founded during the eighteenth century in county Down is relatively small. Seaforde, established in the 1720s by the Fordes, Castlewellan built in the 1750s by the earl of Annesley, Kircubbin, founded ten years later by the Wards and Rostrevor founded at much the same time by the Ross family are four such examples. Most landlord involvement in urban modernisation seems to have been directed towards improving existing settlements – perhaps only founded a hundred years previously – rather than founding new ones. By no means all of the county's landlords had either the opportunity or the desire to promote urban renewal. In all some twenty-seven landed families retained significant urban interests in Down by the mid-nineteenth century, but by this time the value of these holdings showed as great a variation as the value of the associated estates. They ranged from the marquis of Londonderry's £2,843 holding at Newtownards and the earl of Annesley's £1,555 property at Newcastle, to the Mulholland's £74 holding at Millisle and the Whyte's £81 at Loughbrickland. The variation in proportionate terms was just as great, and this had significant implications for the degree to which any one landlord could impose his wishes on any given town. On average, the proportion of the property value owned in the county's towns by their major landlord was 42 per cent, but as table 9.4 shows, individually the figure varied from 89-90 per cent at Groomsport and Newcastle to 20 per cent or less at Banbridge, Downpatrick and Killyleagh. Statistical analysis of these data suggests that pronounced property monopolies, where over half the property value was held by one landlord, were characteristic of smaller and less valuable places.[56] In larger and more complex towns such as Banbridge and Newtownards, where industry and mercantilism had broadened social access to wealth and created an urban *bourgeoisie* increasingly independent of landlord control, the relatively simple polarities of earlier landlord-tenant relations had largely disappeared. In such places even powerful magnate figures such as the marquis of Londonderry were unlikely to retain the monopoly of property enjoyed by their predecessors.

This conclusion points to an interesting paradox which may well explain why the evidence for direct landlord intervention in the remodelling of county Down's towns and villages is not more extensive than it is. In those larger towns which had been sufficiently successful to warrant a high Griffith's assessment, the pattern of property ownership tended to be divided among a variety of individuals, none of whom were sufficiently dominant to impose their own agenda on the community, even though, individually, their holdings may have been valuable and their resources extensive. In smaller villages such as Groomsport or Hilltown, where such monopolies were more likely and the possibility of unilateral landlord intervention theoretically greater, the property base was less valuable and the return on such investment correspondingly less certain. In this situation, some landlords appear to have tried to minimise their own investment and its attendant risks by soliciting the involvement of tenant capital through the medium of building leases. These offered the tenant a favourable term of years and a low rent in return for their bearing the full cost of construction. In some cases, as at Rathfriland in 1762, the leases on offer were perpetuities, that is were for lives renewable for ever, and gave the tenant a virtually inextinguishable interest in the property. The agent's reasoning at Rathfriland was clear enough. Setting the tenements in the town for lives renewable forever would

> induce men of circumstances particularly linen drapers to set there
> and build good houses, as their heirs and assigns will forever
> enjoy the same; and the town parks (which at present pay only
> six shillings per English acre) will then set, the most contiguous at
> twenty shillings an acre....[57]

I ESE of Strangford Lough (Cambridge University Collection of Air Photographs, 1960).

II Corrie, Slieve Commedagh (Cambridge University Collection of Air Photographs, 1971).

III Coast WNW of Kilkeel Valley (Cambridge University Collection of Air Photographs, 1968).

IV NNW of Scarva (Cambridge University Collection of Air Photographs, 1968).

V North from Newry (Cambridge University Collection of Air
Photographs, 1970).

VI NNW of Carrigwilliam Lough (Cambridge University
Collection of Air Photographs, 1970).

VII NNW along the Annalong Valley (Cambridge
University Collection of Air Photographs, 1970).

VIII Strangford Lough north from Downpatrick (Cambridge
University Collection of Air Photographs, 1970).

IX English Mount, Downpatrick.

X Nendrum (Cambridge University Collection of Air Photographs, 1970).

XI Motte east of Hilltown (Cambridge University Collection of Air Photographs, 1970).

XII West from Clough (Cambridge University Collection of Air Photographs, 1971).

XIII Inch Abbey.

XIV Grey Abbey (Cambridge University Collection of Air Photographs, 1970).

XV Downpatrick (Cambridge University Collection of Air Photographs, 1970).

XVI Jordan's Castle, Ardglass (Ulster Museum, W05/03/04).

XVII South front of Mount Stewart (Ulster Museum, W05/53/23).

XVIII Mountain farm near Annalong (Ulster Museum, W05/02/1).

XIX Pulling flax, Dromara (Ulster Museum, W05/43/2).

XX Spreading flax, Dromara (Ulster Museum, W05/43/4).

XXI Retting flax, Ballynahinch (Ulster Museum, W05/10/7).

XXII Flowering linen, Ballynahinch (Ulster Museum, W05/10/1).

XXIII Warrenpoint (Ulster Museum, W05/10/1).

XXIV Holywood (The Ulster Folk and Transport Museum, WAG 791).

XXV Donaghadee (The Ulster Folk and Transport Museum, WAG 942).

XXVI Main Street, Bangor (The Ulster Folk and Transport Museum, WAG 31020).

XXVII Ardglass (Cambridge University Collection of Air Photographs, 1970).

XXVIII Portaferry (Cambridge University Collection of Air Photographs, 1970).

Fifty years later, in 1811, the leases at Hillsborough were shorter – normally for three lives – and the conditions more onerous. Prospective tenants had to submit a plan and elevation of their proposed houses to the agent for approval, and had to agree – on pain of fine – to build these within three years of their taking possession of the tenancies. Once built, they had to white-wash the outside of their dwelling once every two years, and agree to 'preserve and keep their house, outbuildings, fences, orchards, gardens, ditches, hedges, walls, trees, drains and other improvements in substantial order and repair...'.[58]

Similar thinking but a more generous attitude seems to have underlain the marquis of Downshire's strategy fourteen years later at Dundrum. Here the intention was not to promote the linen trade, but to develop the village as a sea bathing resort and grain harbour. The extent of the Downshire's involvement in funding various public buildings and utilities and their wish to invite tenant participation was made clear in an announcement in the *Belfast News Letter* on the 8th November 1825:

....His Lordship has been engaged in the completion of a well considered plan for Dundrum, and already has erected a firmly built and commodious pier of above 300 feet in length, and 50 feet in breadth which has proved of great service to the coasting trade, and very advantageous to consumers in that part of the county. Two large stores have also been finished, with a kiln for drying corn, adjacent to the pier, capable of containing 3 or 400 tons of grain, besides accommodation below on the basement storey for coals, iron, slates and other weightier commodities. An inn and lodging house adjoining are now in progress...which promise... to be as commodious and roomy as any houses that have hitherto been erected in this country, and cannot fail to attract visitors of rank and consideration when they shall be fit for occupation. The warehouses, which have excited a great interest among the grain merchants in various quarters who have been anxious to rent them, have been let to a spirited and wealthy company. The situation of the harbour...and the surrounding country producing the finest grain, make this interesting spot a very desirable settlement and outlet for capital and industry. The lands in Dundrum have been laid out in accommodation for building lodging and other houses....It is intended to erect hot and cold baths on the principle of those most approved in England, and for the use of invalids and other visitors.[59]

In advertising his intentions in this way the marquis was following a

Plate 9.4   Hillsborough court house, as it was rebuilt for the marquis of Downshire probably after *ca*. 1808.

well-worn entrepreneurial route. Advertisements for similar projects connected with the linen industry had appeared in the *News Letter* since at least 1738.[60] His intentions were also fashionable: similar resort developments were being undertaken at much the same period at Ardglass, Rostrevor and Warrenpoint. At Ardglass in 1812

> Mr Ogilvie built entire streets, a church and school house, and an elegant hotel; and also constructed hot, cold and vapour baths; built and furnished lodging-houses for the accommodation of visitors ... (rendering) it one of the most fashionable watering-places in the North of Ireland.[61]

Elsewhere, non-economic motives seem to have been equally important in encouraging landlord involvement in urban improvement. At Hillsborough, for example, the 2nd and 3rd marquises of Downshire combined political objectives, social-consciousness and aesthetic *desiderata* as well as the profit motive in their management of the town between 1793 and 1820.[62]

In fact aesthetics, or more specifically, the desire to create a fashionable and therefore status-enhancing urban environment as a setting for the proprietorial mansion, seem to have figured largely in the design and layout of at least some of county Down's formally

Plate 9.5   'Tudorbethan' estate cottages at Seaforde, built in the 1820s.

planned towns and villages. While some of the regular street plans and uniform plots displayed *ca*. 1840 can be explained as a colonial legacy from the seventeenth century, as for example at Bangor, Newtownards and Donaghadee (table 9.4), other design features can only be accounted for as a deliberate attempt by the landlord to enhance the settlement's appearance for its own sake. Thus the restrained Neo-Classical market house built at Newtownards for the marquis of Londonderry between 1765 and 1771, or the more exuberant Baroque court house rebuilt at Hillsborough for the marquis of Downshire some time after 1808 (plate 9.4) are each in their own way immensely sophisticated buildings, and far more ornate then mere function demands.[63] Similarly, the 'Tudorbethan' revival style adopted for the almshouses and estate workers' housing at Seaforde in the 1820s (plate 9.5) suggest a desire on the part of the Fordes to create an architecturally harmonious environment.[64] In town plans too, we find sophisticated resonances of Renaissance-inspired principles of urban planning, as for example in the conjoined pairs of crescentic 'squares' laid out by the Annesleys at Castlewellan in the 1750s, or the central square and radiating streets created by the Halls at Warrenpoint when they rebuilt the town sometime after 1780.[65] In each of these cases, however, and in numerous other examples, such as the earl of Roden's picturesque Gothick Revival village at Bryansford, rebuilt in the 1820s, or the Banbridge Market House, built at a cost of £2,000 for the marquis of Downshire in 1832, the landlords' evident willingness to invest in 'polite' ornamentation and the complex articulation of architectural space suggests that they were working to their own particular aesthetic agenda – and valued this for its own sake.

Conclusion

In many respects, county Down's landed families emerge as a disparate group, united by their shared status as property *owners*, but divided by the very extent of the wealth which set them apart from the vast majority of the county's population. Few of the county's landowners were of truly magnate status. The Downshires and Londonderrys indubitably were, and possessed wealth and landed acres which set them apart from every other proprietor in the county and placed them on a par with figures such as the duke of Devonshire, the duke of Sutherland or earl Fitzwilliam. Below them, in wealth if not social status, regionally-important families such as the Annesleys, the Fordes and the Perceval-Maxwells maintained a similar lifestyle of status assertion, social obligation and mutual recognition, founded on the possession and management of inherited wealth. Ranked below these again came larger numbers of gentry families, who although they possessed more modest means, were nevertheless also capable of exercising a locally-significant influence over their tenantry and locality alike. By the mid-nineteenth century, each group had succeeded in recreating the geography of the county through their construction of demesnes and country houses and their facilitation of agricultural and urban improvement. Many of these buildings and their surroundings survive to the present day, providing mute but eloquent testimony to a social order which disappeared amid the welter of social and political change in post-Famine Ireland.

References

1. P. J. Drudy, 'Land, people and the regional problem in Ireland' in P. J. Drudy (ed.), *Ireland – land, politics and people – Irish studies ii* (Cambridge, 1992), p. 199.
2. Summarised for Ulster in R. Gillespie, *Colonial Ulster. The settlement of east Ulster 1600-1641* (Cork, 1985), and P. Robinson, *The plantation of Ulster* (Dublin, 1984).
3. R. Mitchison, 'Ireland and Scotland: the seventeenth-century legacies compared' in T. M. Devine and D. Dickson (ed.), *Ireland and Scotland 1600-1850* (Edinburgh, 1983), pp 2-9.
4. E. R. Hooker, *Readjustments of agricultural tenure in Ireland* (Chapel Hill, N.C., 1938); J. E. Pomfret, *The struggle for land in Ireland* (Princeton, 1930).
5. Cited in P. R. Newman, *Companion to Irish history* (Oxford, 1991), p. 106.
6. J. Black, *Eighteenth century Europe 1700-1789* (London, 1990), pp 19-38, 103-117, 208-230.

7.   L. J. Proudfoot, *Urban patronage and social authority. The management of the duke of Devonshire's towns in Ireland 1764-1891* (Washington, 1995), pp 297-325.

8.   L. J. Proudfoot, 'Spatial transformation and social agency: property, society and improvement c. 1700 to 1900' in B. J. Graham and L. J. Proudfoot (ed.), *An historical geography of Ireland* (London, 1993), pp 219-257.

9.   Gillespie, *Colonial Ulster*, pp 113-194; Robinson, *Plantation of Ulster*, pp 91-149.

10.   Robinson, *Plantation of Ulster*, pp 94, 98.

11.   Ibid., pp 52-3.

12.   L. J. Proudfoot, 'Landscaped demesnes in pre-famine Ireland: a regional case study' in A. Verhoeve and A. J. Vervloet (ed.), *The transformation of the European rural landscape: methodological issues and agrarian change 1770-1914* (Brussels, 1992), pp 230-237.

13.   H. M. S. O., *Return of owners of land of one acre and upwards, in the several counties, counties of cities and counties of towns in Ireland* (Dublin, 1876).

14.   T. Jones Hughes, 'The estate system of landholding in nineteenth century Ireland' in W. Nolan (ed.), *The shaping of Ireland. The geographical perspective* (Dublin, 1986), pp 137-150.

15.   W. E. Vaughan and A. J. Fitzpatrick (ed.), *Irish historical statistics, population 1821-1971* (Dublin, 1978), pp 3, 12; H.M.S.O., *Return of landowners*, p. 325.

16.   J. Bateman, *The great landowners of Great Britain and Ireland* (Leicester, 2nd ed., 1971), p. 137.

17.   H. Montgomery Hyde, *The Londonderrys, a family portrait* (London, 1979), p. 39.

18.   A random sample of 26 cases produced a Spearman rank correlation coefficient of +0.892, significant at the 99 per cent confidence level.

19.   E. O'Byrne (ed.), *The convert rolls* (Dublin, 1981), pp 48, 187, 236.

20.   See, for example, W. E. Vaughan, *Landlords and tenants in mid-Victorian Ireland* (Oxford, 1994), pp 103-137.

21.   Proudfoot, 'Spatial Transformation', p. 246.

22.   M. Bence-Jones, *A guide to Irish country houses* (London, 1988), p. x.

23.   A random sample of 30 cases produced a Spearman rank correlation coefficient of +0.86, significant at the 99 per cent confidence level.

24.   Proudfoot, 'Landscaped demesnes', pp 235-6.

25.   Gentleman's almanac for 1789 (Dorse note), P. R. O. N. I., Roden papers, mic. 147 reel 3, vii; memorandum regarding tree planting, n/d but circa 1792, P. R. O. N. I., Roden papers, mic. 147, reel 9, xviii.

26.   Cash Books 1742-1801, P. R. O. N. I., Downshire papers, D. 671/A2/3 – A2/26.

27.   For a useful survey, see J. Black, *Eighteenth century Europe 1700-1789* (London, 1990), pp 208-222.

28.   Bence-Jones, *Guide*, pp xiii-xiv.

29.   Ibid., *Guide, passim*.

30.   S. J. Connolly, *Religion, law and power. The making of Protestant Ireland 1660-1760* (Oxford, 1992), pp 128-143.

31.   R. F. Foster, *The making of modern Ireland, 1600-1972* (London, 1988), pp 176, 194.

32.   A. A. Horner, 'Carton, Co. Kildare. A case study in the making of an Irish demesne' in *Quarterly Bulletin Irish Georgian Society*, xviii (1975), pp 45-104.

33.   Proudfoot, 'Landscaped demesnes', pp 230-237.

34.   W. H. Crawford, 'The influence of the landlord in eighteenth-century Ulster' in L. M. Cullen and T. C. Smout (ed.), *Comparative aspects of Scottish and Irish economic and social history 1600-1900* (Edinburgh, 1977), pp 193-203.

35.   W. H. Crawford, 'Ulster landowners and the linen industry' in J. T. Ward and R. G. Wilson (ed.), *Land and industry. The landed estate and the industrial revolution* (Newton Abbot, 1971), pp 117-144.

36.   Gillespie, *Colonial Ulster*, pp 152-3.

37.   H. M. S. O., *Digest of Land Commission* (Dublin, 1844), i, p. 263; W.A. Maguire, *The Downshire estates in Ireland 1801-1845* (Oxford, 1972), app. iii.

38.   W. H. Crawford, 'The significance of landed estates in Ulster' in *Irish Economic and Social History*, xvii (1990), pp 44-61.

39.   L. Kennedy, 'The rural economy, 1820-1914' in L. Kennedy and P. Ollerenshaw (ed.), *An economic history of Ulster 1820-1939* (Manchester, 1985), p. 38 ff.

40.   W. Bentnick to Lady Clanbrassil, 8 June 1769, P. R. O. N. I., Roden papers, mic. 147, reel 9.

41.   Cash books 1780-1784, P. R. O. N. I., Downshire papers, D. 671/A/2/21-25.

42.   Account of family expenses for the year 1763, P. R. O. N. I., Annesley papers, D. 1854/8/17; T. Getston to Andrew Savage Nugent, n/d but 1826, P. R. O. N. I., Nugent papers, D. 552/A/6/5/9; Miscellaneous accounts, P. R. O. N. I., Forde papers, D. 566/C/1/1-4.

43.   S. Lewis, *A topographical dictionary of Ireland* (London, 1837), i, p. 488.

44.   J. Bardon, *A history of Ulster* (Belfast, 1992), pp 183-239.

45.   And the subject of frequent contemporary comment. See, for example, Arthur Young's comments in *A tour in Ireland,* first published in London in 1780. C. Maxwell (ed.), A. Young, *A tour in Ireland with general observations made on the state of that kingdom in the Years 1776, 1777 and 1778* (Cambridge, 1925), pp 38-47. For contemporary comment, see L. M. Cullen, *An economic history of Ireland since 1660* (London, 2nd ed. 1976), pp 100-103.

46.   See, for example, D. McCourt, 'The decline of rundale 1750-1850' in P. Roebuck (ed.), *From Plantation to partition: essays in Ulster history in honour of J. L. McCracken* (Belfast, 1981), pp 119-139.

47.   H. M. S. O., *Digest,* i, p. 431.

48.   H. M. S. O., *Digest,* i, pp 209-301, 456.

49.   H. M. S. O., *Digest,* i, pp 302-3.

50.   Cited in D. Frey, 'Aspects of agrarian change in the barony of Iveagh Upper, 1815-1880', Unpublished B.A. Dissertation, Dept. of Geography, Q.U.B., 1982, pp 40-81.

51.   Frey, 'Aspects', pp 46-8.

52.   R. B. McDowell, 'Administration and public services 1800-1870' in W. E. Vaughan (ed.), *A new history of Ireland v, Ireland under the Union, I, 1801-1870* (Oxford, 1989), p. 550.

53.   Crawford, 'Ulster Landowners', pp 126-7.

54.   Crawford, 'Ulster Landowners', pp 131-3.

55.   B. J. Graham and L. J. Proudfoot, 'Landlords, planning and urban growth in eighteenth and early nineteenth century Ireland' in *Journal of Urban History*, xviii, No. 3 (May 1992), pp 308-329; L. J. Proudfoot and B. J. Graham, 'The nature and extent of urban and village foundation and improvement in eighteenth and early nineteenth century Ireland' in *Planning Perspectives*, viii (1993), pp 259-281.

56.   A random sample of 20 cases produced a Spearman rank correlation coefficient of -0.4, significant at the 95 per cent confidence level, for the relationship between the percentage of the total property value held by the main landlord and the total Griffith's assessment.

57.   'A scheme for the improvement of the estate and town of Rathfriland (county

Down), 2 March 1764, submitted by the agent, Henry Waring', P. R. O. N. I., McCracken papers, T. 1181/1.

58. P. R. O. N. I., Downshire papers, D. 671/A5/10; D. 671/D8/8/38.

59. *Belfast News Letter,* 8 March 1825.

60. D. G. Lockhart, 'The advertising of towns and villages in the Belfast News Letter, 1738-1825' in *Ulster Folklife,* xxii (1974), pp 91-3.

61. Lewis, *Dictionary,* i, pp 51-2; *The parliamentary gazetteer of Ireland* (London, 1846), i, pp 58-60; ii, pp 192-3, 473

62. Explored in depth in J. Gardiner, 'Landlord motivation for improvement in an Ulster estate town: the case study of Hillsborough, 1780-1820', Unpub. B.A. Dissertation, Depart. of Geography, Q.U.B., 1991, *passim.*

63. Plan of Newtownards Market House c. 1770, P. R. O. N. I., Londonderry papers, D. 654/M36/2; C. E. B. Brett, *Historic buildings ... in the towns and villages of mid Down* (Belfast, 1974), p. 14.

64. C. E. B. Brett, *Historic buildings ... in the towns and villages of east Down* (Belfast, 1973), pp 26-30.

65. P. J. Rankin, *Historic buildings ... in the Mourne area of south Down* (Belfast, 1975), p. 24.

Plate 9.6   Crawfordsburn House, neo-classical, late nineteenth century (Ulster Museum, W05/31/16).

Chapter 10

TREES AND WOODLANDS OF COUNTY DOWN

ROY TOMLINSON

The distribution of woodland in 1996

County Down, in common with Ireland generally, is often described as having little woodland, but until recently the statistical basis for this description was lacking. However, during 1992-4 the land cover of Ireland was mapped from LANDSAT TM satellite data following the European Union CORINE system.[1] Units of land cover greater than 25 ha., including coniferous, mixed and broadleaved woodlands, were delimited and held in a database. Figure 10.1 has been constructed using data derived from this database for county Down, and shows little broadleaved or mixed woodland and few extensive areas of conifers. These types of woodland cover, respectively, 1,320, 274 and 3,014 ha., or roughly between 0.1 and 1.2 per cent of the total county area. These figures are underestimates because of the minimum size rule for mapping (25 ha.), but other recent field-based studies confirm the low woodland cover. For example, in the Mourne and Slieve Croob area of outstanding natural beauty (A.O.N.B.), only 1.2 per cent of the total land area is occupied by private, i.e. non – state woodland, and this approximates to roughly 4 per cent of the land below the present tree line.[2] Even in the Lagan valley regional park (L.V.R.P.), one of the most wooded parts of the county, only 12 per cent of the land area is wooded, and this is low by European standards.[3] In the present day, therefore, woodland is relatively scarce in county Down.

Figure 10.1 reveals that many of the wooded areas are within demesnes and estate lands; those of Tollymore and Castlewellan are well known, but woodland can also be seen around great houses such as Seaforde, Mount Stewart, Castleward and Hillsborough. This coincidence can be shown more clearly by reference to the Mourne – Slieve Croob A.O.N.B. and Lagan valley regional park; in both over 60 per cent of woodland occurs in demesnes, large gardens and as plantations in estates. Figure 10.2 shows the areal importance of these woodland types and their concentration in particular locations, as for example in the valleys around Warrenpoint and Rostrevor. By

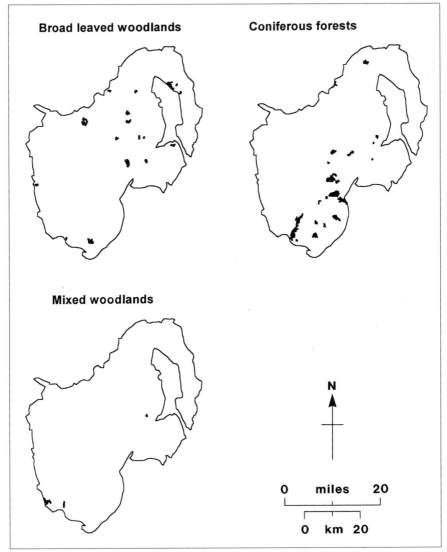

Broad leaved woodlands

Coniferous forests

Mixed woodlands

N

0   miles   20

0   km   20

Fig. 10.1   Woodlands and forests 1990 – derived from the CORINE database. Only those areas greater than 25 ha are shown.

comparison, woodland in more 'natural' situations, such as deeply incised valleys or steep slopes, accounts for only 9 per cent of the total in the L.V.R.P. and 12 per cent in the Mourne – Slieve Croob A.O.N.B. Thus in addition to being relatively rare, the county's present woodland is very much the result of the last 200 years of demesne and estate planting. This chapter examines the reasons for this scarcity, and explores the history of woodland planting in the county and its consequences for the modern landscape.

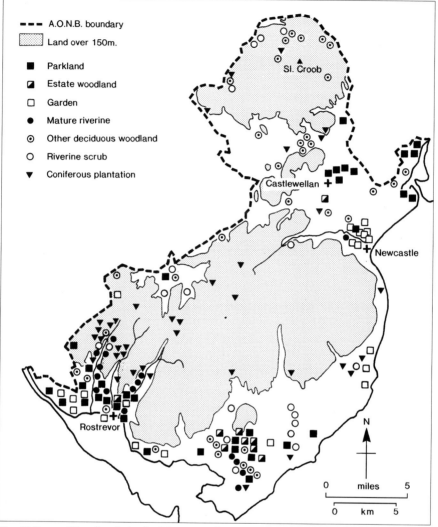

Fig. 10.2   Woodlands in the Mourne – Slieve Croob A.O.N.B.: note the importance
of woodlands in demesnes, large gardens and as plantations in estates.

Woodland development and clearance from the Late Glacial to the Middle Ages

The most usual method of reconstructing vegetation history from late glacial to historic times is by analysing the pollen deposited in successive layers taken from peat bogs and lake muds, but it is difficult to be specific about the evolution of the land cover of county Down using this approach. Despite the frequency of inter-drumlin lakes and peat bogs, few sites have been investigated.[4] Many of the bogs have been cut-over and disturbed or provide information on the past vegetation of their immediate surroundings rather than for the region as a whole. Thus for the present, we have to continue to accept the general picture of the development of Ireland's vegetation, as proposed, for example, by Mitchell.[5]

Mitchell's schema envisages an open landscape during the late glacial (late Midlandian – about 12000 b.p.), dominated by grasses, sedges and mugwort, gradually being replaced by juniper and willow shrubland. In turn, this gave way first to birch woodland and then to the hazel, pine, oak and elm woodland of the Boreal period (about 9500 b.p.). In the Atlantic period (around 7000 b.p.), alder appeared in this assemblage on the wetter mineral soils. Mesolithic people would have been familiar with this wooded landscape and may have played some part in instigating its clearance. Neolithic communities with their agricultural activities certainly began to change it; 'the apparent depression of arboreal taxa around 3000 B.C. (5000 b.p.) marks a "floating" datum which anticipates the eventual relegation of woodland to a minor position in the vegetational landscape'.[6] Indeed, the agricultural activity and the consequent lack of vegetation cover seems to have led to some soil erosion, witnessed, for example, in the clay layer with cereal-type pollen in the peat deposits of Carrivmoragh bog, 5 km. to the northwest of Castlewellan.[7] At the close of the Neolithic there appears to have been some recovery of the woodland,[8] but within about 500 years the clearances of the Bronze Age produced a generally treeless landscape over parts of Ireland. Some of the remaining woods were removed by an upsurge of agriculture during the Early Christian period. For example, at Ballydugan in south Down, there was a marked decline in tree pollen from around 80 per cent of the total terrestrial pollen to about 20 per cent, with an accompanying rise in the pollen of plantains, grasses, bracken and cereals.[9] Holland also indicates Iron Age (120 B.C.) and Early Christian (500 A.D.) agricultural episodes.[10] Later settlement by the Vikings after about 800 A.D. and the Anglo-Normans (after 1169 A.D.) continued this woodland clearance.

Woodland distribution and structure during the plantation period, ca. 1550-1660

Despite this long history of clearance, McCracken estimated that at the beginning of the seventeenth century, woodland occupied 'about an eighth of the whole country' (i.e. Ireland), and that to the south of the River Lagan, between Strangford Lough and Lough Neagh, there were three wooded areas – McCartan's Country, the Dufferin, and Kilwarlin.[11] Some of the densest woodland in Ulster at this time appears to have been in Killultagh, south of Lough Neagh and mainly outside county

Down. Eastward into the county and Kilwarlin and McCartan's Country, this dense cover thinned to patches of trees on the drumlins and shrubby marshland between them. In the Dufferin, McCracken continues, 'oak woodland again appeared on the boulder clay. The woods there were described in 1602 as having the fairest timber trees in Ireland'.

This account of woodland distribution *ca.* 1600 is broadly supported by an examination of contemporary maps, many of which were studied by McCracken and helped form her conclusions, but there are differences between these maps as to the extent of the woodland and its structure. This is to be expected, not only because of limitations of accuracy, scale and knowledge of inland areas, but also because maps were often commissioned for particular purposes so that information could be emphasized or omitted. A map of Belfast Lough of about 1570 shows that north Down had trees along the River Lagan to the south and west of Belfast, but no trees were indicated between Belfast and Bangor.[12] Another, supposed to have been executed in 1572, shows patches of trees on the west side of Strangford Lough, but not elsewhere.[13] This distribution is repeated in maps of around 1580; for example, in one of Ulster containing annotations by Lord Burghley[14] and in another of the east coast from Dublin to Carrickfergus.[15] A map of the east coast of Down from Carlingford Lough to Lecale also shows woodland patches – to the west of Narrow Water Castle, south-west of Dundrum Castle, on the north-east slopes of the Mournes at approximately the present location of Donard Park, and on the hills overlooking the northern shore of Carlingford Lough.[16] It is tempting to link the last with the present Rostrevor oakwoods.

In contrast to the patchy woodland distribution on these maps, another of 1580 showing the coast from county Down to Larne has more extensive trees or, judging from their shape, shrubs, as only rarely are trees of full stature drawn.[17] This 'shrubland' is shown all along the Lagan upstream to Dromore, around Castlereagh and throughout most of the county. Similarly, a map of the north-east of Ireland, drawn *ca.* 1595 made 'especially for that part of Ulster commonly called the Claneboyes and for the great woods of the Dufferin', shows considerable stands of woodland.[18] The 'General Description of Ulster' (thought to be by Richard Bartlett around 1603) also contains prominent woodland patches across a wide area of the county.[19] Meanwhile, on Speed's map of 1610, derived at least in part from earlier unpublished work of 1570-1590, woods are marked only on the northeast slopes of the Mournes, near the present Donard Park.[20] Norden's map of 1610 shows only a little woodland around Blaris (Lisburn) and a small patch in Kilwerty (Kinelarty).[21] In common with many of the other maps, the small scale of the Norden map allows little space to depict woodland; indeed, this may be a cause of the general impression of limited woodland.

In the text accompanying Speed's map the following comment is made about Ulster:

> This equal temperature causeth the ground to bring forth great store of several trees, both fit for building and bearing fruit.

It is unclear whether this describes what was found on the land, in which case it may conflict with the evidence from the map, or whether it is a suggestion that the land is capable of producing such trees. The sentence also raises the distinction between those trees fit for building and others. That is, whether the woodlands contained standards – trees for producing timber – as well as underwood – shrubs and small trees suitable for fuel, fencing and other purposes requiring branches and stems of small diameter. Again, the maps and other documentary sources indicate some disagreement. Hill[22] quotes an explanatory note to a map of the county Down coastline of *ca.* 1566 which makes it clear that the woods it depicted were underwoods of hazel, holly, 'oller' (?), elder, thorn, crabtree, birch and such like, but that there was no great oak or building timber ('great trees' was an earlier term for 'standards').[23] In contrast, on a map possibly published some thirty years later, *ca.* 1590, large woodlands are shown near Belfast and a note appended that along the River Lagan for twenty six miles there was 'much wood, as well as oaks for timber as [well as] other woods'.[24] Bagnall's 'Description of Ulster' of 1586, provides no guidance on the structure of the woodland. Killultagh is described as a 'very fast country full of wood and bog' and Kilwarlin, which bordered it, as 'likewise a woodland and boggy'.[25] Clanbrasil McGoolechan (towards Portadown and the Armagh border) was ' a very fast country of wood and bog' whereas Dufferin was 'for the most part woody'. South Clandeboy also was 'for the most part woodland'. It seems clear that 'wood' was used colloquially rather than as a term of woodmanship, when usually it would signify an area containing trees and shrubs for coppicing as well as standards.[26] In the correspondence deriving from the dispute over lands and woods between Viscount Montgomery and Viscount Clannaboy, woodmanship terms are used; for example, in 1606, in the sale by Con O'Neil to Sir Hugh Montgomery of woodlands growing on four townlands which included 'all the timber, trees, woods, underwoods, and all other trees' but preserved the rights of tenants 'to cut all kinds of timber, oak excepted, necessary for their buildings' and to enter the lands 'for cutting and carrying away the woods and underwoods'.[27] It is not clear from this, however, whether the woodlands were being managed in traditional ways or whether the document was phrased using standard legal practice so as to cover all possible uses.

By 1625, the viscounts' dispute over the woodlands had become so serious that a commission was established to enquire what waste had been committed in the woods in the territory called Slutt Neales (a stretch of country across north- and mid- Down). Of particular interest in attempting to describe the structure of these woodlands is the commission's count of the trees which remained standing or which had been felled in particular lands. The commission

> reported that there were then standing on the lands, of the size of six inches [at least] at the butt [base?], 8,883 trees.....and that there had been cut on these lands, of oak of the same size ..... 11,631 [over the preceding eighteen years]. The commissioners also found that there had been cut for the use of the Lord Chichester, for the building of his houses at Knockfergus and Belfast, upon the lands of Ballynalessan, Ballykoan, Ballykarney, and the towns adjoining, 500 oaks ... The Commissioners also stated that the roofs of the churches of Grey Abbey and Cumber, and a store of timber for the Lord of the Ard's buildings at Newtone and Donaghadee, had been taken from the woods.[28]

Further details are given of the cutting as well as of the townlands apportioned to Viscount Montgomery and Lord Clandeboy, Since the woods apportioned cover a large part of north- and mid- Down, the number of trees counted implies either that their density was low or that woodlands were in small patches, or indeed both. The dimension quoted suggests that the trees were generally small.[29] However, the mention of 500 oaks for building and of roof timbers for churches, indicates that there were some larger trees within the woods, at least in the vicinity of the Lagan valley and within a reasonable distance of Comber, Greyabbey and Newtownards.

Thomas Raven's maps of the Clandeboy or Bangor estates of the Hamilton family also date from 1625-6.[30] On these, lands down the west side of Strangford Lough are frequently shown as wooded, but the symbols rarely indicate mature trees. Instead, the drawings are of a tight, almost conical shape and are more indicative of shrubland than woodland. For example, the Tullachin (Tullykin, Killyleagh parish) map shows this symbol over an extensive area which also contains regular clearings or fields (plate 10.1). A similar pattern is also shown around Comber; the trees or shrubs are scattered but become denser at

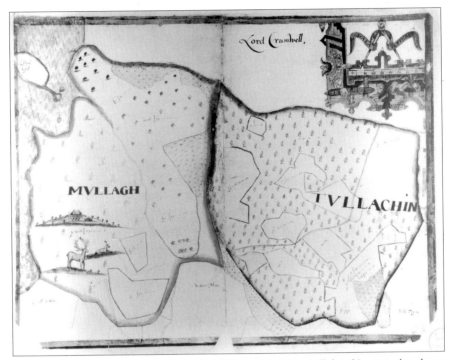

Plate 10.1   Thomas Raven's map of Tullachin (Tullykin, Killyleagh); note the shape
and distribution of the tree or shrub symbols and the clearances.

Ballynickall (Ballynichol) and again this area contains clearances. At
Clonta (Cluntagh, near Killyleagh) the shrubs are widespread and
continue into Killincha (Killinchy – the 'Woods of Killincha' are labelled
and have survived as Killinchy in the Woods townland). Interestingly,
an individual oak is drawn at the junction of Clonta, Killincha and Lord
Cromwell's lands, raising the question of whether it was shown
because it was used as a boundary marker or was used as a boundary
marker because of its rarity. At Ballyhackamore the wood is specifically
named as the 'Shrub Wood of Ballyhackamore' and extends onto the
adjacent Ballymacaret sheet. Similar shrub-like symbols are used on
some bogs where substantial trees would not be expected to grow,
unless the bog had been reduced and become drier through previous
cutting. The general impression given by Raven's maps supports the
view that at this time, the county's woodlands were widely scattered
and comprised largely of shrubs and low trees with numerous
clearances. This interpretation is strengthened by findings from pollen
analysis. Hall noted that at Lough Henney in mid-Down, the pollen
records for the pre-eighteenth century landscapes contain high values
for *Corylus* type pollen so that hazel may have been predominant.[31]

Oak and alder were also present, but not in sufficient quantities to indicate the existence of woodlands which they dominated. She concludes that at Lough Henney the landscape appears to have been one of scrubby woodland with considerable hazel and with frequent cleared areas.

Raven's maps also show deer parks although it is not clear whether these were extant or were in the process of being established. Examples include Mullagh, southwest of Killyleagh, on the site presently occupied by Delamont, while for Killyleagh itself a very fanciful scene is depicted of deer amongst well-grown trees. That the seventeenth century was a period of renewed clearance of the shrubland may be deduced from the 1625 commission, the cleared patches shown on Raven's maps and the probable needs of a growing agricultural economy (as settlers from Scotland and England increased), but there was also the beginnings of planting. Given the scarce documentary evidence, it is uncertain whether this was confined to parks or extended into the surrounding countryside. The only parts of the Civil Survey of 1654-6 to have survived for county Down are the boundary descriptions for the baronies.[32] These give at best only incomplete general accounts of the landscape for some areas. Lecale is described as having 'no wood or timber at all in it' and Kinalearty (Kinelarty) and Dufferin as 'covered with shrubby wood without any timber fit for building or so little that it cannot be estimated'. In Castlereagh barony there were 'few woods left, most of what was, being destroyed by the Rebellion [of 1641]'. These comments provide further support for the conclusions reached earlier concerning woodland distribution and structure in the early 1600s (fig. 10.3), but give little insight into woodland planting and management in the middle and later seventeenth century.

Tenants' planting in the eighteenth and nineteenth centuries

It is clear that by the late seventeenth century there was increasing concern over the loss of woodland in Ireland. In 1672, Sir William Petty suggested that two million trees should be planted in the next fifty years, but his proposal does not appear to have been pursued.[33] However, less than thirty years later, in 1698, the first of seventeen Irish Parliamentary Acts was passed which aimed to promote or enforce tenant planting. The conditions under which this planting took place changed over time, generally to the benefit of the tenant. As the McCrackens have demonstrated, the Act of 1765 was particularly important since it required the tenant to register the trees planted with a justice of the peace.[34] These registrations or affidavits were recorded at quarter sessions and published in the *Dublin Gazette*. Later, the

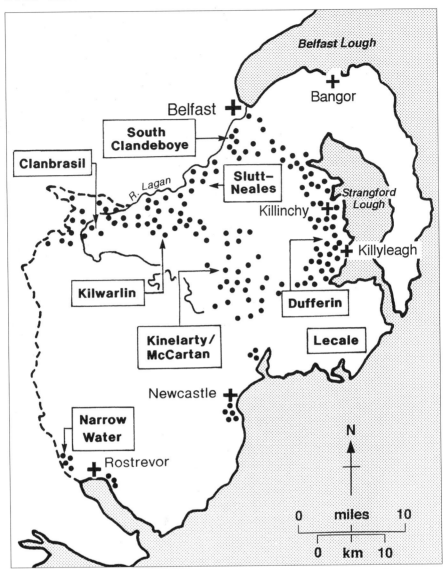

Fig. 10.3   Possible woodland in the late sixteenth and early seventeenth centuries: compiled from sources in the text, but excluding those contemporary maps which show a general expanse of woodland across the county.

affidavits were copied in whole or in part into a ledger for each county. These registers can thus provide documentary evidence of tenant planting and help both the reconstruction of past landscapes and the explanation of present ones.

The records available for county Down are contained in an *Alphabet book of the registry of trees planted according to the Act of Parliament in the [twenty]sixth year of George III* which covers the period 1769-99, and two later volumes covering 1800-22 and 1823-1909.[35] These were acquired by the Public Record Office for Northern Ireland (P.R.O.N.I.) only in 1986, which explains the McCrackens' reference in 1984 to the absence of such records for the county.[36] A further ten original affidavits covering the period 1869-1909 are also in the P.R.O.N.I., but their information is included in the registers. The registers are generally arranged by townland, parish, planter, date and the species and number of trees planted. Normally the information given is straightforward, but there are problems in the use of the registers; for example, the location of the planting may not always be given by townland or the spelling of townland names causes uncertainty as to which is meant. A parish name is important when townlands of the same name occur in separate parts of the county. In a few instances the trees planted are unspecified or two or three species are grouped together. Finally, it is doubtful whether all the tree plantings listed were genuinely by tenants. In total and excluding fruit trees, undershrubs and acorns, the registers show that over 5.13 million trees were planted, a total exceeded only by county Cork in the list of twelve counties published by the McCrackens.[37] Although the registers are a valuable source of information and reveal a considerable scale of planting, their importance should not be overestimated. The seemingly high number of trees planted may be compared with the tens of millions required by modern forestry. Moreover, half of the trees planted were in one area southwest of Newcastle.

Examination of the number of registrations per decade (fig. 10.4) shows that planting was relatively slow between 1769-99, with an average of only five registrations a year. The rate increased in the early part of the nineteenth century, but even at its maximum between 1810 and 1829, the number of registrations only averaged fifteen to seventeen a year. From the mid-1830s the rate of registrations declined sharply and from the mid-1840s fell to one or none a year; indeed, after 1859 there were only nineteen registrations in total. This pattern is very similar to that found for county Londonderry by the McCrackens, where they could offer no clear explanation for the decline in registrations during the 1830s.[38] Imports of timber from the Baltic and North America may have caused people to believe that there was going to be less demand for home-produced timber, but this explanation hardly accords with the trend towards establishing large plantations which developed at this time. The decline began before the famine, so this cannot be regarded as a prime cause, although the contemporary downturn in the agricultural economy may have reduced the tenants' ability to plant. The explanation may lie in the nature of the planting. It

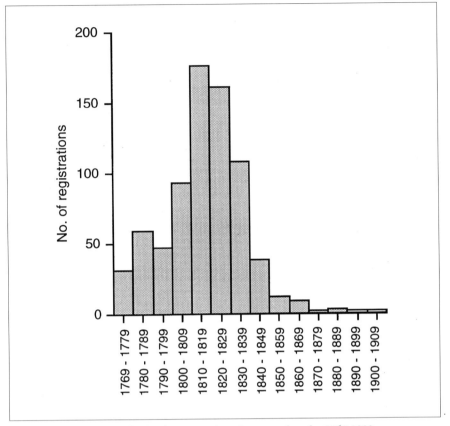

Fig. 10.4   Number of tree planting registrations per decade, 1769-1909.

is probable that most of the trees were never intended for felling, but rather were used to ornament small estates and the grounds around larger farms. Conceivably, by the 1830s much of this had been achieved.

Figure 10.5 shows that parishes in east Down had fewer registrations than those in the west. In particular, there was a belt of parishes with higher numbers of registrations along the county boundary with Armagh, stretching from Tullylish through Dromore and Dromara. These show some coincidence with areas that today have fields of higher quality pasture and arable crops, suggesting that better land quality may have been a factor encouraging the frequency of the original plantings. These parishes were planted throughout the registration period, whereas in the parishes of Kilcoo and Kilmegan, near Newcastle, the high number of registrations was largely a consequence of the large number of plantations established during the 1820s and after. In Knockbreda and Hollywood parishes, most

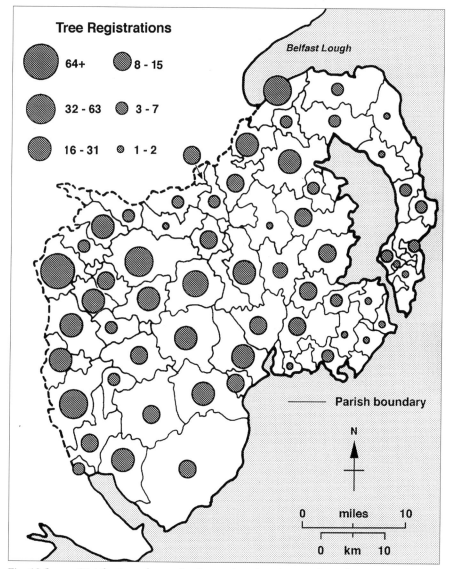

Tree Registrations

64+   8 - 15

32 - 63   3 - 7

16 - 31   1 - 2

Belfast Lough

Parish boundary

N

0   miles   10

0   km   10

Fig. 10.5   Distribution of tree planting registrations by parish, 1769-1909.

registrations also occurred at this time, but were associated with ornamentation rather than plantation. The frequency of the registrations in each parish indicates that this tree planting had – and often retains – considerable significance for local landscapes, especially when the variety of tree species planted and their varying forms and tones are considered (plate 10.2).

More than three-quarters of the trees planted were conifers, and examination of the totals helps to dispel some common misconceptions

Plate 10.2   Belvedere, Lagan valley regional park showing the landscape effects of tree planting. Note how the tones, textures and forms of the trees lend maturity to the view and are in sympathy with the undulating landscape.

about the nature of planting over the last 200 years. For example, ash and not oak was the most commonly planted broadleaf, accounting for 25 per cent of broadleaves or nearly 6 per cent of all trees planted. In contrast, oak constituted only 13 per cent of the broadleaves and 3 per cent of all trees planted. Not only did oak form a low percentage of the overall total, but it was also listed as having been planted in only 32 per cent of all the registrations. In contrast, ash was listed in 80 per cent of all the registrations and of the broadleaves, beech, sycamore, alder, poplars and elms all occurred more frequently than oak.

The high percentage of ash trees may be explained partly by their planned use in hedgerows, where even today ash is the most common tree species. In a recent survey of the Mourne-Slieve Croob A.O.N.B., ash trees were never less than 41 per cent of trees sampled in hedgerows and around Slieve Croob comprised 60 per cent of trees so sampled.[39] The tree registers seldom give the precise location of planting, but some examples show how ash and other species could be used. In 1772, at Cloghanramer, Newry, William Hanna planted a total of 266 ash and 267 sycamore in equal numbers along each of his 'ditches' and to the side of his farm. Similarly, in 1787 at Tullynacross, Lambeg parish, John Hancock planted elm, ash and sycamore of about six years in age 'in hedgerows at the distance [apart] of about 8 feet'. The entry for planting by George Brush in 1773 in Tullynisky, Garvaghy parish, is extremely detailed, although without a contemporary map the ditches specified are difficult to locate. In all 2,035 trees were planted, the vast majority were ash but also included were twelve elm, thirty-four sycamore and 200 alder. Hedgerow planting of ash should not be seen as the only reason for its common occurrence, it was also used as a plantation tree. For example, over 118,000 ash trees were planted by William and Francis Charles Beers on the lower slopes of the mountains southwest of Newcastle, mainly between 1827 and 1838.

Ash was used extensively as a shelterbelt tree around farmhouses, as indicated in the example of William Hanna above, and even in 1985 was present as a single dominant or with other species in 61 per cent of sampled shelterbelts in the Mourne – Slieve Croob A.O.N.B. Sycamore was even more common as a shelterbelt tree, and was found in 71 per cent of the sample. This finding accords with the pattern in the three tree registers. This indicates that sycamore comprised only 5 per cent of trees planted, and with the exception of one notable case near Newcastle, where 10,000 sycamore trees were set, was generally not used as a plantation tree. Over the period of the three registers, 56 per cent of the entries containing sycamores recorded fewer than 100 sycamore trees. Today, most shelterbelts have few tree species; many are single species only, either ash or sycamore, whereas others are merely a mixture of the two. Generally, only the larger houses and farms have a greater species variety, usually including coniferous species and some beech or elm trees. The tree registers have examples of both species-poor and species-rich plantings. Indeed, the latter dominate the registers, possibly because tenant farmers planting only a few trees would not have bothered to register them.

Taking the three registers together, the most commonly planted tree was larch, which accounted for 67 per cent of conifers and 51 per cent of all trees. This species was planted singly or in small groups, but it was also the major plantation tree. The registers record over 2.64 million larch trees with an average of 2,342 per planting. Thirteen plantings contained over 20,000 larch trees while one particular planting scheme contained 400,000. Only 18 per cent of all larch plantings were of less than 100 trees. Larch increased considerably in importance between 1769 and 1909. At the end of the eighteenth century it comprised barely 7 per cent of all trees recorded as planted, but by the latter part of the nineteenth century it constituted 59 per cent of current plantings. This corresponds to patterns in other counties. The McCrackens note that the popularity of conifers grew in the early years of the nineteenth century and that they soon exceeded by a considerable margin the more slowly growing broadleaves. They also note that 'of all the conifers larch was king'.[40]

Scots pine (including undifferentiated 'firs') represented 28 per cent of conifers planted and 21 per cent of all trees in the registers. Although just over one-quarter of the Scots pine plantings contained fewer than 100 pine trees, the species was nevertheless significant in the move towards coniferous plantations in the first half of the nineteenth century. Eight plantings of over 20,000 Scots pine were recorded at this time, and four of these contained over 100,000 trees.

Aside from these two species other conifers were of modest significance. Spruce (mainly Norway spruce) comprised 3.6 per cent of conifers planted and although it was used as a plantation species in the late 1820s and 1830s, nearly half its plantings (47 per cent) were of less than 100 trees. Generally, these other conifers were used to give different forms, tones and textures to the mixed planting.

Although small scale planting around farms and houses continued, the move to plantations from the late 1820s had a major influence on the total number of trees planted and on the character of the landscape in parts of county Down. For example, the 1856 planting by Ross in Ballymoney townland, Kilbroney parish, of 300,000 larch, 9,000 Scots pine, 27,000 oak and 1,000 alder and sally formed the foundation of the present woodland on Thunders Hill. This was continued northward by a subsequent planting scheme – that of Thomas McCartan in 1879 in Drumreagh townland, Kilbroney parish, where 155,000 larch, 800 Scots pine and 200 spruce were planted. One outstanding example of the impact of these plantations is the series of plantings by William and Francis Charles Beers. This took place on the slopes of Drinneevar, Drinnahilly, Thomas's and Millstone mountains to the southwest of Newcastle between 1827 and 1838. Over 2.86 million trees were planted including more than 257,000 broadleaves, not only the ash mentioned above, but also tens of thousands of oak, beech, sycamore and Spanish chestnut. However, larch alone contributed nearly 1.71 million trees, and Scots pine over 844,000 and these, together with spruce, silver fir and a few other pines made up 91 per cent of the total trees planted. The impact on the local landscape may be traced through various editions of the six inch O.S. maps (fig. 10.6) and in the successor forest that can be seen today (plate 10.3).

The impacts of the smaller scale planting recorded in the registers, essentially for ornamentation around substantial houses, may be

Plate 10.3   Donard forest from Newcastle. The coniferous forests are dark and forbidding and their texture rather too even for the mountain slopes. The conical shape of the trees is, however, better suited to the peaks than to more undulating parts of county Down

exemplified by comparing the register entries with the present tree composition at Corry Wood (formerly Wood Lawn), Castlewellan. From a distance, there is little indication of the richness of the species which are still to be found there today. The trees appear to be subsumed within the adjacent Forest Service coniferous plantation and as such add to the overall wooded appearance that lends maturity to the edge of the town. Only the occasional glimpse of large specimens of Wellingtonia towering above other trees at the front of the house provides a hint of what may be found (table 10.1).

Three groups of trees may be identified at Corry Wood: those tree species recorded in 1985 and listed in the plantings of 1815 and 1819; those recorded in 1985 but planted after 1819; and those planted in 1815 and 1819 but not recorded in 1985. The most notable omission in the last group is larch, which comprised 57 per cent of trees planted in 1815 and 1819. This is difficult to explain; either the larch were felled subsequently, or they were planted in the area which is now included in the adjacent Forest Service plantation (which occupies the site of a plantation which existed at the time of the first edition of the six inch O.S. map), and which was excluded from the 1985 survey. The absence of spruce, willows and poplars may be explained in the same

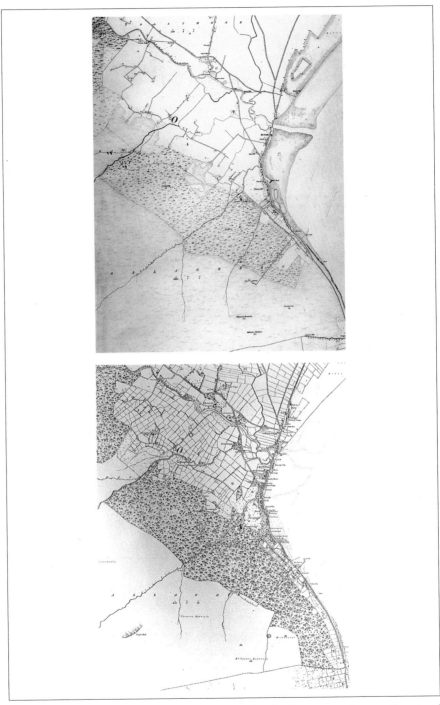

Fig. 10.6   The impact of plantations on the landscape to the southwest of Newcastle, as shown on reductions of the 1834 and 1854 six inch to one mile Ordnance survey maps.

TABLE 10.1

Corry Wood (Wood Lawn) Castlewellan
Comparison of Present Tree Composition with Trees Registered
as Planted in 1815 and 1819.

Species	as % of trees sampled 1985	as % of trees planted in 1815 & 1819 (total 1929)	% 1815 & 1819 excluding larch
Beech	18	7.2	16.9
Lime	13	0.8	1.5
Elm	8	2.3	5.3
Horse Chestnut	5	0.5	1.1
Oak	5	3.0	7.1
Birch	5	1.0	2.5
Sycamore	2	–	–
Silver Fir+	5	1.9	4.5
(Balm of Gilead Fir)+			
Holly	*	0.3	0.6
Service	*	0.1	0.2
Scots Pine	10	–	–
Monterey Cypress	5	–	–
Wellingtonia	5	–	–
Douglas Fir	5	–	–
Atlantic Cedar	2	–	–
Monterey Pine	2	–	–
Austrian Pine	2	–	–
Lawson 'Cypress'	2	–	–
Larch	–	57	–
Spruce	–	10.5	24.4
Weymouth Pine	–	0.3	0.8
Sweet Chestnut	–	0.9	2.3
Mountain Ash	–	0.6	1.4
Poplars	–	5.7	13.3
Ash	–	5.3	12.3
Willow	–	2.4	5.7

* present but recorded as under shrubs.
+ not always separated by planters

way. Ash trees may have been planted at the field boundaries and would not have been included in the 1985 survey. The absence of sweet chestnut and Weymouth pine may result from death or felling over the intervening time. The trees in the second group are a product of later 'Victorian' planting, possibly when the house was modernised between 1835 and 1859. Finally, the diversity of species in the first group (trees listed in 1815 and 1819 and present in 1985), demonstrates the continuing strength of the planting legacy inherited from the earlier period. Beech, oak and silver fir all survived to 1985 with more or less the same frequency they had displayed 166 years earlier.

At Mount Loftus (Lisnascree House), Kilkeel parish, the extensive planting of 1808 can be seen on the six inch O.S. map of 1834. Trees are shown in the grounds around the house, along field boundaries and roads adjacent to the house (5,000 thornquicks are listed in the register), and as orchard. Some of this planting remains as an important element in the modern landscape; the trees occupy a low rise and form a focal point at a junction and major bend on the coastal road. Beech, elm, sycamore and horse chestnut remain, but few survive of the 800 larch, Scots pine, spruce and Balm of Gilead fir that were planted. The nearby hedgerows in particular are devoid of mature trees.

The Lagan valley regional park is one of the most heavily wooded areas of county Down, largely as a result of planting in the eighteenth and nineteenth centuries. Some of this may be found in the registers, for example in Ballynavally and Ballynahatty townlands, where over 25,000 trees were planted between 1793 and 1860. This planting included part of the former demesne of Derramore, now Ardnavally House, as well as adjacent lands. Much of this estate woodland has been lost or replaced, particularly with conifers, but pockets remain; for example, to the north of the present Ardnavally House, around the lodge to the south and along the Purdysburn. These give the locality much of its present graceful character.

Planting in demesnes and around country houses

A considerable amount of the planting evident on the first edition of the six inch O.S. maps is so far untraced in, or was not recorded by, the registers. Belvedere, with its late-eighteenth century house, makes a marked contribution to the wooded appearance of the Lagan valley regional park. When surveyed in 1987, its woodland remained much as it had been in 1832; only one small area in the southwest of the grounds had been lost. There were impressive stands of well-grown beech, sycamore, ash, lime, horse chestnut, birch and elm whose tonal and textural variety enhanced the undulating landscape of the foothills of Drumbo. In addition there were specimens or small groups of sweet chestnut, evergreen oaks, poplars, deodar, walnut, hazel and holly. Similarly, New Grove, also in Drumbo parish, retains much of its original wooded area, although the plantations along the drive were replaced by conifers and mixed stands about fifty years ago. The outer perimeter, as well as some knolls, are dominated by beech, while around the house a diversity of species was recorded in 1987, including sycamore, field maple, hornbeam, sweet chestnut, holm oak and false acacia (*Robinia pseudoacacia*). Over time these and other similar planting schemes around large houses were modified so that the initial concentration on broadleaves, sometimes with a few conifers, gave way in the later nineteenth century to a greater emphasis on conifers, as for example at The Pines, Newtown Lodge and Cedar Hurst in Newtownbreda. Sadly, the sustained expansion of housing in this area over the last few years has led to the loss or depletion of this planting. Until recently it had formed a link between the woodlands of Belvoir Park and those of the Purdysburn and Belvoir Park hospitals and had softened the edge of the built-up area, providing a transition between green belt and townscape.

The great houses and their grounds make a significant contribution to the woodlands of county Down because they assist in defining the soft rolling landscape characteristic of much of the county. Along the Ards peninsula, the landscape would be windswept and open were it not for places like Ballywalter Park, Rosemount (Greyabbey), Portavo, Portaferry House and Mount Stewart. Ballywalter Park was created in the middle of the nineteenth century by the amalgamation of two existing estates, Springvale House and Ballyatwood House, and some of the framework of the original grounds survives in the stands of beeches and oaks planted by Major Matthews around 1800. Most of this formal garden was swept away and replaced by a more heavily-wooded romantic style of landscaped garden dominated by lime trees. In 1846, the new owner, the linen industrialist and former mayor of Belfast, Andrew Mulholland, set about an ambitious plan of reconstruction and within two years over 90,000 trees and shrubs were established. A wind-break of beech was planted at the seaward edge of the grounds and this was followed by plantings of oak, elm, beech, sycamore and some mixed firs.[41] The shelterbelt proved to be insufficient and by the 1870s it had been supplemented by plantings of Corsican, Scots and Austrian pine.[42] At much the same time, specimen conifers were added, including the Monterey pine which presently towers over the other trees.

In 'inland' parts of the county, the parks and woods of great houses such as Seaforde, Hillsborough, Montalto, Mourne Park, Tollymore and Castlewellan continue to form an equally important landscape element. Mourne Park is an outstanding example, and here large wooded areas were already established by 1819.[43] Most of these remain unchanged, despite the extensions and new plantations which continued throughout the nineteenth century. At Mourne Park, particularly in the Beech Wood on the slopes of Knockchree, the trees form an important topographical feature, curving in a broad band around the hill before gradually thinning to moorland up the slope. The forms, textures and colours of the various species blend with those of the land, and draw the eye even when viewed from afar. In similar fashion, the Montalto parkland lends much needed elegance to the southwestern outskirts of Ballynahinch. A somewhat dreary series of bungalow estates is relieved by mature mixtures of mainly broadleaves which sweep round the undulations of the land. Much of the woodland on these slopes originated between 1770 and 1793, when Lord Moira planted over 100,000 trees.

At Tollymore Park, woodland had been established by at least the middle of the eighteenth century; Harris remarks that Tollymore had two deer parks 'or rather one divided in two by a wall through the middle of it, finely wooded, cut into Ridings and Vistoes'.[44] However, it was James Hamilton, enobled in 1756 as the first earl of Clanbrassil of the second creation, who began large-scale tree planting, and he planted between 30,000 and 60,000 trees a year.[45] Larch appears to have been particularly favoured for these plantations and by the 1830s the estate was producing timber from its own saw-mill. In addition, specimen trees were planted in the pleasure grounds around the house, as well as alongside the broad avenue leading from the Newcastle road entrance. Tollymore House was described in the Ordnance survey memoirs as 'delightfully situated, surrounded in every direction by fine wood'.[46] The pleasure grounds now form the arboretum and contain some outstanding mature trees, including Monterey pine, giant redwood, cork and Turkey oaks, sweet chestnut and Douglas fir, as well as the recent specimens planted by the Forest Service. The Forest Service acquired part of the estate in 1930 for afforestation and the remainder in 1941. Since 1955, when the park was opened to the public, many thousands of people have enjoyed the imposing views of nearby mountains and experienced the calm, gentle atmosphere of the wooded walks, especially where old trees arch across the Shimna river.

State forestry

State Forestry began in Ireland with the acquisition of the Avondale Estate, county Wicklow, in 1904. After 1921, forestry in Northern Ireland was transferred to the Forest Service, Department of Agriculture, but the acquisition policy changed little so that many of the older state forests in county Down, as in Northern Ireland as a whole, are based on estates. These include Tollymore Forest, formerly the seat of the earls of Roden; Hillsborough Forest, planted in the Large Park of Hillsborough House; Belvoir Forest, based on the Dungannon estate, and the Castlewellan and Donard Forests, both formerly part of the Annesley estates. Subsequently planted with conifers, these forests retain elements of the originally dominant broadleaves. Indeed, these remnants accounted for most of the 674 ha. of broadleaves and mixed broadleaves-with-conifers recorded in the county's state forests in 1986. For example, at Belvoir Forest the Big Wood remains largely unchanged in outline from its appearance on the 1834 six inch O.S. map. At Castlewellan there are stands of Scots pine on the hill tops; a mixture of beech, ash, and oak at the western end of the lake; a stand of dispersed oak behind one of beech at the north end of the lake, and other scattered stands of beech and larch planted at the beginning of the century. Individual parkland trees, planted perhaps around 1740-60, and an avenue of limes, probably of similar date, adorn the more open areas of the park.

The Forest Service has an important role in recreation and tourism in county Down – in 1995, there were 157,000 paying visitors and 75,000 campers to Tollymore and Castlewellan alone – but it must be remembered that most of its planting is for commercial purposes. By 1986 there were over 4,000 ha. of planted trees on Forest Service land in county Down and of these, 82 per cent was under the more rapidly growing conifers, including larch (about 12 per cent) and Sitka spruce (17 per cent). Although the county has some areas of single species planting, it does not have vast blocks (especially of Sitka spruce) spread over the hillsides – unlike parts of the Antrim plateau and the Sperrins where these 'unnatural' landscapes have been widely criticised. Nevertheless, locally the planting of conifers can still detract from the visual appeal of the scenery, as for example in the contrast between the conifers on the west facing slopes of the Kilbroney valley and the rounded forms and mixed tones of the broadleaves planted in the valley bottom. In 1987 the Forest Service began to change its policy. The first 5 per cent of trees used in any scheme were to be broadleaves, both to soften plantation edges and to increase the wildlife value of the forests, and in general recent afforestation has become more environmentally aware.[47] Forestry will not be extended onto the blanket peatlands and, as enclosed farmland moves out of agriculture, so there may be opportunities for it to move 'down hill' onto better land.

There is encouragement also for the farmer to become more involved in tree planting. There have been grants for farm woodland in Northern Ireland since 1927 but the various schemes met with little success, largely because farmers were required to tie down their land for twenty to forty years without an annual return. In 1988 the farm woodland scheme was introduced to boost the development of farm woodlands and to assist in taking land out of agricultural production. Incentives to farmers included annual payments over the life of the woodland in addition to the original grants given for planting. Higher payments were to be given to schemes using the better land and were offered for longer periods if broadleaves, especially beech and oak, were planted. It remains to be seen whether these initiatives will have a similar effect on the landscape as the trees listed by the registers of the eighteenth and nineteenth centuries. It is certainly to be hoped that they will reverse the general loss of farm woodland that occurred in the county between 1975-86.[48] Recent results from the annual farm census are not promising. Up to 1992 woods and plantations totalled around 2,500-2,600 ha., but in 1993 and 1994 this fell to 1,500-1,600 ha. with a particularly marked decline in the old East Down and Hillsborough rural districts.

Natural woodlands

Throughout this chapter, the present woodlands have been seen as the product of planting over the last 200 years or so, whether by tenant, landlords or the State. However, there are some wooded areas which may be remnants of the primary woodland and others that have developed through 'natural' colonization. Rostrevor national nature reserve (N.N.R.), to the east of Rostrevor town, is an almost pure oak woodland with a holly understorey; plots examined in 1972 showed that 79 per cent of the mature trees were oak with only low frequencies of ash, sycamore, cherry and rowan. Pilcher has suggested that the woodland is derived from regeneration following felling in the 1730s.[49] It appears that on the very steep slopes no period of tillage or pasture intervened between the felling and regrowth, so that it may be regarded as an 'ancient woodland', that is one which predates 1600 A.D. and contains much of the flora and stucture that might have been in a primary woodland. Bohill Woodland N.N.R. is more recent, but the oak, birch, holly, rowan and hazel have regenerated naturally following clear felling. Although tiny, this woodland patch is important as an example of regeneration and because the trees and the ground conditions they create provide habitats for plants and animals that are relatively rare elsewhere.

County Down once had a considerable cover of peat bog, but this declined as peat was cut for fuel.[50] Many of these cut-out areas were reclaimed for agriculture, but others, which became much drier after cutting, provided a habitat in which willows, alders and birches could become established. In parts of the county, as for example near Derryboy, these wooded inter-drumlin sites are an important element in the landscape, and combine with the tree-rich hedgerows to give an overall impression of 'woodedness'. At Hollymount N.N.R. the colonization was different; part of the former marshland is under alder and willow carr which has developed without disturbance since 1745 when a tidal barrage across the Quoile estuary prevented inundation by the sea.[51] This dense carr is possibly the oldest and certainly one of the best examples of this woodland type in Ulster.

Conclusion

This chapter began with a rather depressing statement of the relatively limited extent of woodland cover in county Down at present, and showed how this has resulted from several thousand years of clearance. Woodlands and hedgerows are recent features even on the time scale of the human settlement of Ireland. There has been some contemporary loss of woodlands and treed hedgerows, but county Down has escaped the production of prairie landscapes associated with more arable farming areas. Indeed, despite these losses, there have been encouraging signs of further planting by farmers and landowners. The planting at Tenement Hill, Seaforde, is especially noteworthy insofar as it was supported by an international oil company as part of a scheme to plant a million trees, but in other respects it simply reflects the good practice followed elsewhere in the county. The broadleaves have been planted on a slope adjacent to existing woodland so that when mature they will add to the aesthetic appeal and allow migration of flora and fauna. Renewed environmental awareness, together with changing agricultural policies which now place greater emphasis on support for the maintenance of the rural environment, may ensure that county Down retains and expands its woodlands. Schemes to protect and enhance broadleaf woodlands, with their rounded forms and changing tones, will be to the continued benefit of the rolling landscapes of county Down.

References

1. G. O'Sullivan, CORINE land cover project (Ireland), final report. CEC, DGXI, 1994.
2. R. W. Tomlinson, Mournes – Slieve Croob A.O.N.B. tree survey, report to Environment Service, Department of the Environment for Northern Ireland. 5 vols., 1985.
3. R. W. Tomlinson, Lagan Valley Regional Park tree survey, report to Environment Service, Department of the Environment for Northern Ireland, 1988.
4. S. M. Holland, 'A pollen-analytical study concerning settlement and early ecology in county Down, Northern Ireland'. Unpub Ph.D. thesis, Q.U.B., 1975.
5. F. Mitchell, *The Irish landscape* (London, 1976).
6. K. J. Edwards, 'The anthropogenic factor in vegetational history' in K. J. Edwards and W. P. Warren (ed.), *The Quaternary history of Ireland* (London, 1985).
7. G. W. Pearson and J. R. Pilcher, 'Belfast radiocarbon dates viii' in *Radiocarbon*, xvii (1975), pp 226-38.

8. Holland, 'A pollen analytical study'.
9. G. Singh and A. G. Smith, 'Post-glacial vegetational history and relative land- and sea-level changes in Lecale, county Down' in *R.I.A. Proc.*, lxxiii, B (1973), pp 1-51.
10. Holland, 'A pollen analytical study'.
11. E. McCracken, *The Irish woods since Tudor times* (Newton Abbot, 1971).
12. Map of Belfast Lough showing north Down, P.R.O.N.I., T. 1493/41. Reference numbers and titles refer to the present catalogue of the Public Record Office Northern Ireland. Other maps were consulted in the Map Library, School of Geosciences, Queen's University of Belfast.
13. Printed map of Ireland 'engraved in the reign of Queen Elizabeth 1572 and supposed to be executed for Sir Thomas Smith .... her secretary and governor of the castle of Belfast in that year', P.R.O.N.I., T. 1763/1.
14. Map of Ulster with annotations by Lord Burghley, c. 1580, P.R.O.N.I., T. 1493/6.
15. Map of east coast of Ireland from Dublin to Carrickfergus, county Antrim c.1580, P.R.O.N.I., T. 1493/43.
16. Map of east coast of Ireland from Carlingford Lough to the Barony of Lecale, Downpatrick. c.1580, P.R.O.N.I., T. 1493/45.
17. Map of east coast of Ireland from Dundrum, county Down, to Larne, county Antrim, c.1580, P.R.O.N.I., T. 1493/44.
18. Map of north-east Ireland 'especially the Claneboyes and...the great woods of the Dufferin' c.1595, P.R.O.N.I., T. 1518/6.
19. G. A. Hayes-McCoy, *Ulster and other Irish maps c. 1600* (Dublin, 1964).
20. J. H. Andrews, *Irish maps*, Irish Heritage Series 18, (Dublin, 1978).
21. Map and survey of Ireland by John Norden with list of forts etc. 1610, P.R.O.N.I., T. 1493/1, 11-32.
22. G. Hill, *The Montgomery manuscripts 1603-1706* (Belfast, 1869).
23. N. D. G. James, *A History of English forestry* (Oxford, 1981).
24. E. P. Shirley, 'Catalogue of maps and plans relating to Ireland' in *U.J.A.*, iii (1855), pp 72-6.
25. Reproduced in *U.J.A.*, ii (1854), pp 145-60.
26. O. Rackham, *Ancient woodland* (London, 1980).
27. Hill, *Montgomery maunscripts*, p. 41.
28. Ibid., p. 86.
29. Rackham, *Ancient woodland*.
30. Volume of 79 maps of Clandeboye or Bangor estate of Hamilton family showing town plans of Bangor, Holywood and Killyleagh by Thomas Raven, P.R.O.N.I., T. 870.
31. V. Hall, 'Landscape development in northeast Ireland over the last half millenium' in *Rev. of Palaeobotany and Palynology*, lxxxii (1994), pp 75-82.
32. R. C. Simington (ed.), *The Civil Survey 1654-6*, x (Dublin, 1961).
33. E. McCracken and D. McCracken, *A register of trees for county Londonderry, 1768-1911* (Belfast, 1984).
34. Ibid.
35. P.R.O.N.I., Dow 7/3/2/1-3.
36. McCracken and McCracken, *A register of trees*.
37. Ibid.
38. Ibid.
39. Tomlinson, 1985, Mournes – Slieve Croob A.O.N.B.
40. McCracken and McCracken, *A register of trees*.
41. E. Malins and P. Bowe, *Irish gardens and demesnes from 1830* (London, 1980).

42. Lord Dunleath, 'Not a botanical golf course' in Ulster Architectural Heritage Society, *Ballywalter Park* (Belfast, 1985).

43. Four maps of Mourne Park, Kilkeel. Mainly by John and James Wilson, P.R.O.N.I., D. 3514/1-4.

44. *Down.*

45. Forest Service, Tollymore forest park, Department of Agriculture for Northern Ireland, Belfast, no date.

46. A. Day and P. McWilliams, *Ordnance survey memoirs of Ireland*, iii, Parishes of county Down i, 1834-6; Mid-Down (Belfast, 1990).

47. Forest Service, *Afforestation – the DANI statement on environmental policy*, Department of Agriculture for Northern Ireland, Belfast, 1993.

48. C. Guyer and C. Edwards, 'The role of farm woodland in Northern Ireland: an appraisal' in *Irish Geography*, xxii (1989), pp 79-85.

49. J. R. Pilcher, 'Application of dendrochronological techniques to the investigation of woodland history' in *Irish Naturalists Journal*, xix (1979), pp 377-980.

50. L. T. Brown, A survey of turf working in county Down, Unpub. MSc. thesis, Q.U.B., 1968.

51. Environment Service, county Down nature reserves, Department of the Environment for Northern Ireland, Belfast, no date.

Plate 10.4   Gill Hall House, Coolsallagh, seventeenth century (Ulster Museum, W05/44/14).

Chapter 11

REBELS AND RADICALS: THE UNITED IRISHMEN IN COUNTY DOWN

NANCY J. CURTIN

If the strongest pillar in the United Irish movement was the province of Ulster, the strongest pillar in Ulster was county Down. The county boasted the largest number of sworn United Irishmen (over 28,000 out of a population estimated at about 200,000 in the early 1790s).[1] It was in Down, with its large Catholic minority, that the United Irishmen could test most effectively their claim to unite Catholic and Protestant under the common name of Irishmen. It was in Down, second only to Armagh, where the United Irishmen confronted divisive sectarian hostility in the organization of Defenders and Peep o' Day boys. Approximately half the county's population were Presbyterians, one quarter were Roman Catholic and the remainder were Anglican. The Roman Catholics were proportionately strongest in the southern baronies of Mourne, Lecale and Newry, while the Presbyterians were most numerous in the north and east of the county and the Anglicans most numerous in the west.

At this time, the county also enjoyed an almost unparalleled prosperity, where a relatively even balance existed between agriculture and linen manufacturing. Edward Wakefield observed that 'the land is in a high state of cultivation, and inhabited by a middle class of opulent manufacturers, whose appearance and condition would do credit to any country in Europe'.[2] Presiding over these comfortable farmers and prospering merchants was a sizeable gentry (nearly 100 landlords in 1812), themselves dominated by a handful of rival families like the powerful Hills (marquess of Downshire), the Hamiltons of Killyleagh, the Montgomerys of Newtownards, the Trevors of Rostrevor, the Rawdons of Moira, the Prices of Saintfield, the Wards of Bangor and the Stewarts of Mountstewart. In 1790 these families contested for the votes of 11,000 freeholders, a figure which topped the list of Irish county electorates, and slipped only slightly in rank after the enfranchisement of Catholics in 1793, which led to a registered electorate in Down of 16,000 by the end of the decade.[3]

County Down thus enjoyed considerable diversity in its religious culture, economy and society, and in the politics which provided fertile ground for both the challenge to Protestant Ascendancy and exclusivity in Ireland and its defense. The United Irishmen were able to bustle in a county which already possessed a high level of popular politicisation conducive to radicalization. The county was dominated politically by the Downshire family, but their ascendancy received many electoral challenges. The Volunteers had also been strong in the county, and when the United Irishmen revived the reform movement they incorporated many pre-existing corps. Resurgent sectarianism provoked the emergence of strong bodies of Defenders in the west (along the Armagh border) and in the south of the county. Ideological inspiration emanated from Belfast, particularly through the vehicle of the United Irish newspaper, the *Northern Star*, and leadership came overwhelmingly from radical merchants and Presbyterian ministers.

Certainly Down was a highly politicized society even before the French revolution and its polarizing influence burst on the scene. The initiative of the United Irishmen in uniting Catholic and Protestant behind the twin goals of parliamentary reform and the elimination of confessional distinctions in the exercise of citizenship was a product of a new opportunity rather than new ideas. Indeed, the idea of a union of all Irishmen exerting themselves as citizens was long rooted in the Volunteer tradition, and owes as much to a pervading civic humanist programme which was especially strong in the Scottish universities which educated the professional elite of Ulster society. Civic humanism assumed that corruption, defined as the subordination of the public good to private interests, unravelled the fabric of the commonwealth, and that the only counter to this debilitating disease was civic virtue, the exertion of disinterested citizens assuming their civic obligations.[4] The expression of civic virtue was nowhere more evident than in the formation of an independent citizen militia, the Volunteers. In its earliest incarnation in the late 1770s, the Volunteers followed traditional deferential patterns. Most corps were led by the landed elite and the purpose of the body was to defend Ireland against a French invasion during the American war. The Volunteers became politicized as a fairly united political elite, and demanded commercial and constitutional concessions from a distracted and beleaguered Britain. After the Constitutional Revolution of 1782, volunteering became identified with political reform and the membership declined. The Volunteers persisted after the reform movement died out in the early 1780s, and while some of the corps continued as a gentry-dominated, peace-keeping auxiliary force, many others retained their interest in political questions. At the height of the reform movement, some of these corps admitted Catholics into their ranks, and it was even speculated that only a union of

Catholic and Protestant united by their civic responsibilities could secure a fair and equal representation of the people of Ireland in parliament.[5]

The French revolution translated such speculation into deeds in three ways. First, at a general level, by asserting the sovereignty of the people as a nation of citizens, it democratized the civic humanism which was not only the legacy of Irish radicals, but of their opponents as well.[6] Citizenship had hitherto been closely associated with property; only those with a stake in the society should have a say in its government. The liberal nationalism of the French revolution, however, elided differences in status, class, or confessional allegiance, by proclaiming a sovereign and indivisible people.[7] From indivisible people to United Irishmen was but a short leap, though a momentous one in Ireland, for it required the radicals to discard sectarian suspicions rooted in divergent histories. That this happened was due to the second influence the French revolution had on Irish radicals, especially Protestant ones. The revolution occurred in a Catholic country and proceeded to abolish not only the established church, but all religious disqualifications based on religion. If Catholics in France could act so decisively on behalf of the nation rather than the chapel, could not Irish Catholics do the same? This was one of the key arguments in Theobald Wolfe Tone's widely influential *Argument on behalf of the Catholics of Ireland*, which went far in countering Presbyterian fears and so contributing to the formation of the first Society of United Irishmen in Belfast in October 1791.[8]

Having thus embraced an ideology as well as a strategy which united Catholic and Protestant behind radical reform in Ireland, Irish radicals benefitted, so to speak, from a third influence of the French revolution – war. The continental war which erupted in 1792, and which Britain and Ireland entered in early 1793, provided the context for the spiral of radicalism and counter-revolution that burst at last in 1798. And contemporaries had little doubt that it was an ideological war, whether seen in terms of a conflict between order and anarchy or tyranny and liberty. As an ideological war, it polarized internally as well as externally. The French had their partisans in all the belligerent countries, and certainly the United Irishmen took pride of place among them.

The catalysing effects of war can be seen on many levels. First, the United Irishmen, claiming the side of liberty, denounced the war for its economic consequences, blaming it for unemployment, bankruptcy and the high costs of credit, thus courting popular support.[9] Second, they saw the war as opportunity, initially perhaps in the expectation that war abroad would result in co-opting concessions at home, as happened during the American conflict, but eventually as the opportunity to cement an alliance with a powerful and ideologically compatible republic. But in either case, the United Irishmen emerged unquestionably as a pro-French party, provoking a third effect of the war – government reaction.

War, or the anticipation of war, was responsible for the two initiatives which Thomas Bartlett and Jim Smyth have argued broke down popular deference in Ireland – Catholic relief and the Militia Act.[10] Under British pressure, which in itself was responding to the impending war and Catholic awareness of the price of their loyalty, the Irish parliament was forced to breach the walls of Protestant exclusivity and pass the Catholic Relief Acts of 1792 and 1793. This was the highest price Britain would pay to attach Catholics to the establishment. In return, Catholics were expected to participate in the second initiative, the militia. The militia was to serve in the first instance as an Irish-based force, under direct government control, to serve the military needs of Ireland during the war, thus freeing British regular troops for service abroad. Since this was also the alleged purpose of the politicized Volunteers corps, the militia would in the second instance make the less controllable body redundant and therefore suppressible. Thus Catholics would receive certain significant, if still limited rights (they could vote but not assume high office or seats in parliament), but would be required to accept a corresponding obligation to defend the country and preserve the British connection. The Volunteers, by now a stalking horse for the United Irishmen, would be prohibited. Catholics would become attached to the state while radicals would be isolated.

In the short term, government repression and legal harassment of the United Irishmen, together with concessions to the Catholics, had been relatively successful in stemming the tide of radicalization. But the recall in 1795 of a popular viceroy, Earl Fitzwilliam, proclaimed the limits of Pitt's bounteousness, while an event of the preceding year, the capture of French agent, Rev. William Jackson, combined to transform the United Irishmen into that mass-based citizen army which boasted a half million supporters.[11] By signalling French interest in assisting an Irish insurrection, Jackson's mission provided the radicals with a release from the doldrums of their marginalization – an alliance with the greatest military power in Europe.[12] By dashing any hopes of reform, Pitt's recall of Fitzwilliam convinced the radicals that it would be easier to overthrow the Government than reform it. The war of words, of propaganda and politicisation, merged with a militarized civil conflict. The United Irishman now called for a democratic, secular republic, compromising their lofty ideals at times to court a mass following. The Protestant Ascendancy set itself against this perceived levelling and demagogic movement, and courted its own mass following, given institutional recognition in the Orange Order and the yeomanry corps which emerged in 1796.

The Society of United Irishmen, founded in Belfast in October 1791, called for radical parliamentary reform, Catholic emancipation, and a union of Catholic and Protestant to achieve its aims.[13] Its roots were firmly in the Volunteer reform movement of the 1780s, and although Theobald Wolfe Tone and Dr. William Drennan have both been credited with its inspiration, the true organizers were a secret committee of Belfast Volunteers led by a linen-merchant, Samuel Neilson.[14] The Society was overwhelmingly Presbyterian at its birth, reflecting the confessional demographics of the north-east. The organizational history of the United Irishmen in its early phase was so modest as to appear unremarkable. In November 1791 a Dublin Society of United Irishmen emerged, whose situation in the capital lent it the most public prominence. But in Ulster, which enjoyed the highest number of clubs, there were only nine mentioned in the sources for the early 1790s, one in Armagh, six in Antrim, and only two in Down (at Saintfield and Newry).[15] 'I am somewhat surprised they do not multiply more', observed a puzzled Drennan to his brother-in-law in Belfast, Samuel McTier, 'and I think your societies should exert themselves individually and by circular letter throughout all the towns about'.[16] But there is no evidence that the Belfast society, or even the Dublin one of which Drennan was a member, took this admonition to heart. This was because the societies saw their function as primarily propagandist – to disseminate political information and to co-ordinate whenever possible impressive public displays of the apparently widespread reform sentiment. There was no need to reproduce United Irish societies when Volunteers corps such as those in Downpatrick and Ballynahinch fully endorsed their aims.[17] Not all Volunteers espoused radical positions, but new Volunteers corps were forming which did. 'The patriotic spirit of volunteering daily increases,' the *Northern Star* exalted in July 1792. 'There appears a general resurrection of the Volunteer body throughout the counties of Down and Antrim'.[18]

Reform sentiments were further endorsed by town and parish meetings, Presbyterian congregations, masonic lodges, and freeholders' meetings which culminated in the Dungannon convention of February 1793.[19] The following June the Synod of Ulster held its annual meeting at Lurgan and elected Dr. William Steele Dickson of Portaferry moderator. A member of the United Irishmen and an ardent champion of Catholic rights, Dickson led the assembly in calling for immediate reform of the abuses of government.[20]

Concerned to present the reform movement as irresistible and universal, the United Irish propagandists certainly exaggerated the extent of unanimity in the north regarding reform and Catholic Emancipation. Nevertheless, the mobilization of reformers was as heartening to the radicals as it was alarming to the government. In Down two forces were working to undermine this apparent juggernaut of reformism – the explosion of sectarian violence in the south and west of the county, and the exertions of Lord Downshire to undermine the Volunteers and replace them with the Government-controlled militia.

Downshire himself wrote to the lord lieutenant in May 1792, requesting troops to counter the infection of Defenderism in his county. 'From three to four thousand of those deluded people regularly assemble every day and night in arms, training themselves in the use of them'.[21] Downshire's ally and fellow Down landlord, Lord Annesley, reported his own conclusion about the state of his neighbourhood of Castlewellan. He found 'the papists are getting more insolent every day. . . . The most worthless of the people they have for captains, and a protestant can't go out of the house but the bullets are flying about them'.[22] Lord Lieutenant Westmorland responded quickly to Downshire's request for troops, but was pessimistic about their long-term effect in pacifying the county. Noting that the 'Defenders' spirit spreads very rapidly', he pronounced himself 'convinced that some other mode besides soldiers must be devised to check it, or the effects will be very alarming'.[23]

Other modes were found, and came from an unlikely source. The sectarian disturbances in county Down were certainly embarrassing to Downshire, but perhaps even more embarrassing to the United Irishmen and their allies in the Catholic Committee. While middle-class Catholics and Protestants were proclaiming a brotherhood of mutual affection, lower-class Catholics and Protestants were mobilizing for mutual destruction in south Down. The Rev. Samuel Barber, Volunteer, United Irishman, and Presbyterian minister, arranged a temporary truce after the trouble began in May 1792. But by the next month disturbances were once again assuming alarming proportions, despite the presence of the troops provided by Westmorland at Downshire's request. On July 14 in Belfast, a delegation of Catholic Committee men joined the Volunteers and the United Irishmen in celebrating that dawn of liberty, the anniversary of the storming of the Bastille. The carefully staged event and its resulting declarations proclaimed the amicable union of Catholic and Protestant in Ireland. The participants were only too aware of how this ideal was being compromised in south Down, and a few days later Samuel Neilson proposed that a delegation be sent to Rathfriland to attempt a reconciliation of their lower-class co-religionists. Joining Neilson was the then secretary to the Catholic Committee, Theobald Wolfe Tone, its leader John Keogh, and Alexander Lowry, a local linen merchant who later assumed some prominence in both the Defender and the United Irish organizations. Local Volunteers were enjoined to protect Catholics from Peep o' Day Boy attacks, local magistrates promised impartial justice, and the delegation issued a widely circulated address directed at the Defenders to desist from their mobilization.[24] Such efforts were temporarily successful, although Defenderism itself merely spilled over from Down and Armagh into Louth and Meath, reasserting itself formidably in 1793 and more ominously, coinciding with the militia riots of that year.

While Downshire and the middle-class radicals were equally embarrassed by the resurgence of sectarian disturbances in Down in the summer of 1792, they offered sharply diverging explanations for its occurrence. Downshire and Ascendancy supporters pointed to the levelling principles emanating from Belfast and Dublin, the diffusion of Painite propaganda by United Irishmen, and the civic presumptions of the Catholic Committee. The reformers condemned partial justice, and bigoted landowners and magistrates who encouraged lower-class Protestants and even provided them with that currency of citizenship and status, arms.[25] And yet both sides seem to have agreed that the conflict was fundamentally political, with the Catholic question assuming a democratic character encouraged by the United Irishmen. Lower-class Protestants may have feared the levelling of their own civic status as Catholic relief put them on the same level with lower-class Catholics. How else is one to explain the potent popular defense of the principle of Protestant Ascendancy, articulated by the grand juries in most of the Irish counties in 1792? Taking their cue from the Dublin Corporation, alarmed at both the boldness of Catholic demands and British sympathy for them, Protestant freeholders declared they 'would not be compelled by any authority whatsoever to abandon that political situation which their forefathers won with their swords, and which is therefore their birthright'.[26]

The principle of Protestant exclusivity was breached by the Catholic Relief Acts of 1792 and 1793, which invited Catholics into some of the privileges of citizenship in order that they could undertake one of its chief responsibilities, national defense. The Irish regular military establishment was insufficient to meet the needs of external defense and internal police-keeping expected of it. The Volunteers were becoming more unreliable as they once again surfaced as popular politicians. The Government needed a force that could be directly controlled and Downshire's son, Lord Hillsborough, who in the same year, 1793, succeeded his father to the family title, was instrumental in its formation in county Down, though in the process he succeeded in polarizing the county still further.

The new militia was associated with the Government's assault on organized radicalism in the Volunteer corps, especially the new ones, so firmly rooted in the notion of citizenship. The Volunteers saw themselves as a citizen army, that great safeguard of national liberty, the mobilization of which both signified a free people but also countered the forces of corrupted self-interest in the polity. It was axiomatic in civic humanist discourse that corruption reigned when military obligations were transferred from citizens to mercenaries. Some degree of citizenship was conferred on Catholics in return for their participation in the militia. But by the same token, some degree of citizenship was taken away from the Volunteers when they were thus displaced.

Citizenship was the fundamental issue of the 1790s, and in offering citizenship to all sectors of Irish society, the United Irish succeeded in politicizing all current grievances. Thus, when Hillsborough solicited the co-operation of John Kennedy of Cultra in forming a Down militia, Kennedy respectfully declined:

> Having had the honour of a command in a Volunteer corps for several years past, raised on this part of my estate, consisting of 48 men rank and file, tenants of my own, I cannot think of abdicating a trust reposed in me by so respectable a body, to join any new association by whatever appellation that may be styled. I cannot but consider the Old Volunteers as the natural guardians of our isle.[27]

Nicholas Price complained to Downshire of his difficulties in garnering support for the militia. 'Those scoundrels' were 'busy day and night' turning the popular mind against the measure.[28] John Slade informed Lord Hillsborough that his opponents in his 'own country ring the militia in the ears of the Volunteers to make you unpopular'.[29] The identification of the militia as not only anti-Volunteer but also anti-Catholic was bemoaned by one of the Down's militia own chief officers. Major George Matthews complained that the bigoted Lord Annesley, a colonel of the regiment, was threatening to resign because of the number of Catholics in the ranks. Annesley was 'displeased' about some of the men going to mass, announced his determination not to 'serve in a papist regiment', questioned the loyalty of the regiment, and suggested that he would do better to stay 'at home to defend his property against the papists'. 'No men can behave better',

Matthews maintained, 'if properly treated, but if religious distinctions are kept among them, I am certain it will be attended with bad consequences'.[30] Annesley himself had previously complained that in the Mourne the regiment was enrolling 'a cunning set of Presbyterians, mixed with a set of papists'.[31]

If the militia was politicized at its inception, it remained so throughout its life in the 1790s, at least until the rebellion of 1798 when it proved its loyalty to the state.[32] Until then, however, the corps were always suspect, especially the predominantly Catholic ones, and with some reason. Enrolling poor Catholics meant enrolling Defenders. The irony was that by sending the corps off to serve in other counties, Defenderism was exported as well. By 1796 the United Irishmen were avidly courting militia men, taking pains to exaggerate their success. General Knox in Armagh even threatened to resign when the Irish commander-in-chief, Lord Carhampton, based his deployment of forces on the assumption that the militia, with rare exceptions, constituted a dependable force.[33] Local magistrates, like Robert Waddell in west Down, persistently complained about having to rely on Catholic militia troops, whom they regarded as scarcely distinguishable from the United Irishmen and Defenders.[34] Calling upon the Down magistracy to be vigilant and bold in countering disturbances, Downshire lamented that the Cork and Dublin militia stationed in the county 'are Papists [and] Defenders without much discipline'.[35]

But, as in other areas of Irish society, politicisation of the militia meant not only the infection of Defenderism or republicanism within the corps, but also the entrenchment of loyalism. Major Matthews' dire predictions of the consequences of condoning sectarianism in the Down militia were confirmed a few years later when the Orangemen secured a foothold in the corps. The ringleaders insinuated that Orange lodges enjoyed the approval of Downshire himself. 'There is nothing surer than that Orangemen, if it [sic] goes on, will be the means of making United men'.[36]

The point is that the fundamental issue of contention in Down, as in much of the rest of Ulster, was one of citizenship, and citizenship, because of its association with the civic humanist tradition, was signalled by the bearing of arms. That the militia was successfully introduced, despite strong popular opposition, and the Volunteers were suppressed, meant that the militarisation of politics escalated to a new level. No more could radicals and reformers mobilize in a citizen army sanctioned by a historic, if not very long tradition. Yet the radicals did not abandon the model of the citizen army, nor did the Volunteer corps, suppressed in 1793, just evaporate. Instead many corps simply went underground and were eventually incorporated in the United

Irish network, in effect undergoing an organizational readjustment in the face of government harassment and prohibition.[37]

The militarisation of Europe, therefore, was mirrored by the militarisation of county Down, and perhaps this explains as much as any other single factor the character of politicisation in the county. The virtual exclusion of the popular voice in the established political arena of parliament, or at best its mediation there through a tepid and elitist whiggism, demanded a wider arena for popular political engagement. Thus it was that the United Irishmen emerged as an armed body of citizens, claiming for themselves the virtue of the nation. Even if the spell of the Volunteers had been weaker on the United Irishmen, there were few alternative or practical models for their mobilization. The vehicles of public demonstration or representative convention were denied them, more or less, after 1793. The radical press provided a forum of sorts, a sort of literary anti-parliament in which to engage in political discourse, but the press was subject to constant government harassment, and radical polemics alone were insufficient to move the government to reform itself. But Volunteering did exert a powerful hold over the imagination of the United Irishmen, reinforced by their civic humanism, and when the prospect of French aid emerged after 1794 while the movement was at its nadir, a paramilitary model of organization was embraced.[38]

Prior to 1794 an informal organization of loosely affiliated clubs served the needs of the United Irishmen. Once the United Irishmen adopted an insurrectionary strategy, for which they expected French support, they required a tighter and more hierarchical organizational structure wherein the local societies sent representatives to superior committees at the baronial, county, and ultimately provincial level. This new organizational structure along with a new constitution was formally approved by the representatives of seventy-two local societies (claiming a total of about 5,000 members), mostly from Down and Antrim, on 10 May 1795 in Belfast.[39] A few months later, in August 1795, an Ulster provincial committee was formed, representing over 8,000 United Irishmen from counties Antrim, Down, Armagh, and Tyrone.[40] But at this stage the strength and core of the movement lay within a twenty-mile radius of Belfast, which alone boasted sixteen societies.[41] The primary task of the United Irishmen then was to shore up and organize this base.

Returns of membership at this time seem to reflect only rough estimates of membership, as pre-existing clubs were regulated and absorbed and new societies established. In July 1795, for example, Down claimed 2,000 members, rising to 4,000 the following September.[42] Over a year later, however, a more precise number of

11,016 is offered.[43] This suggests that the new organization was solidly in place by then, and busily expanding into the rest of Ulster. Meanwhile, the numbers of members in county Down steadily rose. In February 1797 the county claimed 15,000 United Irishmen, and by May membership may have peaked at 28,577 and for the first time surpassed the numbers in county Antrim (with 22,716 members).[44] By the end of 1796 the United Irishmen superimposed a military organization on their civil one, preparing for the general insurrection to be co-ordinated with an expected French invasion of Ireland.[45]

Organizational zeal and assiduous propaganda accounted for this growth, but equally important was the appearance of the first fruits of the United Irish alliance with revolutionary France, the appearance of the French fleet in Bantry Bay in December 1796. From October 1796 to February 1797 United Irish membership in Ulster nearly doubled from 38,567 to 69,190, and then nearly doubled again from February to May 1797, when the northern republicans boasted 117,917 comrades.[46] Although the invasion failed, it dramatically proclaimed French resolve to assist an Irish insurrection and gave the United Irish project an aura of inevitability, creating a bandwagon affect.[47]

'Nothing can be more alarming than the present state of the country', a county Down magistrate insisted in April 1797. 'Almost all the peasantry of every description are United Irishmen – multitudes of [the] rich and of the middle class are avowedly of the confederacy; and many of the principal gentry are so much inclined that way that nothing seems wanting but a French invasion to induce the people to rise in mass'.[48] Indeed, United Irishmen permeated every level of Down society. Of the 372 members in the county for whom an occupation can be identified, about 30 per cent worked in the agricultural sector, over 47 per cent in commerce and manufacturing, while 20 per cent could be described as professional. This last category includes forty-two Presbyterian ministers and eight Roman Catholic priests, who were clearly in a position to offer divine sanction for insurrectionary activity.[49] Using the 1821 census figures as a base of comparison, it appears that the agricultural sector was slightly under-represented among the United Irishmen, while commercial, industrial and professional sectors were over-represented.[50] Merchants and ministers certainly dominated the leadership of the movement.[51] It was the 'shopkeepers, petty merchants, and innholders in the county towns', one magistrate reported, 'a set of men more out of reach of grievance and oppression than any other description I know of', who were the principal local instigators of the United Irishmen, encouraged by the 'great democrats in Belfast and Newry, who furnish them with goods for the country and topics for sedition'.[52] A Presbyterian affinity with radicalism and a liberal capitalism associated with this commercial class combined powerfully to challenge Ireland's old regime.

But when the peace of the county was first disturbed in the latter half of the 1790s, it was not through the activities of the United Irishmen. Indeed, the first reference in the Downshire papers to the mobilization of the republicans in Down does not occur until late March 1796, when Downshire's agent, Thomas Lane, reported that 'another body of miscreants are starting up to the northeast of us [Hillsborough] under the denomination of United Irishmen, who mean, as we are told, to neither pay tithes, cess or [sic] taxes'.[53] Of greater concern was the spilling over of organized sectarian warfare from neighbouring county Armagh.

The mid-1780s witnessed the birth of the Catholic Defenders and the Protestant Peep o' Day boys in county Armagh, arguably as a result of a combination of ritualised faction-fighting, the easing of the penal laws against Catholics which alarmed lower-class Protestants, and the exercise of justice on the part of the magistracy.[54] The disturbances were largely confined to Armagh until the early 1790s, when, as we have already seen, sectarianism infected south Down, possibly partly in consequence of the dominance of the Catholic question on the national political scene. The lull in Defender/Peep o' Day Boy activities in Armagh and Down after 1793 was accompanied by an expansion of Defenderism into the midland and western counties in 1794 and 1795. Then, in September 1795, the troubles re-erupted with a vengeance in Armagh, culminating in the infamous battle of the Diamond and the subsequent institutionalisation of the Loyal Orange Order. Receiving covert and sometimes overt support from ultraloyalist magistrates, the Orange Order followed up what they conceived as a divinely sanctioned victory at the Diamond with a concerted and vicious campaign of intimidation against Catholics designed to provoke their departure from the county.[55] The Orangemen succeeded in expelling perhaps 7,000 Catholics from Armagh, but they also provoked a resurgence of Defenderism and provided an opportunity for the United Irishmen, intent on establishing a mass-based organization, to reach out to the Defenders as allies.[56] The history of this alliance is unclear. Earl Camden, the lord lieutenant, assumed a formal compact was entered into in August 1796.[57] But prior to that date the United Irishmen assiduously recruited among the Defenders, employing republican barristers like Thomas Addis Emmet and William Sampson to represent Defenders at the assizes, sending emissaries like Henry Joy McCracken to invite Defender bodies into the United Irish organization, and establishing links between the two organizations through Catholic brethren such as Charles Hamilton Teeling, the son of a Lisburn linen manufacturer, who is said to have assumed chief command of the Defenders in Down, Antrim, and Armagh.[58]

The authorities had suspected, with little foundation, that United Irishmen and Defenders had been in league together since 1792, and they were certainly aware of these efforts to align the two organizations in 1795. Yet it was the outburst of sectarian fighting in the 'linen triangle' in late 1795 and 1796 that claimed the greater attention of those responsible for maintaining the king's peace. The linen triangle, extending roughly from Lisburn to Dungannon and Newry, included the west Down baronies of Upper and Lower Iveagh adjacent to county Armagh, and these districts had the distinction of being the first to be proclaimed under the draconian Insurrection Act of 1796.[59] An extreme and costly measure, the Act was employed only when local authorities acknowledged their inability to restore peace and order through more traditional methods. Local magistrates could petition the lord lieutenant to proclaim a district under martial law with its consequent suspension of conventional civil liberties. In appealing to the government to declare his own neighbourhood in west Down under the Act, Robert Waddell observed that 'there is not a night almost [that] passes without breaking, robbery, burning of houses, sometimes, murder, and very often near it'. But his letter also noted that the United Irishmen, 'going on in their own accursed and evil way,' were not a party to the hostilities.[60] Magistracy reluctance to use the full force of law to quell the disturbances at their earliest outbreak may have been due to some sympathy with the widely acknowledged instigators. Letters to Downshire from Thomas Lane throughout the first half of 1796 describe the Orangemen as the perpetrators of the outrages.[61] But even biased magistrates came to see that the effect of these depredations against the Catholic tenantry was to drive them into the arms of the republicans. Joseph Pollock noted in August 1796 that 'the *discontents* and *fears* of the Roman Catholics there [in county Down] are becoming very great, and that the United Irishmen are increasing *by thousands*'. He especially singled out the neighbourhoods of Dromore, Rathfriland, and Saintfield.[62] By the end of the month, one Down magistrate reported that three-fourths of the people of that county were 'up', or sworn United Irishmen.[63] And throughout the following months magistrates from all over the county were reporting rumours of an imminent insurrection.[64]

The government was facing a truly alarming situation by the end of the summer of 1796. Thousands were joining the ranks of the United Irishmen. The normal judicial channels were proving ineffective to contain the creeping insurgency. Republican and Defender emissaries were boasting of great success in seducing militiamen from their loyalty. A French invasion was expected by the end of the year, and Earl Camden, the lord lieutenant, seriously doubted whether Ireland could be held for the crown.[65] Camden and his chief secretary, Thomas Pelham, blamed the escalating situation on the timidity of the local magistracy, but rousing them to action was a different matter.[66]

It may have been hoped that the mere threat of imposing the Insurrection Act would be sufficient to quell disorder. Camden and Pelham recognized that the Act was controversial and extreme.[67] Local magistrates regarded its implementation in the neighbourhoods as a disgrace.[68] And there was a further problem in resorting to the Act. Some outrageous breach of the peace was required before a district could be proclaimed. This presented the government with a serious dilemma in dealing with the republicans. Where the United Irishmen were strong and well organized, the magistracy was weak and the occasion for disturbance limited. As Camden complained to Home Secretary Portland, 'that part of the country whence most danger is to be apprehended is apparently most quiet and peaceable'. Furthermore, the United Irishmen, as opposed to the Defenders, were, by August 1796, still meeting in small numbers, often at private houses; 'their conduct is cautious and they are never guilty of outrage'.[69] Thus the United Irishmen proceeded steadily in augmenting their numbers and extending their organization, and the authorities were at a loss how to stop them.

The Defenders and Orangemen, however, were a different matter. Orange outrages provoked Defender reactions, often taking the form of raiding the neighbourhood for arms, that highly contested badge of citizenship. The only proclaimed districts in county Down were in the western part of the country, in an area extending roughly from Lisburn to Newry, which formed part of the linen triangle and was the site of revived and intensely violent sectarian warfare.[70] The Act, however, proved ineffective in suppressing or containing the disturbances, as evidenced by the array of successive measures adopted by the authorities to fortify themselves against the onslaught of the republicans. The conflict was becoming, in a sense, more regularized, and the vigilante activities of Defenders and Orangemen flowed into new channels. The Defenders became more closely allied to the United Irishmen and the Orangemen moved from outside the law to within it when the government launched the yeomanry in October 1796.[71]

With a French invasion expected, the government was loath to disperse its scarce military forces among all the neighbourhoods contending with the incursion of the United Irishmen. Magistrates were called to account for their timidity, yet how were they to counter this burgeoning mass movement without calling upon the troops? The militia was regarded as tainted with Jacobinism and Defenderism, and in general unreliable. To root out sedition in the localities, many active loyal magistrates argued, it was necessary to employ and arm local loyalists.[72] The yeomanry was thus conceived of as an armed defense association proclaiming its devotion to the king and constitution. But unlike the Volunteers, the yeomanry would be under direct government control and placed at the service of their local magistrates and military commanders. Camden feared that, under existing circumstances, instituting the yeomanry would be regarded as 'arming the protestants against the papists'.[73] It was inevitable that in the north the new corps would consist in large part of the most violent loyalists, those repelled by the United Irish pleas for radical reform and alarmed by the resurgence of Catholic Ireland represented by the Defenders. The first and most enthusiastic recruits were Orangemen who used their early entry to exclude Catholics from their ranks.[74] The yeomanry corps thus became a haven for Orangemen, and to the United Irishmen and Defenders, the Yeomanry Act merely gave official sanction to continuing Orange outrages.[75] Once again, Downshire was a key figure in instituting the yeomanry, using his own county as the model for other corps.[76] Once again, popular politicisation in county Down was militarized, or rather, the militarisation was intensified and regularized.

The fruits of that French-United Irish alliance, the failed French invasion attempt at Bantry Bay in December 1796, proved a boon not only to republican recruiting efforts, but also to the take-off of the yeomanry corps. A freakish blizzard had foiled the attempt, a Protestant wind loyalists might call it. But Ireland remained vulnerable to foreign invasion and internal rebellion once the initial alarm had passed. The next attempt might, after all, be successful. The government determined that its only defense against such a twin assault was to neutralize the internal threat before the next external one arrived. Bantry Bay was a wake-up call for all loyalists who, recognizing their situation as desperate, began to enrol in the yeomanry corps in droves.[77] The steady rise in yeomanry enrolments and the frequently published expressions of loyalty encouraged the government to take the hitherto dangerous step of disarming and pacifying Ulster.

The United Irishmen were doing more than merely organizing. As the movement extended beyond its tightly organized base around Belfast, and especially as it embraced the more independent bodies of Defenders, the insurgents engaged in a wide variety of activities which called down on themselves a severe government reaction. Recruitment and propaganda may have been the main priorities of the leadership, but local societies were more concerned with establishing dominance in their own neighbourhoods. This involved arming themselves and disarming their opponents, cowing the magistracy and local loyalists into passivity, assuring those of their members who did fall into the hands of the law that they would be acquitted, and generally displaying their strength and discipline. Arms raids were prohibited by the United Irish leaders but local societies casually disregarded orders with which they disagreed.[78] Such activity provided the single best reason for invoking the insurrection act in a district and sanctioning an aggressive magistracy and yeomanry.

Of course it was hoped zealous loyalists might be deterred by intimidation. Magistrates were frequent recipients of threatening letters warning them off the hunt for the seditious. If the warning went unheeded, the threat would be followed through. One such target of republican assassination was the Rev. Philip Johnson, an Anglican clergyman from Lisburn, who was fortunate to survive the attempt on his life. An outspoken advocate of the Orange Order who used his position as a magistrate to offer Orangemen special treatment, Johnson was virulently anti-Catholic and anti-reform, and he very zealously carried out his duties as a magistrate in north Down, provoking the republicans' sanguinary response.[79] Jurors and witnesses were also intimidated, and the authorities found themselves frustrated in the courts when it came to bringing the United Irishmen to justice. Juries at the county Down assizes, Thomas Lane complained to Downshire, 'would not, some durst not, convict, and . . . almost every prisoner was acquitted, let the atrocity of his crime be of what magnitude it would. During the whole week there were but three convicted, and they are not to suffer'.[80] 'No man gives evidence', another Down magistrate complained, 'because they say it is no use risking themselves when no one gets hanged'.[81]

The republican victory in the courts is evidenced by the conviction rate at the Down county assizes during the period from 1796 to 1798. Out of eighty-seven persons tried in 1796, only 19.5 per cent were convicted, 16.1 per cent out of 168 in 1797, and 16.7 per cent out of sixty in 1798. National conviction rates were as follows: 25.6 per cent out of 2,675 in 1796, 24 per cent out of 2,991 in 1797, and 31.4 per cent out of 2,470 in 1798.[82] Thus, the significantly lower conviction rate in county Down suggests the republicans were besting the government in the courts. Indeed, it was the extreme difficulty of convicting United Irishmen which led to the adoption of draconian methods by the government.

The Insurrection Act was invoked to bypass judicial channels tampered with by the republicans. In October 1796 the Irish parliament also suspended *habeas corpus,* thus giving the authorities free reign to arrest well-known United Irish leaders and detain them indefinitely.

Confident that the measure would pass, Camden had already issued orders for the arrest of key northern leaders such as Samuel Neilson, Henry Joy McCracken, and Thomas Russell.[83] The intention was to throw the movement into confusion by removing the heads of the conspiracy. But the organization was so sufficiently advanced that new leaders merely stepped into the position of those arrested.

A mass-based secret society was already somewhat of a contradiction in terms, and the United Irishmen traded absolute discretion for the strenuous assertion of a public presence.[84] While the leaders disapproved of arms raids and other outrages, they encouraged quasi-public demonstrations which served the twin purposes of propagandistically displaying local United Irish strength and drilling the rank and file in assembling at short notice. The arrest of the leaders, for example, provided such an opportunity, as hundreds, even thousands, of United Irishmen were summoned to harvest the potato crops of their incarcerated brethren.[85] Pharis Martin, Jr. described one such crowd of harvesters marching 'through the streets of [Ballynahinch] with their fifes playing and carrying ensigns of rebellion'.[86] Such impudent boldness in associating also characterized the mock funerals conducted by the United Irishmen. Often there would be no body in the coffin which thousands solemnly followed in procession. Rather, it was an occasion for the United Irishmen to practice their drills and show themselves to the public at large.[87] Sporting events such as race meetings or boxing matches were also employed as ostensibly innocuous occasions for the United Irishmen to assemble and intimidate by their very numbers.

The authorities looked ridiculous when they attempted to disperse apparently peaceable citizens engaged in the charitable exercise of raising a poor widow's potatoes. Also eroding the deference expected by the authorities was the pervasive propaganda campaign of the United Irishmen. Songs like those found in the highly popular *Paddy's Resource* explicitly espoused republicanism and derided loyalists, high and low.[88] Handbills and pamphlets spoke to the specific issues of encroaching government tyranny or to the general principles of brotherhood and civic responsibility at the core of United Irish ideology. Most dreaded by loyalists, however, was the United Irish newspaper, the *Northern Star*. Founded by Samuel Neilson in January 1792, the *Star* had a paid subscription of about 5,000, was the focal point for organized oral readings, and permeated the country as far south as Waterford.[89] One of Lord Abercorn's correspondents declared in February 1797 that 'the country [is] completely corrupted or dangerously infected so far as the delivery of the *Northern Star* extends'.[90] George Dallas, while touring Ulster in 1797, observed that 'at every cabin around us you will see them [the lower classes] reading the *Northern Star*'. He often met 'labourers walking to their work and reading this paper as they went along'.[91] Lord Downshire went so far as to order the people of Hillsborough not to subscribe to the *Star*, but to little avail.[92]

County Down, by its proximity to Belfast, was particularly susceptible to the appeal of the *Star*, but some of its most prominent citizens were also major contributors to the paper. Chief among them was a Presbyterian minister, the Rev. James Porter of Grey Abbey. From May to December 1796, Porter contributed a number of columns to the *Northern Star* which were later collected and widely distributed in pamphlet form under the title *Billy Bluff and the squire, or a sample of the times*.[93] The appeal was particularly immediate for residents of north Down, for Porter modelled his characters on easily recognized local dignitaries. Billy Bluff was a farmer engaged by Squire Firebrand to spy on the local Presbyterian minister, R___. The minister, of course, was Porter himself, who espoused the enlightened principles of brotherhood and unity associated with the United Irishmen. The squire was modelled after the Rev. John Cleland, a clerical magistrate and former tutor to Lord Castlereagh. The Squire took his orders from Lord Mountmumble, representing Castlereagh's father, the earl of Londonderry. Irony was the tone of these interchanges between Billy Bluff and Squire Firebrand. In them Porter exposed the bigotry and tyrannical leanings of a knee-jerk loyalism which irresponsibly adopted a strategy of divide and rule. The Squire, for example, accused R___, the Presbyterian minister, of fostering an 'unnatural' friendship when Billy reported his friendly meeting with a Catholic priest.[94] Irony underlay the representation of Firebrand, supposedly a man of God, who interspersed his speech with oaths and curses, and appropriated, as a magistrate, the tools of a corrupt state to suppress the righteous indignation of an aggrieved people. 'There is nothing like making clergyman magistrates', the Squire gleefully proclaimed.[95] Also ironic was the standing of the Stewart family itself in the county. The 1783 general election saw future United Irishmen Samuel Neilson and Dr. William Steele Dickson actively engaged in supporting the failed independent candidacy of the future earl, Robert Stewart. The 1790 election witnessed them backing the successful candidacy of young Robert Stewart, later Lord Castlereagh.[96] But the family's growing identification with the campaign against reform, both in the county and at the national level, made them easy targets for the accusations of hypocrisy and opportunism, accusations underscored and exploited by Porter in his columns for the *Northern Star*. 'The family', one Down magistrate noted, 'is now, I think, the most unpopular in this county'.[97]

Such erosion of popular deference made the resort to coercion even more urgent. Armed with legislation that suspended *habeas corpus,* permitted the exercise of martial law in disturbed districts, and relying on resurgent and increasingly confident loyalist forces, the government launched its counter-revolutionary campaign. On 3 March 1797, chief secretary Thomas Pelham wrote to Gen. Gerard Lake, commanding general of the northern district, ordering him to disarm suspected agitators of the public peace, disperse all seditious assemblies, and to do so 'without waiting for the sanction and assistance of civil authority'. In other words, Lake was empowered to act as if the entire area under his jurisdiction was, in effect, under martial law.[98] Lake responded on March 13 with an order of his own demanding the surrender of all arms and ammunition by non-military personnel.[99] Parties of militia, regulars, and yeomen scoured the countryside over the succeeding months to enforce the order. The sectarianism and anti-republicanism of the Orangemen and yeomen were given full license, encouraged by the sanguinary General Lake himself, whose policy was that only unrelenting force would 'wear these wretches out'.[100] The republicans initially evaded the full force of Lake's onslaught, but by the summer of 1797 his campaign was reaping as much success as terror. 'The practice among them', John McCracken wrote to his incarcerated brother Henry Joy about the disarming parties, 'is to hang a man up by the heels with a rope full of twist, by which means the sufferer whirls round like bird roasting at the fire, during which he is lashed with belts, etc., to make him tell where he has concealed his arms'.[101] 'It is not to be denied', a defensive Camden proclaimed to Pitt, 'that government meant to strike terror'.[102] 'If we treat rebellion as rebellion', Cooke declared, 'we are safe'.[103]

The authorities also took care to weed the militia of sedition, orchestrating elaborate show trials and exemplary executions like those at Blaris Camp in May 1797. Four Monaghan militiamen, selected from over seventy who had been forced to come forward and repent of their involvement with the United Irishmen, were paraded before their assembled brethren at the camp and executed.[104] To assert their newly recovered loyalty, the Monaghan militia wreaked vengeance on republicans in Belfast and were instrumental in silencing the *Northern Star.*[105] While the paper had been attacked before, it failed to recover from this last assault. Castle officials publicly deplored the overly zealous actions of the militiamen, but privately, loyalists were as pleased as they were relieved. 'If the *Northern Star* had continued', Sir George F. Hill wrote to Cooke, 'you never would have broken thro' the ranks of the rebels'.[106]

Momentum was with the government, but the United Irishmen

hoped that at least time would be on their side, the time it would take to launch a successful French invasion. But both sides were racing against the clock. The government was willing to employ the most harsh and brutal means to uproot the conspiracy before the arrival of the French. The republicans merely hoped to preserve their organization against Lake's campaign until it could effectively be unleashed to aid the French. Under such circumstances, the government possessed the advantage, able to charge forward and give their loyalist supporters full encouragement and sanction. The United Irishmen turned against each other. As Charles Teeling observed,

> Prior to 1798 the United Irish system seemed to have reached its acme; indeed, strictly speaking, about that period it might rather have been considered on the wane. . . . The passions of men are not stationary, and having reached the point of elevation, they either recede or burst every barrier opposed to their action. It was impossible that the public mind could have acquired a higher pitch of excitement than was generally experienced in the year 1797. Hence it was naturally lowered, because an immediate appeal to arms was resisted by those who had not formed a just estimate of human nature in the fluctuating passions of the human mind. . . . The result was a less ardent feeling in some quarters, which it was afterwards found more difficult to rally.[107]

Rank-and-file United Irishmen had been told by their leaders since the end of 1796 that they should shortly expect a French invasion force to assist them in the liberation of their country. They were told to wait, to hold themselves ready for immediate action when necessary, to refrain from calling the attention of the authorities to their activities and designs, and to accept patiently the orders delivered from their superiors. In the meantime, however, they saw their neighbours burned out of their homes by government forces. They saw their comrades and, indeed, even the most innocent citizens subjected to every form of brutality at the hands of His Majesty's soldiers, and made victims of floggings, half-hangings, and other forms of barbarous torture designed to extract information about the republican movement. Their houses were searched indiscriminately for arms. Their leaders had fled to avoid arrest. Informers were daily coming forward with evidence implicating members of the organization. This state of affairs kept rank-and-file United Irishmen in eager anticipation for orders to resist, to rise in open rebellion with or without French aid. As James Hope bitterly recalled, 'The people were in daily expectation of being called to the field by their leaders, an intention, as it appeared afterwards, which the leaders had little intention of putting into execution'.[108] Be patient, they were told, and such admonitions encouraged restiveness among the ranks.

The Down United Irishmen were perhaps the most restive. A county committee meeting in Ballynahinch and baronial meetings in Rathfriland and Dromara in May 1797 expressed support for an immediate rising.[109] Appealing to the national executive in Dublin, the northern representatives were rebuffed and resolved that Ulster should go it alone, until they realized that the Antrim colonels refused to act without French aid.[110] The most militant Down leaders, on learning that warrants were out for their arrest, fled the country.[111] The remaining United Irishmen were left to wait upon events. Thus the United Irishmen in the north missed the opportunity to rise from a position of strength.

Lake's policy was driving the United Irishmen underground, making it difficult to assess the ravages actually inflicted on the organization. As 1798 opened Cooke lauded the success of the Ulster campaign, noting that 'no part of the king's dominions [is] more apparently quiet or more evidently flourishing than the north of Ireland'.[112] But apparently and evidently are the key words here, for the authorities were also mindful that apparent peace often signified the strength of United Irish organization in a neighbourhood rather than the lack of it. And in the summer of 1797, the executive directory of the United Irishmen had ordered all committees, from the provincial down to local societies, to suspend their meetings while Lake's troops ravaged the countryside.[113]

While county Down waited out the repression in Ulster, the United Irish organization emerged as a national one as the movement spread south. By November 1797 a national executive was formed representing all four provinces. Leadership also passed from the north to the south, as Ulster chiefs were either imprisoned or fled to avoid arrest. The strategy was to wait for the French, and the only relief offered to the victims of Lake's campaign was largely propagandistic. The United Irishmen sought to expose the savagery of Lake's mobilization and acquired erstwhile allies among opposition politicians in England and Ireland interested in discrediting the Pitt and Camden regime.[114] The earl of Moira, one of the leading landowners in county Down, called for an investigation into what he characterized as a government policy of systematic terror. He presented to both the British and Irish Houses of Lords a catalogue of outrages committed by the government against the people, the information being supplied by the United Irishmen themselves.[115] Moira's motion failed but its introduction was nevertheless embarrassing to both governments. And his lordship's exertion was no doubt encouraging to his tenants in north-west Down, who continued to wait.

Their patience was further tried in October 1797 when the British navy defeated the combined Dutch and French fleets heading for Ireland. Downshire's correspondents jubilantly noted that the towns of Hillsborough, and especially that stronghold of the United Irishmen, Newry, were illuminated to celebrate the victory.[116] It appeared that loyalism was successfully reasserting itself, even in the most republican-contaminated parts of Down. 'The tenants, I think', George Stephenson assured Downshire in May 1798 from Hillsborough, 'in all parts have seen into their folly and knavery, and I trust are returning to their allegiance and industry'.[117]

Government complacency that the United Irishmen in the north, if not new converts to loyalty, were at least cowed into manageable submission, was reinforced by a most valuable informant, a Catholic farmer named Nicholas Magin, colonel in the United Irish army in Down and delegate to the Ulster provincial committee. Recruited by Squire Firebrand himself, the Rev. John Cleland, Magin's motives were not necessarily self-serving. When he first discovered his own distaste for the violent course being taken by the republican movement, Magin merely wanted to retire, but at Cleland's urging he remained as a government agent. By keeping the government informed, he may have wished to prevent a rising.[118] It was Magin who assured the government that the United Irishmen in the north had no intention of rising without the French to spark a national rebellion.[119] Indeed, much of the Ulster committee's attention was given over to organizing a lottery to defray expenses.[120] Caution was the keynote of the Ulster organization, a caution learned as Lake's forces terrorized the republicans into passivity. A policy of patience, awaiting that much-promised French invasion, required keeping the organization intact at all costs. When rebellion erupted in Wexford in May 1798, Ulster leaders had to decide whether or not to risk that organization in action.

'Depend upon it', General Knox wrote from Dungannon on 6 June 1798, 'the Presbyterians will not abet a Catholic plot'.[121] But the next day the United Irishmen and Defenders of county Antrim gathered under the insurrectionary banner of Henry Joy McCracken. What happened was a *coup* against the United Irish leaders. On 23 May 1798 the signal for a national rising was given, and Ulster failed to rise. A provincial meeting held in Armagh on the 29th subjected the timid leadership to charges of cowardice and even betrayal for their inaction. Forced to call a meeting of colonels in Antrim to prepare for a rising, Robert Simms resigned as commanding general in Antrim. The colonels, at a meeting at Parkgate on 1 June, after heated debate, resolved to wait for the French before committing their men to the field. Militant dissidents rallied to Henry Joy McCracken, appointing him the new commanding general, and he proceeded to rally the troops.[122] Not surprisingly, confusion reigned, reflected in county Down when Dr. William Steele Dickson, adjutant-general for the county, was arrested on 5 June. McCracken summoned his colonels, but as James Hope said, they 'flinched'. Three of them informed the new commander of the northern district, General Nugent, of McCracken's plan. To make matters even worse, the messenger McCracken sent to Down announcing his plans, deserted. The Down organization knew nothing of the Antrim rising, with which they were to co-ordinate their own mobilization, until after McCracken's defeat at Antrim town on the 7th. The last word they heard from Antrim was the resolution of the colonels to await the French.[123] The rebel army in Down found itself without a leader and with an organization in disarray. A prosperous linen draper in Lisburn, Henry Munro, was co-opted for the post, despite the fact that he had held no prior post in the United Irishmen's underground army.[124] His inexperience was shared by his subordinate officers, for along with Dickson, and thanks to Magin's information, the whole network of county Down colonels had been arrested.[125]

The first action in Down took place in Saintfield on 9 June, once the rebellion in Antrim was effectively quelled. The battle itself was indecisive, but when the garrison was recalled to Belfast, where Nugent was gathering his concentrated forces, the insurgents occupied the town, sparking off risings in the surrounding countryside. Newtownards fell to the rebels, but local yeomen successfully defended Portaferry. These were minor skirmishes, for both sides were preparing for a great and decisive confrontation at Ballynahinch.

Establishing his camp outside the town, on the estate of the liberal Lord Moira, Munro summoned the United Irishmen from Saintfield and the Ards, bringing the strength of the rebel camp up to 7,000 men, of whom only a small minority were armed. As Nugent's army approached, rebel commanders heatedly debated strategy. Most, like William Fox, urged Munro to play for time, time to discipline their forces and link up with a sizeable contingent from the Mourne. Munro decided to meet Nugent's forces head on, and he occupied Ballynahinch on the 12th of June. Nugent's troops dislodged Munro's advance guard from the town, and then settled down for the night, exhausted from their march, and drunk with the celebration of their small victory. Urged by his subordinates to take advantage of the situation and attack at night, Munro resisted. Hundreds, including a body of some 700 Defenders, deserted his camp in protest and disgust. That morning, on 13 June, the remaining rebels attacked Ballynahinch, outmatched by the well-disciplined and better-armed government troops.[126]

Nugent was no General Lake. As he had done in Antrim, the general offered generous terms of amnesty to all Down insurgents provided they peacefully surrender their arms. Only the leaders would have to account for their actions before a court-martial. Though many refused the offer and joined another body of insurgents in south and central Down, the rebellion in the north was effectively over. Nugent's leniency was in sharp contrast to Lake's reign of terror in the south, but the north still suffered considerable ravages in the aftermath of the rebellion. Undisciplined and vengeful bands of yeoman often ignored their general's orders for clemency. Suspected rebels were burned out of their homes. Hundreds were court-martialled and thirty-four leaders executed.[127] Among them was the Rev. James Porter, who paid with his life for tweaking the nose of the mighty.

The rebels left about 400 dead in the streets of Ballynahinch, with anywhere from 5,000 to 7,000 actually taking part in the battle.[128] An indeterminate number of rebels rose in the Ards peninsula, and Teeling, who was with them, claimed several thousands were waiting and ready in south Down to join Munro's forces for a march on Dublin.[129] Down claimed about 28,000 United Irishmen, and under the most chaotic circumstances, perhaps a third of them actually mobilized. Even more may have assembled to secure their own neighbourhoods only to retire when they heard of Munro's defeat, the last hope of success dissipated. But local authorities remained cautious. 'I am much afraid that all is not yet over', warned Downshire's agent, George Stephenson. 'They must be watched very closely or they will rise again'.[130]

They almost did, in 1803, when the government was not watching and Thomas Russell and James Hope attempted to prepare Down to assist in Robert Emmet's rebellion. When Russell heard that the rising had been aborted, he bowed to the inevitability of a lost cause and gave up further attempts to mobilize the Ulster masses. There had been considerable militant republicanism lingering on in the north, and had Emmet seized Dublin, the north might well have risen formidably again. Even after the failure men were reported to be drilling in Castlereagh, Ballynahinch, Knockbracken and Newry.[131] Russell, however, returned to Dublin in an unsuccessful attempt to rescue the captured Emmet and was arrested himself. Sent to Downpatrick to stand trial for treason in October 1803, he was found guilty and hanged. With bitter irony, he observed that six of the jurors who condemned him had been United Irishmen.[132]

Merchants 'are no great hands at revolution', Tone observed, perhaps meaning that they had much more to lose than their chains.[133] They were also no great hands at soldiering. I have argued here that the civic humanism that pervaded Irish political culture identified citizenship with the bearing of arms. Pride in the citizen army of the Irish Volunteers and its achievements was especially commanding in Ulster, its stronghold. While many factors conspired to challenge ascendancy rule in the 1790s, the character of the United Irish challenge was strongly shaped by the Volunteer precedent. The ideal of the arms-bearing, disinterested citizen was given further resonance by the French revolution, which tended to democratize the notion of citizenship, making it synonymous with the nation. The context of a general European war contributed further to a militarisation of internal politics, as the administration challenged the citizen armies of the Volunteers and United Irishmen with their own, officially sanctioned militia and yeomanry. Downshire's intimate association with both measures provoked an already restive independent political interest in the county. Under the peculiar circumstances of the 1790s, democratic citizenship and its assertion in arms appealed to that huge cross-section of Down society which mobilized as United Irishmen.

The rebellion of 1798 disabused the radical middle-class of their pretensions as citizen soldiers, marking the end of that militarized notion of citizenship associated with their civic humanism. This classical republicanism had provided the most accessible vocabulary for political engagement in the 1790s. Lurking within the conventional lexicon, however, were the ideas of liberalism and individual rights which animated the radical class, but for which they had not yet the words. After the union of 1801 Down republicans could hitch their star to an emerging and eventually triumphant United Kingdom liberalism.[134]

References

1. United Irish membership returns presented at county Down meeting, 11 May 1797, R.C. Lytton White papers, P. R. O. N. I., D. 714/2/1.

2. Edward Wakefield, *An account of Ireland, statistical and political* (2 vols., London, 1812), vol. i, p. 20.

3. Peter Jupp, 'County Down elections, 1783-1831' in *I.H.S.*, xviii (Sept. 1972), pp 178-81.

4. For a discussion of this civic humanism and its adoption by the United Irishmen, see Nancy J. Curtin, *The United Irishmen: popular politics in Ulster and Dublin, 1791-1798* (Oxford, 1994), pp 13-37.

5. For the Volunteers, see R. B. McDowell, *Ireland in the age of imperialism and revolution* (Oxford, 1979), pp 209-326.

6. For loyalist adoption of civic humanist ideas, see Jacqueline Hill, 'The politics of Dublin Corporation, 1760-1792' in David Dickson, Daire Keogh and Kevin Whelan (ed.), *The United Irishmen: republicanism, radicalism, and rebellion* (Dublin, 1993), pp 88-101.

7. For this liberal nationalism, see. E. J. Hobsbawm, *Nations and nationalism since 1780* (2nd ed., Cambridge, 1992), pp 14-45.

8. Theobald Wolfe Tone, *An argument on behalf of the Catholics of Ireland . . . by a northern whig* (Dublin, 1791).

9. See, e.g., *Northern Star*, 20 Feb. 1793.

10. Thomas Bartlett, 'An end to moral economy: the Irish militia disturbances of 1793' in *Past and Present*, 99 (May 1983), pp 115-34; Jim Smyth, *The men of no property: Irish radicals and popular politics in the late eighteenth century* (London, 1992), pp 52-78.

11. See Nancy J. Curtin, 'The transformation of the Society of United Irishmen into a mass-based revolutionary organisation, 1794-6' in *I.H.S.*, xxiv (Nov. 1985), pp 483-92.

12. For the United Irish alliance with the French, see Marianne Elliott, *Partners in revolution: the United Irishmen and France* (New Haven, Conn. and London, 1982).

13. Tone, *Life*, i, pp 141-4; Henry Joy, *Historical collections relative to the town of Belfast from the earliest period to the union with Great Britain* (Belfast, 1817), p. 359.

14. Curtin, *United Irishmen*, pp 42-5.

15. *Belfast News Letter*, 21 Dec. 1792; *Northern Star*, 11, 16 Jan., 4 Feb. 1792; Samuel McSkimin, *Annals of Ulster from 1790 to 1798*, ed. E. J. Crum (Belfast, 1906), p. 5; R. B. McDowell, *Irish public opinion, 1750-1800* (London, 1944), 147; R. B. McDowell, 'The proceedings of the Dublin Society of United Irishmen' in *Anal. Hib.*, xvii (1949), p. 40.

16. William Drennan to Samuel McTier, Nov. 1791, cited in D. A. Chart (ed.), *The Drennan letters* (Belfast, 1931), p. 65.

17. See, e.g., *Northern Star*, 23 May, 23 June, 28 July, 7 November 1792.

18. Ibid., 28 July 1792.

19. See, e.g., Ibid., 28 Nov., 1792; 16, 19, 23, 26, 30 Jan., 1 Feb. 1793; *Belfast News Letter*, 8 Jan. 1793.

20. *Northern Star*, 29 June 1793; William Steele Dickson, *A narrative of the confinement an exile of William Steele Dickson, D.D., formerly minister of the Presbyterian congregation of Ballyhalbert and Portaferry in the county of Down* (Dublin, 1812), pp 23-8.

21. Downshire to Westmorland, 18 May 1792, Downshire papers, P. R. O. N. I., D. 607/B/361.

22. Annesley to Downshire, 1 June 1792, Ibid., D. 607/B/364.

23. Westmorland to Downshire, 25 June 1792, Ibid., D. 607/B/369.

24. Tone, *Life*, i, pp 162-3, 167, 176; for the address, see *Northern Star*, 25 Aug. 1792.

25. 'Extract of a letter from Ireland,' 26 July 1792, P.R.O., HO 100/38/266-8.

26. William James MacNeven, *Pieces of Irish history illustrative of the condition of the Catholics of Ireland, of the origins and progress of the political system of the United Irishmen, and of their transactions with the Anglo-Irish government* (New York, 1807), p. 29.

27. John Kennedy to Hillsborough, 17 Aug. 1793, Downshire papers, P. R. O. N. I., D. 607/B/399.

28. Nicholas Price to Downshire [1793] , Ibid., D. 607/C/22.

29. John Slade to Lord Hillsborough, 3 March 1793, Ibid., D. 607/B/384.

30. Maj. George Matthews to Downshire. 29 June and 3 July 1793, Ibid., D. 607/C/42, 43.

31. Lord Annesley to Hillsborough, 14 April [1793], Ibid., D. 607/B/388.

32. Sir Henry McAnally, *The Irish militia, 1793-1816: a social and military history*

(London, 1949), pp 128-30; see also Thomas Bartlett, 'Indiscipline and disaffection in the armed forces in Ireland in the 1790s' in P. J. Corish (ed.), *Radicals, rebels, and establishments* (Belfast, 1985), pp 115-34.

33. General John Knox to Thomas Pelham, 14 May 1797, Pelham papers, B.L., Add. MS 33104/59.

34. Robert Waddell to Robert Ross, 22 Aug. 1796, N.A.I., 620/24/144.

35. Downshire to John Reilly, 2 Oct. 1795, Downshire papers, P. R. O. N. I., D. 607/C/146.

36. Maj. George Matthews to marquess of Downshire, 4 Dec. 1796, Ibid., D. 607/D/372.

37. See Curtin, 'Transformation'.

38. See *Idem*, 'The United Irish organisation in Ulster, 1795-8' in Dickson, Keogh and Whelan, *The United Irishmen*, pp 209-21.

39. Andrew MacNevin to John Pollock, 9 May 1795, Camden papers, Kent County Archives Office [hereafter Kent C. R. O], U840/O146/7); Robert Johnson to John Lees, 8 May 1795, Ibid., U840/O146/3); Constitution of the Society of United Irishmen, N.A.I., 620/34/59; McSkimin, *Annals*, p. 29.

40. Robert Johnson to John Lees, 8 Aug. 1795, N.A.I., 620/22/28; Earl Camden to Duke of Portland, 25 July 1795, Ibid., 620/22/19; John to Lees, 2 July 1795, Camden papers, Kent C. R. O., U840/O147/17.

41. Earl Camden to Duke of Portland, 25 July 1795, N.A.I., 620/22/19.

42. Ibid.; Capt. ____ Johnson to John Lees, 2 July 1795, Camden papers, Kent C. R. O., U840/O147/17.

43. United Irishmen returns of membership, Oct. 1796, P. R. O. HO 100/62/333-4.

44. United Irish returns of membership, N.A.I., 620/28, 285, 297; 620/30/61; P. R. O. HO 100/71/251-4; R.C. Lytton White papers, P. R. O. N. I., D. 714/2/1.

45. William Torney to Col. ____ Johnson, 2 Sept. 1797, Pelham papers, B.L., Add. MS 33105/73; Information of Edward Newell, 15 Apr. 1797, P. R. O. HO 100/69/202-5.

46. Ibid.

47. Some United Irishmen, notably Henry Joy McCracken and James Hope, lamented the French alliance, which they feared encouraged opportunistic and half-hearted republicans to join the movement. 'The seeds of corruption,' observed Hope, 'were sown in our society', as a consequence of reliance on the French. It was among the 'foreign-aid men' that 'spies were chiefly found'. Quoted in James Hope, 'Autobiographical memoir' in R. R. Madden, *Antrim and Down in '98* (Glasgow, n.d.), pp 105, 107.

48. Extract of a letter forwarded by Sir John Macartney to Dublin Castle, 26 Apr. 1797, N.A.I., 620/29/324.

49. These figures are based on data presented in my chapter on United Irish social composition in *United Irishmen*, pp 126-44.

50. Ibid., p. 129.

51. For a list of Ulster leaders, see the 'Black book of the rebellion, 1798', McCance papers, P. R. O. N. I., D. 272/1.

52. Dr. William Richardson to marquess of Abercorn, 22 Feb. 1797, Abercorn papers, P. R. O. N. I., T. 2541/1B3/6/5.

53. Thomas Lane to Downshire, 24 March 1796, Downshire papers, P. R. O. N. I., D. 607/D/43.

54. See David W. Miller, 'The Armagh troubles, 1784-95' in Samuel Clark and James S. Donnelly Jr. (ed.), *Irish peasants: violence and political unrest, 1780-1914* (Madison, Wis., 1983), pp 155-91.

55. Curtin, *United Irishmen*, pp 148-65.
56. W.E.H. Lecky, *A history of Ireland in the eighteenth century* (5 vols., London, 1898), iii, pp 432-5.
57. Earl Camden to duke of Portland, 6 Aug. 1796, N.A.I., 620/18/11/1.
58. *Belfast News Letter*, 4 Sept. 1795; N.A.I., 620/18/3, 14; William Sampson, *Memoirs of William Sampson, an Irish exile, written by himself* (London, 1832), pp xxii-xxiii; Madden, *Antrim and Down*, pp 13-14; Edward Cooke to Thomas Pelham, 4 Dec. 1795, Pelham papers, B. L., Add. MS 33101/358-9.
59. *Belfast News Letter*, 21 Nov. 1796.
60. Robert Waddell to Edward Cooke, 8 Nov. 1796, N.A.I., 620/26/29.
61. See, e.g., Thomas Lane to Downshire, 13 Mar., 24 Mar., 1 May, 24 May, 26 June 1796, Downshire papers, P. R. O. N. I., D. 607/D/41, 43, 57, 62, 78.
62. Joseph Pollock to Downshire, 2 August 1796, Ibid., D. 607/D/109).
63. Andrew Newton to Dublin Castle, 30 August 1796, N.A.I., 620/23/9.
64. See. e.g., Thomas Higginson to John Foster, 22 August 1796, Ibid., 620/24/156.
65. Camden to Portland, 6 Aug. 1796, Ibid., 620/18/11/1.
66. For these complaints, see Earl Camden to duke of Portland, 6 Aug. 1796, P. R. O. HO 100/64/168-72.
67. Camden to Portland, 21 Mar. 1796, Ibid., 100/62/71-5.
68. See, e.g., Robert Waddell to Robert Ross, 20 June 1796, N.A.I., 620/23/184; Thomas Lane to Downshire, 24 Mar. 1796, Downshire papers, P. R. O. N. I., D. 607/D/43.
69. Camden to Portland, 6 Aug. 1796, P. R. O. HO 100/64/168-72.
70. *Belfast News Letter*, 21 Nov., 5 Dec. 1796.
71. Allan Blackstock, 'The social and political implications of the raising of the yeomanry in Ulster, 1796-8' in Dickson, Keogh and Whelan, *The United Irishmen*, pp 234-43.
72. See, e.g., Thomas Knox to Dublin Castle, 4 July 1796, N.A.I., 620/24/16.
73. Camden to Portland, 3 Sept. 1796, P. R. O. HO 100/62/208-14.
74. Downshire to Dublin Castle, 24, 25 Nov. 1796, N.A.I., 620/26/77.
75. See the United Irish handbill, 'Portrait of a soldier', N.A.I., 620/28/249.
76. Pelham to Downshire, 2 Oct. 1796, Downshire papers, P. R. O. N. I., D. 607/D/213.
77. See, e.g., W. C. Lindsay to Thomas Pelham, 5 Jan. 1797, N.A.I., 620/28/43.
78. Curtin, 'Organisation', pp 213-4.
79. John Goddard to Downshire, 2 Sept. 1796, Downshire papers, P. R. O. N. I., D. 607/D/149; Thomas Lane to Downshire, 23 Sept. 1796, D. 607/D/199.
80. Thomas Lane to Downshire, 1 May 1797, Ibid., D. 607/E/255.
81. James Waddell to Robert Ross, 14 June 1796, N.A.I., 620/23/174.
82. *Commons Jn. Ire.*, xvii, pp 213-4, pp 1,182-3; xviii, pp 348-9.
83. *Belfast News Letter*, 19 Sept. 1796; Lecky, *History of Ireland*, iii, p. 459.
84. See Curtin, 'Organisation'.
85. See, e.g., *Belfast News Letter*, 21 Oct. 1796; De Latocnaye, *A Frenchman's walk through Ireland, 1796-7*, trans. John Stevenson (Belfast, 1917), pp 209-10; Sir George F. Hill to Edward Cooke, [Nov. 1796], P. R. O. HO 100/62/342-5.
86. Pharis Martin, Jr. to R.M.H. McNeill, 11 Nov. 1796, N.A.I., 620/26/40.
87. Dean Richard Annesley to Viscount Castlereagh, 18 May 1797, Ibid., 620/30/104.
88. See Curtin, *United Irishmen*, pp 194-8.
89. John Stewart Hall, 'The Irish press and the French revolution' in *Journalism Quarterly*, 39 (1962), pp 516-17; Isaac Heron to Dublin Castle, 2 Jan. 1797, N.A.I., 620/28/16.

90. Richardson to Abercorn, 22 Feb. 1797, Abercorn papers, P. R. O. N. I., T. 2451/IB3/6/5.
91. [George Dallas] to William Huskisson, 10 July 1797, Huskisson papers, B. L., Add MS 38759/36-54.
92. *Northern Star*, 25 Nov. 1796.
93. Rev. James Porter, *Billy Bluff and Squire Firebrand, or a sample of the times, as it appeared in five letters, with a selection of songs from 'Paddy's Resource'* (1st edn., 1796; Belfast, 1812); Patrick Kennedy to bishop of Ossory, 9 Oct. 1796, N.A.I., 620/25/157.
94. *Northern Star*, 2 Dec. 1796.
95. Ibid., 2 Sept. 1796.
96. Charles Dickson, *Revolt in the north: Antrim and Down in 1798* (Dublin, 1960), p. 83.
97. James Arbuckle to Downshire, 11 Oct. 1796, Downshire papers, P. R. O. N. I., D. 607/D/230.
98. Thomas Pelham to Gen. Gerard Lake, 3 Mar, 1797, Knox papers, N.L.I., MS 56/32.
99. *Belfast News Letter*, 13 Mar., 1797.
100. Lake to Pelham, 13 Mar. 1797, Pelham papers, B. L., Add. MS 33103/220-21.
101. Quoted in Madden, *Antrim and Down*, p. 25.
102. Earl Camden to William Pitt, 3 Nov. 1797, Lords lieutenant correspondence, N. L. I., MS 886/165-81.
103. Edward Cooke to Lord Auckland, Sneyd papers, P. R. O. N. I., T. 3229/2/32.
104. Col. Charles Leslie to Gen. Gerard Lake, 25 Apr. 1797, Pelham papers, B. L., Add. MS 33103/397; Lake to Thomas Pelham, 1 May 1797, Ibid., 33104/3-4; Bartlett, 'Indiscipline and disaffection,' p. 127.
105. Martha McTier to William Drennan, [17 May 1797], *Drennan letters*, 256; Thomas Lane to marquess of Downshire, 25 May 1797, Downshire papers, P. R. O. N. I., D. 607/E/266.
106. Sir. George F. Hill to Edward Cooke [?] June 1797, N.A.I., 620/31/182.
107. Charles Hamilton Teeling, *The history of the Irish rebellion of 1798 and sequel to the history of the rebellion of 1798* (1st edn., 1876; Shannon, Ireland, 1972), p. 70.
108. R.R. Madden, *The United Irishmen, their lives and times*, 3rd ser. (7 vols., London, 1842-5), ii, p. 443.
109. Report of Nicholas Magin, 15 May 1797, R.C. Lytton White papers, P. R. O. N. I., D. 714/2/1; Elliott, *Partners in revolution*, p. 133.
110. Report of Nicholas Magin, 17 June 1797, R.C. Lytton White papers, P. R. O. N. I., D. 714/2/3; Information from Samuel Turner, P. R. O. HO 100/70/339-49.
111. Ibid.
112. Edward Cooke to Lord Auckland, 19 Mar. 1798, Auckland papers, B. L., Add. MS 34454/181-2.
113. Viscount Castlereagh to Thomas Pelham, 11 Nov. 1797, Pelham papers, B. L., Add. MS 33105/204.
114. Curtin, *United Irishmen*, pp 214-18.
115. See *The debate in the Irish house of peers on a motion made by the earl of Moira, Monday, February 19, 1798* (Dublin, 1798); Sampson, *Memoirs*, pp 16-7.
116. Sir George Atkinson to Downshire, 19 Oct. 1797, Downshire papers, P. R. O. N. I., D. 607/E/337; E.V. Mayne to Downshire, 20 Oct. 1797, Ibid., D. 607/E/342.
117. George Stephenson to Downshire, 16 May 1798, Ibid., D. 607/F/169.
118. John Magin to Viscount Castlereagh, 30 June 1800, R.C. Lytton White papers, P. R. O. N. I., D. 714/5/2.

119. Castlereagh to William Wickham, 22 June 1798, P. R. O. HO/100/77/180-1.

120. See, e.g., Magin's reports for 14 Dec. 1797, 7, 27 Jan. 25 Mar. 1798, R.C. Lytton White papers, P. R. O. N. I., D. 714/2/10A-B, 14, 15, 17.

121. Gen. John Knox to Edward Cooke, 6 June 1798, N.A.I., 620/38/61.

122. Report of Nicholas Magin, 29 May 1798, R.C. Lytton White papers, P. R. O. N. I., D. 714/2/23; Madden, *United Irishmen,* ii, pp 444-6; McSkimin, *Annals of Ulster,* p. 70.

123. Hope, 'Autobiographical memoir, in Madden, *Antrim and Down,* pp 123-4.

124. For Munro, see Madden, *Antrim and Down,* pp 227-47.

125. William Fox, 'A narrative of the principal proceedings of the republican army in the county of Down during the late insurrection', N.A.I., 620/4/41.

126. For the battle of Ballynahinch, see Fox, 'Narrative', Ibid.; Teeling, *History of the Irish rebellion,* pp 132-6; Thomas Pakenham, *The year of liberty: the story of the great Irish rebellion of 1798* (London, 1978), pp 263-4.

127. Pakenham, *Year of liberty,* pp 324-5; for the courts martial, see N.A.I., 620/2/9-28.

128. Elliott, *Partners in revolution,* p. 206; Dickson, *Revolt in the north,* p. 155; Lecky, *History of Ireland,* iv, p. 416; McSkimin, *Annals of Ulster,* p. 78; Pakenham, *Year of liberty,* p. 259.

129. Teeling, *History of the Irish rebellion,* pp 201-3.

130. George Stephenson to [Downshire], 4 July 1798, Downshire papers, P. R. O. N. I., D. 607/F/299.

131. For Emmet's rebellion and Russell's activities in the north, see Elliott, *Partners in revolution,* pp 282-322.

132. Madden, *United Irishmen,* ii, pp 261-5.

133. Tone, *Life,* i, p. 241.

134. For the liberalism of the United Irishmen, see Curtin, *United Irishmen,* pp 13-37, 282-9.

Chapter 12

LANDOWNERS AND PARLIAMENTARY ELECTIONS IN COUNTY DOWN, 1801-1921

BRIAN WALKER

The resignation of Lord Arthur Hill in March 1908 from parliament created little stir on the national scene. Lord Hill had held his seat as M.P. for Down West for just over six months, and an examination of *Hansard* reveals that he made few speeches at the House of Commons during this time, although in an earlier parliamentary career Hill had played a more notable role. At a local level, however, his departure from Westminster was a matter of considerable importance. It meant that for the first time in continuous period of nearly a century, a member of the Hill family was no longer returned to Westminster for county Down. From 1817 until 1908, with the exception of the years 1905 to 1907, the parliamentary representation of the county had always included a member of the Hill dynasty, the principal landowners in the county during the nineteenth century. This article on county Down elections during the period of the union will look at the political position of local, influential, landed families, and at how their role in the politics of the county changed dramatically in the course of just under a century and a quarter. Other matters to be investigated include the rise of political consciousness and participation among the electors and the growth of party organisation.

Under the act of union, county Down was allocated two parliamentary seats, as were all Irish counties. As a result of the redistribution of seats in 1884, four parliamentary divisions were established for the county, while a new redistribution act of 1918 increased the Down divisions to five. Besides these seats, some parliamentary boroughs were linked to the county. Downpatrick returned one M.P. from 1801 to 1885 and Newry had one M.P. from 1801 to 1918. As Belfast grew, parts of north Down were included within its parliamentary borough boundaries. This study will concentrate on the elections for the county seats, although reference will be made occasionally to events in the boroughs. During these years laws affecting the franchise and electoral procedures underwent important changes and will be mentioned in the relevant section. We will begin with a survey of county Down elections over the whole period, set in the context of elections elsewhere in Ulster and in the rest of Ireland, and then turn to a more detailed examination of social and political changes.

I

During the first half of the nineteenth century, very few county Down elections, either by-elections or general elections, were contested (five out of twenty-two), and parliamentary representation remained firmly in the hands of a small number of powerful landed families.[1] Such a pattern is also evident in the other Ulster counties, while in the remaining Irish counties there were generally more contests and more representatives from outside the landed gentry, especially among supporters of Daniel O'Connell. Elections were contested in county Down in the 1850s following a rise in tenant unrest, but no contested polls occurred in the next decade, due to the termination of this protest: the principal landed families remained strongly in control. Elsewhere in Ulster county politics followed similar lines. In the other three provinces contested elections were held in the 1850s presaging the rise of an independent political interest, mainly because of agrarian discontent, but the 1860s saw a resurgence of landlord interests. In 1865 landlord parliamentary representation in Ireland was greater than at any time since the 1830s and marked a peak in their political influence.

In the 1870s and early 1880s an upsurge in political activity over the land question resulted in contested elections in county Down as well as in most other counties, both in Ulster and the rest of Ireland. The main landowning interests in county Down lost a seat in 1874 but regained it subsequently and the county proved to be one of the few in Ulster and in Ireland where landlord representatives in 1880 held both seats in face of a powerful liberal or home-rule attack. Numbers of Ulster M.P.s with a landed background fell from twenty-six in 1868 to eighteen in 1874 and to fourteen in 1880 out of a total of twenty-nine. The 1874 general election was the first election in nineteenth-century Ireland when a majority of M.P.s supported home rule or repeal of the union and the 1880 general election was the first when less than half of the M.P.s came from a landed background. Irish landlord M.P.s (from all parties) dropped from seventy-eight in 1868, to fifty-three in 1874 and to twenty-one in 1880, out of a total of 101.[2]

In an almost complete reversal of the trend elsewhere, the heavily contested general election of 1885 returned landed representatives for three of the four county divisions of Down. This pattern was repeated in some other Ulster divisions but practically everywhere else, the new M.P.s, in both unionist and nationalist camps, were mostly from non-landed backgrounds. Between 1885 and 1921 only Down South had regular contests between unionist and nationalist, in contrast to the other Down divisions which were rarely contested and, when they were, it was because of intra-unionist rivalry. Over this period, nonetheless, the number of M.P.s from county Down with a landed background slowly declined so that by 1910 none of the parliamentary representatives came from this class. In other parts of Ulster the number of landed M.P.s also fell. From 1885 onwards very few M.P.s in the rest of Ireland (C.S. Parnell was a notable exception) came from a landlord background.

This survey raises many interesting questions about the political role of county Down landlords in the nineteenth and early twentieth centuries. Why was it so important in the early period and why did it decline? Some commentators, both contemporary and modern, have regarded landlord political primacy as a function of coercive power. Recent research, however, has seen the overall picture in different terms where factors such as deference and social control are more important than coercion. By what means did landlords control political life for so much of the nineteenth century in county Down and how was this control undermined? It is important not just to understand trends which were general to Ireland but also those which were specific to Down. Why did landlords continue to play a role in the politics of county after their influence elsewhere had waned? Why did their domination of the county parliamentary representation finally end?

II

Some comments about the social and economic circumstances of county Down will help to provide a useful context for these elections. At the head of the social apex in county Down, as in other Irish counties during the nineteenth century, were various landowning families with their dependent tenantry. The 1876 parliamentary report on Irish landownership showed that in the county there were twenty-four landlords each with more than 5,000 acres.[3] The largest landowner was the head of the Hill family, the marquis of Downshire, with 64,356 acres (valuation £62,783), who also held substantial property elsewhere, especially in county Wicklow. The Kilmorey estate was 37,454 acres (valuation £13,708) while the Stewart family, headed by the marquis of Londonderry, had 23,554 acres (valuation £34,484). Earl Annesley owned 23,567 acres (valuation £18,886), Col. W.B. Forde of

Seaforde possessed 19,882 acres (valuation £15,404) and Lord Dufferin owned 18,238 acres (valuation £21,043). Apart from these territorial magnates there were a large number of landlords with smaller estates. All told there were eighty-four landowners who held over 1,000 acres. The Delacherois family at Donaghadee for example, owned 2,313 acres while the Whyte family had 1,712 acres at Loughbrickland.

These landowning families played a key role in the social life of the county. As McDowell has commented:

> Land was not only a source of revenue. Its possession conferred a definite social status accompanied by duties and rights; for until well into the nineteenth century it was assumed that the great landed magnates and the landed gentry ought to be largely responsible for the administration of both local and national affairs.[4]

In county Down, as elsewhere in Ulster, they normally acted as magistrates, served as members of the grand juries, and were leading figures in the poor law boards of guardians, on which they sat as ex-officio members. Until the establishment of county councils in 1898 they had the major say in local government and generally played a leading role in voluntary societies and organisations. The vast majority of the landlords in Down were members of the Church of Ireland. Most of the main families persisted throughout the nineteenth century although some new arrivals replaced older families. In the 1840s, for example, the Mulholland family, owners of the successful York Street Flax Mill in Belfast, purchased from the Mathew family, a 6,769 acre estate at Ballywalter, where Charles Lanyon designed a magnificent Italian palazzo-style house for Andrew Mulholland.[5]

Attention must now be paid to those other two elements of rural society in nineteenth century Down, the farmers and the labourers. The census returns show that in 1881 there were 18,469 farmers and 8,275 labourers (cottagers).[6] During the nineteenth and early twentieth centuries there was a steady consolidation of farms and a rise in educational and housing standards. Rising prices for agricultural products from industrial Britain led to growing prosperity for county Down farmers during much of the nineteenth century, especially between 1850 and 1878. In addition, farmers acquired new rights over their land and by the mid 1880s a process had begun which would eventually lead to most farmers in the county owning their own farms by the 1920s. Labourers benefited little from this rise in rural prosperity and the 1883 Labourers' Cottage Act had limited effect on their housing conditions. Of the county's population in 1881, Presbyterians constituted 40 per cent, Catholics 31 per cent, members of the Church of Ireland 23 per cent and others 6 per cent.[7] The proportion of Catholics in the population was highest in the south of the county.

As regards landlord-tenant relations in county Down in the first half of the nineteenth century, we may note from the work of Maguire on the Downshire estates and the evidence of the Devon Commission in the mid-1840s, that relations between the two seem to have been generally untroubled.[8] While the legal rights of most tenants were limited, landlords usually observed customary rights of tenure (often loosely labelled as the Ulster custom) which covered matters of occupancy and rent. The great potato famine did cause distress in some parts of Down, but, thanks partly to the availability of crops such as flax and partly to efforts to provide assistance, the suffering was limited, compared to the south and west of the country.[9] A number of tenant farmer associations were established at the end of the 1840s and the beginning of the 1850s to campaign for tenants' rights, but with the rise in prosperity from the early 1850s most of these organisations collapsed. For the next period of almost three decades landlord-tenant relations in the county continued to be reasonable, by and large, in line with the picture that historians such as Vaughan have drawn for many parts of Ireland in these years.[10] The role of the landlords was generally accepted and deference to them was an integral part of the social norms.

In spite of these generally good relations, however, there were underlying problems in the legal uncertainties over tenants' rights. Ironically, Gladstones' Land Act of 1870 only increased the difficulties because it sought to give legal sanction to customary rights. Landlords and tenants could differ on what these rights were and there followed a number of controversial court cases. From the early 1870s new tenant organisations were established to seek reform but not to overthrow landlordism. A public letter of 1872 concerning the newly formed Down Farmers' Union indicated that this organisation sought to improve the position of the tenant and 'at the same time to secure to the landlord well paid rents and create over the county a prosperous tenantry'.[11] Other tenants' groups were formed in county Down and elsewhere in Ireland in the 1870s. This whole movement, however, took on a radically new impetus in the late 1870s due to a severe agricultural depression caused by a sudden decline in farm prices and a series of bad harvests beginning in 1878. Tenant right organisations in county Down, under a central Ulster association, and in alliance with the Land League (formed in Mayo in late 1879), organised a wave of protest in support of tenants' rights. At a meeting of the Land League at Downpatrick on 6 January 1881, attended by 10,000 people, speakers included Michael Davitt, R.H. Rylett, the Unitarian minister and the Saintfield parish priest, J.P. O'Boyle.[12] In the face of this organised opposition throughout Ireland, Gladstone brought in his 1881 Land Act which legalised fair rent, free sale and fixity of tenure to tenants.

Following the second land act, the land question ceased to be of central importance, although some issues relating to the matter continued to concern local interests. The Ashbourne Act of 1885 began a system of land purchase for farmers while the Wyndham Act of 1903 extended the process to the majority of farmers in county Down as well as elsewhere in Ireland. The 1898 Local Government Act established county councils on a broad franchise, thus transferring power at this level from landlords to farmers. The agrarian revolution of these years from 1879 to 1881 not only undermined the legal and economic position of the landlords in the countryside but it caused a questioning of their status and power which continued afterwards. J.C. Rutherford, in his biography of James Shanks, a tenant farmer of Ballyfounder, Portaferry, noted how: 'The land act of 1881 had given to the farmers a feeling of freedom and independence which they had never before enjoyed. This feeling was manifest in the public boards, and gave a new temper to public discussion'. When Shanks became vice-chairman of the board of guardians at Downpatrick he 'took advantage of the occasion to make a speech against ex-officio members and against landlords'.[13] Another example is that of Major Roger Hall, a landowner from near Warrenpoint, who expressed concern to Sir Thomas Bateson, in a letter of January 1886 which was passed to Lord Salisbury, that a local National League branch had held a lottery for his land: the members first proposed that he should be given a third class ticket to Liverpool but then decided to let him have a cottage and 8 acres.[14] Such forcible seizure did not happen in Warrenpoint or elsewhere but the legal and social undermining of the landlords' position continued.

Any survey of county Down in this period must carry reference to the growing towns and industries of the county. A number of towns, such as Newtownards, Banbridge, Comber and Dromore, underwent considerable population growth primarily because of the expansion of the linen industry which not only benefited existing towns but also created new mill villages such as Drumaness and Shrigley. Besides adding to the general prosperity of the county, this economic growth also led to the rise of a new group of wealthy linen merchants and manufacturers. Families such as the Hursts of Drumaness, the Andrews of Comber and the Browns of Edenderry had emerged as prominent forces by the last quarter of the nineteenth century. Most, but not all of this new group, were Presbyterian.

III

During the first half of the nineteenth century in county Down there were few contested elections and parliamentary representation was dominated by a small group of landed families. Such a tranquil picture, however, disguises the fact that there was often strong political rivalry concerning elections, although it rarely led to a poll, and this family control was only maintained by careful and expensive management, as Jupp has shown in his work on county Down elections, 1783-1831.[15] By 1800 the Hill family, owners of the largest estate in Down, had emerged clearly as the dominant political family. The only serious challenge to their position at this stage came from the Stewart family, which owned the second most valuable estate in the county. In part this rivalry was the result of political differences over the act of union, which had been opposed by the Hills and supported by the Stewarts, especially by their most famous member, Lord Castlereagh. In part also the rivalry may have been caused by personal rivalry between the long established Hills and the more newly arrived Stewarts. A bitter electoral contest of 1790 to the Irish House of Commons had resulted in both families returning one member each for the county and this result was still reflected in the return of the first M.P.s to Westminster in 1801 and in the outcome of the first general election to Westminster in 1802 (uncontested in county Down). On both occasions the M.P.s returned were Francis Savage, a landowner of Portaferry, (representing the Hill interest) and Lord Castlereagh (representing the Stewarts).

This arrangement, however, broke down in 1805. After he was appointed secretary for war in that year, Lord Castlereagh had to vacate his seat. In the ensuing by-election he put his name forward again but now found himself opposed by Col. John Meade, whose family held land around Dromore, and who enjoyed the backing of the Hill interest. Following the death of the second marquis of Downshire in 1801, the marchioness of Downshire had taken control of the Hill estate and by 1805 she was determined to counter Stewart influence. Her reasons were chiefly personal, claiming that Lord Castlereagh had 'long been the inveterate enemy of her family and interests' and that he sought 'to rob the family of its just interests and patronage'.[16] In a bitter, expensive and lengthy poll, Meade defeated Castlereagh by 1,973 votes to 1,481. The Hill influence remained supreme at the next two general elections with the unopposed return of two M.P.s backed by the family, Francis Savage and John Meade. By 1812, however, the marchioness of Downshire had decided against the expense of defending both seats and Lord Castlereagh was again returned for one of the Down seats along with John Meade. Protests by some minor gentry, led by Eldred

Pottinger of Belfast, caused a contest in 1812 but this failed to upset the arrangement between the Hill and Stewart families. Evidence of their hold on county politics can be seen at the next contested election of 1826 when the Stewarts deliberately caused a contest by putting forward a third candidate for the two seats to extend the duration of election so that their main candidate, the new Lord Castlereagh, could attain his 21st birthday and be therefore eligible to sit in parliament. From 1817 a member of the Hill family, rather than a nominee, held one of the Down seats.

At the general elections of 1830 and 1831 a challenge to the Hill/ Stewart control of the county's representation emerged again from the ranks of the local gentry. In 1830 Mathew Forde of Seaforde and in 1831 William Sharman Crawford from Crawfordsburn contested elections but were unsuccessful. Thereafter until the early 1850s none of the elections in county Down were contested. When M.P.s from the Hill or Stewart families resigned, they were replaced by other members of these families. Catholic emancipation and parliamentary reform questions became major political issues in Ireland in the 1820s and early 1830s, but while these issues were raised in county Down in 1830 and 1831, especially by the radical William Sharman Crawford, the local situation remained of greater importance than did ideological differences. Prior to the 1830s, party labels were rarely given to M.P.s who were usually identified politically as either for or against the government. When party labels emerged in 1832, Viscount Castlereagh was described as a conservative while Lord Arthur Hill, who had backed Catholic emancipation, was called a liberal. Hill's successor in 1836, the earl of Hillsborough, however, was a conservative.

This domination of Down politics by the Hill and Stewart families in the first half of the nineteenth century deserves further examination. Jupp has drawn attention to various factors behind the electoral strength of these political magnates. He stresses how important was the individual and general proprietorial strength of both families along with a fairly sophisticated system of electoral organisation.[17] They owned the two most valuable estates in the county and were determined to maintain their electoral interests. In contrast in Downpatrick the principal landlords, the de Clifford family based in England, did not take much interest in the politics of their borough and a number of other landed interests, including the Hill family, put forward candidates for the parliamentary seat which was frequently contested in the first two decades of the century: in 1835, however, the Ker family of Ballynahinch bought the de Clifford estate and a member of that family represented the town between 1835-51, with little sign of opposition.[18] In Newry also, the main landowners, the Needhams, later ennobled as earls of Kilmorey, were not greatly involved in their borough's politics at the beginning of the century, but the return of General Francis Needham to Newry in 1806 marked the beginning of the restoration of that family's influence.[19]

Although the Hill and Stewart families held the major proprietorial interests in the county, their dominance could not be taken for granted. Competition from other large landowners may have been lessened because several of these were able to gain political representation elsewhere. The Needham family dominated Newry politics, the Annesleys held seats in Downpatrick, Great Grimsby and county Cavan, and William Sharman Crawford represented Dundalk (1834 to 1837) and Rochdale (1841 to 1852). The presence of many owners of small estates in county Down, however, meant that considerable effort was required from the Hills and Stewarts to maintain their influence. In 1825 Rev. Mark Cassidy, agent to the Stewart family, advised Lord Londonderry on some of the steps necessary to retain dominance of local politics:

> ... there are so many independent squires and squireens, all of whom, as well as their wives and daughters, require the nicest management. For the marquis to keep up the interests of this family it would be necessary that he should spend as much of his time here as possible, not only entertain the heads of houses, but enter into the most familiar intercourse with them, surprise the breakfast table of one in a morning, the dinner of another in an evening, chat with the ladies, view all the imaginary improvements of the house, farmyard, farm etc., and enter into all the domestic concerns of the whole family. Nor will this be sufficient, the marchioness must also devote much of her time and ease to the same purpose; she must enter into the greatest familiarity with them, be personally acquainted with them all, know the Christian names of the daughters, the policies of the families, the taste of the individuals, balance her attentions with the most scrupulous exactness, so as not to hurt the feelings of one by a greater attention to another, and in all cases appear to think that she is both honoured and gratified by their company in place of appearing to think herself superior.[20]

If the leading landowner could not spend sufficient time on such efforts, good agents were essential.

Besides such attention, families like the Hills and the Stewarts, had both patronage and wealth available to them to keep their supporters faithful. As an example of the relationship between these dominant landowners and the lesser gentry of the county we may note a letter

from Lord Downshire to Nicholas Whyte of Loughbrickland on 5 June
1824:

> I have received your letter of the 30th ult. and shall be happy to
> contribute to the erection of a chapel at L[ough] B[rick] land upon
> your estate and request you will send me the subscription list, that
> I may add my name to it. Having decided to give my support to
> Mr Arthur Montgomery who is a candidate for the vacant office of
> treasurer of the county of Down it will gratify me much should
> your opinion in his favour coincide with mine.[21]

Electioneering required considerable and expensive organisation to
ensure that there was a good turn out. Canvassing, supervision of
polling, transport of electors to the poll and production of election
material had to be organised at the candidate's expense. The Hill bill
for the 1805 election in Down, for example, was put at £30,000.[22]
Attention to registration of electors was an ongoing concern.

What about the electors? During the period 1801-29 possession of a
40s freehold was the principal qualification for voters. Freeholders
qualified to vote numbered 15,000 in 1815.[23] Following Catholic
emancipation the Irish Parliamentary Act abolished the 40s freehold
franchise, leaving the £10 freehold as the minimum franchise
requirement. The Reform Act of 1832 added several minor categories of
leasehold to the county franchise. In 1841 the county Down electorate
was put at 2,215.[24] Because polling was not yet conducted in secrecy
and some poll books have survived for the county, it is possible to
establish how people voted. The evidence shows clearly that in these
first decades of the nineteenth century electors voted overwhelmingly
in support of their landlord's position. In 1830, for example, 96 per
cent of the tenants of the Hill and Stewart families gave both votes to
the two family candidates.[25] Among other estates there is some
evidence that while the first vote was given to their landlord's choice,
the second vote was given to the elector's own preference.

Jupp has examined the close link between landlord interests and the
voting behaviour of tenants. He concludes: 'On the whole it would
seem that deference is a more suitable description than dependence,
although one should not underestimate the ability of landlords to
coerce their tenants'.[26] Election 'persecution' did sometimes occur but it
was rare: tenants may have felt obligated to their landlords because of
their tenurial relationship but landlords were no doubt aware of the
draw backs for their property if otherwise good tenants were evicted or
penalised. What was more important was the strong sense of deference
in rural society. Under the existing social order the role of the landlord

in all matters, political and social, was accepted. While political issues, such as parliamentary reform and Catholic emancipation, assumed some importance in Downpatrick and Newry during the first half of the nineteenth century, they had very limited impact in the county. In Newry concern over such issues led to the election of a Catholic M.P., D.C. Brady, for a brief period from 1835 to 1837, before the influence of the main landowning interests was reasserted. In county Down, however, although some meetings of freeholders expressed their views on political matters, no significant organisation emerged to question the social and political role of the chief landowning families. What remained of radicalism in the county after the 1798 rebellion failed to manifest itself in county politics.[27]

IV

During the period from 1850 to 1885 parliamentary elections in county Down witnessed the rise of a strong challenge to landlord political power. Not only was the deference given to landowners undermined but strong opposition developed in the form of both able rivals at the polls and effective tenant organisations, which could take advantage of these changes. The first manifestation of such developments in the early 1850s, however, had only a limited effect. Following the collapse of much of the Irish rural economy during the great famine and a consequent rise in evictions, tenant protest which was orchestrated by the newly formed Tenant League became widespread in Ireland. William Sharman Crawford, a landowner from Crawfordsburn and former candidate at the Down election of 1831 and now radical M.P. for Rochdale, emerged as one of the main leaders of this movement which sought various rights for tenant farmers.[28] Meetings in support of the Tenant League were held at Banbridge in February 1850 and at Downpatrick in January 1851.[29] By early 1852, Sharman Crawford had come forward as a tenant right candidate for county Down at the forthcoming general election. On 22 May 1852 a Central County Down Tenants' Committee, with representatives from every district, was established to promote his cause.[30] Meetings were held throughout the county and extensive canvassing was organised before the poll in July 1852. Compared to 1831 this election campaign produced a new level both of popular involvement and of political debate.

The election witnessed division in landlord ranks. The Stewart interest had been represented previously by Viscount Castlereagh but he had fallen out with his father, the marquis of Londonderry, over their views on the land question. Castlereagh was obliged to retire.

because of these differences and in February 1852, Lord Londonderry, in a letter which later became public, wrote to D.S. Ker of Ballynahinch: 'You are my eldest nephew, and I willingly offer the first refusal of my interest and means to you, if you will take Castlereagh's position with me in the county seat'.[31] He referred to 'the immense treasure expended by my family in the county seat' and impressed on Ker the need to preserve the family seat. Ker agreed and stood with the other former member, Lord Arthur Hill. The publication of Lord Londonderry's frank admission of his power caused some stir in the liberal press but it did not prevent the defeat of the tenant candidate, Sharman Crawford. Hill won 4,654 votes and Ker 4,117, against 3,113 for Sharman Crawford. This election was the first one contested under the new £12 occupier franchise which resulted in the number of electors for the county growing from 2,446 in 1847 to 10,028 in 1852.[32]

How do we explain the result? Supporters of Sharman Crawford believed that coercive powers of the landlords had a lot to do with the defeat of their candidate. After the election Sharman Crawford claimed that tenants had been punished by their landlords for supporting him. When challenged on this matter, however, he was unable to produce any hard evidence, claiming that his witnesses were too frightened to come forward.[33] Probably there were some examples of such pressure but they were obviously rare, or the liberal press would have given them publicity.[34] What was much more important was the leading role of the landowners in rural society and the acceptance of this position among wide sections of the population, which the new tenant-right movement had failed to radicalise. A strong contemporary defence of landlord influence and attitude is demonstrated in a letter of Lord Dungannon in the *Northern Whig*, 5 August 1852, attacking an election report in the paper that tenants of his had gone to the polls 'looking sadly dispirited, and feeling themselves to be ... the veriest slaves'. He stated:

> I did expect that my views at this moment would influence those of the greater proportion of my tenantry; I have ever made it my endeavour to obtain and merit their confidence and regard; I have ever looked upon their interests as being partially interwoven with my own; I have, in all my transactions with them, adhered to the principle of 'live and let live'; I have never failed, so far as it is in me lay, to promote whatever might conduce to their benefit in their several localities; and if, by the above course of conduct I have been so fortunate as to secure to myself their attachment and confidence, their having, at the recent election, voted in accordance with my wishes and feelings, can hardly be matter of astonishment.

By the next general election, 1857, the land question was no longer as prominent and in county Down the election involved only the main proprietorial interests. By this time D.S. Ker had become a liberal thereby losing the support of his uncle, who now gave his backing to Lt Col. W.B. Forde of Seaforde. Sharman Crawford advised his followers to vote for Ker but this did not prevent his defeat by Forde and the other sitting member Lord Arthur Hill (afterwards Hill-Trevor). Thereafter, in spite of the removal of property qualifications for M.P.s in 1859, opposition to landed interests at the polls largely disappeared, thanks partly to growing prosperity in the countryside and declining tenant protest, and no other contested election occurred in county Down until 1874. By the general election of that year, however, two new factors had altered the situation. First, the Ballot Act of 1872 afforded secrecy at the polls. Secondly, Gladstone's Land Act of 1871 had led to a deterioration in landlord-tenant relations which resulted in the establishment of new tenant associations and a wave of protest meetings involving sizeable sections of the Down tenant farmers.

On 30 January 1874 a large meeting of representatives from all districts of county Down was held to select a candidate to contest the county on liberal and tenant right principles.[35] James Sharman Crawford, a son of William Sharman Crawford, a Presbyterian and an agent on his brother's estate, was chosen. His election address emphasised land reform. From headquarters in Belfast, the solicitor C.H. Brett acted as agent, co-ordinating the work of committees throughout the county, organising canvassing and meetings, and appointing personation and polling agents for election day. Tenant associations gave valuable assistance. From Brett's correspondence we can see that his helpers included farmers' leaders such as Joseph Perry, a farmer of over 100 acres from Downpatrick, William Hurst, a linen manufacturer from Drumaness, and Edward Gardner, a Downpatrick solicitor.[36] The two sitting conservative M.P.s, Lord Arthur Hill-Trevor and Lt. Col. W.B. Forde, stood again, without any form of selection. They issued election addresses, followed up by a letter stating their intention to seek suitable reform of the land act. Local landlords and their agents canvassed tenants in the conservative cause. Col. Forde defended himself over a local court case which resulted from the land act.

The contest saw the return of Hill Trevor with 5,029 votes and Sharman Crawford with 4,814, as against Forde with 4,683. This liberal victory was obviously assisted by effective organisation and the growth of protest over the land question. It is difficult to measure the impact of the Ballot Act because other matters, such as the new rural protest, were very important. Since coercion was not a major factor in local politics the Act was probably not of great significance, although it cannot be entirely discounted. In the other Ulster counties, the land question was of considerable influence but only in counties Monaghan and Cavan did home rule emerge as an issue: elsewhere in Ireland the land question and home rule were important. In the Ulster counties the number of landlord M.P.s fell from twenty-six in 1868 to eighteen in 1874, while in the rest of Ireland there were thirty-five landowning M.P.s returned compared with fifty-two at the previous general election.[37]

The county Down borough seats during the period witnessed both continuity of landlord influence and the rise of a challenge to this influence. When D.S. Ker (first elected in 1859) resigned from Downpatrick in 1867, his seat was taken by William Keown, owner of the second largest landholding in the borough, acquired from the Hill estate in 1818 by his father who had been local agent to the Hills. In 1872, however, the Ker family sold their Downpatrick property to John Mulholland, owner of the York Street Mills in Belfast and a 6,769 acre estate at Ballywalter, and unsuccessful conservative candidate in Belfast in 1868. Keown did not go forward in 1874 and John Mulholland was elected without a contest.[38] In Newry, unrest among Catholic and Presbyterian electors caused strong liberal opposition to the Needham family which resulted in the return of two merchants, William Kirk (1852-59, 1868-71) and Benjamin Whitworth (1874-80), the former a Presbyterian and the latter a member of the Church of Ireland. The general election of 1868 in Belfast witnessed the return of an independent Orange candidate, William Johnston of Ballykilbeg, near Downpatrick, but the indebtedness of his small 866 acres estate would impair his political role and oblige him to seek a government appointment. In 1877 he resigned his Belfast seat on being appointed an inspector of fisheries, at a salary of £700 per annum.[39]

The outcome of the 1874 general election in county Down served to galvanise conservative and landlord forces in the county. Supporters of Hill-Trevor and Forde met on 18 July to set up a county constitutional association with local committees.[40] A similar association was established for county Antrim and a full time political organiser, E.S. Finnigan (born in county Kilkenny and a former school headmaster in Downpatrick), was appointed for both county associations. This new organisation was now put to the test on the death of Sharman Crawford on 29 April 1878. A meeting of delegates of the association on 3 May selected Viscount Castlereagh to run as conservative candidate against the liberal and tenant right candidate W.D. Andrews, a Unitarian barrister from Comber.[41] The result was a conservative victory with Castlereagh winning 6,067 votes against 4,701 for Andrews. While the new conservative organisation may have helped Castlereagh to some extent, what was much more important for Castlereagh's victory was his expenditure of a colossal £14,000 (paid by his father) and a clever political move to win the support of some Catholic electors by a vague promise, which Castlereagh subsequently refuted, to back home rule.

By the 1880 general election, due to the deterioration both in the rural economy and landlord-tenant relations, concern over the land question was at a new peak among the electorate throughout Ireland, including county Down. Representatives of Down Tenants' Union asked Major John Sharman Crawford, a landlord and son of William Sharman Crawford, to stand for the county on liberal and tenant right principles. In his address he declared strong support for legalisation of the 3 Fs. Tenant right meetings were held throughout the county to back his candidature: platform speakers included Presbyterian ministers and Catholic clergy. The Belfast solicitor, Charles Brett, again acted as liberal agent, co-ordinating local committees and supporters. At a meeting of the County Down Constitutional Association in 1880 in Downpatrick, Lord Arthur Hill, second son of the fourth marquess of Downshire, was selected to replace his uncle Lord Arthur Hill-Trevor, and Lord Castlereagh was reselected as the other candidate. Both candidates in their election addresses advocated land reform. For this election a special insight into the conservative organisation can be obtained from the evidence at a subsequent election petition trial in connection with allegations of undue influence and bribery brought against the conservatives.[42]

Under the aegis of the county association there were a number of local committees, providing canvassers, agents and drivers, and organising meetings. Although members of the committees often provided their services free, the other election workers were usually paid; charges that electors were given paid work to secure their votes were not proved in the court. The association helped to bring in volunteers and to involve people in the conservative cause but still the conservatives relied considerably on paid help or landlord assistance; landlords, land agents and bailiffs were frequently involved and acted for the conservatives. At the trial an agent's letter to tenants was read to the court. It stated:

> Believing as I do, most conscientiously, that you will best serve the interests of the tenant farmers of Ireland, and gain for them the same blessings as you yourselves enjoy by voting for Lord Arthur Hill and Lord Castlereagh, I earnestly beg of you to do so ...: Mr Stewart, your landlord, will esteem your compliance with the request herein made, as a personal favour to himself.[43]

It was denied that intimidation was involved and no examples were presented to disprove this denial. Indeed, in their final judgement the judges remarked that throughout the case there was no suggestion that landlords treated their tenants unfairly in electioneering matters.

But while landlord influence in Down was primarily a matter of leadership and advice, there remained a slight coercive element. During the election E.S. Finnigan had made it known that there were ways in which one could find out how individuals voted. He later explained that because of the way votes were numbered and the results announced first by district and then by county, it was possible to have a rough idea of how people voted and tenants may have feared to lose their landlord's good will. The liberals saw this action as a veiled threat although Finnigan stated that he raised the matter in a reforming spirit not as a threat. At the election petition court case one of the judges criticised Finnigan's actions as amounting to a disturbance with the free exercise of the vote, but as the others disagreed and as there was no concrete evidence of an elector being threatened as a result of Finnigan's action, the case against him was dismissed. Although Finnigan was technically innocent of undue influence, it seems fair to accept the view of the first judge that some electors may have been influenced. The whole business served to emphasise the slight element of coercive influence that remained.

The result of the county Down election was Hill 5,873, Castlereagh 5,599, and Sharman Crawford 5,579. This outcome, contrary to the trend elsewhere, needs explanation. First, Finnigan's tactic over the ballot in Down was probably important because, while it may not have affected many, it must certainly have affected twenty voters and this was the size of Castlereagh's majority over Sharman Crawford. Secondly, landlord-tenant relations between the Downshire and Londonderry families and their tenants seem to have been especially good, as several witnesses at the 1881 commission into the land question bore testimony.[44] This fact along with strong declarations of support for land reform from the two candidates was probably helpful. Thirdly, the conservatives had a good organisation under E.S. Finnigan's capable control; their electoral expenditure was higher than in any other Irish constituency. Although the county constitutional association played only a minor role in this election, its emergence was vital in the future development of county politics from a landlord-dominated to a popularly-based conservative organisation. As regards the voting behaviour of the electorate, newspaper reports indicate that most members of the Church of Ireland backed the conservatives and most Catholics backed the liberal while Presbyterians were split half and half between the two sides.[45] Religious issues were not raised during the campaign but Presbyterian and Catholic electors were clearly more prone to join the movement against Church of Ireland landlord M.P.s than electors who shared their religious affiliation.

Elsewhere, landlord parliamentary representation, among all parties, had come under severe attack. In the Ulster counties the number of landlord M.P.s fell from eighteen in 1874 to fourteen in 1880, while in the rest of Ireland only fifteen M.P.s compared to thirty-five in 1874 were landlords.[46] Tenant unrest continued to grow after the general election. In late December, Sir Thomas Bateson, owner of an estate at Knockbreda, warned Lord Salisbury about the situation:

> A few weeks since, the Land League invaded Ulster. Up to that moment rents were well and cheerfully paid without even a murmur. Now all that is changed. The League operates in concert with the Central Radical Tenant Right Association, and the result is a general strike on the part of the tenants; men who voted for the conservatives last April are now openly fraternising with democrats whom six weeks ago they would not have touched with a long pol, and the wave of communism has spread like wildfire. The demand is 25, 30, and in some cases 50 per cent permanent reduction of rents, on the plea of low prices caused by American importation.[47]

In 1881 parliament passed Gladstone's second land bill. Conscious of the strong feelings on the matter, this liberal bill received the support of nearly all the Ulster conservative M.P.s, including the two county Down M.P.s, greatly to the annoyance of the conservative party leadership. This new measure was greeted enthusiastically by northern farmers and tenant right organisations but was rejected by the Land League which was banned subsequently by the government. A new organisation, the Irish National League was formed in October 1882 to seek both home rule and further land reform. By the end of 1881 Protestant involvement in the League had largely disappeared and few Protestants joined the National League. Some issues concerning the land question remained but were now of much less importance for the farming community.

The next election in county Down occurred on 27 November 1884, due to Castlereagh's succession as marquis of Londonderry.[48] On 11 November a meeting of liberal delegates from the various polling districts of county Down selected Arthur Sharman Crawford, another son of William Sharman Crawford, as their candidate. On 14 November a meeting of the County Down Constitutional Association chose R.W.B. Ker, a substantial landowner from Ballynahinch, to stand for the conservative cause. By this stage not only was the land question no longer of central significance but important changes had taken place in connection with the rules governing elections. The Corrupt and Illegal Practices Act of 1883 severely reduced the amount of money that a candidate could spend on electoral expenses which meant that most election work would now be voluntary. Several months prior to the by-election, however, E.S. Finnigan of the County Down Constitutional Association had gone round the county, holding meetings of supporters and initiating or reorganising committees for each district in preparation for any future elections.[49]

Thanks to these efforts Ker now had the support of a well organised election team which conducted an active programme of canvassing and transport of electors, very largely through volunteers. The liberal candidate relied on help from tenant associations and liberal supporters. The result of the election was a conservative victory, with Ker polling 4,387 and Crawford 3,998. Strong conservative organisation seems to have been very important for this outcome, as was the loss of some Catholic support for the liberals, reflecting sympathy for the National League among Catholics and antipathy to the liberal government. In June 1885 another Down by-election was held due to the resignation of Lord Arthur Hill to take up a government position followed by his announcement to re-contest the seat. Presbyterian linen manufacturer, J.S. Brown, failed to unseat Hill, winning 4,696 votes against Hill's 5,099. Again superior conservative organisation and loss of Catholic support for the liberals were important.[50]

Clearly then by mid-1885, in comparison with the situation a decade and a half earlier, the community of interest between landlords and tenants in county Down had been undermined and landlord influence at elections had been reduced. Sizeable sections of the electorate, particularly farmers with Presbyterian or Catholic backgrounds, were voting against landlord candidates. Even those who continued to vote for landlord M.P.s now required them to back measures in the tenants' favour. This political transformation is clearly linked to the change in social relations between landlord and tenant which occurred in the previous decade and a half. While other factors, such as the spread of education among the farming community, no doubt contributed to this new political consciousness, it was the social revolution over the land question which primarily caused this political upheaval.[51] At the same time, the emergence of new professional and merchants groups helped provide leadership for this protest.

Throughout Ireland landlord representation among M.P.s had diminished dramatically and other social groups had asserted their role in the political arena. In county Down, however, the landed interest had faced these challenges quite successfully. Skilful political reorganisation, a determined response to the new opposition and flexibility on the part of the leading landowners enabled representatives from this group to maintain their role in local and national politics. Their success in Down is given emphasis by their failure elsewhere in Ulster. By mid-1885 conservative landlord M.P.s held two seats only in county Fermanagh and even in county Antrim where they had been successful in 1874 and 1880 they lost a seat in a by-election in 1885. Besides Down, Antrim and Fermanagh, their control of parliamentary representation in rural Ulster was reduced to only one seat in counties Armagh and Tyrone, respectively.

V

During the final years of the union from 1885 to 1921, landlord control of the parliamentary representation of county Down collapsed. Paradoxically, this period began with the resounding success of landlord candidates at the 1885 general election in county Down, in spite of the new conditions created by recent changes in electoral law. Yet just over two decades later at the 1906 general election, none of the M.P.s for the county came from a landed background, although Lord Arthur Hill did later represent Down West from September 1907 to March 1908. Elections were now affected not only by the Corrupt Practices Act which limited election expenditure but by two later acts which divided the county into four divisions and greatly extended the franchise to include all adult male householders, thereby increasing the electorate by over 200 per cent between 1884 and 1885 in county Down.[52] Socially, the extension of the franchise was important because it gave the vote for the first time to the labourers. These changes presented all the parties with a considerable organisational challenge.

At a meeting of the County Down Constitutional Association on 22 January 1885 a resolution was passed that the association should restructure its local committees to embrace all classes of believers in the union.[53] Lord Arthur Hill, honorary secretary of the association, and E.S. Finnigan, full-time secretary, were appointed to organise the new committees throughout the county. Speaking at the establishment of one such body at Ballynahinch on 7 May, Finnigan explained that

> It was proposed to form a large committee in each of the polling districts into which the county would be divided, this committee to be composed of the members of the present district committees, together with the representatives of the agricultural labouring class, and those who would have a vote as lodgers,

employees, and servants. The Orange association would have a well defined position. The district master and district officers, together with the master of each of the lodges in the district, would be appointed, or other brethren nominated by them, upon each committee.[54]

This involvement of the Orange Order was extremely important because many of the newly franchised labourers belonged to it.

Under the guidance of Hill and Finnigan, especially the latter, similar local committees were set up throughout the county.[55] Conventions of delegates from these bodies were then held to establish divisional associations and to select conservative candidates, great efforts being made to prevent any group taking individual action on the matter and causing disunity. Lord Arthur Hill, sitting M.P. for the county, was selected on 6 May for West Down, Capt. R.W.B. Ker, the other M.P., was chosen for East Down on 19 September, and Col. Thomas Waring, a prominent landowner at Waringstown, was picked for North Down on 23 September. The local Bangor committee had tried to choose Col. Waring for North Down in May but he declined, saying a representative convention should first be held. In the case of South Down, however, there was difficulty in finding a candidate and only at the end of October was it decided to put forward W.H. Kisbey, a Dublin Q.C.

The effectiveness of this conservative reorganisation in county Down is highlighted when we compare it with what happened elsewhere.[56] Conservative landowners had successfully dominated politics in county Fermanagh until 1885 but they made no real effort to set up local organisations and efforts to organise the pro-union vote in the second half of 1885 were too late to help retain a seat. In county Londonderry conservative landlord influence had collapsed in face of a sustained liberal tenant farmer assault in 1874 and 1880 and only revived in 1885 under pressure from Orange and labourer interests. In Armagh attempts were made to broaden the existing conservative organisation to embrace the new labouring working class vote but because of the insensitive way in which this was done a strong Orange element put forward for North Armagh their own candidate, Major E.J. Saunderson, whom the main body of conservatives had eventually to accept. County Antrim was the only other county to exhibit the same degree of care in the development of the new conservative organisation as found in county Down.

Liberals and nationalists reorganised differently in county Down. On 30 May 1885, a meeting primarily of farming delegates representing different districts in county Down, took place in Newtownards to set up a central committee and make plans for the selection of candidates.[57] In mid-October J.S. Brown, who had been defeated at the 1885 Down by-election, was chosen for North Down. Plans to select candidates for the other divisions failed to materialise, suggesting disillusionment caused by the recent by-election result. Throughout most of Ireland nationalist reorganisation was extensive during 1885 and was based primarily on National League branches with strong Catholic clergy involvement.[58] In the first week of November a convention of South Down National League branches and some Catholic clergy in Newry selected J.F. Small, a local solicitor and M.P. for county Wexford, as nationalist candidate. In keeping with general party policy to only put forward candidates for divisions with a Catholic majority, no one was nominated for the other Down divisions. In early November, J.H. McCarthy, journalist and former M.P. for Athlone, was selected for Newry at an open-air convention held in the town.[59]

The main issue at the 1885 general election was no longer land but the question of the union, and it involved not just conflict between supporters and opponents of the link but also rivalry in the pro-union camp between liberals and conservatives. Nationalists won eighty-five seats in all Ireland including seventeen in Ulster: five nationalist M.P.s were landowners. All the sixteen Ulster pro-union seats were won by conservatives, of whom eight were landowners.[60] Col. Waring won North Down with 4,315 votes against Brown's 2,841 while both Hill and Ker were returned unopposed. In South Down, J.F. Small defeated Kisbey with 4,995 votes against the latter's 3,743 and McCarthy was returned unopposed in Newry. The return of three representatives of the landowning interest, along with others in Antrim was a considerable feat, given the previous developments against their group. Lord Deramore (formerly Sir Thomas Bateson) had no doubt as to why they succeeded. Several years later he declared:

> The Protestant working men are masters of the situation. Under the existing franchise the labourers and artisans control the representation of all the non-nationalist seats in Ulster. The farmers are really nowhere. In 1885, under the lead of the resident gentlemen, the labourers and artisans swept every so-called liberal from the different hustings in Ulster, and sent 16 members to support your government, the bulk of the farmers going for the Gladstone candidates in hope of securing more plunder ...
>
> It is not the farmers who hold Ulster for the Queen, but the labourers and artisans, officered by the landlords.[61]

This view undervalued the importance of the surviving conservative farmer vote, and it ignored the importance of a tactical Catholic vote for the conservatives in some areas in 1885, but it rightly stressed the link between conservative landlords and labourers, through the Orange Order, in the effective new party organisations.

In spite of the success of the landed interest at the 1885 general election, however, their control of the county Down seats would fall from three seats in 1885 to two in 1892 and finally to none in 1906. There are many reasons for this. Income from their estates declined after the 1880s because of a fall in agricultural prices and rents, although thanks to the 1883 Act which limited electoral expenditure, M.P.s no longer required large resources to fund election costs.[62] Concern over land purchase, encouraged by T.W. Russell, caused unrest among tenant farmer electors in the 1890s and the early 1900s, although in keeping with their earlier flexibility the county Down unionist M.P.s all backed compulsory purchase by 1900.[63] Within the unionist camp the landlord M.P.s faced a growing challenge from business and professional elements for the leadership of the party.[64] What was most important in the case of Down, however, was the failure of landed interests in the county to either build on their organisational success of 1885 or to realise that their future strength lay in their ability to recognise and take on board the important changes which had occurred in society.

Initially, the position of the victors of the 1885 general election in county Down seemed to become stronger. When another general election occurred in June 1886, following Gladstone's introduction of a home rule bill to parliament and the consequent split of the liberals into Gladstonian liberals and liberal unionists, the vast majority of liberals in county Down, as elsewhere in Ulster, became liberal unionists and joined their former conservative rivals in a new unionist movement. The three successful conservative candidates of 1885 stood again in 1886 and easily defeated nationalist opponents.[65] In 1892 and 1895 the three unionist candidates were elected without any opposition, care being taken to include both former conservatives and liberals on their nomination papers. But while the 1886 general election saw a re-run of the carefully developed procedure of broadly based meetings nominating candidates and the provision of organisational help by local associations, this procedure in fact had ceased by the general election of 1892 and the conservative associations of 1885-6 mostly seem to have disappeared. Perhaps because of confidence generated by their great success in county Down in 1885-6, the landed leadership now proceeded to dominate parliamentary representation with virtually no effort to consult or involve the unionist electorate.

In 1889 Captain Ker, M.P. for East Down , resigned his seat and was replaced by J.A. Rentoul, a Donegal-born Presbyterian barrister who strongly supported farmers' rights and was an able speaker. He had been asked to go forward for Ker's seat by a number of leading conservatives, including Lord Arthur Hill.[66] No public selection procedure was involved and he was elected unopposed in 1889 and again in 1892. Before the 1895 general election, however, Rentoul was informed by one of his original supporters that the constituency should now be represented by a landlord and his resignation was necessary. In his memoirs published in 1921, Rentoul recalled:

> In earlier days I should have had no option but to retire, for mine was an almost entirely agricultural constituency .... but the times had changed, and landlords, though unaware of the fact were no longer omnipotent ... when my resignation was demanded, in the name of landlordism, I declined to acquiesce.[67]

He then called meetings of electors in East Down and received their support, after which the idea of replacing him was dropped. He was returned unopposed in 1895 and 1900.

No public re-selection of candidates occurred at the 1892, 1895 elections and all three unionist candidates were elected unopposed in North, East and West Down. The local divisional associations and organisations of 1885-6 collapsed, except in South Down where a unionist association backed a candidate unsuccessfully against a nationalist on several occasions. In early July 1898, Lord Arthur Hill resigned as M.P. for West Down. On the same day as the press carried his resignation it was reported that a by-election would occur in a week's time and that his son, Captain Arthur Hill, would be a candidate.[68] An earlier private arrangement between Lord Hill and the marquis of Dufferin and Ava, that the latter would help Hill obtain a colonial governorship in return for Hill promoting Dufferin's son for West Down, had collapsed when it proved impossible to influence the government in Hill's favour.[69] Captain Hill was elected unopposed, although this method of proceeding caused considerable unrest. Concern about lack of consultation and popular involvement received new impetus following the death of Col.Waring, M.P. for North Down, a month later. T.L. Corbett, a London businessman with Ulster connections and unsuccessful unionist candidate in Tyrone on two occasions, now put his name forward for election, claiming, that when his agent approached E.S. Finnigan about the seat, he was informed that a 'stop-gap' candidate was required until Lord Castlereagh became old enough to stand for parliament.[70] Corbett refused to agree to take this position and he stood in opposition to John Blakiston Houston, a north Down landowner, who had the support of Finnigan and the landed interest. Both had their own followers and organisations. Blakiston Houston won the by-election with 3,381 votes against Corbett's 3,107.

When the next general election occurred in October 1900 it was clear that the bad feeling created by the handling of these by-elections had not gone away. Corbett now put himself forward for election again in North Down against Col. R.G. Sharman Crawford, a landowner and son of James Sharman Crawford, who seems to have taken over from Blakiston Houston. Both described themselves as unionist candidates. Corbett had the support of the Presbyterian Unionist Voters' Association which wished to see more Presbyterians elected to parliament, but his campaign emphasised his opposition to all landlords, even the son of a famous radical, and their attempts to control parliamentary representation of the county. A report of one of his speeches in Bangor noted that: 'In conclusion Mr Corbett said it would be observed that he had no landlords on his platform, nor had he any of those who were 'invited to dinner by great landlords.'[71] He deliberately sought the Orange and labouring vote. A resolution of Newtownards Orangemen supported brother Corbett 'in his righteous efforts to put down the tyrannical clique which had been preventing the working men of North Down from having a voice in the selection of a candidate.'[72] The result was a victory for Corbett with 4,493 votes against Sharman Crawford's 3,230.

In spite of public misgivings about the absence of any public selection procedures, the two sitting M.P.s for East and West Down were re-elected without any opposition, as was the sitting nationalist M.P. for South Down. Subsequent by-elections, however, where supporters of T.W. Russell now took the opportunity to promote a radical brand of unionism, would expose the political and organisational vacuum which existed in county Down. In January 1902 Rentoul resigned as M.P. for East Down and within a short time James Wood, a Presbyterian solicitor and supporter of Russell, came forward as a unionist candidate, emphasising a strong policy of compulsory purchase, along with support for the improvement of labourers' conditions.[73] After several weeks delay the name of Col. R.H. Wallace of Downpatrick, who was in service in the war in South Africa, was put forward. Wallace, son of a Downpatrick solicitor with property in East Down, had the support of many of the Ulster M.P.s and local landlords, but in the end he was defeated by Wood who won 3,576 votes against his 3,429. While nationalist support for Wood may have contributed towards Wallace's defeat, what was also fatal for Wallace was the absence of any formal organisation, not only to provide assistance at election time but to make him the official candidate and to draw together the different strands of unionism.[74]

When the next by-election took place in July 1905, following the resignation of Captain Hill, it was evident that the lessons from these defeats of 1900 and 1902 had been learnt. Under the auspices of the newly formed West Down Unionist Association, Henry Liddell, a Presbyterian linen manufacturer from Donacloney, was selected. In his speeches he not only strongly emphasised that he was not a landlord and declared his support for the labourers, but he constantly reminded people that he had been selected by this official body.[75] A.J. Beattie, who had the support of the radical Farmers and Labourers' Union, ran against him but was unsuccessful, winning only 3,015 votes against Liddell's 4,440. By the general election of January 1906 all the Down divisions once more had broadly based unionist associations which selected candidates and provided them with organisational help. In North Down, T.C. Corbett was nominated by the newly formed North Down Unionist Association at a meeting under the chairmanship of Col. R.G. Sharman Crawford, Corbett's opponent in 1900.[76] A.J. Adams, a supporter of T.W. Russell, stood against Corbett but was easily defeated: after the contest Corbett proclaimed his win as a victory for 'organised unionism.'[77] In East Down the candidate of the newly formed unionist association, Captain James Craig, a Presbyterian businessman, defeated James Wood. Henry Liddell was re-selected by his unionist association in West Down and was elected unopposed. A unionist candidate P.K. Kerr-Smiley was unsuccessful in South Down against nationalist Jeremiah MacVeagh.

The 1906 general election marked the effective end of landlord domination of county Down politics. One final effort to assert control, however, would be made by Lord Arthur Hill when in August 1907 he decided to stand in a by-election for West Down against W.J. MacG Macaw, the candidate selected by West Down Unionist Association.[78] After a Russellite candidate, Andrew Beattie, entered the contest Macaw withdrew to avoid splitting the unionist vote and Hill defeated Beattie by 3,702 votes to 2,918. But Hill's actions had won the disapproval of the new Ulster Unionist Council and he now faced continued conflict with his association which caused him to resign in 1908 and to be replaced by Macaw. At the next two general elections in January and December 1910 all the unionist candidates in county Down were selected and promoted by their local associations. The three unionist M.P.s were from business or professional backgrounds and all were Presbyterian. Examination of these associations shows how broad based they were, Captain Craig boasting in 1910 that the delegates of his association had been chosen 'by labourers, farmers, artisans, and in fact all classes of the community.[79] Landowners were still to be found in these organisations but they were no longer in control. Again at the 1918 general election, fought under a new extended franchise and new parliamentary divisions, none of the county Down M.P.s came from a landed background. Finally, however, we may note that in July 1921, at a by-election for Mid Down, after six unsuccessful attempts by his family to win a seat in the county, Colonel R.G. Sharman Crawford was elected unopposed.

This period from 1885 to 1921, began with the landed interest in a controlling position in three out of four county Down seats but ended with its role in county politics greatly reduced. In the face of great changes in the electoral laws, a successful restructuring of party organisations in 1885 left prominent landowners in the county in a dominant political position. Their influence now diminished, mainly because they failed to retain these structures which gave their leadership role legitimacy and broad support in the unionist community. Because of a new level of popular political consciousness, the electorate expected to be involved in procedures of selection and election and when this failed to happen they turned against this landed leadership. Other factors also mattered in the decline of the landed interest in county Down, but its failure to maintain and build on the broad based structures of 1885-6 was the single most important one. An interesting contrast is to be made between the situation in county Down and that in county Antrim, especially in Mid-Antrim. Broad based organisations in county Antrim in 1885 also helped to elect Rt. Hon. R.T. O'Neill for Mid-Antrim. The divisional unionist association for Mid-Antrim did not collapse, however, and, unlike his fellow county Down M.P.s, O'Neill had to go to this organisation for re-election at each general election.[80] Between 1885 and 1906 O'Neill faced a contest on only three occasions and in each he was successful. In 1910 his nephew Capt. Hon. A.E.B. O'Neill succeeded him as M.P. for Mid-Antrim. Similarly in East Antrim where the 1885 association also survived, Captain J.M. McCalmont was M.P. from 1885 until his death in 1913 when he was succeeded by his son Major R.C.A. McCalmont.

The role of landowners at elections in county Down changed markedly during the period of the union. Clearly the state of landlord-tenant relations was important for the electoral influence of the landed interest. At the same time the political response of this group to the social and political changes of the last quarter of the nineteenth century was significant. At first the reaction of county Down landowners to new electoral laws and the dramatic change in political awareness of the electorate was successful, but later they failed to adequately capitalise on their success of 1885. They evolved new political organisations to deal with new circumstances but they failed to maintain these vital links with the electorate. The role of Lord Arthur Hill and E.S. Finnigan seems to have been crucial in these later developments.[81] From the Wyndham Act of 1903 to 1921 most of the big estates in county Down were broken up, but the landed interest had already lost its political dominance. Some former landowners would remain important in the local political unionist associations in county Down post 1921 but they would now share the leadership of the unionist movement with other groups. The only two M.P.s with a landed background in county Down at either the U.K. or Northern Ireland parliament from 1921 to 1969, were Hon. Harry Mulholland and Colonel Gordon. Neither the Downshire nor the Londonderry families again saw members elected for the county although the 3rd marquis of Londonderry would serve in both the Northern Ireland and U.K. cabinets. In the 1920s the Downshire seat at Hillsborough became the official residence of the governor of Northern Ireland and Mountstewart, the Londonderry's home, was acquired by the National Trust in the 1960s. In recent decades a small number from this landed background have been active in politics in county Down, mostly on behalf of the Alliance Party.[82]

References

1. Election results throughout this chapter have come from B. M. Walker (ed.), *Parliamentary election results in Ireland, 1801-1922* (Dublin, 1977).

2. For sources of these figures on the social background of M.P.s see the relevant sections in this chapter.

3. *Return of the owners of land of one acre and upwards in the several counties, counties of cities and counties of towns in Ireland* [c.1492], H.C. 1876, xxx, 61-394.

4. R. B. McDowell, 'The landed classes and the professions' in T.W. Moody and J.C. Beckett (eds, *Ulster since 1800: second series, a social survey* (London, 1957), pp 99-100.

5. *Ballywalter Park* (Belfast, 1985).

6. *Census of Ireland, 1881, i, province of Ulster*, p. 523 [c.964-1 to x]. H.C. 1874, lxxiv, i, 523.

7. W. E. Vaughan and A. J. Fitzpatrick (eds), *Irish historical statistics: population 1821-1971* (Dublin, 1978), p. 58.

8. W.A. Maguire, *The Downshire estates in Ireland, 1801-1845* (Oxford, 1972); *Digest of evidence on the occupation of land in Ireland*, i (Dublin, 1847).

9. See M. P. Campbell, *A history of Tullylish* (Lurgan, c.1984), p. 38.

10. W. E. Vaughan, *Landlords and tenants in Ireland, 1848-1904* (Dundalk, 1984).

11. Quoted in B. M. Walker, *Ulster politics: the formative years, 1868-86* (Belfast, 1989), pp 5-6.

12. *Down Recorder*, 15 Jan. 1881.

13. J. C. Rutherford, *An Ards farmer: or, an account of the life of James Shanks, Ballyfounder, Portaferry* (Belfast, 1913), pp 62-6.

14. Quoted in Walker, *Ulster politics*, p. 22.

15. P. J. Jupp, 'County Down elections, 1783-1831' in *I.H.S.*, xviii, no. 70 (Sept. 1972), pp 177-206.
16. Ibid., pp 184-5.
17. Ibid., pp 181-98.
18. Information on Downpatrick from the entry by P.J. Jupp in R.G. Thorne (ed.), *The history of parliament: the house of commons, 1790-1820, ii, the constituencies* (London, 1986), pp 644-6.
19. Ibid., pp 646-8.
20. Jupp, 'County Down elections', p. 192.
21. Ibid., p. 193.
22. Jupp in Thorne, *House of commons*, p. 643.
23. Ibid., p. 642.
24. Walker, *Irish parliamentary election results*, p. 69.
25. Jupp, 'County Down elections', pp 196-7.
26. Ibid., p. 197.
27. Ibid., pp 199-200; for further discussion on this see A. T. Q. Stewart, The transformation of Presbyterian radicalism in the north of Ireland, 1792-1825, Unpub. M.A. thesis, Q.U.B., 1956.
28. B. A. Kennedy, Sharman Crawford, 1780-1861, Unpub. Ph.D. thesis, Q.U.B., 1953. Paul Bew and Frank Wright, 'The agrarian opposition in Ulster politics, 1848-87' in Samuel Clark and J. S. Donnelly, *Irish peasants: violence and political unrest, 1780-1914* (Wisconsin, 1983), pp 194-200.
29. *Down Recorder*, 2 Feb. 1850, 4 Jan. 1851.
30. *Northern Whig*.
31. Ibid., 23 May 1852.
32. Walker, *Irish parliamentary election results*, pp 76-82.
33. Kennedy, 'Sharman Crawford', pp 424-31.
34. For examples of intimidation see S. M. Stewart, Presbyterian radicalism, landlord influence and electoral politics in county Down in the mid-nineteenth century, Unpub. M.A. thesis, St. Patrick's College, Maynooth, 1981.
35. *Northern Whig*, 31 Jan. 1874. For discussion of land and politics see B. M. Walker, 'The land question and elections in Ulster, 1868-86' in Clark and Donnelly, *Irish peasants*, pp 230-68.
36. For further analysis of this material see Walker, *Ulster politics*, pp 95-6.
37. Ibid., pp 113-6.
38. Ibid., p. 105.
39. Aiden McClelland, *William Johnston of Ballykilbeg* (Lurgan, 1990), p. 79.
40. Walker, *Ulster politics*, pp 117-8.
41. Ibid., pp 123-5.
42. Ibid., pp 138-43.
43. Ibid., p. 140.
44. Ibid., p. 142.
45. Ibid., p. 143.
46. Ibid., pp 149-52. See also C. C. O'Brien, *Parnell and his party 1880-1890* (Oxford, 1857).
47. Walker, *Ulster politics*, p. 7.
48. Ibid., pp 168-70.
49. Ibid., p. 169.
50. Ibid., pp 172-4.
51. See J. H. Whyte, 'Landlord influence at elections in Ireland, 1760-1885' in *English Historical Review*, lxxx (1965), pp 740-60.

52. B. M. Walker, 'The Irish electorate, 1868-1915' in *I.H.S.*, xviii, no. 71 (March, 1973), p. 390.
53. Walker, *Ulster politics*, pp 219-25.
54. Ibid.
55. Ibid., pp 179-80.
56. Ibid., pp 177-92.
57. Ibid., p. 197.
58. Ibid., p. 176 and pp 201-2.
59. Ibid., pp 202-11.
60. Ibid., pp 219-25.
61. Ibid., pp 222-3.
62. For a discussion of the fall in their incomes see Alvin Jackson, *The Ulster party: Irish unionists in the house of commons, 1884-1911* (Oxford, 1989), pp 230-5.
63. For information on Russell's campaign see Alvin Jackson, 'Irish unionism and the Russellite campaign 1894-1906' in *I.H.S.*, xxv no. 100 (Nov. 1987), pp 376-404.
64. Jackson, *The Ulster party*, pp 53-82; David Burnett, 'The modernisation of unionism, 1892-1914?' in Richard English and Graham Walker (eds), *Unionism in modern Ireland* (London, 1996), pp 41-55.
65. Walker, *Ulster politics*, pp 239-43.
66. J. A. Rentoul, *Stray thoughts and memories* (London, 1921), pp 130-3.
67. Ibid., pp 26-7.
68. For criticism of this see the editorial in *Northern Whig*, 19 July 1896.
69. Jackson, *The Ulster party*, p. 220.
70. *Northern Whig*, 1 and 2 Sept. 1898.
71. *Belfast News Letter*, 2 Oct. 1900.
72. Ibid., 28 Sept. 1900.
73. Jackson, 'Irish unionism', pp 376-404.
74. Editorial in *Belfast News Letter*, 7 Feb. 1902 criticises Wallaces' organisation.
75. Ibid., 29 and 30 June 1905.
76. Ibid., 6 Jan. 1906.
77. Ibid., 22 Jan. 1906.
78. *Northern Whig*, 21 and 31 Aug. 1907.
79. Ibid., 8 Jan. 1910.
80. For example, see his reselection in 1895, *Northern Whig*, 10 July 1895.
81. See Jackson, *The Ulster party*, pp 218-22.
82. Examples are the third Lord Dunleath, the fifth Lord Roden, Mr. Patrick Forde of Seaforde and Col. Rowan-Hamilton of Killyleagh.

Plate 12.1   From The province Ulster described, 1610 in John Speed, *Theatre of the empire of Great Britaine* (London 1612).

Chapter 13

THE PROVISION AND PRACTICE OF PRISON REFORM IN COUNTY DOWN, 1745-1894

CAROLINE WINDRUM

The history of parliamentary penal reform dates back to the 1660s,[1] but it was not until the eighteenth century that a sustained intellectual and parliamentary interest in penology emerged. Sparked by concerns for public health and safety within the confines of gaols and beyond, the early prison reformers, products of the Enlightenment such as John Howard, highlighted the widespread human misery, corruption and neglect occurring behind prison walls. Prison administration was poorly developed and haphazard, and was left to a variety of private individuals as well as the local county authorities, the grand juries. In response, the Irish parliament passed a series of acts during the last quarter of the century, which were designed to raise and standardise conditions. While these measures tinkered with the system, legislation passed in 1786 set in place a new prison hierarchy, including an inspector general of prisons, and at the local level made provision for local inspectors and physicians, who were responsible for the improved management of inmates.[2] At a stroke, the basis of future prison reform had been institutionalised. Each county was to have its own gaol[3] where division between the sexes was maintained. A three-tiered class system, separating prisoners according to their crime, was introduced. This differentiated between debtors, who accounted for a significant proportion of the total prison population, and those held on capital and non-capital offences.

During the nineteenth century, the inspection and regulation of prisons became subject to even greater central control. The Prison Act of 1826 advocated a five-fold inmate classification and extended the principles of earlier measures.[4] Prisoners were to benefit from an improved system of moral government and instruction. The lord lieutenant was empowered to appoint two inspectors general who were to survey and report on progress. The pioneering work of Sir Jeremiah Fitzpatrick, the first inspector general, had set a high standard of enquiry. Grand juries were instructed to present higher scaled salaries to prison staff, demonstrating the general movement towards more professional prison management. Turnkeys were to receive uniforms, reflecting their new-found status as public servants.

By the end of the 1830s, a network of newly-constructed or extended prisons existed in much of Ireland. In addition, the numerous county bridewells formed an integral part of the system, acting as temporary houses of correction for disorderly individuals and petty offenders. Prison officials were required to assume greater responsibility for the security of the buildings, as military guards were removed from gaols in 1830. Better organisation and more sophisticated forms of bureaucracy and record-keeping were encouraged. By the 1860s, the prison system was considered too unwieldy and moves were made to strengthen central control. After a number of parliamentary attempts, the General Prison Board was officially established in 1877. The Board quickly rationalised the prison system, closing 114 of the 137 prisons in Ireland.[5]

Throughout this period, prison reform was both informed by, and shaped, the associated developments in law enforcement, poor law and public health.[6] Yet the periodicity and nature of prison reform and its achievements varied considerably at the local level. As part of the national network, county prisons were considered in the broader penal debates, but were also subject to changes in prison law. It is in light of this relationship that this chapter examines the development of prisons within county Down between 1745 and 1894. During the intervening one hundred and fifty years, three successive prisons were located in the county town of Downpatrick. An analysis is presented of their histories based upon the influences and factors responsible for their initial construction, the nature of their evolving administrations and finally, the conditions of their respective managerial regimes. A wide range of contemporary official and private documentation is employed. The grand jury papers for county Down, the annual reports of the inspectors general, the General Prison Board correspondence, press commentaries and related materials provide a comprehensive account of the prisons and the frequent discrepancies between the provision and practice of reform. Before embarking upon this analysis, however, it is appropriate to consider the general composition of the inmate population.

Crime and punishment

Generally speaking, the number of prisoners reflected the state of the country, with increases coinciding with the episodic unrest and economic crises so pivotal to the development of Irish society as a whole. In Downpatrick, committal rates peaked during the 1798 Rebellion, the immediate post-Napoleonic period, and again around the Famine. Conditions were particularly difficult in the 1840s even though county Down escaped the worst ravages of the blight. At this time, a network of over twenty petty session rooms and lock-ups was established across the county to supplement the county goal, while an additional bridewell was built at Newtownards.[7] Earlier, in 1840, the grand jury had financed the building of the Newry bridewell, two years after major repairs to the town's courthouse.

During the post-Famine period, the crime rate in Down gradually declined in line with the national trend, reflecting not only the general demographic downturn but also the creation in 1836 of a national constabulary, and the effects of improvements in the economy. Petty felonies, larcenies and common assaults accounted for the majority of crimes in Down and were geographically concentrated in and around the major towns and villages. In the statistical account of the 311 prisoners held at Downpatrick during 1835, for example, 117 had been found guilty of common assault, thirty-one of riots and breach of peace, and forty-five of simple larceny.[8] Habitual offenders accounted for an increasing proportion of those held in the second half of the nineteenth century, to the dismay of commentators arguing for the reformative qualities of prisons. Many crimes were carried out under the influence of excessive drink. As the grand jury stated, the 'disorderly classes' tended 'to oscillate between the streets, the poor house and the gaol'.[9]

The character and rationale of the punishments handed down by the courts of the petty and quarter sessions changed over time. As in the mid-eighteenth century, the county gaol held many debtors and vagrants, and they were considered to be places of detention where the individual could be held until their trial. Sentences of death or transportation were frequently imposed by the courts. Following the American War of Independence, the British State established new convict colonies in Australia, both to reduce overcrowding in gaols at home and for strong imperialist reasons. Between 1796 and 1830, over four hundred individuals formerly held at Down County Gaol arrived in the rising colony of New South Wales. Petty offenders received seven years while more serious crimes resulted in a fourteen year sentence. Many of the capitally-convicted had their sentences reduced to life transportation. Punishments for those convicted of lesser offences were often exemplary, and were designed to humiliate the offender and deter others. For example, on 12 August 1808, the Hon. Justice Mayne sentenced Thomas Stannage, alias Caldwell, to be 'imprisoned two months, and whipped through Downpatrick one market day in each month' after being found guilty of the intent to pick pockets in Newtownards.[10] Branding or maiming, in turn, stigmatised the offender for life. At a single sitting of the Down Assizes on 27th August 1822, eleven individuals were sentenced to be burnt in the hand along with terms of imprisonment which varied from two to six months.

With the decline of transportation as a penal system in the second half of the nineteenth century, parliament was forced to consider alternatives such as the marks system of penal servitude, which was based on the individual's industry and behaviour. This formed part of the general shift away from physical punishment to more 'humane' methods.[11] In 1818, for example, public whipping of female offenders had been abolished, and by 1866 executions were similarly removed from the public arena. Greater emphasis was thus placed upon the development of the penitentiary, as prisoners had often to be housed for considerable periods of time, and also rehabilitated before their return to society.[12]

The Down House of Correction, 1746 to 1796

The documentary evidence for the history of gaols in Downpatrick dates back to the late seventeenth century. A house of correction existed in Irish Street until 1708, after which the old 'Castle Dorras' was used as a prison.[13] However, a new gaol was opened on the site of the former complex in 1746. Dean Delaney was a prime mover in the grand jury's decision to build 'a new gaol, chapel and bridewell in Downpatrick' although some consideration had been given to the possible renovation of the old building.[14] The cleric had been appalled by the conditions he found during a visit to the old gaol and offered a hundred pounds towards a new building, as well as an annual endowment of twenty pounds for a clergyman to conduct divine service.[15]

Discipline was poor in the new gaol. Some of the prisoners continued to cause a public nuisance during their confinement as they would 'station themselves at windows of the gaol, and by means of a long pole with a hook on the end they frequently managed to steal bundles of yarn, &c. from the assembled rustics'.[16] In addition, begging occurred as inmates lowered small bags from the windows. Such behaviour was not uncommon in Irish gaols. Inmates depended upon charity, as the well-being of prisoners was not part of the county's concern. Prisoners were only permitted to leave the gaol upon the payment of a fee to the gaoler. This practice was open to serious abuse and was heavily criticised in the era of the first prison reformers, when public attention was called to the poor conditions in many of the gaols in Britain and Ireland. John Howard, for example, found that numerous gaols lacked many of the basic conveniences, such as adequate clothing and bedding. Bullying, gambling and bribery of officials was rife. In addition, prisoners could also be cooped up in cells with heavy irons on their feet and robbed of their meagre food rations. Such seems to have been the case in Downpatrick although documentary evidence for the conditions is patchy. A number of escapes occurred,[17] and open acknowledgement was given of the 'disagreeable way' in which prisoners were held.[18] Following an accidental fire in the gaol in the 1790s, in which six prisoners were suffocated, a new sense of urgency was impressed on the issue of prison provision. Dissatisfied with the circumstances of the gaol, the frequent escapes and the increasing political uncertainties of the 1780s, the grand jury purposed to build a new county prison on the principles laid out by John Howard.

Down County Gaol, 1796 to 1831

From the outset, the plans for the new prison were guided by 'a strict sense of public duty', intended to reflect the standing of the county, and by implication, the status of the grand jurors, who were drawn mainly from the leading county families. The jury's decision to provide a new building was in line with the parliamentary guidelines of the 1796 Act.[19] The architect was Charles Lilly, who had previously undertaken repair work at Downpatrick Cathedral. A total sum of £60,000 was presented at the Summer Assizes of 1789, including £233.10.10 towards the purchase of the new site from George Sharrock, a resident of the town. Lilly seems to have altered part of his original plan, as the grand jury agreed to a later proposal 'for the felons' cells [to] be divided into three stories'.[20] It is possible that this architectural deviation was borrowed from a plan devised by the English architect, R.F. Brettingham.

The marquis of Downshire, the earl of Hillsborough, the Hon. Edward Ward and Charles Lilly were appointed to oversee the building program which commenced in 1789 and was completed in 1796.[21] The extensive prison complex covered one acre and contained three main structures. These included the governor's residence and cellblock which were set within a high perimeter wall and fronted by two substantial gatehouses (plate 13.1). The site and situation of the new gaol were central to its security. The newly-acquired location in the Mall, just below the Cathedral and overlooking the town, reflected contemporary thinking. As with contagion, crime was held to spread in poorly ventilated places and thus a site on the marshy lowlands of the meander plain of the River Quoile, for example, would have been unacceptable. The gaol contained all the required facilities, a prison yard, a bath, a privy, a good water pump and a common hall or

Plate 13.1   Down County Gaol, 1796 – 1831 (Source: Down County Museum)

kitchen for each class of prisoner, while its cells were considered dry and airy.

Pressure was placed upon the institution only a short time after its opening when those suspected of complicity in the 1798 Rebellion were confined in the gaol. The Government's concern for the security of the political prisoners held in the gaol led to the heightening of the perimeter wall in April 1798, and the decision to supply stocks and a pillory. By 1803, a gallows costing £100 had been constructed outside the gaol for public executions.[22] It was during this period that the most famous inmate of the prison, the United Irishman, Thomas Russell, was hanged.

The Rev. Arthur Forde, curate of Seaforde, took up the post of local inspector in Down in 1794. He had assumed the role in the House of Correction, two years prior to the opening of the gaol on the Mall. Once the new site was opened he received £20 per annum for most of his eighteen-year term. It was not until 1810 that he received the higher sum of £70, although an additional salary had been paid to him as prison chaplain since 1802. With time, his duties, like those of the other prison officials, became more clearly defined by law. Forde seldom intervened in the gaoler's activities, and displayed more concern for the physical fabric of the building than for the welfare of its inmates. Forde's successor, Dr. Nevin, occupied the post from 1812 to 1820, and maintained the same *laissez-faire* policy. Following Nevin's resignation in 1820, the new appointee, Rev. Richard Maunsell, initiated a number of changes towards the end of his three years as local inspector, including the introduction of more formal schooling arrangements. Sidney Rowan Hamilton replaced Maunsell, but by this time, the board of superintendence, composed of grand jurors, had assumed an increasing role in the upkeep, improvement and operation of the gaol.

Security was the chief concern. To prevent escapes, the gaoler was now a full-time resident of the prison. During Forde's term as inspector, Joseph Robinson held the position, although his suitability was questioned. As gaoler in the old house of correction, he had allegedly accepted bribes from inmates. On 6 August 1804, seven men escaped from the gaol. Robinson placed notices in the *Belfast News Letter* offering five guineas reward for the recapture of each of his charges, two of whom had been convicted of treasonable practises.[23] It is likely that the grand jury thought Robinson culpable, as they replaced him in time for the following Lent assizes. Aware of the need to attract a reputable candidate, the new gaoler, Edward Hamilton, was offered an increased salary of £35 per annum and was permitted to employ an assistant on a semi-formal basis. The new gaoler's career in Down County Gaol did not get off to a good start. In October 1804, eleven men, including a father and son, breached the upper 'flat' of the gaol and descended into the courtyard below by tying sheets together to form a makeshift rope.[24] Reward notices were again posted in the *Belfast News Letter*: ten guineas were offered for each of three of the offenders and five guineas for each of the rest. One of their number, James McKimins, had been involved in the previous breakout. The self-evident organisation behind this successful escape by such a large number prompted an investigation. By the following April, the turnkey, Owen White and three inmates all by the name of Stewart, were tried for assisting the escape. The gaoler's assistant was later acquitted of all charges. Similarly, Hamilton was absolved of any involvement in a later escape in June 1811, when two men, Andrew Callaghan and Thomas Simple, variously indicted on charges of stealing linen cloth and a felony, escaped from the gaol.[25] Both men were quickly recaptured and sentenced to seven years' transportation to New South Wales at the Lent Assizes of 1813.

Edward Hamilton was replaced as gaoler by Hugh Gray in 1815. He held the post until the gaol's closure in 1831. Fears for the security of the building continued. On the 20th July 1817, five men made their bid for freedom through the sewers of the gaol. Four were recaptured immediately, but the fifth, Archibald Lenaghan, held on a charge of having stolen bread in his possession, escaped.[26] An enterprising twenty-two year old from Killinchy, Lenaghan temporarily donned women's clothing to evade detection.[27] During his time on the run, he was suspected together with another escapee of the murder of Adam Heslip. Both were subsequently proved innocent of the crime. Nevertheless, in response to the event, a sub-committee of the grand jurors, including the Rev. Forde, inspected the gaol to determine the need for an under-gaoler, but following Lenaghan's successful recapture, the proposal was quietly dropped.[28] However, a new privy for the felon's prison was presented costing £15.10.0 and arrangements were made to grate the sewers since escapes frequently exploited this weak point in the gaol's security.[29] Even so, some prisoners were not deterred. In September 1820, Patrick Miskelly, a convicted murderer, was detected cutting his way through the prison wall in the gaol yard,[30] and shortly afterwards the grand jury took the decision to employ a full-time turnkey. However, the gaol's record could have been worse: published reward notices suggest that Antrim County Gaol experienced more frequent escapes and lost more escapees than Down.

The prison contained eighteen cells, five day rooms and eight sleeping rooms for an average of 130 prisoners. In practise, the cells were cold, draughty and poorly maintained. There were eighteen 'fires' in the prison but none were located in the cells. Furniture was kept to a bare minimum.[31] Many of the other legislative demands such as the banning of alcoholic drink, the provision of fuel, straw, bedding and clothing were dealt with in an *ad hoc* fashion. Consequently, inadequacies in prison operations came to light at an early stage. In the 1808 annual review, the inspector general, Rev. Forster Arches, lamented that his previous recommendation to prevent conversation occurring between male and female prisoners, namely, an inexpensive alteration to the female ward, had not been made.[32] Time and again, complaints were also raised against the gaoler for failing to implement what had been considered to be 'necessary alterations'.

By the 1810s, prison expenditure fluctuated around £875 per annum, much of it spent on food. A major reassessment of costs came after 1815, following the investigations of the newly-established gaol committee. Expensive 'luxuries', like the supply of a bed and blanket to every prisoner at the cost of £1.12.6 per inmate (in 1814), were to be avoided in the future. Tighter financial control and more rigorous management of accounts and contracts resulted in a saving of £113 in the following annual return to the Jury, despite the fact that £150 was raised 'to provide, and have erected a proper drop or place of execution for criminals at the entrance of the gaol'.[33] Previous poorly staged executions had attracted bad publicity from the press. For example, Patrick Miskelly was sentenced to death for a murder near Lisburn in county Antrim. He was to be 'heavily ironed, and placed in solitary confinement; ...[then to] be taken to the place where criminals are usually executed, and there hanged by the neck until ... dead! .. And after [his] body [was] to be taken to the county infirmary, there to be disected (sic) and anatomised'. The first attempt at his execution failed as he was brought down from the gallows, unbeknown to the crowd and presumably his executioner, prior to drawing his last breath. His revival some moments later caused great alarm. He was not so fortunate the next day when he was finally dispatched.[34]

Attempts to regulate prison standards were characteristically ineffectual. In 1818, ten men from the grand jury were appointed to visit the gaol periodically and report their observations.[35] However, this proposal was greeted half-heartedly and not implemented; thus the general circumstances of the gaol continued to decline. In March 1823, the Hon. Judge Moore in a brief address to the grand jury during the Assizes, highlighted the comments in the inspector's general report for that year. This stated that the gaol 'had been completely neglected; the sewers and yard are out of order, and in a state of dilapidation'.[36] Indeed, Inspector Woodward had added that some of the cells had been used as stores. A dim view was also taken of the gaoler who kept a cow and some pigs on the county ground adjoining the gaol.[37] As the

1820s progressed, the commissioners of work (consisting of ten to twelve men) and latterly the board of superintendence, on which the local inspector held a seat, assumed a greater interest and control over prison developments.

Generally speaking, prior to Maunsell's appointment in 1820, the grand jury's response to new forms of expenditure on the gaol was not enthusiastic, and minor changes or interventions in the pattern of management were generally reactionary in nature. Following the outbreak of typhus fever in the gaol in the summer months of 1817, another committee, including the marquess of Downshire, Earl Annesley and Lord Dufferin, was set up to consider the 'proprietary for making an infirmary'. In the summer of 1818, £500 was given to the new commission for the infirmary. Yet other preoccupations took over and the £500 grant was returned to the grand jury in 1820. Despite the grim medical conditions, the inspector general had urged that education and employment were of greater importance. Most inmates passed the day in idleness, but in 1822 a school was established to occupy the growing numbers, and by 1823, over £300 had been presented by the county for a treadmill.

Other discussions were also taking place at this time. In 1818, up to 230 prisoners had been held at one time, far in excess of the gaol's normal capacity. Consequently, in 1819, the grand jury 'resolved unanimously – .... that the present Gaol is altogether inadequate for the purpose of confinement of prisoners, as well with respect to security as to classification, and that a new Gaol and House of Correction should be built'. As in many gaols, various forms of abuse were common, but an inordinate number of petitions had reached the grand jury that year, drawing members' attention to the practice of 'garnishing'. They recognised the gravity of the situation when the term was defined as a 'kind of entrance money, or black-pot, paid by prisoners to their fellow-prisoners on their committal'.[38]

In August 1819, a committee headed by the marquess of Downshire was appointed to procure plans for a new gaol 'calculated for the most perfect separation, classification and employment of prisoners, amounting to 100 debtors and 150 persons under criminal charges'.[39] Few eligible and cost-effective plans were forthcoming, for later notices in January 1820 extended the deadline for submissions.[40] Fears of unrest ensured that the prison question remained a prominent, although unresolved, issue. In November 1819, Samuel Duncan, a Protestant, was beaten to death following an altercation between two groups near Rathfriland. Whether sectarian differences were the causal factor in the fracas will never be known, but twelve Catholics, allegedly members of the agrarian redresser movement known as the 'Threshers', were indicted for his murder and for causing a riot. Seven were capitally convicted, although two had their sentences commuted to transportation for life; another two were acquitted.[41] As the date of execution drew near, the grand jury communicated their fears of further agrarian unrest to the Dublin administration.[42] Extra militia were drafted into Downpatrick although, in the event, the executions passed without incident. In an act of solidarity, however, 'many threshers attended their funeral ... marching arm-in-arm six abreast – the leading men having white rods in their hands'.[43]

The economic distress of the post-Napoleonic War depression was reflected in prison numbers, and concern over the growing lawlessness of the county was apparent as early as 1816. The grand jury offered £500 for information on those engaged in burnings, outrages, the distribution of threatening letters and other crimes against private property.[44] Nonetheless, while the old gaol was clearly inadequate, the proposal to build a new gaol, which would incorporate the progressive and enlightened views of the prison reformers, was an expensive undertaking and treated reluctantly. In 1821, another committee was raised to investigate whether 'a new gaol, on a smaller scale and less expense, may be advantageously adopted'.[45] Faith in the old building's virtue had also been reinvigorated following the appointment of Capt. Rowan Hamilton, who had convinced the jury that sound management and not additional finance was the key to an effective penal regime. He consolidated and extended the various reforms in discipline, classification, labour and education initiated by Maunsell

From the outset, Rowan instigated a strict code of management. He effected significant reductions in 'the extravagant dietary', substantially lowering the cost of food per inmate. A new system of cooking was organised and supervised by turnkeys, thereby preventing the sort of sale or exchange of food that had happened frequently in the past.[46] A beam and scales were introduced to check on the delivery and distribution of provisions. Prison accounts were audited and thereafter record a general decline in prison expenditure.[47] Rowan's active and interventionist style of management rid the gaol of various practises which were contrary to the spirit of the Prison Act. Turnkeys were no longer permitted to sleep in the chapel, and the gaoler, Hugh Gray, removed his livestock and cleared out cells.[48] As early as the Summer Assizes of 1824, the grand jury unanimously thanked Rowan 'for the great exertion made by him in the execution of his said office, whereby the cleanliness, comfort and regularity of the gaol and prisoners have been much increased, with a greatly reduced expenditure to the county'.[49] The good order of the gaol was also noted by the inspectors general, James Palmer and Edward Woodward, who pointed to the major improvements in staff attitude and support offered by the 'good and reliable Inspector'.[50] In 1825, the jury agreed to the employment of three turnkeys, two earning £30 per annum and the third £20, while the jailer received the much increased salary of £200.

Pressure of numbers, especially prior to the meeting of the Assizes, ensured that a system of classification and separation was difficult to implement, notwithstanding Rowan's efficiency. Seven classes of prisoners had been devised but the assignment of these classes to particular areas of the gaol was difficult to achieve, given that the prison, considered 'old and ill-constructed' by this stage, was badly overcrowded. The inspectors general declared in their 1824 report that it was 'an old prison of the worst description, as applicable to classification and labour', particularly in the female section of the gaol, where the tried and untried mixed freely.[51] In addition, lunatics occupied four large cells in the block by 1826, which was not good for 'the sane's morals or the insane's illness'.[52]

Idleness was the greatest evil within the prison encouraging 'insolent and insubordinate' behaviour amongst inmates, though public debate continued into the practicality, profitability and morality of setting prisoners to work. In Downpatrick, prisoners were not employed prior to 1818. However, substantial strides were made in 1824 when Rowan introduced new work regimes. Male prisoners were employed in stone-breaking and oakum-picking, and learned a range of productive trades which could be carried on after release, including tailoring and shoemaking. Female activities centred around spinning, washing and sewing. Much of the productive effort was geared to prison or county requirements, and a basic prison uniform for the poorest inmates was introduced at this time. As an incentive, inmates received one-third of the profits raised from their work at the end of their sentence. In 1825, the male prisoners produced a gross profit of £10 by breaking stones.[53] In the same year, a treadmill was introduced which accommodated up to eighteen male convicts for routine exercise.[54] As in many other gaols in Ireland, this treadmill performed no other function such as raising water or grinding corn; it simply absorbed time. Subsequently, concern grew over the provision of safety rails and regulators for the treadmill, and the possibly injurious effects it had upon inmates' health following sustained periods on the boards. Shortly after its introduction, the Downpatrick treadmill was relegated to use as a punishment for male inmates for infringing prison rules.

Another aspect of Rowan's successful management concerned the gradual progress made in the schooling of inmates. In common with many of his contemporaries, Rowan believed that ignorance and idleness were the principal causes of crime. By increasing standards of literacy and general education, he hoped that inmates would be encouraged not to return to crime upon their release. Male and female classes were conducted in the dayrooms, where groups of prisoners were educated in hourly shifts. The school master, James Copeland, received £15 per annum and an additional £10 for 'incidental expenses'. The school mistress, Mrs Copeland, adopted the role of matron over the female prisoners and was a permanent resident of the gaol by 1825. Once the new school was established, the administration dispensed with the informal arrangements it had made previously with the Downpatrick Ladies Committee, who had occasionally helped to instruct the women in practical skills such as sewing and spinning.

Despite these significant managerial improvements, an inquiry of 1819 concluded that a new gaol was required for the 'virtues' of security, classification, ventilation, employment, education and solitary confinement. Discussions over the merits, costs and possible location of a new gaol continued for three years.[55] Eventually, in 1824, plans were submitted to the lord lieutenant, who approved an 1820 design by the Edinburgh architect, Robert Reid. Building commenced in that year under the supervision of John Lynn and was completed seven years later.

Down County Gaol, 1831-1894

In January 1831, 131 prisoners and their military guard walked the few hundred yards from their former residence to the new county gaol. The impressive complex was more substantial than its predecessor, and occupied a four acre site in a commanding position over the town.[56] The central hexagonal tower housed the kitchens on the lower floor, the governor's house on the first and the chapel on the top floor. It dominated the four wings which radiated out from this central hub. Male prisoners were housed in these three-storied blocks according to a classification system based on the inmates' legal status and age. Categories included those under charge or convicted of felonies or misdemeanours; those under sentence of transportation; those under sentence of death; and individuals of 'atrocious character' requiring complete separation. The female and debtors' wings, which were similarly classified, lay at either side in front of the governor's residence. Intervening walls screened off the various airing, visiting and inspection yards from each other. Juveniles were separated from adults. The male and female infirmaries were located immediately behind the imposing neo-classical gateway, while the high perimeter wall enclosed the entire area.

The building cost more than £65,000. Up until the 1860s, approximately one-third of the annual gross expenditure was absorbed in staff costs. In addition to the governor and his deputy, there were three chaplains, an apothecary, two matrons, a hospital nurse, a schoolmaster and eleven turnkeys. Prior to the opening, the latter had received instruction in Leitrim Gaol. The medical and educational workers resided in the building, as did the governor and the chief turnkeys. The gaol was 'a building constructed on the best principles, containing all the accommodations which the Prison Act prescribes, and is a very complete specimen of a good county gaol, suited to the wants of an extensive and opulent county'.[57] Uniquely in Ulster at this time, Downpatrick gaol bore a close resemblance to other Irish gaols, particularly those in King's County (Offaly) and Limerick. Within the next two years, aesthetic considerations prompted the grand jury to repair and enlarge the adjacent courthouse and the nearby county rooms.[58]

Capt. Sidney Rowan Hamilton's appointment as governor was unanimously endorsed by the grand jury members. He was a man of strong evangelical Presbyterian convictions. As the only sibling of Archibald Rowan Hamilton, the United Irishman (who had fled to revolutionary France and, subsequently, America, before returning to Ireland following a pardon), Sidney espoused his brother's strong humanitarian principles. An elder in the Downpatrick congregation, Sidney developed a close friendship with the Rev. Henry Cooke. Rowan's nephew and namesake, Sidney, Archibald's second son, had been instrumental in bringing the Rev. Cooke to Killyleagh in 1818.[59] During the last years of the old gaol, Rowan had employed his nephew's tutor, John Waterworth, as a clerk. Waterworth, another Presbyterian from Cooke's congregation at Killyleagh, was now appointed to the new position of deputy governor.[60]

While religious principles were often a motivating factor in penal reform, in Downpatrick an ethos of sober reflection, discipline, work, education, and above all, moral reform was not only inherent within the prison by-laws but was also held by conviction by the chief members of staff. A shared belief in the power of redemptive theology characterised the management of the newly-opened institution. However, Rowan was 'not intolerant of others'[61] and proselytising within the gaol was not permitted by law, as each chaplain had exclusive care over their respective flocks. In any case, Rowan was more astute than to lay himself open to a charge of denominational or sectarian bigotry. Not all possessed his tact. In 1866, the Episcopalian and Protestant Dissenting chaplains became embroiled in a letter writing campaign against each other. The antagonism had been caused when the Presbyterian chaplain, the Rev. White, commented favourably upon 'the comparatively smaller amount of crime in connection with the Presbyterian Church' as against the Established tradition.[62] In turn, White was accused by the Episcopalian chaplain, the Rev. Eager, of representing only his denomination's interests. The longevity of the Presbyterian connection was assured, however, as Waterworth remained deputy governor until December 1882, after a service of fifty-two years.[63] Moreover, another member of the Rowan family held the post of local inspector between 1847 and 1857. After his demise, there was a distinct lack of continuity, as this important position was occupied by various individuals, and was even abandoned briefly in the late 1860s.

Rowan's rigid application of prison rules and strict compliance with the various measures ordered by successive inspectors general ensured that conflicts between the various interests were minimised. Following his death in November 1847 and a funeral service conducted by the Rev. Cooke, a Mr Crookshank took over the running of the gaol. Within three months, he was replaced by George F. Echlin, who was a member of another prominent county Down family, and the youngest son of John Echlin, of Echlinville, Portaferry, who had been appointed high sheriff in 1827. Three years later, in 1851, the grand jury closed ranks to support Echlin against a charge of poor conduct made by the inspector general, James Galway, but they nonetheless set up a committee to investigate his conduct and management.[64] Echlin was subsequently forced to resign following a later incident in 1867, and Major L. J. Thompson assumed the post, having previously acted briefly as local inspector. He, too, received a salary of £200 per annum.[65]

While the prison was greatly admired and subject to numerous visits by officials from neighbouring counties during its early years, the inspectors general became increasingly critical of a number of the grand jury's decisions. As early as 1827, the inspectors general were anxious to commence operations in the partially completed prison, by opening up the new female infirmary to relieve the pressures of overcrowding in the old building. The board of superintendence protested and further delayed the gaol's opening. Three years later, in 1830, the grand jury maintained that there were still serious difficulties in the provision and financing of prison furniture and adequately-trained staff. The tensions continued. The new gaol possessed 150 cells and sixty-seven rooms with beds, providing in all some 201 bedspaces. In theory, each prisoner was to be allocated a separate cell, but in a decision which went against the spirit of the prison ordinances, the board decided to accommodate more than one prisoner in some of the cells. The 'dispute' was exacerbated when the board opted to supply hammocks instead of expensive fixed-iron bedsteads for certain cells in an attempt to cut down on county expenditure.

The new building permitted the classification of prisoners to an extent not witnessed nor practicable previously. Twelve male and four female classes were defined and allocated different spaces within the gaol. Classification ensured that those convicted of lesser crimes were kept separate from those found guilty of graver offences. The aim, the prevention of 'corruption by communication', was underpinned by the notion that immorality could be transmitted between individuals. Equally, it was believed that human nature could be nurtured to a higher moral plane. Thus, criminals could be reformed given the right environment. However, when parliament legalised the strict separation of prisoners in 1840, the grand jury in Down, like most others in Ireland, was faced with the prospect of additional capital expenditure on a building, which in their case, was barely ten years old. Strict separation, it was argued, permitted the moral government of the inmate and simultaneously acted as rational punishment. Joshua Jebb's design for Pentonville prison in north London, opened in the 1840s, was considered the 'model' prison for the separate system. It was based upon Jeremiah Bentham's panopticon plan where all activities, including eating, were done in isolation and staff could view prisoners at all times. The Irish inspectors general embraced its philosophy in order to promote uniformity of standards within local gaols. The county Down grand jury, on the other hand, concurred with a previous criticism made by the inspector general that the 'architect seemed to plan [the gaol] more for security than for moral government'.[66] In fact both the national and local authorities recognised some of the inconsistencies in promoting the separate system. As prisoners were managed in complete isolation and forced to wear masks to hide their identity, the rationale for classification, which was used extensively throughout the country, was substantially undermined.[67] In reality, the 'separate cell system' was adopted to varying degrees and at different rates across the country, and in most cases, classification and separation formed combined themes in prison administration.

The county Down grand jury prepared plans for the adoption of the separate system in the early 1840s and some minor adjustments and alterations were quickly made. Under the new regime, all prisoners were to be restricted to cell-life. Accordingly, the board of superintendence agreed to purchase new fixed iron bedsteads to replace the hammocks and authorised the building of brick partitions in the twenty-six stone-breaking sheds and twenty-three workshops.[68] Other plans to separate prisoners were put into abeyance at least temporarily, as finances had to be redirected to the workhouse and to the provision of lock-ups and bridewells throughout the county as conditions worsened during the Famine.[69]

After a fire at the Downpatrick courthouse in 1855, the renovation and enlargement of that building, including the provision of a connecting underground passage to the county gaol, delayed the planned refurbishment of the prison still further. It was not until 1858 that architectural designs were presented to the grand jury for the renovation of the various wings for male and female prisoners and debtors, and for a new boardroom and laundry area. The cost came to £4,500.[70] The partition walls running longitudinally down the length of each wing represented the main structural deficiency in the existing gaol. Most cells averaged 9.5 by 6.5 feet, and thus fell far short of the prescribed 15 by 7 feet minimum requirement. Similarly, the passage ways and corridors were too dark and impeded the warders' observation of the inmates. During the refurbishment, the interiors of the wings were completely gutted to give a more open aspect to the gaol. New cells were constructed and their enlarged doors were provided with the customary trap-door and inspection hole. New ventilation and heating systems were also installed.

By the early 1860s, an efficient system of separation was in operation. Communal areas such as worksheds, laundry, open-air yards, hospital and toilets were designed to prevent social intercourse and ensure the minimum contact between prisoners. Stalls replaced open forms in the chapel which doubled up as a school. The fixed iron bedsteads were gradually replaced by folding wall-cots which provided more workspace within the cells during the day, as well as reducing the 'opportunity for lounging'.[71] While these improvements effectively tackled the many perceived deficiencies of the prison, one 'major defect in construction remained'. The layout of the various prison blocks was itself a major impediment to the operation of a more efficient separate system, notwithstanding the efficiency, zeal, qualifications and managerial competence of Rowan and his staff. The detached prison blocks required extra personnel to staff each one individually, unlike Pentonville or its modified version at Belfast (officially opened in 1847), where the interlinking of wings to a central area permitted the surveillance of all inmates from a common point.

Despite the physical difficulties, the system of cellular confinement continued. Inmates could expect to spend over twenty hours per day locked up in one of the 200 sparsely-furnished cells. The principles of employment and education were enshrined within the institution. Rowan quickly established a more extensive and rigorous work schedule than the one used in the old gaol. All prisoners undertook some form of industrial labour. Indeed, on various occasions the inspectors general urged other gaol administrations to consider Downpatrick's operation, whereby prisoners were employed in a wide variety of manufacture including tailoring, wheelmaking and carpentry. Women were employed in cooking, cleaning, laundry and sprigging. The treadmill was used for punitive labour but the number of hours a man could expect to spend on the machine were strictly regulated. Under Echlin, this pattern of activity continued, although a capstan mill costing £200 and used to grind wheat when manned by up to forty individuals, replaced the treadmill in 1849.[72] Shot drill was likewise employed from 1850 in an attempt to provide physical activity for the rising numbers held within the gaol. From a daily average of 189 inmates in 1846, numbers had risen to 209 in 1847 and to 236 in 1848 and showed little sign of abating. The prison population peaked in 1851 when up to 214 males and ninety-eight females were held at one point. The total committals for that year were 934 males (including twenty boys aged between ten and sixteen) and 537 females, with re-offenders accounting for approximately one-fifth of the total. Conditions were cramped, rations greatly reduced and discipline was only maintained by the most rigid application of rules. As an interim measure, the administration adopted the 'silent system' to instil discipline and maintain order. Its early introduction owed much to Rowan's preference, and its earlier proven success in American and British prisons and at Derry, where it had been introduced in 1836.[73] Under the circumstances prevailing at Down County Gaol, the separate system was impossible to police as single cells frequently housed more than one inmate. Under the silent system, prisoners could associate with each other but all communication, even non-verbally, was prohibited. As with any disobedience, breaches were severely punished, and offenders were placed in the 'refractory' cells. Advocates of the silent system argued that it was more humane than separation, which was believed by some to cause insanity. The Downpatrick administration were well pleased with the success of the silent system which, as in many other Irish gaols, was used to complement the separate system.

Rowan's insistence on the minimum of disruption by prisoners was severely hindered by one group: the lunatics. Suffering from a range of maladies varying from insanity and epilepsy to deaf and dumbness, they were the proverbial flies in the ointment. Their disruptive behaviour and their constant need for supervision for their own and others' safety created numerous problems, not least because this detracted from the punishment and reform of the other inmates. Nocturnal disturbances were a particular obstacle to the silence rule. One inmate who continually paced his cell had his shoes removed at night. In theory, abuse was minimised, since under the provisions of the separate system, the lunatics and the two prisoners assigned to care for them were isolated from the rest of the prison population.

However, the growing number of lunatics deposited in the gaol meant that prisoners of doubtful character were assigned to their care.[74] As a last resort, some of the worst cases were removed together with their keepers to the old gaol, which had been converted into a military barracks following its closure in 1831. A new wall was constructed at the barracks screening off the old cellblock from the rest of the complex. The practice seems to have originated in the late 1840s under Rowan, who was also captain and paymaster of the North Downshire Militia. The number and proportion of lunatics within the prison population peaked during Echlin's term of office, at an average of around two dozen. Conditions in the old gaol were grim. The windows did not have glass and lunatics slept in damp conditions as no form of heating existed in the cells. As a remedial measure, the grand jury were advised to provide additional blankets and supplements of meat, milk and vegetables for the lunatics' diet. The policy of physically removing 'problem' inmates from the main gaol was not uncommon in Ireland. Leitrim County Gaol at Carrick-on-Shannon resorted to a similar practice. Following the death of three lunatics at Downpatrick in 1863, the grand jury accelerated the building programme of the new Down County Lunatic Asylum as 'the place of confinement for respectable lunatics'.[75] Plans had been approved in 1859 but its construction was a protracted process. By the time the asylum opened in 1870, another six of the thirty-four lunatics held in the prison had died; some from natural causes and others from suicide. It was impossible to prevent such deaths and even with the opening of the asylum, lunatics were still placed in gaol.[76]

In the more favourable economic climate of the late 1850s, the number of inmates at Downpatrick fell considerably and conditions consequently improved.[77] By the 1860s, the building was considered too large. Between 1866 and 1869, the average daily number of inmates dropped from 127 to seventy.[78] Re-offenders figured prominently among this number, and they included some notorious cases. One prisoner with the initials, S.B., had fifty-one convictions for assault and being drunk and disorderly in public streets, while another, M.B., was gaoled twenty times for disorderly and indecent behaviour. Despite the fall in numbers, the cellular arrangement within the different blocks remained, and continued to require a staff of eighteen warders. While the gaol's annual expenditure was lower than in many other counties, the central and local authorities both expressed dismay at the disproportionate amount spent of staffing.

Effective policing of the administrative system was crucial to the smooth running of the institution, and generally speaking, a high degree of discipline and conformity was achieved. Compared to other gaols, relatively few punishments were administered on the authority of the governor or his deputy. However, prisoners found ingenuous ways of by-passing the security system, and wire mesh designed to prevent the passage of goods between visitors and the inmates was not introduced until the 1870s.[79] The most notorious case occurred in 1866. In September, a search of the gaol by three members of the board of superintendence, accompanied by the local inspector, James Stephenson, uncovered a number of luxuries including tea, sugar, candles, letters and books in the cell of William Tennant, who had been convicted of assaulting his brother-in-law. The room was immediately sealed by Col. Forde, one of the board, pending further enquiry into the lapse of prison rules. The board insisted on the involvement of the inspector general, John Lentaigne, in order to secure public confidence in what was to become a lengthy and difficult affair.[80] His investigations generated a considerable amount of interest in both the local and national press. *The Weekly News* carried a damming artist's illustration of the find on its front page, caricaturing Tennant, in the comparative luxury of his cell replete with bath, provisions and bottles of whiskey and rum, juxtaposed to another cell containing a poor Catholic 'wretch'.[81]

A number of irregularities were revealed by the enquiry. Visitors had been able to pass goods to the prisoner. Echlin, the governor for over twenty years, tendered his resignation for this apparently negligent management, although initially it was not accepted. By the end of October, the board had reconsidered their decision and both Echlin and the local inspector, Stephenson, were asked to resign. It was the board's dismissal of the Episcopalian chaplain, the very Rev. Dean of Down, Edward Woodward, which captured the public's attention. The cleric stood accused of supplying Tennant with illegal articles, namely two secular books and some newspapers. In a series of bitter communications between the board and the dean, which appeared in the Belfast and Dublin papers, the cleric sought to vindicate his actions.[82] Woodward claimed that the board had trespassed on his pastoral rights and duties. Moreover, in his opinion, the prisoner, a graduate from Cambridge and member of the English bar, required reading of a secular sort to give 'some mental occupation, not always and exclusively on religious subjects ... [this being] ... absolutely indispensable to preserve him [Tennant] from idiotcy (sic) or lunacy'.[83] The board did not agree and replaced Woodward with the Rev. Eager, an occasional preacher at Down Cathedral. Tennant was fined £8.19.6 and new guidelines were drawn up for the chaplains.[84]

From the late 1860s, during Major Thompson's term as governor, the board of superintendence continued to use the separate system, although the regime became more lax as a large number of the cells fell vacant. During this period, occasional fines were imposed on visitors and turnkeys for smuggling alcohol into the gaol. The board officially relaxed rules on only one occasion, during William Johnston's imprisonment, and then only on the authority of chief secretary, Lord Mayo. Johnston was arrested with two others, William Mawhinney and Thomas Keating, for a breach of the Party Processions Act following their illegal Orange procession from Newtownards to Bangor on the 12th July 1868.[85] Johnston was released five days short of his two month sentence on the order of the government, in an attempt to defuse an already sensitive situation and undermine the Orange demonstration planned for Downpatrick to celebrate his release.[86]

In the early 1870s, there was a notable increase in the number of prison violations, and this led to a tightening up of procedure with regard to prison visits. In 1874, three turnkeys were dismissed for insubordinate behaviour, the third such dismissal since 1861. The first recorded escape attempt occurred in 1873.[87] Anxious to cut down on staff expenditure, the grand jury warmly welcomed the opportunity to close down parts of the gaol in 1874,[88] which by this stage was much in need of repair. The wings were damp and concerns were voiced over the safety of the buildings. These fears were realised when a warder died after slipping on a poorly maintained stairwell in 1878.[89]

The establishment of the General Prison Board in October 1877 set in train many changes for Irish prisons. Newtownards and Newry bridewells were closed the following year,[90] while Downpatrick gaol, which faced the same bleak future, was ultimately converted to convict depot status (along with Maryborough prison) on 1 April 1884, when it acted as an overflow for Mountjoy prison.[91] In 1886, fourteen of Downpatrick's fifty-four inmates were transferred from the latter which, by comparison, held nearly 800 prisoners.[92] During this period, the local character of Downpatrick gaol gradually disappeared. In October 1884, nineteen convicts were sent over from England, including the last eight 'Invincibles' held at Chatham aboard the gunboat *Valorous*.[93] Nor was this the only occasion when the central authorities made use of the peaceable conditions in the gaol and county and the staff's 'loyalty and attachment to the Crown'. In 1866, for example, the board had agreed to hold a number of Fenian prisoners.[94] In the twilight years of the gaol, staff were exchanged with other prisons. In the early 1890s, a number of the Downpatrick warders were sent to Mountjoy, and with the closure of the gaol in May 1891, the remaining warders and their charges were transferred to Belfast. A skeleton operation continued at Downpatrick until 9th March 1894, but by then, the General Prison Board had no further use for the building.

Conclusion

The institutional frameworks within which thousands of people were imprisoned in county Down changed over time. In the second half of the eighteenth century, the house of correction, reputedly established through the humanitarian concerns of a clergyman, soon degenerated into a place of vice and corruption. Encouraged by the parliamentary measures of the latter part of the century, the grand jury opted to build a new prison on the Mall in Downpatrick modelled on the 1786 recommendations. However, the efficiency of any regime is a product of the personnel it employs. Conditions soon deteriorated in this prison after its opening in 1796, as it succumbed to the pressures of overcrowding, an ineffectual jailer, and the intermittent and small-scale improvements financed by the grand jury. Despite the intention to construct a replacement, a reprieve for the old gaol seemed possible when Capt. Rowan, the newly appointed local inspector, instilled a new order in the prison in the mid-1820s. However, a new gaol was opened in 1831. In many ways, the complex was far superior to its predecessor and demonstrated the ideological intentions of the prison reformers. A professional administration drawn from the ranks of the middle classes was appointed, and with the appropriate level of financial resources and grand jury support, an exemplary standard of classification, discipline and reform based on the tenets of education and hard work was established. Pragmatic considerations were crucial in the adoption of the silent system in the 1840s. Nevertheless, as the old gaol demonstrated, once-fashionable designs were quickly outmoded as the pace of penal debate quickened. In the late 1850s, the grand jury could no longer delay the internal refurbishment of various prison blocks that was required to achieve a higher degree of separation among the prisoners. Ironically, the renovations were completed at a time when the rehabilitating claims for the separate system were being abandoned.[95]

In the gradual development of Irish prison management, the *ad hoc* committees of the late-eighteenth and early-nineteenth centuries gave way to the more centralised office of the board of superintendence, established in the 1820s. Both parties were raised from the ranks of the county grand jurors. Prison practice came under the increasing scrutiny and growing authority of the inspectors general. The intrusive central powers set ever higher standards. Inmates at Downpatrick, as in most other Irish gaols, were placed under comprehensive and systematic social control. Their lives were governed by an elaborate system of clocks, bells and regimentation. Unlike the anonymity of earlier gaols, where prisoners were thrown into the 'corrupting mass', the individual gradually became all important under the new regimes. In the collective arrangement of the gaol, each inmate was identified with precision by prison records and staff, and isolated during their incarceration. However, the character of particular institutions was heavily circumscribed by local circumstances. The financial constraints of local administrations, the personalities of key personnel, the desire to attain the organisation and standards set down by parliament, and the penal requirements of the county, were crucial in determining the nature and level of prison reform and management.

Centralisation was reflected in the establishment of the General Prison Board in 1877, which brought nationalisation in its wake. While making a minor contribution to the national scene, Down Gaol, as with most local prisons, closed down in the 1890s. This rationalisation of the prison system ensured growing uniformity of practice in the remaining institutions. In the penal sphere at least, the state had at last wrested power from the localities.

Acknowledgements

I would like to thank the staff and Friends of Down County Museum for funding a one-year fellowship in the Institute of Irish Studies, Queen's University of Belfast, into the history of Downpatrick gaol as part of the Museum's 'Ireland-Australia Project'. The Museum is housed in the former eighteenth century prison. Acknowledgement is also made of the information collected by a previous research fellow, Carrie Wilson, and the Museum's former education officer, Gerry Lennon.

References

1. J. Starr, 'Prison reform in Ireland in the age of Enlightenment' in *History Ireland,* iii (2) (1995), p. 21.
2. 26 Geo. 3 c. 27 (1786).
3. Spelling is standardised as 'gaol' throughout.
4. 7 Geo. iv, c. 74 (31 May 1826).
5. R. B. McDowell, *The Irish administration, 1801-1914* (London, 1964), pp 159-160. The national schema passed to the General Prison Board in 1877 included four convict prisons, thirty-eight local prisons, and ninety-five bridewells.
6. O. MacDonagh, 'Ideas and institutions, 1830-45' in W.E. Vaughan (ed.), *A new history of Ireland: v, Ireland under the Union, 1801-1870* (Oxford, 1989), pp 207-17.
7. Grand Jury papers, Summer Assizes, 1848. The provision included Portaferry, Kircubbin, Killyleagh, Warrenpoint, Dromara and Gilford, P. R. O. N. I., Dow/4/2/11.
8. A. Day and P. McWilliams (eds.), *Ordnance Survey memoirs of Ireland: parishes of east Down iv: 1833-37 East Down and Lecale,* xvii (Belfast, 1992), p. 47.
9. P. R. O. N. I., DOW 4/2/29, Spring 1864, p. 49.
10. *Belfast News Letter,* 19 Aug. 1808, p. 3.
11. An excellent study is offered in M. Foucault, *Discipline and punishment: the birth of the prison* (London, 1977).

12. See, for example, M. Ignatieff, *A just measure of pain: the penitentiary in the industrial revolution, 1750-1850* (London, 1978).

13. According to one commentary, the lower floor of Castle Dorras was still used to hold petty offenders as late as the 1830s. *Ordnance Survey memoirs*, p. 41.

14. *Belfast News Letter*, 12 Aug. 1746, p. 2.

15. Private correspondence of Mrs Delaney writing from Mount Palmer, 10 September, 1744. Quoted in R. E. Parkinson, *City of Downe* (Belfast, 1927), pp 89-90.

16. Ibid., p. 90.

17. *Belfast News Letter*, 23 May 1792, p. 1.

18. Roger Johnson Smyth of Lisburn to marquess of Downshire, 1 Oct. 1795, P. R. O. N. I., D. 607/C/145.

19. *Belfast News Letter*, 3 Mar. 1789, p. 3.

20. P. R. O. N. I., DOW 4/2/1, Summer 1789, no. 43.

21. F. J. Bigger, 'Old County of Down Presentments' in *U. J. A.*, xiii 1907, pp 109-116.

22. P. R. O. N. I., DOW 4/2/5, Lent Assizes 1803, no. 52.

23 James Hayes, James McKimins, Edward Savage, Hugh McCullough, Henry Murray, William Maguire and Edward Hamill. *Belfast News Letter*, 10 Jan. p. 3; 27 Jan. 1804, p. 3.

24. Alexander Stewart, Robert Stewart, Patrick Malone, Patrick McMurray, Henry Henry, Abraham Maginnis, John O'Neill, Patrick Burns, James McKimins, Patrick Maguire and Samuel McAllister escaped. *Belfast News Letter*, 9 Oct. 1804, 16 Oct. 1804, p. 1.

25. *Belfast News Letter*, 23 Mar. 1813, p. 1.

26. Ibid., 5 Aug. 1817, p. 3.

27. Ibid., 2 Sept. 1817, p. 1.

28. P. R. O. N. I., DOW 4/2/9, Summer Assizes, 1817.

29. Ibid., no. 46.

30. *Belfast News Letter*, 5 Sept. 1820, p. 3.

31. 'Report of a committee to inspect gaol accounts at spring assizes,' Summer Assizes, 1828. P. R. O. N. I., DOW/4/2/11.

32. *Prisons of Ireland, report of inspector general*, H.C. 1808 (239), IX, p. 6.

33. P. R. O. N. I., DOW 4/2/6, Lent Assizes, 1815, no. 210.

34. *Belfast News Letter*, 6 Dec 1801 p. 1.

35. P.R.O.N.I. DOW 4/2/9, Summer Assizes, 1818.

36. *Belfast News Letter*, 25 Mar. 1823, p. 3.

37. *Inspector general report .... the prisons of Ireland*, H.C. 1823 (291), x, p. 29.

38. *Belfast News Letter*, 10 Aug. 1819, p. 3.

39. Ibid., 13 Aug. 1819, p. 1.

40. Ibid., 7 Jan. 1820, p. 1.

41. Ibid., 28 Mar. 1820, p. 1.

42. Col. Forde, Downpatrick to Dublin Castle, 27 Mar. 1820, SOC 2187/34.

43. William Paxton, Rathfriland to William Gregory, Dublin Castle, 29 Mar. 1820, SOC 2187/35.

44. *Belfast News Letter*, 5 May, 1816, p. 1.

45. P. R. O. N. I., DOW 4/2/10, Summer Assizes 1821.

46. *Inspector general report .... the prisons of Ireland*, H.C. 1825 (223), xxii, p. 227.

47. P. R. O. N. I., DOW 4/2/10, Summer Assizes, 1821.

48. *Inspector general report .... the prisons of Ireland*, H.C. 1824 (269), xxii, pp 30-31.

49. P. R. O. N. I., DOW 4/2/11, Summer Assizes, 1828, Resolution no. 1.

50. *Inspector general report .... the prisons of Ireland*, H.C. 1824, (269), xxii, p. 268.

51. Ibid., p. 269.
52. *Inspector general report ... the prisons of Ireland*, H.C. 1826-27 (335), xi, p. 40.
53. *Inspector general report .... the prisons of Ireland*, H.C. 1826 (395), xxiii, p. 286.
54. Ibid., pp 286-7.
55. Series of correspondence from Col. Forde, chairman of the grand jury to Lord Downshire concerning the disputes between Reid and Lynn and the financing of the new building, Oct. 1821-Apr. 1822, P. R. O. N. I., D.671/C/12/257, 267, 286.
56. Ulster Architectural Heritage Society, *List of historic buildings, groups of historic buildings, areas of architectural importance in the town of Downpatrick* (Belfast, 1970), p. 31.
57. *Inspector general report .... the prisons of Ireland*, H.C. 1828 (349), xii, p. 349.
58. *Ordnance survey memoirs*, p. 62.
59. F. H. Furey, 'Presbyterianism in Killyleagh prior to 1840' in *Dufferin Chronicles: a publication of the Killyleagh and District Branch*, 2 (1995), pp 18-22.
60. *Downpatrick Presbyterian Church: 150th anniversary, 1827-1977.*
61. J. Thompson Clelland, 'Annals of Downpatrick' (Unpub. manuscript, 1846), transcribed by R. W. H. Blackwood (1923), P. R. O. N. I., T. 2986/1, p. 114.
62. *Downpatrick Recorder*, 27 Mar. 1867, p. 3; 6 Apr. 1867, p. 2.
63. Ibid., 30 Dec. 1882, p. 2.
64. P. R. O. N. I., DOW 4/2/20, Spring Assizes, 1851.
65. P. R. O. N. I., DOW 4/2/34, Spring Assizes, 1868, p. 106.
66. Ibid., p. 121.
67. *Inspector general report .... the prisons of Ireland*, H.C. 1841 (755), xi, pp 788-789.
68. *Inspector general report .... the prisons of Ireland*, H.C. 1842 (117), xxii, p. 367.
69. *Inspector general report .... the prisons of Ireland*, H.C. 1851 (357), xxviii, p. 357.
70. Plans for the architectural refurbishment of Down County Gaol, 1858-1860, P. R. O. N. I., D. 2992/B/6-20.
71. P. R. O. N. I., DOW 4/2/27, Lent Assizes, 1861, p. 60.
72. Prison Accounts sheet, P. R. O. N. I., DOW 4/2/19, Spring Assizes, 1849.
73. *The Ulster Times*, 31 Dec. 1836, p. 1.
74. Criticism concerning a 'most grave offender ... condemned to two years imprisonment, for an indecent assault' being permitted to care for lunatics, *Inspector general report .... the prisons of Ireland*, H.C. 1865 (1), xxiv, p. 171.
75. *Inspector general report .... the prisons of Ireland*, H.C. 1830-31 (269), iv, p. 753.
76. *Inspector general report .... the prisons of Ireland*, H.C. 1867 (1), xxxv, p. 176.
77. This was attributed to the 'peaceful state of the county for some time past', *Downpatrick Recorder*, 7 Feb. 1857, p. 1.
78. *Inspector general report .... the prisons of Ireland*, H.C. 1870 (233), xxxvii, p. 233.
79. P. R. O. N. I., DOW 4/2/40, Spring Assizes 1872.
80. *Downpatrick Recorder*, 15 Sept. 1866, p. 2.
81. *The Weekly News*, 22 Sept. 1866, p. 1.
82. *Belfast News Letter*, 11 Oct. p. 3; 15 Oct. p. 3; 22 Oct. 1866, p. 3.
83. Public letter to Board of Superintendence from Dean Woodward, *Belfast News Letter*, 19 Oct. 1866, p. 3.
84. 'Report of the Gaol Committee presented to the Grand Jury', P. R. O. N. I., DOW 4/2/33, Spring Assizes, 1867.
85. *Downpatrick Recorder*, 4 Apr. 1868, p. 3.
86. Ibid., 25 Apr. 1868, p. 2.
87. *Inspector general report .... the prisons of Ireland*, H.C. 1873 (1), xxxiii, p. 402.
88. *Inspector general report .... the prisons of Ireland*, H.C. 1874 (757), xxix, p. 851.
89. N. A. I., GPB CR 1, Down, 12 Sept. 1878, no. 57.

90. N. A. I., GPB CR 1, Down, 25 June; 6 Aug. 1878, no's. 9, 31.
91. Arrangements for the exchange of staff with Belfast prison. N.A., GPO CR 60, (1891), Down 3514, 9 Apr. 1891; Warders sent to Mountjoy GPO CR 60 (1891), Down 5720, 22 May 1891.
92. *Inspector general report .... the prisons of Ireland*, H.C. 1886 (281), xxxv, p. 281.
93. *Downpatrick Recorder*, 25 Oct. 1884, p. 3.
94. Ibid., 10 Mar. 1866, p. 2.
95. M. Ogburn, 'Discipline, government and law: separate confinement in the prisons of England and Wales, 1830-1877' in *Journal of Historical Geography*, New series, xx, 3 (1995), pp 300-304.

Chapter 14

THE GREAT FAMINE IN COUNTY DOWN

JAMES GRANT

The Great Famine – *An Gorta Mór* in Irish – has been so-called to distinguish it in terms of its severity and duration from the lesser famines which affected Ireland in the early decades of the nineteenth century and before. Contributing to the uniqueness of the Famine was the then unknown cause of the potato blight, the fungus *phytophthora infestans*. It decimated the potato crop in 1845, 1846, 1848 and 1849, with disastrous consequences for a population over half of whom had become dependent on potatoes as their sole or principal item of diet. The historical causes of this dependence have frequently been debated, as have the social, economic and demographic consequences of the catastrophe itself. But surprisingly little has been done to explore the impact of the Great Famine at a local or regional level. This chapter initiates such an exploration for county Down. It is essentially factual, mainly tracing the use in the county of the successive relief measures established by government from 1845 to 1847. Some comparative material is provided as a context within which to assess events in Down, but much more work needs to be done before we can explain adequately why some local economies escaped the Famine, while others suffered severe and prolonged hardship.

Compared to most other counties in Ireland, Down was markedly free from the extreme effects of the Great Famine. This can be demonstrated in a number of ways. The first is the lack of impact of the partial failure of the potato crop in 1845. Then, after the total failure of 1846, only limited use was made of the principal government relief scheme of public works in the autumn and winter of 1846-7. While there was extensive activity by local relief committees, those in county Down were among the last to form. True, workhouses serving poor-law unions wholly or substantially in county Down (Downpatrick, Kilkeel and Newtownards in the former and Banbridge in the latter category) began to fill up, as elsewhere in the country, from October 1846 onwards; but, in general, they succumbed more slowly to pressure of numbers than most. In April 1847, public works gave way to food relief administered through the poor-law system under the provisions of the Temporary Relief (popularly Soup Kitchens or Rations) Act. In common with most of east Ulster, county Down unions successfully restricted their use of the Act and funded the aid they offered under its provisions with considerable independence. Finally, the decline in population in Down between 1841 and 1851 was, at 10.7 per cent in crude terms, markedly below the national (24 per cent) and Ulster (17.3 per cent) averages.

The partial failure of the 1845 potato crop

This is not to say, however, that county Down – generally recognised as one of the more prosperous counties – was impervious to the effects – direct and indirect – of the Famine. The partial failure of between one-quarter and a half of the 1845 potato crop did have its effects in some parts of the county.[1] In Ireland as a whole, the need for extraordinary help did not arise until the late spring – early summer of 1846, when the shortage of potatoes began to push up the prices of all foodstuffs. For example, in Newtownards in April 1846, potatoes were 7d. a stone instead of the usual 2½d. or 3d., while oatmeal, next to potatoes in dietary importance in Ulster, was 2s. a stone instead of the usual 1s.6d. The potato market was in disarray. In Newtownards, the normal export of potatoes had been abandoned, farmers 'throwing' them into the home market and eating them while they were still sound. People in the district were 'abandoning potatoes and going over to oatmeal'. In fact, oatmeal, 'usually eaten during the winter', was being saved for the lean summer months while the available potatoes were used up. People in Newtownards were 'in full and steady employment', yet they were still feeling hardship.[2] In May, an 'increase in paupers' prompted the town's board of guardians to increase their weekly supplies of coarse beef.[3] By early July, on days when potatoes 'cannot be got', brown bread was to be substituted for dinner. Indian meal was already being used for, on the recommendation of the medical officer, the proportion of it in the paupers' porridge was to be reduced to a quarter.[4] Indian meal was also being used in Banbridge workhouse.[5]

Meanwhile, Lord Annesley's trustee, the Rev. J. R. Moore, claimed to have spent 'a large sum of money ... to relieve those persons who had lost their potatoes' in the Castlewellan area of south Down in 1845. He had also been 'selling meal at a reduced rate' since September 1845.[6] While there is shadowy evidence for a relief committee 'sitting in Loughbrickland', there was certainly one active in Ballymacarrett, 'the poorest suburb of Belfast ... densely peopled by the very lowest class of weavers and other operatives'.[7] This committee received two grants in aid for their fund, £100 in June and a further £25 in August, thus marking Ballymacarrett out as the only part of county Down to receive government help following the 1845 potato failure.[8]

Public works, 1846-1847

A large scheme of public works, organised under the Labour Rate Act (9 & 10 Vic. c. 107) was the principal famine measure introduced by the reforming Whigs under Lord John Russell in the autumn of 1846. The Whigs brought a new rigour to relief administration, in contrast to the relaxed approach under Peel in the previous season. Their aim was to prevent waste and so pressurise Irish landlords into providing employment and other relief for their tenants. Waste was to be prevented by placing the whole scheme under the strict supervision of the board of works, which in turn was to be strictly controlled by the treasury. Landlords were to be forced to take their own initiatives by the declaration that all works under the new scheme were to be unproductive.[9]

Only limited use was made of the scheme in county Down, a fact which emerges clearly from the *Analysis of poor employment* covering the period from early October 1846 to late June 1847. The analysis enables us to construct a 'league table' for the thirty-two counties of Ireland, based on the daily average number of labourers employed on the public works. In this table, in which the first eight places are dominated by Munster and Connacht counties (from Cork, with over 42,000, to Kerry, with just under 20,000 employed daily on average), Down comes an insignificant second last – thirty-first out of thirty-two – with a daily average of a mere 335 labourers.[10]

Such a figure is insignificant only statistically. The accounts of the public works in three of the twelve baronies in county Down (Mourne, Upper Iveagh and Newry) reflect the anxieties and uncertainties of the winter of 1846-7 in very striking terms, particularly in Mourne and Upper Iveagh. The occasions when such feelings tended to be given public expression were the extraordinary presentment sessions which, under the public works legislation (9 & 10 Vic. c. 107), were compulsory once the lord lieutenant had declared a barony 'distressed'.

These sessions were often extraordinary in more than the legal sense. They were extraordinary in the excitement, anxiety, menace and even violence they generated; in the crowds which invariably flocked to them; in the often extravagant sums they voted for works, and in that they became veritable battlegrounds for conflicting local interests. Usually, but not exclusively, this involved improving landlords standing against uninterested or careless landlords or against pressure from the mob or others who, for motives worthy or unworthy, were interested only in short-term solutions.

The first extraordinary sessions in Down was for the barony of Mourne, held at Kilkeel on 26 October 1846, with Viscount Newry and Morne in the chair. The first presentment to be discussed was for improvements at Annalong harbour, and these were apparently, approved by the county cess payers. But, when the chairman asked if anyone disagreed,

> a whole host of 'Noes' from the people was the response, the mere putting of the question being sufficient to call forth the angry tumult which was evidently brewing the whole morning.

Anonymous voices from the crowd raised demands, including 'Allow us something on the tops instead of giving all to the lowlands', to which the viscount replied, 'You misunderstand it. If there is distress in the highlands, the trustees will be ready to employ men there in draining', which, according to 'a number of voices', was what they wanted to hear. Several presentments for roads were also passed, but the crowd chanted 'drainage, drainage' on each occasion, once 'in a most ear-stunning manner'. When Viscount Newry and Morne assured the crowd that the Kilmorey trustees had authorised £1,000 for drainage if needed, the meeting ended peaceably.[11] Such chants in favour of drainage and against roadworks were almost universal at extraordinary sessions throughout Ulster, reflecting the condemnation by public opinion of the unproductive character of works under the government's scheme.

Board of works recommendation and treasury sanction for the first batch of works in Mourne was remarkably quick, a mere three weeks, as against a usual delay in Ulster of nearly two months.[12] In early November work began on two road improvements (by far the most common type of work), one new road and one (unspecified) 'town improvement'; a further ten road works and '1 sea wall' followed at the beginning of December.[13] The piecemeal approval of these works meant that, by early January, only 400 were employed, 'which', according to the board of works inspecting officer for the county, Captain Brereton, 'scarcely amounts to half the number of the destitute in the barony on the Relief lists'. The large number of unemployed had caused 'much dissatisfaction' among the people, but they were generally well-behaved.[14] Brereton's figures suggest that between 25 and 30 per cent of the population in the barony were in a state of destitution.

A couple of days after writing this report, Brereton attended Kilkeel Relief Committee and selected thirty extra men for the works, but there were 300 destitute, whose names were on the committee's relief list, anxiously waiting outside for selection:

They were in a very excited state, and on learning that there was no employment for them, they sent a written statement into the Committee "that they were starving and if they were not relieved they would find some other means of supplying themselves with food".

Brereton spoke to them, warning them that if they committed a breach of the peace their names would be struck off the list, and persuading them to disperse with a promise of work in a few days' time. He then pressed upon the board of works that employment must be provided at or near Kilkeel as an absolute necessity if the destitute were to be prevented from committing 'some flagrant outrage'.[15] Reports over the next few weeks were more optimistic, although wages of 1s. a day by task work were clearly insufficient, given 'the very enormous price that oats have arrived at in this locality'. There was 'a wish to have higher wages, and many of the able-bodied labourers [had] gone to the railways in England and Scotland'. Nearby, in Upper Iveagh, the conducting engineer responded to men grumbling about task work, urging them to turn it to their advantage by exerting themselves and earning up to 1s. 9d. per day.[16]

The months of December and January seem to have been particularly appalling in Mourne. The Kilkeel workhouse filled on 30 January, and at the beginning of February, Richard Cooke, M.D., of Kilkeel, provided a strong account to the board of health of the extensive local destitution and related prevalence of 'diarrhoea, dysentery and all forms of bowel affections'. All too often water was both 'the meat and drink' of fever patients, although it was dysentery, 'spreading in ... rapid strides', rather than fever that concerned him. For men on the public works there was but one meal a day and, where families were numerous, that meal was often boiled seaweed.[17] Board of works officials on the spot frequently mentioned in their reports that 'the greater number ... [of small farmers had] already consumed the small quantity [of oats] they had reserved for seed, in order to keep themselves and their families from starvation'.[18]

The extraordinary sessions for the Lordship of Newry, held at Newry on 15 January 1847, seems to have been peaceful. Brereton presented an estimate of between 700 and 800 families (or about 23 per cent of the population) in a state of destitution. The sessions voted works to the value of £2,500 for a two month period, which Brereton then pressed urgently on his superiors. He was particularly worried about the town of Newry itself, where, 'the amount of misery ... arising from scarcity of food and want of employment [was] perfectly frightful'. He paid fulsome tribute to the Newry Relief Committee, without whose exertions destitution would have been far greater than it was. Their fund, from private subscriptions, amounted to nearly £1,000 (it was actually just over £900), with which they were 'relieving from their soup kitchen daily 1,100 individuals'.[19]

The tension at the Mourne meeting at Kilkeel in October was slight compared to the explosive atmosphere of the Upper Iveagh (lower half) sessions at Castlewellan on 9 January 1847. An angry crowd of between five and six thousand had gathered and, but for the presence of a large force of military and police, there might have been serious consequences. The anger of the crowd was due to the popular belief that no money at all would be presented at the sessions because of the opposition to public works (certainly as arranged under 9 & 10 Vic. c. 107) of the marquis of Downshire, one of the most influential landlords in the county.

Downshire's views were well publicised in the press and in broadsheets, in which he called on all ratepayers to be present at the sessions and resist money being voted for useless public works. His opposition was to 'double taxation' and to the compulsory element in the Act which enabled any individual or group, 'no matter what may be their characters, stations or circumstances', to cause a sessions to be held by their representations to the lord lieutenant. There was no obligation on his excellency to inform himself by prior examination whether or not the sessions was required. But once the sessions was appointed, the authority of the lord lieutenant ended. From that point, matters rested exclusively with the ratepayers. Downshire was anxious that they should turn up in large numbers, properly informed, so that on the one hand they would not be overawed or bullied by 'any rabble that choose to assemble' into voting money for public works and, on the other, that worthy landlords who were already providing for their tenants by employment and other private relief efforts should not be forced by unworthy landlords into a share of taxation for baronial works which they did not want and from which they derived no benefit.

While Downshire's views were supported by many landlords in the barony, there was no unanimity among them as to what steps they should take to avoid a presentment. One at least found Downshire's style of opposition to the sessions – the use of rousing broadsheets – distasteful and told him so. Rev. J. R. Moore, trustee for Lord Annesley at Castlewellan, wrote:

> ... pardon me for saying I wish [your notices] had not been published.

He thought the proper way to influence tenants was through one's agents and bailiffs. But Moore also feared that the notices would raise an already high temperature. As he observed to his neighbour, Lord Roden, at Tollymore, 'I cannot think [the notices] judicious ... the sessions will be a *very strong affair*'; and he told Downshire, 'I believe there is such a strong and powerful [feeling] among priests and people that it will be very difficult to stop an assessment'. He was right. The combination of a fundamental lack of unanimity among the landlords, the pressure of popular excitement and the stubborn insistence of the board of works inspecting officer, ensured that Downshire's powerful opposition did not prevail.[20]

Brereton's comments on the Castlewellan sessions put the landlords of the barony in a rather poor light. He felt there was 'a great desire evinced by the landed proprietors to hide the poverty of the people' and he 'was most urgently attacked' by many landlords for bringing the destitution of the barony before them, as his duty required. Brereton's estimate was that about 2,000 families were destitute, about 20 per cent of the population. He succeeded in winning a presentment for the half-barony.[21]

Thus county Down, one of the most prosperous counties in Ireland and one of those least in need of relief works, still had pockets of extensive distress for which, officials believed, the public works were inadequate. The county engineer, John Frazer, set out clearly the extent of the distress. The parts

> that most require assistance for the poor lie in two directions, namely, in a line from Newcastle by the sea, through the barony of Mourne up to Newry; then from the town of Newry up by the towns of Rathfirland [sic] and Hilltown [and] on to Castlewellan, making a bend round by [Dromara], Ballynahinch, Seaforde, and joining in upon Newcastle.

The proprietors of the barony of Kinelarty, Mr. Forde and Mr. Ker, were giving employment in drainage under the board of works. Likewise the marquis of Downshire and the earl of Roden were providing extensive employment out of their own funds, as were many other gentlemen; but still the employment given by all these resources was not sufficient. Fraser suggested 'some large trunk work' that would run right through the poor districts, for instance, a new line of post road from Downpatrick to Newry which was very much needed; there was also a coast road wanted from Newcastle to Kilkeel; from Rathfriland to [Dromara], a district very badly off for employment, there was a road but it was 'notoriously hilly and bad'.[22]

Local relief committees, 1846-1847

While Ballymacarrett and Loughbrickland were exceptions in 1845-6, they were certainly not in the following season, when relief committees were formed all over the county. Down actually had more committees (some thirty-seven or thirty-eight; fig. 14.1) in correspondence with Dublin Castle than any other county in Ulster. Its nearest 'rivals' were Donegal, with thirty committees and Antrim, Armagh, Cavan and Tyrone with twenty-nine each. While extensive activity by relief

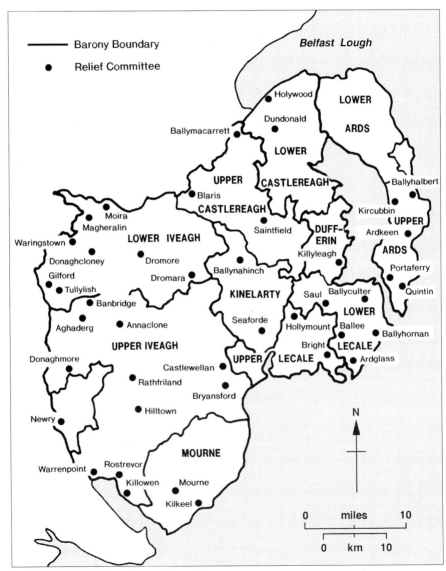

Fig. 14.1   Local relief committees established in county Down, 1846-1847.

committees gave an indication of extreme distress in a county, the important fact about the committees in Down is that they were late to form. Committees corresponded with government if they wished to avail of grant aid or were contemplating doing so. Some shunned involvement with government because it restricted their freedom, particularly in how they used their funds, or simply because of an inbred localism and sturdy independence. It is also possible that some committees felt that local needs were not serious enough to require government help.

In the latter category may have been the three committees on the Ards peninsula, namely Ardkeen, Ballyhalbert and Kircubbin. Other independent committees, reading from north to south in the county, were (with bracketed committees being 'involuntarily' independent because they left their grant-aid applications too late): (Ballymacarrett), Holywood, Moira, Saintfield, Donaghcloney, Killyleagh, (Annaclone), Bright, Ballyculter and Hilltown/Clonduff.[23] Rostrevor/Killowen, one of the most highly organised committees in the county, 'was first constituted as a private committee' with strong landlord support on 8 December 1846, but by early February 1847 had decided it needed government help.[24] Less favoured Annaclone, 'with no resident gentry in the parish', was formed on 7 October 1846. According to their chairman, Rev. Robert Forde, they 'deferred as long as possible applying to the government for some assistance to [their] funds', but were at length compelled to do so on 10 February 1847,

> as the farmers and myself are completely worn out. Famine is now actually staring us in the face. Dysentery has become so prevalent that there is scarce a house in which one or two individuals are not alarming ill [sic.] and several deaths are occurring *daily* ... Unless we can get a donation or relief in some shape, we will soon be as bad as the south.

There is no evidence that Annaclone's application was successful, hence its listing above as 'involuntarily' independent.[25]

Newry was certainly the earliest committee in the county to form, in late September 1846. Annaclone followed in early October. Enquiries were made in the middle of that month from Aghaderg parish (Loughbrickland), but the committee did not begin its operations until mid-December. A public meeting launched the Portaferry/Quintin Committee on 17 November, with Saintfield following in either late November or early December. Holywood and Waringstown began in early December and, from the middle of that month, Banbridge, Aghaderg, Seaforde, Ballynahinch, Warrenpoint (Christmas Eve),

Rostrevor/Killowen and Ballymacarrett commenced. At various dates in January 1847 there followed Ouley (in Newry poor-law union), Moira, Magheralin, Bryansford, Kilkeel, Castlewellan, Ballyhalbert, Kircubbin, Killyleagh, Ballee and Ballyculter. Crobane (near Newry) commenced operations on 3 February, followed by Dundonald, formed at 'a public general meeting' on the 8th of that month; then came Dromore, Dromara, Gilford/Tullylish and Saul. There were several committees whose dates of commencement are unclear, but most of whose first contact with government (through the commissariat relief department under Sir Randolph Routh and his secretary, William Stanley) was late in February; such were Mourne, Donaghcloney, Ardkeen, Donaghmore, Ardglass, Hollymount and Bright.[26] The point should be made that the timing of relief committee activity is a clear indicator of the perception by the leaders of local communities that relief was required.

As elsewhere in Ireland, the districts within which local relief committees functioned varied considerably. According to the government's *Instructions*, published in October 1846, county lieutenants were given great freedom to form 'suitably-sized' districts.[27] The result was that from late autumn 1846 onwards, an almost random patchwork of relief districts developed, consisting of every conceivable territorial arrangement. County Down was no exception. The predominant district was the single parish, of which there were fifteen: Ballyhalbert, Ardkeen (probably), Holywood, Dundonald, Saintfield, Moira, Dromara, Dromore, Gilford/Tullylish, Aghaderg (coterminous with the three electoral divisions of Glaskermore, Loughbrickland and Scarva in Banbridge poor-law union), Donaghmore (encompassing two electoral divisions in Newry union), Ballyculter, Bright and Saul. A further fourteen districts consisted of one or more electoral divisions of various poor-law unions: Blaris (Lisburn union); Donaghcloney, Magheralin and Waringstown (all Lurgan); Killyleagh (Downpatrick); Hilltown/Clonduff (two divisions of Newry union); Rostrevor/Killowen (likewise, Newry); Seaforde (three electoral divisions, namely Seaforde, Dunmore and Rosconnor and part of a fourth, Clough, all in Downpatrick union); Hollymount, on the outskirts of Downpatrick was probably a division of that union; likewise, Kilkeel and Mourne were divisions of Kilkeel union and, finally, Crobane, Newry (though there was a dispute about it) and Ouley were each relief districts consisting of a single electoral division within Newry poor-law union.

In between these groups of parish and electoral division districts were miscellaneous ones like Warrenpoint, which consisted of two parishes (Warrenpoint and Clonallon) and one townland, Ballyagholy, 'belonging to the same Union district', while Portaferry/Quintin contained no less than five parishes, namely Ardquin, Ballyphilip, Ballytrustan, Slans and Witter. Banbridge was made up principally of the parish of Seapatrick, but with a townland and bits of two others from adjoining parishes tacked on. In Lecale barony, the Ballyhornan, Ballybeg and Tullamgrange Committee, despite its long name, confined its activities to the three townlands so named. Finally, Ardglass and Ballee committees divided the electoral divisions of Ardglass (Downpatrick union) between them, Ballee accounting for 18¼ townlands and Ardglass the remainder. Such idiosyncrasies were, no doubt, like Warrenpoint's, explicable by local custom and perfectly understood by Viscount Castlereagh, the lieutenant of the county, because he sanctioned the local arrangements.[28]

Nevertheless, in a few instances, Castlereagh's lack of clarity about the extent of relief districts caused serious problems for local committees. The most conspicuous difficulty occurred at Newry, where he sanctioned a committee for 'Newry', without any qualification.[29] The problem about Newry only surfaced after the relief committee had obtained an equal donation in aid of their fund of £782. The chairman, William Thompson, claimed that the donation had been made to the Newry Soup Kitchen Committee whose activities were strictly confined to the town. There was a flurry of protest to Routh from gentlemen subscribers residing close to the town, who claimed that the committee had been appointed for the electoral division of Newry, which embraced rural areas like theirs. Their view was supported by the committee secretary, Rev. Daniel Bagot, vicar of Newry, who, in a much-underlined letter to Routh, insisted:

> ... His Excellency the Lord Lieutenant has granted £782 to the *relief committee* for the *electoral* division of Newry'. The electoral division included not only the town, but also three or four townlands around it, yet the grant had been 'merged into the funds of the *Newry Soup Kitchen*'; one of the rules of the soup kitchen was that no person could receive relief from it 'who was not an actual *resident in the town* on 14th December 1846'.

Bagot demanded that, if necessary, 'a peremptory instruction' should be sent to his chairman that the grant must be applied to the whole electoral division or that the Newry soup kitchen must extend its operations to the whole electoral division.[30]

Castlereagh created similar problems for the Rathfriland General Relief Committee. Evidently he had nominated a large relief district for the Rathfriland area, but failed to define it clearly, for although it embraced the parishes of Clonduff, Garvaghy and Drumballyroney, 'doubts were entertained about the legality of the parish of Drumgath being included ...'. The problems did not become apparent until several sub-committees attempted to obtain government grants in aid of their funds, when Routh required them to provide certification from the chairman and treasurer of the general committee. In the ensuing correspondence, the secretary of the general committee informed Routh that the relief district was, 'owing to its size and other causes ... totally unmanageable ...' and, further, that the committee 'has done and can do nothing'; it was 'useless', and existed 'in mere name'.[31] When pressed by Routh for further information about the Clonduff Sub-Committee in particular, the secretary told him that no such sub-committee had ever been formed. But the vicar of Clonduff, Rev. Richard Archer, who was applying for a government donation for his sub-committee, argued strenuously for the formal recognition by Routh of what were evidently widespread informal practices by self-appointed sub-committees: '... we conceived what was done by a portion of the committee under the implied sanction of the General Committee was done by all ...'.[32]

But another cause (one of the 'other causes' mentioned by the secretary) of confusion appears to have been landlord involvement, if not interference, in the funding of relief in the area. Rev. J. R. Moore, uncle and agent to the young Earl Annesley was, it seems, genuinely concerned for the welfare of the tenants of the estate, provided he controlled both the money and the mechanism of relief. He explained what he called his 'plan' to Rev. Richard Archer. He gave money to local committees in areas where there were Annesley tenants,

> provided that I was allowed to name the agent Mr. Shaw with myself as a sub-committee to give out the meal .... I appoint a farmer out of each townland, a Roman Catholic a Church of England a Presbyterian [sic]. I meet them, consult their local knowledge, refer to the relief lists and with my own I have some knowledge of the existing distress and I give out meal accordingly.

He proposed to send a subscription of £21 to 'Rathfryland Relief Committee', of which Rev. Archer was to get £14 for Clonduff and Rev. Garstin £7 for Drumballyroney. With a government donation added, Archer would have £28 and Garstin £14, and Archer was told: '... you would stipulate with the Relief Committee, that you were both in the proportions I have mentioned to be dispensers of money on Lord Annesley's property ...'.[33] It is distinctly possible that such conditional help from landlords pressurised clerical members of local committees like Rathfriland to disengage themselves and their efforts from the main committees and concentrate on their immediate concerns, as Rev. Archer had evidently been doing, thereby weakening the committee to the extent that it became utterly impotent.

Outside influences, like the arrangements of the county lieutenant, were not the only sources of vexation for committees. These could arise within the membership itself, either through a clash of strong personalities or, perhaps, as a reflection of long-running local disputes. Killyleagh and Ballynahinch had their own vexations.

The Killyleagh dispute was between A. R. Hamilton, Esq., of Killyleagh Castle and the rector of the parish, Rev. Dr. Edward Hincks. At the inaugural relief meeting in early January 1847, Hincks proposed a large district comprising the whole barony of Dufferin. But an amendment was carried 'that each electoral district look after is own poor'. Hincks wanted a larger committee, 'under the direction of government', to embrace the electoral division of Crossgar, part of his parish in which, he said, 'very great distress exists', but the majority preferred an independent committee. The reason for the distress in Crossgar – and lack of provision for it – was that the division consisted of

a number of townlands belonging to different proprietors, many of them being subdivided, so that there are about 40 proprietors in all .... From these causes it has been found impossible to do anything for the relief of the existing destitution by voluntary efforts.

And to make matters worse, 'there [was] no magistrate nor unemployed gentleman resident in the Division and only one clergyman of any domination'.[34]

Here were juxtaposed two widely contrasting electoral divisions within the same parish: Killyleagh, 'which is', in Hincks' words, 'wealthy and where there has been a large voluntary subscription, while the distress is comparatively small', and Crossgar, with much and increasing distress and in need of substantial funds which were not forthcoming because there was no resident 'unemployed' gentleman to organise them, if that were possible with such a complexity of forty landlords (in a division of 6,335 statute acres).[35] It provides a classic illustration of an 'abandoned' district alongside a well-endowed one, where the resident and active landlords (including, besides Hamilton, the marquis of Dufferin and William Sharman Crawford) were determined not to be drawn into a wider relief provision where they would be liable for the destitute of careless proprietors.

In Ballynahinch the vexation had a different source, although the participants had similar interests to those in Killyleagh. Rev. Charles Boyd, vicar of Magheradroll, saw himself – justifiably, it seems – as the champion of the destitute against William R. Anketell, the newly appointed agent to the principal landlord, David Ker, M.P. Anketell, in Boyd's words, 'rules the committee in a very arbitrary manner', so that 'their object seems to be to economise their funds at the expense of life. Mine to feed the hungry according to the benevolent regulations of government'.[36] The point at issue was the interpretation of government regulations, which, according to Boyd, 'direct[ed] the *gratuitous issue* of meal to *destitute cases'*. Boyd had devoted his best attention to the destitute, especially in early March, when there were a 'number of deaths' in the district. But at this very time he found himself obstructed by the committee secretary 'under mistaken views upon the subject of "gratuitous issues"', particularly when sixty tickets which he made out for the destitute were all refused at the committee's meal store.[37] The episode seems ultimately to have hinged on landlord control of a committee and its fund (to which Ker and his family were the majority donors). It also suggests, as a possible landlord objective, the clearance of unwanted destitution, for the local union workhouse, at Downpatrick was full at the time. It must be said that Ker and his neighbour, Rev. W. B. Forde, had met with their tenants the previous December and had agreed to lend money to small farmers for drainage at 5 per cent, to be repaid in ten years. They believed that drainage was the best thing that could be done 'for the small farmers and labourers in the present emergency'.[38]

These views were compatible with current ideas of political economy, and while many in Ulster might have held them themselves, in practice the predominant attitude among members of local relief committees was much more humane. There was a particularly widely-held opinion that normally decent, hardworking labourers or small farmers should not be reduced to destitution before being helped. This can be amply illustrated from county Down.

The Rev. H. Smyth-Cumming proposed to Routh a hypothetical case of a tenant in the Seaforde area ('there may be 300 more like him') with, say, thirteen acres of £12.10s. annual valuation. After providing for himself and his family for three months prior to December 1 out of his corn crop (that is, since the potato failure), he had ten hundredweight of oats left:

> He has of stock one cow, one heifer and one horse. Are we, I would ask, to wait until this man and his family has consumed the ... oats and, it maybe has sold ... his ill-fed stock before we can give him or his children remunerative employment and thus have increased the already alarming mass of hopeless, helpless paupers on the land?

Smyth-Cuming would have such a man given work, would leave him his oats for seed time and the milk of his cow to provide income to pay his bills, 'thereby preserving the man's independence of spirit and ... [enabling] him to keep his position in society ...'.[39] Similar views were expressed by the chairman of the Newry Relief Committee, although his committee was divided on the issue of giving relief to small farmers, 'say holding 5 or even 10 acres to enable them to leave the public works and to put in their crops'. Some thought not; such farmers were not destitute; 'they should sell or part with the land'. But the chairman believed 'this ... would be the means of increasing paupers to a great extent'; committees were intended 'to forward as far as possible the cropping of the land with the least possible delay'.[40]

Rostrevor/Killowen, one of the best organised committees in the county, was also anxious 'to assist the small farmers by grants of food, so as to enable them to support themselves while preparing their ground and putting in their crops'. They wanted to give similar 'aid by food towards the subsistence of cottiers and labourers who have no land ...', whose only labour was from the small farmers, but they 'are unable to give them any wages'. The official government position, insisting that the only relief 'to those capable of labour' should be by sales of food, was unhelpful: 'if rigidly adhered to [it] would render the fund inapplicable to the relief of a large class of the most destitute around us', namely, the small farmers and the landless labourers. In addition, Rostrevor/Killowen was one of the very few committees in the county giving agricultural employment.[41] 'Our trust', wrote the secretary of the Blaris Committee, 'is that, by good management of our funds and proportionate help from government, we may ... carry the distressed population through this calamitous period without any assessment or taxation involving struggling householders and small farmers'.[42]

Bryansford committee used their fund in giving food to the most destitute and 'in cheapening it to those whose wages ... cannot enable them to purchase provisions at the exorbitant rates of the markets and the huxters [sic] ...'.[43] Ballee had a similar approach,

> to assist with a comfortable meal three days in the week to [sic] each family gratis and let them depend on their own exertions for the remainder. ... With us, the able-bodied labourer has full employment but their wages are not sufficient to maintain their families.[44]

A humane approach was not the same as careless indulgence. Many committees indicated to Routh that they had systems of visitation or inspection. To quote but two examples, the first from Portaferry/ Quintin: 'Every applicant must be recommended by a subscriber, he is then brought forward personally and examined by the committee', which consisted of the chairman and principal landlord, John Nugent, and 'the Protestant, Presbyterian and Roman Catholic clergymen and several of the most respectable inhabitants'. The weekly allowance of meal to those working but unable to support their families, was only 'sufficient to keep off the pangs of hunger'.[45] In Dundonald and Blaris, all applicants were 'personally visited by the committee'.[46]

On the evidence of the extensive correspondence from the local relief committees to the commissariat relief department at Dublin Castle between September 1846 and April 1847 (but especially from December to March), we must conclude that there was considerable destitution in many parts of county Down. Even if we take the cynical view that most letters from committees were 'begging' letters, seeking grants in aid of local funds, the tone of too many letters is too serious and the anxiety is too consistent for their sincerity to be doubted. Furthermore, the same consistently serious tone is evident in letters from independent committees.

The Temporary Relief Act, April-August 1847

Relief by food, through 10 Vic. c. 7 (the Temporary Relief or Soup Kitchens or Rations Act), replaced the public works scheme in April 1847. A new temporary relief commission under Sir John Burgoyne was established, but, since the relief was to be mainly funded out of the poor rates, its organisational framework was the poor-law system. Where necessary, local committees were reorganised into relief districts consisting of one or more electoral divisions of a poor-law union and they were strictly controlled by a small union finance committee. In addition to poor rates, the balance of the funds of the 'old' committees could be used to purchase food, and government agreed to continue to grant aid local voluntary subscriptions.[47]

There was widespread opposition in principle to the new relief, particularly in east Ulster. Many boards of guardians feared it as a great experiment in outdoor relief, with possibly nightmarish financial implications. It was the east Ulster unions of Antrim, Belfast and Newtownards which, alone of the 130 unions in Ireland, avoided the Act completely, although Newtownards had dallied with the prospect of using it.[48] Individual electoral divisions within unions could also opt out. Of the 229 in the whole of Ireland which did so, 186 were in Ulster unions (including forty-seven in the unions of Antrim, Belfast and Newtownards).[49] But the vast majority adopted the Act because they were unable or unwilling to continue local voluntary subscriptions.

The comprehensive statistics for the operation of the Temporary Relief Act provide a useful profile of the pressure points of distress in Ireland at large during the period of its operation. They also afford us comparisons, often quite marked, between poor-law unions and between electoral divisions within unions, which support Cullen's observation that the Great Famine was 'less a national disaster than a social and regional one'.[50]

One set of figures within the statistics which provides a particularly useful comparator is the 'maximum number on rations in any one day' during the operation of the Act, expressed as a percentage of the population of the union or electoral division. If we arrange, in descending order of magnitude, the percentage figures for the 127 unions using the Act, we find the upper half of the list dominated by Connacht and Munster unions, the lower half by those of Leinster and Ulster. Baillieborough union (substantially in county Cavan) is the highest placed Ulster union (forty-ninth in Ireland), with a maximum of 39 per cent of its population on rations. The highest placed county Down union (108th in Ireland) is Banbridge, with 13.3 per cent on rations; Downpatrick (114th) had just over 9 per cent and Kilkeel (125th) 2.1 per cent. Newtownards, of course, did not use the Act.

These union figures conceal considerable variations from one electoral division to another. For example, of the twenty-three electoral divisions in Banbridge union, seven had between 20 and 30 per cent of their population on rations, while at the lower end of the spectrum, a further eight divisions were below the union average with figures of between 13 and 9 per cent. Banbridge, Tullylish and Mullahead divisions, on the other hand, did not use the Act, the first two certainly because the balances of their 'old' funds, carried over, were sufficient to fund their relief needs between April and August 1847. Similar differences existed in Downpatrick union. Only two of its twenty-four divisions, had more than 20 per cent of their population on rations, while a further eight had between 10 and 20 per cent (table 14.1) and six did not use the Act at all. The latter comprised Inch, Killinchy, Kilmore, Leggygown, Portaferry and Quintin. The latter pair benefited from the balance of the 'old' fund of the Portaferry/Quintin Relief Committee, which had been the sixth largest in the county; the others avoided the Act because landlords and tenants combined voluntarily to provide for relief. Kilkeel union had ten electoral divisions of which only three availed of the Act. They were Greencastle (6.4 per cent), Kilkeel (5.7 per cent) and Mourne Park (4.7 per cent). Altogether, Kilkeel union's involvement with the Act was nominal.[51]

The Temporary Relief Act was an unqualified success. Admittedly, it had the great advantage of coinciding with a dramatic slump in food

TABLE 14.1

Banbridge and Downpatrick unions
Sample variation in the percentage of population on rations by electoral division
April-August 1847

Banbridge		Downpatrick	
Glaskermore	29.35 per cent	Hollymount	23.6 per cent
Crossgar	28.62 per cent	Downpatrick	22.6 per cent
Loughbrickland	26.0 per cent		
Skeagh	25.8 per cent	Ardglass	17.8 per cent
Scarva	21.8 per cent	Raholp	16.2 per cent
Ardtanagh	21.35 per cent	Killough	15.66 per cent
Tyrella	15.0 per cent		
Ballyward	13.0 per cent	Castlewellan	14.4 per cent
Tirkelly	13.0 per cent	Crossgar	12.2 per cent
Mullaghbrack	12.4 per cent	Strangford	11.4 per cent
Ballybrick	11.6 per cent	Clough	11.0 per cent
Moneyslane	10.4 per cent		
Ballyshiel	9.65 per cent		
Magherally	9.5 per cent		
Balloolymore	9.1 per cent		

prices. Indian corn from America was at a high of £19 a ton (ex Liverpool) in February 1847; by the end of March it had dropped to £13 and by the end of August to £7.10s.[52] Three million people were fed at one third of the cost of the public works scheme.[53] Reports from all over the country about the improved appearance of the people verged at times on the euphoric. One area reported on to the government was Banbridge union, where 'the industrious poor were left on stoppage of relief in a more comfortable position than they [had] been for any period during the last two years ...'.[54]

The poor-law system

The influx into the workhouses in Ulster seems to have begun in October 1846, 'no small evidence', in the words of Rev. James Disney of Charlemont in county Armagh, '... of the destitution which exists, as the most unreasonable reluctance prevails in these parts ... to taking shelter in the [poor] houses'.[55]

Most workhouses experienced a great surge in admissions in December 1846 or January 1847. By the turn of the year, twenty-one of the forty-three Ulster unions were filled to more than their capacity, seven others were close to it, while fifteen reported no pressure. While it is difficult to generalise, it can be said that most workhouses catering for the larger centres of population were nearly or over full, such as Belfast, Londonderry, Armagh, Newry, Lisburn, Ballymena, Omagh and Cavan. Among the fifteen reporting no pressure were Downpatrick and Kilkeel in county Down. However, Newry was full on 30 January 1847 and Downpatrick was full before the end of February.[56]

The initial pressure on the workhouses, which became more critical in the new year, brought a series of major problems for the boards of guardians. The first and most obvious was accommodation. Second, there was the problem of provisioning. Third, while none of the unions wholly or substantially in county Down experienced the epidemics which struck most workhouses in the spring and early summer of 1847, there was still the acute problem of the care of the sick and the constant fear of epidemic conditions. Finally, an enormous and prolonged financial problem dogged most boards of guardians; it was exacerbated by the expense, first, of the Temporary Relief Act in the period from April to August 1847 and, more seriously, of the introduction of unwanted outdoor relief under the extended Irish poor law from August 1847 onwards.

As workhouses filled up, all kinds of devices, most of them temporary, were employed to extend accommodation. The most usual was the erection of 'sleeping galleries' around the larger common rooms such as dining halls, dormitories or wards. Wooden sheds, for which plans were available from the poor-law commissioners, were erected in workhouse yards. They were already in use by the turn of the year in Belfast and Banbridge and were being organised in Newtownards.[57] Guardians could rent houses or other buildings near the workhouse as temporary accommodation. Occasionally, workhouse buildings were converted; in others, the problem was solved for a time by moving people around the existing accommodation. Newry, for example, was planning a sixty-bed fever ward, whereas Newtownards arranged to move the 'small number of fever patients' into a temporary building, while erecting sleeping galleries in the boys' dormitories and fitting up beds in the probationary wards.[58]

Pressure for admission to the Banbridge workhouse was by far the most dramatic of the county Down unions. It began in earnest, as it did virtually everywhere in the county, in October 1846, when an unprecedented 165 people were admitted. Similar numbers were admitted in November, then a huge leap brought 401 in December, the house reaching and passing its complement of 800 on the day after Christmas. By the turn of the year there were 900 inmates.[59]

The medical officer had reported to the poor-law commissioners his strong objections to allowing more than 800 in the house, at a time when 'whooping cough, influenza and dysentery [were] prevalent'. The commissioners agreed and, because the medical officer was so emphatic in his attitude, the board of guardians 'very reluctantly refused to grant any further admissions for the present'.[60] As the workhouse filled up with the destitute and starving, so the risks of infectious diseases increased. The numbers of deaths rose alarmingly from twenty-nine in December 1846 to eighty-nine in January 1847; there were sixty-four deaths in February and seventy-two in March 1847. In November, the medical officer had noted 'measles very prevalent'; in early January, 'whooping cough, influenza and dysentery prevalent', and, on 27 February, 'dysentery prevalent and fever on the increase and .... small pox ... beginning to break out about the town', with twenty-six deaths the previous week. On the same day, the workhouse master reported that the water supply would not meet present consumption; the board ordered that 'another well be forthwith sunk'.[61] Fever cases continued to increase, until, at the beginning of May, it was found necessary to add 'a temporary wooden house to the fever hospital', which was ready for occupation on the 29 May.[62] Fortunately, while numbers of patients in fever (and a parallel number convalescing from it) continued to run in the forties and fifties throughout the year, with a peak of sixty on Christmas Day, there was no uncontrolled epidemic in Banbridge. We must assume that the main factors behind this were the insistence of the medical officer that admissions should be regulated and the strict adherence to the one aspect of fever treatment which was well understood at that time, namely the need for isolation.[63] But there was also the availability of two temporary fever hospitals, one at Tanderagee in the Armagh end of the union and the other at Dromore. They provided an extra 220 beds, which placed Banbridge fifth among the Ulster unions (after Lurgan, Cavan, Armagh and Enniskillen) in emergency fever provision in the summer of 1847.[64]

When the guardians accepted the curtailment of admissions, their first response was to turn out the fifty-four paupers who had been provisionally admitted, but not before each was given a dinner. Their next step was to seek extra accommodation. An approach was made to a Mr. Murray of Lurgan for the hire of part of his brewery in Banbridge, currently unoccupied, as a temporary workhouse.[65] Meanwhile sheds, in course of erection in the men's and women's yards were ordered to be 'raised from one to two storeys' and it was decided to install (sleeping) galleries 'in all parts of the workhouse'.[66]

Despite the provision of extra accommodation, severe pressure continued on the workhouse throughout the spring and summer months of 1847. Furthermore, the guardians' minutes frequently record large numbers of applicants turned away for lack of room. The fifty-four turned out on 2 January have already been mentioned. An identical number was refused admission on 23 January, while 106 were refused entrance on 13 February, ninety-two on 27 February and 170 on 13 March, when the workhouse master reported 'great difficulty' with this large number, because many of them refused to leave the workhouse gate when ordered. He was informed he could call in the constabulary if necessary. On 10 April, sixty-two were turned away, 'although', as the minutes record, 'all the applicants exhibited symptoms of starvation and some even of death'. On 1 May, 110 were rejected and 130 on 29 May.[67]

On these occasions, the board of guardians usually ordered the rejected applicants to be given a dinner or 'dinner and one half lb. of bread to reach their respective residences', or 'some portion of food' to enable them to get back home, since many of them had come 'from a distance of 9 miles and all in a state of extreme destitution'.[68] While the poor-law commissioners warned the guardians several times that the law did not permit such food donations out of the poor rates, the board continued the practice, 'feeling convinced that at this particular crisis of distress ... the ... Commissioners would not object when the motions which actuate the Board ... are taken into consideration'.[69]

If admissions to Banbridge workhouse were the most dramatic of the county Down unions, the most carefully monitored by the local press were those to Downpatrick. Built to contain 1,000 paupers, it was the largest in the county. In the opinion of Assistant Poor-Law Commissioner Edward Senior, who was responsible for the twenty unions in counties Antrim, Londonderry, Tyrone and Down, Downpatrick was the 'most favourably circumstanced union he knew' (fig. 14.2).[70]

From October 1846, the local press began to document the 'expected influx' to the workhouse. In the first week of that month, eleven paupers were admitted; in the third week, forty-one, and in the second week of November, fifty-one ('chiefly women and children'), This brought the number in the workhouse to a record. 'There are now 523 paupers in the house', noted the *Downpatrick Recorder*, 'being 18 more than the largest number ever on the books at one time before'.[71] At the first meeting of the guardians in December, 'the admission of paupers was the principal business'.[72] The press, like the guardians, paid close attention to able-bodied workmen entering the house. Among the forty-one admitted in the third week of October were some weavers, 'who stated they were able to earn but 4s. a week', a reminder of the serious slump in the linen trade, which continued throughout 1847.[73]

Another record for Downpatrick was set in the week before Christmas, when ninety-five paupers were admitted, the highest number ever in one week.[74] Over the next few weeks admissions were

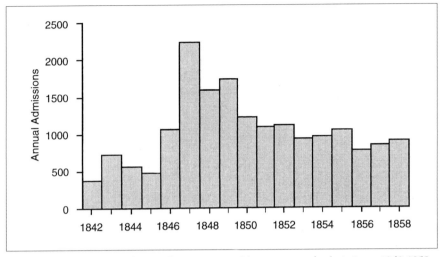

Fig. 14.2   Downpatrick poor-law union workhouse: annual admissions, 1842-1858.
Source: Indoor registers, BG XII/GA/1, 2 & 3 (P.R.O.N.I.).

in the sixties per week.[75] At this point a smallpox epidemic broke out, the guardians removing themselves for their weekly meeting on 9 January from the workhouse to the grand jury room in Downpatrick courthouse. There were six deaths from smallpox in the first week of the new year, even although it was described as a mild form, with some thirty-three cases confirmed.[76] The house was closed to new admissions for some weeks, but, before the end of February, it was full.

The numbers admitted to Downpatrick workhouse were modest compared not only to Banbridge but also to Newtownards. In October 1846, 102 paupers were admitted there, followed by 148 in November and 331 in December, by which time the house was filled to its complement of 600 and beyond. By the middle of February 1847, there were 832 in the house and admissions during the following twelve months continued to run at over 300 a month, with peaks of 416 and 602 in March and June 1847 respectively. Only in February 1848 did admissions begin to fall below 200 a month, a trend which continued throughout that year. Thereafter, except for seasonal increases from November 1848 to May 1849 and again during the following winters, numbers quickly fell back to pre-Famine levels.[77] On this evidence, Famine-related hardship in the Newtownards union was sharp but comparatively short-lived (fig. 14.3).

By contrast, pressure was sustained in Banbridge to such an extent that by the end of November 1847, the house was once again full to its newly-enlarged complement of 1,200. The poor-law commissioners

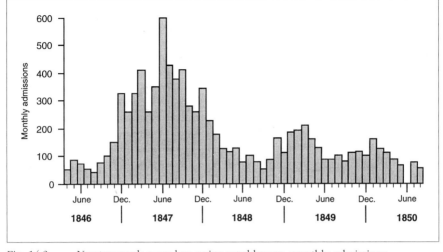

Fig. 14.3   Newtownards poor-law union workhouse: monthly admissions,
             1846-1850.
             Source: Board of guardians' minute books, BG XXV/A/1 & 2 (P.R.O.N.I.).

called on the guardians 'at once to commence the outdoor relief' now
allowed by the new Irish poor law of August 1847 (10 Vic. c. 31,
Sect. 1), finally threatening that if the board did not commence outdoor
relief immediately, the commissioners would intervene and do it for
them.[78] Numbers remained high during the whole of 1848 and well into
1849, reaching a peak of nearly 1,500 in February of that year. Only by
September 1849 were they below 800 (the original complement) and
falling.[79]

Kilkeel was unique among the county Down unions. It was the
smallest in area, by far the most sparsely populated, had the smallest
workhouse (built to contain 350), and yet proportionately, its poor-law
relief capacity was almost as favourable as Downpatrick's, which was
the best in the county. Kilkeel mirrored most other Irish unions insofar
as it experienced a surge of applications around the turn of 1846-1847
which quickly filled it to capacity. But this did not last long. So low-key
were matters in the union that, on board day, 10 March 1847, at a time
when great anxiety pervaded numerous parts of the country, no
guardians turned up for the weekly meeting.[80]

The Irish Poor-Law Extension Act, August 1847

The parliamentary passage of the new Irish Poor-Law Bill occurred at a
politically opportune time for the government, when the Temporary
Relief Act was operating successfully. As a result, there was only a
token resistance in the lords. But the implementation of the Act had no

such congenial environment. There was a profound anxiety among all boards of guardians about the uncalculated cost of the new poor law, which allowed outdoor relief for the first time and required the appointment of salaried relieving officers in each union to administer it, with a house to serve as a depot and, if necessary, a servant to cook food, for cooked food was the chosen medium of relief. The number of relieving officers was to be negotiated between the poor-law commissioners and each board of guardians.[81]

The *Belfast News Letter* reported – accurately – that 'many Boards of Guardians, especially in counties Antrim and Down have determined to resist the order of the Commissioners to appoint relieving officers on the ground that outdoor relief is not necessary'. The government, considered the newspaper, had committed 'a very serious mistake' in applying the principle of outdoor relief to every union in Ireland, 'no matter how different the circumstances of some unions may be from those of others'. While it was willing to admit the necessity of outdoor relief, 'in many of the distressed districts of the south and west', yet in other districts it was 'an expensive farce'.[82] Of the ten unions shown in a 'Return of Relieving Officers' not to have made any appointments by November 1847, six were from east Ulster, namely, Antrim, Downpatrick, Kilkeel, Larne, Lisburn and Lurgan.[83]

It is surprising that Newtownards is not included in the list, because a majority of its board of guardians conducted a vigorous, even truculent campaign against both the principle of outdoor relief in the new law and its mechanism, the relieving officer. With serious discourtesy to the poor-law commissioners and a disregard for their authority, 'which would seek to force Newtownards into the same category as Skibbereen', with an extravagant approval of the 'old' Irish poor law against the new and an obsessive self-congratulation on Newtownards' ability to avoid the Temporary Relief Act, they only succeeded in embarrassing the minority on the board. The latter, although opposed – except for one *ex-officio* guardian, Robert Nicholson of Balloo – to the new arrangements in principle, realised that the law had to be obeyed. In various attempts to bring the majority to reason, all the principal office-holders resigned their offices (including William Sharman Crawford, M.P., the chairman), and formally disassociated themselves from the majority.[84]

The rate in aid issue, 1849

The financial burdens of the Irish poor-law system in the summer of 1847 were frightful. With full workhouses, which a year earlier had been nearly empty, with a great proportion of the inmates ill, and with the added expenses of the Temporary Relief Act, outdoor relief and the relieving officers, rates were struck on an unprecedented scale, often being trebled, quadrupled or even more in comparison with pre-Famine years. It is not surprising that many boards of guardians failed to bring in the rates, even when hard-driven by a zealous administration. Between 1847 and 1849, forty-two of the 130 boards in Ireland were 'dissolved' by the commissioners and replaced by full-time vice-guardians. Despite such radical treatment, twenty-three unions, all in Connacht and Munster with the exception of Glenties in Ulster, were still bankrupt in early 1849. The government then took the drastic and, to many in Ireland of all political persuasions and religious creeds, unconstitutional step of requiring the solvent unions to submit to a special 'rate in aid' to bail out the bankrupt. The legislation for this was rushed through parliament in March 1849, and authorised the Irish poor-law commissioners to impose a special rate, not exceeding 1s. in the £, on all poor-law unions (in practice, on the solvent unions). In the event, a rate of 6d. in the £ was levied in June 1849 and a final one of 2d. in the £ in December 1850.[85]

Ulster opposition to the rate was led by two county Down M.P.'s, Viscount Castlereagh and William Sharman Crawford (then member for Rochdale, but no less committed to Irish matters), assisted by some Dublin Tories. This opposition was so vehement that the matter became regarded in parliament as 'the Ulster question'.[86] Downpatrick Board of Guardians was possibly first to over against the proposed rate when, on 27 January 1849, they prepared a petition to parliament, insisting that 'each union should support its own poor'. In mid-February, they urged Viscount Castlereagh to call 'a County meeting on an early day'.[87] Ulster opposition was stimulated by the widespread conviction among local boards of guardians that they had managed the Famine crisis well, while boards in the south and west had mismanaged it badly. These local perceptions were shared – and publicly acknowledged – by the senior poor-law administrators in Ireland. The poor-law boundary commissioners of 1848-49 were similarly complimentary, while Ulster M.P.'s had no doubts about the superiority of their local guardians. The proposed rate was doubly unconstitutional. It violated the political union of 1801 and it dishonoured poor-law theory and practice whereby relief and rating were always local, never national, concerns.[88]

Sharman Crawford set out the substance of the Ulster opposition in an amendment he moved in parliament on 1 March 1849, to the effect that

> it is unconstitutional and unjust to impose on Ireland separate national taxation for the wants of particular localities, so long as the public general revenue of Ireland is paid into an imperial

treasury and placed at the disposal of an imperial legislature for the general purposes of the United Kingdom.[89]

Castlereagh emphasized Ulster's loyalty, but warned that, if the rate were enacted, 'he would not give one month's purchase for [Ulster's] tranquillity'. But, lest this should be interpreted as incitement, he quickly added: '... they should not burst into an outbreak, but they would resist the levying of the rates by every constitutional means in their power'.[90]

Thus was generated an Ulster propaganda within parliament whereby the (misleading) impression was conveyed that the rate would bear more heavily on Ulster than on any other province. The parliamentary campaign was supported by a vigorous programme of public meetings at home, although there is evidence to suggest that this programme was not as successful as had been hoped, because the 'heads of society' in the province failed to provide sufficiently vigorous leadership.[91] The government had its way, supported by a 'famine fatigue' in English public opinion. But many Ulster boards of guardians carried out the threat of passive resistance to the rate in aid which the campaign had adopted.[92]

Conclusion

There is no doubt that, compared to virtually every other county in Ireland, Down survived the Great Famine remarkably well. Yet, as this account has shown, there were localities in which people suffered great hardship. This is best illustrated by the poor-law union of Kilkeel – and the surrounding barony of Mourne – which needed the various schemes of relief in a very limited way. The poor-law resources were hardly strained, there was just a token use of relief by food, and the principal landlords seemed aware of tenant needs and became involved in providing for them; yet the need for extraordinary public works in the winter of 1846-47 was an indication that employment was seriously insufficient. The accounts of those present show that, for at least a few months, there was appalling destitution, affecting around 20 per cent of the population in this otherwise favoured area.

Banbridge poor-law union seems to have been the worst affected part of the county. The statistics for the use of the Temporary Relief Act indicate a number of electoral divisions with close to 30 per cent of their population requiring food, with large numbers of destitute, starving and ill people turned away from the workhouse in the first half of 1847.

Even in districts where full employment was acknowledged, so also was the inability of working men to earn enough to feed their families, especially if large, so high were the prices of foodstuffs. Such circumstances applied equally to 'urban' areas like Ballymacarrett and rural parts like Ballee.

While local relief committees were much later starting in county Down than elsewhere, except county Antrim, they were very numerous, a clear indication of very deep local concern. The accounts they have left behind in their correspondence are sober, occasionally tragic, and, certainly, leave no room for retrospective complacency.

This account has focussed largely on the period up to the summer of 1847. The sources of evidence up until then are varied and informative. Thereafter, with the concentration of all relief in the poor-law system from August 1847 onwards, the sources narrow considerably, with the boards of guardians records in particular, being often unyielding in their blandness. But one has only to look, for example, at the admissions records of Downpatrick union (Senior's 'best circumstanced union' in east Ulster) in the decade after the Famine, to see that even here, its grave effects were slow to clear.

References

1. J. S. Donnelly, 'Famine and government response, 1845-6' in W. E. Vaughan (ed.), *A new history of Ireland, v. Ireland under the union, i, 1801-70* (Oxford, 1989), p. 277.

2. *Northern Whig*, 16 Apr. 1846.

3. Minutes, Newtownards' board of guardians (hereafter Mins BG), 20 May 1846, P. R. O. N. I., BG XXV/A/1.

4. Ibid., 8, 15 July 1846.

5. Mins Banbridge BG, 6 July 1846, P. R. O. N. I., BG VI/A/5.

6. Rev. J. R. Moore to Mr. Duffin, 25 Feb. 1847, Annesley MSS, P. R. O. N. I., D. 1854/6/3.

7. John Doran, P.P. Aghaderg, to Routh, 18 Oct. 1846, relief commission papers (hereafter RCP), (county Down) II/2A/6440; Rev. John Boyd to Routh, 16 April 1847, ibid., II/2a/19326; *Northern Whig*, 2 and 9 April 1846.

8. *A Statement of sums issued, by order of his excellency the lord lieutenant, as donations in aid of subscriptions raised by relief committees for the purchase of food in Ireland*, H. C. 1847(735), xxxvii, pp 235-242.

9. T. P. O'Neill, 'The organisation and administration of relief, 1845-52' in R.D. Edwards and T.D. Williams (ed.), *The great famine. Studies in Irish history 1845-1852* (Dublin, 1956), pp 23-28.

10. *Analysis of returns of poor employment under 9 Vic. c. 1 and 9 and 10 Vic. c. 107 from week ending 10 October 1846 to week ending 26 June 1847*, H. C. 1852 (169), xviii, p. 595.

11. *Belfast News Letter*, 31 Oct. 1846.

12. J. Grant, The great famine in the province of Ulster 1845-49 – The mechanisms of relief (hereafter Famine Ulster), unpublished Ph.D. thesis (Q.U.B. 1986), pp 151-2.

13. *Number and description of works applied for, recommended and sanctioned in each district of Ireland in the year 1846*, H. C. 1847(764), 1, pp 523-559.

14. Extracts from the journal of Capt. Brereton, inspecting officer, county Down (hereafter Brereton journal), for the week ending 9 Jan. 1847, H.C. 2847 (797), lii, p. 91.

15. Entry for 16 Jan. 1847, Ibid., p. 92.

16. Extracts from the report of Mr. John Frazer, conducting engineer for county Down, in *App. F to report of commrs public works for Feb. 1847*, ibid., pp 205-6.

17. Richard W. Cooke M.D. to sec. board of health, 2 Feb. 1847, RCP county Down, II/2a/10009.

18. Brereton journal, week ending 20 Feb. 1847, H. C. 1847 (797), lii, p. 240.

19. Brereton journal, week ending 9 Jan. 1847, ibid., p. 92.

20. Moore to Lord Downshire, Moore to Lord Roden, both dated 2 Jan. 1847, Annesley MSS, P. R. O. N. I., D. 1854/6/3; Printed notice, ibid.

21. Ibid.

22. Report of Mr. John Frazer, conducting engineer for county Down on the baronies of Mourne, lower half of Upper Iveagh and Newry, in *App. F to report of commrs public works for Feb. 1847*, H. C. 1847 (797), lii, pp 205-6.

23. RCP (county Down), II, *passim.*

24. Edward John Evans, vicar of Kilbroney, sec., to Wm. Stanley, 12 Feb. 1847, ibid., II/2b/10962.

25. Rev. John Forde, rector of Annacloan [sic.], to the commissary general, 10 Feb. 1847, ibid., II/2a/10718. Forde was one of the few correspondents to mention growing lawlessness: 'petty robberies are becoming prevalent and I had a sheep stolen from myself a month ago ...'.

26. Ibid., *passim.*

27. *Instructions for the formation and guidance of committees for relief of distress in Ireland consequent on the failure of the potato crop in 1846,* H. C. 1847(764), l, pp 104-7.

28. RCP (county Down), *passim.*

29. Lord Castlereagh to Routh, 28 Jan. 1847, ibid., II/2a/9812.

30. Wm. Thompson (chairman of the relief committee) to Routh, 22 Jan. 1847, ibid., II/2b/9812; Hugh Boyd to Routh, 4 Feb. 1847, ibid., II/2a/10146; W. I. Corry (n.a.), 4 Feb. 1847, ibid., II/2a/10155; Daniel Bagot (Vicar of Newry) (n.a.), 5 Feb. 1847, ibid., II/2a/10249.

31. Rev. R. A. Agar to the relief commission, 12 Mar. 1847, ibid., II/2a/13920.

32. Rev. R. A. Agar to Stanley and Rev. Richard Archer (vicar of Clonduff) to Routh, both 30 Mar. 1847, both ibid., II/2a/16277.

33. Rev. J. R. Moore to Rev. Mr. Archer, Hilltown, 18 Mar. 1847, Annesley MSS, P. R. O. N. I., D. 1854/6/3.

34. A. R. Hamilton to Stanley, 15 Jan. 1847, RCP (county Down), II/2a/9182; Hincks to Stanley, 13 Feb. 1847, Ibid., II/2a/11044.

35. Hincks to Stanley, 17 Feb. 1847, Ibid., II/2a/11370.

36. Capt. Boyd, Magheradroll Vicarage, to the commissary general, 16 Mar. 1847, Ibid., II/2a/14382; *Belfast News Letter,* 22 Dec. 1846.

37. Capt. Boyd to the commissary general, 10 Mar. 1847, RCP (county Down), II/2a/unnumbered.

38. *Belfast News Letter,* 15 Dec. 1846.

39. H. Smyth-Cuming, sec. Seaforde Relief Comm., to Routh, 18 Dec. 1846, RCP (county Down), II/2a/8324.

40. Wm. N. Thompson, chairman, to Routh, 10 Mar. 11847, ibid., II/2a/13553.

41. Edward John Evans, vicar of Kilbroney, sec., to Stanley, 22 Feb. 1847, ibid., II/2a/11711; Same to same, 12 Feb. 1847, ibid., II/2b/10962.

42. Rev. Henry Henderson to Routh, 29 January 1847, ibid., II/2a/10078.
43. Wm. S. Hills, chairman, to Routh, 22 Jan. 1847, Ibid., II/2a/9425; Same to same, 25 Mar. 1847, Ibid., II/2b/15637.
44. Thos. Gracey to Routh, 20 Feb. 1847, ibid., II/2a/11671; Thos. Gracey to Stanley, 11 Mar. 1847, Ibid., II/2b/13714.
45. [John Nugent to Routh], 9 Mar. 1847, Ibid., II/2b/13364.
46. Cover note to Dundonald subscription list, 8 Mar. 1847, ibid., II/2b/13723; Rev. Alexander Henderson, sec., Blaris, to Routh, 27 Feb. 1847, ibid., II/2b/12347.
47. O'Neill in Edwards and Williams, *Great famine,* p. 237.
48. Mins Newtownards BG, 17 Feb. 1847.
49. *Supplementary appendix parts II and III to 7th report relief commissioners,* H. C. 1847-8(956), xxix, pp 23-81.
50. L. M. Cullen, *An economic history of Ireland since 1660* (London, 1972), p. 132.
51. All the foregoing statistics (including those in table 1) are derived from *Supplementary appendix parts II and III to 7th report relief commissioners,* H. C. 1847-8 (956), xxix.
52. C. Woodham-Smith, *The great hunger: Ireland 1845-49* (London, 1962), p. 293.
53. O'Neill in Edwards and Williams, *Great famine,* pp 234, 241.
54. *Supplementary appendix parts II and III to 7th report relief commissioners,* H. C. 1847-8(956), xxix, p. 7.
55. James Disney to the commissary general, 26 Dec. 1846, RCP (county Armagh), II/2b/8541; Sir James Stewart to Routh, 22 Jan. 1847, RCP (county Donegal), I/2a/9536.
56. *Statement showing the amount of workhouse accommodation in Ireland, the number of inmates on the 9th January 1847 etc* (hereafter *statement*), H. C. 1847 (790), lv, pp 7-13; *13th annual report of poor law commissioners,* 1 May 1847, H. C. 1847 (816), xxviii, pp 27-8.
57. *Statement*, mins Newtownards BG, 16 and 30 Dec. 1846.
58. *Statement*, mins Newtownards BG, 9 and 16 Dec. 1846.
59. Mins. Banbridge BG, Oct. to Dec. 1846, *passim.*
60. Ibid., 2 Jan. 1847.
61. Ibid., Nov. 1846 to Mar. 1847, *passim.*
62. Every workhouse was required to have a fever ward, often referred to as a hospital because it was built at a distance from the main workhouse. Typically such wards contained about forty beds.
63. Mins Banbridge BG, Dec. 1846 to Dec. 1847, *passim.*
64. Grant, Famine Ulster, p. 278.
65. Mins Banbridge BG, 2 Jan. 1847; it was November before the brewery was hired and 300 boys were moved there in December, ibid., 20, 27 Nov. and 18 Dec. 1847.
66. Ibid., 16, 23 and 30 Jan. 1847.
67. Ibid., 16, 23 and 30 Jan. 1847.
68. Ibid., 30 Jan., 13 Mar., 10 and 27 April 1847.
69. Ibid., 27 Feb., 13 and 20 Mar. 1847.
70. *Downpatrick Recorder,* 3 Oct. 1846. Senior was the younger brother of the English political economist and poor-law reformer, Nassau William Senior.
71. Ibid., 10 and 31 Oct., 2 Nov. 1846.
72. Ibid., 12 Dec. 1846.
73. Ibid., 31 Oct. 1846.
74. Ibid., 16 Jan. 1847.
75. Ibid., 2, 9 and 16 Jan. 1847.
76. Ibid., 16 Jan. 1847.

77. Mins Newtownards BG, 1846-51, *passim*, P. R. O. N. I., BG XXV/A/1 & 2.

78. Mins Banbridge BG, 27 Nov. 1847, and 1 and 8 Jan. 1848, P. R. O. N. I., BG VI/A/7.

79. Mins Banbridge BG, 1847-49, *passim*, P. R. O. N. I., BG VI/A/7 & 8.

80. Mins Kilkeel BG, Oct. 1846 to Jan. 1849, *passim*, P. R. O. N. I., BG XVI/A/3, 4 & 5.

81. Circular of poor law commissioners on relieving officers, no. 340/M/47, 16 July 1847, summarised in Mins Belfast BG, 21 July 1847, P. R. O. N. I., BG VII/A/6.

82. *Belfast News Letter*, 21 Sept. 1847.

83. *Return of relieving officers*, H. C. 1847-8(963), liv, pp 29-31; *First annual report of Irish poor law commissioners*, 1 May 1848, H. C. 1847-8 (963), xxxiii, pp 394-5.

84. Mins Newtownards BG, 21 July 1847 to 5 Jan. 1848, *passim*. Col. Ward, *ex-officio* for Kircubbin, resigned his membership of the board in protest against the majority.

85. Grant, Famine Ulster, pp 309, 440-1.

86. The phrase was the earl of Lincoln's, *Hansard*, 3, ciii, 295 (6 Mar. 1849).

87. *Northern Whig*, 30 Jan. and 20 Feb. 1849.

88. Grant, Famine Ulster, chapter 7.

89. *Hansard*, 3, ciii, cols. 48-51 (1 Mar. 1849).

90. Ibid., cols. 78-9 (1 Mar. 1849).

91. *Northern Whig*, 24 May 1849, speech of David Ross of Rostrevor.

92. Grant, Famine Ulster, chapter 7.

Chapter 15

POPULATION CHANGE IN COUNTY DOWN 1841-1911

L. A. CLARKSON

'The early-modern period [in Ireland]', Líam Kennedy has written recently, 'witnessed the interplay of three vital forces: colonialism, religion and ethnicity'.[1] The outcomes of this interplay were still working themselves through in the nineteenth century, and nowhere more so than in county Down. A consequence of colonisation was settlement and population growth and the rhythm of demographic change has imparted to Irish social history a distinctive pattern ever since 1600. A further consequence, in Ulster at least, was ethnic and religious divisions which likewise have persisted into present times.

The size of the population in Ireland in 1600 can only be guessed at; it can hardly have been more than one million. In 1700 it was probably less than two million. Growth was spasmodic during the first half of the eighteenth century, but thereafter the population grew more rapidly than anywhere else in western Europe, touching two per cent per annum in Connaught and averaging 1.6 or 1.7 per cent for the whole country between 1750 and 1820. On the eve of the Great Famine the population of Ireland was at least 8.2 million.[2] At the end of the nineteenth century the population of Ireland was 4.5 million and it continued to fall into the twentieth century. It is against this background that the population history of county Down should be viewed.

Changing demographic patterns

On the eve of the Great Famine the population of county Down exceeded 368,000. In 1911 it was 204,000. Over a period of sixty years the county, excluding that part of Belfast that lay within its boundaries, lost 45 per cent of its population (see appendix, table 15.1). This was in line with Ireland as a whole although a little less than the historic province of Ulster where – again excluding Belfast – population fell by 49 per cent. If we restore Belfast, the population of which increased fivefold (from 75,000 to 387,000), to the province, Ulster suffered only a three percent reduction in population between 1841 and 1911.

The largest losses in Ulster were experienced by the south-western counties and the smallest in the north and east, including county Down. The broad picture of Ulster is set out in table 15.1. Since this essay is about population change it can hardly avoid being quantitative in approach, but in order not to impede the flow of the narrative, the statistical material has been sited in the appendix. Unless otherwise stated the statistics are taken from the database of Irish historical statistics held in the Department of Economic and Social History at The Queen's University of Belfast and derived ultimately from the censuses of Ireland from 1841 to 1911.[3]

At different times the census commissioners used two administrative units in which to group the inhabitants of counties: baronies and poor law unions. Baronies were the ancient divisions of counties and were employed for census purposes until 1891. There were approximately 320 baronies in Ireland in the mid-nineteenth century. In county Down nineteen baronies existed between 1841 and 1891 but not all were in use throughout the period. Four – Ards, Iveagh Lower, Iveagh Upper and Lecale – existed only in 1841 and were thereafter split into two. The areas of baronies also changed over time, although in a major way only in the case of Belfast. Population data at barony level were not given in 1901 and 1911.

Poor law unions were created by the Poor Law Act of 1838 and from 1840 they gradually replaced baronies. Initially there were 130 poor law unions in Ireland but their numbers increased to 163 over time. There were eight poor law unions covering county Down. Only three – Downpatrick, Kilkeel and Newtownards – lay wholly within the county; the other five extended into other counties. The greater part of Banbridge union was in county Down, and there was a small portion also in county Armagh. Lisburn union was split geographically, more or less half and half, between counties Antrim and Down, with the urbanised part in county Antrim. Lurgan union was spread across three counties; the greater part was in county Armagh and a small piece was in county Antrim, leaving a predominately rural portion in county Down. The union of Newry straddled counties Armagh and Down.

Because poor law unions extend for a longer time in the context of published census data and – with the exception of Belfast – remain almost unchanged in size, they have been used as the major unit of analysis in this essay. Population totals for the county Down parts of the eight poor law unions are presented in table 15.2. Barony totals are also given for the sake of completeness in table 15.3. There was little difference between the county totals in the period from 1841 to 1891 based on either unions or baronies: throughout there was a small surplus in favour of the latter.

Table 15.2 shows that during the Famine decade from 1841 to 1851, all unions except Belfast shed population. County Down as a whole lost roughly 10 per cent of its population. Of the nine counties of Ulster, the population of county Antrim (excluding Belfast) also fell by 10 per cent as a direct consequence of the Great Famine; at the other extreme, Cavan and Monaghan, in the west of the province, both suffered losses of around 30 per cent.[4] In county Down the biggest falls during the Famine decade were experienced by the relatively remote unions of Kilkeel, Downpatrick and Banbridge, and the smallest by the unions that abutted areas of urban growth.

After 1851 the population of the county continued to decline, albeit at a slower rate. Nevertheless, all the county Down unions, apart from Belfast, continued to lose population until 1891. Thereafter, in Newtownards union there was a modest recovery of roughly 3,000 over the next twenty years. The populations of Kilkeel and Newry unions also increased slightly between 1891 and 1901 (by 3,400 between them), before falling again by 2,100 in the next decade. In general, the smallest falls over the period from 1841 to 1911, were sustained by the unions in the north and the south of the county and the largest losses occurred in the centre. The exception was Lisburn union where the rural part of the union (i.e. the part in county Down) lost population to the town of Lisburn which doubled in size (from 6,200 to 12,400) between 1841 and 1911.

The presence of Belfast in the northern corner of the county slightly complicates any discussion of population change in the county as a whole. Table 15.4 shows that the geographical area of the Belfast barony fluctuated as the boundaries of the city were periodically redrawn. The barony population, on the other hand, increased during every decade between 1841 and 1891. The union population increased throughout the nineteenth century, with the exception of the aberration in 1861 caused by a mistake made by the census commissioners. The population totals for Belfast poor law union suggest that we should add around 15,000 to the county population in 1841 and 57,000 in 1891. Thereafter, because of a re-alignment of the boundaries of Belfast in 1898, the addition to the county total in 1901 and 1911 should be around 10,000. These additions make little difference to the general picture of a falling population, although they moderate the rate of decline, particularly before 1900.

As the population of the county fell, so the density declined (see table 15.5). Overall, by 1911 the density of population in county Down was about 60 per cent of what it had been in 1841, but that figure was boosted by the Belfast union. The smallest decreases occurred in the Newtownards union where population density fell by a quarter, and in

Kilkeel and Newry where it was 40 per cent, or less. The biggest falls, of 45, 47, and 48 per cent were in the contiguous unions of Lisburn, Banbridge and Lurgan in the west of the county. Some of the rural population of the Lisburn and Lurgan unions were probably being sucked into the towns of those names, both of which lay outside the county and which grew in size during the period.

Some other features of the demographic picture are worth noting. Ages are available only at the county level and are set out in table 15.6. Over time, the average age of the population rose. In 1841, 38 per cent of the population was under 15 years of age and 5 per cent 65 or older. In 1911 the proportions were 30 per cent and 10 per cent. These changes were concentrated towards the end of the nineteenth century and were the cumulative product of long-term emigration and declining fertility.

Turning to sex ratios, during the second half of the century females outnumbered males in county Down. The largest female's surpluses were in the Newtownards and Newry unions (see table 15.7). There is little sign in county Down of the balance swinging towards a surplus of males before 1911 as it did in many western parts of Ireland. A move in favour of males, nevertheless, can be seen by concentrating attention on the population aged over 14. In county Down, the male/female ratio for the over-14 year olds rose from 0.79 in 1871 to 0.91 in 1911.[5]

Throughout the province of Ulster there were marked inter-county differences in the sex ratios, with the western counties exhibiting male surpluses by the beginning of the twentieth century. At the other extreme, the borough of Belfast had a substantial surplus of females. These differences reflected a general tendency throughout Ireland during the late-nineteenth and early-twentieth centuries for females to leave the countryside in greater numbers than males in order to find work in urban industry or domestic employment.[6] The relatively high proportion of males in the unions of Belfast, Lisburn and Lurgan – all on the fringes of developing industrial towns – were probably the result of females going to the towns in order to find work. The county Down sex ratios, in general, corresponded to the pattern found on the eastern side of Ulster which had the largest towns and the greatest proportion of non-agricultural jobs.

Down was one of the more urbanised counties of Ireland, even excluding the Belfast section. In 1841, 12.3 per cent of the population of county Down lived in towns of at least 2,000 people, compared with an Ulster average of 9.5 per cent. By 1911, 25.9 per cent of the county's population was urbanised. This figure was almost identical to those for counties Antrim (excluding Belfast) and Armagh but was exceeded in county Londonderry (36.3 per cent); at the other extreme, the proportions in Donegal were 3.8 per cent, in Cavan 6.5 per cent, and in Fermanagh 7.8 per cent.[7]

The towns of county Down were generally small (below 10,000) but most of them grew in size between 1841 and 1911. Table 15.8 shows the population of those towns that had populations exceeding 2,000 at some point during the period. Newry had been an important port in the early-nineteenth century but stagnated under the impact of competition from Belfast, although it more or less held on to its population. The trade of Donaghadee suffered even more severely from the development of Belfast (and of Larne in county Antrim) and Portaferry was another small port that lost much of its importance as the century progressed. Newtownards flourished as an important centre of regional trade and was stimulated by its proximity to Belfast. Downpatrick and Rathfriland, on the other hand, were not well located to benefit from the demands of Belfast. The remaining towns grew, either as linen-producing centres or as satellites of Belfast.

Finally, in this survey of demographic features, we turn to the denominational breakdown. During the later-nineteenth and early-twentieth centuries the proportion of Roman Catholics in the population was stable at just over 30 per cent for the whole county and the combined Protestant population just under 70 per cent.[8] Denominational distribution is available at the barony level for 1861 and is shown in table 15.9 and fig. 15.1. The highest Roman Catholic proportions were in baronies in the southern half of the county and the highest Presbyterian proportions were in the north. The Church of Ireland population was more evenly spread, except for a cluster in Iveagh Lower Upper in the west of county Down. These patterns had been created at the turn of the sixteenth and seventeenth centuries by English and Scottish settlement in east Ulster and have persisted ever since.[9]

The mechanics of demographic change

Population trends are the product of variations in fertility, mortality and migration. The first, fertility, is the outcome of changes in marriage behaviour, fecundity and fecundibility. Together, these three fs help to determine the birth rate, although the latter is influenced also by the age and sex structure of the population.

The birth rate, compiled from the registrar-general's statistics, is given for county Down for the period from 1864 to 1911 in table 15.10, together with those for Ulster, Belfast and Ireland as a whole. The quality of registration was poor in the years immediately after 1864 and the apparent rise in the county Down birth rate during the 1860s has more to do with the improvement in registration than any increase in

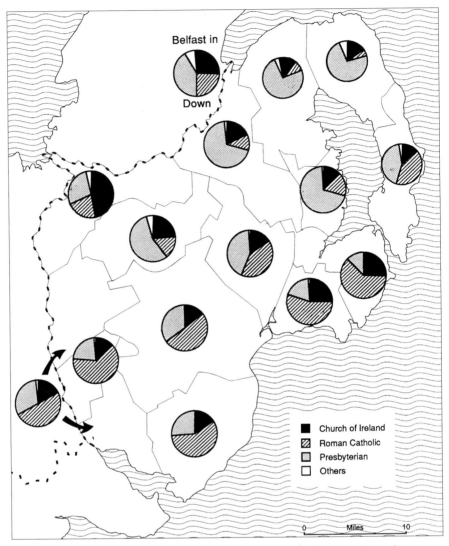

Belfast in

Down

Church of Ireland

Roman Catholic

Presbyterian

Others

0   Miles   10

Fig. 15.1   Denominational distribution by barony, 1861. (Source: Census).

the virility of the county's inhabitants.[10] The decline in the early-twentieth century was caused largely by the removal of Belfast (county Down) from the county figures. The Belfast birth rate was persistently above the county rate. Without Belfast, it is probable that the birth rate in county Down had been falling since 1880.

There are two issues relating to nuptiality in later nineteenth century Ireland that interest demographers. The first is the retreat from marriage after the Great Famine. A useful measure is to focus on the 45-54 age cohort, on the assumption that if a person had not married by then, he or she was likely to remain unmarried. It can be seen from table 15.11 that the proportion of males in this age band who were unmarried rose from 18 to 24 per cent between 1871 and 1911 and the proportion of females from 22 to 29 per cent. Comparable figures for earlier decades are difficult to calculate because different age cohorts were used, but in 1861 the proportions were probably around 14 per cent for males and 16 per cent for females. The proportions immediately before the Great Famine were probably little different.

As with so many measures, the Belfast poor law union is a special case. Until 1891 the proportion of males who remained single was low: such was the surplus of females in the city that men had little difficulty in finding marriage partners. Conversely, the proportion of unmarried females in Belfast aged 45-54 was substantially greater than that of males, although lower than in other poor law unions. The marked change after 1901 reflected the redrawing of boundaries in 1898 that left the remaining part of the Belfast union behaving like rural county Down. Elsewhere in the county the female proportion who remained unmarried was usually a point or two higher than the male, with a slight tendency for the gap to widen over time. Throughout the period from 1871 to 1911 Lisburn had a high proportion of unmarried adults, but the biggest changes over the period occurred in Downpatrick, where the male proportion of unmarrieds rose by 64 per cent and the female proportion by 38 per cent. The growing aversion by females in particular to marriage was important since their failure to enter the breeding population depressed general fertility, even though, among married women, fertility remained high. This proposition rests on the assumption that births – and for the most part conceptions – occurred within marriage. There is no evidence that county Down deviated in any degree from the general Irish pattern of low levels of illegitimacy.

The second issue that attracts demographers is an upward shift in the age at marriage. According to one version of Irish social history, the country was marked by widespread youthful marriage in the early nineteenth century and by a more restricted and elderly marriage regime at the end of the century. The Great Famine was the watershed dividing these two patterns; to mix the metaphor, the Great Famine was the trigger that propelled Ireland from the old pattern of young marriage to the new pattern of delayed marriage.[11] In reality, it is unlikely that marriage ages in pre-Famine Ireland were ever as low as the stereotype suggests, and in the east of Ireland the mean age at first marriage was already rising before 1845.

In the absence of direct information about ages at first marriage, a reasonable guess can be made by calculating the singulate mean age at marriage. This is done by examining the proportions of single and married males and females in successive age cohorts from 15-19 to 50-54.[12] Between 1871 and 1911 the singulate age for males rose by two years but scarcely shifted for females (see table 15.12). However, there were large upward movements in the female age in the Belfast and Lurgan unions. It is difficult to measure the singulate mean age for the years before 1871 because of the way that ages in the census data were grouped. Nevertheless, we can reorganise the age cohorts in the 1841 census to correspond approximately to the cohorts of later decades; this produces a singulate mean age at marriage of 28.0 years for males and 25.7 years for females. The calculations suggest that, if people in county Down had once married very young, they were already moving towards older marriages before the Famine, although we should remember that a relatively high mean age is perfectly compatible with a low modal age. The calculations also indicate that women in 1841 were then marrying, on average, two years younger than their granddaughters (or great granddaughters) did seventy years later. This may seem a small difference but it was enough to reduce completed fertility by up to one birth per family.

The consequences of the joint effects on general fertility of declining nuptiality and rising mean age at marriage can be simply illustrated. In 1911 completed family size in Ireland was 6.8.[13] This was high by comparison with other regions of western Europe at that time and also when compared with the experience of pre-contraceptive societies at earlier periods. In England, for example, women marrying at age 25 gave birth on average to six children over their reproductive lives.[14] Nevertheless, let us assume that in 1841, 84 out of every 100 women who lived to age 54, married and that they each produced eight children (i.e. one more than did their descendants in 1911). A cohort of 100 women, therefore, gave birth to 672 babies. In 1911, 71 per cent of women living to age 54, married and produced, on average, seven children: that is, a total of 497 children. General fertility measured in this way thus declined by 26 per cent.[15] Assuming a smaller completed family size of 7.5 in 1841 implies a fall in general fertility by 1911 of 21 per cent.

A decline in general fertility is perfectly consistent with a stable or even rising age-specific marital fertility rate; the former is determined mainly by the proportions of women staying out of or delaying entry into the breeding population whereas the latter is the outcome of the behaviour of couples within marriage. Marital fertility – defined as the number of births per 1,000 married women aged between 15 and 44 – remained high in Ireland during the later-nineteenth and early twentieth centuries. Indeed, in county Down, marital fertility increased by 6 per cent between 1871 and 1901.[16] This may have been the consequence of a sharp decline in emigration rates after 1891 leaving more of the young female breeding population at home. Alternatively there might have been changes in fecundity or fecundability working to keep marital fertility high, although it seems unlikely.

Fecundity refers to the physiological capability of a man, woman or couple to produce a live birth. R.E. Kennedy has argued that fecundity throughout Ireland rose during the post-Famine decades and that it increased still further in the twentieth century because of improvements in nutrition.[17] The argument is unconvincing. The potato-dominated diets widespread throughout Ireland before the Great Famine were nutritious and conducive to high fecundity. Hunger and starvation between 1845 and 1849 probably reduced fecundity by interrupting the menstrual cycle and lowering libido. As the Famine receded so nutritional status recovered in the short run and fecundity presumably rose. However, as the century progressed, nutritional standards fell rather than improved, although never to levels that impaired fecundity, as the population abandoned potatoes, oatmeal, and buttermilk in favour of white bread, sugar, tea and fatty American bacon.[18] Much more a threat to fecundity was the upward shift in the mean age at marriage since the ability of women to bear children falls with age. In short, once the trauma of the Great Famine was past, there are no grounds for believing that fecundity rose in county Down or anywhere else in Ireland.

Fecundability is a measure of the probability of conception in one menstrual cycle among women who menstruate regularly but who do not practise contraception. The chief influence here is the frequency of intercourse, although age, foetal mortality and post-partum non-susceptibility also have an effect. More reliable food supplies after the Famine possibly contributed to more regular menstruation and more frequent intercourse, but since the coital history of Ireland remains to be written we simply do not know. Studies in non-Irish societies reveal a considerable variation in fecundability that may or may not have existed in Ireland.

There remains a further possibility: the restriction of fertility within marriage. If it occurred, the most likely explanation was extended lactation. The potato and milk diets of the pre-Famine period had permitted early weaning. The shift away from potatoes and milk during the later-nineteenth century possibly resulted in babies being kept longer at the breast, in which case the period of post-partum non-susceptibility would be extended. Other forms of birth control, stopping short of mechanical devices, included abstinence. Ireland did not share in the demographic transition of the late-nineteenth century experienced in other parts of western Europe except in a very muted way.[19] We are left with the conclusion that general fertility in Ireland, and by implication in county Down also, declined because of a retreat from marriage rather than because of any measurable changes in reproductive behaviour within marriage.

The second demographic variable to consider is mortality. Death rates for county Down, Ulster, Belfast (including the greater part in county Antrim) and Newry are shown in table 15.13. The apparent increase between the 1860s and 1870s is of little moment since it reflects an improvement in registration and not a real change. Thereafter two features are noteworthy. The first is that mortality in county Down was higher than the Ulster average throughout the period. One reason for this was the relatively urbanised condition of the county, particularly that part of Belfast in county Down. It is noticeable that the exclusion of Belfast from the county average after 1901 reduces the county Down rate. The second feature is that between 1871 and 1911 (and probably between 1851 and 1911) the death rate remained stubbornly high. In the two decades before the Great Famine the all-Ireland death rate was 23 or 24 per 1,000, little different from that in England and Wales. During the Great Famine it rose to 53 per 1,000, and then dropped back, probably to around 18 or 20.[20] County Down mirrored these changes, although probably in a less extreme fashion. Thereafter death rates in Ireland showed little sign of falling, whereas in England and Wales the rate was 15.4 per 1,000 in 1901-11.

There are two likely reasons for the continuity of the death rates. The first is the ageing of the population. We have already noted that the population of county Down was growing older: a greater proportion was moving into the age bands that possessed the greatest propensities to die. The second was urbanisation. County Down had a greater share of town dwellers, even excluding the south-eastern fringes of Belfast, than many Irish counties. One of the risks of urban living was urban eating. Post-Famine Ireland experienced rising living standards but falling standards of nutrition as the old pre-Famine staples of potatoes and milk were discarded.

What did people die of? As table 15.14 shows, between 25 and 30 per cent of deaths annually were the result of tuberculosis and respiratory diseases, with comparatively little variation over time. Diarrhoea diseases, fevers, measles, whooping cough, and diphtheria brought the proportion to around one-third, with some tendency for the proportion to decline over time. The remaining deaths were caused by the ailments of old age, heart and circulatory problems, cancers, influenza, and the like.

The patterns revealed in table 15.14, particularly the importance of tuberculosis and respiratory diseases as killers, were similar to those found in other parts of the United Kingdom.[21] Tuberculosis was on the decline in Britain during the late-nineteenth century for reasons that are, even today, obscure, but which are probably related to improved living and nutritional standards.[22] In Ireland – and in county Down – deaths from tuberculosis remained high until 1900 and this may be linked with urban growth and a deterioration in diets. Any slight slack in tuberculosis deaths was taken up by other respiratory infections.

The other causes of death identified in table 15.14 reflect the concerns of the third quarter of the nineteenth century. This explains, for example, why smallpox appears in the table, even though it caused so few deaths. Compulsory vaccination after 1867 virtually eliminated what had once been a major killer.[23] During the 1860s and '70s smallpox still made its mark. There were at least 100 deaths in county Down during the first two years of – very defective – registration in 1864 and 1865. Between 1872 and 1875 there were 121 recorded smallpox deaths. Thereafter, years passed often with no smallpox fatalities. Between 1876 and 1911 there were only eleven years that experienced a total of thirty-four deaths from smallpox.

Deaths from typhus behaved in a similar way to those from smallpox: they were initially high and then dwindled away. Typhus and typhoid were distinguished in 1869 (before they had been grouped together by the registrar-general as 'fevers'). The former was a disease of hunger, poverty and crowding and conveyed from person to person by the body louse. Typhoid was a water-borne disease. Deaths from typhus in county Down numbered in the twenties and thirties a year during the 1870s, fell to single figures during the 1880s and '90s, and all but disappeared after 1900, when the Belfast statistics were separated from the county total. Diarrhoea and dysentery, whooping cough, scarlet fever, measles and diphtheria were principally diseases of childhood. Unfortunately the data do not permit the calculation of age-specific death rates from selected diseases at county level, but it is reasonable to assume that the prevalence of such afflictions were responsible for keeping infant and child mortality high.[24]

The third influence on population change is migration. County Down shared with other parts of Ireland losses of population during and after the Great Famine. The degree of poverty may have been less extreme than in other counties; against that, Belfast was an accessible and powerful attraction. In 1841 more than 5,500 inhabitants of Belfast had been born in the 'counties adjoining' (i.e. Antrim and Down) implying that these two counties were the reservoirs replenishing the city's population. Between 1841 and 1911 the census authorities, when identifying places of birth of people living in Belfast, grouped the city and counties Antrim and Down together; except for 1841, when the figure was 85 per cent, the proportion ranged from 73 to 78 per cent.[25]

Emigration statistics are even more frail than other demographic measures because of the manner by which they were gathered.[26] For this reason, Ó Gráda has devised a means of estimating emigration based on age-cohort depletion rates.[27] The results of applying that method to county Down, together with recorded emigration, are presented in table 15.15. There is not a great difference between the estimated and recorded rates, except in the decade 1891-1901 when, one suspects, the expansion of Belfast across the river Lagan made the northern part of the county an area of in-migration. The redrawing of the city's boundaries after 1898 removed this distorting influence. The recorded figures also demonstrate a cyclical pattern of emigration, whereas the rates derived from cohort analysis show that there was a gradual tapering away of emigration from the high levels of the post-famine decade.

Emigration rates from county Down were in line with those for Ulster as a whole, although lower than those found in the west of the province, especially in the earlier years. We cannot be sure where the men and women who left the county went, except that many of them found their eldorados in Belfast rather than in Liverpool or Boston.

Influences on demographic change

The consequences of birth, death and emigration in county Down are summarised in table 15.16. A gently declining birth rate, a more or less constant death rate, and an emigration rate that halved over fifty years, created a demographic deficit in the decades during and after the Great Famine. Individuals can choose whether or not to enter the breeding population, and whether to stay put or to pull up their roots and quit the places of their birth, although they have less control over the manner and time of their dying. Fertility and emigration rates were the products of personal decisions. But behind these human events were economic and social forces making for change. This final section considers, briefly, a few of the broader influences on personal behaviour.

A simple economic explanation of the persistent decline of population in county Down after 1851 is that the county slowly lost one of its more labour-intensive occupations. Around the time of the Great Famine, agriculture had accounted for roughly 36 per cent of the recorded occupations in the county. By 1891 the proportion had fallen to 31 per cent. In the early twentieth century the figure apparently rose to 37 per cent, but this was because the extension of the boundaries of

Belfast removed a substantial chunk of industrial employment from county Down.[28] It may also be the case that the fall in the emigration rate at the end of the nineteenth century actually swelled the numbers of people seeking their living from the land.

The proportion of the population employed in farming tells only part of the story of the upheavals in rural society. After the Great Famine there were important changes in the structure of agriculture and a decline in the numbers and proportions of farm labourers. In 1841 there had been 186 farm workers to every 100 farmers in the county; by 1911 there were only 125, as farmers came to rely, increasingly, on family labour rather than hired help.[29] Accompanying these developments were changes in the composition of farm output. These are summarised in table 15.17. Between 1852 and 1911 the acreage under grain halved while that under potatoes declined substantially after 1861. On the other hand the area of land used for animal feed and rearing livestock increased. Except for the very substantial increase in poultry numbers, farming in county Down was shifting away from those forms of production that generated large-scale employment. Between 1852 and 1871, to take another measure, the number of small holdings of five acres or fewer declined by 14 per cent.[30]

What were the labourers surplus to agricultural needs to do? There was, of course, industry. Domestic spinning and weaving of linen had been an important prop of the rural economy for generations, but the mechanisation of linen manufacture from the end of the 1820s pulled production into the towns, most of which lay beyond the borders of county Down. Belfast offered higher earnings as well as the less tangible pleasures of urban life. It was easy to get to and it readily soaked up the diminishing surpluses between births and deaths.[31] County Down was more prosperous in the second half of the nineteenth century than counties in the west of the province. Nevertheless, in the decades before Partition it could not hold sufficient of its population to prevent the persistent fall in numbers.

We have identified here only economic influences on population trends. But there were others. More than thirty years ago K. H. Connell stressed psychological and institutional forces in post-Famine Ireland leading to an apparent aversion to marriage.[32] Much earlier, writing of rural-urban population movements in late nineteenth-century England, Sir John Clapham reflected on 'Buckingham men immobile in vale and beechwood, and Oxfordshire men tied, by affection surely not by inertia, to the valleys of the Windrush and the Evenlode'.[33] County Down had its own vales and woods, its drumlins and its Mournes to hold the affections of its men and women. There were influences on marriage and migration beyond those of economic calculus. Without them, perhaps, county Down might have lost even more of its people between 1841 and 1911 than in fact it did.

Ultimately demographic history is the product of the decisions of hundreds of thousands of individuals to marry, to raise children, to stay close to their roots, or to seek the allures of green fields – or grimy streets – in distant parts. By 1911 individuals even had some control over the manner of their dying, since the greater prosperity that accompanied the population decline of the second half of the nineteenth century gave them more choice in the ways of their eating, living and working. The consequences of such choices became even more obvious during the twentieth century.

APPENDIX

TABLE 15.1

Population change in Ulster 1841-1911 (1841=100)[34]

Year	Antrim	Armagh	Belfast	Cavan	Donegal	Down	Fermanagh	Londonderry	Monaghan	Tyrone
1841	100	100	100	100	100	100	100	100	100	100
1911	68	52	516	37	57	55	40	64	36	46

TABLE 15.2

Population change in county Down, by poor law union, 1841-1911

		POPULATION							
Poor law union	Area	1841	1851	1861	1871	1881	1891	1901	1911
Banbridge, county Down	107,139	72,387	63,762	61,398	56,259	47,569	40,598	36,206	34,381
Belfast, county Down	*	15,522	15,607	8,276	27,275	36,237	57,264	8,045	9,245
Downpatrick	147,360	77,167	63,770	57,969	54,644	49,139	43,236	38,869	39,196
Kilkeel	81,829	28,638	24,761	22,614	21,426	19,877	18,181	19,131	18,077
Lisburn, county Down	71,642	44,626	40,489	38,505	33,062	29,345	26,574	21,203	20,070
Lurgan, county Down	27,274	22,099	21,221	20,535	18,213	15,286	12,981	11,022	10,550
Newry, county Down	65,557	47,419	42,283	36,577	34,339	31,733	26,989	29,493	28,444
Newtownards	93,850	60,285	56,861	53,428	48,231	42,921	41,286	41,920	44,340
Total		368,143	328,754	299,302	293,449	283,439	267,109	205,889	204,303
Total, excl. Belfast		352,621	313,147	291,026	266,174	235,870	209,845	197,844	195,058

* See Table 15.3.

	INDEX							
	1841	1851	1861	1871	1881	1891	1901	1911
Banbridge, county Down	100.0	88.1	84.8	77.7	65.7	56.1	50.0	47.5
Downpatrick	100.0	82.6	75.1	70.8	63.7	56.0	50.4	50.8
Kilkeel	100.0	86.5	79.0	74.8	69.4	63.5	66.8	63.1
Lisburn, county Down	100.0	90.7	86.3	74.1	65.8	59.5	47.5	45.0
Lurgan, county Down	100.0	96.0	92.9	82.4	69.2	58.7	49.9	47.7
Newry, county Down	100.0	89.2	77.1	72.4	66.9	56.9	62.2	60.0
Newtownards	100.0	94.3	88.6	80.0	71.2	68.5	69.5	73.6
Total	100.0	89.3	81.3	79.7	77.0	72.6	55.9	55.5
Total, excl. Belfast	100.0	88.8	82.5	75.5	66.95	9.5	56.1	55.3

TABLE 15.3

Population change in county Down by barony, 1841-1891

	1841	1851	1861	1871	1881	1891
Ards	46875	–	–	–	–	
Ards Lower	–	28519	27458	24258	21598	21564
Ards Upper	–	15650	13988	12639	10980	10164
Belfast, county Down	6697	7936	9378	16155	23917	43051
Castlereagh Lower	27567	25312	25375	26893	26048	27256
Castlereagh Upper	32252	28795	26703	24086	21893	20031
Dufferin	9410	7504	7721	7916	7221	6030
Iveagh Lower	70146	–	–	–	–	–
Iveagh Lower Lower	–	26364	25932	23239	19787	17003
Iveagh Lower Upper	–	38889	·37021	32113	26749	23273
Iveagh Upper	87349	–	–	–	–	–
Iveagh Upper Lower	–	39814	36854	33707	28485	24102
Iveagh Upper Upper	–	35147	31519	29725	26826	22997
Kinelarty	20895	17050	15594	13944	12398	10947
Lecale	31776	–	–	–	–	–
Lecale Lower	–	10467	9084	8512	7662	6459
Lecale Upper	–	15638	14033	13255	12172	10973
Lordship Of Newry	18907	17843	14950	14419	14680	12337
Mourne	16269	13825	13070	12588	11691	10872
Total	368143	328753	308680	293449	272107	267059
Total, excl. Belfast	361446	320817	299302	277294	248190	224008

TABLE 15.4

Population of Belfast in county Down, 1841-1911

Year	Barony area (acres)	Barony population	PLU area (acres)	PLU population
1841	576	6697	16477	15522
1851	576	7936	16477	15607
1861	1319	9378	15157	17654a
1871	1668	16155	17033	27275
1881	1668	23917	17033	36237
1891	1668	43051	17033	57264
1901			12602	8045
1911			12609	9245

a   This figure includes the population of the electoral district of Ballymaccarret, which was on the county Down side of the River Lagan and which in 1861 was erroneously excluded from the county Down portion of the PLU.

TABLE 15.5

Population density by poor law union. 1841-1911 (population per acre)

Union	1841	1851	1861	1871	1881	1891	1901	1911
Banbridge	0.68	0.60	0.57	0.53	0.44	0.38	0.34	0.32
Belfast	0.94	0.95	0.55	1.60	2.13	3.36	0.64	0.73
Downpatrick	0.52	0.43	0.39	0.37	0.33	0.29	0.26	0.27
Kilkeel	0.35	0.30	0.28	0.26	0.24	0.22	0.23	0.22
Lisburn	0.62	0.56	0.54	0.46	0.41	0.37	0.30	0.28
Lurgan	0.81	0.78	0.75	0.67	0.56	0.48	0.40	0.39
Newry	0.72	0.64	0.56	0.52	0.48	0.41	0.45	0.43
Newtownards	0.64	0.61	0.57	0.51	0.46	0.44	0.45	0.47
Total	0.66	0.61	0.53	0.62	0.63	0.74	0.38	0.39

TABLE 15.6

Age cohorts, county Down, 1841-1911

Age cohort		1841	1851	1861	1871	1881	1901	1911
					Year			
Under 1	Males	4343	3738	3532	3326	2425	2022	1972
	Females	4140	3677	3529	3282	2344	1973	2003
1-4	Males	18464	14001	14767	13530	11428	8654	8247
	Females	17872	13405	14208	13338	10780	8346	8037
5-9	Males	23179	19398	17069	16306	14238	10545	10365
	Females	22640	18769	16640	15608	13897	10196	10142
10-14	Males	22658	20327	16070	15866	14632	10640	10301
	Females	21949	19622	15458	14963	13942	10081	9819
15-19	Males	19203	17600	15178	12980	12405	9704	9654
	Females	20811	19758	17240	14358	13096	10080	9484
20-24	Males	14858	13639	12366	9467	9202	8307	7998
	Females	18389	17746	16995	13011	11825	10170	8896
25-29	Males	11951	9875	8907	9467	6687	6953	6531
	Females	14449	12627	12753	13011	9314	9021	8343
30-34	Males	9253	8918	7995	7727	6185	6274	6503
	Females	12625	10963	10657	10524	8432	7574	7453
35-39	Males	8149	7752	6433	6268	5630	5385	6118
	Females	9222	8771	7821	8137	7289	6251	7117
40-44	Males	9339	8410	7522	6577	6587	5346	5592
	Females	11103	9530	9056	8237	8634	6166	6350
45-49	Males	6570	5872	6217	5371	4934	4395	4817
	Females	7185	6351	6950	6333	5952	5167	5282
50-54	Males	6816	7421	6949	6301	5695	4726	4490

TABLE 15.6 *(Continued)*

Age cohorts, county Down, 1841-1911

		Year						
	Females	8022	8370	7698	7214	6744	5716	4972
55-59	Males	4414	4088	4366	4671	3667	3510	3529
	Females	4665	4512	4525	4873	4136	3925	3799
60-64	Males	4884	4736	5864	5272	4756	4297	3244
	Females	5976	5845	6594	5919	5500	5143	3572
65-69	Males	2587	2481	2630	5272	2801	2469	3069
	Females	2822	2738	2954	5919	2991	2773	3574
70-74	Males	2487	2205	2589	3095	2771	2339	2996
	Females	2749	2617	2941	3530	3040	2698	4056
75-79	Males	1354	1084	1321	1357	1560	1163	1489
	Females	1362	1245	1405	1512	1481	1296	2036
80-84	Males	978	783	875	977	1028	806	695
	Females	1281	1023	1146	1161	1300	1009	951
85-89	Males	232	237	235	316	257	248	247
	Females	295	279	294	330	269	299	329
90-94	Males	96	83	86	88	95	73	82
	Females	118	111	137	129	113	106	111
95-99	Males	34	24	23	31	22	10	12
	Females	46	39	47	48	31	25	20
100 plus	Males	0	4	15	5	6	5	0
	Females	1	12	13	13	11	5	6

TABLE 15.7

Male-female ratios 1841-1911

Union	1841	1851	1861	1871	1881	1891	1901	1911
Banbridge	0.94	0.94	0.92	0.90	0.90	0.89	0.88	0.92
Belfast	0.90	0.89	0.85	0.86	0.91	0.91	0.95	1.01
Downpatrick	0.91	0.89	0.85	0.87	0.89	0.90	0.91	0.96
Kilkeel	0.92	0.87	0.87	0.88	0.88	0.90	0.99	0.94
Lisburn	0.98	0.95	0.94	0.93	0.93	0.93	0.96	0.94
Lurgan	0.99	1.00	0.99	1.00	0.96	0.96	0.95	0.96
Newry	0.91	0.91	0.88	0.89	0.89	0.88	0.87	0.90
Newtownards	0.87	0.86	0.83	0.85	0.86	0.86	0.86	0.86
County average	0.93	0.91	0.89	0.90	0.90	0.90	0.92	0.94

TABLE 15.8

Population of towns in county Down, 1841-1911[35]

Towns	1841	1851	1861	1871	1881	1891	1901	1911
Banbridge	3324	3301	4033	5600	5609	4901	5006	5101
Bangor	3116	2849	2531	2560	3006	3834	5903	7776
Comber	1964	1790	1713	2006	2165	2051	2095	2589
Donaghadee	3151	2821	2671	2226	1861	1886	2073	2213
Dromore	2110	1862	2531	2408	2491	2359	2307	2364
Gilford	643	2814	2892	2720	1324	1276	1199	1117
Holywood	1532	1408	2437	3573	3293	3389	3840	4035
Newry	11972	13435	12179	13364	14808	12961	12405	11963
Newtownards	7621	9566	9542	9562	8676	9197	9110	9587
Portaferry	2107	2074	1960	1938	1647	1624	1514	1518
Rathfriland	2183	2053	1916	1827	1572	1461	1294	1365

TABLE 15.9

Denominational distribution by barony, 1861

	Church of Ireland	Roman Catholic	Presbyterian	Other
Ards Lower	15.0%	5.7%	72.7%	6.6%
Ards Upper	12.9%	41.4%	43.1%	2.6%
Belfast	27.2%	24.2%	41.3%	7.3%
Castlereagh Lower	13.5%	8.4%	74.3%	3.8%
Castlereagh Upper	17.8%	11.1%	69.0%	2.1%
Dufferin	12.3%	17.0%	69.4%	1.3%
Iveagh Lower Lower	22.8%	15.7%	56.1%	5.3%
Iveagh Lower Upper	46.6%	21.5%	28.0%	3.8%
Iveagh Upper Lower	13.7%	51.5%	34.3%	0.5%
Iveagh Upper Upper	16.6%	50.2%	31.5%	1.7%
Kinelarty	15.7%	40.1%	43.1%	1.1%
Lecale Lower	25.4%	61.7%	12.6%	0.3%
Lecale Upper	25.4%	55.1%	18.5%	1.0%
Lordship of Newry	13.0%	63.3%	22.4%	1.4%
Mourne	14.4%	58.3%	26.6%	0.7%

TABLE 15.10

Birth rates per thousand, 1861-1911[36]

	1864-71	1871-81	1881-91	1891-1901	1901-11
County Down	24.8	26.2	25.4	26.6	22.7
Ulster	26.3	25.4	22.3	22.4	22.6
Belfast		33.1	30.7	32.9	30.6
Ireland		26.2	22.8	22.1	22.4

TABLE 15.11

The proportion of the population aged 45-54 who remained unmarried

Union	1871 Males	1871 Females	1881 Males	1881 Females	1891 Males	1891 Females	1901 Males	1901 Females	1911 Males	1911 Females
Banbridge	21.78%	21.22%	20.48%	22.58%	20.43%	24.36%	24.00%	26.80%	24.90%	30.65%
Belfast	6.22%	16.90%	7.86%	16.05%	7.40%	13.76%	18.98%	27.83%	16.49%	25.93%
Downpatrick	18.61%	22.80%	24.08%	29.92%	24.99%	30.33%	30.11%	33.45%	30.64%	31.43%
Kilkeel	18.52%	20.39%	19.26%	24.47%	22.88%	26.03%	22.14%	26.23%	21.06%	25.38%
Lisburn	24.68%	24.09%	21.49%	23.22%	20.24%	24.70%	26.17%	30.43%	26.81%	30.86%
Lurgan	18.77%	18.42%	21.63%	20.00%	25.35%	17.36%	23.41%	25.39%	22.24%	29.41%
Newry	20.28%	21.78%	21.37%	23.21%	25.02%	26.40%	27.76%	26.99%	27.47%	26.65%
Newtownards	16.14%	27.14%	15.63%	25.73%	16.77%	25.05%	17.41%	27.26%	18.45%	28.13%
Average	18.12%	21.59%	18.98%	23.15%	20.38%	23.50%	23.75%	28.05%	23.51%	28.55%

TABLE 15.12

Singulate mean age at marriage, 1871 and 1911

Union	1871 males	1871 females	1911 males	1911 females
Banbridge	28.6	27.6	30.7	27.7
Belfast	27.3	25.6	30.3	28.0
Downpatrick	29.7	30.2	30.6	27.2
Kilkeel	30.2	29.0	32.0	27.7
Lisburn	27.7	27.2	29.4	27.3
Lurgan	28.7	22.8	30.6	28.3
Newry	29.3	27.4	30.7	28.4
Newtownards	27.9	27.2	29.3	27.3
County Down	28.5	27.5	30.5	27.6

TABLE 15.13

Death rates county Down, Ulster, Belfast and Newry (per 1000)[37]

	1864-71	1871-81	1881-91	1891-1901	1901-11
County Down	16.3	19.4	19.1	19.4	18.0a
Ulster	15.9	17.4	17.2	18.4	17.7
Belfast		24.1	23.5	23.4	20.0
Newry		18.6	18.7	19.6	19.2

a Excluding Belfast.

TABLE 15.14

Causes of death, county Down, 1875-1910[38]

Year	TB	Respiratory diseases	Diarrhoea & dysentery	Whooping cough	Scarlet fever	Measles	Diphtheria	Typhus	Smallpox	Sum
1875	14.2%	12.1%	1.8%	1.7%	6.6%	1.3%	0.6%	0.4%	0.2%	38.7
1876	15.2%	13.8%	1.9%	1.9%	2.5%	0.6%	0.5%	0.5%	0.0%	36.9%
1877	15.2%	14.4%	1.8%	1.0%	2.1%	1.0%	0.5%	0.7%	0.0%	36.8%
1878	14.8%	12.4%	1.6%	1.3%	1.7%	0.5%	0.5%	0.2%	0.1%	33.0%
1879	12.8%	16.1%	0.9%	1.4%	1.1%	0.1%	0.2%	0.3%	0.0%	33.0%
1880	15.0%	12.9%	2.0%	2.6%	0.6%	0.3%	0.5%	0.2%	0.0%	34.0%
1881	15.0%	14.3%	1.5%	2.2%	0.3%	0.4%	0.7%	0.2%	0.0%	34.4%
1882	15.8%	13.5%	2.0%	0.5%	1.5%	0.7%	0.4%	0.3%	0.2%	34.6%
1883	12.8%	15.3%	1.6%	1.7%	5.0%	0.7%	0.4%	0.1%	0.0%	37.6%
1884	15.3%	14.1%	1.4%	1.8%	1.5%	0.1%	0.3%	0.2%	0.0%	34.6%
1885	15.0%	16.0%	1.9%	1.3%	1.0%	2.1%	0.4%	0.1%	0.0%	37.7%
1886	15.7%	15.2%	2.2%	1.2%	0.6%	0.1%	0.3%	0.1%	0.0%	35.4%
1887	13.7%	16.9%	2.6%	2.2%	1.5%	0.4%	0.3%	0.1%	0.0%	37.6%
1888	13.6%	16.6%	1.5%	1.8%	0.8%	2.7%	0.8%	0.1%	0.0%	37.9%
1889	13.7%	15.5%	2.2%	1.5%	0.3%	0.8%	0.6%	0.1%	0.0%	34.8%
1890	13.4%	15.0%	1.5%	1.5%	0.2%	1.7%	0.8%	0.1%	0.0%	34.1%
1891	13.2%	17.2%	1.7%	2.0%	0.2%	0.3%	0.5%	0.1%	0.0%	35.2%
1892	12.4%	16.4%	2.1%	2.3%	0.3%	2.9%	0.6%	0.1%	0.0%	37.0%
1893	13.0%	15.7%	4.0%	1.0%	0.6%	1.0%	0.8%	0.0%	0.0%	36.3%
1894	12.3%	15.8%	2.4%	2.3%	0.7%	3.1%	1.0%	0.2%	0.0%	37.7%
1895	12.7%	16.3%	3.9%	1.4%	0.7%	1.1%	0.5%	0.0%	0.1%	36.7%
1896	14.4%	14.5%	3.1%	1.6%	1.5%	1.5%	0.7%	0.1%	0.0%	37.4%
1897	13.2%	15.9%	3.2%	2.8%	0.5%	0.8%	0.5%	0.0%	0.0%	36.9%
1898	13.0%	15.6%	3.9%	1.0%	0.2%	0.6%	0.8%	0.0%	0.0%	35.2%
1899	12.3%	16.7%	3.6%	1.3%	0.5%	0.8%	0.9%	0.0%	0.0%	36.1%
1900	11.9%	16.8%	3.3%	1.2%	0.4%	0.9%	0.9%	0.0%	0.0%	35.5%
1901	11.5%	15.2%	2.4%	0.7%	0.2%	0.7%	0.7%	0.0%	0.0%	31.5%
1902	12.6%	16.3%	1.4%	1.2%	0.2%	0.3%	0.4%	0.0%	0.0%	32.5%
1903	13.1%	14.7%	1.3%	1.0%	0.1%	1.8%	0.5%	0.0%	0.0%	32.5%
1904	12.1%	15.7%	1.5%	2.0%	0.2%	0.2%	0.6%	0.0%	0.2%	32.3%
1905	12.7%	13.7%	1.2%	1.3%	0.4%	0.8%	0.4%	0.1%	0.0%	30.6%
1906	12.4%	13.8%	1.4%	1.4%	0.6%	0.6%	1.4%	0.0%	0.0%	31.7%
1907	10.4%	19.0%	0.8%	0.6%	0.1%	0.4%	0.6%	0.0%	0.0%	31.8%
1908	10.5%	15.5%	0.8%	0.6%	0.2%	1.0%	1.1%	0.1%	0.0%	29.8%
1909	10.1%	15.3%	0.8%	0.9%	0.2%	0.1%	0.7%	0.2%	0.0%	28.4%
1910	9.0%	15.8%	1.1%	2.6%	0.4%	0.7%	0.8%	0.0%	0.0%	30.4%
Average	13.2%	15.3%	2.0%	1.5%	1.0%	0.9%	0.6%	0.1%	0.0%	34.6%

TABLE 15.15

Recorded and estimated emigration rates (per 1000) from county Down, 1851-1911[39]

	1851-61	1861-71	1871-81	1881-91	1891-1901	1900-11
Recorded	15.5	9.8	11.9	10.0	3.6	7.7
Estimated	14.4	13.7	13.4	12.6	10.3	6.3

TABLE 15.16

The balance of birth, death and emigration, 1864-1911

	1864-71	1871-81	1881-91	1891-1901	1901-11
Birth rate	+24.8	+26.2	+25.4	+26.6	+22.7
Death rate	–16.3	–19.4	–19.1	–19.4	–18.0
Emigration rate	–13.7	–13.4	–12.6	–10.3	– 6.3
Balance	– 5.2	– 6.5	– 6.3	– 3.1	– 1.6

TABLE 15.17

The composition of farm output, 1852-1911[40]

Year	1852	1861	1871	1881	1891	1901	1911
Grain, acres	237218	227388	206256	167536	145992	130706	113867
Potatoes, acres	64636	87953	86710	70747	64934	54665	52156
Flax, acres	26033	34636	32585	34218	14754	10924	15867
Meadow, hay, fodder, forage crops, acres	70815	84911	112032	113922	115734	121192	129831
Cattle, numbers	163580	175752	189888	180378	211429	223150	162828
Sheep, pigs, goats, numbers	139976	126049	170664	130969	311955	201933	207003
Horses, etc., numbers	43835	49554	44784	46857	49108	55878	52670
Poultry, numbers	546697	573900	683901	888288	1015139	1463981	1900276

References

1. Liam Kennedy, 'Colonialism, religion and nationalism: an introduction' in Liam Kennedy (ed.), *Colonialism, religion and nationalism in Ireland* (Belfast, 1996), p. xi.

2. Joel Mokyr and Cormac Ó Gráda, 'New developments in Irish population history' in *Economic History Review*, 2nd series, xxxvii (1984), pp 475-6.

3. Full references to the censuses are not given here. They can be found in W. E. Vaughan and A. J. Fitzpatrick (ed.), *Irish historical statistics: population, 1821-1971* (Dublin, 1978).

4. L. A. Clarkson, 'Population change and urbanization 1821-1911' in Liam Kennedy and Philip Ollerenshaw (ed.), *An economic history of Ulster, 1820-1940* (Manchester, 1985), p. 139.

5. B. M. Walsh, 'Marriage rates and population pressure: Ireland, 1871 and 1911' in *Economic History Review*, 2nd series, xxiii (1970), p. 155.

6. Vaughan and Fitzpatrick, *Irish historical statistics*, pp 10-13; R. E. Kennedy, Jr., *The Irish; emigration, marriage and fertility* (London, 1975), p. 69.

7. Clarkson, in Kennedy and Ollerenshaw, *Economic history*, p. 140.

8. Ibid., p. 155.

9. Raymond Gillespie, *Colonial Ulster: the settlement of east Ulster 1600-1641* (Cork, 1985), pp 57-63; Philip Robinson, *The plantation of Ulster: British settlement in an Irish landscape, 1600-1670* (Dublin, 1984), pp 42-50.

10. Walsh, 'Marriage rates and population pressure', p. 150.

11. The arguments are summarised by L. A. Clarkson, 'Marriage and fertility in nineteenth-century Ireland' in R. B. Outhwaite (ed.), *Marriage and society: studies in the social history of marriage* (London, 1981), pp 237-55.

12. The technique is described in John Hajnal, 'Age at marriage and populations marrying' in *Population Studies*, vii (1953), pp 111-36.

13. Liam Kennedy and L.A. Clarkson, 'Birth, death and exile: Irish population history, 1700-1921' in B. J. Graham and L. J. Proudfoot (ed.), *An historical geography of Ireland* (London, 1993), p. 169.

14. For a general discussion see E. A. Wrigley and R. S. Schofield, *The population history of England 1541-1871* (London, 1981), pp 228-36, 254-7. See also Roland Pressat, *The dictionary of demography*, ed. by Christopher Wilson (Oxford, 1988), p. 37.

15. This is not a conventional way of measuring general fertility. See Pressat, *Dictionary*, pp 81-2.

16. Clarkson, in Kennedy and Ollerenshaw, *Economic history*, p. 150.

17. R. E. Kennedy, *The Irish*, pp 177-9.

18. Kennedy and Clarkson, *Economic history*, p. 171. Dietary changes are discussed more fully in L.A. Clarkson and E. Margaret Crawford, *Food in Ireland, 1600-1920: a social history*, Oxford, forthcoming.

19. Kennedy and Clarkson, 'Birth, death and exile', pp 163-4, 168-9.

20. Ibid., p. 171.

21. Compare Michael Flinn (ed.), *Scottish population history from the seventeenth century to the 1930s* (Cambridge, 1977), pp 398-9.

22. For a brief discussion see Robert Woods, *The population of Britain in the nineteenth century* (London, 1992), pp 61-7.

23. F. F. Cartwright, *A social history of medicine* (London, 1977), p. 90.

24. See Kennedy and Clarkson, 'Birth, death and exile', p. 172; Flinn, *Scottish population history* , pp 404-5; F.B. Smith, *The people's health 1830-1910* (London, 1979), pp 65-6, 85-111.

25. *Census of Ireland, 1911. Province of Ulster* (London, 1912). City of Belfast, table xxv, p. 31.

26. S. H. Cousens, 'The regional variations in population changes in Ireland, 1861-1881' in *Economic History Review*, 2nd series, xvii (1964), p. 307.

27. Cormac Ó Gráda, 'Some aspects of nineteenth-century Irish emigration' in L. M. Cullen and T. C. Smout (ed.), *Comparative aspects of Scottish and Irish economic and social history 1600-1900* (Edinburgh, no date [1977]), pp 65-73.

28. These proportions are derived from the census data contained in the database of Irish Historical Statistics. They have to be treated with caution because of changes in the methods of classification over time; in particular the occupational figures for 1861 and 1871 (not included here) were gathered in a different manner from preceding years. The proportions given in the text are robust enough for our purposes.

29. David Fitzpatrick, 'The disappearance of the Irish agricultural labourer, 1841-1912' in *Irish Economic and Social History*, vii (1980), p. 88.

30. All these figures are derived from the agricultural statistics stored in the database of Irish Historical Statistics, Q.U.B.

31. See Liam Kennedy, 'The rural economy' in Kennedy and Ollerenshaw, *Economic history*, pp 5-10, 44-48; and Philip Ollerenshaw, in Kennedy and Ollerenshaw, *Economic history*, pp 69-79.

32. K. H. Connell, 'Catholicism and marriage in the century after the Famine' in K. H. Connell, *Irish peasant society: four historical essays* (Oxford, 1968), pp 114-7.

33. Sir John Clapham, *An economic history of modern Britain, iii, Machines and national rivalries (1887-1914)* (Cambridge, 1938), p. 98.

34. Adapted from Clarkson, in Kennedy and Ollerenshaw, *Economic history*, p. 135.

35. Vaughan and Fitzpatrick, *Irish historical statistics*, pp 28-9.

36. Clarkson in Kennedy and Ollerenshaw, *Economic history*, p. 149; R. E. Kennedy, Jr., *The Irish*, p. 213. Note that registration of births, deaths and marriages did not commence until 1864.

37. Clarkson, in Kennedy and Ollerenshaw, *Economic history*, p. 148.

38. This table is based on the detailed analysis of the tables of the registrar-general carried out by my colleague, Dr Margaret Crawford.
39. Clarkson, in Kennedy and Ollerenshaw, *Economic history,* p. 146.
40. This table is constructed from the agricultural statistics for Ireland held in the database of Irish Historical Statistics.

Chapter 16

THE HERRING INDUSTRY IN COUNTY DOWN 1840-1940

VIVIENNE L. POLLOCK

As a hunting activity based on the extraction of a renewable food resource from its natural habitat, the seafishing industry has certain individual characteristics which local studies help to define. Historically, commercial seafishing functioned with little regard to regional or national boundaries. Production was governed by sea-based effort, with access to the fishing grounds determined by the audacity and competence of fishermen. The disposal of catches was similarly sea-defined: the distance from the fisheries to the quayside markets was one of the central factors in the organisation of distribution networks. Because the economic success of seafishing ventures was supported by structures of remarkable geographic fluidity, their local progress was underpinned by an extremely complex relationship of cause and effect. In county Down as elsewhere, changes in local circumstances were often initiated by events in fisheries far away.

This chapter examines the nature and composition of the herring industry in county Down during the hundred years after the Famine, a period of enormous change within the commercial seafisheries as a whole as new technologies developed, and new markets and new patterns of demand emerged for fresh and processed fish. The ways in which these innovations became part of the local fabric of seafishing depended ultimately on the combination of chance and common practise which provided the traditional framework for local fishery pursuits. This framework was itself shaped by wider forces. Chief amongst these were the opportunities offered by accessible resources. These determined not only what type of fish were available but also when, where and in what manner catches were won and fish landed and sold. We begin, therefore, with a brief analysis of the adjacent maritime ecology and its potential for the establishment of an economically viable fishery enterprise.

The maritime resource
The population and species dispersal of fish stocks is primarily

determined at base by factors of marine ecology: by water depth, salinity and temperature; by the physical properties of the seabed; and by the abundance of food, the basis for which in a saltwater environment is phytoplankton. In the north-east Atlantic, these factors combined to produce a fertile and varying marine habitat supporting vast numbers of the world's most important commercial food fishes. Ireland as a whole enjoyed a prime position in relation to this unrivalled resource base. The existence of a narrow surrounding continental shelf meant that Irish fishing boats did not have to travel far to reach marginal ocean areas where deep-water fish like ling and hake could be taken alongside shallower-water species like cod and haddock. To the east lay the Irish Sea, a region of traditional richness with a long-standing reputation as a breeding ground for plaice. The rocky, indented shoreline common to much of the Irish coast provided a prime habitat for crabs and lobsters, while productive oyster and scallop beds, succoured and scoured clean by Atlantic and Irish Sea currents, occurred naturally in estuarine waters. Indigenous mussel, winkle and whelk beds also occurred in abundance around the Irish coast; these were an important source of bait for line fishing as well as a source of saleable food for export or local consumption.

Seafish are classified biologically on the basis of their lifestyle as either demersal or pelagic species. Demersal fish, such as cod, hake, haddock, whiting, and the flat fishes, are bottom living and feeding, solitary and generally sedentary species. While spawning migrations occur to a certain extent in all free-swimming families of seafish, these are less pronounced among demersal species, and, on the whole fish of this type remain in the same sea area throughout their life. Thus, demersal species provide a localized resource base, theoretically available for exploitation all the year round. In fishery terms, enterprises based on the capture of demersal species are usually grouped together under the heading of 'whitefisheries'.

Pelagic species, on the other hand, are surface-swimming and shoal-forming, appearing periodically in huge numbers in the coastal waters where they gather to feed and to spawn. Their main food source, plankton and plankton-eating species, is found in the greatest abundance where the ocean's surface is stirred and oxygenated by the meeting of currents of different temperatures. Two such interfaces exist in coastal waters in the north-east Atlantic: one to the north of the British Isles, where the Atlantic Drift meets currents flowing southwards from the Arctic, and one to the south, where the Gulf Stream collides with cold water moving south through the North Sea. Ireland's position relative to the European land mass (which directs the course of these currents) allowed large-scale visits from two of the most valuable pelagic species. Shoals of herring and mackerel gathered on grounds all around the Irish coast at their appropriate spawning times, with mackerel, which prefer slightly warmer water to herring, arriving in the greatest numbers in southern inshore waters. The commercial significance of pelagic fish derived from their habit of forming huge, homogeneous shoals at given times in certain regions, thus enabling the capture of massively large numbers of fish of uniform type and quality at relatively predictable times and locations. One corollary of this, however, was that the same habits of shoaling and free migration also led to enormous and at times apparently inexplicable fluctuations in both the short- and the long-term availability of local pelagic resources.

Ireland's fishing grounds thus contained a wide range of commercially important seafishes. As a result, opportunities existed for several types of fishery pursuit – from land-based operations involving the capture of crabs and lobsters to highly productive seasonal pelagic fishing, with sedentary species such as cod, whiting and flat fish providing a year-round demersal fishery. The economic potential of a maritime resource did not, however, rest solely on the volume and value of commercial species it contained. Two other factors underpined its exploitation.

First, the fishing grounds had to be reached. A country needed to enjoy maximum access to adjacent waters if their maximum benefit was to be extracted. Ireland was completely surrounded by sea, with over 2,500 miles of coastline. Furthermore, a great part of this coast line was endowed either with sandy beaches or rocky, natural harbours, both of which offered shelter for fishing boats without the need for heavy expenditure in artificial harbour construction. Second, the fish which were caught had to be sold. The presence of an internal market, together with the availability of export outlets for fresh or processed fish was of vital importance for commercial fishing. Ireland's population had a long tradition of fish consumption, related not only to their religious affiliation but linked also, perhaps, to their historic reliance on primary animal protein staples, such as meat, milk and butter. Recent historical studies indicate that even in the eighteenth and early nineteenth centuries the Irish diet contained many 'primitive' features, including a per capita consumption of fish that was significantly higher than in England.[1] Moreover, home demand could be supplemented by supplying an external demand which, thanks to Ireland's close proximity to mainland Britain and continental Europe, could be met within advantageously short distances.

The factors which governed the potential strength of regional commercial seafishing were essentially the same as those which underpinned its national success: namely, the extent and benevolence of coastlines, the fecundity and reliability of reachable fishing grounds and the proximity of central marketing and distribution arenas. County Down was relatively well favoured in all these respects. Although the county area was small (extending for only forty-nine miles at its longest and twenty-five miles at its broadest) its county seaboard stretched for over 100 miles from Newry in the south to Belfast in the north. Furthermore, unlike the long cliff-coast of its northern neighbour, county Antrim, the Down coast was liberally punctuated by sandy beaches and natural harbours. In addition, it encompassed not one but three tidal loughs – Belfast Lough, Strangford Lough and Carlingford Lough, all of which were home to important populations of valuable sea- and shellfish. Most significantly of all, the county Down seaboard formed part of the western littoral of the Irish Sea, a shallow, saucer-shaped depression whose productivity has only recently been challenged by pollution and over-fishing.

The region was, moreover, effectively separated from the rest of Ireland by the trading corridors of the upper Bann valley – which led southwards between the Mourne Mountains and the Keady Mountains in county Armagh – and the Lagan valley, which led south-westwards between the Castlereagh Hills and the Antrim Plateau. From Belfast and Newry, cross-channel and coastal links extended to connect not only county Down but also Ulster with the rest of Ireland, the British mainland, the Continent and the Americas. At the same time, the county's agricultural prosperity was reflected in the significant number of smaller local ports. These included Killough harbour, built under the direction of Alexander Nimmo (from 1821-1824), and Donaghadee and Ardglass, where construction was supervised by Sir John Rennie in the 1820s and 1830s.

As in Ireland generally, therefore, opportunities existed in county Down for several types of fishery enterprise. Diversification of effort was clearly possible. Indeed, the local seafishing industry traditionally contained various specialised branches which were followed both within and beyond the region at a variety of different commercial levels. This chapter concentrates on herring fishing, one of the key sectors of the county Down seafishing industry in terms of its local and national importance, and examines the nature, shape and development of what was essentially a regional manifestation of a nation-wide enterprise.

The county Down herring industry

Although some fishermen maintained that on parts of the Down coast herrings could be found all-year-round, three distinctly separate herring seasons, based on the arrival of the fish, existed: a summer season from about May or June, when the fish swarmed to spawn in Dundrum Bay and along the outlying east coast; an autumn season from early September, when the shoals came very close to the county's southern shores; and a short and comparatively unpredictable winter season when shoals were occasionally discovered in the county's three sea loughs in January or February. The latter fishery existed very much on an *ad hoc* periodic basis, and was worked, in the twentieth century at least, in a mainly opportunistic fashion. The autumn fishery was of considerable local significance, but was essentially a small-boat enterprise, exploited by south Down men in skiffs, many of whom were fishermen only when the herrings were in the area. The summer fishery, however, was a cosmopolitan affair, patronised by travelling boats from the four corners of the British Isles and followed as part of a peripatetic fishery which circled the Atlantic, Irish and North Sea, and English Channel coasts.

These fisheries were of enormous productivity and value for a concern that was pursued at most for only five or six months of the year. According to official figures, between 1864 and 1919 over 225,000 tons of herring, worth more than £1,500,000 in quayside sales alone, were landed at county Down ports, giving an average annual return for the fishery of over 4,000 tons of fish worth over £30,000 in quayside value. The prominence of the Down herring fisheries in national terms is also indicated in the official records which reveal that during these years, one-quarter of all the herring landed in Ireland and almost one-third of the total Irish revenue from herring sales was won from the county's ports.[2]

The structure of the herring industry in county Down makes it likely, however, that these figures under-represent the full extent of the local fishery. In the first place, they take no account of boats which fished from the county's harbours but landed their catches elsewhere. As James Murphy, explained in 1866, boats employed in local summer herring fishing went to sell their fish 'to Howth, to Scotland, to Ardglass and to other places'.[3] While this use by local boats of 'better markets'[4] outside Down and even outside Ireland remained a regular feature of the local herring fisheries throughout the period under review here, substantial amounts of herring were also transmitted from fishing boat to central markets by 'buying' boats working from the fishing grounds. In 1868 John Brophy, one of the travelling Irish fishery inspectors, visited Ardglass at the height of the summer herring and reported that while fish valued at £28,000 had been returned as sold in the port, there was also:

> a large quantity of fish carried away from the fishing ground of which no account could be taken. Two steamers from England

and one from Scotland attended the greater part of the season for the purpose of conveying the fish away to Liverpool, to Holyhead, to Workington and to Glasgow ....[5]

Figures for local landings also ignore the earnings of those local boats and crews which were working as well as landing fish elsewhere. The travelling fleet was an important source of employment for fishermen who may, indeed, have found themselves sailing to and fishing from home ports during their time as migrant workers. In 1858 it was reported that:

> for the last five or six years about twenty of the young fishermen [from Newcastle and Annalong] get employment for the months of June and July in Anstruther in Scotland to assist in the herring fishery; they each get a share, one-twelve, in a boat. Some few of them made the acquaintance of the Scotch fishermen while working on a railroad and since then they have been written for annually.[6]

Similar arrangements pertained in the pelagic Irish mackerel fishery. In 1899 the Isle of Man boats which attended this fishery at Kinsale were 'to a considerable extent manned by Irish fishermen [who] join the boats at the Isle of Man and assist in fitting them out'.[7]

As the herring industry in county Down developed during the late nineteenth century, some local fishermen participated in the wider fishery by becoming part of the crew of larger boats for the high season before returning to their own smaller boats for the autumn inshore season. When the Northern Ireland fishery department tried in the 1920s to contact Kilkeel fisherman John Teggarty regarding his loan of £115 for a new herring skiff, engine and nets, they were told that he could not be reached as he was 'employed on the *Lull* at the minute, as master or second mate, for the Dunmore East herring'.[8] The *Lull* was a Scottish steam drifter owned for a time jointly in Belfast and Buckie, when her master was a Buckie man, George Slater.[9] County Down travelling boats were also involved in the Irish Sea industry. Chambers McBride, a Kilkeel fisherman of some local prominence described the fishing year in this sector thus:

> We went to Dunmore about Patrick's Day to the herring fishing and came home about the middle of June to drift for herring at Kilkeel until the first week of September. Then we fished in the skiffs for the spawning herring with anchored or trammel nets. We then returned to the big boats and went drifting for herring at Balbriggan and Dundalk to the end of February.[10]

In 1927, the advisory committee on fishery development defined the Irish Sea herring fishery in less personal terms as:

> summer herring first, at Dunmore East early in May, then a few weeks later the main herring fishery starts at Ardglass, till October, the grounds bounded approximately at four corners by the harbours of Howth, Ardglass, Holyhead and Peel .... the Irish Sea shoals disappear in October and November; the fishery is continued in Maryport by local boats, and a number of Northern Ireland boats. At the same time the harvest herring appears [sic] of the south Down coast, which is followed by Kilkeel and adjacent harbours.[11]

Although herring were traditionally followed from harbours along the length of the Down coast, their main visits favoured the county's southern shores. As the Irish Sea fishery expanded after the mid-nineteenth century, three ports emerged as key centres of the industry. The first of these was Ardglass. Although this port had been famous as a fishery harbour since at least the fifteenth century, it owed its nationwide reputation as one of the foremost of the nineteenth-century Irish Sea herring stations almost entirely to the fact that it was the only non-tidal port on the Irish east coast between Kingstown (now Dun Laoire) and Belfast. By the early twentieth century Ardglass had no large-boat fishing fleet of its own, and maintained its prominence solely through the busy patronage of visiting boats from other ports in county Down, Ireland, Scotland, England and the Isle of Man (plate 16.1). In contrast to Ardglass, Kilkeel developed as a fishing port as well as a fishery harbour, and was home to the greater part of the travelling south Down herring fishing fleet. The other southern centre for the herring fishery was Annalong, which shared many of the characteristics of Kilkeel while never quite matching it in overall stature.

It was in these three ports that the county's herring curing industry was based. The importance of this sector to the local development of herring fisheries reflected centuries of necessity and practise. Because herring was not only an exceptionally mobile fish but also an extremely perishable one, it had to be 'processed' for market within a very short time of being caught. Thus, the wealth of herring fishermen and herring merchants had traditionally rested on the trade in cured fish. The first travelling commercial herring fishing vessels, such as the big Dutch bussess of the fifteenth and sixteenth centuries, were equipped both for catching and curing, but in later years sea-going herring boats served a shore-based curing industry. In the case of the British Isles, this developed when changes in the broad pattern of

Plate 16.1   Scots steam drifters at Ardglass in the 1920s (Source: Welch collection, Ulster Museum).

herring movements in the early eighteenth century enabled contracted fishermen to work from port on a daily basis.

The functional separation of the catching and curing sectors began in the mid-eighteenth century, when existing government bounties designed to stimulate British trade in herrings were extended to provide payments for the export of cured herring without regard to the size or type of vessel which landed the raw fish. This enabled curers to obtain herring from small-boat fishermen without losing the bounty on their final product. As a result, quayside markets were freed for both seller and buyer, creating the conditions in which the British Isles herring industry developed in the nineteenth century as a loosely-structured network of seasonally-defined landing places, served by both travelling and home-based large- and small-boat fleets. The increasing use of auctions rather than of sales by prior agreement finally severed the last formal link between supplying boats and buyers, and set the final seal on the independence of local fishermen. For the first time, more or less, they were able to sell on equal terms with visiting boats in their home markets, thereby forcing curers to obtain supplies of fish by competing actively with other buyers in boatside markets.

Whilst various reports submitted to the 1836 commission on the state of the Irish seafisheries referred to the previous presence of Scottish dealers in the major county Down herring port of Ardglass 'to buy and cure herrings',[12] by the time the commission sat, the bulk of the herring landed on the Down coast was sold and eaten as fresh fish. And, while some isolated incidents of curing were recorded during the remainder of the nineteenth century, the overwhelming feature of the herring industry in Ireland in general and in Down in particular during this period was its emphasis on fresh fish. This was due primarily to the buoyancy of demand for county Down herring in the valuable fresh markets in mainland Britain and Ireland, which elevated its quayside price to a level where curers either could not or would not compete with fresh buyers.[13] There was, however, a further problem for local curers: county Down summer herring were alleged to be too fat to be cured to the standards of 'the brand'.[14]

Despite the Irish fishery inspectors' efforts to stimulate interest in the re-establishment of the herring curing industry in Ireland after the Famine, it was not until the inauguration of the Congested Districts Board in the late nineteenth century (coupled, it should be pointed out, with a contemporary decrease in the quayside price of Irish herring), that any firm steps were taken in this direction. The first mention of the export of cured herring from Ireland in the twentieth century referred to a congested district, when it was noted that an 'eminent' New York firm had praised Downings Bay herrings (from county Donegal) as having 'a flavour which was preferred by the majority of the trade to Scotch herrings'.[15] In every respect other than place of processing, however, Downings Bay herrings could be quite properly described as 'Scottish' cured herrings. For the outstanding feature of the early development of the Irish curing industry, first in Donegal and then five or six years later in county Down, was the extent to which production in all sectors of this enterprise involved the work of Scottish men and women.

Herring curing, like herring fishing, was an extremely mobile operation. It required no permanent industrial structures, and all the material equipment, in the shape of salt, barrels and timber, was easily shipped from region to region. All a firm needed locally, except, of course for a regular supply of suitable fish at a reasonable price, was a small piece of land on which to erect a coopering shed and gutting troughs. An agreement between Davidson, Pirie and Co., Leith, and the Northern Ireland ministry of commerce for land leased in Ardglass in 1925 shows how cheaply this could be found. Three plots on the harbour cost this firm only £22 10s. (or £7 10s each) without taxes for a year which ran from 1 June to 31 May.[16]

The curers also needed two types of skilled worker to produce their fish to brand standard – coopers and gutters. The coopers were versed in the highly specialised craft of making the barrels in which fish were cured for export. This art had been lost in Ireland during the nineteenth century and for most of the Ardglass high-season production, barrels were imported by sea, with the port of Belfast supplying 'some thousands each year'.[17] At the same time, curers working locally employed a managing cooper from Scotland 'but Scottish coopers [had] to be employed in any case, by reason of local substitutes being unavailable'.[18] Over time, Down developed its own skilled coopers, many of whom, like their Scottish counterparts, were directly linked with the curing business. For example, one of the largest Kilkeel cooperages of the inter-war period belonged to a prominent local family called McKee, whose members were involved with a number of curing operations in the port and throughout Britain and Ireland.[19]

The other expert workers in the curing industry were the women who gutted and packed the herring. At Ardglass, this labour was not local,[20] despite the opportunities which must have mushroomed as the local curing industry developed apace after its hesitant start in 1907 (plate 16.2). In 1909 nearly 9,000 barrels and 3,000 half-barrels of cured fish left Ardglass harbour, most of which was produced in a short, six-week season by Scottish firms with labour hurriedly sent in from

Plate 16.2.   Curing herring at Ardglass (Source: Green collection, Ulster Folk and Transport Museum).

Donegal and Peterhead.[21] The success of the first major Ardglass curing season hit even the city press, and the *Belfast News Letter's* unusually detailed coverage of that year's fishery gives some idea of the organisation and atmosphere of this new trade. By the end of September, five firms in all, each employing 'about eighteen girls or ninety women gutting and packing' were hard at work; the first bulk shipments had been sent out; and the quay 'daily [presented] an animated appearance such [had] not been seen since the opening of the railway to Belfast'.[22]

The herring girls who worked in Ardglass came mainly from Scotland and the outlying western coasts of Ireland. In 1926, for example, 150 women workers were employed in curing in the port, of whom half came from Scotland and half from the west of Ireland.[23] It appears, however, that Donegal was the chief, immediate Irish source for this labour. *Circa* 1925 the fishery inspectors noted that in Ardglass:

> curing was largely in the hands of Scottish curers, [who use] labour recruited in Scotland and Donegal. Three Northern Irish concerns were also involved. Their employees were recruited mainly in Donegal.[24]

One of these Northern Irish concerns appears, incidentally, to have belonged to the above-mentioned McKee's, who ran several operations in Killybegs after the First World War and who were also responsible for organizing women workers to come from there to county Down in late summer.[25]

The curing industry in the McKee's home port of Kilkeel, and in the other regular local curing port of Annalong, operated along quite different lines from the Ardglass enterprise. For a start, it was smaller, with the two ports together handling only about 15 per cent of the county's annual herring cure. It was established much later in the season, and was much more localised in organization, with curers tending to produce predominantly for domestic markets and to buy their supplies of fish from local boats. As far as the curing firms themselves were concerned, there is no record of Scottish interests working in either of the southern centres, and in both the custom was to use Irish or county Down workers as gutters and packers of herring.[26] In 1925, for example, three firms were stationed at Annalong, where 'all the labour employed .... was employed locally'.[27]

From its slow beginning in 1907, herring curing in Ardglass rapidly grew into a major export-based industry. In 1909, five curing firms worked in the port to produce 7,870 barrels and 2,240 half-barrels of fish to send to Russia. The Russian agents who had organised the trade remarked that 'they were greatly pleased with the quality of the fish and [expressed] their intention of again visiting the place'.[28] In 1911 the crown brand was introduced. Fish sold with this mark of quality fetched 'very satisfactory prices' and gained a 'generally favourable opinion' amongst its continental buyers.[29] In 1912, just under 30,000 barrels of fish, with an estimated fresh weight of about 5,600 tons were exported from county Down.[30]

The loss of continental European and Russian markets during the First World War was a severe blow to the British curing industry generally. However, compensating markets were found in America, where Ardglass herring enjoyed 'a very high reputation and [met] with ready sale'.[31] Although the revolution in Russia in 1917 meant the end of the export trade with that country, trade with and through Germany was resumed after the end of hostilities. In 1926 herring cured in Ardglass was 'eagerly bought up on the spot by the U.S.A. and Germany'.[32] In the same year, fourteen curing firms worked in the port, where 'all available space .... was occupied as curing plots'.[33]

The establishment of a major curing industry in county Down did not mean the end of the original fresh fish trade. The resurgence of the Irish east coast herring industry in the mid-nineteenth century occurred at a period when national domestic markets for fresh fish were being consolidated. British demand for fresh herring was vital for this fishery, with the English market generally taking three-quarters of the Irish catch[34] in a trade which was based at the big herring stations of Howth, Ardglass, Kilkeel, Arklow and the Skerries. In 1878, it was noted that at these 'great centres ... the fish is sold by auction immediately after being caught, and paid for on the spot, and are immediately dispatched to England by special steamers employed for the purpose'.[35] But Ardglass also supplied fresh herring to other inland and local Irish markets. In 1902, for example, the first year for which a detailed breakdown of the distribution of herrings is available, Ardglass exported just under 80 per cent of its herring to fresh distant markets; the rest was sold locally, apart from about 280 cwts (about 500 barrels) which was cured.[36] The size of this local market for fresh herring should not be underestimated. In 1923, the fishery development commission was advised that in Ardglass alone, 'twenty tons of herrings can be disposed of daily ... for sale as fresh herrings to Belfast and throughout Ulster, distribution being effected by means of rail and motor lorry and to convenient agricultural communities by means of hawkers' carts'.[37]

Regional production of herring was governed by two factors. While the local abundance of fish was obviously a prime determinant, the number of vessels also affected the level of landings. Fleet complement, and therefore catch capacity, was not evenly sustained in county Down for the entire duration of the local herring fishery. It expanded as the season progressed, and local boats were joined by travelling drifters from many parts of the British Isles. Although the evidence is difficult to evaluate, the pattern of port use during the local season invariably took the form of a gradual escalation of activity which reached its peak several weeks after fishing commenced. It was this escalation which heralded the annual establishment of the herring curing industry, and the effective split of the county Down summer herring fishery into two seasons: an early 'freshing' season, when herring were bought for the fresh fish trade, and a 'main' curing season, when these buyers were joined by buyers of herring for the cured fish trade. Although the break between the two was generally assumed to coincide with the the local 'Twelfth' holiday, in practise the actual date varied from year to year according to the arrival of the visiting fleet. For example, in 1926 curing began in Ardglass on 23 June, 'several weeks earlier than usual',[38] while in 1928 it did not start until the first week in August when 'steam drifters arrived from Shetland and north Scottish grounds'.[39]

Visiting drifters were attracted to a given region by a combination of reliable fishing and good quayside demand. The free exchange of information between herring fishing areas resulted in any local changes in either of these factors being rapidly reflected in the number of participants in the fishery. In 1903, the major herring fishing stations on the four coasts of Ireland were linked by an official 'telegraphic intelligence system',[40] modelled on the information network introduced into the Irish mackerel fisheries a year earlier. In the first year of the herring scheme's operation, about twenty thousand telegrams were dispatched,[41] an information flow which not only reflects but which must also have greatly influenced the movement of traffic within the Irish industry. The statutory supply of information was maintained after partition in a system which linked ports in Down with those in the rest of Ireland and the Isle of Man in an exchange of local news regarding landings, quayside prices and the location of the Irish Sea shoals.[42] Its efficiency was recorded in 1926 by the fishery inspectors, who noted that:

> the early intimation to boats of the high prices being made to fishermen as a result of intensive curing operations at Ardglass attracted to that port many boats which would have otherwise have landed their catches elsewhere.[43]

That year was exceptional for the herring industry in county Down.

The quantity of herring landed in the region very nearly equalled the amount brought in in 1912, a year which itself had seen the greatest volume of local landings since 1878, while the local curing industry also surpassed itself by creating 'a new record .... for this district'.[44] These high levels of production depended on the early abundance of high-quality fish in adjacent grounds. This brought first the visiting boats and then, in force, the visiting curers, who created the buoyancy in the local market which attracted further vessels. This increase in capacity was sustained by the continued fruitfulness of local herring grounds, and absorbed by the increased efforts of the curers, which in turn maintained quayside demand at a level which supported the enhanced fleet. But that was not the whole story. The same year (1926) also saw the General Strike with its attendant coal shortages at many British ports. Ardglass, however, had a quayside advantage in the form of a ready supply of cheap fuel for the steam drifters. This was due to the canniness of local coal merchants, who arranged for the cargo vessels arriving to take cured herring to Hamburg and the Baltic ports to bring continental coal with them as ballast for their outward journeys.[45] This advantage ceased by 1927, when over a hundred fewer visiting boats worked from the port, despite the fact that both local demand for fish and the state of the local fishery differed little from their condition twelve months previously.

The 1926 coal strike was just one of many factors affecting the progress of the herring industry in county Down. Ecological variables, such as the short-term deterioration of local grounds, comparatively better or worse conditions in other areas, the quality of locally-available stocks, and the timing of the arrival of the shoals all combined to create either a benign or malign context for the local industry. In addition, the nature of quayside demand for locally-landed herring changed dramatically in the nineteenth and twentieth centuries. This involved the expansion and contraction of the fresh trade and the establishment of a local market for herring for curing.

In the 1860s and 1870s the herring industry in county Down was supported by an enormous expansion in the national demand for fresh fish. The region's advantageous position relative to wet-fish markets for herring was reflected in the prominence of this enterprise in local ports during these decades. Although the continued acceleration of activity in off-shore whitefishing substantially reduced the importance of the short-lived herring fishery generally in fresh markets, the county's fishery was sheltered to a certain extent because of the early arrival of herring in the region. Thus although locally-caught herring was forced into growing competition with other species of fish in retail outlets, it remained largely free from competition with herring from other regions of the British Isles. At the same time, county Down's location enabled buyers in the region to represent both British and Irish domestic markets.

This privileged position did not last for ever. Very low levels of production in the county in the 1890s coincided with a general contraction in demand for herring, and increasing competition from fresh herring from other Irish grounds. Yearly Irish exports of herring to British mainland markets declined from an average of over 100,000 boxes in the 1870s to just under 85,000 in the 1880s and to just over 65,000 in the 1890s, a decrease of, approximately, 20 and 25 per cent respectively. In comparison, county Down's contribution to the Irish herring fishery fell from just over 30 per cent of total yield in the 1880s to just under 20 per cent in the 1890s, and fell again in the next decade, despite local improvements in both total yields and total values. Nevertheless, this sustained fall in local quayside demand was instrumental in attracting the herring curing industry to the region. This more than compensated for the reduction in demand for fresh herrings. Indeed, it was probably the local emergence of this new market for herrings which accounted for the increase from 1910 in county Down's share of total Irish landings, and the re-appearance of the region as one of the key herring areas on the Irish Sea coasts. This revival was itself short-lived, and by the 1920s and the 1930s the industry in the county was once more in decline. This time, however, the collapse can be associated with a fundamental shift in the economic, rather than the ecological, viability of herring fishing.

This is not to deny the impact of the increasing unreliability of local grounds. The failure of usually productive herring fishing areas during this period was reported with depressing frequency by the Northern Ireland fishery inspectors. The succession of poor fishing years after 1928 culminated in 1934 in a season which was so bad that the government allowed the introduction of an unprecedented scheme of weekly payments to local herring fishermen, 'to enable them to continue operations in the hope that the situation would improve as the season advanced'.[46] It did not, and in that year only 8,000 cwts of herring were landed in Northern Ireland, a pitiful result which constituted, in the words of the inspectors, 'a new low record in the decline which during recent years has been recorded'.[47]

Whilst the prolonged deterioration of local fish stocks was obviously a matter of concern, much greater damage was caused by the collapse of quayside demand for herring in the British Isles as a whole in the aftermath of the First World War. The immediate post-war period was not a good time for herring fishermen in county Down. The end of war-inflated food prices caused a sudden steep decrease in the local value of herring, from 28s (average price per cwt.) in 1918 to just 9s 6d in 1923. At the same time the local industry was further reduced by the refusal of the government to extend to Ireland the guaranteed markets for herring which it had granted to England and Scotland in 1919, a move which indicates conclusively the general lack of demand for this fish at national level after the war. .

The return of the curing industry to county Down in 1924 revitalized local quayside markets, and for the rest of the 1920s the prospect for herring fishermen in the region looked bright. But a series of substandard yields from the start of the 1930s made the county profoundly unattractive for curers. By mid-decade, they were beginning to see their own markets shrink under the weight of import quotas and exchange restrictions on the continent. Thus, when catches started to improve at least in quantity as the 1930s drew to an end, county Down was left struggling to attract and keep sufficient curing firms to deal with gluts of landings. In 1937, only four firms took spaces in Ardglass, compared with the 'six or eight with good staffs of workers'[48] which opened in Peel on the Isle of Man. The county Down curers were so stretched that 'on several occasions herring had to be roused (i.e. salted temporarily) overnight and worked up the following day, and there were several instances when the work of curing was carried on till after midnight, the gutting and packing of herring being done by the aid of flares'.[49] Finally, the firms were forced to tell fishermen that they could not guarantee to take their fish any longer.[50] The following year, the curers flatly refused to start work before August 'unless guaranteed against loss'.[51] This was not forthcoming, and within ten days of their arrival, quayside markets had become 'so saturated with herring' that catches amounting to 160 crans (about 28 tons of fish) had to be dumped.[52] County Down was, in fact, over-supplied with herring for almost the entire season – to such an extent, indeed, that local ports closed on three occasions, the last being forced by the insistence of representatives of Portavogie fishermen, who wired Ardglass and Peel 'on their own responsibility'.[53]

Pressure on local markets for herring in 1938 was compounded by a general lack of demand for herring on the British mainland. This did not affect county Down fishermen directly, as they had ceased to compete in that trade after the first World War, but it did force them into competition in Ireland with herring from cross-channel sources, in particular from Scotland. Once again, Portavogie fishermen went for direct action, and at the very beginning of the season sent a deputation to the ministry of commerce to request that the import of Scottish herring be stopped, or, if not, that curers be guaranteed against loss if the surplus early herrings were cured and sent to the Continent.[54] So squeezed was the British market for herring in 1938 that even Belfast featured as a herring port, when Scottish herring drifters made direct landings there from Clyde grounds following the imposition of landing quotas at the Clyde herring ports.[55]

That year was a miserable one for herring fishermen in county Down. Lack of demand, coupled with improvements in the yield from herring fisheries elsewhere, resulted in markets being almost permanently over-supplied with fish for the whole of the local season. By late July, their plight was so severe that the department decided to implement a subsidy scheme, 'similar to that given in 1934'.[56] In one fundamental respect, however, these subsidies were not at all similar. The first decision to provide aid for fishermen had been taken because there were no fish to be caught. The second was taken because no markets could be found. The seventy-year cycle of the post-Famine herring industry had drawn to an end.

Local effects of the collapse of the curing industry

After the end of the first World War, the commercial importance of herring fishing in county Down largely resulted from the presence of the herring curing industry. While this sector was seriously affected by the failure of local herring grounds from the 1920s, these local reductions in supply did not by themselves undermine the national viability of British curing enterprises. It was not isolated dearths of herring but the general dearth of overseas demand which initiated the decline of the British curing industry and caused the whole fabric of the British herring industry to crumble. The fading post-war success of commercial herring fishing in county Down was part of this wider process.

This loss of demand was a major blow to herring fishermen everywhere and it would be foolish to argue that county Down fishermen did not also suffer from it. However, several factors combined to prevent the national contraction of the curing industry from being as damaging an event in local terms as might first appear.

First, a large part of the commercial activity in this sector traditionally consisted of externally-based enterprises which impinged little if at all on the local economy. Any expansion in herring fishing was geared to overseas trade, much of which was conducted without recourse to local marketing networks. The export of fresh herring from county Down to the British mainland, which had been a crucial element in the mid-nineteenth-century growth of the local fishery, was undertaken by visiting buyers; even the vessels which carried fish away from local ports tended to be from the 'sister country'. A similar situation pertained in the later curing industry, where finished fish was bought 'on the spot' by foreign buyers, and conveyed out of port by steamers with names like the *Ilse* or the *Marta Schroeder*.[57] Even the selling of fresh fish was not confined to local traders: in 1927 three of the four salesmen required to handle county Down landings came from Northern Ireland. The other came from Scotland.[58]

The service sector for this enterprise also saw a substantial proportion of its revenue go to external interests. According to official sources, the foreign fishing vessels which visited Ardglass brought with them 'a considerable proportion of the supplies they need, i.e. salt and barrels'.[59] Although it was conceded at the time that the importation of coal and salt, and the reloading of coal into the drifters 'gives a great deal of employment',[60] careful examination of the final figures for the 1925 season reveals that the related financial value of servicing this fishery was indeed slight. In this year, expenditure on railway fares, barrels, freightage, ground rents and storage, wages to local workers in cartage and curing and 'miscellaneous' other expenses represented a gross income of about £7,000. Moreover, this sum should be compared with the estimated loss to the region of £4,400 which resulted from visiting drifters and their crews 'going home at the weekend because of lack of facilities'.[61]

The extensive external involvement in the county Down herring fishery resulted from the peripatetic nature of the herring industry. To a large extent, the selling of herrings and the servicing of the fleet were not exclusively local responsibilities but functions which were fulfilled either by representatives who travelled with the producing sectors, or by local agents of the various participant vessels. The wider significance of county Down is not denied by this argument; its geographic position and maritime facilities combined to ensure the region's vital position in the Irish Sea herring industry. But the major local port of Ardglass was not the sole platform for this activity. It should be regarded instead as a seasonal, east coast work-base for travelling British and Irish fishermen. It was to a certain extent inevitable that the lion's share of the wider benefits of herring fishing in the Irish Sea should be dispersed to the regions which were represented at the heart of the enterprise. It was these areas, rather than county Down, which were hardest hit by its decline.

The effects of the collapse of the wider herring industry were also not as detrimental to local herring fishermen as might at first appear. Because herring landings in county Down traditionally represented the combined efforts of a largely cosmopolitan fleet, a substantial proportion of 'local' income from herring fishing invariably went to fishermen from outside the region. The failure of local grounds and the subsequent deterioration of local fishing opportunities obviously affected local fishermen. However, declining local fortunes were also accompanied by reductions in the numbers of visiting boats. Whilst the supporting statistics are difficult to read and reproduce, they suggest that a drop in the overall value of local herring fishing did not necessarily result in a reduction in individual returns. For example, the fishery inspectors themselves noted in 1927 that, whilst overall landings had fallen from the previous year 'the average per boat [at Ardglass] approximated fairly closely to the average in 1926'.[62] In fact, closer examination of the returns reveals indicates that average individual quayside sales stood at £303 per vessel in 1926 but at £315 per vessel in 1927.[63] Thus, in this case a decrease in overall capacity was related to an increase in average return.

The existence in county Down of two herring industries – one freshing and the other curing – further sheltered local fishermen from the wider effects of the industry's general decline. As noted above, the brunt of the post-war collapse in the commercial herring fisheries was borne by the curing industry, which in county Down was dominated in all its branches by outsiders. Even the fishing boats which supplied the curers with fish tended to be visitors, with curing rarely beginning until the local fleet had been supplemented by the arrival of drifters from other areas.

The contraction of the curing industry in county Down certainly hit supplementary trade, such as coopering and the importation of salt. At the same time, however, secondary activity associated with curing had failed to penetrate the local economy to any great extent. While reductions in curing capacity and the patronage of foreign boats had a direct impact on the volume and value of herring landings, the fact that a large part of herring fishing activity in the county was conducted by visiting vessels to supply visiting curers meant that purely local operations were not profoundly disadvantaged when these enterprises failed.

Indeed, falling production often worked to the benefit of local fishermen. For although local vessels tended to serve fresh markets and travelling vessels rather than the curing industry, there was no compulsion for boats to sell exclusively to either sector. Although curers did try as far as possible to avoid bidding in fresh markets, they would do so when need drove them. Thus in 1932, the normal seasonal decline in quayside prices as the season progressed was completely reversed. Unusually light landings during the 'main' fishery forced curers 'to compete not only with each other but also with fresh buyers in a effort to keep their workers employed'.[64]

This boost to prices during times of dearth offered local fishermen some respite when catches were light. At the same time, the ability of the curing industry to absorb large quantities of herring also enabled unusually heavy catches to be disposed of at satisfactory prices – curing firms already in the area could be persuaded to extend their operations, or additional curing firms could be tempted to come in. But the fact that it was the visiting boats which provided these large quantities of fish provided a further opportunity to protect prices during times of glut. When markets were in danger of becoming saturated, access by travelling boats to local ports could be restricted.

This action was made possible by the split in the local fishery into a 'main' and an 'early' fishery. The early season, which was pursued almost exclusively by local vessels, was of tremendous importance to county Down fishermen. In 1930, herring worth £6,928 was sold at Ardglass and Portavogie during this period, giving local fishermen 'almost £200 a head'[65] outside their earnings for the remainder of the fishery. The local fresh market was extremely inelastic in comparison with the cured market, and the monopoly of local boats to supply it was jealously guarded. County Down fishermen may have been powerless to prevent the direct importation into Northern Ireland of foreign herrings for fresh consumption, but they were remarkably successful in preventing foreign vessels from working from local ports 'before the time that curing might be expected to begin'.[66] This was achieved by a directive of 1936 which restricted until 12 July each year the number of herring vessels working from county Down ports to forty-five, and the method of fishing they employed to drift-netting.[67] As the fishery inspectors noted at the time:

> with landings [thus] confined to local boats, the requirements for the fresh market created keen competition ... In this respect, the operations of the Directions in practice [were] all to the benefit of local fishermen, although not entirely favoured by the freshers who attended at Ardglass and who were at times unable to fulfil their orders.[68]

Conclusion

Taken as a whole, the period 1860-1939 was one of progress for local fishermen. It witnessed a general strengthening of the infrastructure of their industry: new steam links were established between the region and the British mainland, road and rail communications were extended to fishing centres and fishery harbours, harbours themselves were rebuilt and repaired, and major efforts were made both to initiate new markets and to increase the supply of fish to existing ones. On the operational, or 'catching' side of commercial seafishing, a widespread improvement took place in capital equipment, the standard of the fleet rose notably, and the old unsteady dependence on sail was broken by the introduction of motor power. As for the fishing population itself, there was a pronounced shift towards professionalism, a discernible improvement in income from individual fisheries and a marked intensification in fishing effort amongst individual fishermen.

The initial basis for these improvements was undoubtedly the revival at the opening of this period of the summer herring fishery. The local benefits of its consequent expansion were enormous, both in the short and the long term. Part of its significance lay in the revenue raised by fishermen in quayside and boatside sales, and in the trading profits of the agents who handled the fish for wider markets. But the presence of a buoyant herring industry secured a new foundation for local commercial seafishing as a whole as capital which derived from herring fishing was injected into general fishing operations. Moreover, the local effects of the subsequent decline in this sector were limited. In the first place, much of the loss this represented was sustained by outsiders. In the second, the physical manifestations of the previous success of the herring fishery survived in the shape of restored harborage and an improved fleet. Finally, the home market for fresh and cured herring, whose supply was almost exclusively the preserve of local fishermen, remained viable until the closing years of the inter-war period.

Furthermore, the local whitefisheries had been growing steadily in stature and importance since the turn of the century. The growth and increasing stability of the returns from this sector compensated greatly for the fluctuating success of the herring industry. Indeed, many improvements in the latter had been initiated (at least in part) by contemporary reductions in the value of pelagic fishing. Most significantly of all, the barren years of the inter-war herring industry saw a new demersal fishery in county Down based on the introduction of a winter seine-net fishery for whiting. This grew steadily during the 1920s and 1930s, and by the end of this period, had assumed supreme importance in the region.

This shift resulted in a number of local changes in the direction of fishery activity. Commercial herring fishing was a summer affair, taking place in the locality from about April to September. Whiting were caught in the winter months, in a season which lasted from November to March. Pelagic herring were taken in stationary drift nets; demersal whiting were captured by Danish seines, active, sea-based adaptations of the old shore seine. The two fisheries therefore demanded different organisation, different equipment, different skills and technical knowledge and a different awareness of resource behaviour.

However, the structure of commercial seafishing in county Down enabled the move to Danish seining to take effect with the minimum of disruption. The prevalence of combination fishing in the region ensured that most local fishermen were masters of several arts, so that knowledge of whitefishing extended to fishermen who were neither primarily nor exclusively involved in that sector. Crucially, reliance on a diversity of fishing activity also aided the introduction of new forms of fishing by reducing the actual and perceived risk of displacing existing fishing techniques. The key features of the development of Danish seining in the region were the initial adoption of the device as an adjunct to herring fishing, and the extent to which the initial expansion in its use was governed by the fortunes of that fishery. Indeed, although the example of Portavogie boats was undoubtedly instrumental in advertising the efficacy of the new method to many other fishermen in county Down, it was not until 1938 that Portavogie fishermen themselves were prepared to regard whiting fishing as 'their main source of earning a living, even more so than herring fishing'.[69]

Much of the vigour of the county Down fisheries resulted from the easy way in which commercial information and ideas flowed from region to region. But the strength of local seafishing also rested on the existence of not one but two fishing industries. Down possessed an indigenous, home-based seafishery but was at one and the same time a centre for the wider, sea-based seafisheries. These existed simultaneously, creating a situation in which small-scale and large-scale commercial enterprises could complement as well as compete with one another. Great structural flexibility ensued, which allowed a wide range of fishermen to participate on common terms in different ventures. This was the cornerstone of the industry in the county, and enabled the maximisation of available resources, both capital and natural, within a framework of independent local activity. The success of the county Down whiting fishery in the 1930s was undoubtedly due in large part to the local adoption of modern technical systems and the local exploitation of wider markets. But the enterprise of the county's fishermen who secured the new methods and seized the new opportunities was firmly rooted in the past and in the traditional structures which obtained in their industry.

References

1. L. M. Cullen, *The emergence of modern Ireland 1600-1900* (1981), pp 154, 187.
2. Unless otherwise stated, all statistics quoted in this chapter have been abstracted from the relevant annual reports of the Irish and Northern Irish fishery boards. Full statistical abstracts are available in V. L. Pollock, 'The seafishing industry in co. Down 1860-1939', unpub. Ph.D. thesis, University of Ulster, 1988.
3. *Report of the commissioners appointed to inquire into the seafisheries of the United Kingdom, i, report and appendix,* P.P. (1866) xvii [hereafter *1866 R. C.*], evidence James Murphy, p. 1072.

4. *Report of the inspectors of Irish fisheries, 1871*, P.P. (1872) xvi, 505, p. 538.
5. *Report of the deep sea and coast fishery commissioners, Ireland, for 1868*, P.P. (1868-9) xv, p 577 [hereafter *R. I. F. B. 1868*], p. 591
6. *Report of the commissioners of fisheries, Ireland, for 1858*, P.P. (1859, sess 2) xiv, p. 798.
7. *Report of the inspectors of Irish fisheries, 1899*, P.P. (1900) xii, p. 316
8. Steven to Tallent, P. R. O. N. I., COM 43/1/26 and 27.
9. Belfast district registers of fishing boats (held at Belfast Custom House), Book 3, f. 95. The *Lull* was built in Aberdeen in 1918 and registered in Belfast in 1924 as a steam schooner, owned by Wallace Orchard and Arthur Tempest of Strandtown, Belfast, and William and George Slater of Buckie, Scotland. Her captain was named as George Slater. See also P. R. O. N. I., COM 43/3/2, wherein the Lull was named as one of the 'visiting' vessels in Ardglass in 1923 and 1924.
10. Chambers McBride, quoted in Mourne Observer, *Sailing ships of Mourne: the co. Down fishing fleet and the Newcastle Lifeboat* (Newcastle, county Down 1971) [hereafter *Sailing ships*], p. 41.
11. *Report of the departmental advisory committee on the development of fishery harbours in Northern Ireland* (H. M. S. O., Belfast, 1927) [hereafter *1927 S. C.*], p. 9.
12. *Report of royal commissioners of inquiry into the state of the Irish seafisheries, with minutes of evidence and appendices, i, report and appendix*, P.P. (1837) xxii, 1 [hereafter *1836*], oral evidence Ardglass, p. 51.
13. Pollock, 'Seafishing', pp 203-205.
14. *Report of the inspectors of Irish fisheries, 1914*, P. P (1914-16) xxii, p. 440. The crucial importance of crown branding to the nineteenth-century British curing industry was another legacy of the government bounty system. Its significance dated from 1808 when a new system of payments was granted in Scotland provided that herring was cured and packed in accordance with regulations laid down by the herring board. Originally intended as a device against fraud, the crown brand came to be seen by buyers as a mark of assured quality and was maintained as such by Scottish curers after the bounty payments were withdrawn in 1830.
15. *Report of the inspectors of Irish fisheries, 1900*, P. P. (1901) xi, p. 313.
16. P. R. O. N. I., COM 43/3/2.
17. Herring fishing, Ardglass, 1926, P. R. O. N. I., COM 42/7.
18. P. R. O. N. I., COM 43/2/4.
19. Oral evidence, E. More, Kilkeel; tapes and transcriptions held by author.
20. P. R. O. N. I., COM 42/1.
21. *Belfast News Letter*, 23 August 1909, p. 12.
22. Ibid.
23. *Sailing Ships*, p. 44.
24. P. R. O. N. I., COM 42/7.
25. Oral evidence, E. More, *op. cit.*
26. See Pollock, 'Seafishing', pp 217-22, for a more detailed examination of these differences.
27. P. R. O. N. I., COM 42/1.
28. *Report of the inspectors of Irish fisheries, 1909*, P. P. (1910) xxx, pp 547-8.
29. *Report of the inspectors of Irish fisheries, 1911*, P. P. (1912-13) xxvii, p. 13.
30. This weight is based on an estimation of 1,000 fish to one barrel of cured herring. Conversion from barrels to weight uses the formula barrel x 1,000 = fish; fish – 625 = mease; (mease x 7) – 3 = cwt.
31. *Report of the inspectors of Irish fisheries, 1916*, P. P. (1918) x, p. 43.

32. *Report of sea and inland fisheries of Northern Ireland 1926* (Belfast, 1928) [hereafter *R. N. I. F. B. 1926*], p. 7.
33. *Ibid.*, p. 10.
34. *Report of the inspectors of Irish fisheries, 1875*, P. P. (1876) xvi, p. 601.
35. *Report of the inspectors of Irish fisheries, 1878*, P. P. (1878-9) xvii, p. 581.
36. *Report of the inspectors of Irish fisheries, 1902*, P. P. (1903) xiii, p. 563. A total of 41,351 cwts. of herring was landed in Ardglass during the season, of which 33,005 cwts. was sold fresh in distant markets, 8,160 cwts. was sold fresh locally, and 500 barrels (or *ca.* 286 cwts) was cured.
37. P. R. O. N. I., COM 43/4/4.
38. *R. N. I. F. B. 1926*, p. 6.
39. *Report on the sea and inland fisheries of Northern Ireland, 1928* (Belfast, 1928), p. 5.
40. *Report of the inspectors of Irish fisheries, 1903*, P. P. (1904) xi [hereafter *R. I. F. B. 1903*], p. 325.
41. Ibid.
42. *R. N. I. F. B. 1926*, p. 2.
43. Ibid.
44. Ibid., p. 6.
45. Ibid., p. 7.
46. *Report on the sea and inland fisheries of Northern Ireland 1934* (Belfast, 1935) [hereafter *R. N. I. F. B. 1934*], p. 29.
47. Ibid.
48. Ardglass 1937, P. R. O. N. I., AG 6/6/5.
49. Ibid.
50. Ibid.
51. Ardglass 1938, Ibid.
52. Ibid.
53. Ibid.
54. Portavogie 1938, Ibid.
55. Belfast 1938, Ibid.
56. Portavogie 1938, Ibid.
57. P. R. O. N. I., COM 42/7.
58. *Report on the sea and inland fisheries of Northern Ireland, 1927* (Belfast, 1928) [hereafter *R. N. I. F. B. 1927*], p. 6.
59. P. R. O. N. I., COM 42/11.
60. Ibid.
61. Ibid.
62. *R. N. I. F. B. 1927*, p. 8.
63. Figs from *R. N. I. F. B. 1926* and *1927*; full comparisons are:

	1926	1927
Value of Ardglass fishery	£58,941	£43,500
No. participant vessels	£194	£134
Average return per boat	£303	£313

64. *Report on the sea and inland fisheries of Northern Ireland, 1932* (Belfast,1933), p. 7.
65. *Report on the sea and inland fisheries of Northern Ireland 1931* (Belfast, 1931), p. 8.
66. Portavogie 1936, P. R. O. N. I., AG 6/6/5.
67. Ibid.
68. Ibid.

Plate 16.3   The Long Hole, Bangor (The Ulster Folk & Transport Museum, WAG 3392).

Chapter 17

THE IRISH LANGUAGE IN COUNTY DOWN

CIARÁN DEVINE (CIARÁN Ó DUIBHINN)

The Gaelic languages are conventionally divided into Irish, Scottish-Gaelic and Manx, and form one branch of the modern Celtic languages; the other branch consists of the British group, containing Welsh, Cornish and Breton. I will use the name Gaelic interchangeably with Irish, to emphasize the similarity of the three members of the Gaelic group, especially in such contact areas as county Down, Galloway and the Isle of Man.

Gaelic was the sole or dominant language in county Down from the earliest recorded times (seventh century AD) until the plantation at the beginning of the seventeenth century, and remained strong in the southern half of the county for a further two hundred years. Between 1750 and 1900, as happened in large parts of Ireland and Scotland, Gaelic in county Down was steadily replaced by English. Its more tangible legacy today includes almost all our placenames,[1] and a high proportion of our surnames.[2] And folk memory has not entirely forgotten Boirche, the shepherd and piper of the benns; Domhanghort, the eponymous hermit of Slieve Donard; or Deaman, the king whose name occurs in Rademon near Crossgar.[3]

A summary linguistic history of county Down to 1600

One of the earliest known events of Irish history is the defeat of the Ulaid (Ulstermen) by southern invaders known as the Oirghialla, and the destruction of their leading site, Eamhain Macha, in the fourth or early fifth century AD. The Ulaid (also known as Clanna Rudhraighe) now retired eastwards to the modern counties of Down, Antrim and Louth, while central and southern Ulster was ruled by the Oirghialla. At around the same time, another southern group, the Uí Néill, took over the north-west and made their base at Aileach. Within East Ulster, a group called the Cruithin are also distinguished.

Although we thus have four identifiable population-groups in Ulster at this time, all of them were Gaelic-speaking at least by the time of the earliest written records in the seventh century AD. Foremost amongst these early texts is the *Táin Bó Cuailgne*, thought to date from the eighth century, which deals with conflicts between the Ulaid and their southern neighbours, supposed to have taken place around the start of the Christian era. While it is just possible that the Cruithin, and even the Ulaid, originally spoke a British (i.e. Welsh) form of Celtic, or (less likely) were not Celtic in speech at all, no traces of any pre-Gaelic language have survived. Gaelic was also the language carried into Scotland by the Dál Riata of north Antrim from the late fifth century onwards.

By the fourth-fifth century AD the main tribes or clanns in the county Down area were the Uí Echach Cobha (of the Cruithin) in the west; the Dál Fiatach (of the Ulaid) in the east, but extending westwards to the Bann in the north, with their capital at Dún Dá Leathghlas ('English Mount', Downpatrick); and the Dál Araidhe (of the Cruithin) in the far north, as well as in much of modern county Antrim.

With the coming of Christianity, monasteries were founded, of which the principal in county Down by the sixth century were Dún Leathghlaise (Downpatrick), Aondruim (Nendrum), Magh Bhile (Movilla, Newtownards), Beannchair (Bangor), Rath Murbholg (Maghera), Druim Mór (Dromore), Domhnach Mór (Donaghmore) and Linn Duachaill (Magheralin).[4] It was in seats of learning such as these that the great manuscript compilations of Latin and Gaelic literary, genealogical and historical material were made, over the succeeding centuries.

From the sixth century, the kingship of Ulster (i.e. of counties Antrim and Down) was shared between the Dál Fiatach and the Dál Araide and occasionally with the Uí Echach Cobha. Around the eighth century, the Dál Fiatach expanded northwards into the south of county Antrim at the expense of the Dál Araide and established a new capital at Duneight in the ninth century. From 972, the kingship of Ulster remained with the Dál Fiatach.

Viking incursions began at the start of the ninth century – Bangor was attacked in 810, and Movilla was plundered in 824. The final defeat of the Vikings in Ireland is traditionally assumed to have come at Clontarf in 1014. The Vikings spoke Norse, which contributed a quantity of loan-words to Gaelic, but in Down almost the only toponymic record of their presence is the name of Strangford (though the lough continues to be known in Irish as *Loch Cuan*). This is in contrast to the extensive place-name landscape which they bequeathed to northern and western Scotland and the Isle of Man, and to the possible persistence of their spoken language until Norman times in some small areas of southern Ireland.

The Uí Néill had meanwhile spread across central Ulster from the west, gaining control over the ecclesiastical centre of Armagh and moving their principal sites to Tulach Óg and Dungannon. The demise of the Vikings perhaps mattered less to the Ulaid than the relentless pressure of the Uí Néill. Nonetheless, the first quarter of the twelfth century saw an Irish renaissance. When the lands associated with the various monasteries were consolidated into larger dioceses at the Synod of Rath Breasail in 1111, their boundaries reflected the contemporary Irish tribal territories, with the lands of the Uí Echach Cobha forming the diocese of Dromore, those of the Dál Fiatach forming the diocese of Down, and those of the Dál Araide forming the diocese of Connor.[5] Bangor monastery was restored in 1124 and brought under Augustinian rule in 1137, and new monasteries were founded, including that of the Cistercians at Newry in 1144.

The Normans under Strongbow came to southern Ireland in 1170, and John de Courcy arrived in Ulster in 1177. The Normans were composed of both French and English speakers, with the former socially dominant. They too added to the quota of monasteries, including Blackabbey (St Andrew's, Ballyhalbert), Inch, Greyabbey, Comber and new Benedictine and Franciscan establishments in Downpatrick. The king of Dál Fiatach, Ruaidrí Mac Duinn Shléibe, was slain by de Courcy in 1201.

At its greatest extent, the Norman earldom of Ulster covered the former territories of the Dál Fiatach, the Dál Araide and the Dál Riata, or at least their coastal areas, as well as the north coast of the present county Derry.[6] The only groups east of the Bann who maintained an independent existence in the interior were the Uí Echach Cobha and, in county Antrim immediately to the north of Lough Neagh, the Uí Thuirtre, a group of the Oirghialla who had earlier been located in south Derry, and some of whom later appear as the O'Flynns of the Ards Peninsula.

The Normans in east Ulster gradually faded out in the fourteenth century, and left little permanent linguistic effect in county Down, whereas their language extensively influenced the Irish dialect of Munster. In Ulster the return to Gaelic is well documented in place-names; in the Ards, for example, Philipstown and Talbotstown of the fourteenth century had become Baile Philip and Baile Thalbóid by the early seventeenth century, whence modern Ballyphilip and Ballyhalbert.[7]

At this period surnames are coming into use, as we have already seen with Mac Duinn Shléibe (McAleavey, Dunleavy) of the Dál Fiatach, whose power was effectively ended by the Normans, although the name continues until the late thirteenth century as king of the 'Irish' of Ulster. Some of this family later attained prominence as physicians to the O'Donnells, and in Donegal they were given the sobriquet 'Ultach', whence possibly Mac an Ultaigh (McNulty). The surname Mac Duinn Shleibe is also common in Argyll, where it may be shortened to 'Mac a' Léigh' and is anglicised to Livingstone. The Mac Giolla Mhuire (Gilmore) name is also of the Dál Fiatach.

By the fourteenth century, the Mag Aonghusa (Magennis) and Mac Artáin (McCartan) families had emerged from the Uí Echach and their territories are reflected in the extent of the later baronies of Uí Echach (Iveagh) and Cenél Fhaghartaigh (Kinelarty), respectively.[8] The Mac Aonghusa clann seem to have had a ceremonial centre at Knockiveagh near Rathfriland,[9] while the Mac Artáin lands contained the ecclesiastical site of Loughinisland. Names such as Savage and Fitzsimons attest to the assimilated Norman presence in the east of the county.

But it was a branch of the Uí Néill, the Clann Aedha Buidhe (Clandeboy), who took over from the Normans in north Down, moving down both sides of Belfast Lough by the fourteenth century. There must have been many smaller population movements too, one of which concerns the Uí Thuirtre (with their principal surname Ó Floinn), who are found from the fifteenth century in Inishargey parish in the Ards.[10] Also worthy of mention is the twelfth-century migration of the Mugdorna, a tribe of the Oirghialla, from Cremourne in county Monaghan to the south of county Down, where they gave to the Mourne Mountains their name in English.

Down was once again entirely Irish-speaking at the close of the sixteenth century, on the eve of Plantation.[11]

Plantation

In most parts of the island where the Normans remained, they became, in the famous phrase, 'more Irish than the Irish themselves', but in the area known as the Pale, around Dublin and northwards along the east coast to Dundalk, the Norman colonies formed a bridgehead for continuing English involvement in Ireland.

Ulster was considered to be now the most Gaelic of all the provinces, and the most resistant to English rule. The English of the Pale mounted many expeditions against it and finally defeated the Gaelic forces under Ó Néill and Ó Domhnaill at the Battle of Kinsale in 1601. This defeat broke the old order in Ulster, terms were agreed in 1603, and in 1607 the chiefs of the leading Ulster clanns emigrated to the continent in the 'Flight of the Earls'. Ulster was now wide open to the plantation schemes of James I, whereby loyal English and Scots were settled on the confiscated lands of the native clanns in the escheated counties of Armagh, Tyrone, Derry, Donegal, Fermanagh and Cavan.

We should recall that large-scale population exchange between Ulster and Scotland was nothing new. Under the Gaelic order it was rather the norm. The Scottish bardic families of the MacMhuirichs and Morrisons, for example, were of Irish origin; while in the other direction, Scottish *gallóglaich* participating in the Irish clann wars came to form important clanns themselves, including the MacDonnells in Antrim and the MacSweeneys in Donegal. But these Irish and Scots shared a common Gaelic culture, whereas the intent of the Jacobean plantation was to destroy the Gaelic culture and replace it with an English one. To the plantation mentality, highland Scotland was no less barbarous than Ulster.

Down and Antrim already shared ongoing diffusion of population with Scotland and these counties were not included in the Jacobean plantation. An abortive English attempt had been made to plant the Ards in 1571, but then, beginning in 1605, Montgomery and Hamilton, two Lowland Scots from northern Ayrshire, came to an agreement with Conn O'Neill by which they took over the Great Ards and half of Conn's Castlereagh estates in return for getting him a royal pardon, and over the next few years Conn sold off most of his remaining lands.[12] Montgomery got Newtownards, Greyabbey, Comber and Donaghadee, while Hamilton got Bangor, Holywood, Killinchy and Ballyhalbert and settled them mainly with Lowland Scots in 1606-7. Hamilton also acquired the Dufferin estate around Killyleagh from the Anglo-Norman Whites in 1610.[13]

English estates in county Down included those of the Hills (Downshires), who acquired Hillsborough and much of northern Uí Echach from Mac Aonghusa, and continued to encroach on Uí Eachach throughout the seventeenth century, as far south as Newry. Newry itself had been granted to the English Bagenals in the mid-sixteenth century. Lecale was another centre of English settlement: Downpatrick, Ardglass and Strangford 'reverted to the crown' in 1599 and eventually found their way into the possession of Mountjoy. The Cromwells had holdings including the abbey lands of Down, Inch and Saul acquired from Mountjoy, which passed to the Southwells in 1687; and in 1636 they sold Dundrum to the Blundells, from whom it passed by inheritance to the Downshires. The Cromwells obtained one-third of Cenél Fhaghartaigh from Mac Artáin, and this passed to the Fordes in 1637. The Conways, whose main estates were in south Antrim, owned Dromore in 1635, and a corner of county Down around Moira.[14]

The Little Ards and parts of Lecale were still held by Gaelicised Anglo-Norman families, including Savage (Portaferry), Fitzsimons (Kilclief) and Audley (Strangford). Savage married Montgomery's daughter and converted to Protestantism. The Fitzsimons sold their holdings piecemeal. In 1643 the Audleys sold part of their Strangford lands to the Wards, who acquired the remainder two centuries later. The Russells lost most of their estates around Downpatrick in Oliver Cromwell's time. The southern part of county Down remained in the Mac Aonghusa family. Mourne was held by Anglo-Normans, with some Welsh and Scots settlement.[15]

The efforts of the natives to recover lost ground only resulted in further land confiscations. After the failed uprising of 1641, losses included the lands of the Laverys at Moira,[16] and the Mac Aonghusa and Mac Artáin lands were mostly granted to new Cromwellian settlers. Mac Aonghusa regained his title, but not his lands, after the restoration of the English monarchy but the title was finally forfeited after the Williamite Wars in 1691. It has been estimated that as many as 80,000 Scots settled in Ulster in the years following 1690.[17]

Petty's 'census' of 1659 gives the numbers of 'English, Scots and Irish', but in county Down the English and Scots are counted together. The percentages of English/Scots in some baronies of county Down are as follows:[18]

TABLE 17.1

Percentage of English/Scots in Down baronies in 1659

Barony	% English/Scots
Lecale	40
Upper Iveagh	17
Lower Iveagh	49
Newry	17
Kinelarty and Dufferin	48
Castlereagh	59
Ards	60

These figures illustrate that many natives still remained as tenants in all areas at this period.

It is far from clear whether Petty's classification is made on the basis of country of origin (as is ostensibly the case), or of language, or of religion, or of political sympathy. In most cases these factors will correlate highly, but not always: in analysing the 1659 data for the Ards and Castlereagh, Adams tries to interpret the census in linguistic terms, so that he can compare it with the virtually monolingual English situation in the same baronies around 1760, but he is forced to acknowledge the problems posed by the classification of Gaelic-speaking Lowland Scots, and likewise of the Gaelic-speaking Manx element.[19]

The question of the extent of Gaelic-speaking amongst the incomers is an interesting one. Highland Scots, including those of Kintyre, would have been thoroughly Gaelic-speaking, but in county Down it is to be supposed that most of the settlers came from the western part of the Lowlands: Renfrew, Ayr and Galloway. A good deal has been written about the survival of Gaelic in Galloway and Carrick (the southernmost part of Ayrshire), and the general opinion seems to be that Gaelic was extensively spoken in the area in the mid-sixteenth century, but to have died out around 1760 (late speakers are located to Cultezron near Maybole; and to Glenapp, the glen where the road from Stranraer to Girvan leaves the coast).[20] So it is likely that the south-west contained substantial Gaelic-speaking and bilingual areas at the beginning of the seventeenth century and anyone from these areas settling in county Down would have had little difficulty in understanding the Gaelic of their adopted county.

Adams notes that some Manxmen were settled round the coast of county Down from Mourne to Belfast in the seventeenth century, and he lists Manx surnames found in county Down as including Crangle, McKisack, Quail, and Quekett.[21] The Isle of Man would have been solidly Gaelic-speaking at this time, and even in 1861 there were many monglot Gaelic speakers there. In the census of 1911, Man was still 4.3 per cent Gaelic-speaking, while in 1901 the overall figure was 8.1 per cent with the west coast of the island ranging from 11 to 23 per cent.

Religion and language: converting the Irish

The Church of Ireland, from Elizabethan times right through the seventeenth century and well into the eighteenth, had difficulty in deciding whether to use Gaelic in working with the native population, or whether cultural conversion should go hand-in-hand with religious conversion. Among the achievements of the party who favoured using Irish, the New Testament was translated under Bishop Daniel of Tuam in 1608, and the entire Bible in Irish was produced by William Bedell, bishop of Kilmore and Ardagh, and belatedly printed in 1685. Bedell 'had the Book of Common Prayer read in the Irish tongue in the church of K[ilmore, County Cavan] for the benefit of those that he had brought from popery, but understood not the English tongue'.[22]

The Presbyterian Church, with its strong Scottish connections, had no reservations about the use of Gaelic. The Belfast Synod of 1710, for example, sent out six ministers and three probationers to preach in Irish all over Ulster. Interestingly, they also arranged that congregations who wanted Irish-speaking ministers 'are to exchange members with those who can speak Irish'.[23] Restricting consideration to county Down and neighbouring areas, we may note that Rev Patrick Simpson from

Islay was in charge of a school in Dundalk to train ministers in the use of Gaelic, and in 1717 he was instructed 'to preach in any place of the County of Down where he may have an Irish congregation and audience'.[24] Adams records Methodist preaching in Gaelic in the market place in Lisburn in the second half of the eighteenth century.[25] It was said of Rev Moses Neilson, minister of Rademon near Crossgar and of his congregation in 1784: 'The Dissenters and Papists of this parish mostly speak in that language [Irish], and his prayers and discourses are made in it.'[26] In 1798 his son Rev William Neilson (of whom more later) was arrested after preaching in Gaelic there.[27] And the Rev William Laing, a native of Perth, preached in Gaelic in the Newry district from 1780 to 1806, as well as to the Kintyre settlers about Ballymascanlon.[28]

Public preaching may be directed to any and all sections of the population, but the use of Gaelic inside Protestant churches can only mean that a large part of those particular congregations were Gaelic speakers. Were they planters who came from Scotland already speaking Gaelic; or planters who came speaking English but adopted the language of the natives; or Irish-speaking natives who converted to Protestantism in the early days of the plantation? It is probable that all three explanations are involved. We have already considered the first, and two pieces of evidence bearing on the second are the remark just quoted about the people of Rademon in 1784; and also an incident related by Ernest Blythe when a Presbyterian relative from Castlewellan visited Blythe's mother's family in the early years of the nineteenth century: his English was odd as he usually spoke Irish.[29]

Regarding the conversion of native Irish to Protestantism, certainly Adams' 'spot-check' on the surnames of the Saintfield First Presbyterian congregation of 1969-70 points in that direction; as he says, 'one can change one's religion in a year or two but it takes a generation or two to change a family's language.' He concludes:

> a considerable part of the old Irish population [in east Ulster] seems to have been absorbed into one or other of the reformed churches, usually into presbyterianism, which in the seventeenth and early eighteenth century must have had a considerable Irish-speaking membership. The association of Irish language survival with strongly Roman Catholic areas belongs to a later period and to central and west Ulster.[30]

In an article devoted to this subject, de Blacam writes: 'The schism of the sixteenth century cut geographically across the Gaelic world. Scotland and that part of Ulster which was infiltrated, not planted, became Protestant even before the plantation of Ulster.'[31]

The response of the Catholic Church to the use of Gaelic by the Protestant Churches varied. In the early seventeenth century, a programme of Catholic religious publication in Irish was undertaken: Keating's *Eochar-Sgiath an Aifrinn* appeared in 1615, but the main centre of activity was Louvain, where the Franciscan college of St Anthony issued three major works between 1611 and 1618. The third of these, *Scáthán Shacramuinte na hAithridhe*, is of particular interest to us, as its author was Aodh Mac Aingil, from county Down, whom we shall mention again. Two centuries later, Protestant Bible societies employed many native scholars, including Hugh Gordon of Loughinisland, to teach the people to read the scriptures in Irish.[32] In some areas, such as Antrim and Cavan, the result was that Catholics acquired a distrust of anything written in Irish.

Irish literature in county Down: bardic poetry

Since around 1200, the chief literary genre in Gaelic had been 'bardic poetry', which is poetry in elevated language and strict metre, often in praise of clann chiefs. There were hereditary bardic families, often associated with a particular clann, but not confined to writing in its praise alone. As well as poetry, the poets were expected to be well versed in genealogy and history, and much material of this sort has also survived, in the form of pedigrees and annals.

One of the bardic families in county Down were the Ó Ruanadha (O'Rooney) family, a number of whom were 'pardoned' in 1602.[33] The name of Ballyroney comes from this family. The Ó Ruanadhas were mainly associated with the Mac Aonghusa clann, but poems in praise of Mac Aonghusa also survive from many other pens, including those of Feargal Óg Mac an Bháird (fl. *c.* 1600) from the Donegal bardic family, and of Fear Flatha Ó Gnímh (before 1629).[34]

Not exactly in the native bardic tradition, but none the less interesting for that, was Rev Patrick Dunkin, Episcopalian vicar of Donaghmore parish (county Down) in 1649, who was banished to the Isle of Man by puritan reformers around the year 1650. He composed the song *Truagh mo thuras ó mo thír* on the occasion. He returned to Ireland after the Restoration, around 1666, when he became precentor of Armagh and rector of Killeavy.[35]

The Gaelic scholar and collector of manuscripts Énrí Ó Muirgheasa gave a list of Ulster poets and scribes,[36] and his earliest writer with county Down associations is Rev Cathal Mac Ruadhraigh of Drumgooland, who lived about 1650 according to O'Reilly (who calls him 'Thomas McRory').[37] He is the author of *Do chaill Éire a céile fíre*, a lament for Eoghan Ruadh Ó Néill, which was translated into English in 1701 by the Hon. Arthur Brownlow of Lurgan.

In 1680, the chief of Clann Aedha Buidhe, Cormac mac Áirt Óig, ordered a collection to be made of the genealogies and praise poems connected with his clann.[38] Many of the pieces had been composed over a period of three centuries by members of the east Ulster bardic family of Ó hEachaidhéin (Haughian), who also wrote for the Mac Aonghusas.

Ó Muirgheasa also mentions Diarmuid mac Lughaidh Mac a' Bháird, a native of county Down according to O'Reilly, who places his *floruit* in 1690.[39] Hughes counts this Diarmuid 'among the last of the great classically-trained Irish poets' in an article in which he points out that the bardic tradition lasted longest in east Ulster and in the highlands of Scotland.[40] It is possible that Ballyward may be named from this family.

Irish literature in county Down: popular verse

The social dislocation of the native Irish in the seventeenth century meant that by *ca.* 1700 the clann chiefs were no longer in a position to maintain family bards and the market for praise poetry had dried up. With the demise of the bardic order, versifiers would henceforth write in simpler forms and would use the language of the common people, who were now their only audience. One of the new breed was Colla Mac Seáin (Johnston) of Mourne, whom O'Reilly dates to 1726.[41] From the same period, and presenting both sides of the story, is a humorous but moving poetic contention between Donnchadh Mór Ó Labhraidh and Giolla-Mhuire Caoch Mac Artáin. Ó Labhraidh, a worldly farmer, mocks the art of the blind harper with country wit: 'Cé an traona seo sa ghort?', while Mac Artáin hits back at the materialism of 'Donnchadh na mbó'.[42]

Although south-eastern Ulster was a centre of Gaelic literary activity in the eighteenth century, the nearest Down can come to claiming one of the major poets is the case of Pádraig Mac a' Liondain (1665-1733). O'Reilly says he hailed from the Fews in county Armagh, but Ó Muirgheasa doubts this: 'There are no Mac Alindons in the Fews to-day, while they are plentiful in Co. Down around Hilltown, Rathfriland and Mayobridge, and Irish was spoken in this district until quite recently.' One of Mac a' Liondain's compositions is in praise of a Sliabh Crúb, and certainly the best known mountain of that name lies in county Down. Despite these indications, later scholarship supports the Fews theory.[43] By the same token, county Down would seem to lose its claim on Mac a' Liondain's daughter Máire, who engaged in a poetic contest with the county Armagh poet Peadar Ó Doirnín, and possibly on Feargus Mac Bheathaigh (McVeigh), who wrote Mac a' Liondain's grave-lay, though once again Ó Muirgheasa is correct in saying that McVeigh is a county Down surname.[44]

One surprising omission from Ó Muirgheasa's list is Micheál Ó hÍr, who is named in a manuscript of Art Mac Bionaid's as the author of *Seachrán Chairn tSiadhail*, the song of an itinerant journeyman. The song travelled as widely as its author and gathered new verses wherever it spread, so that no less than twenty-eight stanzas, ranging from Omeath to Donegal, were printed in a monograph by Seosamh Laoide.[45] The location in the title is Carnteel in county Tyrone and Laoide suggests that Ó hÍr may have come from the neighbouring part of county Armagh. Nevertheless a Down association is possible since the name O'Hare is a common one in the county.

Irish literature in county Down: scribes

The popular Gaelic literature of south-east Ulster in the eighteenth century spawned a scribal tradition which continued through the third quarter of the following century. We now mention some scribes with Down connections, but this list is likely to be very incomplete.

The last name on Ó Muirgheasa's county Down list is that of Pádraig Ó Pronntaigh (Patrick O Pronty), 'a great Irish scribe, but also wrote a few religious poems'. Ó Casaide notes that his mss. date from 1732 to 1763, and that he was probably of Fermanagh extraction and was probably living at Ballymascanlon, county Louth about 1738. But he finds no evidence to connect him with another Louthman, Hugh Prunty, whose son Patrick (born 1777, between Rathfriland and Loughbrickland) was the father of Charlotte, Emily and Anne Brontë.[46]

Eoin Ó Gripín, of Ballymagreehan in Drumgooland has a number of extant manuscripts including some dated between 1796 and 1799. He may have been a hedge-schoolmaster in the area. Seosamh Laoide had at one time in his possession a manuscript of an Ossianic tale rewritten in Ballymagreehan.[47] Two scribes from Newry are named by Ó Casaide as Aodh Ó Néill (mss. 1785, 1806), and Pádraig Ó hEithir (mss. 1795, 1797).[48]

The Ó Loingsigh (Lynchy or Lynch) family of Loughinisland were also of the scholarly and scribal tradition, and ran a school which was famed for Irish and classical learning. The last of the Lynchys was Pádraig Ó Loingsigh, some of whose Irish manuscripts still survive in various libraries. He is found teaching Irish in Belfast Academy in 1794, and taking private classes. His pupils included Thomas Russell, 'the Man from God knows where', who was working in the Linenhall Library. Some of Ó Loingsigh's work found its way into print, though not bearing his name, including Irish conversations in a magazine called *Bolg an Tsolair* (1795), and a phonetically-written translation of St Luke's Gospel (1799). He seems to have returned to Loughinisland about 1801, but in 1802 he made a celebrated trip to Connacht to obtain the words of Irish songs for Edward Bunting, and gathered more than three hundred of them. In 1803, Ó Loingsigh was made to testify at the trial in Downpatrick of Thomas Russell, who was hanged for high treason. No more is heard of Pádraig Ó Loingsigh after this, but it is thought he may be buried in Loughinisland.[49] The Patrick Lynch who was secretary of the Gaelic Society in Dublin in 1806 is shown by Ó Casaide to be a different person.[50]

Irish literature in county Down: religious literature

Turning from poetry to religious literature, the seventeenth-century translations into Gaelic of the New Testament by Daniel, and of the complete Bible by Bedell, have been mentioned earlier. We now return to that period for the first of two county Down authors of religious works.

Aodh Mac Aingil (Hugh McCawell) was born in Downpatrick or possibly in Saul in 1571. He was educated locally and in the Isle of Man, and returned to Ireland about 1592 as tutor to the two sons of Hugh O'Neill in Dungannon. He accompanied Henry, the elder of the two boys, to Salamanca University in 1600, where they both studied. Aodh entered the Fransciscan order there in 1603. He was made a professor at the newly-founded College of St Anthony in Louvain in 1605, and in 1618 he published his major work, *Scáthán Shacramuinte na h-Aithridhe*, a treatise on penance. Mac Aingil's prose style has been highly praised. In 1623 he moved to Rome, where we may imagine that he often visited the grave of Hugh O'Neill who had died there in 1616. He was appointed archbishop of Armagh in 1626, but while he was preparing to return to Ireland to take up the post he contracted a fever and died on 22 September, and was buried in Rome. Besides the *Scáthán*, Mac Aingil is the author of a number of theological works in Latin, and of several religious poems in Irish, most notably of the Christmas carol *Dia do bheatha, a naí naoimh*.[51] A short anecdote from the *Scáthán* is given in appendix 17.1 (a).[52]

Rather more than a century later, we encounter Dr James Pulleine (or Séamus Mac Póilín). The date and place of his birth are unknown, but he was dean of the Catholic diocese of Dromore in the middle of the eighteenth century, and lived at Clonduff or Annaclone.[53] The text has been preserved of an oration in Gaelic which he delivered on the grave of Owen O'Neill of Bannvale, of the Clann Aodha Buidhe, who was drowned in the river Bann in 1744.[54] He also wrote an Irish catechism, *An Teagasg Críosdaidhe Angoidhleig*,[55] of which editions were published in 1748 (anonymously) and in 1782. He died around 1776.[56]

Pulleine has also been suggested as the author of the manuscript translation dated 1762 of the *Imitatio Christi* by Thomas à Kempis *Tóruidheacht na bhFíreun ar Lorg Chríosda* – although some believe a Franciscan friar (perhaps of Drumnaquoile) to be a more likely candidate.[57] Of the language of the *Tóruidheacht*, Ó Mordha says (my translation): 'It could be said that the Irish in the Tóraidheacht is a mixture of literary Irish and of the translator's dialect, but the work bears throughout a strong dialect flavour.'[58] The *Tóruidheacht* was published in 1915, edited by An tAth. Domhnall Ó Tuathail.[59] A short extract from the introduction is given in appendix 17.1 (b).

Irish literature in county Down: William Neilson and his grammar

Our next writer may be said to inherit both the religious prose tradition and the secular scribal one which we left with Patrick Lynch. William Neilson was the son of Rev Moses Neilson, who had come as a Presbyterian minister from the Strabane region to Rademon near Crossgar in Kilmore parish in 1767. Moses Neilson was an Irish speaker, and used Irish in Rademon, as already noted.

William was born in 1774. He was schooled first by his father, and later by Lynch at Loughinisland. He attended Glasgow University from 1789 until 1791, and became a minister in 1796. He spent the years from 1797 to 1818 in Dundalk, where he is known to have preached regularly in Irish. His arrest in 1798 after preaching in Irish during a visit home has already been mentioned; he was released from Downpatrick court the following day. He went on to become a professor in the Belfast Academy from 1818 until his death in 1821, and one of his pupils there was Robert McAdam. We can thus trace a line of academic descent from Pádraig Ó Loinsigh, through William Neilson, to Robert McAdam.

In 1769, Moses Neilson began to compile a book on Irish grammar, and this work was taken over and completed by William, leading to the publication of *An introduction to the Irish language* in 1808. This famous book consists of three sections: grammar; phrases and conversations; and extracts from the ancient books. The conversations are the most valuable part of it, and are reported to be partly based on those published earlier by his old teacher Lynch, though it has also been suggested that they have an even longer history.[60] A second and somewhat altered edition of the book was published in 1843, long after the author's death. A facsimile reproduction of the first edition has recently appeared.[61]

The preface to the first edition contains the following:[62]

> It is, particularly, from the **absolute necessity** of understanding this language, in order to converse with the natives of a great part

of Ireland, that the study of it is indispensible. If Irish be no longer the language of the court, or the senate, yet the pulpit and the bar require the use of it; and he that would communicate moral instruction, or investigate the claims of justice, must be versed in the native tongue, if he expects to be generally understood, or to succeed in his researches. In travelling, and the common occurrences of agriculture and rural traffic, a knowledge of Irish is also absolutely necessary.

The book was not sufficiently classical to please John O'Donovan:

This grammar is the joint production of Dr Neilson and Mr Patrick Lynch ... Mr Lynch had a good practical knowledge of the dialect of Irish spoken in the east of Ulster but was a rude scholar. The orthography, however, and grammatical rules, are adapted to this dialect, and not to the general language. The arrangement of the work is excellent, but it is to be regretted that the examples given to illustrate the rules are, for the most part, provincial and barbaric.[63]

From an opposite viewpoint, at the beginning of the revival, Dubhglas de híde said of William Neilson that he was the only person who had done anything for the common speech of the people.[64]

Neilson certainly set out to describe contemporary spoken Irish, but insofar as his book may happen to contain the Irish of east Ulster, this appears as much a natural result of circumstance as a deliberate objective. The quotation from the preface above shows that Neilson's horizons were not narrowly local, and he reveals his position on dialect matters when he mentions

the provincial accents, which vary in Irish, as in all other living languages; and the only remedy for which is a careful attendance to those rules, which are framed conformably to the orthography, and founded upon the authority of the ancients, in whose time the language was cultivated and refined infinitely beyond the modern manner of expression[65]

and 'attending to the various inflexions of nouns, in the different parts of Ireland ... would be descending to the sanction of provincial barbarisms'.[66]

This regard for the 'authority of the ancients' led Neilson to praise east Ulster Irish when it remained consistent with the established orthography (in respects where the spoken Irish of other parts had changed, as in the pronunciation of broad 'bh' and 'mh'), whereas some cases where Ulster Irish itself deviated from the norm simply fail to be witnessed in his spelling. For example, he consistently writes the word for daughter as *inghean*, but remarks in a note that 'it is pronounced in Scotland, and the North of Ireland, nian.'[67] Other words where Neilson's spelling disagrees with Ulster pronunciation include: *bosga, caiptin, bhur, tre/trid*; whereas he employs spelling in accord with Ulster pronunciation in other cases, e.g. *Gaoidheilg, nuaidheacht, pighin, ponta, seort, go de, asteach, astigh, tuit.*

Whatever about their language, Neilson's nine dialogues are certainly not parochial in their subject matter, and in the last of them the action ranges from Downpatrick, Dundrum and Annahilt all the way to Knockmoy, Gort and Kiltartan in county Galway. A short extract from that dialogue, *Teach oidheachta tuaidhthe* or 'A country inn', located somewhere in the midlands, where two men from near Dundrum ('laimh re traigh dùn droma'), called Mac Gabhann and O Ruanadh, arrive on their way to the fair of Ballinasloe, and get into conversation with another traveller ('duine uasal'), who asks them about the antiquities in their part of the world is reproduced in appendix 17.2.[68]

Language shift and survival: Census figures 1851-1911

A new source of information becomes available to us with the Census of Ireland of 1851, in which a language question was included for the first time. This was largely due to the prompting of Belfastman Robert McAdam, and the question was included in every census from 1851 until 1911, that is, every ten years during that time.

The census data is presented on a county basis, and it is well at this point to recall the statement of Eóin Mac Néill that 'the county divisions of Ireland have no sanction in tradition or history save that of the Sheriff and the Hangman for whose duties they were introduced.' For as long as the boundary between county Down and county Armagh approximated to that between Mac Aonghusa's domains and those of the O'Hanlons and others, it had some cultural significance in the Gaelic world, and served to demarcate a Gaelic-speaking area stretching from south Down, through south Armagh, south Monaghan, north Louth, north Meath and east Cavan. This area is generally referred to as Oirghialla, from the tribe who occupied the greater part of it at a much earlier period; by the 1850s it no longer had internal boundaries of any social consequence.

Oirghialla was now cut off from other Gaelic-speaking areas, e.g. from the Sperrins to the north or Connacht to the west. It continued to be squeezed from both sides and eventually eliminated by the forces which had isolated it: Ulster English from the Lagan and Blackwater valleys on the one hand, and southern Hiberno-English from the former Pale on the other. County Down was a peripheral area within Oirghialla, and by the 1850s Gaelic was already in terminal decline there. Table 15.2 lists the number and percentage of the county population who declared themselves able to speak Irish in the period from 1851 to 1911 – including both urban and rural areas but excluding any part of Belfast from consideration:

TABLE 17.2

Number and percentage of Irish-speakers in county Down 1851-1911

	1851	1861	1871	1881	1891	1901	1911
Number of speakers	1153	767	338	880	590	1411	2432
Percentage of population	0.36	0.26	0.12	0.35	0.27	0.69	1.19

These figures show surprising fluctuations and have to be carefully considered, but they are of the utmost interest all the same. The problems with the language question were many. The question simply asked whether the subject spoke Irish – how well, or whether as one's first language, was simply not asked. Varying social pressures also affected the responses. This is how MacAdam describes the attitude prevailing in 1851:

> In various districts where the two languages coexist, but where English now largely predominates, numbers of individuals returned themselves as ignorant of the Irish language, either from a sort of false shame, or from a secret dread that the Government in making this inquiry (for the first time) had some concealed motive, which could not be for their good. Their native shrewdness, therefore, dictated to them that their safest policy was to appear ignorant of the unfashionable language.[69]

The upturn in 1881 is doubtless due to the fact that the language question had been until then merely a footnote on the census form, and could easily be ignored by the enumerators. In the last two censuses we see the effects of the Gaelic revival – the Gaelic League was founded in 1893, and people began in numbers to learn Irish as a second language.

Adams makes a useful distinction when he divides Irish-speaking as reported in these censuses into three categories: *survival Irish*, the original Irish of the district, on which I will be focusing; *immigration Irish*, due to inward population movement from Irish-speaking districts elsewhere, as we might expect to find in urban centres, in particular, in Newry and Warrenpoint; and *revival Irish*, learned as a second language in classes, which may be quite different from the original local form, and which dominates the 1911 figures for county Down.[70]

The original forms for the 1901 and 1911 censuses are available for public inspection, though those for earlier censuses have been lost. When the forms for 1901 are examined, even greater doubt is cast on the meaning of the published figures. I had planned to identify the 1,411 speakers of Irish in county Down in the 1901 census, and count them by ded, parish and barony, while looking at factors which might be indicators of survival Irish, such as county of birth, acquisition of Irish from parents, and degree of education. However it proved impossible to determine which individuals were included as Irish speakers in the published table.

This was because the responses to the language question were in many cases amended, whether by the householders, by the enumerators, or by the census staff. There may be several layers of amendments on one form, making the response practically illegible. It can also happen that the reply is ambiguous, for example, when it is filled in for the head of household only, with dots or ticks for the other members. Even the clear responses are often absurd, such as when a family is made to consist of a number of Irish-speaking monoglots together with a number of English-speaking monoglots. But most perplexing of all is the large number of Protestant families who claimed to be monoglot Irish speakers, from their oldest to their youngest member. Catholic Irish-speakers, on the other hand, almost always claimed to be bilingual, and rarely included children. It seems clear that the Protestant families who returned themselves as monoglot Irish speakers misunderstood the question; perhaps they took the 'Irish language' to refer to Hiberno-English, or perhaps they did not see the question in linguistic terms at all.

The forms have been subjected to a systematic attempt to delete those 'Irish' and 'Irish and English' responses which may be regarded as errors. The response is most likely to be cancelled for Protestants, for whole families, for those below middle age, for those claiming to be monoglots, and for those born in county Down. However I cannot relate the published figures for the county districts to the forms, either before or after emendation, and thus I cannot further analyse those published figures. The district which I examined most closely was Banbridge Urban District, and, allowing for illegibility and ambiguity, I judged that 196 persons in that area were returned as Irish speakers on the forms, the great majority of them as monoglots – whereas the official total is 52 bilinguals and no monoglot Irish speakers. Again, by my reckoning, the systematic amendment process reduced the number of Irish speakers in the Banbridge Urban District to a mere 8. I can find no way to identify the 52 who were admitted to the published table.

Thus the responses to the language question, at least in this area in 1901, are seen to be very unreliable. In the published tables, some allowance has been made – in a way which I do not currently understand – for spurious reporting of ability in Irish, but we must remember that other factors were at work to cause the real Irish speakers to under-report themselves, and no attempt was made to compensate for these. McAdams's description of the suspicions of the respondents in 1851 has already been quoted, and would not have been lessened by the use of policemen as enumerators. Other respondents may have lacked the confidence to declare a knowledge of Irish if, for example, they had not spoken it for a long time, or were not completely fluent in it, or were living away from their native place. They might feel in these circumstances that their Irish was not worth recording in comparison with that found in other parts of Ireland.

Taking the published census figures as we find them, we may try to analyse them by breaking them down either by age-group or by locality, as far as the tables allow. Neither method proves very illuminating, however. Table 17.3 lists the number of Irish speakers in each decadal age-group, but any attempt to follow a ten-year group of people through successive censuses is hopeless.

TABLE 17.3

Number of Irish-speakers in county Down 1851-1911, by decadal age-group

Age-group	1851	1861	1871	1881	1891	1901	1911
0-10	5	41	2	6	59	84	186
10-20	74	79	19	48			
20-30	148	127	43	87	70	578	1429
30-40	156	108	45	108			303
40-50	188	107	41	135	234	515	
50-60	215	83	56	119			329
60-70	202	113	59	164			
70-80	109	73	47	134			
80-90	46	31	22	68	127	234	185
90-100	8	3	3	10			
over 100	1	2	1	1			
unknown	1	2	0	0	0	0	0

Things are only slightly better in a spatial analysis of the figures. The figures were tabulated by baronies until 1891, and by county districts (urban and rural districts) from 1901. The numbers and percentages are as given in table 17.4a.

TABLE 17.4a

Number and percentage of Irish-speakers in county Down 1851-1891, by barony

Barony	1851	1861	1871	1881	1891
Lower Ards	17 (0.06)	14 (0.05)	30 (0.12)	32 (0.15)	52 (0.24)
Upper Ards	10 (0.06)	23 (0.16)	5 (0.04)	14 (0.13)	4 (0.04)
Lower Castlereagh	21 (0.08)	14 (0.06)	27 (0.10)	72 (0.28)	116 (0.43)
Upper Castlereagh	18 (0.06)	34 (0.12)	13 (0.05)	24 (0.11)	28 (0.14)
Dufferin	4 (0.05)	3 (0.04)	6 (0.08)	5 (0.07)	4 (0.07)
Lower Lecale	14 (0.13)	5 (0.06)	13 (0.15)	11 (0.14)	17 (0.26)
Upper Lecale	27 (0.17)	26 (0.19)	5 (0.04)	10 (0.08)	23 (0.21)
Kinelarty	8 (0.05)	13 (0.08)	5 (0.04)	12 (0.10)	34 (0.31)
Lower Iveagh (L)	14 (0.05)	8 (0.03)	12 (0.05)	13 (0.07)	30 (0.18)
Lower Iveagh (U)	31 (0.08)	12 (0.03)	19 (0.06)	62 (0.23)	61 (0.26)
Upper Iveagh (L)	347 (0.87)	203 (0.55)	108 (0.32)	231 (0.81)	71 (0.29)
Upper Iveagh (U)	168 (0.48)	184 (0.58)	51 (0.17)	144 (0.54)	89 (0.39)
Lordship of Newry	453 (2.54)	220 (1.47)	36 (0.25)	238 (1.62)	18 (0.15)
Mourne	21 (0.15)	8 (0.06)	8 (0.06)	12 (0.10)	43 (0.40)

Note: Towns are here included with the surrounding barony. In three cases a town for which separate figures were returned lay on the boundary between two baronies, and its Irish-speakers have been here divided in proportion to the number of Irish-speakers already in those baronies:

Newtownards (1851), 14:	Lower Ards, 6;	Lower Castlereagh, 8
Newtownards (1861), 2:	Lower Ards, 1;	Lower Castlereagh, 1
Rathfriland (1851), 1:	Upper Iveagh (L), 1;	Upper Iveagh (U), 0

TABLE 17.4b

Number and percentage of Irish-speakers in county Down 1901-1911, by rural district

Rural district	1901	1911
Newtownards Rural	87 (0.21)	124 (0.28)
Castlereagh Rural	44 (0.55)	97 (1.05)
Hillsborough Rural	50 (0.24)	40 (0.20)
Downpatrick Rural	227 (0.58)	897 (2.29)
Moira Rural	15 (0.14)	43 (0.41)
Banbridge Rural	287 (0.79)	313 (0.91)
Newry No 1 Rural	575 (1.95)	725 (2.64)
Kilkeel Rural	126 (0.66)	193 (1.07)

Note: Urban districts have been here included with the surrounding rural districts.

TABLE 17.5

Baronies of Upper Iveagh (lower half), Upper Iveagh (upper half) and the Lordship of Newry: percentage of Irish-speakers in decadal cohorts 1771-1871, estimated from the 1881 census (from Fitzgerald, 1984). In brackets, percentages actually reported in the 1851 census.

born in:	Upper Iveagh (lower half)	Upper Iveagh (upper half)	Lordship of Newry
1771-1781	11 (4)	10 (3)	9 (9)
1781-1791	11 (4)	10 (2)	9 (9)
1791-1801	9 (2)	5 (1)	6 (6)
1801-1811	5 (1)	3 (1)	4 (5)
1811-1821	3 (1)	2 (0)	4 (4)
1821-1831	1 (0)	1 (0)	4 (2)
1831-1841	0 (0)	1 (0)	3 (1)
1841-1851	0	1	3
1851-1861	0	0	1
1861-1871	0	0	0
Overall in 1881	0.81	0.54	1.62

We might wish to study for each barony what proportion of people born in each decade spoke Irish, and in this way form an idea of when Irish ceased to be the first language of children in different areas. The figures from the earliest language census, that of 1851, allow this but their acknowledged inaccuracy casts doubt on the value of the exercise.[71] The more accurate figures of 1881 suffer from the problem that different geographical units are used for the age-distribution of the general population (dispensary districts) and for that of the Irish-speakers (baronies). However, Fitzgerald managed to perform such an analysis of the 1881 figures, on the basis of reasonable assumptions, and also using the earlier censuses to extrapolate backwards.[72]

Fitzgerald regards his figures for the proportion of Irish speakers born in each decade between 1771 and 1881 as minimum estimates, which may be understated for a number of reasons. He concludes with regard to county Down that only in Upper Iveagh (both halves) and the Lordship of Newry did the figure exceed 2.5 per cent even in 1771-1781. His estimates for these three baronies are given in table 17.5.

The relative slowness of the decay in the Lordship of Newry is probably due to continued replenishment from south Armagh and north Louth, and the same may be true to a lesser extent of the urban areas of Upper Iveagh (upper half) which comprise Warrenpoint, Banbridge and the greater part of Rathfriland. Survival of true county Down Irish

TABLE 17.6

Percentage of Irish-speakers among over-40 age-group in 1911 census: highest-scoring deds in selected areas outside county Down

County, etc.	DED	%
Oirghialla survival area:		
Armagh	Killeavy	38.3
Monaghan	Crossalare	44.1
Louth	Drummullagh	60.7
Meath	Ballinlough	14.0
Cavan (East)	Virginia	24.8
Other east Ulster survival areas:		
Tyrone	Fallagh	90.7
Derry	Bancran	35.4
Antrim (Glens)	Red Bay	46.4
Rathlin		82.6
Ulster salient of Connacht area:		
Fermanagh	Lattone	17.1
Cavan (West)	Derrynananta	59.7
Leitrim	Yugan	50.6

should be sought in Upper Iveagh and especially in the lower half.

Baronies and county districts are too large for meaningful study of geographic distribution. Finer grain was provided, for the first and only time, in the 1911 language figures, which were published for the smaller 'district electoral divisions' (deds), which average about 1,000 in population and are thus considerably more extensive than the townlands from which they sometimes take their name. Table 17.6 illustrates the state of Gaelic in 1911 in certain parts of Ulster and neighbouring counties.

These figures represent, in Adams' terminology, mainly survival Irish. However in county Down, where the highest-rated ded is Rossconor at 4.3 per cent, survival Irish is very scarce by this time and what Irish is found there is mostly revival Irish. In studying the 1911 census in county Down, we are basically studying the distribution of revival Irish, and I will not repeat here my previous analysis.[73]

Language shift and survival: the state of Gaelic in county Down

The census data provides a background against which various statements about the condition of Gaelic in county Down may be evaluated, and I give a collection of such statements in appendix 17.3, where full references will also be found.

Language shift, even under the most favourable circumstances, takes several generations to complete. At some point in time, the children of a particular area will cease to be raised bilingually with English and Irish, though this will not occur at precisely the same time for all families. The last children to be raised bilingually, that is, the last fluent speakers of Irish, will have little opportunity to use the language as adults, but some of them will still be alive seventy years later. Children raised in houses where these last fluent speakers passed their old age may be expected to pick up words and phrases from them, and traces of native Irish may thus linger for their lifetime also. Thus, in exceptional circumstances, these traces could be found as much as a century and a half after the language has ceased to be generally used, though perhaps half that time is a more likely limit in general.

Fitzgerald's analysis suggests that practically no children were raised speaking Irish in county Down after 1821, but that in the decade 1781-1791 at least 10 per cent of Upper Iveagh was still Irish-speaking in this sense. A period of 150 years would bring us then almost to the middle of the twentieth century. Appendix 17.3 contains reports of persons purported to be native speakers as late as the 1940s, and there is every reason to suppose that the number of such reports could be multiplied on further enquiry. However, it is difficult by that stage to distinguish bearers of the last traces of native Irish from the much more numerous group who learned some Irish in class as teenagers as much as forty years earlier – both are simply 'old Irish speakers'. The distinction is further obscured by the likelihood that those possessing remnants of native Irish would have participated in revival activities as well. It must be assumed that, in the majority of these cases, Irish was acquired through classes, unless – as is true in a few cases – there is convincing evidence that we have a native speaker.

There is fair consistency among the major statements about the decline of Irish. Laoide claims that it was widely spoken south of a line from Scarva to Portaferry 'in Neilson's time', say around 1790. The next areas to lose Irish seem to have been the Upper Ards, Lower Iveagh and the parish of Aghaderg – the latter two were stated in 1834 to have had Irish spoken in them within living memory, and all three appear to be excluded from the area described as Irish-speaking in 1820 by Hume ('from Ballynahinch to near Newry and Newcastle' – though Lower Lecale should probably be added to that). Hume's area can in turn be subdivided at the time of O'Donovan's visit in 1834 into areas where Irish was spoken only by extremely old people (Lecale, and the parishes of Kilmore, Drumballyroney and Donaghmore) or by those above middle age (the parishes of Annaclone, where some children born in the 1770s were raised with Irish, and Clonallan), and areas which were still generally Irish-speaking (the parishes of Drumgath, Clonduff, Kilcoo, Drumgooland, Kilmegan and Loughinisland). It is also possible that the more mountainous parts of Kilkeel were still Irish-speaking, but firm evidence either way is lacking.

How long did Irish last in its county Down heartland? Hume's relatively precise statement has been generally accepted as meaning that it had gone by 1874, and Laoide opts for 1890, while Piatt claims that it held out until almost 1930, though his anecdotes may refer to speakers of no great fluency. He argues that a casual enquiry may easily elicit the information that some individual, living or recently deceased, is 'the last speaker' when they are in reality one of a number who, being house-bound, no longer meet each other; such statements then propagate through written sources. I interpret the various remarks quoted in appendix 17.3 as showing that Irish was still widely spoken in Drumgath and Loughinisland in the 1830s; in Drumgooland in the 1840s; in Kilmegan in the 1850s and possibly later; and in Kilcoo in the 1860s and probably considerably later. In Clonduff, where information is fullest, it is clear that children born before 1840 were generally raised with Irish; Irish was still quite widely used in the 1880s; fluent speakers were not difficult to find in the 1890s, and at least one man knowing some words of native county Down Irish was living as late as 1945.

County Down Irish: the nature of the dialect

It is hardly surprising that Down was the earliest Ulster county to lose the continuous thread of native Irish over its whole area when we consider how it is situated near to major commercial centres and trade routes. The Mourne Mountains failed to protect the language as effectively as did more modest hills elsewhere in the province. Irish in county Down did not survive until the age of sound recording: I do not know of a single word of it on tape or on record. It did not survive into the golden age of folklore collection: little of it has been noted in the form of popular stories, songs or proverbs. It did not survive into the age of descriptive linguistics, when a scholar could write down a scientific description of speech which would enable another to recreate it at a later time. Given another fifty years, all of these things would have been different. In spite of all this, we still know something of the nature of county Down Irish, for example, from the consideration of placenames, and from its evident similarity to the longer-lived Irish of adjoining counties.

Ulster Irish occupies a central position in the Gaelic world made up of Ireland, Scotland and the Isle of Man.[74] Within Ulster, the main subdivision is into Donegal Irish and east Ulster Irish, the latter spoken until recent times not only in Oirghialla but in Inishowen, the Sperrins, the Antrim Glens and Rathlin Island. Being spread over such a relatively large area, east Ulster Irish must necessarily contain some variation, but nevertheless exhibits many consistent features.[75]

One of the most striking differences between east Ulster Irish and Donegal Irish is the pronunciation of the vowel written 'ea' (e.g. *fear*, a man, pronounced 'far' in most of Ireland, but as 'ferr' in east Ulster). Examples seen in English include the pronunciation of 'Crossgar' as 'Crossgerr', or 'Kilfedder' for 'Giolla Pheadair'. J. J. Kneen comments that 'it is interesting to find that Manx agrees with Scottish Gaelic and the Irish of County Down in retaining the short e sound in a word like "fer", whereas elsewhere in Ireland it becomes â.' Colm Ó Baoill shows that an e-sound (open or closed) is common all over east Ulster.[76]

Another interesting case of the pronunciation of 'ea' is the name *Seán* – earlier spelled *Seaghán* – which is pronounced 'Shawn' in Munster, 'Shaan' in Donegal, but 'Shane' in east Ulster, whence anglicisations like Shane O'Neill, Shane Bernagh, Shane Crossagh, MacShane, Glenshane, Broughshane, and so on. Likewise *Eachach*, giving *Loch nEachach* (Lough Neagh), *Uibh Eachach* (Iveagh). The pronunciation of the second syllable of 'Lecale' seems to suggest that 'a' could be raised even after a non-palatal consonant; it may be no more than coincidence that this happens in south-west Scotland in words such as *math*, and is considered nowadays to be a characteristic of Islay Gaelic.

Cathal and *Eachach* also show that 'th' or 'ch' in the middle of a word tends to disappear and leave a single long syllable. Wagner adds the examples *droichead* and *frithir*, and Neilson advances *athair* and *máthair*, where the 'th' is omitted 'in most of the counties of Ulster, and the east of Leinster',[77] At the end of a word too 'ch' can be very weak: *ach* (ah), *fliuch* (flooh), *bocht* (bot, as in Ballybot). Neilson says this last case occurs 'in all the country along the sea coast, from Derry to Waterford'.

Neilson also states that 'the ancient pronunciation' of broad 'bh' and 'mh' as 'v', especially at the beginning or end of a word 'is still retained in the north of Ireland, as in Scotland, and the Isle of Man', whereas 'throughout Connaught, Leinster and some counties of Ulster, the sound of "w" is substituted'.[78] An tAth. Mac Thréinfhir cites a county Down place-name, *Páirc a' Bhóthair*, which supports this. Neilson admits that broad 'bh' or 'mh' may become 'w' in the middle of a word, e.g. *leabhar*, but criticises dropping them in 'the south' in *foghmhar* and *faobhar*, which he says should have a 'v' sound.

Medial 'ng' is vocalised, e.g. in *ceangail*. *Deartháir* is shortened to *dreár*.

In the field of grammar, *cha* was universally used for negation in east

Ulster, at least orally, though Neilson and the *Tóruidheacht* (in the manuscript) generally avoid it. Typical east Ulster forms of prepositions which turn up in the *Tóruidheacht* include *ann a dteampoll* (i dteampall), and *roimhe leis an bheathaidh* (roimh an bheathaidh). A characteristic east Ulster plural termination is found in *tonnógadh*, *scológadh*, and so forth.

Vocabulary items generally associated with east Ulster include *coinfheasgar* (tráthnóna, evening), *tonnóg* (lacha, duck), *ársuigh* (innis, tell), *frithir* (nimhneach, sore), *corruighe* (fearg, anger), *práinn* (deifir, hurry), *go seadh* (go fóill, yet), *márt* (bó, cow), *toigh* (teach, house).

A number of the peculiar features of east Ulster Irish are in agreement with the Gaelic of Scotland and of the Isle of Man. It has long been argued whether Rathlin Gaelic should be classed as Scottish or Irish, and Robert McAdam stated of Antrim Gaelic in 1873: 'having myself conversed with both Glensmen and Arran men I can testify to the absolute identity of their speech'.[79] A similar relationship must have held between the Irish of the Ards and the Gaelic of Galloway, and between the speech of Lecale and that of Man, but by and large county Down Irish may be taken as closely resembling the dialects of Armagh and Louth, where Irish was spoken well into the twentieth century on the very borders of county Down. Similarity with Omeath Irish has been directly reported by Mac Gréacháin.

County Down Irish: *Gréasaí as Co an Dúin*

We have earlier seen some examples of written Irish from county Down, from the eighteenth and early nineteenth centuries. Now we turn to the very small quantity of material from county Down which has come down to us in the oral medium. As already pointed out, native Irish disappeared in county Down before the folklorists had a chance to collect it, and so we are dependent on material collected in adjacent counties but clearly originating in county Down.

In 1902, Seosamh Laoide published a song entitled *Bóthar an Mhaighre*, which he had obtained some years previously from Máire Ní Cheallaigh (or Mrs Larkin) of Carraig na gCailleach in south Armagh. She had learned it in Mayobridge about fifty years earlier.[80] Although Irish was no longer spoken in Mayobridge, Laoide comments that 'the piece ... is still current in the neighbouring counties of Armagh and Louth' and refers to other versions or fragments from Lislea (county Armagh) and from Omeath.

Another version, entitled *An Cailín ó Chonndae Lughmhaigh*, was obtained from near Dromintee in south Armagh by Énrí Ó Muirgheasa, via Tomás Mac Cuilleanáin.[81] Yet another version was collected by Lorcán Ó Muireadhaigh from Mrs O'Hagan of Ballinteskin, Omeath, whose mother was a county Down woman, and who is probably the same Mrs Betty O'Hagan (née Connolly) of Knocknagorran or Ballinteskin whom Michael J Murphy notes in 1957 (in correspondence with Harry Tempest) as one of the last Omeath native speakers, then aged over 90.[82] A version from Virginia, county Cavan was noted about 1910.[83]

The song's content leaves no doubt that it is of county Down origin. It tells of a shoemaker from county Down whose travels take him through the Moyry Pass to county Louth, where he engages a young girl in conversation and wastes no time in asking her to marry him. She replies that she has no interest in himself or in county Down. The shoemaker seems oblivious to any personal insult in this, but takes ill to the criticism of county Down, and spends the remaining two verses pouring insults on the girl and on her native place. By contrast, county Down people are sociable and generous, and the county abounds in all kinds of plenty! His greatest praise is bestowed on 'An Gleann', which Laoide identifies (not altogether convincingly) with Glenn, a few miles north of Newry towards Loughbrickland.

Bhí me lá beag aerach ag dul Bóthar an Mhaighre,
'Sé chas damh an spéir-bhean as Conntae Lughmhaighe;
D'fhiosruigheas féin di, ag iarraidh téamfaidh,
An bpósfadh sí gréasaidhe as Conndae an Dúin.

Tá tú ag pléideadh 's char bh'áil liom féin thú,
Cha rabh mo spéis ariamh in bhar nDún;
Tá an t-arán daor ann, 's char chleacht mé féin é;
Ba mhíle b'fhéarr damh i gConndae Lughmhaighe.

A chailleach tútach de threibh na mbrúideadh,
Nach dtuigeann súgradh, 's nach n-aithigheann greann!
Cha rabh mise acht 'súgradh, is cha n-olc liom diúltadh,
'S a liacht sin cúilfhionn beag deas 'sa' Ghleann.

Bíonn min agus plúr ionn, agus ubhla cumhra,
I n-áit na gcrústa bhíos agaibh ann;
Nuair a bhéidheas na doirse dúnta ar dhruim an diúltaidh
Béidh fáilte dhúbalta síos fá'n Ghleann.

Another song with county Down credentials is *Gadaí an tSléibh' Ruaidh*, collected by Donn Piatt from Ned Gréasaí (Éamonn Ó hAnnluain) of Óméith. According to Piatt, the *Sliabh Ruadh* in question was north-west of Warrenpoint.[84]

I now suspect that the poem *Lá Bealtaine*, which I included as an appendix in a previous work on Irish in county Down[85] may be a composition of An tAth. Domhnall Ó Tuathail. I have found no proof of this as yet, apart from a probable reference to it under the name *A Mháire bhig*.[86] Ó Tuathail's teaching method, 'Módh na Ráidhte', was in vogue at the period in question, when he was himself based in Downpatrick. The saying about the doctor and the priest which I also included in that appendix[87] is definitely attributable to Ó Tuathail, being part of an *agallamh* in which speaker 1 is suffering from a sore head:[88]

2. Cha dtigidh leis a bheith dochrach frithir, nuair nach rabh tú aig an Dochtúir.
1. Bhí mé aig an tSagart; agus b'fhéarr liom a lámh naomhtha, ná an buidéal is fhéarr a rinne Dochtúir suas ariamh.
2. O! seadh! Is saoire lámh an tSagairt ná buidéal an Dochtúra!

The revival of Irish

We have hitherto been preoccupied with the native Gaelic of county Down, and its demise. But this is not to say that Irish is dead in county Down, for, at the same time as native Irish was on the wane, efforts to conserve and perpetuate the language were gathering strength, with the result that not a few people in county Down today speak Irish.[89] We have seen the effects of Gaelic League activity on the censuses of 1901 and 1911, and there have been references to revivalism among the reports on the state of Irish in county Down.

The revival of Gaelic predates the Gaelic League however. The first moves had more to do with Irish music than language, and took place in Belfast at the end of the eighteenth century. They included the organisation of the Belfast Harp Festival of 1792, and the consequent efforts of Edward Bunting to collect Irish songs, on which Patrick Lynch was employed, as already mentioned. However the Irish language was also being taught in Belfast: Lynch had been engaged in this activity in 1794, and William Neilson was to teach Irish in the Royal Belfast Academical Institution during his time there as professor of Classics and Hebrew (1818-21).

Although it had existed informally for some time, the year 1830 saw the official foundation in Belfast of *Cuideacht Gaedhilge Uladh* (The Ulster Gaelic Society) 'for the preservation of the remains of ancient Irish literature, maintaining teachers of the Irish language where it most prevails, and publishing useful books in that tongue.'[90] Leading .members included Dr James McDonnell, Rev Dr R.J. Bryce, and Robert S. McAdam. The president was the marquis of Downshire.

Robert McAdam (1808-1895) was the most active of the members. He had attended the Belfast Academy and very probably learned Irish from William Neilson. He was a founding partner in 1835 of the Soho foundry in Belfast's Townsend Street, and this was his employment for most of his life. But the Irish language was his great interest. He amassed a great collection of manuscripts, and employed individuals such as Peadar Ó Gealacháin and Aodh Mac Domhnaill from Meath and Art Mac Bionaid from South Armagh in writing and copying material in Irish. McAdam himself compiled manuscripts of Irish materials which he encountered in his travels to all parts of Ulster, including a large manuscript dictionary.[91] The definitive account of this period of Irish language activity in Belfast has been written by Ó Buachalla.[92]

The *Cuideacht Gaedhilge Uladh* was not merely academic in its approach to Irish, but actively promoted the use of Irish, for example, by sending teachers of Irish to Gaelic-speaking areas such as Ballinascreen in county Derry. However its activities were confined to Ulster, and it never envisaged the possibility of reviving Irish among the common people in areas where it had been dead for several generations. Yet this was to be the ambitious aim of an organisation founded in 1893, two years before McAdam's death – *Connradh na Gaedhilge* or the Gaelic League.

This was a period of heightened nationalistic awareness, led by young and vigorous organisations, such as the Gaelic League and the Gaelic Athletic Association in the cultural sphere, and Sinn Féin and the United Irish League in politics. In this atmosphere the language revival became a mass movement, capable of capturing the popular imagination, and people of all ages began to learn Irish as a second language in evening classes run by branches of the Gaelic League.

County Down was to the fore in Gaelic League activity in the early years of the twentieth century. The first Gaelic League branch in the county was founded in Newry in September 1897.[93] The following branches are mentioned as preparing for the first *Feis an Dúin* in 1902:[94] Leitrim, Clanvaraghan, Drumaroad, Newcastle, Magheramayo, Kilcoo, Castlewellan, Bryansford, Glassdrummond, Shanrod, Dechomet, Annaclone and Magherill; while branches were also active in Newry, Mayobridge, Killowen, Portaferry and Ballyvarley, at least. The comparatively good showing in the language question of the 1911 census by Moneyreagh, situated well to the north, was apparently due to Gaelic League classes organised there by Rev Richard Lyttle, who had died in 1905.[95]

In the years from 1911 to 1915 Downpatrick was the home of An tAth. Domhnall Ó Tuathail, the author of the teaching method known as *Módh na Ráidhte*, whom we have already mentioned on several occasions.[96] In that short time he made a considerable impact on the revival in east Down, and was instrumental in founding the short-lived Irish College at Rossglass in 1921.[97]

A detailed history of the Gaelic League in county Down has yet to be written. I give, in appendix 17.4, brief biographical details of some figures prominently involved in those early days. The list is necessarily selective and the details are very partial in most cases.

The success of the Gaelic League had some consequences for the kind of Irish which was promoted. In the early days especially, Irish had to be taught by whoever was available and able to teach it. In Ulster generally, and in county Down in particular, these were usually members of the teaching profession or customs and excise officials, very often from the south or west of Ireland. Naturally enough, they taught the dialect of Irish with which they were most familiar. In county Down, where native Irish was on the point of extinction, they could not be expected to know the local variety.

Moreover, nationalist philosophy provided a rationale for a centralised view of Irish and for discounting Gaelic in Scotland as something external, although it must be said that individual Gaelic Leaguers were enthusiastic supporters of Gaelic contacts with Scotland. The centrist trend met with opposition, and the 'dialect wars' raged fiercely in Belfast between the rival colleges of *Coláiste Chomhghaill*, run in the main by Munstermen living in Belfast, and *An Árd-Scoil Ultach*, which insisted on Donegal Irish as the best-known variety of Ulster Irish. The point had earlier been diplomatically expressed by Séamus Ó Ceallaigh:

> Ulster has many Munster and Connacht teachers, and they are nearly all giving instructions in Irish, *bail ó Dhia orthu*, but the blessing is not an unmixed one. It is easy to see that all attempts to rehabilitate the language in any district should be made from a basis of local usage in the matter of pronunciation. The gap between the Irish-speaking mother and her English-speaking child is so big already that nothing in our methods should tend to widen it. And should not the implied principle be observed as far as possible even where Irish has died out.[98]

A simple but typical illustration is provided by Adams, commenting on Pulleine's oration for Owen O'Neill, where the Irish name of Holywood is given as *Ard Mhic Criosg*: 'about the middle of the eighteenth century there were enough Irish speakers around north Down ... to know its proper pronunciation in the original Irish dialect of the area, which is more than can be said for many bilinguals in the area nowadays who have acquired Irish as a second language.'[99] It is not the abilities of learners which are being criticised here, but rather, an unconscious lack of concern with the local dimension of Gaelic.

The view that Irish should be uniform throughout Ireland and that Gaelic outside of Ireland is of no relevance has been formalised in the definition of official standard Irish, which now dominates Gaelic education and publishing in Ulster as it does elsewhere in Ireland, to the detriment of Ulster Irish. Comhaltas Uladh, the semi-autonomous Ulster regional organisation of the Gaelic League which was founded in 1925 with the specific object of fostering Ulster Irish, made representations when standard Irish was being designed in the late 1940s and 1950s, but these went unheeded.

As a popular expression of Irish culture, the Gaelic League has been rather eclipsed for most of its history by another organisation founded at around the same period, the Gaelic Athletic Association (GAA). Though perceived primarily as a sporting organisation, the aims of the GAA include the fostering of Irish culture generally. In the early days, both organisations had a good part of their membership in common, and were often confused in the popular mind, with the result that the activities of one were sometimes attributed to the other.

The GAA appoints Irish-language officers to encourage use of Irish, but its promotion of Irish suffers from the difficulty that purely recreational activities – such as Gaelic games, Irish music, and Irish dancing – are more easily approachable and pay quicker dividends than re-learning a language, and may be enough in many cases to satisfy the demand for cultural expression. However, by maintaining a positive attitude to things Irish, the GAA has helped to create a situation which is at least passively favourable to the Gaelic language. The influence of the GAA has spread widely as a result of the spectacular sporting successes of the 1960s, now being repeated in the 1990s. It is paradoxical, though, that by basing its most prestigious competitions on the county unit, it has created passionate allegiances to those artificial administrative divisions, which, unlike baronies or dioceses, have no historical basis. The GAA celebrated the centenary of its foundation in 1984, and this was the occasion for much historical reflection, which in county Down resulted in a number of club histories, as well as a comprehensive county history.[100]

Acknowledgements

My best thanks are due to Pádraig Mac Thiarnáin and Cumann Gaelach Leath Chathail who encouraged and published the original version of this essay, and to the following for discussion and information: Séamas Mac Diarmada, Méadhbha Uí Chriagáin, Cathal Ó Baoill, Colm Mac

Eoin, Séamas Mac Giolla Fhinnéin, Danny Murray, Fintan Mussen, Charlie Cunningham, Willie McGreevy, Ruairí Mac Gráinne, Peter Milligan, Austin Morgan, Ben Mac an Bháird, Aodán Mac Póilín, Sean Mackin, Pádraig Mac Giolla Ruaidh, Ellen Gracey, Bridie Lennon. Also to the staff of Queen's University Library, Belfast Central Library, the Linenhall Library, the Public Records Office of Northern Ireland, the South-Eastern Education and Library Board, Ballynahinch, St Patrick's College, Drumcondra, and the College of Saint Teresa Archives, Rochester, Minnesota.

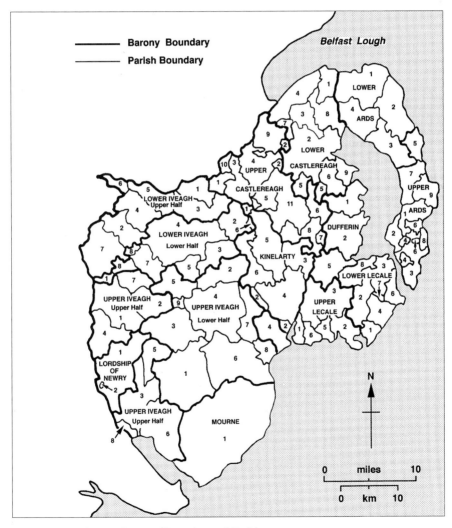

Fig. 17.1   County Down – Baronies and Parishes.

CO. DOWN – BARONIES AND PARISHES

UPPER IVEAGH
Upper Half
1. Aghaderg *pt of*
2. Annaclone
3. Clonallan
4. Donaghmore
5. Drumgath
6. Kilbroney
7. Seapatrick *pt of*
8. Warrenpoint

UPPER IVEAGH
Lower Half
1. Clonduff
2. Dromara *pt of*
3. Drumballyroney
4. Drumgooland
5. Garvaghy *pt of*
6. Kilcoo
7. Kilmegan *pt of*
8. Maghera
9. Newry *pt of*

UPPER LECALE
1. Ballykinler
2. Bright
3. Down
4. Kilmegan *pt of*
5. Rathmullan *& detached portion*
6. Tyrella

LOWER LECALE
1. Ardglass
2. Ballee
3. Ballycutter *& islands*
4. Dunsfort *& islands*
5. Inch *& islands*
6. Kilclief
7. Rathmullan *& detached portion*
8. Saul & islands

MOURNE
1. Kilkeel *& islands*

LOWER IVEAGH
Lower Half
1. Aghaderg *pt of*
2. Annahilt *pt of*
3. Dromara *pt of*
4. Dromore
5. Garvaghy *pt of*
6. Magheradrool *pt of*
7. Magherally
8. Seapatrick *pt of & detached portion*

LOWER IVEAGH
Upper Half
1. Blaris *pt of*
2. Donaghcloney
3. Hillsborough
4. Magheralin *pt of*
5. Moira
6. Shankill *pt of*
7. Tullylish

UPPER ARDS
1. Ardkeen *& islands*
2. Ardquin *& islands*
3. Ballyphilip
4. Ballytrustan *& detached portion*
5. Ballywalter
6. Castleboy *& detached portion*
7. Inishargy *& islands*
8. Slanes
9. St. Andres *alias* Ballyhalbert *& islands*

LOWER ARDS
1. Bangor *pt of & islands*
2. Donaghadee
3. Grey Abbey *& islands*
4. Newtownards *pt of*

UPPER CASTLEREAGH
1. Blaris *pt of*
2. Comber *pt of*
3. Drumbeg *pt of*
4. Drumbo
5. Killaney
6. Killinchy *pt of*
7. Killyleagh *pt of*
8. Kilmore *pt of*
9. Knockbrea *pt of*
10. Lambeg *pt of*
11. Saintfield

LOWER CASTLEREAGH
1. Bangor *pt of*
2. Comber *pt of*
3. Dundonald
4. Holywood
5. Killinchy *pt of*
6. Kilmood
7. Knockbrea *pt of*
8. Newtownards
9. Tullynakill

LORDSHIP OF NEWRY
1. Newry *pt of*
2. Tideway

KINELARTY
1. Annahilt *pt of*
2. Kilmegan *pt of*
3. Kilmore *pt of*
4. Loughinisland
5. Magheradrool *pt of*
6. Magherahamlet

DUFFERIN
1. Killinchy *pt of & islands*
2. Killyleagh *pt of & islands*

APPENDIX 17.1

(a) Extract from the *Scáthán* by Aodh Mac Aingil
(Hugh McCawell)

Do bhí Bráthair Mionúr tuata do chlainn ar naomhathar S. Proinnsias 'gá raibhi beatha bheanduighthe dhiadha 'na chomhnuidhe a mainisdir dár n-órd san Spáinn san chathraigh dárab ainm Samora (do bhádhus[s]a féin san mainisdir). As í bá oiffig dhó bheith 'na spinnséir [sin, riarthóir na bialainne]. Do-chuaidh i ccumann lé Bráthair Preidsiúr tuata, spinnséir mhainistreach S. Doimnic san chathraigh chédna. Do ghealladar an dís se dá chéili, gibé dhíobh do-gheabhadh bás ar tús, go ttiocfadh d'fhios an fhir eile do thabhairt sgéul na tíre thall dhó, dá bhfhaghadh cead ó Dhia chuige. Fuair an Bráthair Mionúr bás, agus, iar mbeith dá chompánach san phroinntigh ag déanamh a oiffige, tháinig chuigi. Do labhradar sealad ré chéile agus do innis an marbh neithe iongantacha don bhéo ar phíantuibh purgadóra agus go raibhi féin ionnta. Do fhiafruidh an béo dhe créd fa raibhe 'a bpurgadóir. Adubhairtsean nách raibhe d'fhiachuibh air achd, an uair do bhíodh ag roinn a ccoda ar an ccoimhthionól, nach déineadh na coibhrinn cothrom, achd go mbíodh barr ag cuid aca ar a chéili, agus 'na éiric sin go raibhe a lámh dheas ar dearglasadh, agus, dá dhearbhadh sin, do bhúail ar an mbórd í agus do loisg áit na ccúig méor go domhuin san cclár ndarach lé teine agus lé géire na lasrach do bhaoi asda. Agus atá lorg na láimhe sin aniogh go hiomlán san mbórd soin dubh-loisgthe agus pláta airgid 'gá fholach ar a bhfoil glés osgailti dá thaisbénadh do dhaoinibh onóracha, ór, suil do cuireadh an folach air an ccuid sin don bhórd, do bhriseadh na daoine thigeadh dá fhéchuin ní éigin don chronn dhóite, dá bhreith riú dá mbrosdughadh dochum lóirghníomha do dhénamh ina bpeacadhuibh ré mbás; agus as iomdha duine bhrosduigheas aniogh féin chuigi so an lorg sin amháin na láimhe d'fhaicsin dubhdhóite.

(b) Extract from *Tóruidheacht na bhFíreun ar lorg Chríosda*

A luchd annsachd an chrábhaidh, aig seo agaibh leabhrán ceirt-bhriatharach, deagh-chomhairleach, binn-fhoclach darab ainm 'Tóraidheachd na bhfíreun air chéim lorg Chríosda', noch do sgríobhadh ó thús san teangaidh Laidne le brathair ainglighe oirirc do Órd Bheannuighthe St. Auguistín; anois air na thairbhirt dhíbh ann so i ndeilbh, i n-éideadh agus i líbhrea mur dtíre féin, eadhon san teangaidh ghaoidheilic.

Is fada ó do dheallruigh téasdas agus deagh-chlú an ughdair bheannuighthe air feadh na cruinne, air mhodh gur bhreathnuighdear luchd eagna agus mór-eolais air chrábhadh, nach rabh amach ó'n Sgrioptuir Dhiadha én leabhar amháin is dísle, dhiadha, dheagh-chomhairlighe nó é; agus uime sin, is cian ó do ghabhadar saothar daoine foghlumtha gach én tíre an leabhar diadha-sa a chur a dteangaidh agus a gcanamhaint dhúthchasaigh a mathara agus a dtíre féin, air mhodh go bhfuil sé le faghail, ní hé amháin san teangaidh Laidne, Eabhra, Ghréigis, agus Arabaic; ach fós ann gach cainnt agus ann gach ceileabhar choitcheannta eile air feadh réagunaibh imchiana choigchricheacha choimhigheacha an domhain mhóir. Agus, ar an ádhbhar sin, do tógadh dhamhsa mar an gceudna, saothar do ghabhail a chur a gcló agus a gcainnt ár dtíre féin, eadhon, sa teangaidh ghaoidheilc; agus cé go bhfuil sé anois neóin agus deireadh an lae, ní bhfuil sé go fóill ro-mhall an maith do dhéanamh uair ar bith, óir a deir Críosda féin san t-Soisgeul linn go bhfuair an mhuinntir, a tháining go mall san fhíneamhain, mar fuair an luchd oibre a tháinig go moch, eadhon, an tuarasdal agus an luach-saothair céadna.

APPENDIX 17.2

Extract from Neilson's *Teach oidheachta tuaidhthe,* a dialogue in *An introduction to the Irish language*

D. U. An bhfuil mòran de lorg na sean fhoirgneadh, no oibreacha cian arsaigh eile, le faiceal in bhur dtirse?

O R. Ta fuighill sean-chaislean, sean-chealla, agus sean toìr cian àrsaigh go leor ann.

Mac G. D'ar ndoigh go bhfuil; agus gur arsaigh an obair na ratha, 's na huaimhneacha, 's na leaca liteardha a fuaras ionnta.

O R. B'fheidir gur sinne na cloch-oir, 's na charnain, 's na cromleaca, na iad sin fèin.

Mac G. Is doiligh radha ciaca is sinne.

D. U. Ca bhfuaras na leaca liteardha, a deir tu?

Mac G. Aithreasa me dhuit, a dhuine uasail. Fa mhìle d'on ait, a mbion sinne nar gcomhnaidh, fuaras uaimh, air leathmalaigh chnuic, le fear a bhi ag tochailt fa chloich, a dtimchioll deich mbliadhna o shoin. Ni raibh smuaineadh, no fios ag neach beo go raibh a leithid ann, no go dtarla a fhaghail mar sin; na h uaimh fhada, chaol, gan chnamha, gan taise, no lorg ni ar bith ann; achd ballaigh folamha, air na bhfollach do leaca mora. Bhi seomra bheag, dheas, chruinn cumpa, indeilbh chiseán bheach, air leath taobh na huamhcha sin; agus doras beag, cumhang a dol innte, falamh fòs, mar an gcuid eile. Achd chèanna fuaras aon leac, leabhar, leathan, a mullach na haitese; agus, air an taobh iochtarach d'on leic sin bhi tri line grabhthalta, do ghlan litreachaibh cheart chumpa; nach fuaras aoinneach ariamh o leith, a bhfeadfadh an sgrìbhìn sin a leaghadh, no a mhìneadhadh.

O R. Nil aon fhocal breige ann. Oir chonnairc me fèin an uaimh, 's an leac, 's an sgrìbhin, an uair a fuaras è.

D. U. Nil amhras air bith agam ann. Oir chonnairc mise fòs tuairisg na huamhcha sin, a deir tu: agus mac samhuil na litreach ceadna clo bhuailtè, igclair umha, ann nuadh stair chondae an Duin.

Mac G. Thainig duine uasal foghlumtha ann sin, o Atha na hilide, a chomharthaigh sios air chairt è.

D. U. Nach bhfuaras cromleac, faoidh charn, laimh leis [an] ait sin?

Mac G. Fuaras, go deimhin, fa dha mhìle dho sin, (a dtimcioll seacht mbliadhna roimhe sin), leac aidmheil mor, leathan, comhthrom, leabhair, comh mìn le cloichin cois thragha; go gcreidim nach bhfuil cromleac ann Eirin comh deas leis; reir mar dhubhairt an duine uasal sin, a thainic 'ga fheacuin.

Bhi fàl de leaca fada, cothroma, na seasamh ceart suas air a gceann thort timchioll fan chromleic mhòir, an uair a fuaras i; faoidh charnan mhòr, do mhion chlochuibh.

D. U. Nar togbhadh na leaca fada sin?

Mac G. Nil aoin diobh nachar tugadh chum oibre a bhi 'ga dheanamh laimh leis an àit.

D. U. Niar bhriseadh an uamhaigh mo dhoigh.

Mac G. Do briseadh, is milleadh i; agus niar fàgadh aoìn leac, no cloch, a bhfiu an dadamh, nachar togadh air shiubhal, an nòs ceadna.

D. U. Is iongnadh liom gur briseadh an uaimh.

Mac G. Dar ndoigh go leagadh go talamh an tòr-cruin aig Dùn phadruic. Agus shaoilinnse, a dhuine uasal, nach mbiadh se sona bainte le na leithid.

D. U. Nil mise 'ga radh go bhfuil se mioshona; ach togar dhamh gur naireach dho dhaoinibh uaisle, foghlamtha, gan cion no meas a bheith, air bhfuighioll oibreach arsaighthe na tìre.

APPENDIX 17.3

Some observations on the state of Irish in county Down

Many of these statements have been previously published by Ó Casaide.[101] A particularly important class of observations are those made by John O'Donovan in 1834, when he visited county Down in connection with his place-names work for the Ordnance Survey.[102] Since the statements may be mildly contradictory, it seems best to facilitate comparison by presenting them in a geographical arrangement, beginning with statements relating to the county as a whole, and then giving those which are specific to a barony or parish.

The county
Harris (1744) remarks that 'the Irish tongue is in a manner banished among the common people, and what little of it is spoken can be heard only among the inferior rank of Irish papists; and even that little diminishes every day by the great desire the poor natives have that their children should be taught to read and write the English tongue in the Charter or other English Protestant schools, to which they willingly send them'.[103] However, this statement is at variance with the other evidence as to the extent of Irish in county Down.

Dubourdieu (1802): 'The English language is so general [in County Down] that every person speaks it; but, notwithstanding, the Irish language is much used in the mountainous parts, which in this, as well as in most other countries, seem to have been the retreat of the ancient inhabitants.'[104]

Whitley Stokes, in a tract printed in 1806, giving information on the prevailing language in certain counties, brackets Down together with Antrim and Armagh under the comment '[Irish] spoken by a few'. This is certainly intended to mean less than half, but more than in other areas where Irish is described as 'spoken by very few' or 'scarcely any'.

Wakefield's *Statistical Account of Ireland* (1812) says of counties Antrim, Down, Armagh and Derry that 'the people who reside in the mountainous districts retain the ancient Irish language, and to them it is chiefly confined.'

Rev. Dr Graves estimated the 'relative proportion of those who daily speak Irish' around 1820 in certain areas, and gives a ratio of two Irish speakers to five English speakers for Armagh and Down, considered together.

The remarks of Stokes, Wakefield and Graves above are quoted by Christopher Anderson (1846), who further applied Graves' proportions to the county populations from the 1821 census. He concluded that, in the case of County Down, 92,974 people spoke Irish daily in 1821, out of the county population of 325,410, but this is certainly an over-estimate.[105]

John O'Donovan visited county Down in 1834 and refers to Rathfryland, Castlewellan, Clough and Downpatrick as the Irish district, 'from Slieve Donnard to Slieve Croob', centred on Castlewellan, and extending no further north than Loughinisland.[106]

Mr and Mrs S.C. Hall (1843): 'Until about a century ago, an extensive "Irish-speaking" population existed near Downpatrick; but they have all disappeared; and the only traces of the language are to be found in the mountainous districts, where the people are almost exclusively Irish, or in the neighbourhood of Carlingford Bay at the south.'[107]

O'Donovan, writing in 1857: 'In the Glens of the Co Antrim it [the Irish language] is a good deal spoken; it is also very much spoken in the County Donegal and in the mountainous parts of Londonderry, Tyrone and Down, particularly along the Mourne Mountains ... Very little [spoken by the middle classes]; generally by the lower classes.'[108]

Abraham Hume (1874): 'So late as 1820 ... the Irish language was spoken, along with English, from Ballynahinch to near Newry and Newcastle ... An intermediate period occurred and thirty years later nothing but popular Irish expressions were known, while the number who employed them was greatly reduced. To-day, there is little to be found of it beyond single words, and a strongly marked Hibernic pronunciation or "brogue".'[109]

Alexander Knox (1875) says that Irish 'is understood by many, especially in the hill country of Mourne and Iveagh, in common with English, which is now in universal use all over the county.'[110]

In a manuscript dated 1 March 1876, Proinsias Ó Catháin (Francis Keane) writes: 'To some extent a dialect of the language still lingers in the Mourne districts of Down and in the Glens of Antrim'. Ó Catháin also quotes figures for each Ulster county which may be compared with the 1871 census but cannot be entirely derived from it: he says that County Down has 339 people who speak Irish and English, but no Irish-speaking monoglots; only 2 people read Irish, while no-one writes it.[111]

In *Irisleabhar na Gaedhilge* of 1895-96, Seosamh Laoide states that 'a vein or thread of Irish' was spoken from Westmeath to Louth 'and also, it is said, in a very small district of the Mourne Mountains.' Laoide does not disclose his source for this information, but he adds in a footnote that 'this is doubtful; County Down may now be styled a *condae gallta*, or thoroughly Anglicised county.'[112]

In *Irisleabhar na Gaedhilge* 1897, H Boyd states that 'at least part of the Lord's Prayer ... exists [in Irish] among the very few here (Co Down).'[113]

In *Irisleabhar na Gaedhilge* 1902, of which Laoide was by now editor: 'It would seem that the last native of Co Down who could speak Irish died only ten or twelve years ago or so. In the time of Neilson, the grammarian, probably the bulk of the population of the baronies of Lecale, Kinelarty, Iveagh, Mourne, the Upper Ards, and the Lordship of Newry – that is, of the extent of territory south of a line drawn from Portaferry to Scarva – were Irish-speaking.'[114]

Aodh Mac Gréacháin, writing in 1912: 'We must realise that the old native speakers of Irish are rapidly disappearing in Louth and Armagh, as they have almost disappeared in County Down ... Judging from the remnants of Co. Down Irish which I have collected, it differed little in idiom, vocabulary or pronunciation from Omeath Irish.'[115] Mac Gréacháin's evidence is particularly significant, as he was not only a competent Gaelic scholar but must have been well acquainted with the local situation. His remarks indicate that by 1912 there were few if any fluent speakers remaining, but there were still people who could recite scraps which they had heard from native speakers. After another generation, say, by 1935, these too must almost all have gone.

Séamus Ó Néill (1910-1981), a native of Clough, writes in 1936 that 'about a century ago, Downpatrick was the heart of a large Gaelic-speaking area, which included the outlying districts of Castlewellan, Clanvaraghan, Rathfriland and even Ballynahinch.' And later in the same article: 'I am acquainted with a gentleman who heard Irish spoken by a native speaker of county Down not longer than forty years ago.'[116]

Donn Piatt states in 1932 that 'Irish lingered in County Down until within the last few years'. His evidence though is generally vague with regard to identities and even localities. One claim which does not stand up to scrutiny is where he says that Lorcán Ó Muireadhaigh obtained the county Down song *An Cailín as Conndae Lughmhaighe* in the Mourne Mountains in 1912, whereas Ó Muireadhaigh himself says he obtained it in Omeath.[117] Piatt's other evidence is worth reproducing here: 'About the same time [1912] Seán Mac Maoláin spoke to Irish speakers in County Down. In 1925 a girl student told me she had got a few lines of a song that very summer in the Mourne Mountains. In 1930 another student reported that Irish was just gone, within a few miles of Sliabh Crúb. Irish lived near Castlewellan, Newry, Hilltown, and Banbridge well into the present century, although written authorities, and Séamus Ó Casaide's valuable study evidently based on such authority, make it die about the seventies of the last century.'[118]

Specific civil parishes or baronies
Aghaderg

Dr Arthur McArdle, the parish priest of Aghaderg from 1816 to 1838, told O'Donovan in 1834 that there was no Irish speaker left in the parish though in his time there were numbers of old men who understood it well.[119]

Dr Mac Domhnaill told Bunting around 1839 that 'Miss Reilly of Scarvagh is the only person who he [Pat Byrne, a harper] knows now living who was taught to play [the harp] through the Irish language'.[120]

Some old people in the hilly country east of Kernan Lough (where Aghaderg parish meets Tullylish and Seapatrick) spoke Irish, or so a Gilford man told Adams around 1940.[121] Note however that an early Gaelic League branch had been active in nearby Ballyvarley: its president, James McGrath, stated in 1905 that 'the Irish language has taken a good hold in the district, although it was not an Irish-speaking district.'[122]

An Irish-speaking old woman in the Scarva area was known to the mother of Jackie Quinn, who worked at Scarva railway station as a young man during the Second World War. This instance is unlikely to pre-date 1890, but nothing is known of the speaker's origins.[123]

Annaclone

Dean Arthur McArdle, referred to under Aghaderg, was a native of Annaclone, and was born around 1770. He 'speaks Irish very well', according to

O'Donovan. His sister, Mrs Con Magennis of Ardbrin 'understands Irish very well, and is now the only repertory of the traditions and legends of Iveagh. She gave me [O'Donovan, 1834] all the Irish names of townlands in the parishes of Annacloan and Drumballyroney'.[124]

Fr James McKey, born in Annaclone around 1774 and P.P. of Annaclone when visited by O'Donovan in 1834, was an Irish speaker. He died in August 1834.[125]

Drumballyroney

A farmer named Hennan, of the townland of Lisnacroppan, in Ballybrick ded, nearly 90 years of age, said to O'Donovan (1834) that Irish was the first language he ever spoke.[126]

Donaghmore

In the parish of Donaghmore O'Donovan (1834) found a man who was 100 years old, blind and dying, but who gave him the ancient name of every townland in the parish.[127]

Newry

When James Boswell was travelling on the road from Newry to Dundalk in 1769, one of the party fell off his horse about two miles past Newry, and this necessitated a visit to a nearly farmhouse ... 'a neat highland house and all the people spoke Irish, though they could speak English too'.[128]

O'Donovan was told (1834) that there was no person a native of the lordship of Newry who could speak Irish, but was eventually brought to the oldest man in the lordship or parish of Newry, old McGilvoy, 84 years of age, who gave the pronunciation of the townlands 'as he heard them in Irish' and their meanings.[129]

'As recently as the youth of the present writer's father, Protestants in Newry (an industrial Ulster town where complete anglicisation might be expected) talked Irish to the incoming country folk on market days, and many were proud of whatever Gaelic they knew – few seemed to have regarded it as "not theirs"' – Aodh de Blacam (1891-1951) in 1934.[130]

The hinterland of Newry on the county Armagh side contained large numbers of Irish speakers until well into the twentieth century. In 1898, for example, a group from the Newry branch of the Gaelic League spent a day visiting 'the Irish-speaking districts of Meigh and Killeavy... From the time we left Clohogue until we came to Ballymacdermot on our return we had plenty of Irish ... Every grown person in that great tract of country seems to understand it, though only the middle-aged and old people speak it habitually'.[131]

Clonallan

The McGarveys had a school in Aughnagon in the early eighteenth century.[132]

James Downey is mentioned by Harris (1744) for reasons unconnected with language. He 'lives in the parish of Clonallen and townland of Bavan, being born somewhere thereabouts ... he speaks good Irish, but very little English'.[133]

A song in Irish was noted down some years prior to 1902 from Máire Ní

Cheallaigh (Mrs Larkin) of Carraig na gCailleach near Slieve Gullion, who had learned it at Mayobridge, county Down, about fifty years before. 'She stated that at the time she resided in Mayo Bridge Irish was spoken there only by the old people'.[134]

An tAth. B. Mac Thréinfhir's grandmother (born 1858, Burren district, a couple of miles north of Warrenpoint) knew the days of the week in Irish.[135]

Kilbroney

Maggie Cull of Knockshee remembered her father talking Irish to a cousin from Scotland around 1914.[136] Her father was probably Stephen Cull, born around 1850, living in Ballintur townland in 1901.

Glenshass and Slieveroosley are said to have had an element of Irish-speakers in the early years of the century, and to have received the attentions of the *múinteoirí taistil*.[137] The name Glenshass is not commonly found on modern maps, but is well-attested in Irish literature (Gleann tSeaghais) and appears to refer to the valley of the Kilbroney River.

Kilbroney is one of the few parishes in county Down where there is evidence of revival activity in the 1901 census. There are a significant number of teenagers claiming to speak Irish and English, particularly in the area of Drumsesk townland, though their parents do not profess to speak Irish.

Kilkeel

'Attical ... is the last area where Irish was spoken in Co Down', according to Pádraig Ó hEithirn, a teacher living in Rostrevor, speaking around 1980.[138]

Jimmy Nevin, born in 1862 in Moneydarraghmore, a seaman by occupation, had Irish words, which he must have acquired orally as he was not literate. His mother was a Sloan from Attical.[139]

The last 'natural' Irish-speaker in the Kilkeel area was Michael (or Patrick?) Burns, of Carrigenagh, who died around the early 1940s, and was probably born around 1880. He came from a family who were basket-makers.[140]

'Old timers recall people like "Eddie Poland" and Mary McGreevy conversing in Irish at Glasdrumman chapel in the early 1920s.'[141] Edward Poland was a committee member of the Glassdrummond Gaelic League branch from its inception on 21 April 1902 and at Glassdrummond Feis held on 16 November 1902 he won a prize for singing the test piece *An Spailpín Fánach* and was highly recommended in 'senior books, O'Growney'.[142]

Drumgath

Dr James McKnight (1800-1876), the champion of the rights of tenant-farmers, writes in a letter quoted by Séamus Ó Néill that 'my father had an enormous store of scraps of this kind [Irish melodies], and when a child he used to sing them to me in Irish.' His father was a Presbyterian farmer in the Rathfriland area, and an Irish speaker.[143]

Clonduff

John McLindon a farmer gave O'Donovan (1834) a list of the Irish names of the mountains of Clonduff.[144]

'There are a good many Irish-speaking people in the neighbourhood of Hilltown, but I think nearly all of them can speak English; when, however, they frequent fairs in the upper parts of Co Armagh, for instance at Newtownhamilton or Crossmaglen, they meet numbers of people who speak English very imperfectly, and with these people the Down men converse altogether in Irish' – a correspondent of W. H. Patterson, 1880.[145]

R.L. Praeger – a nephew of Patterson – writes in 1941: 'When I first knew Hilltown, fifty years ago, you could still hear Irish spoken if you knew where to find it.'[146]

Manuscripts of Francis McPolin from 1943-45 contain mention of Irish speakers in the Clonduff area.[147] On 14 November 1943, McPolin writes of Ann Savage, aged 95, of Goward: 'Ann can still bless herself in Irish. Her father and mother always gave out the Rosary in Irish at night, and often spoke Irish to each other. If the young ones wanted to go out on their céilidhe at night the old pair always spoke a few words together in Irish before letting them go.'[148] Michael J. Murphy obtained folklore in English from Ann Savage.[149]

Murphy met Ann Savage through Patrick Rooney, who was out looking for sheep near the Spelga Pass around 1944 when Murphy encountered him: 'when he found out what I was after he began to fling phrases in Gaelic at me'.[150] McPolin states that Rooney lived with Ann Savage in Goward, was aged 65 in 1945, and 'belongs to the Mayobridge district', but his grandmother was from Tamary, on the boundary of Clonduff and Drumgath parishes.[151]

McPolin reports that 'Mr Fitzpatrick (95) told me Nov. 1943 that in his boyhood days Mr and Mrs Stephen Gribben of Ballygorian could speak Irish. He well remembers calling in their house one day (doing a message, I presume). When he was there they began speaking Irish to each other, and he, thinking they were planning to murder him, ran out and away.'[152]

On 11 March 1945, McPolin re James Cowan, farmer, Stang, aged 60: 'Traditional Irish: Cowan was able to repeat a number of phrases in Irish which his grandmother who knew the language taught him when he was a child, e.g. bless himself, count from one to ten, and such phrases as "shŏwitchshough". At the same time he says his mother knew no Irish. She apparently was born about the transition period when parents did not wish their children to learn Irish. That would be about 1840-50 in this district. Cowan's granny belonged to Drumboniff; she was born in the place where Barney Murnin now lives.'[153]

McPolin gives the following cure for a stye, from Clonduff: pluck nine jags (spíon) of a gooseberry (spíonóg) and point each three times at the sufferer's eye, saying 'Speena, speena, huggarth (chugat) the cript; cript, cript, huggarth the speena'. Then throw the thorn over your right shoulder.[154] McPolin gaelicises 'cript' as cruibh. O'Neill-Lane (1918 edition) gives craobh fhabhra for 'stye', with Oriel provenance.

Patrick McPolin of Ballykeel, aged 80, told Francis McPolin on 7 January 1946: 'Yes, my father knew a great deal of Irish. He learned a lot from his mother, for she knew nothing else but Irish. I remember Fr Kearns speaking some words of Irish to him (wherever *he* learned it) but my father not only answered him but came out with some more. "Oh Pat", says Fr Kearns, "that is going too far for me."[155] Fr Kearns was born in Seagoe in 1846 and was in Clonduff from 1881 until 1923, becoming parish priest in 1891.[156]

Kilcoo

'During the earlier years of his episcopate [Patrick McMullan, bishop of Down and Connor, 1793-1824] the examination by the bishop of the children was in the native language wherever the Irish language was spoken, as in Kilcoo, the lower side of Lecale and the Glens of Antrim'[157]

Patrick Darby was born in the house of his grandmother (Rose McAllister) in Clanawhillian (Clonachullion) in 1874, and was brought up in Fofanny. He became a cattle dealer and later owned a public house on the Springfield Road in Belfast. Although he did not speak Irish, he had a cure for sprains in Irish, which passed from father to daughter and from mother to son. He had six daughters but the one who inherited the cure (Alice) did not marry and is now deceased. His relatives recall only the last piece of the cure:

> *fear atá ag baint na mónadh,*
> *tabhair an leonadh leat.*[158]

This is enough to show that it was a form of *Ortha an Ghortuighthe*.[159]

Joe Charleton, whose mother was a Byrne from Kilcoo, describes visits to his grandmother in the 1920s, and reports that the old people especially spoke Irish 'naturally', and that everyone had spoken Irish in his grandmother's youth. Her own mother did not know 'even her prayers' in English. A monthly fair was at one time held in Downpatrick for Irish speakers from the Mournes who preferred not to do their buying and selling in English in Castlewellan or Burrenbridge or Rathfriland.[160]

A woman from Tullyree who died around 1942 is said to have turned to speaking Irish towards the end of her life, and a woman from Omeath had to be brought in to act as interpreter. This is a strong indication that Irish was her first language, but I have been unable to contact the source of this information, and in the absence of further details there is a possibility that she too may have been a native of Omeath or south Armagh. However, all the female inhabitants of Tullyree in the 1901 census were natives of county Down, except for one who was born in England.

There is a tradition that the last Gaelic speaker in the Clonachullion/ Moyad/Fofannybane area was a fiddler around the 1940s period.[161]

Drumgooland

Fr Patrick McKey, parish priest of Upper Drumgooland (or Leitrim) 1785-1808 was described as the last of the Irish-speaking priests in that parish.[162]

We have already mentioned Eoin Ó Grípín of Ballymagreehan, the scribe of a number of manuscripts in Irish around 1800.[163]

In 1847, a James Paxton was murdered at his dwelling-place in Dechomet, off the Katesbridge-Castlewellan road.[164] A local man called Rooney came forward as an eye-witness, but his testimony was difficult to understand as he had only a little English.[165]

Breggie McCartan of Leitrim, believed to be a native speaker, died around 1925.[166]

Thomas McClean came to Ballymaginthy from Burrenbridge in the 1930s. He died in the 1950s and is buried in Leitrim. Although not a highly-educated man, he was a good Irish speaker, and is thought by some to have been a native speaker. He gave Irish names to his fields.[167]

Kilmegan

The Franciscans of Downpatrick took refuge in Drumnaquoile around 1630. The last member of the community seems to have died between 1796 and 1800, having remained alone there for perhaps forty years, teaching in the adjoining school. 'According to local tradition he spoke only Gaelic and of course Latin'.[168]

Ernest Blythe relates the impression created when a Presbyterian relative from Castlewellan visited Blythe's mother's family in the early years of the nineteenth century: 'his English was strange as he usually spoke Irish' (translation).[169]

Castlewellan was described by O'Donovan in 1834 as 'the very centre of the Irish district'.[170]

The 'Ballach Murrays' removed from Carrickmannan (Killinchy parish) around 1820 to upper Clanvaraghan and Crocknafawil. 'Another Ballach Murray remembered was Francey Murray – he had a daughter Eliza who married Felix Downey and spoke Irish in their lifetime up to 1910 ... another Gaelic-speaking family was Tarry McElroy from Fermanagh who was married to a sister of Pat Morgan and lived where Eamon McKinney lives now'.[171]

The Gaelic League organiser Tomás Ó Conceanainn, visiting the Castlewellan area in 1901, comments favourably on the numbers and enthusiasm of the learners but makes no mention of native speakers and it may be safely inferred that he was unaware of any. He makes an explicitly negative statement in the case of Clanvaraghan – the learners there had 'no speaker of the language among them'.[172]

Mrs Catherine Murphy of Annsborough, born in Castlewellan town around 1840, had some Irish prayers, words and phrases when visited by Ernest Blythe in 1914. 'A good deal of Irish was spoken in her father's house during her youth, and the rosary was usually said in that language' (translation).[173]

Loughinisland

Here was located Lynch's school, which Neilson attended. Pádraig Ó Loingsigh must have left the place before 1794, for he is teaching in Belfast that year. Hugh Gordon, also an Irish scholar, was teaching in Loughinisland c. 1824-1827.[174]

In 1834, Loughinisland was the northern limit of the 'Irish district'.[175]

Magheradroll

George Kelly from Drumaness told Adams that 'none of his grandparents (born around the 1840s) could speak Irish, though it was remembered that it was spoken by some of their relatives of one generation before that'. He also remembered an old woman living there early in the twentieth century whose first language was Irish, but he thought she came from further west in the county.[176]

Kilmore

Moses Neilson was accustomed to give sermons in Irish in Rademon, where he was minister from 1767 to 1823.

In the townland of Clontaghnaglar, O'Donovan (1834) met an old man named Killen who gave him the Irish names of three or four parishes.[177]

A journalist was told by Denis Cahill, a schoolteacher in Teconnaught, that it was not so very long since there had been Irish speakers in Annacloy.[178]

Lecale

In 1793 and the years immediately following, Irish was still spoken in the 'lower side of Lecale' and was used by the bishop of Down and Connor in examining the children – fuller quotation under Kilcoo above.[179]

'Up till some forty years since, the familiar language of the "lower side of Lecale" was genuine Irish' – J. W. Hanna in 1853.[180]

O'Donovan (1834) was told by John Martin of Downpatrick that there was hardly any Irish speaker in the barony of Isle Lecale, unless about Ardglass, but in Downpatrick Gaol he found an old man from the parish of Saul who could speak Irish, confined for debt in the 89th year of his age. Another 85-year-old man in Saul also helped with the place-names, and O'Donovan obtained the old Irish names of townlands in the neighbourhood of Kilclief and Ardglass, but his conclusion was that 'Irish is nearly fled out of Lecale'.[181]

A Scottish minister preached in English and Gaelic to Scottish fishermen at Ardglass in 1872.[182]

Irish was reported to be still spoken in the 1880s in Cariff, near Kilclief.[183]

At an *aeraidheacht* held on Killard Banks on Easter Sunday 1903, an *Irish News* correspondent encountered an 'Irish-speaking old man … accompanied by an old woman and a young girl. Both the old people conversed in *Ar dTeanga Fein*, but the girl apparently knew nothing save *Beurla*.'[184]

An Irish-language summer college was held at Rossglass (near Killough) from 1921 to 1923, though the area could not be described as Irish-speaking.[185] One of the Irish-speaking families visited by the students were the Murphys (Mac Murchaidh) of Minerstown.[186]

Ards

Andrew Savage of Portaferry, the head of the leading family in the Upper Ards, was married to Margaret Nugent, of Dysart, County Westmeath, who died in 1741. Their son Patrick (1739-1797) was to become High Sheriff of county Down in 1763. In a letter to Andrew Savage dated 21 August 1744, his wife's sister, Mrs Barbara O'Reilly, living at Ballinlough, county Westmeath, writes of Patrick: 'Patt is very forward, I think 'tis very early for him to read. My little boy speaks nothing but Irish, which I fear will prevent his being a scholar so soon.' Stevenson assumes that the last sentence quoted applies to Patrick Savage too, but it seems to me more likely to refer to Mrs O'Reilly's eldest son, Hugh (her second child, Andrew, was just over one year old at this time).[187]

It is reported by a colleague that some of his grand-uncles on the maternal side called Heaney were fluent speakers who used to speak Irish regularly. This may be dated to around 1920, and they were around 50 years of age at the time. He believes them to have been native speakers, and possibly to have originated in the Ballyhalbert area.[188]

Castlereagh
Adams records Methodist preaching in Irish in the market place in Lisburn in the second half of the eighteenth century. He concludes that at the very least there must have been old people who spoke Irish in the country districts around the town and who would visit it on fair days. The hinterland would of course include some of Castlereagh and Lower Iveagh.[189]

In Holywood around 1815, 'The Irish is unknown except to a few individuals, and these not natives of the parish.'[190]

In 1834, the oldest man in the parish of Knockbreda, O'Gara (84), told O'Donovan that no Irish was spoken in his time.[191]

Lower Iveagh
In Dromore, O'Donovan found (in 1834) that the last person in the neighbourhood who knew Irish was a very old woman who had died a few years previously.[192]

In Magheralin in 1834, the schoolmaster, Robert McVeagh, a native of the parish, told O'Donovan he remembered when Irish was spoken but that 'there is not one now in the neighbourhood who understands a sentence of it'.[193]

In Aghagallon, from an Ordnance Survey manuscript of 1838: 'The Irish language too prevailed to a great extent throughout the Parish about 40 years back, particularly in the Montiaghs. A few settlers from other Districts still speak Irish, but none of them are natives of the parish.'[194]

APPENDIX 17.4

Some early Gaelic League activists in county Down

An tAth. Aodh Ó Raghallaigh (Fr. Hugh O'Reilly). Born in Dechomet, Drumgooland parish, where his father was a teacher, on 24 January 1863. A member of the Royal Irish Academy, and President of St Colman's College, Newry, 1896-1915. Died at Rostrevor on 19 January 1927, buried in Kilbroney. Founder member of Newry Gaelic League branch, 19 September 1897. President, Craobh an Iubhair, *c.* 1905.[195] Member of the Coiste Gnó of the Gaelic League.

Aodh Mac Seagháin (Hugh McShane). Member of Craobh an Iubhair 1905. Teacher at St Colman's Pioneer Temperance branch, *c.* 1905.[196] Published some fragments of south Armagh Irish obtained from Séamus Ó Fágáin in *An Claidheamh Soluis* in 1909.[197]

An tAth. Pádraig Ó Grianáin (Fr Patrick Greenan). Born at Ballynanny in Clonduff parish around 1862. Died at Dromore on 22 April 1931.[198] Joint treasurer of Coláiste Bhrighde, Ó Méith in 1912. Member of the Coiste Gnó of the Gaelic League.

Aodh Mac Gréacháin (Hugh Graham). Born on 18 November 1878, parents James (a farmer) and Ellen (née Burns), probably at Kilkinamurray near Katesbridge, where the family were living in 1901. Trained as a teacher at De La Salle College, Waterford, 1896-98. Won first prize for a collection of place-names at Feis Ó Méith 1901.[199] Principal of boys' school, Ballynahinch 1904-17. B.A. from Royal University in 1907. Married Susan McKay, Dromara on 17 August 1909. Member of east Down Coiste Ceanntair, 1912.[200] Member of committee of Coláiste Bhrighde, Ó Méith, 1912, and taught there that year.[201] H.Dip.Ed. from Queen's University Belfast 1914-16. In 1917, emigrated to America, where he taught English and Maths in 1917-18 in St Thomas' College, St Paul, Minnesota, which An tAth. Lorcán Ó Muireadhaigh left at around the same time to return to Ireland. Wife died 16 November 1919, leaving two children. Married Margaret Teresa Meagher of Halifax, North Carolina on 18 September 1922. Obtained M.A. in 1919 and Ph.D. in 1927, both from University of Minnesota. Published *The early Irish monastic schools* in 1923. Pursued a career in the Catholic educational sector in Winona (Minnesota), in St Louis, and from 1930 as Head of Department of Education, John Carroll University, Cleveland, Ohio. Died 2 May 1952.[202] Collected some remnants of county Down Irish, untraced.[203]

Máirtín Mac Eachmharcaigh (Martin McCafferky). Born Ballaghaderreen, county Mayo on 11 December 1874. Qualified as a teacher and came to Ballykinler National School, county Down, in February 1898. Became headmaster of St Malachy's, Castlewellan in April 1900. Married Catherine Nic Aoidh, from Doire Bán, county Armagh, also a teacher, on 25 October 1910. Founded and taught in Gaelic League branches in Castlewellan area, and organised local *feiseanna* for over forty years. Died 10 May 1948, buried in Ballaghaderreen.[204]

Séamus Ó Murchadha (James Murphy). The first *múinteoir taistil* in

Castlewellan district was James Murphy, of Kirkdale Road, Liverpool, originally from Macroom, county Cork, appointed at a meeting on 10 November 1901. He left about a year later, to return to Cork.[205]

Domhnall Ó Baoighill (Donal O'Boyle).Gaelic League organiser and teacher around 1912. Taught at Coláiste Bhrighde, Ó Méith, in 1912.[206]

An tAth. Aodh Ó Brolcháin (Fr Hugh Bradley). Played a major part in founding the Irish College at Rossglass. Founded Coláiste Phádraig, Rann na Feirste. Latterly lived in Newcastle. Died in Bangor on 7 October 1972.[207]

An tAth. Roibeard Fullerton (Fr Robert Fullerton), B.D., B.C.L. Native of Maghera, county Derry. Spent most of his life in Belfast, where he lectured in Irish history at the Árd-Scoil. On staff of Coláiste Bhrighde, Ó Méith, in 1912. Also involved in the Rossglass Irish College. President of Down and Connor Historical Society from its foundation on 7 June 1926 until his death in 1938.[208]

Henry Murphy, Annsborough. Born around 1874. His mother, a native of Castlewellan, had some phrases of county Down Irish.[209] Committee member of Castlewellan Branch of Gaelic League in 1902.[210] Also active in GAA (county secretary in 1909-10 and 1915) and in Sinn Féin.[211] Died 28 March 1919.[212]

John McCourt. Born May 1886. Solicitor's apprentice. Taught Irish in 1903-5 in Banbridge, Loughbrickland and Ballyvarley. Won a court case against the Catholic clergy in 1905 over remarks made about him during a sermon. Active in GAA, especially Clann na Banna club, Banbridge. Secretary of County Board of GAA in 1905.[213]

Stephen McGeown. Born 21 January 1882 at Dromena in Kilcoo parish; youngest of six boys and three girls; parents Neal (a farmer, whose people may have come from the Lurgan area) and Susan (née McPolin).[214] Became joint secretary of the Kilcoo Gaelic League branch on 20 October 1901.[215] Teaching assistant in St Malachy's School Ballymacarrett from 1896; attended St Patrick's College Drumcondra 1902-3.[216] Represented Glenshesk on the council of the first Feis na nGleann (county Antrim) in 1904.[217] Taught in St Mary's Boys' Public Elementary School, Dunsfort around 1912, where he provided voluntary Irish classes for the combined boys'and girls'schools, for half an hour in the afternoon, three days a week.[218] Secretary of Shane O'Neill branch of the Gaelic League, Ardglass, in 1912.[219] Later taught for a time in Portaferry (1916-23), where his pupils included Joseph Tumelty, and also taught Gaelic League classes there.[220] Played the violin, and was a keen golfer and gardener. Did not marry, and died 7 June 1959 at St Joseph's Convent of Mercy Warrenpoint where he had been resident for some time (assisting with their book-keeping), and is buried in Kilcoo.[221]

Micheál Mac Uiginn (Michael Davitt McGuigan). Holder of teaching diploma from Coláiste Chomhghaill (Belfast) and certificate from Cloghaneely College. Gaelic League district organiser for east Down in 1912. Lecturer in Coláiste Chomhghaill from 1912. Secretary of County Down Feis, Ardglass, 1912. Living in Ballynahinch, 1912. Married Annabella Fitzsimons, Strangford on 12 June 1912, but she died in 1922 (buried in Drumaroad). Moved to Belfast before 1917 and taught for many years in the Christian Brothers there. Connected with St Malachy's College, Rathlin in 1919.[222]

Thomas Cahill, Teconnaught. Teacher, died 20 May 1929. Much involved in Gaelic League activities.

Brian Mac Cathbháid (Brian McCavitt). Born Shanrod, Katesbridge on 25 January 1902, son of Alexander McCavitt, a national schoolteacher and a native of Dromore. Lived in Belfast and Gortahork and qualified as a vocational teacher. After teaching in various localities, became director of Comhdháil Náisiúnta na' Gaeilge in 1944. Retired from this post in 1957 and moved to Bundoran, where he died on 10 February 1973. Member of Comhaltas Uladh and of the Coiste Gnó.[223]

Feidhlim Mac Aonghusa. Born Newry, 1902. Educated at Newry Christian Brothers' School and University College Dublin. A mainstay of the Gaelic League in Newry until his death in 1956.[224]

References

1. See Gerard Stockman (general editor), *Place-Names of Northern Ireland*, i: Newry and South-West Down (G. Toner and M.B. Ó Máinnín), Belfast, 1992; ii: The Ards (A.J. Hughes and R.J. Hannan), Belfast, 1992; iii: The Mournes (M.B. Ó Máinnín), Belfast, 1993; iv (Baronies of Toome, county Antrim, P. McKay) and v (Northwest Down/Iveagh, K. Muhr) forthcoming.
2. See Robert Bell, *The book of Ulster surnames* (Belfast, 1988); Edward MacLysaght, *The surnames of Ireland* (3rd ed., Dublin, 1972); George F. Black, *The surnames of Scotland* (New York, 1946); J.J. Kneen, *The personal names of the Isle of Man* (London, 1937).
3. See for example Michael G. Crawford, *Legendary stories of the Carlingford Lough district* (Warrenpoint, 1913; recently reprinted).
4. Reeves, *Ecclesiastical antiquities*, pp 141-55, 303-8.
5. For the diocesan boundaries, see for example the map in Mallory and McNeill, *Archaeology of Ulster*, p. 275.
6. *Archaeology of Ulster*, including map of later thirteenth-century Ulster on p. 251.
7. Hughes and Hannan, *Place-Names* ii, pp 41-2, 103-4.
8. See Bríd Ní Chonghaile, 'Cúige Uladh roimh an Phlandáil' in *An tUltach*, lviii, no. 1 (January 1981), pp 4-6; idem, 'Mac Artáin Chineál Fhaghartaigh' in *An tUltach*, lviii, no. 3 (March 1981), pp 4-6; idem, 'Mag Aonghusa Uíbh Eathach' in *An tUltach*, lviii, no. 7 (July 1981), pp 4-7; Séamus Ó Néill, 'Muintir Mhic Artáin – cine is mór cáil' in *Inniu*, 1 May 1964, p. 5.
9. See An tAth. B. Mac Thréinfhir, 'Cnoc Uibh Eachach' in *An tUltach*, xxxvi, no. 12 (December 1959), pp 3-4; *Place-Names of Northern Ireland*, i, pp 47-8.
10. Hughes and Hannan, *Placenames*, ii, p. 83.
11. For map of sixteenth-century Ulster clann territories, see *Archaeology of Ulster*, p. 300.
12. D.A. Chart, 'The breakup of the estate of Conn O'Neill, Castlereagh, county Down, temp. James I' in *R.I.A. Proc.*, xlviii, C (1942-3), pp 119-51.
13. J. Braidwood, 'Ulster and Elizabethan English' in G.B. Adams (ed.), *Ulster dialects* (Holywood, 1964), pp 1-109, at 17-21.
14. Ibid., pp 13-14, 19, 20.
15. Ibid., pp 19, 20, 21.
16. Ibid., p. 14.
17. Ibid., pp 16-17.

18. Seamus Pender (ed.), *A census of Ireland circa 1659* (Dublin, 1939), p. xiii.

19. G.B. Adams, 'Aspects of monoglottism in Ulster' in *Ulster Folklife*, xxii (1976), pp 76-87, reprinted, slightly abridged, in Adams, *The English dialects of Ulster*, ed. M. Barry and P. Tilling (Holywood, 1986), pp 113-24.

20. James B. Johnston, *Place-names of Scotland* (Edinburgh, 1892), p. xxxiii; James Ferguson, 'The Celtic element in Lowland Scotland' in *Celtic Review* i (1905), pp 246-60 and 321-32, at 322-4; W.J. Watson, *Bàrdachd Gàidhlig* (Inverness, 1918), p. 21; W.L. Lorimer, 'The persistence of Gaelic in Galloway and Carrick' in *Scottish Gaelic Studies*, vi (1949), pp 114-36 and vii (1951), pp 26-46; John MacQueen, 'The Gaelic speakers of Galloway and Carrick' in *Scottish Studies* xvii (1973), pp 17-33; Adams, 'Aspects of monoglottism', p. 85 note 15.

21. Adams, 'Language and man in Ireland' in *Ulster Folklife*, xv/xvi (1970), pp 140-71, note 152, reprinted in Barry and Tilling, *English dialects*, pp 1-32; Adams, 'Aspects of monoglottism', p. 81.

22. Quoted in N.J.A. Williams, *I bprionta i leabhar* (Dublin, 1986), p. 50.

23. John Thompson, *An abstract of the laws and rules of the General Synod of Ulster from June 15th 1694 to June 1800* (Dublin, 1803), p. 15.

24. W.T. Latimer, *History of the Irish Presbyterians* (Dublin, 1902), p. 293.

25. Adams, 'Aspects of monoglottism', p. 83.

26. Colin J. Robb, 'A famous Irish grammar' in *Irish News*, 9 January 1946, p. 2.

27. Séamas Ó Saothraí, *An ministir Gaelach Uilliam Mac Néill* (Dublin, 1992), pp 33-4.

28. Pádraig Mac Con Midhe, 'Gaeilge an Dúin, II' in *An tUltach*, xlv, no. 12 (Nollaig 1968) pp 3 and 7; Maolcholaim Scott, 'Ballymascanlon and Irish links with Gaelic Scotland' in *Cuisle na nGael*, vii (1991), pp 132-3.

29. Earnán de Blaghd, *Slán le hUltaibh* (Dublin, 1970) p. 68; idem, *Briseadh na teorann* (Dublin, 1955) p. 100.

30. Adams, 'Aspects of monoglottism' p. 84.

31. Aodh de Blacam, 'The other hidden Ireland', in *Studies*, xxiii (1934), pp 439-54, at pp 441-2.

32. Breandán Ó Buachalla, *I mBéal Feirste cois cuain* (Dublin, 1968), p. 103 including note 2.

33. T.F. O'Rahilly, 'Irish poets, historians, and judges in English documents, 1538-1615', *R.I.A. Proc.*, xxxvi, C (1921-4), pp 86-120, at p. 109.

34. Edward O'Reilly, *A chronological account of nearly four hundred Irish writers ... to 1750* (Dublin, 1820), p. 159; A.J. Hughes, 'The seventeenth-century Ulster/Scottish contention of the Red Hand: background and significance' in D.S. Thomson (ed.), *Gaelic and Scots in harmony: proceedings of the second international conference on the languages of Scotland* (Glasgow, 1990), pp 78-93 at p. 82.

35. Williams, *I bprionta*, pp 57-8; Énrí Ó Muirgheasa, *Dhá chéad de cheoltaí Uladh* (Dublin, 1934, 1969), pp 13-6.

36. E. Ó Muirgheasa, 'The Oireachtas country' in *An Claidheamh Soluis*, 17 July 1915, p. 7; and 24 July 1915, supplement, p. ii.

37. O'Reilly, *A chronological account*, pp 194-5.

38. Tadhg Ó Donnchadha (ed.), *Leabhar Cloinne Aodha Buidhe* (Dublin, 1931).

39. O'Reilly, *A chronological account*, p. 201; A.J. Hughes, 'Fuar leam longphort mo charad' in *Celtica*, xix (1986), pp 61-74.

40. Hughes, 'The contention of the Red Hand', p. 90.

41. O'Reilly, *A chronological account*, p. 220.

42. Séamus Ó Casaide, 'The Irish language in Belfast and county Down 1600-1850' in *Down and Connor Historical Society Journal*, ii (1929), pp 4-63, at p. 12; that

article also published in book form (Dublin, 1930); Ó Muirgheasa, *Amhráin Airt Mhic Chubhthaigh* (2nd ed., Dundalk, 1926), part ii, pp 23-9 and 63-6.

43. O'Reilly, *A chronological account*, p. 222; E. Ó Muirgheasa, 'The Oireachtas country', part i, p. 7; Seosamh Mag Uidhir, *Pádraig Mac a Liondain, Dánta* (Dublin, 1977).

44. Ó Muirgheasa, 'The Oireachtas country', part ii, p. ii; Ó Casaide, 'The Irish language', p. 9.

45. Seosamh Laoide, *Seachrán chairn tSiadhail* (Dublin, 1904).

46. Ó Muirgheasa, 'The Oireachtas country'; Ó Casaide, 'The Irish language', p. 20; B. Mac Thréinfhir, 'Athair na mBrontes' in *An tUltach*, xxxiv, no. 3 (March 1957), pp 4 and 14.

47. J.B. McAleenan, *Teagasc Críostaí Uí Ghripín*, unpub. M.A. thesis, University of Ulster, Coleraine, 1990; Ó Casaide, 'The Irish language', p. 24; Laoide, 'Úr-Chill an Chreagáin' in *An Claidheamh Soluis*, 31 October 1908, p. 7.

48. Ó Casaide, 'The Irish language', p. 15.

49. Information from Ben Mac a' Bháird, Newcastle.

50. Ó Casaide, foreword to Charlotte Milligan Fox, *Annals of the Irish harpers* (London, 1911) p. x; idem, *Patrick Lynch of county Down, Irish scholar* (Dublin, 1927); idem, 'Memoir of Patrick Lynch' in *Journal of the Irish Folksong Society*, xxii-xxiii (1927), pp xvii-xxv; idem, 'Patrick Lynch of Castlebar' in *Irish Book Lover* xvi (1928), p. 70; idem, *Irish in Belfast and county Down*, pp 13-40, esp. p. 39; idem, 'The two Patrick Lynches' in *Irish Book Lover* xxii (1934) p. 118; Cathal O'Byrne, 'Patrick Lynch of Loughinisland' in *As I roved out* (Belfast, 1946), pp 385-9.

51. Tomás Ó Cléirigh, *Aodh Mac Aingil agus an scoil Nua-Ghaeilge i Lobháin* (Dublin, 1935, 1985); Anraí Mac Giolla Chomhaill, *Bráithrín bocht ó Dhún* (Dublin, 1985); Patrick Kearns, *Down's angelic genius* (Newry, 1985); Williams, *I bprionta*, pp 40-1.

52. In this and in other extracts, the original spelling and language are retained; this may give the texts an unfamiliar appearance compared with abbreviated spelling and normalised grammar, but to convert them to some such standard form would make it pointless to offer them as linguistic examples.

53. B. Mac Thréinfhir, 'An tAthair Pulleine' in *An tUltach*, xl, no. 7 (July 1963), pp 6 and 18; and xl, no. 8 (August 1963), p. 7; Kearns, 'James Pulleine, an eighteenth-century dean of Dromore' in *Seanchas Árd Mhacha* (1984), pp 70-9.

54. Douglas Hyde, 'An Irish funeral oration over Owen O'Neill, of the House of Clanaboy' in *Ulster Journal of Archaeology*, iii (1896), pp 258-71; and iv (1898), pp 50-5.

55. Francis McPolin, 'An old Irish catechism from Oriel' in *Irish Ecclesiastical Record*, lxix (1947), pp 509-17.

56. Information from Séamas Mac Diarmada, Newcastle.

57. Séamus P. Ó Mordha, 'Údar Thóraidheacht na bhFiréin' in *Stud. Hib.*, iii (1963), pp 155-72; Anselm Faulkner, 'Tóruidheacht na bhFíreun air Lorg Chríosda (1762): the translator' in *Éigse*, xv (1973-4), pp 303-11.

58. Ó Mordha, 'Údar', p. 157.

59. *Tóruidheacht na bhfíreun ar lorg Chríosda*, ed. Domhnall Ó Tuathail (Dublin, 1915); James O. McDermott, *Transcribing and editing the Tóraidheacht*, unpub. M.A. thesis, Queen's University Belfast, 1979; Dermot Devlin, *Toruidheachd na bhFíreun*, unpub. Ph.D. thesis, University of Ulster, Coleraine, 1989.

60. Terence P. McCaughey, 'Muiris Ó Gormáin's English-Irish phrasebook' in *Éigse* xii (1968), pp 203-27.

61. Rev William Neilson, *An introduction to the Irish language* (Dublin, 1808; facsimile reproduction, Belfast, 1990); for fuller information on William Neilson, see Ó Saothraí, *An ministir Gaelach*; idem, 'Cúlra Gaelach William Neilson' in *An tUltach*, lvi, no. 9 (September 1979), pp 9-12; idem, 'William Neilson, D.D., M.R.I.A., 1774-1831' in Mac Giolla Chomhaill (ed.), *Meascra Uladh* (Belfast, 1974), pp 80-8. O'Donovan, p. 65.

62. Neilson, *Introduction*, p. x.

63. John O'Donovan, *Irish grammar* (1845), quoted in Ó Casaide, *Irish in Belfast and county Down*, p. 40.

64. Dubhglas de hÍde, *Mise agus an Connradh* (Dublin, 1937), p. 11.

65. Neilson, *Introduction*, part 1, p. 144.

66. Ibid., part 1, p. 145.

67. Ibid., part 1 , p. 157.

68. Ibid., part 2, pp 64-8.

69. Ó Buachalla, *I mBéal Feirste*, pp 216-7.

70. Adams, 'The last language census in Northern Ireland' in Adams (ed.), *Ulster dialects* (Holywood, 1964), pp 114-5.

71. G.B. Adams, 'The 1851 language census in the north of Ireland' in *Ulster Folklife*, xx (1974), pp 65-70 contains barony-level maps based on the 1851 census for those born 1761-1791 and 1791-1821.

72. Garret Fitzgerald, 'Estimates for baronies of minimum level of Irish-speaking amongst successive decennial cohorts: 1771-1781 to 1861-1871' in *R.I.A. Proc.*, lxxxiv, C (1984), pp 117-55.

73. Ciarán Ó Duibhín, *Irish in county Down since 1750* (Downpatrick, 1991), pp 8-13; for other work on the 1911 census, see Adams, 'Last language census', for maps of six-county area at ded level for whole population, and for those born before 1871; G.B. Adams, 'Language in Ulster 1820-1850' in *Ulster Folklife*, xix (1973), pp 50-5, for map of eleven-county areas at dispensary district level for those born before 1851.

74. For general information, see T.F. O'Rahilly, *Irish dialects past and present* (Dublin, 1932, 1972), chapter xvii; Colm Ó Baoill, *Contributions to a comparative study of Ulster Irish and Scottish Gaelic* (Belfast, 1978); Cathair Ó Dochartaigh, *Dialects of Ulster Irish* (Belfast, 1987); and, for more specific information: Mac Thréinfhir, 'Gaeilge chontae an Dúin theas'; Mac Con Midhe, 'Gaeilge an Dúin, II'; Dónal Mac Aonghusa, 'An Ghaeilge i gcondae an Dúin' in *Lá*, 25 March 1993, p. 20.

75. A number of the examples which follow are taken from a radio broadcast by Heinrich Wagner, date unknown.

76. Ó Baoill, *Contributions*, p. 303.

77. Neilson, *Introduction*, part 1, p. 143; Wagner, loc.cit.

78. Neilson, *Introduction*.

79. Quoted in Patterson, p. xi.

80. Laoide (?), 'A song from Iveagh (county Down)' in *Irisleabhar na Gaedhilge*, xii (1902), pp 152-4.

81. E. Ó Muirgheasa, *Céad de cheoltaí Uladh* (Dublin, 1915), pp 99, 256-7, 337; new edition by T.F. Beausang (Newry, 1983), pp 98, 239-40, 292.

82. An tAth Lorcán Ó Muireadhaigh, *Ceoltaí Óméith* (Dundalk, 1920), p. 15.

83. Úna Ní Fhaircheallaigh, 'Dánta a conndae na Midhe' in John Ryan (ed.), *Féil-sgríbhinn Eóin Mhic Néill* (Dublin, 1940), pp 97-100.

84. Donn Piatt, in *Fáinne an lae*, 29 August 1925; idem, 'Gaeilge Óméith' in *An tUltach*, xliv, no. 8 (August 1967), pp 10-11.

85. Ó Duibhín, *Irish in county Down*, pp 39-40.
86. Gearóid Mac Giolla Domhnaigh, 'Dónall Ó Tuathail, sagart na ráite' in *An tUltach*, lxxi, no. 12 (December 1994), pp 8-14, at p. 12.
87. Ó Duibhín, *Irish in county Down*, p. 40.
88. An tAth Domhnall Ó Tuathail, 'The phrase method' in *An Claidheamh Soluis*, 29 January 1916, p. 6.
89. In the 1991 census, local government districts wholly contained within county Down (North Down, Castlereagh, Ards, Down) returned a total of 9,908 people with a knowledge of Irish, while districts partly in county Down (Lisburn, Banbridge, Newry and Mourne) returned a further 22,378 such individuals.
90. Ó Casaide, *Irish in Belfast and county Down*, p. 49.
91. A work on McAdam's dictionary by Colm Beckett is due for publication in the near future.
92. Ó Buachalla, *I mBéal Feirste*; in English, see Pádraig Ó Snodaigh, *Hidden Ulster* (Dublin, 1973).
93. Mac Con Midhe, 'Thall a's i bhfus' in *An tUltach*, xxviii, no. 3 (March 1951), pp 5-6; Mac Giolla Domhnaigh, 'Conradh na Gaeilge 1893-1993?' in *Cuisle na nGael*, ix (1993), pp 1-4.
94. *Irish News*, 5 September 1902, p. 6; *Feis an Dúin* is an event, still held annually, comprising competitions in language, music, dancing and sport, organised by the Gaelic League with the co-operation of the Gaelic Athletic Association.
95. Adams, 'Last language census', p. 139.
96. Mac Giolla Domhnaigh, 'Sagart na Ráite'.
97. Anon., 'Maighréad Nic Eoin', in *An tUltach*, xl, no. 5 (May 1963), p. 2; Aedín Ní Choirbhín, 'Coláiste Bhríde, Ros Glas' in *An tUltach*, lvii, no. 7 (July 1980), pp 3-4.
98. *An Claidheamh Soluis*, 6 June 1903, p. 3.
99. Adams, 'Aspects of monoglottism', p. 83.
100. Sighle Nic an Ultaigh, *An Dún – ó shíol go bláth – the GAA story* (Newry, 1990); for list of club histories, see p. 661 therein.
101. Ó Casaide, 'The Irish language'.
102. John O'Donovan, *Letters containing information relative to the history and antiquities of the county of Down*, published as a supplement to *An Leabharlann*, Dublin, *c.* 1906.
103. Harris, *Down*, p. 109.
104. John Dubourdieu, *Statistical survey of county Down* (1802), quoted in Ó Casaide, 'The Irish language', p. 47.
105. Christopher Anderson, *The native Irish and their descendants* (3rd ed., London, Dublin and Edinburgh, 1846).
106. O'Donovan, 'Letters', pp 50, 70, 79, 88.
107. Ó Casaide, 'The Irish language', p. 55.
108. Ibid., p. 58.
109. Ibid., p. 55.
110. Alexander Knox, *A history of the county of Down* (Dublin, 1875), p. 48.
111. Proinsias Ó Catháin, Essay on the present state of the Irish language and literature in Ulster, 1 March 1876 (RIA, MS 12.Q.13 pp. 1-91 [128-218], at p. 3 [130]; I am indebted to Tomás de Bhaldraithe for this reference.
112. Seosamh Laoide, 'Irish in Monaghan county' in *Irisleabhar na Gaedhilge*, vi (1895-96), pp 145-52, at pp 145, 151.
113. H. Boyd, 'Notes and queries, no. 220' in *Irisleabhar na Gaedhilge*, viii (1897), p. 124.

114. Laoide (?), 'Song from Iveagh'.
115. Aodh Mac Gréacháin, 'Coláiste Bhrighde', *Irish News*, 8 August 1912, p. 7.
116. Ó Néill, 'County Down and the native tongue', *Irish News*, 3 January 1936, p. 4.
117. Ó Muireadhaigh, *Ceoltaí Óméith*, p. 15.
118. Donn Piatt, 'Re the last Irish-speakers of Leinster' in *Irish Book Lover*, xx (1932), pp 122-4.
119. O'Donovan, 'Letters', p. 42.
120. Ó Casaide, 'The Irish language', p. 29.
121. Adams, 'Last language census', p. 139; Anon (?r B. Mac Thréinfhir), 'County Down Irish' in *Score* (Official magazine of Down GAA), no. 6 (1978), p. 10.
122. *The Aghaderg story 1903-1984* (Newry, c. 1984), pp 6, 8-9.
123. Information from Pádraig Mac Giolla Ruaidh, Belfast, who also worked at Scarva station at the time.
124. O'Donovan, 'Letters', pp 42, 62-3; Rev Edward Campbell and Padraic Keenan, Some notes on the clergy of Dromore from the earliest times to the present day, 1952, updated 1954, typescript in PRONI CR 2/5/1, pp 4-6.
125. O'Donovan, 'Letters', p. 55; Campbell and Keenan, notes, p. 14.
126. O'Donovan, 'Letters', pp 61-2.
127. Ibid., p. 49.
128. F. Brady and F.A. Pottle, *Boswell in search of a wife 1766-1769* (Melbourne, 1957), pp 219-20; Candida, 'An Irishwoman's diary', *Irish Times*, 25 July 1977, p. 9.
129. O'Donovan, 'Letters', pp 45, 46.
130. de Blacam, 'Hidden Ireland', p. 451.
131. Quoted by Ó Saothraí, 'John Francis Small: an fear a scríobh stair an Iúir' in *An tUltach*, liv, no. 1 (January 1977), pp 6-8 and liv, no. 2 (February 1977), pp 10-12, at no. 1, p. 7.
132. Mac Thréinfhir, 'An tAthair Pulleine', first part, p. 6.
133. Harris, *Down*, p. 254.
134. Laoide (?), 'Song from Iveagh', p. 153.
135. Mac Thréinfhir, 'Gaeilge Chontae an Dúin Theas' in *An tUltach*, xl, no. 3 (March 1963), p. 6; Chronicler, 'The Irish language in county Down' in *Score*, no. 8 (October 1978), p. 9.
136. Candida, 'An Irishwoman's diary', *Irish Times*, 24 March 1980, p. 9; Aodán Mac Póilín drew my attention to this information.
137. Information from Ruairí Mac Gráinne, Dublin and Colm Mac Eoin, Downpatrick.
138. Candida, 'An Irishwoman's diary'.
139. Information from Charlie Cunningham, Annalong.
140. Information from Charlie Cunningham, Annalong and Willie McGreevy, Glassdrummond.
141. 'An Ghaeilge ar an Ghlasdromainn' in *Pobal Ruairí*, i, no. 1 (March 1988), p. 3.
142. *Irish News*, 23 April 1902, p. 3; 20 November 1902, p. 3; 18 December 1902, p. 7; there is a photograph from the late 1920s of a Mary McGreevy, Glassdrummond (with her mother Eliza, outside their cottage) on the cover of *Twelve miles of Mourne*, v (1992).
143. Ó Néill, 'James McKnight' in *Irish Times*, 7 May 1976, p. 10; idem, 'James McKnight an Preisbitéarach' in *Inniu*, 22 January 1960, p. 3; Ó Saothraí, 'William Neilson, D.D., M.R.I.A., 1774-1831', at p. 80.
144. O'Donovan, 'Letters', p. 65.
145. W.H. Patterson, *A glossary of words in use in the counties of Antrim and Down* (London, 1880), p. x.
146. R.L. Praeger, *A populous solitude* (Dublin, 1941), p. 63; Aodán Mac Póilín drew

my attention to this.

147. I am grateful to Fintan Mussen, who has custody of the Francis McPolin manuscripts, for allowing me to examine them; the two copybooks here quoted from are identified by their types as 'S.O. Book 127' (SO) and 'Educational Book-keeping Exercise Book' (EB); McPolin (SO, pp 112, 172) records an interesting tradition that Leitrim townland in Clonduff (not to be confused with Leitrim in Drumgooland parish) was settled by families from south Armagh and north Louth, who found a refuge there under O'Neill of Bannvale in the eighteenth century; he cites the surnames Carroll, Hanlon, Matthews and McAtee.

148. McPolin, SO, p. 36.

149. Michael J. Murphy, *Ulster folk of field and fireside* (Dundalk, 1983), p. 17 and photograph opposite p. 39.

150. Ibid., p. 17.

151. McPolin, SO, pp 119, 121.

152. Ibid., p. 47.

153. Ibid., pp 64-5.

154. Ibid., p. 68.

155. McPolin, EB p. 11.

156. Padraic Keenan, *Brief historical sketch of the parish of Clonduff* (Newry, 1941), pp 19-20; Campbell and Keenan, notes, p. 46.

157. O'Laverty, quoted in Mac Con Midhe, 'Gaeilge an Dúin, II'; Mac Con Midhe, 'An Ghaeilge i gco and Dúin' in *An tUltach*, xlv, no. 11 (November 1968), p. 15 further quotes O'Laverty to the effect that McMullan was born in Loughinisland in 1752 and was educated at the Lynch school there.

158. Information from Cathal Ó Baoill, Newcastle.

159. For a version from the Sperrins, see Éamonn Ó Tuathail, *Sgéalta mhuintir Luinigh* (Dublin, 1933), p. 136.

160. Joe Charleton, 'Lough Island Reavy' in *Kilcoo, a Gaelic and social heritage* (Newry, 1986), pp 466-7; idem, 'Na cainteoirí dúchais ó thuaidh', *Sunday Press*, 18 May 1986, p. 23.

161. Information from Austin Morgan, Newcastle.

162. McAleenan, *Teagasc Críostaí Uí Ghripín*, p. 25.

163. Ibid., p. 18 and passim.

164. *Belfast Newsletter* 14 May 1847, p. 2; 3 August 1847, p. 1; 7 March 1848, p. 2; *Down Recorder*, 15 May 1847, p. 2; 22 May 1847, p. 4.

165. Information from Sean Mackin of Savanaghan, Dungannon, a native of Annaclone, who heard it related around 1934-5 by Ned Norris, then aged around 80; Norris had travelled as a carter with his father Pat and his grandfather between Castlewellan and Banbridge, and had heard the story from his grandfather when they passed the cross-roads in question.

166. Information from Colm Mac Eoin, Downpatrick and Séamas Mac Giolla Fhinnéin, Leitrim.

167. Information from Séamas Mac Giolla Fhinnéin.

168. G. Park, *Drumaroad and Clanvaraghan* (Castlewellan, c. 1984), p. 16.

169. de Blaghd, *Slán le hUltaibh*, p. 68; idem, *Briseadh na teorann*, p. 100.

170. O'Donovan, 'Letters', p. 70.

171. Park, *Drumaroad and Clanvaraghan*, p. 123.

172. Tomás Ó Conceanainn, 'Mr Concannon in Down', *An Claidheamh Soluis*, 14 December 1901, supplement, p. 2.

173. de Blaghd, *Slán le hUltaibh*, p. 68.

174. Ó Buachalla, *I mBéal Feirste*, p. 103.

175. O'Donovan, 'Letters', p. 88.
176. Adams, 'Last language census', p. 140.
177. O'Donovan, 'Letters', p. 88.
178. Candida, 'An Irishwoman's diary', *Irish Times*, 13 March 1978, p. 9.
179. O'Laverty, quoted in Ó Casaide, 'The Irish language', p. 23.
180. J.W. H[anna], 'The Anglo-Norman families of Lecale' in *U.J.A.*, i (1853), pp 92-100, at p. 95.
181. O'Donovan, 'Letters', pp 79, 80, 85, 86.
182. *Down Recorder*, 20 July 1872, p. 2.
183. Nic an Ultaigh, *An Dún – the GAA story*, p. 18.
184. *Irish News*, 13 April 1903, p. 8; Nic an Ultaigh, *An Dún – the GAA story*, p. 46.
185. See note 97.
186. Information from Ruairí Mac Gráinne.
187. John Stevenson, *Two centuries of life in Down* (Belfast, 1920; new edition, 1990); A.P.W. Malcolmson, Introduction to catalogue of Nugent papers, P.R.O.N.I., D.552, drawing on the works of G.F. Savage-Armstrong; John Lodge, *The peerage of Ireland* (rev. ed., London, 1789) i, *sub* Nugent.
188. Information from Dr Peter Milligan, Belfast.
189. Adams, 'Aspects of monoglottism', p. 83.
190. Rev. W. Holmes (*c.* 1815) in W. Shaw Mason, *A statistical account, or parochial survey of Ireland drawn up from the communications of the clergy*, three vols (Dublin, 1814), iii.
191. O'Donovan, 'Letters', p. 8.
192. Ibid., p. 18.
193. Ibid., p. 15.
194. Quoted in Ó Buachalla, *I mBéal Feirste*, p. 58, note 13.
195. Mac Giolla Domhnaigh, 'Conradh na Gaeilge'; James McCavitt, '80 years ago', in *Cuisle na nGael*, i (1985), pp 25-8; Campbell and Keenan, notes, p. 100.
196. McCavitt, '80 years ago'.
197. Aodh Mac Seagháin, 'Dornán Sean-Rannta' in *An Claidheamh Soluis*, 30 January 1909, p. 5; 13 February 1909, p. 12; 27 February 1909, p. 5; 6 March 1909, p. 5; 13 March 1909, p. 5.
198. Keenan, *Clonduff*, p. 27; Campbell and Keenan, 'Some notes on the clergy of Dromore', p. 71.
199. *An Claidheamh Soluis*, 21 September 1901, p. 28.
200. *Irish News*, 11 June 1912, p. 7.
201. Seán Crawford, 'The Gaeltacht at my door' in *Mourne rambles*, a supplement to *Cuisle na nGael* x (1994), pp 52-4.
202. *The American Catholic who's who*, vi, 1944-45 (Detroit), p. 171; *Who was who in America*, iii, 1951-60 (Chicago, 1963), pp 338-9.
203. Mac Gréacháin, 'Coláiste Bhríghde'.
204. Pádraig Mac Con Midhe, 'Thall a's i bhfus' in *An tUltach*, xxvi, no. 6 (June 1949), p. 3; Anon., 'Pósadh' in *An Claidheamh Soluis*, 5 November 1910, p. 2.
205. *Irish News*, 13 November 1901, p. 7; *An Claidheamh Soluis*, 30 November 1901, supplement, p. 2; *An Claidheamh Soluis*, 14 December 1901, supplement, p. 3; Mac Con Midhe, 'Thall a's i bhfus' in *An tUltach*, xxx, no. 2 (February 1953), p. 3.
206. *Irish News*, 15 July 1912, p. 6; Crawford, 'The Gaeltacht at my door'.
207. Mac Con Midhe, 'Thall agus Abhus' in *An tUltach*, xlix, no. 11 (November 1972), p. 18; photograph, *An tUltach*, lxix, no. 7 (July 1992), p. 11; see also note 97.
208. Proinsias Mac an Bheatha, 'Timpeall' in *An tUltach*, lxii, no. 9 (September 1985),

p. 10; notice in *Journal of the Down and Connor Historical Society*, ix (1938), p. 81.

209. de Blaghd, *Slán le hUltaibh*, p. 68.

210. *Irish News*, 28 May 1902, p. 3; *Irish News*, 13 June 1902, p. 6.

211. Nic an Ultaigh, *An Dún – the GAA story*, pp 68, 83, 535, 598-600.

212. *Frontier Sentinel*, 5 April 1919, p. 5.

213. *The Aghaderg Story*, pp 6, 8-9; Nic an Ultaigh, pp 50-1, 57, 59, 600.

214. Information from Mrs Bridie Lennon, Castlewellan, a niece of Stephen McGeown.

215. *Irish News*, 13 November 1901, p. 7; *An Claidheamh Soluis*, 16 November 1901, p. 571; *Irish News*, 12 December 1901.

216. Records of St Patrick's College, Drumcondra, Dublin.

217. Jonathan Bell, 'Intelligent revivalism: the first Feis na nGleann, 1904' in A. Gailey (ed.), *The use of tradition* (Holywood, 1988), pp 3, 11; another link between Feis na nGleann and Ardglass at the time is provided by Francis J Bigger.

218. Information from Ellen Gracey, Ballynahinch.

219. *Irish News*, 18 March 1912, p. 8; 11 June 1912, p. 7.

220. *Fáinne an Lae*, 16 March 1918, p. 2; *Irish News*, 6 December 1922, p. 6.

221. Information from Mrs Bridie Lennon.

222. *Irish News*, 17 January 1912, p. 7; *An Claidheamh Soluis*, 27 January 1912, p. 11; *Irish News*, 9 May 1912, p. 8; *Irish News*, 22 June 1912, p. 1; *Fáinne an Lae*, 14 June 1919, p. 2; *Irish News*, 17 January 1922.

223. Donncha Ó Laoire, 'Slán le Brian Mac Cafaid' in *An tUltach*, xxxiv, no. 9 (September 1957), pp 8 and 12; Pádraig Mac Con Midhe, 'Thall agus abhus' in *An tUltach*, no. 4 (April 1973), pp 15-6; Anon., 'Canon T.G. Pettit agus an Ghaeilge' in *Cuisle na nGael* vii (1991), pp 57-8.

224. *An tUltach*, xxxiii, no. 7 (July 1956), p. 8; *Cuisle na nGael*, ix (1993), pp 25-7.

Plate 17.1   The Square, Rostrevor (Ulster Museum, W05/85/3).

Chapter 18

RELIGION AND SOCIETY: PROTESTANTISM IN NINETEENTH-CENTURY COUNTY DOWN

MYRTLE HILL

Religious faith plays an important part in the lives of individuals. It not only supports and sustains many through the various crises of life, it helps also to shape their perceptions of themselves, and to determine their role in personal relationships, in the family, and in society generally. In a broader sense too, the religious affiliations and allegiances of any community are vitally important in determining its social, cultural and political ethos. During this period, which begins in the immediate aftermath of the United Irish rebellion and ends with the Home Rule crisis, the links between constitutional politics and religion have been clearly identified. However, religious organisations of all kinds were also affected by less dramatic events in the secular world such as demographic change, urbanisation and the gradual rise of democracy. This chapter explores some aspects of the changing nature of Protestant religious experience during these years, both personal and institutional, and examines the relationships between the churches and society and between church and meeting house, in and around county Down.

One of the immediate difficulties posed by county history is, however, the arbitrary nature of the boundaries imposed upon the area under discussion. The lines of division between counties Down, Antrim and Armagh, drawn up for administrative purposes in the sixteenth and seventeenth centuries, do not relate to human, ethnic or cultural factors, and nor therefore to either the concepts or practice of faith. Thus one would expect to find similarities and parallels in religious experience between towns and villages in adjoining counties, while perhaps noting diversity caused by other factors. One could suggest for example that proximity to Belfast may have been a significant factor in determining experience in both Newtownards and Lisburn, with the industrial centre increasing its influence over its hinterland during the course of the nineteenth century. On the other hand, how similar were religious experiences in the industrial suburb of Ballymacarret, the fishing village of Killyleagh and the market-town of Banbridge?

Moreover, the geographical boundaries created by the religious institutions themselves further complicate the picture, making denominational comparisons particularly difficult. The two Church of Ireland dioceses of Down and Dromore, for example, take in the whole of county Down, but the diocese of Down was united with that of Connor which embraces most of county Antrim, while that of Dromore was a separate ecclesiastical unit until 1842 (fig. 18.1). Until 1873, the Lordship of Newry and Mourne was also an independent jurisdiction. County Down also contains seven presbyteries, the local organisational units of the Presbyterian Church in Ireland, although two of these, Belfast and Newry, reach into the counties of Antrim and Armagh respectively. Methodism operates a circuit system which forms an overriding element linking independent communities; and the nineteenth-century circuits of Belfast and Newry both included parts of county Down. All three systems co-exist within the single geographical area of the county, and reflect the differences of organisation and administration which are only the most obvious distinctive features of each denomination.

From the mid-seventeenth century the four north-eastern counties of Ireland – Antrim, Down, Armagh and Londonderry – have represented an area in which religious belief is fundamentally different from the rest of the island. Within this region an overall Protestant majority of almost two-thirds (65.7 per cent) has produced a distinctive social and cultural climate, which in turn has led to political singularity. However, while its majority status did much to determine the character of Protestantism in this area, the relationships and interactions between different denominations were also of significance. The 1861 census shows that almost one half (44.6 per cent) of the Protestant population were Presbyterian; members of the Established Church made up 20.5 per cent, with a mixture of smaller denominations, headed by Methodism, accounting for the remainder.

While the local predominance of Presbyterianism reflected both the close links between the north-east of the island and its Scottish neighbour and a strong regional identity, Anglicans and Methodists too were intensely conscious of their distinctive historical origins. Each denomination was thus separated from the other by social, cultural and political factors as well as by theological distinctions, and the relative strengths and weakness of their constituencies was an important factor in determining the social and cultural ethos of the community.

Presbyterianism

The history of county Down is inextricably bound up with the history

Fig. 18.1   The ecclesiastical province of Armagh, 1800: diocesan boundaries.

of the Presbyterian Church in Ireland, which by 1800 was long-established and well-organised. But although its leaders frequently stressed the distinction between themselves and other 'dissenters', the Presbyterian community was not entirely homogeneous. Individual Presbyterians could choose between several distinct and rival varieties of the faith, imported as a result of continuing interaction between the peoples of Ulster and Scotland. At the head of the numerically strong and geographically concentrated Presbyterian community was the Synod of Ulster, the provincial church government which attracted the loyalty of the vast majority of Ulster Presbyterians throughout the eighteenth and nineteenth century. Other significant minority groups included the Covenanting or Reformed Presbyterian Church, which had originated in the second Scottish Reformation of 1638-49 and had put down somewhat delicate roots in Ulster during the troubled years of the mid-seventeenth century. By 1800 only three itinerant preachers were employed by the Covenanters, but these 'fiery preachers' covered large geographical areas.[1] William Staveley, for example, who organised several reformed congregations, including that in Rathfriland, county Down, was said to have a parish which 'extended from county Down to the counties of Armagh, Monaghan and Cavan'.[2]

The Associate Synod, or the Seceders, a Scottish breakaway sect which began to make an impact in Ulster in the 1740s, was numerically stronger than the Covenanters and was particularly successful in competing with mainstream Presbyterianism. Combining conversionist zeal and a strong emphasis on fighting sin with rigid orthodoxy and strict discipline, the Seceders had organised a total of sixteen congregations in county Down by 1818.[3] While an energetic and assertive outreach programme goes a long way to explaining this rapid expansion during the course of the eighteenth century, it was also to some extent a consequence of the perceived shortcomings of the Synod of Ulster. A few local examples will serve to illustrate both the problems within mainstream Presbyterianism and the opportunism of the newcomers.

In purely practical terms, the provision of new meeting-houses often filled an existing gap in the church structure. At a time when travel was slow and difficult, the distance from home to meeting house was often a critical factor in attracting potential worshippers. One mid-century parliamentary report indicated that, given good roads and weather, people would travel a mile to church but probably no further,[4] so that in places like Boardmills, where there had been no meeting-house in an area of ten by eleven miles, the Seceders' provision of both a building and a form of worship acceptable to the local Presbyterian community was particularly welcome.[5] Similarly, the Synod of Ulster's lengthy delay in filling the vacancy brought about by the death of their minister provoked the congregation of Drumgooland to apply instead to the Seceding Church, resulting in the establishment of a rival neighbouring congregation. Ballycopeland's Secession church was formed as the result of similar frustration.[6] Numerous examples suggest that the Seceders, like the Covenanters, provided an acceptable alternative within the broad Presbyterian movement for those who disagreed with mainstream Synod of Ulster theology or practice, and offered an outlet for evangelical fervour in a period of growing religious enthusiasm.

Numerous doctrinal disputes and divisions within the Synod of Ulster itself also contributed to dissatisfaction amongst the Presbyterian laity in the late eighteenth and early nineteenth centuries. These disputes were largely due to what has been described as 'the inherent tension of Presbyterianism, between traditional ecclesiastical orthodoxy and the right of private judgement'.[7] In this period the major disputes were connected with the ideas of Arianism and subscription to the Westminster Confession of Faith. Arianism constituted a rejection of the traditional Christian doctrines of the divinity of Christ and the Trinity – a view offensive to more orthodox laity, and was capable of creating acrimonious divisions. Although the importance of this brand of theological liberalism has probably been exaggerated, county Down provides many examples of congregations divided by competing orthodox and Arian candidates, with ministers like the Rev. Josiah Kerr in Ardglass finding that a declaration of Arianism could cost him his job.[8] The subscription issue, although frequently merging with accusations of Arianism, was in fact a separate, equally contentious debate. To the orthodox, those who refused to subscribe to the Westminster Confession of Faith were as heretical as Arians, while for non-subscribers the demand to conform to 'man-made' confessions was regarded as an unreasonable restraint on individual conscience.[9]

While Presbyterian democratic tradition ensured that the Synod of Ulster was prepared to embrace a range of theological opinion if supported by a synodical majority, at congregational level differences of opinion frequently erupted, resulting in public dissension and community division. During the ministry of James Neilson (1792-1838) in the county town of Downpatrick, for example, a section of the congregation 'impatient with lack of clear positive preaching', simply withdrew from the meeting house. In Ballynahinch in 1774 a portion of the local Synod of Ulster congregation, dissatisfied with their minister, formed a new congregation under the seceding Presbytery of Down. When the Synod of Ulster withdrew the licence of the Reverend J. Gibson who had been called to Ballywalter church, his supporters took possession of the meeting house and declared themselves 'Independents'.[10] The frequency with which congregations took issue with each other, their ministers, or the synod over such matters, and the consequent forming of breakaway groups, suggests a degree of disharmony at grassroots level which could not only divide communities, but significantly affect the cause of Presbyterianism in a locality,[11] and was to build to a climax which split the church in the 1820s.

Congregational disharmony was not, however, confined to doctrinal matters. The inherent power of the congregation in the government of its own church could give rise to considerable tension on a wide range of issues, and in all branches of Presbyterianism lay authority was frequently exercised over local ministers. Thus, in 1809, Isaac Allen of Garvaghy was charged by the elders with 'marrying a couple on one day's proclamation, going to a play that was acted in the neighbourhood and with being too much given to farming'.[12] On the other hand, William Skelly of Donaghadee, deposed *sine die* for alleged immorality in 1821, was nonetheless able to organise a second congregation in the area, which he served until 1856, when he was restored to the General Assembly.[13] The strong bonds of loyalty and affection formed between individual ministers and their congregations was obviously an important factor in close-knit communities. Following the death of the popular Reverend Samuel Edgar of Ballynahinch in 1826, a majority of his congregation wished his son to take his place. However, as David Edgar was then a probationer, with two years at college to finish before his ordination, a minority of the congregation broke away to form a third Presbyterian church in the area. When the Reverend S. J. Moore of Donaghmore accepted a call to Ballymena in 1850, his congregation, which had flourished during his ministry, put up a strong resistance, drawing up a list of Eleven Reasons of Protest.[14] The strong self-governing tradition within the Presbyterian tradition ensured that the Synod of Ulster employed much time and diplomacy in mediating in such local conflicts. While there were clearly defined lines of authority between synod, presbytery and congregations, decisions taken by one body were not always acceptable to the others.

Frequently, one important source of unity between a congregation and its minister was their shared social background. As Megahey points out, Presbyterianism embraces a fairly narrow social spectrum, with its main strength made up by the commercial and business classes and tenant farmers who were the dominant social and political grouping in county Down.[15] The dramatic developments within Ulster Presbyterianism in the fifty years after 1800 reflect the growing interconnections between religious belief and the social and political aspirations of these 'middling men'. In the aftermath of the United Irish Rebellion and the French Revolution, this community found it necessary to reassess its traditional toleration of dissent. This was particularly relevant to county Down, which, together with Antrim, had been the main focus for political radicalism in the North. Indeed, from a total of thirty ministers and eighteen probationers from the different branches of Presbyterianism implicated in the disturbances, A.T.Q.

Stewart lists eleven ministers and five probationers from county Down.[16] The executions, imprisonments and forced emigrations which followed had a strong impact on the local community. And while it is true that many county Down Presbyterians also fought on the government side in '98,[17] the visible leadership provided to the rebels by so many of its clergy was a major source of embarrassment for the governing body of the church.

At its autumn meeting in 1798, the Synod of Ulster was anxious to clear itself from the suspicion under which it was placed, and in the following year repeated it denunciation of Presbyterian rebels:

> On the whole of this melancholy and most painful subject, while the Synod reflects with sorrow, on the Scandal brought upon its Reputation, by the Indiscretion and misconduct, of a few misguided and unworthy Individuals; It feels Confident in declaring that there is no ground for suspecting its Loyalty, as a Body ....[18]

On its part, the government, concerned to encourage a more respectable, more conservative and more loyal dissenting leadership, responded with the offer of an increased and differential annual payment to the Irish Presbyterian Church.

In the years following the rebellion and the Act of Union, a combination of disillusionment, fear and a growing awareness of the steady progress of Catholicism helped to accelerate the demand for greater doctrinal orthodoxy and a stricter religious lifestyle within the Presbyterian community. A perceived, though erroneous, link between religious and political radicalism also influenced change, and that link was perhaps most ardently promoted and disseminated by Henry Cooke in the first decades of the nineteenth century (plate 18.1). Cooke was to leave his stamp on Irish Presbyterian history, and a focus on the fishing village of Killyleagh, where he took up his second ministry in 1818, sheds some light on the influences affecting the course of local and national politico-religious developments. In this particular dispute, different varieties of Presbyterianism, local personalities, and the context of a changing political climate all played their part.

On, indeed before, his arrival in Killyleagh, Cooke had been supported and befriended by Captain Sidney Hamilton Rowan, whose father, Archibald Hamilton Rowan was the local landlord, and whose family was strongly influential in the Killyleagh area. A. H. Rowan had been a rebel in '98 and leaned towards the radical in all aspects of life, including his religious beliefs,[19] but Captain Rowan had undergone a classically emotional conversion while attached to the militia, and since

Plate 18.1   The Reverend Henry Cooke, D.D. LL.D (Source: Ulster Museum).

his return to Killyleagh in 1814 was a ruling elder in the church, enthusiastically evangelical, and conservative in politics.[20] As Finlay Holmes points out, the differences between father and son illustrate the changes which were taking place in the convictions and outlook of many Irish Presbyterians.[21] Although there was clearly some support for A. H. Rowan's Arian views in Killyleagh, his son was to play an increasingly active role in establishing evangelical orthodoxy in the area.

It was the visit of a Unitarian missionary to the village in 1821 which provoked a public debate on Presbyterian doctrine and first brought Henry Cooke to the fore as the major spokesman for Presbyterian orthodoxy and conservatism. The anti-Trinitarian views of the Reverend J. Smethurst, whose tour to the North of Ireland had been funded by the English Unitarian Fund, were publicly challenged by Sydney Hamilton Rowan and his minister, with the latter devoting his next Sunday service in Killyleagh to a full denunciation of Unitarian theology. Cooke then pursued his quarry, delivering his own response to Unitarianism in every town and village on Smethurst's lecture tour.[22] This was followed in the Newry synodical meeting of 1822 by a claim that Arianism was being taught by the Presbyterian ministers and professors of the Belfast Academical Institution, and for the next seven years Cooke's demand for uniformity and orthodoxy within the Synod of Ulster dominated not only the church government, but the proceedings of congregations, presbyteries and the popular press. Cooke's argument centred on the question of subscription, for if all members were required to subscribe to an agreed orthodox formula, the whole problem of heresy could be eradicated. Despite a strong opposing argument for the retention of flexibility and variety, the increasingly heated dispute resulted in the withdrawal of the liberal non-subscribing section, who went on to form their own 'Remonstrant' synod in 1830.

Cooke was later able to claim, in defence of his views on Protestant opposition to Catholic Emancipation, that 'there is not a man in Ulster, who has better means of knowing the state of mind of the common people among ordinary Presbyterians than I have',[23] and clearly his 'plain and powerful' speaking as he travelled on foot and horseback through Ulster won him acceptance at the popular level. His campaign brought issues which had long troubled the Synod of Ulster to the surface, and made complex doctrinal niceties a matter of often over-simplified public debate. For, despite claims to the contrary, Cooke's rhetoric carried a highly political and topical message, with the threat to Presbyterian orthodoxy linked to a more general threat to Irish Protestantism. Cooke's associations with evangelical members of the ascendancy, such as the earl of Roden, whose home in Tollymore, county Down, he visited frequently, gave both a sense of urgency and a stronger political slant to his theological stance. For men like these, religious, social and political convictions were inextricably intertwined.

The increasing confidence of the Catholic community, clearly visible in new chapels and rising numbers of priests, and given political force by the campaign for Catholic Emancipation, was thus met with a Presbyterianism strengthened by orthodoxy, revitalised by evangelical theology, and forsaking its traditional liberalism for a more rigid conservative position. In the following years it was Cooke who led the Presbyterian challenge to the system of national education, and who called for co-operation between Presbyterian and Episcopal Protestants to ward off the growing threats from Catholicism and liberalism. Frequently by the side of the staunchly conservative earl of Roden, Cooke's stance was not always appreciated or approved by his colleagues in the synod, but he did represent the increasingly strong view- that in political matters Protestants of all creeds had more to unite than to divide them.

But what did the subscription controversy actually mean for the Presbyterians of county Down? The split of 1829 involved seventeen congregations, but, given the internal dynamics of congregations we have already noted, it was never likely that this situation would be resolved without acrimonious disputes. Many local congregations suffered disruption or complete division, with Remonstrant ministers sometimes retaining the loyalty of part of the congregation, and with individual loyalty sometimes overriding matters of doctrine. Thus in Ardglass, a majority of the congregation of David White followed him to the Remonstrant synod; when the minister at Greyabbey, John Watson, and a section of the congregation made a similar move, 100 seat holders remained. In Kilmore, the Reverend Arthur Neilson took his congregation from the Synod of Ulster, but following his death in 1831, many of the people returned to their original allegiance.[24] Such incidents were not only disruptive in terms of the running of congregational matters, but could also lead to considerable financial hardship. When the non-subscribers from Clough held on to the meeting-house following their secession to the Presbytery of Antrim in 1829, it took the newly-installed minister of the remaining congregation seven years to legally recover the building.[25] A similar case in Killinchy in 1835 resulted in the local Synod of Ulster Presbyterians worshipping in a grain store until their property was eventually restored to them.[26]

In Killyleagh itself, as in many areas, the debate did not go away, but rumbled on for several years, with Cooke regarded as a hero of national proportions by one section of the Presbyterian community, while the demonstrations of his opponents also raised considerable enthusiasm. For several years the main focal points were the neighbouring townlands of Derryboy and Raffrey, in which each side wished to erect a congregation. The battle to win sufficient adherents to make a congregation financially viable included large outdoor meetings in Derryboy and Greyabbey.[27] Ministers from Down Presbytery periodically conducted sermons in a schoolhouse in Raffrey, but it was 1843 before a congregation was established. Following Cooke's removal to Belfast at the end of 1829, the two generations of the Hamilton Rowan family continued to contest each other's views in the choice of a successor, with the followers of the evangelical captain eventually securing victory. Although the debate between Presbyterians in Killyleagh focused on doctrinal differences, there were evidently other complicating factors at work.

Representative of a more orthodox and evangelical tradition of Presbyterianism, the new alignment of forces in the Synod of Ulster led to its union with the Secession synod in 1840. On the formation of the new General Assembly, only seven Secession congregations chose to maintain their separation from the mainstream body – although there were the inevitable internal divisions. For example, when 1st Boardmills attached itself to the new assembly, some of the congregation objected and seized the meeting house. The resulting financial and practical difficulties were only resolved after a hostile struggle and the personal mediation of Lord Downshire.[28]

The evident concern of the laity over the choice of their minister reflected the importance of the churches' guidance and leadership in many aspects of everyday life. At the local level, the session, made up of the minister and elected elders, played an important role in determining the social and moral tone of the community. Monthly meetings were held to deal with financial arrangements, almsgiving and the exercise of discipline, with elders responsible for overseeing the social and religious needs of the surrounding neighbourhood. Each elder reported on the spiritual and moral welfare of the congregation in the quarter or district for which he was responsible, bringing any wrongdoing to the attention of the session. Fornication seems to have been the most frequent social misdemeanour coming before the session courts, and this was absolved by 'outward signs of inward repentance' – public confession before the congregation, though less serious cases could be heard by the session itself. Once the 'sinner' expressed repentance, he or she was rebuked and admonished and after prayer, restored to the privileges of the church. The session minutes of Loughaghery Presbyterian Church, near Hillsborough, for example, record that Mr. Brown of Ballycreen, after acknowledging the evil of 'having a Freemason's dance last winter in his barn' was admonished and restored.[29] It is difficult to gauge the response of individuals to this type of spiritual and moral disciplining; much would depend on the depth of individual commitment and on the nature of the 'sin'. One 1840 report, from the Secession congregation in Castlewellan, suggests that in previous years many of those whose behaviour received such public censure simply left the congregation.[30] Although the minutes go on to state that 'latterly discipline was submitted to generally', public disciplining as a means of moral control does appear to have been on the decline in the second half of the nineteenth century.

But so long as the rituals of birth, marriage and death required the sanction of religion, at least an outward conformity to the rules of session was advisable. Equally, such occasions could be used to pull backsliders into line. Thus, a couple belonging to Loughaghery Presbyterian church, wishing their child to be baptised, had first to undergo public censure and rebuke for bad attendance at public worship, ignorance of the principles of the gospel, and irregular conduct in returning from a funeral on the Lord's day.[31] Increasingly too, minister and session expressed unwillingness to baptise children in private houses on Sundays. As the minister of Millisle and Ballycopeland Church explained,

> the collection of friends which sometimes takes place at a baptism and the conversation that commonly occurs, [is] inconsistent with the sanctification of the sabbath, nor will he continue to baptise children to such parents as willingly neglect the observance of the sacrament of the Lords supper or public worship[32]

– although an 1871 report from Portaferry Presbytery indicated that strong feeling on this matter could lead individuals to forsake their congregation for one with less rigid conditions.[33]

In the case of marriage, it was probably a lack of clarity regarding the official legal position of the Dissenting Church which accounted for the frequency with which ministers and couples were rebuked for 'clandestine' or irregular marriages in the late eighteenth and early nineteenth centuries. Although Presbyterian marriages were 'countenanced' the law itself was unclear, and it was possible for them to be declared illegal. The synod was therefore understandably scrupulous in ensuring that before the marriage ceremony was performed, the approval of session and the permission of parents had been obtained, and that the banns had been proclaimed for three consecutive weeks. This particular issue was resolved following a contentious and highly publicised case in 1844. The general tightening-up on regulations and behaviour within Presbyterianism was part of an overall raising of standards in churches of all denominations in Ulster in the second half of the nineteenth century.

The resolution of internal difficulties ensured that nineteenth-century Presbyterianism – more confident, outreaching and assertive – gathered fresh impetus in the formation of congregations, supplemented by building programmes and increases in the number of services as well as a stronger emphasis on the importance of domestic and foreign missions. This new religious vigour reinforced the inherent political strength of the Presbyterian community, with its most ardent spokesmen perceiving secular and religious positions as inseparable.

The Church of Ireland

As part of the constitutional establishment, the Church of Ireland operated within a different, and often difficult, framework, its pastoral relationship with its parishioners complicated by tasks of civil administration. The parish, operating as a kind of unofficial local parliament, was responsible for the upkeep of church buildings, schools and roads; for the burial of the destitute; for the welfare of deserted children; and for looking after the poor. Those in the latter category who were unable to work would have been granted badges or licences to entitle them to beg – ensuring that only the 'deserving' poor were a charge on their parish. The vestry minutes thus reflect the material rather than spiritual concerns of the locality, as rates were levied for these purposes.

Such responsibilities ensured that Anglican clergy had considerable influence within the community, a situation reinforced by the strong ties they frequently developed with local gentry in the course of their work. And while the Church attracted a wide social range of adherents amongst landlords, the professional and business classes and labouring families, the clergy themselves were most likely to come from gentry or professional backgrounds. Gamble's praise of the northern clergy during his tour of Ireland in 1812 reflects this socio-political aspect of their work:

> ... the clergy of the Established church in the north of Ireland are a virtuous, charitable and useful body of men. In many parts they are almost the only resident gentry, and diffuse, by their example, and that of their families, a spirit of order, decorum, and gentleness in their neighbourhood.[34]

Both the local and national power of the Church placed it in a position of privilege in relation to other religious denominations. Presbyterians, who were numerically stronger than Anglicans in the north, particularly resented having to pay for the maintenance of the parish church, while tithes were a source of controversy and difficulty until resolved by government intervention in 1838.

Representative of only a tiny minority in Ireland as a whole, it is not surprising that the Established Church was the target for much hostile criticism in this period, but complaints also focused on the pastoral role of the Church and its ministers, with pluracy and non-residence cited as particularly problematic areas of apathy and neglect. As might be expected, conditions in the more prosperous and substantially Protestant north-east were generally better than in the south and west of the country. This trend was evident even within the province of Armagh, where, of the 110 unions reported in 1823, only five were in the diocese of Dromore and seven in Down.[35] There was much local variation in the condition of the thirty-four churches, with many populated areas lacking access to worship, and there was also a severe shortage of parsonage houses. Indeed, the united diocese of Down and Connor was one of only two in Ireland where the bishop himself had no fixed official residence during much of the nineteenth century. The Church's material and administrative inadequacies most obviously affected the services offered to the community, and the frequency with which divine service was held, communion celebrated and confirmations performed, was regarded as insufficient in many areas. Under pressure from an increasingly unsympathetic legislature, and under the critical scrutiny of the Presbyterian community, the Church of Ireland in county Down could not afford complacency.

There were also those within its own ranks who were concerned to strengthen the role of their Church and to reinvigorate the spiritual life of their parishioners. One of the most prominent Anglican figures in Ulster evangelical circles was Thomas Tighe, whose appointment to the parish of Drumgooland in 1778 has been regarded as marking the beginning of evangelicalism within the Irish Church.[36] Tighe, together with B. W. Mathias who was his curate from 1797 to 1804, injected vigour and enthusiasm into the religious life of county Down, winning the confidence and respect of both his congregation and fellow preachers of all denominations.[37] Tighe and Mathias, perhaps influenced by the work of Peter Roe in Kilkenny,[38] set up a clerical association in Dromore as a forum for discussion and support in which a more pious and zealous type of religious leadership was encouraged. At one such meeting, in 1802, Mathias gave his views on common abuses of clerical duty:

> What opportunity, O what desire for watching over his flock can that clergyman have whose hours are employed in the routine of the drawing room or assembly, at the receptions of the great, in political studies and parties, at the hunt or the racecourse ... whose days are dedicated to the business of their farms or the pursuit of philosophy and 'belle-lettres'? Such persons may be polite gentlemen, they may be good jockies [sic] and farmers, they may be deep philosophers or elegant poets; but they are not, they cannot be Watchmen.[39]

At sermons preached out of doors on Sunday evenings, these committed young men stressed the importance of sabbitarianism, regular prayer and bible-reading, and strove to instil in their listeners new standards of personal behaviour and family duty. There is no doubt of the important stimulus given to religious activity in the area by these men; while Tighe was cautious not to offend church discipline, he does appear to have given support to early missions to the area initiated by interdenominational English-based societies.[40] His blend of Anglican orthodoxy and evangelical zeal was to be an inspiring example for later churchmen. As one religious historian puts it, Tighe's forty-three years of incumbency in Drumgooland

> show(ed) the new standards of pastoral faithfulness that the revival was bringing back to the church. For, supremely, Thomas Tighe was the prototype of the 19th century evangelicals who, as preachers and pastors in the parishes of rural Ireland, were so markedly to improve the condition of the church and to influence the life of the nation.[41]

Evangelical self-confidence could, however, take on an appearance of spiritual arrogance which not everyone found acceptable. During the late 1780s a public row erupted in Bangor between the Reverend Smyth and Lord Bangor. The latter complained to the bishop of the diocese, accusing Smyth of highly unorthodox preaching methods because he held services in private houses and was known to be openly sympathetic to Methodism. He was undoubtedly however also incensed by Smyth's public censorship of his personal behaviour. The ecclesiastical authorities were compelled to take action, and a contentious court case resulted in October 1778.[42] Although the case against Smyth was dismissed, his licence was later revoked, and, an outcast from the establishment, he later managed to estrange the Methodist body also.[43] The lives of Smyth and Tighe exemplify the best and worst of early Anglican evangelical activity in the county, and indicate the potential it had for both progress and disruption.

Local clergy were of course subject to the guidance and discipline of the church hierarchy, and their relations with their bishop was thus significant. Tighe had been encouraged and supported by Bishop Percy of Dromore (1782-1802), who was himself cited as a fine example of local leadership. One Church historian drew attention to his constant residence, his unremitting attention to the poor, his vigilant superintendence of the diocese, and his personal piety, liberality and benevolence.[44] The importance of such commitment was highlighted during the tensions of the late eighteenth century when Percy's influence, residence and example was felt to have contributed to the absence of rebellion in his own parish. However, as he remarked in June 1798, this was by no means a common response to the crisis, noting that in the general panic and alarm, all his fellow bishops were sending their families to England, and that his neighbour, the bishop of Down, had already gone.[45]

The leadership provided by Richard Mant – Bishop of Down and Connor for twenty-five years from 1823 (during the last five of which he was also bishop of Dromore) – illustrates the response of the Church to changing times, and provides an interesting example of the relationship between bishop, clergy and laity. An Englishman, with no knowledge or experience of the region, Mant had just spent two years as bishop of Killaloe. On receiving news of his transfer to the north, he acknowledged that while his new see was 'one of the most eligible in the country', he had to admit to being 'a perfect stranger, except from books and conversation, to that part of the country where my official duty lies'.[46] His first impressions of his new diocese were very favourable; county Down, he wrote,

> bears an appearance very considerably resembling that of many parts of England, to which on the whole it more nearly approaches than to the south of Ireland.[47]

On taking up residence in Holywood, the new bishop did not let his inexperience prevent him from exercising his authority.

The contrast between Down and Connor and Killaloe was of course very striking, and was most immediately obvious to Mant in the much larger numbers of people coming forward for communion or confirmation. But much remained to be done to bring the local Church up to the new standards of Anglican churchmanship which both the English and Irish hierarchy sought to impose on their clergy, and Mant set about his task with enthusiasm. After visiting several parishes, he observed the good understanding between Anglicans and

Presbyterians; however he found it difficult to accept all aspects of his clergy's behaviour. When he discovered, for example, that his clergy sometimes co-operated with the local meeting house in the timing of services, the announcement of activities or the contents of sermons, he determined to put a stop to such mutual accommodation. He expressed a fear that his clergy were 'compromising their principles' in order to conciliate their Presbyterian counterparts.[48] In an area where the relationship between church and meeting house was of particular significance, his intervention in long-established traditions – unwelcome to some – can be seen as part of a wider campaign to reassert hierarchical authority, internal discipline, and distinctive church forms.

Such strict adherence to the distinctive principles of the establishment tended to clash with the promotion of the wider evangelicalism which was coming to characterise all denominations in this period, and which was now clearly evident in the actions of many lower-ranking Church of Ireland clergy. Apart from interdenominational activities, Mant was also concerned with laxity in matters of discipline, which he saw expressed in some of his clergy's criticism of church leaders and in their practice of extemporaneous prayers. His Charge of 1834 also focused on the Home Mission set up by a group of Anglican evangelicals and operating in rural areas.[49] While Baptist Noel, a visitor to Kilkeel in 1836, praised the work carried out by the mission,[50] Mant found its intrusions unacceptable.

But even the most dedicated of churchmen recognised the need for positive action on the part of the establishment to fill the gaps within its structure, and under pressure from local clergy, Mant took steps to permit the extension of their labours outside the rigid boundaries of existing parish churches. Thus, in the late 1830s, a network of diocesan societies was established to deal with the problems of outreach and church extension in Down and Connor.

The Clergy Aid Society was a fine example of evangelical initiative harnessed to the cause of the Church. Formed in 1837 to increase opportunities for worship in places where these were most deficient, the society had a considerable impact on county Down. After obtaining the permission of the parochial minister, preachers were supplied on a monthly basis to 'stations' in outlying areas. In March 1838, such 'stations' were in operation at Hillhall and Clogher, Hillsborough, Killinchy, Bangor, South Tyrella and Ballyphilip. Sunday evening stations were also held to reach the summer visitors in Dundrum and Castlewellan.[51] The 1839 report reiterated that this system of 'occasional supply' was continuing to work well, recording that services in Mr. Martin's mill, in the parish of Killyleagh, were attended by 250, at the school-house Crossgar by sixty-five, and that the schoolroom in Dundrum was not big enough for all who wished to attend.[52]

This more accessible and flexible approach to provision at the local level was also developed by the Church Accommodation Society.[53] Of twenty grants distributed by it in the united diocese, county Down received seven, which provided for the rebuilding of the parish church at Holywood, a new church at Tyrella and the Chapel of St. James near Hillsborough as well as endowed chapels at Hollymount, Kilwarlin and Groomsport. The laity also made a significant contribution to these improvements; landlords concerned to provide places of worship for their tenantry, facilitated the building of chapels of ease, or made handsome contributions towards the costs of churches for their parish. These patrons included Lady Harriet Forde at Hollymount, the marquis of Downshire at Hillsborough, and Mr. Waring Maxwell at Groomsport (plate 18.2). Lady Annesley endowed £1,250 for the building of a church on her estate at Castlewellan in 1840, and Lord Roden's chapel at Tollymore was the object of much praise. Robert Ward of Bangor castle provided the funding for a new chapel of ease at Kircubbin, while the primate, Archbishop Beresford was responsible for the church at Carrowdore.[54] Thus, a mixture of private benevolence and evangelical zeal, overseen by the bishop, considerably improved the local profile of the Church.

In other matters, however, Mant's lack of experience of local sensitivities brought him into direct conflict with clergy and laity alike. His purpose in forming the Church Architecture Society in 1842 was 'to give a more appropriate appearance to the houses of God..and to improve the style of churches'.[55] While this sounds harmless enough, the new society became the focus of great bitterness, with local clergy equating their bishop's 'high church' sensibilities with Puseyism and Romanism. While much of the hostility was probably a reflection of Mant's insistence, both from the pulpit and in the press 'that nothing without the bishop was allowed', the perception that he was introducing 'popish novelties, under the guise of antiquities', indicates a more serious cultural gap between the Englishman and his Ulster parishioners.[56] Their anti-Catholic convictions grounded in local realities, Mant's clergy regarded his scholarly attributes and high-minded Anglican subtleties as inappropriate and, with the Church Architecture Society associated with Tractarianism, even dangerous. In 1843 the bishop was presented with a memorial from the clergy and laity of his diocese, requesting his withdrawal from the society. The 1,300 signatures included official dignitaries and representatives of the legal and medical professions, as well as private gentlemen, merchants, bankers, tradesmen, artisans and yeomen and the petition reflected the

Plate 18.2   Groomsport Church of Ireland church (Source: Welch collection, Ulster Museum).

genuine concern of men who feared the steady encroachment of Catholicism in every aspect of political and social life. Mant, however, indignantly refused to 'be placed under the ban of any of his clergy' and in the event it was not the Church Architecture Society, but the highly successful Church Accommodation Society which was dissolved as a result of this episode.

Archdeacon Many, rector of Hillsborough, was also accused of 'indulging in Puseyite practices'. On this occasion the marquis of Downshire called a meeting of the principal members of the church, who resolutely condemned the action of 'the very reverend dignitary'.[57] Parishioners in Donaghcloney, Dromore Diocese, complained of their curate, the Reverend Lucius Arthur's 'over-scrupulous and unedifying regard to the observance of fasts, festivals and saints days', and alleged that in his sermons he gave 'peculiar prominence to one of the most monstrous of Rome's erroneous doctrines – exclusive salvation'. While Mant approved their bringing the matter to his attention, he defended the curate's position and rebuked his clergy for the hint of rebellion he detected in their memorial.[58]

Fears of Roman influence were to continue to disturb Anglican evangelicals throughout the century, and this debate illustrates again the ways in which local political concerns were closely interwoven with matters of faith and worship. But, despite these hiccoughs, the Church of Ireland continued to consolidate its position, strengthening both its physical presence and its pastoral role. Bishop Knox, Mant's successor in Down, Connor and Dromore, was a more quiet and restrained figure than his predecessor, and though one historian notes that he 'maintained his whig principles in an unsympathetic environment', he avoided major clashes with his clergy.[59] Annual church gatherings at which papers on church questions were read and discussed, brought bishops, ministers and laity together, and provided an important forum for the exchange of a range of representative views.

During Knox's tenure the building of churches continued and new parishes were also formed. A more general commitment to the spread of the gospel, both within Ireland and further afield, was evident in the development of church home and foreign missions. Fund-raising, charity sermons, and the provision of material as well as spiritual aid to parishioners all testify to the expanding role of a more dynamic institution. Ironically, by the time Gladstone disestablished the Church of Ireland in 1868, it had – in Ulster at least – become a more effective and efficient body. Disestablishment was the logical outcome of the programme of reform undertaken at the beginning of the century, a process which entailed the gradual separation of the Church's pastoral and political roles, and dramatically changed its position within the community, limiting its influence to those who adhered to the principles and practice of Anglicanism.

The most immediate practical crisis prompted by the Irish Church Act was that of finance, and fund-raising campaigns in the county again revealed the vital contributions made by individuals. In Dundonald, for example, the patronage of the two local 'big houses' was crucial in securing the future of local Anglicanism: John Cleland contributed £1,000, the Gordon family £700, Dr. Cassidy £100 and the Reverend Cleland £30; collections from 'others' totalled £5 – all of which supplemented the income from the new Church Commissioners.[60] Bazaars, fairs and legacies also played an important role, particularly before the setting up of diocesan schemes.[61] The move from established to voluntary status in many ways completed the transformation undergone by the Church of Ireland in the course of the century, with the pastoral and spiritual care of its parishioners now firmly at the top of its agenda. The 1886 parochial report for the diocese of Down and Dromore noted that all but two of the eighty-one churches were in good order, that all but a tiny minority held divine services twice on Sundays, and that communion was frequently celebrated.[62] Although the numbers of communicants varied considerably, and never included more than a portion of the congregation, the distinction thus revealed between 'serious' church-goers and those for whom the parish church represented their social and cultural identity, was a realistic reflection of the Church's role in the community.

Methodism

In the earliest years of its development Methodism was a term interchangeable with evangelicalism, but in Ireland, as throughout Britain, the new sect quickly established its own organisational and theological boundaries. Breaking free from Anglican rigidity, the flexibility of itinerancy was its greatest asset, with preachers prepared to deliver sermons wherever they found a crowd: by the roadside, in markets, fields or barns. Although sometimes invited by local evangelicals, Methodist preachers frequently drew the hostility of more orthodox churchmen. Bishop Percy, for example, refused the use of the market house in Dromore to itinerants, while John Wesley himself was refused the use of the church in Moira by the local rector.[63] Happily, the earl of Moira, who was Wesley's host, was able to undermine clerical influence, sending his bell-man to summon the people. Such differences of opinion between lay and secular authority on the treatment of travelling preachers were not at all uncommon in this period, when many societies were founded as a result of personal invitations by local families. In Ballykeel, near Dromore, for example, a young man who had been converted by his aunt, opened his house to the preachers and a class was formed which the young convert was to lead for sixty years.[64]

The flexibility of Methodism was clearly attractive to parishioners in Anglican areas where the lack of buildings, or the means to dress in a way deemed appropriate, prevented church attendance, and in the early period, open-air sermons and meetings in homes and barns can be seen as supplementing the parochial structure at its weakest points, rather than as attempts to replace it. Presbyterians were slower to respond to the new sect, but, no doubt encouraged by congregational divisions in the pre-Cooke era, interest soon picked up. By 1819 about 40 per cent of Ulster Methodists were Presbyterian, although many of these continued to attend their own church as well as the local society.[65] In 1822, Methodist missionary Matthew Lanktree reported from the Downpatrick circuit

> This is a populous country, composed very much of the middle classes of society, remarkably intelligent and industrious. The majority of them are Presbyterians, many of them, as well as their Ministers, Arians. Their prejudices against Methodism are greatly diminished, so that we have but seldom to preach to small congregations. I cannot state after all, that 'the fields are white to the harvest', but in several places, where the good seed has been sown, it has sprung up, and much has been done 'to prepare the way of the Lord'.[66]

The revivalist tendencies of the new sect introduced important elements of emotion and excitement into contemporary religious expression, and played a critical role in spreading the new faith. One Methodist preacher, Mr Ridgeway, in the last month of the old century, gives a graphic illustration of the sense of drama which could lead to the formation of new societies or the rejuvenation of existing ones:

> The work of God among us broke out first upon us in Newry. I went there hoping to catch some of the holy fire, and saw eight converted the first night, and four the night following. Each week brought fresh accounts of the increase of the work in Newry, and we were all looking and longing for the flame to reach us. We agreed, therefore, to set apart a day for fasting and prayer, which was faithfully observed by all the neighbouring circuits.[67]

Local revivals were often prompted by charismatic itinerant preachers, such as Lorenzo Dow, an American, whose visit to

Downpatrick in 1807 led to a doubling of the number of members in the local society.[68] The preaching of women, a novelty confined to the early period of Methodism, was also a guaranteed crowd-puller. One of the best known was Anne Lutton, a native of Moira, county Down. Born in 1791, of a respectable religious family, Anne underwent a classic religious conversion in 1815, following a Methodist class meeting. Although the propriety of female public preaching was disputed amongst Methodists, many supported her position that the individual who was compelled by God had no choice but to obey. She took care that her meetings never clashed with church services, and only addressed groups of women, and only one Anglican minister, in Dromore, seems to have spoken out against her. Between 1818 and 1831 she presided at large crowded meetings throughout the North, a rare example of public female piety in this period.[69]

Physical crises also acted as a stimulant to religious behaviour. During the cholera epidemic of 1832, the Methodists in Donaghadee noted that 'Pressed by the messenger of death, and unknowing who next might be summoned to the cholera house, or the grave, a general concern for eternal life pervaded the community'.[70] But while the establishment of new classes and the building of galleries in the local Methodist church testified to the truth of this statement, Methodists were also vulnerable to negative influences such as emigration, with the statistics of local societies providing evidence of local social and economic dislocation.[71] This problem was not so severe in Down as in the western and southern counties, but small societies, such as that in Donaghadee, for example, noted a steady trickle of emigrants from the area.

In 1816 the division of Methodists into the Primitive Wesleyans, who retained the position of original Methodism and operated as a religious society, and the Wesleyan Methodists who ordained their own preachers and were thus able to offer the sacraments, also led to a decline in numbers.[72] As a voluntary body, it was easier for the former to co-operate with other religious denominations, and there are many examples of mutual assistance facilitating worship. In the new Methodist meeting house erected in Ballyphilip in 1830, for example, it was reported that 'in the morning only Primitive Methodists are admitted, (the average number that attend, thirty) in the evening persons of all persuasions are admitted, generally from forty to fifty are in attendance'. And when a Primitive Wesleyan chapel opened in Comber in 1820 on a site provided by the marquis of Londonderry, valuable help was given by the local clergy and laity of different denominations. Similarly, Presbyterian congregations in Newcastle and Killyleagh had the use of the Methodists' buildings while their own meeting houses were being built.[73] These examples reflect the willingness of both clergy and people to engage in interdenominational co-operation in the wider interests of Protestantism. One of the most popular Wesleyan Methodist preachers, Gideon Ouseley, was received with great cordiality at the home of the earl of Roden, and also had the use of the Presbyterian meeting house in the area. Like Roden and Henry Cooke, Ouseley saw political as well as religious dangers in the rise of Catholicism; he praised Cooke's work for orthodoxy and was a regular contributor to the anti-Catholic rhetoric of the period.[74]

Methodist leaders had always placed a strong emphasis on personal morality and attempted to influence the day-to-day behaviour of their flock. Members of the Strangford society who joined in the plundering of a ship wrecked off Kilkeel in 1779, for example, were individually denounced from the pulpit – a tactic which seemed to work, as many of the stolen goods were subsequently restored.[75] At Drumcree, near Downpatrick, local Methodists claimed that their influence brought about the closure of the local dancing school and the desertion of the public house, with membership of the society substantially increased. Comments from many observers, however, suggest that such improvements were not limited to Methodism, but that the moral basis of society as a whole was undergoing significant change. Thus, it was reported from Blaris parish as early as 1834 that 'dancing, hand ball play and different other amusements were practised here about forty years back, but these have been subsequently relinquished and religious practices substituted in their stead'. In Downpatrick around the same period the 'prevalence of the religious principle' was praised, as was the sobriety of the lower orders, with 'an intoxicated person scarcely ever to be seen'.

While changing trends in popular culture were perhaps not so dramatic as these reports suggest, it does seem that a combination of secular and religious influences was affecting behavioural patterns. Changes in farming methods, urbanisation, industrialisation, and a shift to a monied economy all led to the greater regularisation and organisation of leisure time. The increasingly evangelical ethos adopted by the Churches was also significant, with ministers of all denominations intervening to impose certain standards of behaviour on their communities. Thus, the General Assembly in 1862 protested against the county Down railway operating a Sunday service, 'as an aggravation of the evil of violating the sanctity of the Sabbath, as inflicting great hardship and wrong on the officials, rendering it impossible for them to unite in the public worship of God'.[76] The women who traditionally sold light refreshments outside the meeting-house gate on Sundays were removed by an irate Henry Cooke, though 'with considerable difficulty'. Cooke also strove to put an end to the practice of visiting the local pub between the two mid-day services. Indeed, the drive against alcohol can be seen as the most persistent campaign waged by religious leaders in this period.

The formation of local temperance societies was result of the initiative of John Edgar of Belfast, and after some initial resistance from middle-class congregations, spread through the north-east with rapidity. By 1833, 150 societies, boasting 150,000 members were established in Ulster alone. These were supported by both secular and religious leaders, and great claims were made of their success. However, Baptist Noel, reporting on the short-lived nature of good intentions in the town of Rostrevor, suggested that there was much exaggeration:

> The clergymen were, with Mrs Ross and some others, endeavoured to establish a temperance society. The meeting was crowded. The labourers were delighted with the speeches of Professor Edgar, many names were given; and there the matter ended. The members were unfaithful to their resolutions, and the puncheon and the spirit seller triumphed. At Warrenpoint, as I was assured by a gentleman, out of eighty houses about forty sell spirits.

While this campaign was unlikely to have reformed hardened drinkers, what is perhaps more significant is the evidence of the Churches' growing concern with social behaviour, and their recognition that to engage successfully in competition with popular cultural activities it was necessary to provide not only morally, but socially acceptable alternatives. In the course of the century a christian subculture of church-based societies provided their members with tea-drinking rooms, reading rooms, processions, excursions and parties. Although these had probably a fairly limited appeal for non church-goers, such recreational activities were important in binding the Church closer to the community which it served. For example, annual congregational soirees, such as that held in 2nd Saintfield Presbyterian church in 1842, combining talks by visiting ministers and the singing of psalms with a tea party, were an opportunity for social intercourse which emphasised the common faith and way of life shared by clerical and lay members of the community.[77]

Probably the most successful of all the Churches' nineteenth-century achievements was the development of Sunday schools. The first one in Ireland was established in Bright church, county Down by the Reverend Kennedy during a local revival in the 1770s. Although the whole island was to participate in the movement, the north-east of

Ulster saw the greatest concentration of such schools. All denominations recognised the importance of such work, and the annual reports of the Hibernian Sunday School Society, a co-ordinating body formed in 1809, record its particular appeal to the Protestants of Antrim, Down and Derry (table 18.1). By 1831, one in every eleven children in county Down was attending on Sunday mornings or afternoons, not only to be inculcated with the doctrines and deliberations of the church, but to learn to read and write – perhaps the only opportunity to do so for young girls engaged in textile production. For many children the schools were also a rare place of warmth and comfort, with prizes to be won for attendance and biblical knowledge (ranging from bibles and instructive books to 'plain useful clothing or a testimonial on leaving the school'). Add to this the fun (and food) provided by annual parties and excursions, and it becomes clear that Sunday schools not only brought a new generation into the churches, but evolved as an important aspect of popular culture, reinforcing habits of Sunday attendance and 'respectable' behaviour. As such they were greatly encouraged by the middle-classes of the county, who provided the strong network of support necessary for their success, in the form of patronage and by offering their services as teachers and inspectors.

TABLE 18.1

Sunday Schools, 1860

County	Population	Schools	Scholars	Teachers
Antrim	358,503	455	53,286	4,806
Armagh	196,420	166	18,755	1,481
Cavan	174,303	94	6,518	496
Down	**317,778**	**372**	**41,157**	**3,926**
Donegal	254,288	161	8,999	806
Fermanagh	115,978	101	7,769	637
Londonderry	191,744	198	19,794	1,692
Monaghan	143,410	76	6,096	451
Tyrone	251,865	20	17,014	1,444
ULSTER	2,004,289	1,823	179,388	15,739
IRELAND	6,515,794	2,686	230,668	20,873

Source: Records of the Sunday School Society of Ireland.

Indeed, for many middle-class young women, the Churches' new emphasis on outreach provided a welcome opportunity to engage in 'acceptable' work outside the home. Nor should the significance of their input to local religious life be undermined. Whether it was as Sunday school teachers, sextons, leaders of girls' religious organisations, administrators in auxiliary societies, selling their own goods at fund-raising bazaars, writing letters on behalf of female missionaries, or teaching needlework to young girls, women made a considerable contribution to Church life.[78] It is perhaps unsurprising that this female activism received little official acknowledgement other than general expressions of gratitude. Despite a widespread recognition of the significance of women's role in almost every sphere of religious life, a combination of religious conservatism and institutional bureaucracy resulted in their continued exclusion from participation in the major administrative or decision-making bodies. Not until the emergence of the Deaconess' Guild in 1908, was women's work recognised in a full-time paid capacity within Presbyterianism, while their ability to act as ruling elders was agreed only in 1926. A similar situation persisted within the Anglican Church, where a bill for the admission of women as members of church vestries was defeated in 1916, but passed in 1920. According to a speech made by the dean of Armagh in 1892, the 'silencing' of women over such a long period was bound to have detrimental effects:

> I know more than one parish in which troubles and agitations would have much more speedily [been put] down if our franchise had been regulated by the principle that 'in Christ Jesus there is neither male nor female, but Christ is all, and in us all'. ... (having regard to the great zeal, the practical efficiency, and the success of female energy, both in the mission field and in such organised and priceless work as, for example, the Girls' Friendly Society performs at home) I am persuaded that the time is ripe for some step toward the recognition of women in the franchise of our own church.[79]

The 1859 Revival
The full extent of evangelical influence was perhaps most clearly reflected in the great revival of 1859 – a mid-century outpouring of religious feeling which swept across the province of Ulster, but whose greatest concentration could be detected in the Presbyterian counties of Antrim and Down. Despite contemporary explanations of the phenomenon as dramatic and spontaneous, it is clear that decades of evangelical preaching ensured that the church-going population was both receptive to and well-prepared for such an event. The first incidents of religious excitement in county Antrim were linked to the holding of prayer meetings amongst the laity, with conversions at times

accompanied by extreme examples of 'hysteria' or 'physical prostration'. Promoted by a combination of popular preachers, landlords and employers, revivalist enthusiasm reached the towns and villages of county Down by early summer. Boardmills, Ballynahinch, Banbridge, Comber, Dromore, Downpatrick, Newtownards and Saintfield were all affected, while in the seaside holiday resorts of Donaghadee and Millisle, Sunday night open-air meetings attracted large crowds.

Local interest was often sparked by the emotional speeches of converts. In Rathfriland, for example, a young Belfast convert attracted a huge gathering which he had only begun to address when a man swooned, then

> sudden as a gunshot, a strong woman sent forth an unearthly scream ... In a moment she was upon her knees, crying, as she clapped and wrung her hands alternately in wild excitement, 'Oh! my heart. Oh! my hard heart'. The crowd was convulsed, and shook like aspens in the breeze. The voice of the speaker was soon drowned amid the shrieks; the air was filled with groans and screams for mercy. Crowds gathered and pressed around to listen to the lamentations, and here and there to the fervent appeals of the awakened. It was not till long after nightfall that a large portion of the helpless mourners were carried to their homes.[80]

Open-air sermons and emotionally-charged prayer meetings were also frequently the scene of physical disorientation, which awakened awe and anxiety amongst the watchers. While there is little doubt that such incidents sustained the momentum of the movement, and were perhaps frequently exaggerated for that reason, they also provoked alarm, criticism and scepticism amongst observers. In Downpatrick, the local newspaper, the *Recorder,* published the dean of Down's opposition to the revival, in which he was supported by the Anglican minister of nearby Killyleagh in a pamphlet entitled *God's works and Satan's counterworks as now carried on in the north of Ireland.* Both men regarded the excesses of the revival as satanic intervention. The Presbyterian minister of Killyleagh responded vigorously to these literary denunciations, replying to the dean of Down in an address in his own church, and to Hincks in a pamphlet on *God's work in the north of Ireland and especially at Killyleagh, county Down, vindicated.* Like other supporters of the movement, he focused on the divine nature of events.[81]

The Killyleagh pamphlet debate reflected the difficulties faced by the Churches which, having prayed for revival, needed to contain and control what many regarded as its excesses. The Presbyterian General Assembly pronounced itself satisfied that the revival was 'a great blessing from God', although its clergy were urged to use caution. In the Anglican community, top-level support came from Dr. Knox, who, after inviting his clergy to breakfast to hear their opinion on the revival, gave his support. The dean of Dromore participated by holding united prayer meetings in Newry,[82] an example of interdenominational co-operation which was repeated in many areas. The Anglican rector of Killinchy worked closely with his Presbyterian counterpart and informed Knox that 'most satisfactory fruits have followed the widespread confession of sin and profession of repentance which attended the ministrations of the gospel in this neighbourhood'.[83]

While there is no doubt of the general rejuvenating affect of the revival on the religious community, it is more difficult to measure its success statistically. Some ministers reported a considerable increase in the number of communicants: from fifty to 102 in Dundonald; from 'scarcely twenty' to 150 in Ballymacarret, and a rise of 100 in Castlereagh.[84] Gibson, the revival's first historian, calculated the number of Presbyterian congregations visited by the revival and of individuals added to the Church in Ulster (table 18.2).[85] Presbyterianism was undoubtedly affected more strongly than other denominations, and thus counties Down and Antrim not surprisingly recorded the greatest impact. Close analysis of denominational statistics reveals, however, that most increases were short-lived, and indeed mainly confined to those already on the periphery of local religious life.[86]

TABLE 18.2

Presbyterian congregations visited by the 1859 Revival

County	Congregations	Additional Communicants
Antrim	81	4,353
Down	**69**	**2,132**
Londonderry	36	1,258
Tyrone	42	118
Armagh	26	6
Donegal	23	502
Monaghan	18	412
Cavan	10	169
Fermanagh	1	21

Based on 307 out of 460 Ulster congregations in connection with the General Assembly. W. Gibson, *The year of grace: a history of the Ulster Revival of 1859* (Jubilee Edition, London, 1909), p. 256.

Revivalist leaders also claimed that the movement dramatically affected moral behaviour; in Carryduff it was reported that all four public houses had closed down; in Banbridge whiskey dealers were said to be giving up their business, and strong drink was apparently no longer consumed at Protestant funerals.[87] No doubt small communities may have been affected by the drama of the summer's events, but claims of a general moral transformation cannot be substantiated. The revival's main significance lies in its clear articulation of the values of Evangelical Protestantism, closely linked to the social and cultural ethos of the community.

The enthusiastic involvement of the laity was an increasingly common feature of the period – the interest of the earl of Roden in a range of socio-religious ventures has already been mentioned. One visitor to his Tollymore estate, which boasted a depot of bibles, Sunday schools and a domestic chapel where he officiated as pastor to his family and neighbours, considered it 'part of his stewardship to save the souls of his tenantry'.[88] In benevolent gestures such as the provision of clothes for the poor, special charity services and the teaching of local children, church and laymen worked closely together in the mutual interests of the community. Similarly, while clergy of all denominations had to respond quickly and effectively to the demands of a people who perceived that their political vulnerability could only be safeguarded by a more confident and assertive Protestantism, political leaders were frequently called upon to 'defend the faith' – a call to which Roden in particular was quick to respond.

At times of tension, at both the local and national level, Protestants of all creeds united against the perceived threat from Catholicism. Thus the disestablishment of the Church of Ireland, long desired by many dissenters, became for some a symbol of dangerous liberalism. Henry Cooke headed the emotional display of Protestant solidarity in Hillsborough in 1867 which was one of the major demonstrations against Gladstone's Act.[89] And in the midst of much greater tension in 1886, a Methodist newspaper reported that all doctrinal distinctions had been temporarily suppressed in the face of more urgent matters.

> The relations of the Protestant churches in Ireland to each other were never so sympathetic as at present. Their unanimity of judgement and identity of attitude towards 'Home Rule' afford happy illustration of the solidarity of Protestantism, and herald a brighter future for their common work.[90]

On the other hand, the underlying anti-Catholicism which pervaded Evangelical Protestantism also rose to the fore at times of stress – as at

Dolly's Brae in 1849, Ballykillbeg in 1867 and Belfast in 1886 – allowing religious differences to spill over into violent sectarian confrontation. Thus the religious leadership displayed, whether from Sunday morning pulpits or the speakers' platform at the Great Protestant meetings in Hillsborough, carried a weighty responsibility, often determining the nature of local community relations.

Conclusion

While such instances of solidarity temporarily transcended narrower theological distinctions, the main Churches in the county had, as we have noted, significantly developed their denominational distinctiveness. While serving the wider interests of Protestantism, Presbyterians and Anglicans in particular, continued to influence the dynamics of local life. As the century progressed, church leaders shifted their concern from attendance figures to ways of interacting with and influencing the community – from the cradle to the grave (and of course, beyond). For a majority of people the church or meeting house remained the venue for the ceremonies and rituals which marked out the major passages of life, and, particularly in the pre-war period, the Churches' progressive and positive steps in establishing social funds, events and facilities, were vitally important in terms of welfare provision.

Religious faith consists of more, of course, than the considerations of material benefits, theological distinctions or even political identity covered by this chapter. In this area, more than any other, public and private worlds come together, with the dynamics of emotion and intellect, knowledge and aspirations, circumstances and heritage moulding the experience of individuals and community. Reflecting and determining cultural, political, social and spiritual values, Protestantism in nineteenth-century county Down encompassed the richly diverse and often contradictory values of Church and people.

References

1. P. Kilroy, *Protestant dissent and controversy in Ireland 1660-1714* (Cork, 1994).
2. A. Loughridge, *The covenanters: a history of the Reformed Presbyterian Church of Ireland* (Belfast, 1984), p. 28.
3. David Stewart, *The seceders in Ireland, with annals of their congregations* (Belfast, 1950).
4. R. Currie, A. Gilbert and L. Horsley, *Churches and churchgoers: patterns of church growth in the British Isles since 1700* (Oxford, 1977), p. 59.
5. Stewart, *Seceders*, p. 62.
6. The opportunism of the seceders is discussed in J. Thompson, 'The inter-relationship of the Secession Synod and the Synod of Ulster', Unpub. Ph.D thesis, Faculty of Theology, Q.U.B., 1980.

7. A. T. Q. Stewart, *The narrow ground* (London, 1977), p. 98.
8. *Records of the General Synod of Ulster, 1691-1820* (hereafter *R. G. S. U.*), 3 volumes, iii, p. 354; *A history of the congregations in the Presbyterian Church in Ireland 1610-1982* (Belfast, 1982).
9. Stewart, *Narrow ground*, pp 77, 110.
10. *History of congregations*, pp 397, 91, 101.
11. Ibid., p. 267.
12. Ibid., pp 492-3.
13. Ibid., p. 382.
14. J. Davison, *An ancient Irish parish past and present, being the parish of Donaghmore, county Down* (London, 1914), pp 275-6.
15 A. J. Megahey, 'The Irish Protestant Churches and social and political issues 1870-1914', unpub. Ph.D thesis, Q.U.B., 1969.
16. A. T. Q. Stewart, 'The transformation of Presbyterian radicalism in the north of Ireland 1792-1825', unpub. M.A. thesis, Q.U.B., 1956.
17. Peter Carr, *The most unpretending of places: a history of Dundonald county Down* (Belfast, 1987); Trevor McCavery, *Newtown: a history of Newtownards* (Belfast, 1994), pp 95-6.
18. *R. G. S. U.*, iii, p. 221.
19. A. H. Rowan to Dufferin, 7 December 1817 and 21 December 1817, P. R. O. N. I., Correspondence of Baron Dufferin, D.167/D/C/41/4.
20. W. H. Drummond, *Autobiography of Archibald Hamilton Rowan* (Dublin, 1840).
21. R. F. G. Holmes, *Our Irish Presbyterian heritage* (Belfast, 1985), p. 100.
22. J. S. Reid, *History of the Presbyterian Church in Ireland*, 3 vols. (2nd edn., London, 1853), iii, p. 474.
23. J. L. Porter, *The life and times of Henry Cooke* (Belfast, 1875), p. 68.
24. *History of congregations*.
25. *Authentic report of the speech of the Reverend Henry Cooke, on the case of the congregation of Clough (county Down) at the meeting of the General Synod of Ulster in Coleraine 1831* (Belfast, 1832).
26. A. McCreery, *The Presbyterian ministers of Killyleagh* (Belfast, 1875), p. 261.
27. Ibid., pp 256-8.
28. *History of congregations*.
29. 9 May 1806, P. R. O. N. I., Loughaghery Presbyterian Church register, CR.3/8/1.
30. Castlewellan visitation, December, 1840, P. R. O. N. I., Minutes of the presbytery of Down, Secession Synod, 1827-41, D.1759/1D/20, 20.
31. Loughaghery Church register, 1818.
32. T. Kilpatrick, *Millisle and Ballycopeland Presbyterian Church* (Newtownards, 1984), p. 28.
33. Portaferry visitation report 1871, P. R. O. N. I., D.2709/2/11.
34. J. Gamble, *View of society and manners in the north of Ireland in the Summer and Autumn of 1812* (London, 1813), p. 291.
35. W. R. Mant, *Bishop Mant and his diocese* (Dublin, 1857).
36. D. H. Akenson, *The Church of Ireland: ecclesiastical reform and revolution 1800-1885* (London, 1971), p. 132.
37. A. R. Acheson, 'The Evangelicals in the Church of Ireland', Unpub. Ph.D. thesis, Q.U.B., 1967. See also, 'Extracts of a tour through the north of Ireland, under the patronage of the Evangelical Society of Ulster in the Summer of the year 1800', p. 15; and, H. B. Swanzy, *Biographical succession lists of Dromore diocese* (Belfast, 1933).
38. S. Madden, *Life of Peter Roe* (Dublin, 1842).

39.   Acheson, 'Evangelicals', p. 12.

40.   F. E. Bland, *How the Church Missionary Society came to Ireland* (Dublin, 1935), p. 32.

41.   Acheson, 'Evangelicals', p. 27.

42.   Anon., *An account of the trial of Edward Smyth, late curate of Ballyculter* (Dublin, n.d.).

43.   C. H. Crookshank, *History of Methodism in Ireland*, 3 vols (London, 1885-8), i, p. 452.

44.   Mant re bishop Percy.

45.   Letters of Bishop Percy to his wife, June 11th and 13th 1798, B. L., Ad. Mss. 32,335.

46.   Mant, *Bishop Mant*, pp 156, 157.

47.   Ibid., p. 158.

48.   Ibid., pp 159, 181-2.

49.   Charge of 1834.

50.   B. Noel, *Notes of a short tour through the midland counties of Ireland, in the Summer of 1836, with observations on the condition of the peasantry* (London, 1837), p. 387.

51.   *Account of the proceedings of the Down and Connor Clergy Aid Society for the year ending Sept. 1838* (Belfast, 1838).

52.   *The Down and Connor Clergy Aid and Additional Curates Society Report, July 1839* (Belfast, 1839).

53.   *Fourth and final report of the Down and Connor Church Accommodation Society, Jan 19 1843* (Belfast, 1843).

54.   Ibid.

55.   W. A. Phillips, *History of the Church of Ireland*, 3 vols (Belfast, 1934), iii, p. 356.

56.   July 1842, P. R. O. N. I., Downshire correspondence, D.671/C/188/40-42; J. Barry, *Hillsborough: a parish in the Ulster Plantation* (Belfast, 1962), p. 27.

57.   Hugh McCall, *The house of Downshire; a sketch of its history 1600 to 1868* (2nd ed., 1881), p. 95.

58.   E. D. Atkinson, *Dromore, An Ulster diocese* (Dundalk, 1925), pp 152-6.

59.   R. B. McDowell, *The Church of Ireland 1869-1969* (London, 1975).

60.   Carr, *Unpretending*, pp 158-9.

61.   E. D. Atkinson, *An Ulster parish: being a history of Donaghcloney* (Dublin, 1898), pp 68-9.

62.   Parochial reports for the dioceses of Down and Dromore, 1886, P. R. O. N. I., D.1.0.1/15/1, D.1.0.1./15/3.

63.   Crookshank, *Methodism*, ii, p. 259.

64.   Ibid., ii, p. 124.

65.   Ibid., ii, p. 466.

66.   Matthew Lanktree, *Biographical narrative* (Belfast, 1836).

67.   Ibid., pp 106-7.

68.   Crookshank, *Methodism*, ii, p. 289.

69.   J. H. Wescott, *Memorials of a consecrated life: compiled from the autobiography, letters and diaries of Anne Lutton of Moira, county Down* (London, 1882).

70.   Crookshank, *Methodism*, ii p. 175.

71.   See the printed annual *Minutes of the Methodist Conference in Ireland*.

72.   J. R. Binns, 'A history of Methodism in Ireland from Wesley's Death in 1791 to the reunion of Primitives and Wesleyans in 1878', unpub. M.A. thesis, Q.U.B., 1960.

73.   A large number of examples are cited in Crookshank, *Methodism*.

74.   P. R. O. N. I., Ouseley Collection, CR6/3.
75.   Crookshank, *Methodism*, i, p. 330.
76.   Minutes of the General Assembly, iii, p. 161.
77.   G. Bowsie, *Carryduff Presbyterian Church 1841-1983* (Belfast, 1983), p. 24.
78.   D. Hempton and M. Hill, *Evangelicalism in Ulster society 1740-1890* (London, 1992), pp 129-42.
79.   Rev. A. Lockett (ed.), *The official report of the Church Conference* (Dublin, 1892).
80.   W. Gibson, *The year of grace: a history of the Ulster Revival of 1859* (Jubilee edition, London, 1909), p. 132.
81.   McCreery, *Killyleagh*, p. 306.
82.   N. D. Emerson, *The Church of Ireland and the 1859 Revival* (Dublin, 1959).
83.   Gibson, *Year of grace*, p. 117.
84.   M. Hill, 'Ulster Awakened, The '59 Revival reconsidered' in *Journal of Ecclesiastical History*, xli, no. 3 (July, 1990).
85.   Gibson, *Year of grace*, p. 256.
86.   Hill, 'Ulster Awakened'.
87.   J. Edwin Orr, *The Second Evangelical awakening in Britain* (Edinburgh, 1949), chapter 8.
88.   C. E. Tonna, *Letters from Ireland* (London, 1837).
89.   *The great Protestant demonstration at Hillsborough, 30 October 1867* (Belfast, 1867).
90.   *Christian Advocate*, 19 February, 1886, quoted in Megahey, 'Irish Protestant Churches', p. 39.

Chapter 19

THE CATHOLIC CHAPEL AND THE CATHOLIC COMMUNITY: OBSERVANCE AND TRADITION IN NINETEENTH-CENTURY COUNTY DOWN[1]

OLIVER RAFFERTY, S.J.

Catholic identity within the Irish context arguably depends on two inextricably linked factors. The first is the practice of Catholicism itself which has been grafted onto the attendant cultural accoutrements of the Gaelic outlook and way of life.[2] The second is the long history, since the Reformation, of the struggle to survive as a religious and political force against a background of official hostility. In the context of county Down we must also take account of the specific circumstances of Ulster, and in particular of the enormous success and prevalence of Protestantism, especially in its Presbyterian hue, in east Ulster. It is true that (in some respects) Presbyterianism produced a number of the more radical and liberal elements in Irish Protestantism,[3] but that community has also had its share of some of the most reactionary individuals in that tradition. It is against this background that the Catholic community in the nineteenth century developed its self-understanding, and fostered its relationships with the Presbyterian and Episcopalian communities.[4]

The Catholic community in nineteenth-century Down, whilst labouring under the constraints common to Irish Catholicism as a whole, was none the less acutely aware of its peculiar difficulties as an impoverished and disadvantaged minority in a largely Presbyterian setting. Yet, as we shall see, that very setting came to shape its identity. Moreover it was dependent on the more benevolent elements within the Protestant communities for its survival and expansion, at least in the public aspects of its life and worship.

The historian of Catholicism in Down works under a number of disadvantages. Many of the extant records are either official ecclesiastical or government papers. Such sources arguably skew the perspective on the community in too much of an official direction, and make it difficult to know precisely how 'ordinary' Catholics viewed the events which shaped their lives. In the nineteenth century hostility between the Catholic and Protestant communities was constantly growing, especially after the Catholic Emancipation Act led many Protestants to again see Catholicism as a political threat. Many of the public records therefore focus on inter-communal strife, the sheer vividness of which overshadows more subtle complexities of the relationships between the communities.

Finally, county Down is divided between two Catholic dioceses: the united diocese of Down and Connor, which incorporates most of east and north Down, and the diocese of Dromore, which includes large tracts of south and west Down with small outposts in Antrim and Armagh. We must also reckon with the influence of Belfast which, after the Famine, had overtaken Dublin as the industrial capital of Ireland, and which in ecclesiastical geography is in the diocese of Down. However in the interests of focusing what follows on Down itself, I have tried as far as possible to abstract the urban reality of Belfast with its peculiar pastoral difficulties, and I discuss that area only when it is absolutely necessary for a full appreciation of the challenges facing Catholicism in the century as a whole.

The Catholic community in Down in the nineteenth century exhibited many of the general features of Ulster Catholicism. At the beginning of the period it was a relatively weak and disparate group with an underdeveloped sense of religious identity and little political power. By the end of the century the community exhibits what we have come to expect as the marks of a quintessentially Catholic ultramontane nationalist community.[5] That process is perhaps one of the most fascinating adjustments in nineteenth century Irish history. Nevertheless, the persistence of Catholicism in Down was in many respects a haphazard affair. It was one of two Ulster counties to have the lowest percentage of Catholics in the general population. The concentration of Catholics in specific areas was at times due to specific religious factors. Walter Harris, for example, noted in the eighteenth century the prevalence of Catholics in Downpatrick because of the town's proximity to a centre of pilgrimage, St Patrick's wells at Struell.[6] By contrast the northeast of the county had very few Catholics.[7] In Donaghadee, the first mass since the seventeenth century was celebrated only in 1805, and by 1884 the Catholic electorate in the Ards and Castlereagh area accounted for just six per cent of the total.[8]

Perhaps not surprisingly, the Catholic community in the early years of the century shared some of the features of its larger Presbyterian neighbour. Patrick MacMullan, the bishop of Down and Connor, writing from Downpatrick in 1814 to the authorities in Rome, acknowledged that a number of parishes in his diocese maintained what they took to be a right to 'call' their own priests. The parish in Belfast elected a committee of more prominent members to help in the administration of the congregation, and these were known by the Presbyterian title of elders. MacMullan was determined to resist such, in his view, dangerous tendencies, and to reassert full episcopal authority.[9] This relative independence of the laity in ecclesiastical affairs was also apparent in Newry, which in the early nineteenth century had the largest population of urban Catholics in Ulster. Bishop Michael Blake complained to the primate, archbishop Thomas Kelly of Armagh, that the church committee in the town repeatedly refused to pay the salaries of the curates and to supply the other needs for worship. Blake sought to impress upon the committee that they had no rights independently of the bishop. To this end he deprived it of one of its traditional functions, that of collecting money after mass on Sundays, and instead organized his own collections. The committee in reaction was to accuse him of insulting the Catholics of Newry.[10]

By mid-century Belfast was beginning to be an important centre of Catholic population[11] and a number of Catholics were emerging as substantial businessmen. For the most part, however, Catholics in Down were at the lower end of the social spectrum as labourers or as the poorer sort of tenant farmer, although generally speaking they were, in common with Catholics elsewhere in east Ulster, better off than their co-religionists in other areas.[12] Where, as in the linen triangle, Catholics did enjoy the benefits of greater economic security, their social life was not vastly different from that of their Protestant neighbours.[13] Mother Emmanuel, of the Convent of Mercy in Newry, the sister of Lord Russell of Killowen, recalled for Russell's biographer that on Sundays after dinner 'each one of us had to read a chapter of the bible aloud while mamma and dada listened respectfully'.[14]

Such sabbatarianism had perhaps in itself little to do with the content of Catholicism, or with how Catholics saw their role in Ulster life, but it is a significant indicator of the influences upon Catholic practice from a perhaps unexpected quarter. Another aspect of this close proximity of the different religious traditions was that Catholics imbibed something of the Protestant work ethic, and consequently took less time off to observe religious festivals and holy days, a practice which was, so we are informed, 'so inimical to industry in the southern part of Ireland'.[15]

The practice of Catholicism

From the closing decades of the eighteenth century, Catholics had been free to practice their religion openly and without hindrance. Consequently an enormous amount of church building was set in progress in the period up to the Famine. One of the features of church building in rural areas early in the century was that much of the heavier work, such as drawing stone from quarries, was carried out by parishioners themselves free of charge.[16] Cornelius Denvir, bishop of Down and Connor 1836-1865, declared in his report to Rome on the state of his diocese in 1845 that there was at least one chapel in every parish and that in the greater number there were two, many of which were substantial and newly built.[17]

The growth of what we might call the Catholic infrastructure would not have been possible without Protestant benefactions. The Protestants of Belfast not only gave the land for a new Catholic chapel to be built in 1842, but also contributed a further £800 to the cost of building. Thomas McGivern, the future bishop of Dromore, when parish priest of Drumgath in the 1870s, obtained from Lord Downshire land for a Catholic cemetery near Rathfriland.[18] A previous marquis had granted to Hugh Smith, the parish priest of Lisburn, an acre and a half of land on which to build a church. Similarly Patrick Curran the parish priest of Newtownards and Holywood, and a former tutor to the marquis of Londonderry, used his influence with the Castlereagh family to obtain the site in Newtownards on which he built a Catholic church in 1813. The Londonderry family maintained a benevolent interest in Catholic affairs in their area late into the century; the dowager marchioness built the third church for the Holywood parish in 1875 (plate 19.1).[19] Such examples could be multiplied many times over.

Despite a growing confidence about their position in Ulster society, Catholics still harboured a sense of the burden of their history. Addressing a St Patrick's day banquet in Belfast in 1853, James Killen, the parish priest of Holywood, said that for nearly 300 years the clergy had suffered persecution, and were willing to suffer again with their people.[20] Such sentiments were not entirely the product of an over-active imagination. Until 1871 a marriage between a Catholic and a Protestant, if conducted by a Catholic priest was invalid in the eyes of the law. For having conducted just such a service in Loughinisland the local Catholic curate, Fr. Bradley, had a warrant issued against him in 1829 at the behest of the Church of Ireland rector, James Stannus. When the Sisters of Mercy opened their convent in Downpatrick in 1855 there was much opposition. The local newspaper accused them of trying to win converts to Rome, and urged Protestants to greater zeal in visiting the poor and sick of the area as a means of trying to counter the baneful influence of the nuns.[21]

At the same time bishops and priests stressed the rapid progress the Church had made since the turn of the century. By 1835 in the Down portion of the Down and Connor diocese there were 58,405 Catholics worshipping in thirty-seven chapels. For the Dromore diocese the

Plate 19.1   The Catholic parish church, Holywood. Built by the dowager marchioness of Londonderry in 1875, the church was one of many examples of Protestant aid for Catholic church building. It was subsequently destroyed by fire in 1994. (Source: Green collection, Ulster Folk and Transport Museum).

figures were 76,275 worshipping in thirty-four chapels.[22] Although sometimes compared unfavourably with Catholicism elsewhere in the country measured by such factors as the ratio of priests to people and attendance at mass, county Down by early mid-century fared better than many areas. In Dromore there were seventeen parish priests, including the bishop, and ten curates, which gives a ratio of one priest for every 2,825 Catholics. In the rest of Down there was one priest for every 2,085 Catholics, one of the best ratios in the whole country.[23]

An analysis of the returns of those attending mass is broadly in line with work done elsewhere.[24] It is difficult to be absolutely precise since the returns are incomplete, but it is possible to suggest that in Dromore diocese, 25,000 people or roughly 32.77 per cent of the Catholic populace attended mass on Sundays and holidays, while in the rest of Down, the figure was 19,902 or approximately 34 per cent.[25] Some attempts have been made to claim that this rather low indication of practice cannot be accurate. P. J. Corish suggests that allowance must be made for the fact that the figures are based on the Church of Ireland parish unit, that they are concerned with only the main service each Sunday, and for the fact that children under seven and the elderly and sick had no obligation to attend mass.[26] Perhaps one of the most significant aspects of the debate is that raised by Ambrose Macaulay concerning the lack of episcopal injunctions on the issue. Had bishops believed that Catholics were especially neglectful in this matter they would undoubtedly have pronounced upon the question.[27] These low figures have been adduced as evidence for the claim that 'native Irish culture is not the source and strength of modern Irish piety'.[28] On the other hand, to take but one indicator, if the county Down experience is representative we can see a lively and profound outpouring of piety at a popular level, associated with such pilgrimages as the annual Hilltown gathering to commemorate the killing of a priest and his congregation in 1643, and the holy wells at Struell. The latter was a subject of much controversy. From 1836 the clergy annually railed against the pilgrimage, but these protestations were ignored. The *Downpatrick Recorder*, in unusual alliance with the Catholic priests, regularly denounced such gatherings and in 1860 reported that the numbers taking part had fallen considerably. The pilgrims, however, fought back. Two years later when two priests from Downpatrick went out to the well to disperse the pilgrims 'many were heard to speak in bitter terms of the interference of the priests, which they seem to regard in something of the light of an outrage'.[29]

Clerical opposition to such popular practices is indicative that reform was under way in Catholic piety. The effect of this reform was to move the centre of religious activity from the home to the often newly built chapel. That transition gave an enhanced role to the position of the Maynooth-educated priest. Bishop Denvir believed that the ministry of these 'well disciplined and zealous clergy' had 'done much to restore religion' after centuries of persecution. The aim of all this was to give a better understanding of Catholicism, and to foster devotions which were under the control of the priests, and thus less open to superstition.[30] After his appointment as bishop, Michael Blake introduced to Dromore such 'modern' features as the Sodality of the Sacred Heart, the Purgatorian Society, and the Confraternity of Christian Doctrine. The latter was also an important society for catechising in the rest of Down, as the Down and Connor diocesan regulations of 1834 make clear.[31]

It must not be thought, however, that the clergy were uncritical promoters of ultramontane popular piety. In complaining of the writings of St Alphonsus Ligouri, especially of tomes such as *The glories of Mary*, Blake asserted that 'fanatics will avail themselves of his works... to represent the Catholic Church as an encourager of the most shameful corruption of morals and the rankest superstitions'.[32] Reform notwithstanding the home still remained an important centre for religious practice. The statutes of the province of Armagh, 1834, made the holding of stations compulsory, however by the end of the century there were very few places in which it was customary to have mass said in private houses.[33]

Parish missions became increasingly popular from the mid-century on, and at an emotional level fulfilled something of the same function as 'revival' meetings among Protestants. They were also a means of raising money. At the famous Lisburn mission in July 1853, admission charges to high mass ranged from one shilling to sixpence, and the evening services cost the devotees between three and six pence. At times these missions had something of an ecumenical flavour with Protestants of the more 'respectable classes' attending in order to listen to the sermon. Of course, there could also be sectarian overtones to such gatherings, and the rioting which accompanied the Lisburn mission was blamed by the *Northern Whig* on the parish priest, John McKenna, on the grounds that he had staged the event to coincide with the Boyne commemoration festivities.[34]

There were other indications of reform. Diocesan administration became more formal, with annual or triennial visitations of each parish by the bishop, during which the conduct of the clergy was scrutinized, first communions administered, children and adults confirmed, and catechism examined.[35] The renewal of Catholic religious life, 'the devotional revolution' so called, was well under way before Paul Cullen's return to Ireland in 1850, but from that time onwards one can detect a more determined political aspect to Catholicism within the state. Despite Cullen's distrust of the institution, Maynooth College did instil a more robust political sense into its graduates in comparison with the clergy of a previous generation. By the mid-century the old style continental trained priests, and the cisalpine product of Maynooth were rapidly dying out. The Church of Ireland rector of Donaghmore in the late 1860s could, however, describe his Catholic equivalent, Fr. Felix McLaughlin as 'a most kind, good-natured priest of the old school', in spite of his Maynooth education.[36]

Measured by external ultramontane criteria, Catholic religious life in Down by the end of the century was in an expansive and exuberant mood. Clerical numbers were increasing; Belfast, Downpatrick and Newry could boast of Catholic schools, orphanages, and a hospital. Priests from the Passionist, the Redemptorist and the Jesuit religious orders had made their appearance for the first time in Ulster, either in Belfast or county Down (the Jesuits only briefly), and the Dominicans re-established themselves in Newry for the first time since the Reformation. The laity were worshipping in churches in unprecedented numbers. There remained however a sense of nostalgia for the past. In 1897 Pope Leo XIII issued an encyclical letter on the rosary. In commenting on it, the Belfast *Irish News*, in triumphalist vein, declared that 'In all our vicissitudes Irish Catholics can still claim to have preserved in a great measure the love of their forefathers for the pious and efficacious practice of which the Holy Father writes so eloquently'.[37] This new found confidence linked as it was to a sense of grievance about past persecutions, inevitably affected the community's relationship with its Protestant neighbours, who tended to see any form of Catholic advancement as a setback for Protestants.

Education

One of the fields in which Catholics made considerable gains was in education. Although by the end of the century Catholic illiteracy rates still tended to be higher than those of Protestants, the general educational standing of the community in Down had made enormous progress. There is some suggestion that Catholic priests in Ulster were less concerned about specifically Catholic provision in education than their colleagues in other areas of the country.[38] Leading churchmen could certainly see some advantage in having Catholic and Protestant children educated together. William Crolly, then bishop of Down and Connor, testifying before the education commission of 1825, declared that he believed 'mixed education' was an effective means of suppressing party spirit provided some precautions were taken to ensure that no undue influence was exercised by one particular religious tradition.[39] Indeed before the setting up of St Malachy's College in Belfast in 1833, Crolly used to prepare his seminarians for Maynooth by sending them to the Presbyterian Belfast Academical Institution for their secondary education.[40]

The early years of the operation of the national school system were marred by opposition from Ulster Presbyterians, in many instance led by the indomitable Henry Cooke. On several occasions the more redoubtable opponents of the system resorted to violence. In 1836 the Rev. James Porter of the secession church at Drumlee in county Down allowed his school to be affiliated to the national system. The school was attacked by a Presbyterian mob and both Porter and his school master were assaulted.[41] By contrast Catholics in Down were anxious supporters of the system. The first clergyman to apply for a school grant under the terms of the national schools provisions was Thomas Kelly, then bishop of Dromore and subsequently archbishop of Armagh. Within the first two years of the system's operation many of the parishes of Down had applied for grants, the applications, as was required, carrying the signatures of both Catholics and Protestants. Perhaps most remarkably of all, the system was also supported in these early years by Paul Cullen, then rector of the Irish college in Rome, who was eventually to become one of its sternest critics.[42]

Michael Blake, who succeeded Kelly as bishop of Dromore, showed some hesitation about the system, but he was won over to it largely through assurances given by Daniel Murray, archbishop of Dublin. His main complaint then became the fact that the commissioners were slow to supply the necessary funds, and that his people were thus becoming frustrated since there was a great need of education for the poor of his diocese.[43] Blake's concern for adequate funding was also shared by Cornelius Denvir,[44] bishop of Down and Connor, who was an enthusiastic supporter of the system to the extent of becoming a commissioner for education. However he resigned from this post in 1857, owing to pressure from other members of the Irish hierarchy.

It is also clear that where Catholics had control over schools they were concerned to ensure that the board's regulations were duly observed. Robert Stuart Currie, a district inspector of education, remarked in his 1864 report on the convent school in Downpatrick that the Sisters of Mercy were scrupulous in this regard, lest infringement of the regulations might 'prevent the school from recommending itself to persons of different religious denominations, or in any way lessen its usefulness and circumscribe its influence'.[45] The glowing testimony Currie gave of the benefits of convent education in Downpatrick contrasts sharply with that of D.C. Richmond, the education inspector for the Armagh and Belfast areas, the latter including north Down, before the Powis commission four years later. Whilst Currie praised the nuns for the quality of the education provided, Richmond testified to the 'marked inferiority of convent to ordinary national schools'.[46] Although by this stage the Irish bishops were more aggressive in their demands for a Catholic education system spearheaded by nuns and Christian Brothers, Richmond saw such schools in less benevolent terms. In his view the Catholic system produced 'true and earnest adherents of the Church, but is opposed to the formation and independence of character which a method of greater freedom tends to produce. In this respect the Christian Brothers and the nuns are entirely at one'.[47]

Bishop Denvir's association with the education commission was publicly opposed by a number of priests and prominent lay people in his diocese. By the time he was forced to resign as bishop in 1865, the *Catholic directory* had drawn attention to the unsatisfactory level of provision for Catholic primary education in the diocese of Down and Connor. This meant, according to the *directory*, that Catholic children were required to attend national schools 'in which the course of religious instruction is highly perilous to the faith of such catholic children'.[48] This reflected the view of Patrick Dorrian, Denvir's coadjutor bishop and successor, that because of Denvir's neglect many Catholic children had to attend Presbyterian schools where there was danger of proselytism.[49] On the other hand the Powis commission recorded that Denvir in 1854, and Dorrian's own testimony before it in 1868 had stressed that they were both satisfied that the national system was not being used for proselytizing purposes.[50]

It is perhaps possible to detect here not so much antipathy to the system as such but rather a desire on the part of the hierarchy to have a greater influence on Irish society as a whole. For social and economic reasons it was impossible for the Church in Down to maintain a comprehensive provision for Catholic education at the elementary level. By 1868 the attendance of Catholic children at schools run by nuns or Christian Brothers was a mere 228. The foundation of institutions for post-primary education in Belfast and Newry earlier in the century was in the first instance to provide for the training of priests. It was probably a growing sense of political power rather than a fear of the consequences of mixed education that determined the increasingly militant attitude of Catholic churchmen to the question.

Writing in 1851 George Crolly, a county Down man and a professor at Maynooth, defended the national system, and rejected what he took to be the assumption too often displayed by 'popular newspaper writers' that mixed education was 'essentially bad'. Quoting from a bull of Pope Gregory XVI issued in 1841 he pointed out that during the first ten years of its existence 'the Catholic religion had suffered no injury' from the system.[51]

For his part Bishop Michael Blake specifically rejected the idea that the schools as such posed any threat to Catholicism. At a meeting of the hierarchy in 1839 he complained about several bishops who saw the schools as part of a larger conspiracy against the Church and who 'dwelt on the dangers to which the Catholic religion is exposed in Russia and Prussia, as if there were any parity between the government of Great Britain and Ireland and those despotic monarchies'.[52]

From 1845 onwards the bishops also confronted the problem of the Queen's Colleges. Cullen, writing from Rome to Blake, informed him that the Government's aim of educating Catholics and Protestants in the same universities would be fatal to Catholic interests. Naively he believed that if the bishops kept aloof from them the Government would 'in the end make the colleges Catholic'.[53] For their part, Blake, Crolly and Denvir to varying degrees all supported the Queen's Colleges while seeking various adjustments to make those institutions more Catholic. Conversely neither Denvir nor Blake would allow the collection for the Catholic university to be taken up in their dioceses on St. Patrick's day 1851. Blake however underwent several changes of mind on the colleges issue. He told Cullen that he was pleased that the pope did not approve of the Colleges Act. On the other hand he declared that 'I would not be anxious to see [the pope], the head of a state, in public opposition to the minister of England'. At the same time he assured Cullen he did not see the necessity of a solemn public condemnation of the colleges by the pope.[54]

It would however be misleading to conclude from all this that the episcopal leadership of the Catholic community in Down in the first half of the century was unconcerned about specifically Catholic education provision. The Rev. John Keenan founded a school in Newry under the direction of Bishop Thomas Kelly in 1823 which subsequently became St. Colman's College. Bishops MacMullan, Lennan, and Blake all left money in their wills for purposes of Catholic education. Furthermore Blake's opposition ensured that the standard religious textbooks of the national system, *Introductory lessons on christian evidence* and *scripture lessons*, were not used in the Newry Model school when it opened in 1849.

It is equally clear that prior to 1831, Catholics and Protestants enjoyed the benefits of mixed education without too much complaint from either side. By 1824, 6,000 Catholic children in Down were attending schools conducted by the various Protestant educational societies.[55] Dr. James Neilson, a Presbyterian minister, conducted a school in Downpatrick which had the distinction of producing three Catholic bishops: Crolly, Denvir and Dorrian.[56] Mason's *Parochial survey* and the *Ordnance survey memoirs* give abundant evidence of the fact that Catholic and Protestant children were taught together. Let me take two random examples. In the parish of Kilcoo, which included Newcastle, Lord Annesley had two schools built which were attended by children from Episcopalian, Presbyterian and Catholic families.[57] In the parish of Killinchy in north-east Down, the Kildare Place Society ran a school which was visited by the clergy of all denominations, all of whom, according to the day book, were satisfied with how the school was conducted. In this instance the master, John Murray, was a Catholic, and of 181 children taught there ninety-eight were Presbyterians, three were Church of Ireland and eighty were Catholics.[58]

This is not to suggest that there were no complaints arising from mixed education. We have some evidence that organisations such as the Kildare Place Society did see one function of their schools as a means of converting Catholic children from popery. On the other hand, the Catholic authorities obviously believed that it was possible to minimise and counteract such threats. However, once the government became directly responsible for education in the period after 1831, Catholic churchmen began to become increasingly uneasy that the schools, coupled with other developments such as the 'godless colleges' and the operations of the Charitable Bequests Act, might be used as an instruments of state policy for the subversion of Catholicism.[59] One aspect of the issue was the question of government interference in what was seen as a parental and ecclesiastical responsibility. This was an enduring consideration. When the 1892 Education Bill proposed compulsory attendance at school the bishops objected on the grounds that this restricted the freedom of choice of parents with regard to the education of the children. Patrick McAlister, bishop of Down and Connor, wanted a papal condemnation of the proposal of such an 'infidel system'.[60]

Developments elsewhere also had an influence on the attitude of Irish churchmen to the education question. The struggles over education in Italy, France, and Germany,[61] the hardening of attitudes in Rome to all social change in the aftermath of the 1848 revolutions, and the failure of many Roman officials to fully comprehend the position of Ireland as a largely Catholic country within the essentially Protestant United Kingdom – all these combined to ensure that the care and subtleties needed to deal objectively and fairly with the Irish education question were not always in evidence.

As with so many other questions facing Irish society, the post-Famine period saw a hardening of opinion in Catholic demands and expectations. Although Blake and Denvir remained at the helm of Catholic church leadership in Down for more than a decade after the Famine, both had less flexible assistants, who eventually succeeded them.[62] As the clergy in general became more ultramontane in attitude, they became more antagonistic both to government initiatives and to Protestant influence.

Perhaps, however, the single most important factor conditioning Catholic attitudes in the great debates on education was the increased militancy of the Presbyterian Church. Led in the matter by Henry Cooke, the Synod of Ulster skilfully manipulated the provisions of the 1830 Act and prevailed upon the government to change the system so as to favour Presbyterian interests. The resultant Catholic frustration found expression in a 1859 declaration by the bishops. Although they were reconciled to the system because of the circumstances of the country, it was nonetheless objectionable in several respects, particularly in that the 'changes made to its rules from time to time, having been adverse to Catholic interests, have increased the distrust of the Catholic episcopacy'.[63]

Given their disadvantageous numerical position in Down, not even the most militant members of the Catholic community could afford to maintain too great an hostility to their Episcopalian and Presbyterian neighbours. This might go some way towards explaining the relatively moderate stance taken by most of the leading churchmen in Down on the education question in the nineteenth century. No such constraints operated on Catholic opinions in other regions of the country. Tom Garvin's observations regarding a later period are equally applicable to the situation of Catholics in the mid-decades of the century. 'Far from Ulster physically and psychologically, the southern counties of Ireland were as insensitive to Protestant fears as they were immune to Orange threats'.[64]

There can be no doubt that the growth in the Catholic presence in areas such as Belfast threatened Protestant sensibilities, and stimulated Protestant hostility to Catholic political pretensions. The struggle over education and Catholic determination to assert as much control as possible in the education process is perhaps best seen as part of a wider shift in the relationships between the two communities. Whereas Down Presbyterians in 1826 were supportive of Catholic aspirations over emancipation, the 1830s and 1880s saw particularly bad inter-community violence, and when the offer of Home Rule appeared to satisfy Catholic political ambitions, it met with outright Protestant rejection.

Catholic-Protestant relations

It is tempting to try to understand inter-community hostilities in Ireland in terms of a simple correlation between Catholic political advance and Protestant fears of domination.[65] However one cannot neglect the role of specifically religious beliefs in the mutual antagonism between Catholics and Protestants. Upon his nomination as bishop of Down and Connor in 1895, Henry Henry wrote to the rector of the Irish College in

Rome that he was deeply conscious of the burden laid upon him 'in this heretical diocese ...'.[66]

A soiree in the Orange hall in Downpatrick on 6 December 1870 heard the leading county Down Orangeman, Matthew Skillen, denounce the errors and dogmas of Rome. He asked rhetorically how many masses it would take to get a soul out of purgatory? 'Just as many as it would take snow-balls to heat a bakers oven'. He reminded his listeners that Orangemen existed to protect the Protestant community against the errors he had just parodied.[67] By contrast Henry Cooke told a meeting in Belfast in July 1840 that his politics were inseparable from his religion and that he got them both from the bible.[68] William Johnston of Ballykilbeg was yet another political figure able to combine his political with his religious beliefs. His biographer assures us that 'a violent hatred of popery' was imbued virtually with his mother's milk and from this he derived the conviction, from which he never wavered, that the Church of Rome 'was the enemy of freedom'.[69] At the same time Johnston wanted to maintain a distinction between Catholics as individuals and their Church. As if to emphasise this Johnston affected astonishment when the parish priest of Downpatrick, Bernard McAuley, urged his flock at the 1857 by-election to vote for Johnston's opponent, Richard Ker. Johnston declared that his fight was not with Catholics but with 'the Church that degrades and enslaves them'.[70] This distinction was for the most part lost on the Catholic community.

In so far as one can separate out the religious and political factors in the relations between the two communities one can discern that Catholics moved gradually from a position of support for the Union in the early nineteenth century, through a period of disenchantment, to a favouring at the end of the century of some measure of Home Rule within the Empire. Arguably, Protestant antagonism to Catholicism was the largest single influence on that process.[71] For his part, in demonstration of his loyalty to Queen and constitution, Bishop Denvir was one of the minority of bishops who presented a loyal address on behalf of his clergy to Victoria and Prince Albert on their visit to Ireland towards the end of the Famine in 1849.[72] Such commitment to the established order was noticed a decade and a half later by Jeremiah O'Donovan Rossa, who was disgusted with the lack of nationalist spirit among Catholics in north Down during his Fenian recruitment tour in Ulster.[73]

In spite of the widespread contact through mixed education, and even some common agitation on the question of land reform, inter-community hostility was an enduring feature of the second half of the century. The inability of many Protestants to differentiate between Catholics who were loyal and those who wanted radical political change was doubtless one factor in the growing sectarianism in east Ulster, whereby Catholicism itself became the focus of hostility. This is not to imply that intolerance was a one way street. The sentiments, if not all the details, of the Ordnance Survey memorialist in 1838 could have been written at almost any point in the century.

> During the last thirty-five years, orangeism (under the appellation of loyalty) has prevailed to a considerable extent in this part of the country, from which some of the foulest crimes have originated though chiefly owing to the retaliation of the papists ... Half the murders are owing to party zeal. However, it is greatly allayed at present, yet such has been its baleful effects on that portion of society that even the infant children of these deluded people are taught to hate each other merely because one is born a protestant and the other a papist.[74]

The resurgent sectarianism in Down in the 1840s was also fuelled by renewed tension between the Orange Order and revived Ribbonism.[75] However if the sectarian riots in Belfast[76] at various points in the century, the Dolly's Brae affair in 1849,[77] and the riots at Crossgar in July 1857[78] poisoned the relations between the two communities in Down, the phenomenon itself was not new. On the other hand a long history of antagonism may well have been given added edge because of specific political fears at various points in the century.

Drilling in Ballynahinch and Newry presaged the hopeless attempts at rebellion in 1803. At a meeting in Belfast in August that year, resolutions were passed condemning the 'despicable number of insignificant traitors' who had taken part in the fiasco at Loughinisland.[79] Attention was yet again directed to the rebellious Catholics. As if to make amends, Patrick MacArtan the parish priest of Loughinisland, testified against Thomas Russell who, along with Michael McGuire, was sentenced to death. Furthermore MacArtan addressed a letter to the local landowner, which was signed by 1320 of his parishioners, declaring the intention of the Catholics in the area to defend 'the present order of things as by law established'. For this proof of their loyalty the Catholics asked only 'the protection of the laws, and the confidence of our Protestant brethren'.[80] MacArtan also reminded Forde how in the 1798 rising he had prevented a single one of Forde's Catholic tenants from joining that affray. All this despite the fact that his church had been burnt on several occasions, and he had been personally man-handled by Orangemen.[81]

At times of relative political instability Catholic clergy often remarked on the friendliness which existed between the communities. At the jubilee celebrations of his episcopal consecration Patrick Dorrian acknowledged that it had been his great fortune to live in friendship and harmony with Presbyterians and Protestants (Episcopalians), who had always dealt fairly with him.[82] This was more than simply the maintenance of friendly individual relations at a time of community distance.[83] There is no doubt, however, that by the 1880s the interests of both communities were so clearly at variance that religious differences were exploited for political ends. This had not always been the case. In the early years of the century the legacy of the United Irishmen did indicate to some degree that it was possible for Catholics and Protestants to share the same ideological platform. We have seen how the social *mores* of both communities were relatively similar. With the coming of the Second Reformation however, and the agitation over Repeal, the stage was set for the two communities steadily to draw apart.[84] Ironically one element in fostering inter-community strife was the spectacle of public disputations on matters of theology between Catholic and Protestant clergy, such as that in Downpatrick at the end of April 1828[85] associated with the attempts of the British Reformation Society to open a branch in the town. Contemporary commentators noted that such encounters did much to sour relations between Catholics and Protestants.[86]

Another area of contention, and one of the features of the Second Reformation, were the attempts to induce Catholics to convert to Protestantism. When Fr. George Dempsey, the administrator of Bryansford, tried to embarrass Lord Roden and his parson, the Rev. A. W. McCreight, by displaying in Downpatrick the clothes and other articles which they had used to try to bribe Catholics into conforming to the Established Church, Roden served him with a notice to quit. Roden, however, who had a reputation of generally being kindly to his Catholic tenants, later dropped the case,[87] his general aim was to try to show that prosperity was linked with Protestantism.[88]

The Revival of course not only consolidated the emergent sense of Protestant identity in Ulster; by the 1880s its effects also had definite political overtones, as the Protestant community set its face resolutely against Home Rule.[89] By then the alliance between the Church of Ireland and the Presbyterian Church, based on shared political and religious interests, was well cemented. Since the 'banns of marriage' had been declared by Cooke in October 1834, Presbyterian and Episcopalian interests had steadily coalesced. Rome and its clergy were seen as the common enemy of all shades of Protestant opinion.

Not all Catholic observers, however, saw the Revival in menacing terms. At the Down assizes in 1859, the Catholic Chief Baron, Pigott, concluded that the Revival had 'extinguished party animosity and produced the most wholesome moral results'.[90] At the beginning of that decade, Protestant resistance to Catholic expansionism was clearly demonstrated in the opposition which was provoked by the restoration of the Catholic hierarchy in England. Even then, however, there were surprising instances of accommodation. The parishioners of Dromore were joined by Episcopalians and Presbyterians when they petitioned the Catholic M.P. for Lancashire South, Alexander Henry, himself a native of county Down, to vote against Lord John Russell's response to the restoration, the Ecclesiastical Titles Act. A similar petition was sent to Sharman Crawford by the Catholics of Garvaghy.[91] Crawford and Lord Castlereagh both spoke against the measure. Castlereagh was thunderingly rebuked by the *Downpatrick Recorder*, which reminded him that he would have to answer to the Protestant electorate of Down for this instance of betrayal.[92]

The internal dynamics of Catholicism also contributed to heightened tension. Ultramontane Catholicism had its own distinctive political agenda. The issue here was not so much the espousal of any one political platform but rather the tendency to seek to control the political process as such. If the Belfast *Ulsterman* at its foundation could declare that its intention was to be a journal which by its honesty, intelligence, and national feeling might truly 'represent the Catholics of Ulster',[93] that representation would have to conform to what the clergy determined was truly in the interests of the community. Bishop Henry in later years was bitterly to regret that some of his people were putting nationality before religion by resisting his political posturing in Belfast.[94] Here of course the problem had been exacerbated by the Parnellite split. It is a mark of how the Church's role had changed that the clergy could confidently predict the end of Parnellism. Archbishop Michael Logue thus wrote to Tobias Kirby in Rome that 'the north, priests and people, is solid against Parnell. A small clique in Belfast and Newry[95] are trying to make a noise, but nobody heeds them. I am hammering away on the subject on every available occasion'.[96] As part of the same hammering process Bishop Patrick McAlister was determined to counter the pro-Parnellite *Belfast Morning News* in the name of morality. By founding his own newspaper, the *Irish News*, he effectively emasculated the opposition and forced his rival out of business.[97]

Such clerical politicking was by no means new. The *Newry Commercial Telegraph* had complained sixty years earlier of clerical interference in elections, despite the assurances given in the run up to Emancipation that priests would be happy to abandon politics and concentrate on their pastoral duties.[98] The authorities in Rome had also rebuked the Irish bishops because of clerical political activity.[99] A problem in the earlier decades was the fact that however much they asserted their compliance to papal strictures, bishops in the earlier decades such as Blake were too wedded to O'Connell to surrender all political ambitions. Although the bishops had agreed under pressure from Rome to forbid the use of church property for party political purposes, Blake held a demonstration in the grounds of his own church in Newry to raise a tribute to the Liberator.[100] Crolly, however, would not allow the O'Connell rent to be collected at the chapels in his diocese. The Whiggish tendencies of Crolly and Denvir found an echo in Patrick Dorrian, who in a speech for St. Patrick's day in the mid-1870s, declared that he would not like to see Home Rule if he thought it would lead to religious bitterness or to decline in trade or agricultural production.[101]

Conclusion

There can be little doubt that the Catholic community in Down in the nineteenth century for the most part saw its social salvation as linked with the fortunes and general prosperity of the United Kingdom as a whole. In its religious life the community shared the growing ultramontane and Italianate tastes of mainstream Irish, and indeed British, Catholicism. Like the Catholic community in the other northeast counties of Ulster, it had an almost schizophrenic attitude to Protestantism. Although dependent on the generosity of wealthy Protestants for its rapid growth and development, its very success encouraged an alienation between the two communities which progressively obliterated common liberal political objectives.

It is, however, important not to be seduced into too ready an acquiescence in the idea of inter-community harmony in the early years of the century as compared with the barely concealed contempt at the end. Even in the more tolerant days of 1817 the president of the Belfast Academical Institution, the Rev. Dr. William Bruce, could write, under the pseudonym Zwinglius, that

> Every intelligent protestant must know, that this infallible and immaculate guide which assumes the title of THE CHURCH, is tainted with errors more numerous than the most ignorant and fanatical protestant sect, or than all our sects together.[102]

By contrast, as we have seen, in the middle of the penultimate decade of the century, Patrick Dorrian could attest that throughout his ministry in county Down and in Belfast, he had always lived in friendship with his Protestant neighbours, and he respected their religious convictions although he disagreed with them.[103]

In a very real sense, the Church had no particular political ambitions.

The concern of ecclesiastical authority was to secure the most favourable conditions possible within which to conduct the Church's work. That work was inner directed towards the spiritual needs of Catholics, and to that extent its political purposes were not intrinsically linked to growing Irish nationalism. Protestants, however, were correct in discerning that one of the features of ultramontanism was the desire to control political activity. Many elements in the Catholic community in Down resisted such encroachments, but not on such as scale as to reassure Protestants of Catholic benevolence should Catholics ever gain the upper hand socially or politically.

What is perhaps significant was the capacity of the Catholic community to shed its residual resemblance to the culture around it, to absorb the extraneous elements of ultramontanism, and therefore to distance itself from its own past. To that extent one can talk just as much of dislocation from, as of continuity with, its inherited traditions. Such a phenomenon affected both communities. Catholics and Protestants in Down were equally caught up in political and religious developments originating elsewhere. Owing to the historical antagonisms between the two communities, the Second Reformation and the Revival, the struggles over education, and the growing political tensions which arose from Repeal and Home Rule, all revived in a more vehement strain inter-religious hostility. One effect of all this was to make Catholicism in the Ulster context more inward looking and more preoccupied with its distinctive characteristics, forcing it in the twentieth century into flirtations with radical politics and violence, as it sought to channel the renewed energies of prejudice and sectarianism.

References

1. I wish to thank Roy Foster and Ambrose Macaulay for their comments on an earlier draft of this paper.

2. This, of course, is not to deny the influence of English and continental Catholicism upon it.

3. At a dinner in 1828 the bishop of Down and Connor, William Crolly, declared that 'if Presbyterianism be a name liberality must be its surname'. Quoted in *Northern Whig*, 10 Jan. 1828.

4. The usage 'Catholic, Protestant and Dissenter' remained widespread well into the nineteenth century.

5. S. J. Connolly, *Religion and society in nineteenth century Ireland* (Dundalk, 1985), p. 35, sees this process, at least at a religious level, as making fairly rapid strides in the early decades of the century. There are good reasons, however, as we shall see, for concluding that the process was slower in Ulster than in the rest of the country. P. J. Corish, *The Irish catholic experience: a historical survey* (Dublin, 1985), pp 166 & 184, emphasizes that even by the mid-century Catholics in Ulster were, despite their relative prosperity, 'deprived' so far as their religious life was concerned. James Boyle, Catholic bishop of Kildare and Leighlin, told a

select committee on tithes that northern Catholicism was slow to respond to developments within Catholicism in the period after the Union. See *First and second reports from the select committee, lords, on tithes in Ireland*, H. L. 1831-2 (663) xxii, p. 278.

6. *Down*, p. 35.

7. The north-west of the county was also sparsely populated with Catholics. By 1812 the parish of Annahilt in the Dromore diocese had only twenty Catholics, who had recently arrived. They worshipped with their co-religionists at Ballynahinch. See W. S. Mason, *A statistical account or parochial survey of Ireland*, ii (Dublin, 1819), p. 18.

8. P. Bew and F. Wright, 'The agrarian opposition in Ulster politics' in S. Clark and J. S. Donnelly Jnr. (ed.), *Irish peasants: violence and political unrest 1780-1914* (Manchester, 1983), p. 212.

9. MacMullan to Rev. John Connolly, 12 Oct. 1814, Archives of the diocese of Down and Connor (hereafter A. D. D. C.), B14/3.

10. 28 June 1833, Blake Letter Book, p. 7, P. R. O. N. I., DIO(RC) 3/1.

11. Until 1825 it was customary for the bishop of Down and Connor to live in Downpatrick. Upon his appointment as bishop, William Crolly petitioned Rome for permission to move the administrative centre to Belfast, attesting to the growing Catholic importance of the town for Catholics.

12. H. D. Inglis, *Ireland in 1834*, ii (London, 1835), p. 215, shows that employment was more constant and wages were up to 4d. more per day than elsewhere in Ireland.

13. D. Kennedy, 'The Catholic Church' in T. W. Moody and J. C. Beckett (ed.), *Ulster since 1800: a social survey* (London, 1957), p. 174.

14. R. Barry O'Brien, *The life of Lord Russell of Killowen* (London, 1901), p. 23. Even further down the social scale it is clear that Catholic priests tried to instil a sense of solemnity in their congregations. J. H. Williams in his 1836 return for the parish of Kilbroney records that 'crowded meetings for the purpose of amusement do not take place as formerly, such meetings being opposed by the Roman Catholic clergy'. See A. Day and P. McWilliams (ed.), *Ordnance survey memoirs of Ireland: parishes of county Down I, 1834-6*, iii (Belfast, 1990), p. 30.

15. A. Day and P. McWilliams (ed.), *Ordnance survey memoirs of Ireland: parishes of county Down III, 1833-8*, xii (Belfast, 1992), p. 7.

16. Compare A. Day and P. McWilliams (ed.), *Ordnance survey memoirs of Ireland: parishes of county Down I, 1834-6*, iii (Belfast, 1990), p. 77 and *idem, Ordnance survey memoirs of Ireland: parishes of county Down II, 1832-4, 1837*, vii (Belfast, 1991), p. 10.

17. Denvir to Paul Cullen, 20 Dec. 1845, Cullen Papers, Irish College Rome (hereafter I. C. R.).

18. *Newry Telegraph*, 27 Nov. 1900.

19. J. O'Laverty, *An historical account of the diocese of Down and Connor, ancient and modern*, ii (Dublin, 1880), pp 142-7. Estyn Evans points out that the ornate Gothic style of many such churches demonstrated little concern for continuity with regional tradition. See E. Estyn Evans, *Mourne country* (3rd edition, Dundalk, 1978), p. 201. Contemporary critics questioned the advisability of lavishing scarce resources on such buildings in the face of often overwhelming poverty, a view shared by some Catholic observers. See H. Plunkett, *Ireland in the new century* (Dublin, 1904), p. 107. Compare M. J. F. McCarthy, *Priests and people in Ireland* (Dublin, 1902), *passim*. More recently Liam Kennedy has argued that the church building in its own way contributed to some economic development. See

L. Kennedy, 'The Roman catholic church and economic growth in nineteenth century Ireland' in *The Economic and Social Review*, x no. 1 (1978), p. 56.

20. *The Ulsterman*, 19 Mar. 1853.

21. *Downpatrick Recorder*, 5 May 1855. The accusations of proselytism became a common theme, 12 April 1856 and 12 Dec. 1857. The situation improved, however, with the passing of the years, and upon the death of Mother Borgia, the superior of the convent, in 1864, Protestants turned out in force to mourn her. See *The Catholic directory* (Dublin, 1865), p. 351.

22. *First report of the commission of public instruction Ireland* (45 and 46), H. C. 1835, pp 18-19.

23. These figures are also based on the 1835 House of Commons report, pp 230-39 and pp 243-61. Using the same report Sean Connolly gives a somewhat different picture. See S. J. Connolly, 'Catholicism in Ulster 1800-50' in P. Roebuck (ed.), *Plantation to partition: essays in Ulster history in honour of J. L. McCracken* (Belfast, 1981), p. 159, table 1. Connolly suggests for Dromore that there was one priest for every 2,934 Catholics. However, in his calculations he fails to take account of the fact that the bishop of Dromore also acted as parish priest of Newry. His figures for the rest of the county are combined with those of Antrim to give one priest for every 2,654. If, however, we take only the county Down section of the diocese of Down and Connor, the ratio is as I have indicated. By 1871 there were still only twenty-eight priests in that part of Down, a figure which had remained fairly constant since 1733, despite the fact that the Catholic population had increased threefold. See A. Knox, *A history of county Down* (Dublin, 1875), p. 159.

24. D. W. Miller, 'Irish Catholicism and the Great Famine' in *Journal of Social History*, ix (1975), pp 81-98.

25. Ibid., p 86. Miller indicates that in the environs of Newry, mass attendance was in the region of 46-51 per cent.

26. Corish, *Irish Catholic experience*, pp 166-7, 186-7. In fact Miller does make allowance for these figures, something Corish accuses him of not doing. Miller, 'Irish Catholicism', p. 84.

27. A. Macaulay, *William Crolly: Archbishop of Armagh, 1835-49* (Dublin, 1994), p. 111.

28. Miller, 'Irish Catholicism', p. 87.

29. *Downpatrick Recorder*, 28 June 1862.

30. Day and McWilliams, *Parishes of county Down III*, p. 32, unusually for Down, indicates the prevalence of superstitions such as 'belief in fairies, elves and the visitation of departed spirits'.

31. *Statuta diocesana in episcopo [sic] Dunensi et Connoriensi [sic]*, A. D. D. C., C34/1.

32. Blake to Cullen, 27 Jan. 1842, Cullen papers, I. C. R.

33. Drumgooland was one of the very few places in Down where the custom still obtained. See Rev. John Green to Rev. Michael Kelly, 29 Aug. 1896, Kelly papers, I. C. R. The gradual abolition of 'stations' was one of the reforms that Paul Cullen had set in motion on his return to Ireland. There were many allegations of sexual abuse and avarice connected with stations.

34. *Northern Whig*, 6 July 1853. McKenna's reply rejecting the accusation appeared in *The Ulsterman*, 9 July 1853.

35. Michael Blake gives such details of episcopal pastoral practice. See Blake to Cullen, 10 Feb. 1846, Cullen papers, I. C. R.

36. J. Davidson Cowan, *An ancient Irish parish past and present being the parish of Donaghmore county Down* (London, 1914), p. 348.

37. *The Irish News*, 4 Oct. 1897.

38. Connolly, 'Catholicism in Ulster', p. 162. Equally, there are many indications to the contrary, see for example the *Catholic directory* (Dublin, 1851), p. 210. Henry Cooke gave evidence before the select committee on Ireland in 1825 that in the Poor school conducted by his congregation at Killyleagh in county Down, in some instances the priests had withdrawn the children from the school at least on Sundays. See *Report from the select committee on the state of Ireland*, P. P. 1825, viii, p. 363.

39. *Appendix to the fourth report of the commissioners of Irish education*, H. C. 1826-7, (89) xiii, p. 182.

40. Macaulay, *Crolly*, p. 105.

41. D. H. Akenson, *The Irish education experiment* (London, 1970), p. 170.

42. Macaulay, *Crolly*, p. 189.

43. Blake to Murray, 3 and 10 Mar, 1838, in M. Purcell (ed.), 'Documents: Dublin diocesan archives; Murray papers' in *Archiv. Hib.*, xxxvii (1982), pp 81-2.

44. Denvir to Murray, 11 Mar. 1838, Murray papers, Ibid., p. 92.

45. *Downpatrick Recorder*, 13 Aug. 1864. Bishop Blake made a similar point to the education office in Dublin thirty years earlier, concerning the convent school at Newry. See Blake to Thomas Kelly, 26 May 1833, Blake letter book, P. R. O. N. I., DIO (RC) 3/1.

46. *Report from the commissioners of primary education (Ireland)*, H. C. 1870 xxviii pt 1, App. 3, p. 557.

47. Ibid., p. 554.

48. *The Catholic directory* (Dublin, 1865), p. 164.

49. Dorrian to Archbishop Joseph Dixon, 2 June 1864, Dixon papers, Archives of the archdiocese of Armagh.

50. *Report from the commissioners of primary education (Ireland)*, H. C. 1870 xxviii pt 1, App. 3, p. 585.

51. G. Crolly, *The life of the Most Rev. Doctor Crolly, archbishop of Armagh, and primate of Ireland [sic]* (Dublin, 1851), p. lii. The archbishop himself had told the Pope in 1838 that if the system was condemned it would outrage the best government Ireland ever had, and religion would suffer not only in the British Isles but also in the British colonies.

52. P. MacSuibhne, *Paul Cullen and his contemporaries with their letters from 1820-1902*, ii (Naas, 1962).

54. Blake to Cullen, 8 Oct. 1846, Cullen papers, I. C. R.

55. *Second report of the commissioners of Irish education inquiry*, H. C. 1826-7 (12), xii, pp 36-7.

56. Crolly was to describe Neilson as one of the most liberal and respectable clergymen in county Down. See Crolly to Rev. Hugh McConville, 11 Mar. 1825, Dromore diocesan archives. Neilson also employed at least one Catholic teacher in his school, a Mr. Doran who spent some time in prison owing to his activities with the United Irishmen. See Crolly, *Life*, p. 30.

57. Day and McWilliams, *Parishes of county Down III*, p. 30.

58. Day and McWilliams, *Parishes of county Down II*, p. 92.

59. Blake in one of his periods of discontent maintained that these measures together with the increased Maynooth grant were intended by the Government to cause 'alienation of the people from their pastors and finally the triumph of heresy and infidelity', the result of which would be to 'enslave our religion and our country to the British Government'. See Blake to Cullen, 12 Dec. 1845, Cullen papers, I. C. R.

60. McAlister to Tobias Kirby, 14 Feb. 1892, Kirby papers, I. C. R. In a subsequent note, McAlister told Kirby that if the new system 'be forced upon us it will be disastrous in this diocese where it will [be] entirely managed by anti-Catholic bigots', Ibid., 15 Mar. 1892.

61. See the relevant sections in H. Jedin (ed.), *Handbuch der Kirchengeschichte*, vi/2 (Freiburg, 1973 and London, 1981).

62. John Pius Leahy was assistant bishop to Blake from 1854 and succeeded in 1860. He died in 1890. Patrick Dorrian was coadjutor bishop of Down and Connor in 1860-65, and bishop in his own right between 1865 and 1885.

63. *The Catholic directory* (Dublin, 1860), p. 239.

64. T. Garvin, *Nationalist revolutionaries in Ireland, 1858-1928* (Oxford, 1987), p. 52.

65. This is precisely the charge levelled by Protestant clergymen during the debate over the Disestablishment of the Church of Ireland. See the address of the Rev. Robert Hannay at Greyabbey, June 1868, in the *Downpatrick Recorder*, 6 June 1868.

66. Henry to Michael Kelly, 1 Sept. 1895, Kelly papers, I. C. R.

67. *Downpatrick Recorder*, 10 Dec. 1870.

68. A. T. Jackson, *Friends and acquaintances of Henry Cooke* (Belfast, 1985), p. 5.

69. A. McClelland, *William Johnston of Ballykilbeg* (Lurgan, 1990), p. 5.

70. Ibid., pp 17, 57. McClelland insists, however, that Johnson maintained friendly relations with his Catholic neighbours.

71. This is not to deny that from the Protestant perspective, fear of Catholicism was combined with a fear of what one might call 'political Catholicism', and in particular the political ambitions of the Pope as a temporal ruler.

72. Daniel Murray to Denvir, 10 Aug. 1849, A. D. D. C., D. 49/29.

73. Jeremiah O'Donovan Rossa, *Recollections* (New York, 1898 and Shannon, 1972), p. 289.

74. Day and McWilliams, *Parishes of county Down III*, p. 31.

75. One effect of the Famine was to see an increase in Ribbon activity in the county. See *The Weekly Vindicator*, 17 Feb. and 24 Mar. 1849.

76. The city was as Hepburn has described it, 'truly the cockpit of community conflict in late nineteenth-century Ulster'. See A. C. Hepburn, 'Catholics in the north of Ireland, 1850-1921: the urbanisation of a minority' in A. C. Hepburn (ed.), *Minorities in history* (London, 1978), p. 85.

77. Several magistrates, including Lord Roden, were dismissed for their failure to protect Catholics on that occasion, and for refusing to take evidence in order to apprehend those responsible for the affray. See *Papers relating to an investigation at Castlewellan into the occurrences at Dolly's Brae on 12 July 1849*, H. C. 1850 (1143) li, p. 331 ff. The Party Procession's Act was the parliamentary response to the affair.

78. See for example the accounts in the *Downpatrick Recorder*, 11 and 18 July 1857.

79. *Belfast News Letter*, 9 Aug. 1803.

80. O'Laverty, *An historical account*, i, p. 100.

81. Ibid., p. 98; P. Killen (ed.), *St. Macartan's Church Loughinisland: bicentenary 1787-1987* (1987), p. 48.

82. *Belfast Morning News*, 20 Aug. 1885.

83. K. Theodore Hoppen, *Elections, politics, and society in Ireland 1832-1885* (Oxford, 1984), p. 266.

84. According to Finlay Holmes, the Catholic Church emerged from the Protestant crusade 'stronger and more intolerant of Protestantism than it had been before'.

See F. Holmes, *Our Presbyterian heritage* (Belfast, 19-), p. 114.

85. The more than 300 pages of these debates can be read in *An authentic report of the discussion which took place at Downpatrick on the 22, 23, 24, 28, 29 and 30 April 1828, on six points of controversy between the Church of England and the Church of Rome* (Belfast, 1829).

86. *Northern Whig*, 8 May 1828. Not all clergy rose to such challenges. Catholic missionaries in Newry refused an invitation to engage in such debates on the grounds that they did not advance the cause of religion. See *The Ulsterman*, 12 Mar. 1853.

87. O'Laverty, *An historical account*, i, pp 59-63.

88. D. Hempton and M. Hill, *Evangelical protestantism in Ulster society, 1740-1890* (London, 1992), p. 88.

89. Ibid., p. 167.

90. J. Bardon, *A history of Ulster* (Belfast, 1992), p. 344.

91. *The Catholic directory* (Dublin, 1851), p. 251.

92. *Downpatrick Recorder*, 29 Mar. 1851.

93. *The Ulsterman*, 17 Nov. 1852.

94. Henry to Michael Kelly, 14 Nov. 1897, Kelly papers, I. C. R.

95. Reminiscent of the independence of the laity we saw at the beginning of the century.

96. Logue to Kirby, 5 Dec. 1891, Kirby papers, I. C. R.

97. McAlister to Kirby, 18 April 1891, Kirby papers, I. C. R. McAlister asked for the pope's blessing for his paper which would 'serve the cause of religion in Ulster'.

98. *The Newry Commercial Telegraph*, 16 Jan. 1835.

99. There are numerous examples of such rebukes. See for example the letters of Cardinal Giacomo Fransoni in J. F. Broderick, *The Holy See and the Irish movement for the Repeal of the Union with England, 1829-47* (Rome, 1951), pp 61-2.

100. Blake claimed, however, that he contributed to the tribute because of the services O'Connell had rendered Catholicism and not in order that 'we may obtain Repeal'. See undated memo, 'For the meeting of the inhabitants of Newry', Blake letter book, P. R. O. N. I., DIO(RC) 3/1, p. 29.

101. *Belfast Morning News*, 18 Mar. 1874.

102. *Belfast News Letter*, 27 May 1817. See also Macaulay, *Crolly*, p. 33.

103. *Belfast Morning News*, 20 Aug. 1885.

Chapter 20

BELIEFS IN COUNTY DOWN FOLKLORE

ANTHONY D. BUCKLEY

The *Concise Oxford dictionary* defines folklore as 'the traditional beliefs and stories of a people'.[1] Accordingly, this chapter examines some of the stories and explores the nature of 'belief' in the folklore of county Down. It uses materials[2] which were collected in different parts of the county to examine, specifically, belief in fairies, ghosts and cures.

If someone were to ask, 'Do you believe in fairies'? we might take this to be both a factual but also a rather abstract question. It would be as though, for example, we had been asked if we believed in evolution; or if we thought the world was round; or if we believed it would rain today. We would give our opinion based on the evidence available to us. If, however, someone were to say that he had *seen* a fairy, and he then asked the question, 'Do you believe in fairies?', this would be a proposition of quite a different kind. He would be asking not only for a general opinion about the existence or non-existence of fairies, he would also be asking us to express an opinion of him, of his experience, and of what he had *said*. His claim to have seen a fairy would transform the discussion. No longer would the debate concern merely *fact*, the central question would now be one of veracity and trust. Was the man telling the truth, or was he mistaken, or mad, or a liar? Similarly, when we consider the nature of belief in folklore, questions which are about *fact* often turn into questions of *trust*. We are invited not so much to judge an opinion, as to judge whether a person (and what he says or does) is to be trusted.

Much of what is called folklore has three inter-related elements. First, folklore frequently affirms the truth of the non-rational. Many things held to be 'true' within folkloric discourse flatly contradict the judgements of science, or, indeed, of common sense. In some ways, much folklore directly subverts common sense realities. Because of this, many beliefs of folklore tend to be eccentric and marginal. If the study of folklore is the study of 'beliefs', then it is paradoxical that most of the beliefs studied by folklorists are those which very few people consistently believe in.

Second, much folklore affirms truths which are supposed to belong to 'ordinary people'. As such it contradicts those truths which are the assumed property[3] of intellectual or other elites. The challenge to rationality found in folklore sometimes also challenges those who have control over that rationality. Notably, it is doctors who are challenged, but so also are other professionals.

Third, there is a strong emphasis in folklore relating knowledge to inter-personal relationships and especially to relations of trust. In this, folkloric beliefs contrast heavily with those other forms of knowledge which are legitimised by more impersonal criteria. This third point takes the discussion of belief in folklore close to the idea of religious belief. Many beliefs of folklore are not simply an affirmation of fact, they are more an acknowledgement of trust. This trust may be in the person telling a story, or in the broad traditions of the populace, or, indeed, in the power and person of God.

At this point, we should perhaps clarify what is meant by folklore. Despite the dictionary definition, few folklorists confine their researches to beliefs alone. Most also include practices. Such customs as wake games or the mummer's play, for example, or more practical knowledge relating to domestic or agricultural life, do not always seem to have had any major component of belief. Even here, however, what folklorists tend to study in Ireland is not a cross section of the actual beliefs and practices of any given set of people. Rather, it is a somewhat skewed sample of these beliefs and practices.

A good starting point for the study of Irish folklore is the book which has become the very bible of Irish folklore studies, Seán Ó Súilleabháin's *Handbook of Irish folklore*.[4] Ó Súilleabháin's book is a practical guide. It is intended to help the folklorist to ask the right questions and to raise correct issues with informants as he sits in a farmhouse or cottage, collecting information. Ó Súilleabháin does not in fact guide collectors entirely towards 'beliefs'. His check-list includes topics such as practical farming techniques, patterns of rural and urban settlement, care and management of livestock, blacksmithing, sports and pastimes and countless others, many of which are firmly rooted in the common sense practice of everyday life. On closer examination, however, we discover that his seeming preoccupation with the everyday is, nevertheless, slightly eccentric.

In particular, Ó Súilleabháin places an emphasis upon the continuity of contemporary belief and practice with the past, and its reliance upon tradition. This emphasis has a strange effect. It ensures that the topics he recommends for study are those which are rather peripheral to the concerns of the informants themselves. One cannot even attribute all the skewing of the sampling to the idea of continuity. When Ó Súilleabháin refers to religious belief, for example, he directs attention to the fasting and prayers before and after the Mass and to accounts of the Holy Communion species being lost.[5] He does not deal directly with the Mass which is at the heart of the Catholic faith.

This preoccupation with the peripheral is one that is found in the work of many folklorists. The main journal of Irish folklore is *Béaloideas*, and many of its articles focus upon matters which are extraordinarily marginal to the beliefs and practices of everyday life. Often the beliefs examined are those which contradict the common sense of ordinary people. Matters which are at the centre of life, the economy, politics, the family, religion, are mostly ignored.

Folklore exists as a special category of popular thought largely because it is a form of knowledge which is at the edge of the everyday concerns of the people who espouse it. When contrasted with other more dominant or more prevalent forms of knowledge, folklore can be considered as an alternative or residual form.[6] As such it is sometimes, though not always, subversive of both science and common sense. To an extent too it is subversive of more orthodox forms of religion. However, it shares with much religion a concern for that which cannot be contradicted by argument or by evidence.

Occasionally, anthropologists have suggested that not every religion is constituted by belief.[7] Tooker has argued, for example, that, for many peoples, religion is more a matter of allegiance to gods and to social groups, with little or no element of 'belief' in religious doctrines.[8] Few religions in the world have a creed. The implication of these studies is that christianity is unusual in that membership of the religious group, depends on a willingness to believe certain doctrines or propositions. The suggestion here is that while both orthodox and folk beliefs found in Ireland involve assenting to particular propositions, the idea of belief is rather more complicated than this. Also involved is the notion of trust. While belief may include, to some extent, intellectual assent, it also embraces interpersonal trust. Since trust is an essential element in maintaining allegiances, the gulf between christianity and other 'non believing' religions may, therefore, not be so great as these anthropologists think.

This chapter does not shrink from the emphasis found more generally in Irish folklore studies on peripheral beliefs and practices. Indeed, it concentrates entirely on matters of belief and especially on those elements within folklore which contrast with the norms of science and of common sense. The aim here is to explore the curious quality of much folkloric belief, using certain beliefs found in county Down. The argument focuses particularly upon narratives about fairies and ghosts, and the practice of making 'cures'.

Fairy and ghost belief in county Down

There have been no significant published studies of the folklore of county Down. Collections of folkloric materials exist, however, in both the Department of Irish Folklore, University College Dublin and in the Ulster Folk and Transport Museum, where there are major archives. The archive at University College has its origin in the impulse, after independence, to create a repository of national culture, and much of this material, Ireland-wide, was collected in the Irish language. The sound archives of the Ulster Folk and Transport Museum began in the 1960s and the pace of collection increased in the 1970s. Although there are undoubtedly regional variations, an impressionistic investigation of these sources as they relate to county Down does not reveal anything in the general spirit of the county's folklore which differentiates it sharply from that of other parts of Ireland. There are materials on ghosts and fairies and on banshees and seasonal customs, as well as information which might more properly be described as oral history.

There are, of course, many kinds of narrative found in county Down as elsewhere, but much of it is beyond the scope of the present chapter. One common form of narrative is the joke. Jokes have always been common, and the stories which are nowadays told as part of the modern storytelling revival usually take the form of a joke. This chapter concentrates on that non-joking form of narrative which folklorists call 'märchen', and especially upon stories of ghosts and of fairies. In this kind of narrative, there is a strong element of non-rationality, on belief in that for which there is little or no evidence. This emphasis leads eventually away from the idea of belief as an intellectual assent to certain propositions and towards the realm of faith, where belief has within it a major component of interpersonal trust.

The basis for this discussion has been well established by Ballard.[9] This is the idea that such stories, however strange or unlikely, are told as 'true' stories. The narrator invites the listener to believe that the events told in the story did in fact take place. Ballard has shown that nearly all fairy and ghost stories are presented as though they were true. I want to suggest further that this is not, however, accidental. It is often the apparent truthfulness of the incident described, that gives the *genre* its charisma or point.

Fairy stories, differ, for example, from the wholly fictional joke, 'there was this man ...'. In the joke, the point of the joke lies in some form of surprise, occurring in the punch-line. The surprise may be in the unusual events described in the narrative, or (as in puns) in the words themselves, or, as in many dirty jokes, in the transgression of some conversational norm. Often, the joke is rather like a conjuring trick. The observer is led to believe that he understands what is going on, interpreting the events described in one framework. Then suddenly, by surprise, his understanding of the situation changes and he finds he did not comprehend it at all.

In the fairy or ghost story, the nature of the narrative is quite different. Here the tension in the story lies in whether the unlikely events described should be believed or not. A punch line – i.e. the surprising turn of events at the end of the story – is not necessary. What is necessary, however, is that the story be told as though it were true, or as though somebody, for example, the person who originally told the story, believed it to be true. If there is no tension between belief and unbelief in the fairy or ghost story, then the story loses its force. It may have to be rescued by being turned into some other *genre*. It may have to be turned into a joke by giving it a punch line.

The non-rationality of fairy and ghost narrative is most obvious in the simplest of stories. In Portaferry, for example, a schoolchild told me of a man who was playing cards with his grandfather. During the game, the grandfather noticed that the other card player had a cloven hoof (and was, therefore, the devil).[10] Lurking in this story is perhaps, as a moral sub-text, a puritanical warning against the playing of cards. Its narrative structure, however, its dynamic, its point, is constituted by the tension between two elements. First, there is the fact that, by the criteria of common-sense rationality, the story cannot be true. But second, the story was first told as a first hand experience to a child by his grandfather. We must therefore take the story as having been intended as an account of true events. At the heart of the narrative, therefore, is the question of whether it ought to be believed. But the question of belief turns into one of trust. Ballard draws attention to a common word used in this context. We want to know if the man is lying.[11] Would a grandfather *really* deceive his grandson? Is the grandfather, we wonder, to be trusted?

A friend from Killydressy in the Ards told me a typical ghost story. He told of an acquaintance who saw a light as he walked along the road from Six Roads to Rubane. The ghost was one of Nancy Clint, a woman who once owned a shop there. She haunts the place and sometimes she jumps out at the cars.[12] Here again, there is the same tension. The story cannot, by normal standards of reason, be true, but the story was told to my friend as a first hand experience. The question of whether to believe the story, therefore, transforms itself. No longer is it merely a question of intellectual assent to some matter of fact. What is also at issue is whether my friend's acquaintance (and, therefore, my friend) is to be trusted.

Another informant, a retired labourer, formerly of Kearney village on the Ards, full of stories and a writer of occasional poems, told me of the fairies:

I was working at Cyril Lord's factory at the time, and two men ... I'd say one was maybe sixty and the other one might have been fifty-eight, but (it was) wonderful how serious they were, mind you.

I'd more or less gone down the toilets to have a smoke, you know, and I was just standing, with the door ajar a wee bit, having a smoke. And these two boys came in, two men, aged men. And they stared talking about fairies, aye, a big thorn bush that was growing away about half a mile off the factory.

And one of the boys says to the other (and I was taking the whole thing as a joke. I was laughing, but I didn't let them see me). And he said, "Do you see that? Do you see that bush up there boy?" he says to the other fellow. "Aye," he says, "that's a fairy bush. That's a fairy bush." .... So the one started to tell the tale, and I can tell the tale effectively, I think.

He says, "I worked the building site", he says, "thirty five years ago, and", he says, "there was a fairy – a tree – just the same as that there, one lone thorn tree and there weren't another within, well", he says, "a mile of it, over a mile of it. It was sitting there on its own".

"And the contractor came", he says "And, of course, he says that this whole site has to be levelled for these new houses to go on. And", he says, "I know the man well that was asked to go and cut the thorn down, and he wouldn't do it".

"Now", he says, "remember. I'm talking about the days", he says, "when you'd have done anything to hold your job.... This fellow wouldn't go to cut it... And none of them {would} go".

"But", he says, "there was a young boy", he says, "he was about twenty-one or twenty-two years of age, and I can remember it because – I can even see him", he says, "tonight, a big strong young man", he says, "and he had black curly hair. A 'terror of the devil' sort of type, you know.

Oh, he would knock the thorn over. He wasn't afeared of fairies, you know. So he went out and he took a saw with him, and he sawed the tree down and these other boys looked on and, 'the hell,' he says, 'that bush has to come down. Somebody's got to take it down'".

"Aha", he says, "You done wrong. You shouldn't have taken that down"....

"And", he says, "it's as true as I'm standing, as soon as he emerged from the thorn at all, all of a sudden", he says, "that young fellow that cut down the thorn – nothing wrong with him, but he couldn't go on to do a day's work for the rest of the day".

"Well the next morning he came in. Now", he says, "this is just the way it was, and that's the truth. I was one of the boys that witnessed it". (And that boy was actually serious. Although I, I didn't swallow it you know.) He says, "The young man came walking in the next morning, and they were all talking at the hut ready (for the boss hadn't come in) to start the work, you see, and he's coming down the road, and", he said, "he walked forward", he says, "(and I) just stood speechless", he says, "looking at him. He's black curly hair. And there wasn't a hair on his head that wasn't as white as snow. A head of white coloured hair. And," he said, "it wasn't grey. It was white".

And he turns round to this boy and he says, "What happened to your hair overnight", he says. Or "God What did you do"?

"I done nothing", he says, and he was a perplexing sort of boy with it.

And the old boy says, "Well, I'll tell you", he says, "you cut down the fairy thorn".

And that was the tale they're telling: that he's a black curly hair one day and the next day, after they cut the thorn down, his hair was just a mass of white curls where they were black.[13]

The same man told me too of how he came across some fairy pipes near to Kearney.

I remember ... that very old woman telling me. Mrs Donnan sent me and another fellow round. "Go to the fairy bush and you'll dig up clay pipes". Well, you know, we were only ten years old. You know, we were silly enough to go, which I can remember so vividly clear in my memory.

And we went, and we dug at the bottom of this thorn bush. A big thorn it was. And we got several small pipes. Like, I've saw them since, you know, but I don't think they were manufacturing them in them days. Well, it was just about the size of the joint of my finger, and the shanks {stems} on all on them. About half a dozen of them.

And we ... thought the fairies, for that was a fairy bush. But then, when I thought back, when I got older where did they come from, these pipes? Or had it been an old custom to bury the pipes and make somebody like me think they were fairy pipes? I don't know.[14]

His story was later corroborated by a neighbour.

Well we used to go along to the fairy bush ... There was a stile there. There was a stile that comes right across the fields right to the top on Dooey Hill there. And they called that the Piper stile. And it was the next stile into the next field. You turn right, and there was a wee bush. I mind when we were small, we used to go in and scrape the soil away and we got the wee pipes – wee small pipes ... And the bush is there yet.[15]

Another man, more sceptical, said that he thought these pipes were used by children to smoke the herb coltsfoot. Coltsfoot (*Tussilago farfara*) is a small plant with yellow flowers used sometimes as an ingredient in commercially-made herbal tobacco. He said that one place where such pipes were found was in a spot where children used to walk to school. He said, with a smile, that it was 'like opium'.[16] Even this attempt to rationalize and discount the story heightens an element common to all the stories. In all of them, a central feature is that the events are in doubt. By the standards of scientific or common sense knowledge, the events could not possibly have taken place.

We are not speaking here of skilful storytelling (though some of my informants were entertaining). Again it is useful to contrast these stories with the joke. In the joke, as in conjuring, there is an element of surprise. The surprise comes in part from the nature of the tale, and in part from the skill of the performer. The emphasis on skilful performance and verbal dexterity is also absent from the fairy or the ghost story. It was suggested above that folkloric kinds of knowledge or 'belief' are often founded in trust. The fairy or ghost story depends upon the story seeming to be truthfully told. At the very least, the storyteller will look to the authority of the person from whom he first heard it (or from whom that person first heard it). In contrast to the joke or the conjuring trick, a lack of skill in the performer can actually enhance the power of the fairy or ghost story. My poetic informant from Kearney once spoke of a man who told him he had seen a fairy. The man, he said, was 'a harmless sort of a man who would not tell a lie'. Unlike the joke, the authenticity of the tale is increased and not diminished by this lack of skill. This is because the element of truth so vital to the fairy story is entwined with the element of trust. These stories are only successful when at least somebody seems to believe them to be true. And this then requires that the listener must decide whether to put his trust in the narration.

County Down cures

The denial of the importance of skill and knowledge, the emphasis on non-reason and the subversion of rationality, and finally the emphasis on trust is even more apparent in matters of the cure. But there is another element here. This is the similarity with religion. With the cure, the beliefs in question are again not merely forms of propositional knowledge. When we say we believe in a cure, we are saying that we are prepared to put our trust in it. This may imply that we will put our trust in the traditional knowledge of the other person. It may imply that we trust in the traditional knowledge of our own community. Frequently, however, with the cure, we must also put our trust in God. The cure, therefore, dramatizes a faith in a relationship either to another person or to the divine. Belief in a cure is not merely a belief in an impersonal technology.

Cures are a practical activity, but there are also narratives about the practice. The narrative generally tells the tale of how a little man or woman with his non-rational practices can do what the doctor cannot. He or she can cure an illness 'when the doctors couldn't do anything for it'. First let me speak of the practice, by beginning with an anecdote of my own.

In 1978, it so happened that I had a torn cartilage in my right knee. For some time, whenever I walked along, my knee would give a sickening 'crack'! It would thus become painful and misshapen so that I could not walk until I had paused to push the joint back into shape.

Then, I found myself in the home of an elderly couple near Hilltown in the Mourne Mountains. Someone had told me that the old gentleman had a cure for the sprain. Seizing my opportunity, I thought it might be interesting to get myself the cure for my sprained knee.

The old man asked me if I were a Catholic or a Protestant. This was important, he said, it affected the manner in which the cure was performed. I replied that I was 'brought up in the Church of England'. He then knelt down on the flags in the kitchen, asked me to roll up the leg of my trouser and he began his cure.

First, he blessed himself. Then he ran his hands over my knee from top to bottom, stroking it. With his thumb, he made a small sign of the cross on the top right (his top left) of my knee. He made a second cross below it on the same side of my knee, and a third cross was placed below that. He then went on to make a set of three crosses down the centre of my knee. And then he made yet another set of three crosses down the left side of the same knee. While his hands were not busy making the signs of the cross, he ran his right hand over my knee. When he had completed the crosses on my knee, he put some crosses on the floor. All this time, he prayed visibly but not audibly.

Abruptly, he looked up and explained that he would do the whole thing three times, Because, he said, I lived so far away, this would be easier for me. In normal circumstances, I would have to return on three consecutive days, or in the morning, afternoon and evening. It would save me a lot of bother if he did it all in the one go.

When he had completed his prayers and the crosses on my knee, he blessed himself, climbed off his knees and stood up. He explained that the cure might take perhaps two weeks to work. It might even seem for a time to get worse. As it healed, it might give me pain, particularly at night.[17]

This is, in many ways, a typical cure found in county Down but also elsewhere in Ireland. The essence of the cure is a technique, usually, as here, a prayer, which the healer has learned from somebody else. The technique is secret and its transmission is carefully restricted. Here, as often happens, the cure must be passed from a woman to a man or from a man to a woman.

Many cures are similar to this. I met a man in Leitrim near Hilltown who had a cure for the heart. His cure was a secret prayer. It had the additional feature that the sick person had to place a cup of oaten meal against his or her chest to test whether the cure had been successful. If it had been successful, then a depression or hole appeared in the oaten meal in the cup. If, on the other hand no depression appeared then the cure would have been unsuccessful. I was told locally of a man who went to get this cure, and for whom the oatmeal failed to move in the necessary manner. He died of heart failure some short time later.[18]

Cures for ringworm are common enough. One man had a black, rather evil smelling ointment consisting of three sorts of fat which he applied to the ringworm. He instructed his patients to leave it on for a week before washing it off.[19] Another man, living near to Kilkeel, also had an ointment. He told me that ringworm was highly infectious. It can lie, he said, in ditches for up to seven years. You can also catch it from money. Whole housing estates can get it. It seems to appear, he said, 'in the spring of the year and in the fall of the year, when the blood changes'. The man learned his cure from his mother and because the cure is so popular and because he is away such a lot being by trade a haulier, he has passed it on to his wife.[20]

I met a woman in Portavogie who had a cure for bleeding. She inherited it from a male relative and must pass it on to a male relative. As with the cure for the sprain, it is a 'religious' cure, consisting of a silent prayer. She can give this cure over the telephone. The sufferer must not even thank her for the cure. She had to forcefully prevent people from saying thank you. Often she had to put the phone down suddenly or slam the door because people find it difficult not to say thank you.[21]

A blacksmith near Annalong told me of how his grandfather was cured of excessive bleeding by similar means:

> The brother and I were building a house, building a shed ... It was a tin roof we were putting on. So this evening I had to go away, and he had to go away, so we just left it till tomorrow or next day. But my grandfather, he went out and, you see, ... we had this roof half tinned, and there was this loose rafter here, and he gets up on a ladder and puts his hand on the loose rafter, and the loose rafter comes down this way and his head takes the tin; splits him straight across here.
>
> Well ... the blood run from that couch ... out through that door and out through there. And the doctor had his head stitched and all, and couldn't get the blood stopped.
>
> This man came in. "Did you not get the cure of the stopping of the blood?"
>
> "No", my granny says, "no".
>
> He jumped on the bicycle. He was back in fifteen minutes and the blood was stopped ...
>
> Now two years ago, Mervyn Gordon got the horns taken off a bullock. And the bullock was lying in the field and the blood was running out of him ... And (an acquaintance) got on the phone and he rang a man in Portadown.
>
> And the man (on the other end of the phone) said, "that's all right"...
>
> Mervyn Gordon told me, he says "Would you believe that"?
>
> I said, "I can believe that, for it happened to my grandfather twenty-five years ago"...
>
> He stopped the blood over the phone![22]

Cures of this kind, which are the property of particular people, are usually secret. One woman, explained why she could not tell me the details of her cure for the sprain. She said that if she told me then I would be the one who could use it and that the cure would no longer work for her.[23]

Not everybody takes this view, however. The owner of a ringworm cure passed the cure on to his wife, while continuing to use it himself. He thought that sometimes if you 'broke' a cure (i.e. revealed the secret), then it would be the patient that suffered. The illness would return even worse than before. As he said this, he had in mind another cure he knew of for toothache. This cure consisted of a prayer written on a piece of paper which the sufferer had to carry with him on his person. Somebody he knew cured his toothache with this medicine, but, when he opened up the tied-up piece of paper, the toothache suddenly returned and he had to go immediately to the dentist, so great was the pain.[24]

Cures are administered sometimes to animals. One hears, for example, of individuals who can whisper into the ears of horses and heal them of stiffness of the joints.[25]

Not all cures are the outcome of particular techniques. Many are attached to particular types of people. First, and most common of all these types of person are those women whose maiden name is identical with their husband's surname, as, for example, when a Miss Jones marries a Mr Jones. (Some people also insist that there must be no blood relationship between the couple). Such a woman will usually have the cure of either jaundice or whooping cough. Second, a child whose parents have the same surname (whose mother, therefore, has a cure) will also have a cure. A girl will, in general, have the same cure as her mother. The son will usually have a cure for the inflammation known as erysipelas, also called 'wildfire' or 'the rose'. Third, posthumous sons (I met two posthumous sons in county Down, never daughters) have the cure of the mouth infection called thrush. Finally and famously, although I never met any who were native to county Down, seventh sons of seventh sons can cure any illness.

I encountered individuals with these kinds of cures in a single working-class street in Newry.[26] In all, though I met only four of the individuals in 1978, there were, then, five people with the cure in this street. They were almost, I thought, a group practice. One lady has the cure of whooping cough. When a child is brought to her suffering from whooping cough, she gives it bread, butter and sugar. Her maiden name was the same as her married name which is why she has the cure. When she married, it was her sister-in-law who told her that she would have the cure, and that bread, butter and sugar is what she should give the children. The cure should be repeated three times. On the day of my visit, she was sending, through the post, the last instalment of her cure to a man in Lurgan, a bank manager, who is her daughter's boss. This lady has a relative in the same street who also has the cure for whooping cough, by virtue of being married to a man with the same surname. She too gives her patients, bread, butter and sugar.

Living next door to the first lady is a man who has a cure of the mouth infection called thrush. This ailment causes blisters to appear in the mouth. He has this cure because he is a posthumous son – his father was dead when he was born. He has been practising the cure from as early as he can remember, perhaps since he was three years old. His cure takes the form of giving a cup of tea to his patients. Later, I was told that some posthumous sons cure the thrush by breathing into their patients' mouths.

In the same street, I found an eighteen year old girl who cured bad backs. In a similar way to the man who could cure thrush, she has been curing bad backs since she was a very small baby. To effect the cure, she places her feet upon the sufferer's bad back. The reason she has this cure is that she is a seventh daughter. I have not heard elsewhere of seventh daughters having a cure and the belief is no doubt related to the widely known idea that cures can be effected by seventh sons of seventh sons.

In Portaferry lives a lady whose parents had the same surname. Like her mother, this woman has the cure for jaundice. She gives bread or a biscuit to sufferers. Her brother has a cure for erysipelas. This he cures by bathing the affected part in tap water.[27]

Sometimes the remedy is quite simple. In other cases it is more complicated. My friend who came from the village of Kearney in the Ards, told me of how someone cured his jaundice:

> I myself was cured of jaundice, so like I've no doubts. That's one thing I don't intend saying, "Well I have my doubts about it". I've no doubts about it, because I went to the doctor. I was really, real bad, so I was, but I told him only once, just once. I wasn't eating one bite. Oh, I was awful sick of it, for a fortnight maybe. I couldn't even take a sup of milk, a drink of milk. I couldn't even take a drink of water. And I was the colour of an orange. And I went to her (the woman with the cure) and she said, "Willie dear, you've got it bad". And the doctor was giving me this and giving me that in the end till I wasn't getting anywhere with it. They were going to send me to the hospital. I went into this old woman away down the road house in Ballygelagh. And I'd heard tell she had the cure of the jaundice and I went in till her and I came home. I felt that much better the next day, (in) three days time, I was back at my work. The whites of my eyes was yellow as soon as I went and the whites of my eyes started getting white again. Oh I was cured of the jaundice! She had the cure for it....
>
> Now I'm a non-believing – I tell myself – I like the proof of a thing. But she had a one wee piece of bread, lovely home-baked bread, you know this home-baked country soda bread...
>
> "One wee piece", she says, "Willie, take that at dead hour of midnight. No not a minute after. Take it at twelve o'clock", she says. "Put it in your mouth. Chew it. Swallow it. Forget about it".

The same man also told me of the same woman's cure for erysipelas.

> She cured it with bog water. She would have taked you down there and she would have bathed whatever you had maybe in your jaw or in your leg or your arm where you'd got it. You've got to go to the bog twelve o'clock either twelve in the day or twelve in the night for bog water out of the drain, boggy, muddy water.
>
> She'd wait until the water showered down to the bottom of that in the dish and she would have said to you, "Lean over that dish dearie. Lean over it. Do you see your face in that? No? Well in a long while when you look – can you see your own face in –"
>
> "Aye I see my face in it".
>
> "Now, you see, the water all settled down". The water became clear and you could see your face, reflection. And she'd start bathing your face with that bog water with just a rag just, not sponge, just a piece of rag.
>
> I mind I took a boy down to get a cure. She said, "Oh no. Don't dry it. "No", she said, "don't dry it". He went to dry it off with his wrist.
>
> "Oh don't dry it", she said. "Don't dry it. Never dry it. Let it dry itself".
>
> It wasn't a very long time drying before the heat was on it, a tremendous heating and flame, you know. Oh, it hurt that much! And that boy came up, and he was back he had to go at twelve o'clock the next day.[28]

Yet other cures do not really belong to anybody at all. In Warrenpoint, I was told of several such cures. The swellings of mumps should be rubbed with red flannel; a stye should be rubbed with a gold ring; or else it should be jabbed nine times with a rose thorn.[29] In the Ards, someone told me how his grandmother cured a stye by sticking a gooseberry jag into it nine times and throwing the last one over the shoulder.[30]

A secretary in the Ulster Folk and Transport Museum, told me of several other cures. Hives, she said, were caused by the blood becoming 'fired' and this in turn was caused by eating too many oranges or other citrus fruit, or by eating duck's eggs. She thought a poultice of damp baking soda, or camomile lotion or docken leaves could cure hives. Docken leaves, she said, were also a cure for nettle stings. And one can cure a headache by standing on one's head. She said too she could remember syrup of figs and castor oil being 'poured into her' when she was a child.[31]

Occasionally, the cures which belong to particular people are nevertheless not secret. One man in the Mournes showed me his cure for warts. To make the cure, he takes a piece of cotton and ties it in a loop. He then slips the loop over the wart as though to tighten the knot over the wart. As the knot tightens, he allows the wart to slip off the knot. The knot is then pulled tight and it is taken away and buried in the garden.[32]

And finally, there are holy wells. The one I am most familiar with is St. Cooey's wells on the Ards peninsula. These wells are associated with a local saint and what is supposed to be the ruin of his hermitage. The well has been tidied up and transformed into an attractive shrine by the local Catholic parish and it now receives many visitors. There, spring water feeding into a stream forms itself into some small rock pools allowing those who wish to wash in the water or use it to drink. The man who first showed me the wells likened them to the waters at Lourdes. There, as a younger man, he had helped the infirm to make use of the water. He said that it was your faith that cured you, and that if you believed in something enough, it would work for you.[33]

There is in all of this a sense that the cure is available when the doctors let you down. Certainly, as I became interested in cures, I found myself approached by many people with chronic or terminal illnesses who needed cures. Many clung to the hope that 'doctors' or 'the medical profession' might not know everything there was to know about healing. And behind this was also an idea that in these residual forms of knowledge, lay truths that the medical and other authorities resisted. For example, there was a cure for skin cancer in the Mourne Mountains. It consisted of a plaster containing some herbal ingredients, including, I understand, some dangerous drugs, which 'drew out the cancer by the root'. Here, the healer fell foul of the law. One is not, of course, allowed to administer dangerous drugs without proper authority. Some detectives from Newry, therefore, came to his house and took away everything connected with the cure.

When I spoke to the owner of this cure, his main complaint was that 'collar and tie men' or 'educated men', among whom he singled out doctors and vets (but among whom, I suspected, he might easily include me) prevented people from doing things themselves. A man could not use his cure because only the doctors knew how to cure people. A man could not castrate his own animals because only the vet knew how to do that. And they charged a fat fee for doing it.[34]

This complaint against orthodox medicine is found quite generally among those who heal. One man in Rostrevor told me how for many years he kept a billy goat to ward off abortion (brucellosis) in cattle. Every year, from November onwards, the goat would go into the rutting season. It would start to drink its own urine, and in no time would smell abominably, apparently to attract female goats. My informant told me that this powerful smell would communicate itself to the soil and it kept the cattle free of disease for a whole year. The smell would still be in the soil until the next November when the rutting season began again. He no longer kept a he-goat, he said, but he did still have the leather strap which he had used to tether it. The odd thing was, he said, that during the rutting season, the strap always began to smell. Like the man with the cure for cancer, he was annoyed at the attitude of the authorities. He had written to an agricultural research establishment to tell them about the effect of billy goats on cattle disease. Apparently, they were not very impressed. These people, he said with mild irony, were experts and he was not. 'After all', he said 'I've only been working with animals for thirty years'.[35]

In all of this there is a strong element of the non-rational. If the treatment works, then the knowledge of its efficacy does not form part of any theory of the human body and its workings. This unofficial healing sharply contrasts with the official practices of doctors and hospitals, where medicinal practice is, at least in principle, enshrined in theories of the human body. In orthodox medical practice, the *ad hoc* treatments that do still exist will, it is hoped, one day be integrated into such theories. In contrast, the cure is almost a celebration of the *ad hoc* remedy. The seventh son, or the woman with the same surname as her husband has the cure for no good reason that anybody can articulate. The best that anyone can say is that the cure 'seems to work'. All that is required is that the patient believe.

Conclusion

This chapter has emphasized here the coincidence of the idea of belief with that of trust. The two concepts are, at first sight, quite different, but on closer examination, they merge. In this context, the idea of 'belief' is essentially one derived from religious practice, and here there is an essential ambiguity. Many churches have a creed which lists a whole series of rationally formulated propositions to which church members are supposed to give assent. In contrast, however, for many religious people, this aspect of belief is less important than one might expect.[36] For many people, the term 'belief' refers less to doctrinal propositions and more to trust. When a person says that one must 'believe in the healing power of God' in order to be saved, he is speaking as much of trust as of intellectual assent. Alternatively, his beliefs may also include the trust that they have, whether this is in the Bible, in the Church, in a priest or minister or in God.

Folkloric beliefs have the same kind of ambiguity. A person will say that he thinks a cure will work if the sick person believes that it will work. Such a belief does, of course, assent to matters of fact, but it is much closer to an act of trust. My argument has been, however, that this element of trust is a central element in much of what is called folklore. Folklore often tells of inexplicable events, events which could not happen. So when we hear of such events, we can only rely (or choose not to rely) on the good faith of the original narrator.

To an extent, however, fairy and ghost belief and the cure represent a symbolic act of 'rebellion'.[37] The rebellion in question is against the forms of everyday thought. Folk belief is opposed to the tyranny of orthodoxies and the tyranny of reason. The rebellion, we should note, is not a radical repudiation of common sense, reason and science in favour of non-reason and anti-science. Nevertheless, by espousing belief in fairies and ghosts and cures, or at least by playing with such ideas,[38] there arises the possibility of avoiding more dreary and threatening aspects of life conjured up by reason.

While fairies and ghosts do this in a rather abstract manner, cures touch on more vital issues. Sometimes, the scientific reasoning of doctors can sound like a sentence of death. In such a case, the phrase that one hears in stories of successful cures can offer the prospect – however remote – of healing. When 'the doctors can't do anything with' the ailment, the notion that there are alternate realities and alternate cures can be a beacon of hope. It is not uncommon for an individual to express scepticism of unofficial healing, and, then in the next breath, tell how he was himself cured.[39]

In a Bangor hotel, I interviewed the most famous healer in Ireland, Finbar Nolan. He is the seventh son of a seventh son, and, like many others who have the cure by virtue of being a particular type of person, he has been practising his cure from an early age. He is an exceedingly persuasive man, whose company I enjoyed. As our interview ended, he asked me whether I agreed that his form of healing might work. I hesitated to give a clear opinion, but he insisted on his question.

Finbar Nolan 'Well, listen, if you were sick, would you go to a healer? On the evidence that you've seen?'

Tony Buckley 'If I was very sick?'

Finbar Nolan 'Suppose a doctor said, "Listen, I can't do any more for you". From your experience of what you've seen?'

Tony Buckley 'I suppose it's one of those questions I've tended to put off ....

Finbar Nolan 'But would you go?'

Tony Buckley 'I might come and see you actually.'

Finbar Nolan 'Would you go and see any of the other people that you've spoken to?'

Tony Buckley 'It's difficult to say.'[40]

My equivocation shows how attractive alternative and residual ways of thinking can become when science, common sense and rationality fail. For most of the time, we find common sense realities useful and comforting. Sometimes, however, we are also pleased that other more residual realities might just possibly be found lurking behind a hedgerow.

References

1. R. E. Allen (ed.), *Concise Oxford dictionary of current English* (London, 1991).
2. These materials were collected on behalf of the Ulster Folk and Transport Museum and are lodged, in the form of tape recordings, transcripts and fieldnotes, in the Museum's archives.
3. S. Harrison, 'Ritual as intellectual property' in *Man* (new series), xxvii (1992), pp 225-44.
4. S. Ó Súilleabháin, *A handbook of Irish folklore* (Dublin, 1942).
5. Ibid., p. 151.
6. R. Williams, 'Culture' in D. McLelland, *Marx, the first 100 years* (London, 1983).
7. R. Needham, *Belief, language and experience* (Chicago, 1972); D. E. Tooker, 'Identity systems of Highland Burma: belief, Akha Zán, and a critique of interiorized notions of ethno-religious identity' in *Man* (new series), xxvii (1992), pp 799-819.
8. Tooker, 'Identity systems'.
9. L. M. Ballard 'Ulster oral narrative: the stress on authenticity' in *Ulster Folklife*, xxvi (1980), pp 35-40. See also L. M. Ballard, 'Tales of the troubles' in P. Smith (ed.), *Perspectives on contemporary legend* (Sheffield, 1982).
10. A. D. Buckley, Fieldnotes 1976-79, Ulster Folk and Transport Museum, p. 178.
11. Ballard, 'Ulster oral narrative', p. 37.
12. Fieldnotes, pp 272-3.
13. Tape C77.99, Field recordings 12, pp 86-7.
14. Tape C77.89, Field recordings 12, p. 19.
15. Tape C77.108, Field recordings 12, pp 183-4.
16. Fieldnotes, pp 75, 83.
17. Fieldnotes 1976-79, pp 250-52. To my surprise, my knee did, indeed, get better. As he predicted, for several days, my knee itched and felt uncomfortable. Thereafter, and for about a year, though I continued to feel a weakness in it, I had no recurrence of the dreadful 'crack', and I had no more need to push my knee back into shape. Then, about a year later, and with no warning, I bent over to pick up something from the floor. My knee collapsed and I was rendered completely immobile. In considerable pain I was driven to the hospital, where it took an operation to make it better.
18. Fieldnotes, pp 254-5; see also tape C77.10.
19. Fieldnotes, p. 263.
20. Fieldnotes, pp 264-5; see also tape C78.17.
21. Fieldnotes, pp 274-5; see also tape C78.32.
22. Tape C78.20.

23. Fieldnotes, p. 271.
24. Fieldnotes, pp 264-5; see also tape C78.17.
25. Fieldnotes, p. 253.
26. Fieldnotes, pp 285-8.
27. Fieldnotes, pp 273-4; see also tapes C78.31 and C78.32.
28. Tape C77.100; Field Recordings, pp 12, 114-6.
29. Fieldnotes, p. 246.
30. Fieldnotes, p. 232.
31. Fieldnotes, pp 261-2.
32. Fieldnotes, pp 278-9; see also tape C78.33. My informant practised the cure on a wart that I had on my own finger. The wart eventually did go, but sadly it was many years later.
33. Fieldnotes, pp 92 ff.
34. Fieldnotes, p. 265; see also tape C78.17.
35. Fieldnotes, pp 257-58; see also tapes C78.10 and C78.11.
36. A. D. Buckley and M. C. Kenney, *Negotiating identity: rhetoric and social drama in Northern Ireland* (Washington, 1995), chapters 7 and 8.
37. M. Gluckman, *Rituals of rebellion in south-east Africa* (Manchester, 1954).
38. Buckley and Kenney, *Negotiating identity*; see chapters 8-10 for a discussion of the idea of play.
39. Fieldnotes, pp 252-53.
40. Tape R84.7.

Plate 20.1   Rippling flax, Dromara (Ulster Museum, W05/43/5).

Chapter 21

RURAL PATHS OF CAPITALIST DEVELOPMENT: CLASS FORMATION, PATERNALISM AND GENDER IN COUNTY DOWN'S LINEN INDUSTRY

MARILYN COHEN

For approximately two centuries, linen yarn and cloth were produced in great abundance in the Upper Bann Valley in county Down, during which time the industry dominated the economy of the county, as it did in much of east Ulster. This chapter will focus on the period between 1700-1900 when capitalist relations of production became dominant in all branches of linen production. Such relations are characterised by a class of producers or proletariat who are dependent upon a capitalist class who owns privately the strategic resources necessary for the workers' survival. Working class survival depends upon their ability to exchange their capacity to work for wages. The specific paths of capitalist development in each process are analysed, using particular firms located in the county as typical examples.

Several points will frame the analysis. First, capitalist development in county Down's linen industry was linked to political and economic processes beyond its boundaries at the regional, national and international level. Second, there was no simple linear process of capitalist development with rates and paths of class formation and mechanisation diverging along sub-regional, occupational and gender lines. Third, uneven capitalist development requires analysis of regionally specific conditions in which the multiplication of small as well as large units of capital can occur. These conditions are affected by class and gender relations at both ends of the social pyramid and by the availability of labour and sources of power. The specific challenges to securing both faced by early Victorian linen capitalists in rural industrial regions of county Down were distinct from those in urban Belfast, and resulted in linen-dominated villages and towns bearing the heavy imprint of paternalism. Throughout, I will emphasise the specific 'connections between and among structures, processes of change, and human action' which together sustained the growth and dominance of linen.[1]

The eighteenth-century linen industry in Down, 1700-1825

> To the north of these (Mourne) mountains, and on the Western side of it, comprehending Hillsboro', Banbridge, Moyallon and round towards Newry, the land is in a high state of cultivation, and inhabited by a middle class of opulent manufacturers, whose appearance and condition would do credit to any country in Europe ... The whole tract is embellished with plantations; and whether owing to the wealth created by the linen manufacture, or the trade carried on at Belfast and Newry, everything exhibits evident signs of increased population and industry. The banks of the rivers Bann and Lagan are covered with Bleach fields, and present that cheerful pleasing scenery which characterises a manufacturing country and excites in the mind an idea of improved civilisation.[2]

By the time of Edward Wakefield's enthusiastic account in 1812, the linen industry in county Down had been flourishing for nearly a century. Its expansion had been dependent upon deliberate encouragement by the English state which granted Irish linen duty-free access to English markets. Linen from Ireland and Scotland largely supplanted continental suppliers stimulating the production by Irish weavers of broader cloth suitable for export.[3]

Another English policy which helped lay the foundation for the linen industry in Ulster was the Cromwellian Settlement, which stimulated increased immigration from Britain. Immigrants from central and southern Scotland settled in north Ulster, while those from northern England settled in mid-Ulster, especially in the Lagan Valley and north Armagh. Here the linen industry developed along commercial lines based on the imported skills of the Northern English linen weavers, who originated from areas dominated by weaving and small-scale commercial agriculture. These weavers brought with them the ability to weave coarse cloth, such as was woven in north Yorkshire and parts of Cumberland, and fine linen which was woven in Manchester.[4] Since immigrants usually sponsored themselves, their capital was insufficient for large scale investment in land. Consequently, they sought to diversify agriculture with textile production.[5]

A significant group who emigrated from northern England during this period were the Quakers. They settled in small groups or as individual families on land leased to them as a result of negotiations between proprietors and the Society of Friends as a corporate body from the 1650s onward. The areas where they chose to settle were Lisburn, Lurgan, Magheralin, Banbridge and Moyallon. Scholars have shown that Quaker contributions to the formative stages of the linen industry came fifty years before the arrival of Protestant Huguenots led by Louis Crommelin.[6]

Class strategies to promote the linen industry: the elite bloc

The strategies of those seeking to profit from the linen industry thus built upon the foundation laid by the English state but also reflected their particular class interests. By the mid-eighteenth century, the fortunes of landlords, bleachers and drapers in county Down were interconnected and dependent upon the continued expansion of the linen industry. Within this tripartite 'elite' bloc, the class interests of landlords lay principally in increasing their ground rent and political influence, and in securing a stable tenantry. Consequently, large landlords in county Down, such as the marquis of Downshire, supported the linen industry by providing good market facilities, improving infrastructure, serving on the Linen Board, providing spinning wheels, and by granting favourable terms of tenure to bleachers, drapers and weavers which encouraged them to settle, populate and invest capital on the landlord's estate. The activities of small landlords, such as the Johnstons of Gilford, were less direct and therefore less well documented. Their contribution to the linen industry chiefly consisted in facilitating capital investment through granting favourable terms of tenure. Consequently, according to Dubourdieu, by the end of the eighteenth century most of the land in county Down was held in fee simple or leased for long terms of lives and years renewable forever.[7]

Until the mid-eighteenth century, landlords were the most powerful group in this elite bloc for cultural and economic reasons. Land was the principal source of influence, respectability and status. The reason for the positive influence and encouragement of landlords in the promotion of the linen industry was that it provided the opportunity for enrichment through an increase in the value of their land. In the second half of the eighteenth century, land values soared (especially in areas located close to good market towns), and the small holdings demanded by an increasing population of linen producers brought increased rent revenues to landlords.

Low rent payments by large tenants ensured that the profits returned on capital investments in linen were not wholly absorbed by landlords. As a result, by the end of the eighteenth century, an 'energetic and independent middle class' emerged who were powerful enough to weaken the control of landlords over their estates.[8] An example are bleachers who benefited enormously from favourable tenure arrangements with landlords. Although the interests of landlords and bleachers could be in conflict over attempts to alter the physical environment to ensure sufficient water power, landlords usually encouraged bleachers' efforts to invest capital on their estates.[9]

Bleachers were the linen industry's first centralised capitalists. They invested substantial sums of money to provide waterpower, erect mills and mechanise phases of production. Which sources provided the initial capital required by bleachers? In addition to grants from the Linen Board, Crawford suggests that an important source of capital came from mortgaging property titles. Since land was the principal source of credibility, and social and financial status, it was the major security for raising loans. For example, John Nicholson, owner of a large bleach yard at Hall's Mill, mortgaged a variety of holdings and obtained at least £15,000, which he probably invested in the construction of a drying house, and for purchasing two large coppers, eight kieves, a wringing engine and cold press to develop the bleachgreen.[10]

By the early eighteenth century, the ten mile stretch along the Bann between Gilford and Banbridge had become renowned for its numerous bleachyards.[11] In north-west Down and bordering county Armagh, a large segment of this powerful and wealthy group of bleachers was comprised of Quakers. Quakers in this region were very active in the early history of Ireland's linen industry, helping to establish diaper and damask production in north Down and making major contributions to the bleaching process.[12] For example, in 1675, a Scottish Quaker named Alexander Christy came to the townland of Moyallon in Tullylish, acquiring it from landlord John Magill in 1685. Christy is thought to have introduced the linen industry to the Moyallon district.[13] Christy's five grandsons (fig. 19.1) were prominent in the bleaching of linen both in Scotland and Ireland. Two of his sons, James and Thomas, lived at Stramore and Moyallon respectively. By 1765, over one quarter of Moyallon's 404 acres was owned by the Christy family including part of the east bank of the Newry Canal and part of the new dam located there.[14]

Bleachers in county Down were not simply noteworthy for their number or wealth. Time had always been the principal problem in bleaching since whitening linen was a very lengthy process. In the early eighteenth century, machinery for washing, rubbing and finishing linen was perfected. Bleachers along the Upper Bann in county Down, including Thomas Christy, are credited with adapting woollen tuck mills for use as linen washmills. Thomas Christy is also credited with inventing the drying house where cloth was dried after starching and blueing, thus eliminating some of the time and risks involved in open-air drying.[15] Bleachers in county Down were among the first to make use of sulphuric acid or Vitriol which reduced the bleaching process

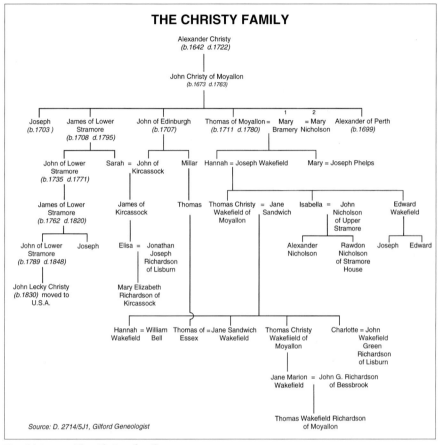

Fig. 21.1   The Christy family tree.

from seven or eight months to four.[16] James Christy, a man who was 'always alert to technical changes' and who had himself 'made many advances in the art', was a leading partner in the Moyallon vitriol company, set up in 1786 to meet the demand from local bleachers for this chemical.[17] Finally, by 1801, Thomas Christy Wakefield of Moyallon made use of a hydrometer to determine the strength of the alkali used in the bleaching process. Prior to this, testing the alkali's strength was left to the foreman bleacher who reached his conclusion 'by tasting the liquor', an uncertain method which could result in costly accidents.[18]

Bleachgreens became increasingly concentrated geographically and socially. By 1800, their construction required a capital outlay of £2-3,000.[19] By 1783, the twenty bleachgreens between Gilford and Banbridge bleached 90,000 pieces of linen annually, an average of 4,500 each rising, according to Thomas Christy Wakefield, to 8,000 pieces fifteen years later.[20] By this time, yard wide linen cost 8s and cambrics 7s yielding a profit of 8⅓ per cent.[21] Crawford suggests that by 1803, the sixty-six bleachgreens in county Down bleached 238,000 pieces of linen a year.[22] If we multiply Wakefield's 8,000 pieces by twenty, the bleachers between Gilford and Banbridge alone bleached a total of 160,000 pieces annually or 67 per cent of county Down's total capacity.[23]

In the early eighteenth century, drapers and bleachers were distinct categories, but as the century progressed they tended to merge as wealthy bleachers expanded their activities into the sphere of circulation. A heterogeneous group ranging in wealth from small draper/weavers to large draper/bleachers, drapers were dealers who purchased brown linens and sent them as white linen after bleaching to be sold either in Dublin's White Linen Hall or to English factors. Usually drapers held between ten and twenty acres of land and spent most of their time travelling, attending markets, and making trips to Dublin.[24] The activities of drapers first brought about the emergence, growth and regulation of the brown linen markets which replaced the older fairs. Drapers, who increasingly took over the marketing of linen, accumulated profits later to be invested in mills and factories.

Sider has called for a 'more historically dynamic perspective on merchant capital and the social worlds that have formed under its dominance'.[25] Such a perspective requires historically and regionally-specific class and gender analysis. It is argued elsewhere that small drapers or manufacturers, who were a petty capitalist class, are part of a full explanation of expanding capitalist relations of production in the Irish linen industry.[26] Emerging from the ranks of weavers, manufacturers purchased a few looms and a small stock of yarn, and provided these to a few (maybe as few as one or two) cottier weavers who worked together rather than separately. Since cottier weavers held only tiny parcels of land or 'cot-takes' under one acre, they were dependent, like other proletarians, upon wages to survive.

Following Gray, the accumulation of capital by small manufacturers and large merchants in the core linen weaving region in north-east Ulster is held to have been dependent upon the exploitation of female yarn spinners in the peripheral yarn counties in the west of Ireland.[27] Due to the low wages earned by spinners, small manufacturers were able to save on capital outlays for yarn. They thereby accumulated enough capital to increase the size of their holdings, set up cottier weavers in small cottages on tiny plots and provide raw materials (yarn) for their employees. These manufacturers were thus early putters-out who were no longer engaged in weaving themselves. Instead, like wealthier drapers, they took the cloth produced by their employees to brown linen markets and sold it, thus dominating their cottier employees at both the points of production and exchange. By 1800, manufacturers formed the majority of 'weavers' selling yarn and cloth in brown linen markets.[28]

These manufacturers, who did not have large reserves of liquid capital, nevertheless took risks to obtain profits. If the market turned down, their small capital, which was tied up in stocks of yarn, could be wiped out. This is what occurred after 1825 when higher priced handspun yarn could not compete with cheaper millspun yarn.[29] Manufacturers are significant because they are a regionally-specific example of producers evolving into merchants and capitalists, able to extract profits at both the points of production and exchange.[30] Draper/ bleachers are another example. Those drapers who operated purely in the circulation sphere extracted merchant's capital (buying cheap and selling dear) by paying producers of yarn and cloth low wages, since producers partly provided their own subsistence through farming small plots of land. However, to the extent that drapers large and small began to provide yarn for weavers, they began to exert dominance over the production process, thus decreasing the producer's control and valued independence.

Many such enterprising drapers dominated Banbridge market and were quick to realise the significance of changing the linen trade's organisation. Prior to 1825, they were aggressive in seeking to overcome trade barriers and the competition posed by British mill-spun yarn by extending the putting-out system.[31]

> Between Banbridge and Guilford some of the first manufacturers who invested large capital in the linen trade established themselves and here the great experiment of placing the linen trade of Ireland on a new foundation was tried.[32]

Banbridge provides a clear example of how eighteenth-century commercial urbanisation might reflect the unified interests of the local elite. Part of the explanation for Banbridge's growth from a small village in 1690 to one of the principal linen market towns by the early nineteenth century lies in the alteration made to its built environment to meet the commercial needs of linen drapers. As early as 1744, the town held 'some of the greatest Fairs for Linen Cloth ... five times a year, constantly attended by Factors from England'.[33] The town's expansion was greatly facilitated by the alterations after 1750. Its four principal streets were widened and its landlord, the earl of Hillsborough, encouraged building by granting leases at nominal rents. His heir, the 3rd marquis of Downshire, also stood to gain in terms of tolls and rents from encouraging trade at Banbridge, and built a market place in 1815 for meal and grain, a brown linen hall in 1817, and a market house for linen yarn and cloth in 1834.[34]

In 1817, James Corry, secretary of the Linen Board, described Banbridge as the largest linen market in county Down with annual sales of brown linen valued at £53,976. Although this figure was well below those for the markets at Armagh, Dungannon and Lisburn, it rivalled the longer established market at Lurgan and surpassed Newry (table 21.1).[35]

TABLE 21.1

Value of linens sold at various linen markets in county Down, 1816

Market	Weekly Sales (£ s d)	Annual Sales (£ s d)
Banbridge	1,038 0 0	53,976 0 0
Newry	922 0 0	47,944 0 0
Downpatrick	750 0 0	39,000 0 0
Kilkeel	400 0 0	20,800 0 0
Kircubbin	300 0 0	7,800 0 0
Rathfriland	66 0 0	3,432 0 0
Ballynahinch	17 0 0	884 0 0
Hillsborough	8 0 0	416 0 0

Source: F.W. Smith, *The Irish linen trade handbook,* p. 65.

Domestic producers of linen yarn and cloth

Shifting our attention to the producers of yarn and cloth, weavers in north-west county Down produced fine linen cloth such as cambric, lawn, linens, diaper, damask and chequers. Those who produced this cloth divided their time between agriculture on small plots of land and textile production. Rent was paid through the sale of yarn and cloth, and since weavers were not dependent on farming for their living, only small plots of land needed to be leased – if at high rents per acre – to each household. Small plots served both to keep wages down and to deter proletarianisation, or full dependence on wage labour, as did owning looms and spinning wheels. Producers were thereby able to retain considerable control over their work.

Although the distinction between men's work (weaving), and women's (spinning and winding) was rigid, household composition was flexible, and included itinerant and related spinners and apprentice weavers to extend its productive capacity.[36] By the early-nineteenth century, however, this rigid division of labour was beginning to 'soften'. McKernan has shown how the flying shuttle, introduced at the end of the eighteenth century, drew increasing numbers of females into weaving. She also draws an important connection between the expansion of the putting-out system, in which yarn was supplied to weavers, and the appearance of female weavers.[37] This insight is relevant to the region between Gilford and Banbridge where the putting-out system expanded prior to mill-based spinning.

The interdependence between land tenure practices, the linen industry, subdivision, subletting and population growth are well established. Contemporaries, such as Dubourdieu, stressed subletting of land to undertenants and the provision of a share to each child at marriage as the chief reason for the growth in the number of small farms in county Down.[38] In the late eighteenth century, Down experienced rapid population growth. According to Dubourdieu, the number of houses rose from 19,270 in 1751 to 38,351 in 1791, an increase of 4,817 houses every ten years.[39] The 1821 census, which included 1813 aggregate statistics, shows that the number of houses in the county rose to 53,310 in 1813 and to 62,425 in 1821. The population rose correspondingly from 287,290 in 1813 to 329,348 by 1821. With 544 square miles, and 598 inhabitants per square mile, an average of only 5⅘ acres was held per household. This population density was surpassed in Ireland only by counties Dublin, Louth, Armagh and Monaghan.[40]

The complex differentiation between categories of textile-producing households in county Down is also well documented. At the bottom of the social ladder were cottiers, a proletarianised group of part-time weavers or agricultural labourers, whose existence depended on 'a patch of land, a crudely built cabin, and sometimes supplies of yarn'.[41] Independent farmer/weavers ranked above cottiers in their standard of living due to their autonomy, which stemmed from their leasing larger five to ten acre plots of land and providing their own flax and yarn. Although these were the most numerous group of weavers in the eighteenth century, as a group they were not homogeneous: weavers of fine linen earned more than weavers of coarse linen.[42] Fine linen weavers, who were prevalent in north-west Down, had more varied diets and lived in stone houses, many of which had a kitchen, dairy, several small bedrooms, and a workshop 'remarkable for comfort and cleanliness'.[43]

Independent weavers were the 'core of the oral and literary cultures of the communities in which they lived'.[44] In many areas, including Banbridge, male weavers founded reading societies or clubs where books were purchased by subscription and shared, where poetry written by local 'bards' was supported, and where debates on political, economic, and religious issues flourished. The Banbridge Reading Society was founded in 1795 with a monthly subscription of one shilling, a total membership of 120, and a catalogue of 568 books.[45]

Such participation suggests that independent weavers earned enough for discretionary spending and exercised considerable control over the labour process. Indeed, independent weavers controlled the allocation and continuity of work tasks within their household, and often marketed their own webs. Household members generally produced yarn and cloth under the direction of the male head, while wives and other females provided the other domestic services. Weavers could relax and work at a slower pace just after market day and increase their pace as the next market day approached. Under pressure, weavers were known to work all night. They also worked hardest in the first half of the year. After June, when prices dropped, some worked in bleachyards or tended their plots before returning to the loom.[46] This independence was integral to the culture of the common people of north-east Ulster, and encroachments via the putting-out system were resisted.[47]

Although the men's high cultural and leisure pursuits depended upon the provision of essential services by women, we know little about the private forms of women's work culture at this time. Eighteenth-century women were responsible for domestic work and spun yarn only when they had 'spare' time. The rhythm of women's work was distinct from the men's and reflected the continuous nature of domestic tasks. Male public arenas for socialising such as book clubs, hunts or pubs were not open to women. In ways similar to handspinners from the Caux region in France, Irish spinners 'gathered to work not to relax'.[48] Wakefield's description of women's 'work' is blurred with 'amusements', suggesting a lack of distinction between work and leisure which was characteristic of precapitalist work generally. It also provides an historically and gender-specific example of task orientation.

> The women in the weaving districts are much accustomed to visiting each other, and these visits are called keating. A young female, with her spinning wheel on her head travels a considerable distance to the house of an acquaintance, where others are assembled, who spin, sing, and converse during the whole evening ...[49]

In sum, on the eve of the huge transformation to factory spinning which occurred after 1825, regions in north-west Down along the Bann Valley were 'economic nerve centers of proto-industry'.[50] In this region geographical, technical, organisational, and marketing resources were concentrated and 'major possibilities for capital accumulation' existed.[51] Accumulation of capital in small and large units by classes, ranging from small manufacturers to large drapers and bleachers, occurred. Although leasing land – however small – helped sustain the independence of producers, by the end of the eighteenth century weavers in the Banbridge vicinity were becoming proletarianised as they increasingly abandoned their holdings and concentrated solely on weaving. Thus, both linear models of capitalist development and 'mode of production' models based upon assumptions of 'natural economy' or simple reproduction among peasants cannot adequately explain early capitalist development in county Down. If we eliminate the theoretical possibility of accumulation among peasants they are rendered passive, only appearing as 'prey' rather than as active agents in their own right.[52] Henceforth, the development of a capitalist linen industry in Down was as much related to external technological imperatives emanating from England as internal forces associated with an emerging capitalist class structure.

The nineteenth-century linen industry in Down, 1825-1914

The process of transition from domestic production to factories was conditioned, according to Hudson, by a number of factors which differed from one industrial region to another. Such change depended on the degree of proletarianisation, the extent of agricultural involvement on the part of workers, the nature of the competitive response, the power and influence of merchant and landowning capital, and technological imperatives.[53] To this extensive list we may add cultural conceptions of gender since, 'gender is a pervasive symbolic system which inheres in all social relations, including economic relations ...'.[54]

The expansion of the domestic Irish linen industry depended on the exploitation of cheap female handspinners whose wages were kept low by their retaining small plots for food and flax. The first objective of machine flax spinners in the late 1780s was to displace the coarse yarns produced by handspinners. Fine yarn was safe for the moment, but after 1825, all but the finest handspinners were driven out of the market in Ireland and in the linen districts in Europe. Irish handspinners could only produce one bundle of yarn every four weeks as compared with four bundles per week per person in a spinning mill. Further, by the mid 1830s, one bundle of 100 leas yarn spun in a mill cost about 2s 4½d as compared with just under 4s 10d by a handspinner in her home. Consequently, handspinners were forced to sell their yarn far below cost to compete with mills resulting in wage reductions of up to 90 per cent between 1815 and 1836.[55]

Boyle has documented the rapid mechanisation of yarn spinning in Ireland after the abolition of legislation affecting the importation of

British and foreign yarns. By 1835, there were twenty-two spinning mills in Ireland and by 1845 these had increased to sixty. While mechanised spinning initially affected all linen producers, its effect in the long term was more regional. In the peripheral yarn-producing counties in the north and west of Ireland, rural industry collapsed. Mill-spinning concentrated the linen industry in the north-east, especially in the greater Belfast region. By 1835, at least ten of twenty-two flax spinning mills were within a twenty-two mile radius of Belfast. Outside Belfast, flax mills were heavily concentrated in counties Armagh and Down, and in south Antrim and east Tyrone.[56]

The core linen district in east Ulster was closer to the sources of the more easily woven mill-spun yarn.[57] In these regions, large numbers of women and children turned to handloom weaving as wages, status and independence in weaving declined. Another option for displaced handspinners in areas close to mills was to work as winders of yarn. In the parishes of Seapatrick and Tullylish, many women were employed as winders either for their husbands, putters out, or for the thread manufacturers setting up in the area at this time. The importance of winding as a source of employment for displaced spinners in Seapatrick was emphasised by the Rev James Davis in 1836:

> ... In this parish in which there is so much employment given to women and children in the winding of yarn, their earnings would be more than in many others; if women have no employment but the spinning of yarn they will not make more, on the average, than 2d or 2½d per day, and possibly their children nothing; a very middling winder of yarn will make 3½d per day, a good one 4d or 5d, when diligently employed all the time ...[58]

In north-west Down, where women were employed as winders, female proletarianisation, or dependence upon wage labour, revealed both the complexity and unevenness of the process. If employment in the new spinning mills was available, displaced spinners joined the ranks of the new industrial proletariat adjusting to new relations of production and working conditions. Where they worked as winders for putters-out, they were essentially proletarianised since they exchanged their labour for a wage. However, while they remained at home, they were not subject to factory-based working conditions and discipline. Winders, who were still part of a disintegrating domestic system, enabled manufacturers to squeeze additional profits from employees who partly absorbed the costs of sustaining themselves. Last, if women worked within the domestic system as winders for their husbands, who were, in turn, employed by putters-out, they were part of the process by which capitalist work relations were penetrating the production process, albeit indirectly.

Although industry blossomed in much of north-west Down after 1825, there were significant sub-regional differences. For example, a comparison can be made between the baronies of Lower Iveagh, where frenetic capitalist investment ensued, and Upper Iveagh, which did not industrialise. In 1836, labourers in Upper Iveagh interviewed by poor law commissioners voiced concern that their wives could not earn more than 1d per day at handspinning since the opening of the new spinning mill at Castlewellan. Like their husbands, who were once farmer/weavers, these women turned to agricultural pursuits such as selling eggs to supplement their household income.[59]

Whereas mill-based spinning radically affected the whole organisation of linen production, linen weaving remained unmechanised. Instead, what spread was the putting-out system. Men with capital such as bleachers and drapers bought mill-spun yarn from mills and employed weavers at an agreed price. Within fifteen years of the introduction of fine mill-spun yarn, the majority of Ulster's weavers were employed by manufacturers and many brown linen markets withered. It is not surprising that many weavers in county Down who were independent considered their circumstances to be much worse under the putting-out system. The words of the Rev. Davis mirrored the sentiments of weavers in his parish: 'The operatives in the linen trade are becoming more and more dependent, the money is leaving the hands of this useful class of men, and is accumulating, to an immense extent in the hands of their employers'.[60]

After 1825, the capital which had been accumulated by merchants, bleachers and drapers during the eighteenth century was invested in a variety of manufacturing establishments. The 1834 Ordnance Survey memoirs for the parishes of Tullylish and Seapatrick mention nineteen bleachgreens, four flax scutching mills, one spinning mill, one vitriol works, four corn mills and two flour mills along the Bann.[61] Only three years later in 1837, Samuel Lewis's description of Tullylish mentions a thread manufactory at Milltown which employed 170, a spinning mill at Coose employing 200, and a large spinning mill under construction at Gilford.[62]

The accumulation of capital by the county's entrepreneurs resulted in a concentration of wealth and power which was mobilised collectively and individually to alter the physical environment. For example, in 1836, the numerous mill owners along the Bann endeavoured to maintain and increase their profits by forming a joint stock company. Since the principal source of power was the Bann, members sought to supply their mills more effectively with water power. The Bann

Reservoir Act, passed in 1836, empowered these capitalists to raise the money required for building a reservoir by means of £50 shares, and allowed them to levy a rate not exceeding £10 per annum on each foot of occupied fall. Three reservoirs – Lough Island Reavy near Castlewellan, Deer's Meadow and Corbet Lough were authorised, although Deer's Meadow was abandoned.[63]

Early Victorian linen capitalists along the Bann

The challenge of millspinning was taken up early in north-west Down by several capitalists in the 1830s. The first spinning mill on the River Bann was built about 1834 at Hazelbank by Samuel Law, a bleacher. Law employed William Fairbairn to put up one of his iron breast-shot water wheels, which had first been used for driving beetling engines. The 1834 Ordnance Survey memoir describes Law's bleachgreen as having two large water wheels, one of which turned machinery for spinning linen yarn. The mill's machinery consisted of 3,000 mule spindles operated twelve hours a day, nine months a year by 143 females and forty-two males.[64]

Another example was William Hayes, who came to Banbridge in the late eighteenth century, taking over the Millmount bleachgreen owned by the McClelands as well as land at Edenderry.[65] William also acquired glebe land at Seapatrick where he established his third son Frederick W. Hayes. Frederick was a pioneer of both power spinning and weaving. In 1826, he was given a grant of £500 by the Linen Board for machine spinning fine yarn, probably by the older dry spinning method. By 1835, Frederick was also weaving linen and cotton union cloth on 100 powerlooms at Seapatrick, at a time when there were only a few hundred powerlooms in all of Ireland producing cotton fabric. Seapatrick was the first powerloom factory on the Bann, and perhaps the first in the Irish linen industry.[66]

For about ten years, Hayes concentrated on weaving union cloth, but ultimately turned to the manufacture of linen thread, a branch of the industry growing in importance in the Banbridge area. Hugh Dunbar was another early thread manufacturer. He was son of the linen draper Robert Dunbar, who manufactured linen thread at Huntley Glen. In 1824, Hugh Dunbar was listed in *Pigot's directory* as a thread manufacturer, but he was also a successful linen manufacturer. Acquainted with the trade since 1805, he employed 1,700 handlooms by 1839.[67]

Thread manufacture, like yarn spinning, was revolutionised by the wet spinning process. In 1834, the competition from mill-spun yarn compelled Hugh Dunbar to build his own spinning and twisting mill. Since Dunbar did not possess sufficient capital for such an undertaking, he formed a partnership in 1834 with W. A. Stewart of Edenderry, Banbridge. Dunbar chose Gilford for the site of his new spinning mill, where an established bleachgreen with considerable water power already existed.[68] After two short-lived partnerships between 1836 and 1839, Hugh Dunbar formed a lasting partnership with John Walsh McMaster of Armagh and James Dickson, another son of a linen bleacher and manufacturer. The yarn and thread mill was completed in November, 1841. In 1843 the firm divided into two, trading under the name of Dunbar McMaster & Co. for flax spinning and linen thread production and Dunbar Dickson & Co. for the manufacture of brown linen.[69]

The strategies of rural capitalists: employer paternalism

Rural industrial capitalists such as Hayes and Dunbar confronted challenges which were distinct from those in urban Belfast. Most of them were dependent upon water power, were further from ports, warehouses and sources of credit generally, and needed to attract and control a labour force. Mid-Victorian employer paternalism was a hegemonic solution which combined economic, political and cultural forms of domination to address both these labour recruitment challenges and the need for security by a 'green' or newly formed working class wholly dependent upon earning wages.[70] Numerous paternalistic employers built company towns and mill villages or hamlets in county Down.

One of Ireland's earliest and most significant company towns was Dunbarton at Gilford, built by Hugh Dunbar (plate 21.1). Dunbar's attempts to build a community at Dunbarton coincided with the demographic upheaval precipitated by industrialisation and compounded by the Great Famine. Prior to the opening of the new spinning mill in 1841, the population of Gilford was 643. In the decade between 1841 and 1851, the population exploded to 2,814. By 1846, Dunbar employed about 2,000 workers, making Dunbar McMaster & Co. the largest spinning mill in Ireland. In that year, factory inspector James Stewart noted the breadth of his paternalism:

> No expense is regarded that can promote the happiness or comfort of the workers. The medical attendant is there allowed a salary of £180 a year. A very superior school is attached to the factory, free of charge to the workers and their families with a library; the working hours are limited to 11 hours a day and no reduction in wages.[71]

The concentration of workers in factories and surrounding settlements rather than in dispersed cottages posed an immediate problem

Plate 21.1   Gilford, *ca*. 1831 and 1861 (Source: Six Inch Ordnance Survey Maps).

for those creating these built environments: how were workers to be housed in the right locations? Capitalists in county Down and elsewhere initially sought to resolve this problem by building rows of company-owned tenements close to the mill gates.[72] Hugh Dunbar began building houses for his workforce almost immediately after leasing the necessary land in the 1830s. He continued building them rapidly until 1862, and sporadically thereafter. These workers' houses were more typical of urban terraces than rural cottages, with many having no land and some with no rear access. The houses owned by Dunbar and his successors were inspected monthly, limewashed annually and repaired at the firm's expense.

Dunbar retained exclusive ownership of the workers' houses until his death in 1847. He also built a fever hospital, donated land on Castle Hill for the Roman Catholic Church and built a school which opened in 1846 with three separate infant, male and female departments.[73] Dunbar was succeeded by his partner, John Walsh McMaster, who exceeded his predecessor's paternalistic endeavours. McMaster's efforts between 1847-61 are especially noteworthy as Gilford's population peaked at 2,892 due to the contemporary Famine-induced demographic disruption. Although 200 houses were built between 1836 and 1862 at a cost of £10,000, supply did not meet demand. In the worst year, 1851, 466 households occupied 220 second class houses (the classification given to the vast majority of factory owned houses); 122 households lived in sixty-three third class houses; while forty-nine households were pressed into twenty-nine fourth class houses.[74]

This revival of social and economic paternalism in the mid-Victorian period looked backward to the patriarchal family, suggesting that the model for harmonious class relationships was that of father and child. Consequently, feminist scholars have stressed how gender distinctions were integral to this ideology, which built upon the reconstitution of older patriarchal relations characteristic of domestic workshops within the factory and its surrounding community.[75] Lown argues that textile mill owners, who were dependent upon female labour, had to reconcile this dependency with the widely-held norm that adult men should function as breadwinners supporting their wives and children. Employers attempted to address this contradiction partly through rigid occupational sex segregation and unequal wages.[76] With the one exception of doffing mistresses, who supervised young women and children, all supervisors and managerial positions in spinning mills, bleachgreens, and later, in powerloom weaving factories, were male. Furthermore, Victorian cultural assumptions about mechanical aptitude and strength associated these traits with masculinity determining that all skilled workers were male.

Such cultural assumptions regarding masculinity and femininity were, however, necessarily modified by the labour requirements of rural capitalists. Because men were less likely to find alternative sources of employment outside the linen industry in rural industrial regions, employers tended to hire more of them than did employers in urban Belfast. As table 21.2 shows, proportionately more adult males and fewer women over the age of eighteen were employed at Dunbar McMaster & Co. than in Belfast.

TABLE 21.2

Age and gender breakdown of workers at Dunbar McMaster & Co (1867)*, Belfast (1866)** and Ulster exclusive of Belfast (1886)**

Workers	Dunbar McMaster Co	Belfast	Ulster
Men	369 = 23.1%	853 = 13.8%	1939 = 18.3%
Lads	262 = 16.4%	576 = 9.3%	1660 = 15.7%
Boys	31 = 1.9%		
Total Males	662 = 41.4%	1429 = 23.1%	3599 = 34.0%
Women	541 = 33.9%	3661 = 59.1%	4689 = 44.3%
Women < 18 yrs	341 = 21.3%	1103 = 17.8%	2305 = 21.8%
Girls	54 = 3.4%		
Total Females	936 = 58.6%	4764 = 76.9%	6994 = 66.1%
Total Workers	**1598**	**6193**	**10593**

Source: *Paris universal exhibition, 1867; ***Returns of labour statistics from the Board of Trade, Industrial Relations: Wages,* IUP ser (1887-92), xx, p. 483.

For the next thirty years following the Great Famine, the linen industry along the Bann expanded rapidly, generating enormous wealth among capitalists. For example, the combined business of Dunbar McMaster & Co. and Dunbar Dickson & Co. 'flourished beyond measure ... and the firm made money in tubfulls.'[77] The firm added a bleachgreen in 1849 and built a warehouse in Belfast in 1856. The partners built or purchased large mansion houses, while the world famous threads produced by the workforce won awards at international exhibitions at home and abroad. During the 1860s, the linen industry boomed in response to the increased demand for linen cloth brought about by the 'cotton famine' – a sharp decline in supplies of raw cotton, itself the result of the American Civil War.

Evidence suggests that the McMaster's accumulation of great personal wealth did not temper their paternalism. Their long paternal arm extended deep into the community, affecting all aspects of life in

Gilford/Dunbarton. In the 1850s and 1860s, a local co-operative society was established together with a sick fund, to which the owners contributed £250 annually and workers £350, as well as a penny bank and a savings fund. The owners provided land for all the Christian denominations and made a substantial contribution to Gilford's new Church of Ireland church and Sunday school. Self improvement was encouraged through the provision of infant, day and evening schools, a Young Men's Mutual Improvement Society, a news room, library, public lecture room and a Temperance Society. Recreational activities included cricket, boating, handball, football clubs and gymnastics.[78]

Bleaching along the River Bann

Since bleachgreens were considerably smaller than spinning mills, they did not form the core of complex company towns such as Dunbarton. The settlements surrounding bleachgreens were villages and hamlets with company-owned housing and, occasionally, a shop or a school. Employers might have a sick fund for their employees and provide coal at a cost deducted from their wage. Typical of the county Down bleachgreen was Banford bleach works near Gilford (plate 21.2). Continuously owned by Quakers, Banford was built on the site of what was probably the oldest bleach mill on the Bann, owned originally by John Nicholson. By 1814, Nicholson's business had faltered and it was purchased the following year by a linen draper, Benjamin Haughton. Haughton was typical of bleacher/manufacturers who employed handloom weavers, thus profiting from control over production in both weaving and bleaching. Haughton subsequently invested in several bleaching and finishing mills in Tullylish.

Haughton's two sons, Thomas and Samuel, followed in their father's footsteps. In 1863, Benjamin and Thomas joined with Daniel Jaffe to form Banford bleach works. In 1883 John Edgar bought out Benjamin Houghton's interest and he and Thomas ran the business on the 177 acre site. Finally about 1890, Frederick Sinton bought the business and it remained in the Sinton family until it closed.[79]

During the company's peak years, between 1862 and 1872, most of the linens and union cloth it bleached came from Belfast, Manchester and London, although local linen manufacturers such as Dunbar Dickson & Co. were also suppliers. While the various greens along the Bann must have competed with one another to some extent, parliamentary and oral evidence suggests that they tended to specialise. For example, in the 1850s, Uprichard's bleachgreen at Springvale already specialised in diaper and damask, continuing thereafter to specialise in heavy linens such as damask and sheeting. In the 1850s, Banford was described as a 'general linen bleachers', bleaching cambric

Plate 21.2   Bleach green development in the Bann valley: Banford *ca*. 1831 and
1861 (Source: Six Inch Ordnance Survey Maps).

as well as other lighter and narrower types of linen. Banford also specialised in bleaching union cloth for its English customers. Both firms relied on similar techniques and retained the older open-air processing method. While this open-air method took longer, it preserved the strength and quality of the cloth more effectively.[80]

There was also variation in the size of the workforces employed in the bleachgreens along the Bann and in the stock of housing built by employers to accommodate them. In 1865, the partners of Banford bleach works owned only thirteen houses but they increased these to thirty-two by 1886. The Uprichards, owners of two bleachgreens, built more houses: ten in Knocknagore, fifteen at Mill Park, and twenty-two at Coose. The largest bleachgreen at Milltown, owned by the Smyths, formed the basis of a substantial village with a school and seventy-two houses in Drumnascamph and Lenaderg.[81]

In contrast to spinning mills, there was considerable similarity between patriarchal familial norms which stress a male breadwinner and the labour force requirements of bleachgreen owners. Unlike other branches of the linen industry, the workforce at bleachgreens was predominantly male, and fewer bleachers' wives worked outside the home. Such work required skill, strength and night shifts, all of which were considered to be masculine traits. In fact, we know from parliamentary evidence collected in the 1850s, that Haughton & Fennel at Banford and J. & W. Uprichard never employed substantial numbers of women, although firms bleaching cambric such as Banford tended to employ female labour.[82] In 1863 to 1865, a time of rapid growth, the wage books indicate only eight women were employed at Banford. In 1909, at a time of contraction, only twelve women were employed, ten of whom worked in the stockroom and two as markers.

Retention of the open-air bleaching method and rapid technological innovation during the nineteenth century in the bleaching industry slowed the interrelated processes of mechanisation, deskilling and feminisation which had occurred comparatively quickly in the spinning and weaving phases of production. Deskilling involves the breakdown of whole work processes and craft knowledge retained by workers as a result of mechanisation and the separation of planning (management) from execution (workers). This process has frequently been associated with increases in the number of female employees, loss of wages and status.[83] The early twentieth-century bleaching process bore a remarkable similarity to late eighteenth-century methods, despite an overall extension in the use of chemical bleaching agents which reduced the time linen was exposed to the atmosphere. As proletarians, bleachgreen workers were dependent upon wages and did not control their hours, rates of pay or exposure to hazardous chemicals and noise.

Nevertheless, they retained craft knowledge, a key element of skilled work which was strictly a male preserve.

Further, given the predominance of a male workforce, it is not surprising that the family labour system based upon recruitment of kin, which was prevalent throughout the linen industry, was strongest at bleachgreens. Bleachgreens were relatively good places to work, earning men higher wages and subjecting them to less dangerous health hazards than spinning mills. Although bleachgreen workers were not labour aristocrats, since their wages did not permit significantly higher standards of living or opportunities for vertical class mobility, most were able to keep their wives at home, better emulating middle class values regarding proper gender roles.

Powerloom weaving factories along the River Bann

Handloom weavers in county Down were able to compete with powerlooms until the 1880s. However, both the numerical decline among handloom weavers after the Great Famine and the increased demand for linen in the 1860s and 1870s during the cotton famine were powerful stimulants to the spread of powerlooms and proletarianisation. Although official statistics for handloom weavers in county Down in 1898 underestimated their numbers, aggregate census data between 1861-1901 confirms their decline. Between 1861 and 1911, county Down lost one third of its population and one fifth of its houses. Areas specialising in handloom weaving such as the electoral division of Tullylish in Lurgan poor law union, lost population in even greater numbers due to the industry's decline.[84]

Although the powerloom weaving of linen did not begin in earnest until the 1860s, powerloom weaving of cotton and union cloth had been present in county Down since the 1830s. Of the 1,516 powerlooms in Ireland in 1836, one third were in county Down. Shrigley cotton mill had 425 powerlooms and 100 were located in Hayes' mill in Seapatrick. When the cotton industry declined after 1850 these powerlooms disappeared.

When investment in powerlooms resumed in the 1860s, eight weaving factories were built in county Down increasing the number of powerlooms to 930. By 1868, the number of powerlooms in Ireland was almost equal to Scotland and far ahead of England, with 8,971 of the 12,149 located in counties Down and Antrim. Finally, by 1905, there were twenty weaving factories in county Down with 5,286 powerlooms.[85]

Hazelbank Weaving Co. at Coose near Lawrencetown was an example of a powerloom factory with a long history. The factory had been owned by the Law family since the early-nineteenth century. It was formerly the site of perhaps the earliest spinning mill on the Bann and it had continued to produce yarn until at least Samuel Law's death in 1867. Law had also built thirty-six workers' houses at Coose known as 'Law's Row', and another nineteen in Drumnascamph.

Between 1875 and 1879, Thomas Dickson and William Walker purchased the spinning mill and most of the houses, and established the Hazelbank Weaving Co. By 1879, powerloom factories provided fertile investment opportunities for entrepreneurs. Dickson increased the number of powerlooms from seventy-five to 200 and built two preparing sheds where he employed 200 people. The workforce at powerloom weaving factories was predominantly female, the 'daughters of small farmers residing at a convenient distance from the factory'.[86] Many of these small farmers were also domestic weavers, and as powerlooms encroached upon their craft, employment opportunities requiring lesser skills for their daughters and, to some extent, their sons, expanded. Again, since limited employment opportunities for men existed, more male weavers were hired in weaving factories outside Belfast than by those in the city to fill typically female jobs including weft winders, pirn cleaners, and givers-in.[87]

Powerloom weavers were paid by the piece according to a scale of prices which made their pay nearly equal whether they wove fine or coarse linen. This was in contrast to handloom weavers, whose wages could vary substantially according to the type of cloth woven. Generally, piece-rate workers earned slightly better wages than time workers, and this resulted in slightly higher wages and status for female weavers and winders compared with spinners.[88]

However, the wages of weaving factory workers were often held down through fines. Although these were generally small, they could amount to a considerable deduction from the worker's weekly wage. All linen industry workers could be fined for late attendance, reelers were fined for reeling either too much or too little (short or long count), and weavers were fined for damaged webs. The 1896 Truck Act attempted to control and regulate fines and most spinning mills and weaving factories posted a contract notice showing the various deductions that could be made.

The Truck Act could be evaded, however, by designating as a 'bonus' a certain part of the sum contracted to be paid to the worker and attaching certain conditions to its payment. Usually a bonus ranged from 6d to 1s per week, but amounts varied. In spinning mills, the bonus was a time bonus or an amount given for making full time in a week. Since this sum formed part of the sum contracted to be paid, workers considered the bonus to be part of the wage. Without it, wages were too low to sustain the worker. In the majority of mills,

workers who were not at the entrance gates at the exact commencement time or after meal hours were locked out until the next meal
time, losing both wages and bonus. This applied even in the case of
illness.[89] Although there was slightly more leniency for weaving factory
workers who arrived a few moments after commencement time, they
lost half the bonus if late once, and all of it if late again. Weavers also
lost the bonus if the cloth passer found flaws in their cloth.

Fining poignantly illustrates the deskilling process in weaving where
a relatively skilled, autonomous, and largely male workforce of
handloom weavers was feminised and degraded as they were stripped
of their craft knowledge and control over the production process. As
Patterson argues, 'mechanisation allowed an influx of women and
young girls into weaving. This meant that the weaving trade began to
suffer a lowering of status as it became defined as "women's work"'.[90]
Weavers received their work in the shape of a beam of warp or vertical
threads which was divided into so many 'cuts' or lengths of cloth to be
woven. The management of the labour process in powerloom weaving
factories bore remarkable similarity to the 'scientific management'
movement at the turn of the twentieth century associated with
Frederick Winslow Taylor. The number of cuts varied considerably, and
with each beam weavers received particulars stating the number of cuts
and the length of time each cut should take to weave. Note was made
of the time when weaving began indicating that powerloom weavers
made few independent decisions during the production process.
Instead, a number of men – tenters, cloth passers and managers – were
responsible for overseeing productivity and quality control.

The end of linen production : making-up

The final stage of production located in county Down was hemstitching
which, again, employed mostly women. Hemstitching was a branch of
the sewing and making-up end of linen production which employed
between one in four and one in nine working women and girls in
Ulster between 1850 and 1914. According to Collins, the Irish sewing
industry evolved out of the short-lived cotton industry and remained
firmly connected to the west of Scotland. Both cotton weavers and
embroiders of muslin obtained their work through the highly
developed putting-out networks concentrated within thirty miles of
Belfast in county Down. The county was the site in the 1820s of the
first Irish firm, Cochraines at Donaghadee, dealing solely in sewn
muslins. However, 'although the sewing industry was originally situated
in county Down, its rapid expansion in the 1840s involved a once and
for all shift to the north-west counties of Donegal, Londonderry and
Tyrone'.[91]

More than any other branch of linen production, sewing and making-up did not conform to the centralisation process, and this has resulted in its neglect by scholars. These branches were distinguished by production being split between processes performed inside and outside factories. The women employed inside hemstitching factories occupied the highest-status female occupations in the linen industry, since the work was clean, dry and quiet.[92] The lack of concern shown by factory inspectors for inside stitchers was matched by the intense preoccupation among lady inspectors and school attendance committees over the sweated labour of female outworkers and their children.

From the mid-nineteenth century, making-up in north-west Down consisted largely of hemstitching handkerchiefs. A typical example of a hemstitching factory is Blane's in Ballydugan, started in 1910 by Christopher Blane and his son James. In 1912, Blane introduced two Swiss embroidery machines and opened the first of two Swiss embroidery schools in Ireland, the other being at Maghera. Swiss embroidery was a skilled occupation and predictably, the machinery was operated by an adult male with three female assistants. All were taught their skills in the 'Theory Room' or school by an experienced Swiss instructor. Hemstitching factories paid their workers piece-rates, and in the case of Swiss embroidery, the wages of the female assistants depended on the speed of the male embroiderer. A proficient embroiderer could produce as many as thirteen dozen handkerchiefs at one time.[93]

Wage books between 1899 and 1900 from another hemstitching firm in Banbridge, John Johnson Hemstitcher, provide evidence relating to the distinct patterns of employment for women employees. Inside stitchers were single women who were paid regularly by the piece. On 16 November 1900, wages paid to twenty-five inside stitchers varied between 3s 5½d to 12s 3d with an average of 6s 4d. They were fewer in number than the outside stitchers, who included a large proportion of married women. Outside workers were intermittently paid, indicating that these women worked when they could find time in their daily domestic routine. Outworkers either picked up their work at the factory or had it delivered by pony and trap. For example, for the week of 5 January 1900, thirty-seven outside stitchers were on Johnson's wage books. The wages paid to the outside stitchers ranged more widely from 2s 5d to £1 0s 9d. Only fifteen were paid that week, and of the fifteen, eleven were paid more than once that month. Eleven of the thirty-seven were married women, but only three of these were paid more than once that month.[94] Although the number of hours outside stitchers worked is unknown, the small piece rate of 1½d per dozen must have compelled them to labour long hours. Women were frequently assisted by their children both during and after school hours with negative affects on attendance and achievement.

Conclusion

In conclusion, following Harvey, 'money creates an enormous capacity to concentrate social power in space'.[95] In county Down, particularly along the Bann, the linen industry generated money capital for two centuries. Investment strategies by capitalists in the industry were often defensive, meaning that large capital investments in machinery or buildings were resisted until they became imperative. Thus, the mechanisation of the various processes in linen production was uneven. It began with bleaching, which required long periods of time, and ended with fine linen weaving after the Great Famine pushed up handloom weavers' wages and the cotton famine stimulated demand for linen and other alternatives to cotton cloth.

The distinct challenges to labour recruitment and stability faced by rural capitalists were frequently met by varying degrees of paternalism. As a managerial strategy, paternalism reproduced patriarchal familial deference and dependence upon male factory owners in the workplace and community. Whether the scope of factory culture was small, as in the case of hamlets surrounding bleachgreens, or extensive, as in Gilford/Dunbarton, paternalistic employers wielded enormous social power over their workforces who were dependent upon them for wages and housing. Although these settlements were centred around distinct phases in linen production, they displayed similar factory cultures with relatively minor distinctions in living standards and life chances among the working class. The ideology of the capitalist as benevolent distant patriarch, encapsulated in the term 'linen lord', partly served to legitimise rigid class and gender inequality and was reinforced by an increasingly deskilled and female workforce.

By the early twentieth century, after twenty years of decline in the linen industry, the narrow economic base of county Down's linen-based communities was cracking. Just as the transformations in the production of linen yarn and thread ushered paternalistic industrial capitalism into this region, decisions made by the owners of the oldest yarn and thread spinning mills at Gilford and Seapatrick spelled the decline of family-dominated factory cultures. After the initial merger led by William Barbour in 1898, both Hayes and the McMasters joined the Linen Thread Company Ltd.[96] While employer paternalism did not end immediately after this amalgamation, the omnipresent 'linen lords' in the region began to recede after World War I along with the industry which had provided fortunes for a few and narrowly constrained livelihoods for the many.

References

1. L. Tilly, 'Connections' in *The American Historical Review*, lxxxxix, no. 1 (Feb, 1994), p. 3.
2. E. Wakefield, *An account of Ireland, statistical and political* (London, 1812), p. 22.
3. W. Carter. *A short history of the linen trade, i: to the time of the industrial revolution* (Belfast, 1952); W. H. Crawford, *Domestic industry in Ireland: the experience of the linen industry* (Dublin, 1972), p. 1; L. M. Cullen, *An economic history of Ireland since 1660* (London, 1972), p. 53.
4. W. H. Crawford, 'Ulster landowners and the linen industry' in J. T. Ward and R. G. Wilson (ed.), *Land and industry* (New York, 1971), p 118; W. H. Crawford, 'Drapers and bleachers in the early Ulster linen industry' in L. M. Cullen and P. Butel (ed.), *Negoce et industrie en France et en Irland aux XVIIIe et XIXe Siècles/Actes du Colloque Franco Irlandais de Historie, Bourdeaux-Mai, 1978* (Paris 1980), p. 113; W. H. Crawford, 'Economy and society in eighteenth century Ulster', unpub. Ph.D. thesis, Q.U.B., 1982, p. 82.
5. P. Gibbon, *The origins of Ulster Unionism* (Manchester, 1975), p. 14.
6. Carter, *A short history*, p 6; Crawford, 'Drapers and bleachers', p. 113; Cullen, *An economic history*, p. 60.
7. Rev. J. Dubourdieu, *Statistical survey of the county of Down* (Dublin, 1802), p. 30; Wakefield, *An account*, pp 255-256; W. A. Maguire, *The Downshire estates in Ireland 1801-1845* (Oxford, 1972), pp 110, 118.
8. Crawford, 'Ulster landowners', p. 118.
9. P. R. O. N. I., mic. 102/1.
10. Crawford, 'Drapers and bleachers', p. 116; J. W. McConaghy, Thomas Greer of Dungannon, 1724-1803, Quaker linen merchant, unpub. Ph.D. thesis, Q.U.B., 1979, p. 112; P. Hudson, *The genesis of industrial capital* (Cambridge, 1986), p. 19.
11. *Down*, pp 105-106.
12. Crawford, 'Drapers and bleachers', p. 114; M. Cohen, 'Peasant differentiation and proto-industrialisation in the Ulster countryside: Tullylish 1690-1815' in *The Journal of Peasant Studies*, xviii, no. 3 (Apr., 1990), pp 425-26.
13. Gilford Genealogist, P. R. O. N. I., D. 2714/5J1; Crawford, 'Bleachers and drapers', p. 115; J. M. Richardson, *Six generations of Friends in Ireland* (London, 1894), p. 184; G. R. Chapman, *Historical sketch of Moyallon meeting*, Preparative Meeting Clerk, Friends Meeting House, Moyallon, p. 3.
14. Copy of Francis Atkinson's survey of Moyallon, 23 November, 1764, P. R. O. N. I., Burgess estate papers, D. 1594/115.
15. E. R. R. Green, *The Lagan Valley* (London, 1949), p. 69; Crawford, 'Drapers and bleachers', p. 115; Crawford, 'Economy and society', p. 91; Cohen, 'Peasant differentiation', p. 426.
16. W. Charley, *Flax and its product in Ireland* (London, 1862), pp 3-5; A. Young, *A tour in Ireland* (London, 1892), p. 131; J. Curry, *Elements of bleaching* (Dublin, 1779); S. H. Higgins, *A short history of bleaching* (London, 1924), p. 63.
17. Young, *A tour*, p. 131; McConaghy, 'Thomas Greer's', p. 69; Crawford, 'Drapers and bleachers', p. 115; Cohen, 'Peasant differentiation', p. 426.
18. Wakefield, *An account*, p. 693.
19. C. Gill, *The rise of the Irish linen industry* (Oxford, 1925), p. 246; Green, *Lagan Valley*, p. 62.
20. Crawford, 'Economy and society', p. 103.
21. Wakefield, *An account*, p. 693.

22. Crawford, 'Economy and society', p. 103.
23. Cohen, 'Peasant differentiation', pp 426, 430.
24. Crawford, 'Economy and society', p. 92; Gill, *The Rise*, pp 149, 151.
25. G. Sider, *Culture and class in anthropology and history* (Cambridge, 1986), p. 191.
26. Cohen, 'Peasant differentiation', pp 419-20, 427.
27. Jane Gray, 'Rural industry and uneven development in Ireland: region, class, and gender, 1780-1840' unpub. Ph.D. thesis, John Hopkins' University, 1991, p. 237; 'Rural industry and uneven development: the significance of gender in the Irish linen industry' in *The Journal of Peasant Studies*, xx (1993), pp 590-611.
28. Crawford, *Domestic industry*, p. 6.
29. *Pigot's provincial directory* (London, 1825), pp 385-86. See also H. McCall, *Ireland and her staple manufactures* (Belfast, 1870), p. 209, where he states, 'The effect of centralising the manufacture of linens was most unfavourable to many small capitalists. Makers who only had a few weavers at work would not compete with the extensive men in the trade'.
30. K. Marx, *Capital* (New York, 1974), pp 334-36.
31. S. Lewis, *A topographical dictionary of Ireland* (London, 1837), p. 177; *I.A.C.D.*, p. 6.
32. *Reports of assistant commissioners on handloom weavers, industrial revolution: textiles*, IUP ser., 1839-40, ix, p. 659.
33. *Down*, p. 83.
34. W. H. Crawford, 'The evolution of Ulster towns' in P. Roebuck (ed.), *Plantation to partition: essays in honour of J. L. McCracken* (Belfast, 1981), p. 146; Lewis, *Topographical dictionary*, p. 177.
35. W. S. Kerr, 'Section on the linen trade' in Capt. R. Linn, *A history of Banbridge* (Banbridge, 1935), p. 166.
36. B. Collins, 'Proto-industrialisation and pre-Famine emigration' in *Social History*, vii, no. 2 (May, 1982), p. 134.
37. A. McKernan, 'The dynamics of the linen triangle: factor, family and farm in Ulster, 1740-1825', unpub. Ph.D. thesis, The University of Michigan, 1990, p. 269.
38. Dubourdieu, *Statistical survey*, pp 39-40; Wakefield, *An account*, p. 363. See McKernan, 'The dynamics', for a more complex discussion of subdivision on the nearby Richill Estate in county Armagh.
39. Dubourdieu, *Statistical survey*, p. 243.
40. *Abstract of the population of Ireland*, xiv, 1822, p. xiii.
41. L. Kennedy, 'The rural economy' in L. Kennedy and P. Ollerenshaw (ed.), *An economic history of Ulster 1820-1939* (Manchester, 1985), pp 32-3.
42. Dubourdieu, *Statistical survey*, p. 238.
43. C. Coote, *Statistical survey of the county of Armagh* (Dublin, 1804), pp 133-34; Crawford, *Domestic industry*, pp 26-7.
44. Gibbon, *Ulster unionism*, p. 30.
45. J. Hewitt, *The rhyming weavers and other country poets of Antrim and Down* (Belfast, 1974), p. 32.
46. Crawford, *Domestic industry*, pp 33-4.
47. Gray, 'Rural industry', pp 178-183; Jane Gray, 'Gender and plebeian culture in Ulster' in *Journal of Interdisciplinary History*, xxiv, no. 2 (Autumn, 1993), pp 252-53.
48. G. L. Gullickson, *Spinners and weavers of Auffay* (Cambridge, England, 1986), p. 84.
49. Wakefield, *An account*, p. 739; Gray, 'Rural industry', pp 151-52; Gray, 'Gender and plebeian culture', p. 260.

50. Kennedy, 'Rural economy', p. 14.

51. Ibid.

52. S. W. Mintz, 'A note on the definition of peasantries' in *The Journal of Peasant Studies*, i, no. 1 (1973), p. 94.

53. Hudson, *The genesis*, p. 13.

54. S. Rose, *Limited livelihoods* (Berkeley, 1992), p. 9.

55. E. J. Boyle, 'The economic development of the Irish linen industry, 1825-1913', unpub. Ph.D. thesis, Q.U.B., 1977, p. 48.

56. Ibid., pp 34, 51.

57. See Collins, 'Proto-industrialisation', pp 138-39 and E. L. Almquist, 'Mayo and beyond: land, domestic industry and rural transformation in the Irish west', unpub. Ph.D. thesis, Boston University, 1977, for analyses of the regional impact of mill spinning.

58. *Reports from commissioners; poor inquiry Ireland, 1836*, App. D, H.C. 1836, xxxi, Evidence of the Rev James Davis, p. 335.

59. *Poor law inquiry*, App. D, pp 67, 91; M. Cullen, 'Breadwinners and providers: women in the household economy of labouring families, 1835-6' in M. Luddy and C. Murphy (eds.), *Women surviving* (Dublin, 1989), p. 104.

60. *Reports from commissioners; poor inquiry (Ireland)*, App. E, H.C. 1836, xxxii, p. 335.

61. 20 October, 1834, P. R. O. N. I., O.S.M., MIC.6/173,170.

62. Lewis, *A topographical dictionary*, p. 658.

63. J. F. Batemen, 'Description of the Bann reservoirs, county Down, Ireland' in *Minutes of the proceedings of the Institution of Civil Engineers*, xii, (1848), pp 251-53.

64. Parish of Tullylish, Fieldbook, P. R. O. N. I., val. 1B/350; *I.A.C.D.*, pp 7, 19-20; Millbook 5, c. 1836, P. R. O. N. I., Valuation of mills in county Down.

65. *I.A.C.D.*, p. 18.

66. Ibid., p. 18.

67. Pigot, *Directory*, p. 334.

68. H. C. Lawlor, 'Rise of the linen merchants in the eighteenth century', P. R. O. N. I., Beck Notebooks, D. 1286/1, ii, no. 2 (February, 1942), p. 91.

69. Lawlor, 'Linen merchants', P. R. O. N. I., Beck Notebooks, D. 1286/1, p. 91; Notes on Dunbar McMaster & Co of Gilford, P. R. O. N. I., Genealogist Gilford Area, D. 2714/8F.

70. P. Joyce, *Work, society, and politics* (New Brunswick, 1980), p. 146.

71. *Half yearly reports by inspectors of factories, report by James Stewart, industrial revolution: factories*, IUP ser. (1842-47), xii, p. 24.

72. D. Harvey, *The urbanisation of capital* (Baltimore, 1985), pp 22-23.

73. D. S. MacNeice, 'Factory workers' housing in counties Down and Armagh', unpub. Ph.D. thesis, Q.U.B., 1981, pp 18-31; *Reports from commissioners: Paris universal exhibition*, H.C. 1967-68, xxx, pp 60-63; M. P. Campbell, 'Gilford and its mills' in *Review Journal of the Craigavon Historical Society*, iiii, no. 3 (1981-82), p. 36; M. Cohen, 'Paternalism and poverty: contradictions in the schooling of working class children in Tullylish, county Down, 1825-1914' in *History of Education*, xxi, no. 3 (1990), p. 6.

74. Census of Ireland, 1851, P. R. O. N. I.

75. Rose, *Limited livelihoods*, p. 37; Judy Lown, *Women and industrialisation* (Minneapolis, 1990), p. 3.

76. Lown, *Women and industrialisation*, p. 8.

77. Notes on Dunbar McMaster & Co. of Gilford, P. R. O. N. I., D. 2714/8F; Lawlor, 'Linen merchants', p. 92.

78. *Paris universal exhibition*, pp 60-83.

79. *I.A.C.D.*, p. 21.

80. *Report of the commissioners appointed to inquire how far it may be advisable to extend the provisions of the acts for the better regulation of mills and factories to bleaching works established in certain parts of the United Kingdom of Great Britain and Ireland*, H.C. 1854-55, xviii, p. 77; Interview with A. Uprichard, former bleachgreen owner, July, 1883.

81. Griffith's valuation for the Parish of Tullylish, 1865, P. R. O. N. I.; Banford bleach works, wages book no. 4, 1863-65, P. R. O. N. I., D. 1136/FA/1; G. H. Bassett, *The book of county Down* (Dublin, 1888), p. 261.

82. *Report of the commissioners appointed to inquire how far it may be advisable to extend the provisions of the acts for the better regulation of mills and factories to bleaching works established in certain parts of the United Kingdom of Great Britain and Ireland*, H.C. 1854-55, xviii, p. 77.

83. H. Braverman, *Labor and monopoly capital* (New York, 1974).

84. Census of Ireland, 1841-1911, P. R. O. N. I.; W. H. Crawford, 'A handloom weaving community in county Down' in *Ulster Folklife*, xxxix, 1993, p. 5.

85. *I.A.C.D.*, p. 261.

86. Bassett, *County Down*, pp 270-71; Griffith's valuation, 1865, P. R. O. N. I., val. 12 B/16/25B, 1879-1886; History of flax spinning mills in Ulster, P. R. O. N. I., Beck Notebooks, D.1286/2/4.

87. *Return of labour statistics from the board of trade, part II, industrial revolution: wages*, IUP ser., 1887-92, xx. Weft winders were operatives who wound yarn onto 'pirns' or bobbins on a winding machine. Full bobbins were taken to weft offices to be distributed to the weaving room. Since the quality and cleanliness of weft were essential to weavers' earnings, bobbins needed to be kept clean by pirn cleaners. Vertical parallel warp threads were wound onto the weaver's beam in sufficient number and length for a web of cloth. These warp threads were then passed by drawer-in through the heddle and reed, mechanisms which raised and lowered the warp and determined the closeness of the warp threads respectively.

88. B. Messenger, *Picking up the linen threads* (Belfast, 1979), p. 161.

89. *Annual report of the chief inspector of factories and workshops for the year 1906*, H.C. 1907, x, pp 240-242; H. Martindale, *From one generation to another* (London, 1944), pp 138-41.

90. H. Patterson, 'Industrial labour and the labour movement, 1820-1914' in L. Kennedy and P. Ollerenshaw (ed.), *An economic history of Ulster* (Manchester, 1985), p. 160.

91. This paragraph is drawn from B. Collins, 'Sewing and social structure: the flowerers of Scotland and Ireland' in R. Mitchison and P. Roebuck (ed.), *Economy and society in Scotland and Ireland 1500-1939* (Edinburgh, 1988), pp 242-254; and B. Collins, 'The organisation of sewing outwork in late nineteenth-century Ulster' in M. Berg (ed.), *Markets and manufacture in early industrial Europe* (London, 1991), pp 139-156. The quote is taken from p. 141.

92. N. Connolly O'Brien, *Portrait of a rebel father* (Dublin, 1975), p. 124; Messenger, *Linen threads*, p. 162; M. Cohen, 'Working conditions and experiences of work in Tullylish, county Down' in *Ulster Folklife*, xxx (1984), p. 15.

93. Cohen, 'Working conditions', p. 15; Valuation revision list, Tullylish, 1909-1920, P. R. O. N. I., Griffith's valuation, val.12B/21/8/E.; Crawford, 'A handloom weaving community', pp 7-8.

94. Cohen, 'Working conditions', p. 15; J. Bourke, *Husbandry to housewifery* (Oxford, 1994), p. 122.

95.   D. Harvey, *Consciousness and the urban experience* (Baltimore, 1985), p. 12.
96.   The linen thread company Ltd., *The faithful fibre* (Glasgow, n.d.), p. 33.

Plate 21.3   Bangor Bay (Ulster Folk and Transport Museum, WAG 399).

Chapter 22

COMMUNICATIONS IN COUNTY DOWN

FRED HAMOND

Social interaction, commerce, trade and industry all depend on an effective communications network. Over the past three hundred years, as Ireland's economy has slowly modernised and its population grown and then, in the 100 years following the Great Famine, more dramatically declined, so the roles played by successive forms of communications have changed, both in response to and as instigators of the broader processes of economic modernisation. Although the pace of change has not been even either at a national or regional level, the story has – more or less – been one of a progressive improvement in the speed and efficiency of transport, with a consequent shrinkage in journey times and costs. In effect, distances in Ireland have 'shrunk' as previously remote districts and communities have been brought within a progressively better integrated and, in the twentieth century at least, more centralised space-economy.

Although hardly remote by the standards of Connacht or west Munster, county Down witnessed these sorts of changes, in large part as a result of Belfast's burgeoning nineteenth-century growth as Ireland's major industrial city. By the mid-eighteenth century, the county already possessed a highly developed road network, and over the next hundred years numerous improvements were made to this, while canals were constructed and many piers, quays and harbours were built around the coast. In the period between the Famine and the First World War, however, the emphasis switched to railways, and in common with Ireland generally, their construction in county Down had profound consequences for existing methods of inland transport. In particular, the new railway systems emphasised Belfast's growing supremacy as Ulster's regional capital, the foundations for which had been laid much earlier in the town's charter of incorporation of 1613.[1] By the end of the seventeenth century Belfast was Ulster's main port, and its subsequent growth owed much to the willingness of its merchant and industrial community to invest in improving the city's communications both within and beyond its immediate hinterland. Of especial significance was the opening of the Lagan Navigation between

Belfast and Lisburn in 1763, and its extension by canal to Lough Neagh in 1794; the construction of Ulster's first railway to Lisburn in 1839; and the cutting of a deep water approach from the Pool of Garmoyle to the quays between 1839 and 1849.[2] These and other improvements greatly strengthened the social, industrial and commercial ties between Belfast, Ulster and Britain and this was reflected in the exponential growth of vessel tonnage to and from the port. This rose from 50,000 tons in 1800, to 3.4 million tons by 1914, when Belfast was the largest port in Ireland.[3]

The developments which took place in county Down's communications thus occurred as part of a process of growing regional integration and centralisation upon Belfast as Ireland's northern economic hub. This chapter explores these developments on a thematic basis, discussing successively the evolution of the county's road network and the legislative provisions made for its improvement; the modernisation and extension of its fishing and other ports; and the growth of its canals and railways. The emphasis throughout is on the local processes of modernisation and their social, economic and spatial consequences.

Roads

Prior to the eighteenth century, roads evolved between settlements as the need arose; travel by foot over relatively short distances was the norm, while horses and pack animals were used for longer journeys. The first attempt to address the issue of road development in Ireland came in 1615, when the Irish parliament took over responsibility from Britain for the country's roads.[4] This work was delegated to the parishes and administered by their respective church vestries. Each parish's inhabitants were legally required to provide six days' unpaid labour for the maintenance of the roads between the market towns and from these to the sea. In 1634, further legislation was enacted for the erection and repair of bridges, fords and causeways, but in contrast to the roads, this work was to be administered by the county grand juries, the costs being met by a levy on the relevant barony or county at large.[5]

Given the expense of bridge construction, it was invariably only the larger rivers, such as the Lagan, Bann or Quoile, which were spanned; elsewhere fords and ferries were employed. Timber, being cheaper than stone, was frequently used, and wooden bridges are recorded at Belfast, Lisburn, Dromore, Banbridge, Gilford and Downpatrick prior to 1700. The most remarkable work of this period was undoubtedly the Long Bridge across the mouth of the River Lagan at Belfast. This twenty-one arch structure, described as 'one of the most stately bridges in the kingdom', was executed in Scrabo sandstone between 1682 and 1689 at a cost of around £10,000.[6]

Despite the piecemeal and often unco-ordinated nature of these projects, an impressive road network had evolved in the county by the early eighteenth century (plate 22.1). Then (as now), the main trunk route ran between Belfast, Newry and Dublin, and the road was turnpiked by the Government in 1733 between Dundalk and Banbridge and between Banbridge and Belfast.[7] Tolls were collected on each of these sections to pay for maintenance and improvement. The road was progressively upgraded under the aegis of these turnpike trusts in order to cope with the increasing volume of traffic. Between 1739 and 1755, for example, substantial improvements were made between Hillsborough and Dromore. These developments encouraged the initiation of a regular coach service between Dublin and Belfast in 1740, and of a mail coach service in 1789. The latter provided a fast and regular method of transport, albeit at greater expense than the privately-run coaches. Post-chaises and horse-drawn cars also served areas off the main routes.

Although most of the county's towns and villages were interconnected by the 1720s, this was not always by the most direct route. Downpatrick, for example, could only be reached from Belfast via Lisburn or Comber. Further government legislation in 1739 enabled the construction of new, more direct roads between market towns.[8] These roads required a greater degree of planning and co-operation than was possible at parish level, and recognising this need for regional co-ordination, the government transferred responsibility for the main roads from the parishes to the county grand juries in 1765.[9] The unpopular labour impost was abolished in favour of the presentment system. Under this, a panel of jurors was appointed by the county sheriff to levy taxes on the inhabitants of the barony in which the road lay. Anyone interested in carrying out road construction, for which minimum standards were laid down, could apply to the jury for his costs. If the scheme was approved, the contractor's expenditure was repaid on completion of the work. The juries also issued maintenance contracts for roads and bridges. An early example of this sort of 'presentment road', built in the late 1760s, runs over the Mournes between Hilltown and Rostrevor.

Numerous other 'direct alignment' roads were constructed in county Down during the mid-eighteenth century, including those between Ballynahinch and Hillsborough, Dromore and Killyleagh, Downpatrick and Strangford (via Saul), and Belfast and Newtownards. Although initially relatively cheap to construct, the disregard of gradient posed increasing problems as the volume of wheeled traffic and the distances

Plate 22.1   County Down roads ca. 1714 (Source: H. Moll, *A new map of Ireland*).

travelled both increased in the later 1700s. The steep gradients on some roads became so inconvenient that they were eventually re-routed to avoid the obstacles concerned.[10] This happened, for example, on the road between Banbridge and Loughbrickland in the 1790s. Thereafter, most new roads were contoured rather than directly aligned.

Despite the inevitable abuse of the presentment system by some landowners and contractors, it proved remarkably successful. An analysis of county maps suggests that between 1739 and 1810 there was a threefold increase in road mileage, from 550 to 1,600 miles.[11] Writing in 1802, Dubourdieu noted:

> The roads of this county [Down] are in general allowed to be excellent; the soil is dry, the country neither flat nor shaded with

hedgerows, the materials for making them good, and the gentlemen very careful in keeping them in repair, and anxious to have the money granted for them honestly accounted for.[12]

The Irish post office was also instrumental in promoting road improvements. The Act which created the post office in 1784 also specified that new post roads were to have a minimum width of 42 feet and a maximum gradient of 1 in 35. Following detailed surveys of the entire Irish post road network, the postmaster general requested that county grand juries initiate presentments for their upgrading, and a number of schemes were begun in Down. Between Hillsborough and Lisburn, for example, a new turnpike and bridge were constructed in the 1820s in order to avoid a steep hill on the old road at Bridge Street, Lisburn. At the same time, the direct road between Belfast and Newtownards was realigned to the north via Bradshaw's Brae. Perhaps the most notable scheme was the reduction in the gradient of the road immediately north of the River Bann at Banbridge. Here the 'Cut' was excavated and a new bridge erected over the river in the early 1830s (plate 22.2).

During the first half of the nineteenth century, the grand jury authorised a number of new road schemes in county Down. The existing Newry to Clough road via Hilltown and Bryansford, for example, was superseded by one via Rathfriland and Castlewellan. New turnpikes were also made between Moira, Lisburn and Belfast (via Dunmurry). The Irish Board of Works, set up in 1831, also financed various schemes in the county. These included contouring the Dromara to Dundrum and Downpatrick to Strangford roads in the 1840s, and part-funding the replacement of the Long Bridge by the Queen's Bridge in 1843.

As elsewhere in Ireland, the systematic upgrading of the county's roads was mirrored by the increasing sophistication of bridge design. Prior to 1800, bridges were invariably of rubble stone construction, with simple semi-circular arches and minimal decoration. Some were also characterised by their narrow carriageway, humped-back profile and pedestrian refuges along the parapet walls. After 1800, increasing use was made of wide-span segmental arches, regularly-coursed dressed stone and decorative embellishment. Examples of such bridges were to be found in most of the main towns, including Belfast, Lisburn, Dromore and Newry. Standards were also maintained by the appointment of a county surveyor from 1834 onwards.

The volume of traffic carried by these roads varied considerably in different parts of the county. The largest flows occurred in Belfast's hinterland. In 1835, for example, a census of public transport recorded an average daily passenger flow between Lisburn and Belfast of over

Plate 22.2   The Cut at Banbridge in the early 1900s (Source: Green collection, Ulster Folk and Transport Museum).

2,000 people, compared with around 500 between Belfast and Holywood and just under 400 to Newtownards. Elsewhere the flows diminished rapidly with increasing distance from Belfast. On average, fewer than 250 people travelled by public transport as far as Newry, while less than half that number travelled to Portaferry, Saintfield or Downpatrick. Generally speaking, the coastal areas of Ards, Lecale and Mourne had comparatively few roads, necessitating or perhaps reflecting a greater reliance on sea communications.[13] In the early 1840s, the county's road mileage had increased to 2,560 miles, the third highest county total in Ireland after Tipperary and Cork.[14]

The era of major road construction came to an end around 1850. Thereafter, the rate of road building declined despite a steady increase in expenditure (fig. 22.1). The focus was now on making minor improvements to the main roads, and improving the minor roads linking them. Various factors may have prompted this change in emphasis. The fall in population after the Famine may have reduced the demand for new roads, while the development of the railways provided an effective alternative to the turnpikes, the control of which reverted to the grand juries in 1850s. Moreover, the county's high road mileage also meant that an increasing proportion of revenue had to be spent on maintenance. The presentment system persisted to 1898, when the county council assumed responsibility for all public roads and bridges.

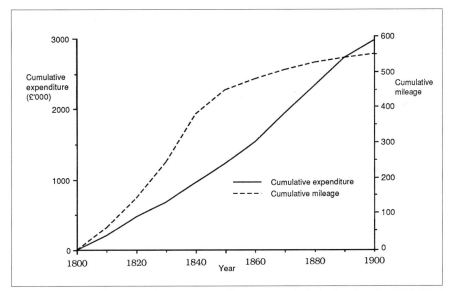

Fig. 22.1   Road construction in county Down, cumulatively by decade, 1801-1900 (Source: Fulton, *Roads of Ireland*).

Sea communications

Arguably, Down is one of the most advantaged of Ireland's coastal counties in terms of its sea communications. The loughs of Belfast and Carlingford give shelter, good inland access, and are within easy reach of Britain. Between them is a long indented coastline which affords many opportunities to construct piers and quays. Although a good road network existed by the mid-eighteenth century, surfaces were unconsolidated and methods of transport were still relatively primitive, particularly for the carriage of raw materials and finished goods over long distances. Shipping provided an economically viable alternative for these over certain routes, and this encouraged the development of harbour facilities for the movement of people and freight around the coast and to Britain and beyond (fig. 22.2).

Of particular significance in promoting these changes were the new trading conditions which obtained during the Napoleonic War (1793-1815). Deprived of easy access to its traditional overseas suppliers of foodstuffs, Britain increasingly relied on Irish farmers to supply the shortfall, particularly in grain and dairy products. In many areas, arable cultivation for cereals expanded at the expense of grassland, and in traditional corn growing areas such as Lecale in east Down, the resulting boom conditions led to an intensification of cereal exports through existing or recently constructed ports, especially once the Anglo-Irish corn trade had been relieved of all restrictions in 1806.

County Down ports

It is against this background that the development of county Down's minor ports must be seen. Prior to 1700, the most significant ports in the county were Strangford and Ardglass, both of which were of medieval origin, when Ardglass in particular was of national economic significance.[15] The onset of greater political stability in the early-eighteenth century, coupled with improved economic conditions, encouraged many landowners to petition parliament for finance to build piers and quays in order to develop the agricultural and industrial potential of their estates. Piers erected in this way included Downpatrick (1717), Killough (1730s), Bangor (1757), Killyleagh (1768), Donaghadee (1785), Rostrevor (1795) and Dundrum (1809).[16]

Killough typifies the prosperity which could result from such investment. The new quay was erected by the leading local landlord, Michael Ward, and was used to import coal and rock salt and export barley and refined salt. Adjoining it, Ward built lime and corn kilns, warehouses and salt pans. He also laid out a road connecting the port to his country house at Castleward, eight miles to the north.[17] Throughout, Ward's purpose was to enhance the local agricultural

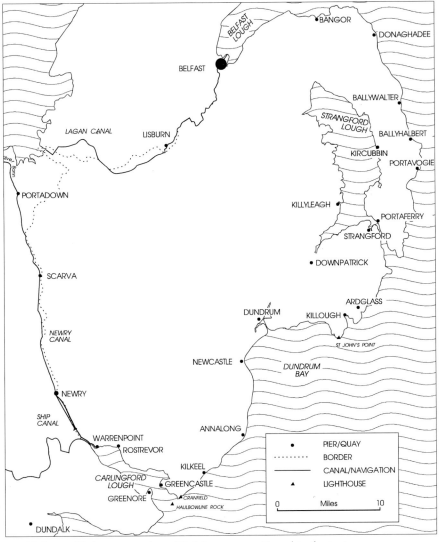

Fig. 22.2   Harbours, canals and lighthouses mentioned in the text.
(Source: *I.A.C.D.*).

economy, and thus the profitability – and rentable value – of the farms and other commercial properties on his estate. Across Strangford Lough, the relative landward isolation of the Ards Peninsula meant that this area too depended crucially on the development of its harbour facilities for further economic growth. For example, Portaferry, which had been a small trading port since the early 1600s, was greatly developed by the Nugent family in the late 1700s, when trading links were established as far afield as Sweden and Norway.[18] A quay was also built at Kircubbin around the same time.[19] The limited number of ports around Strangford Lough and their absence altogether at Comber and Newtownards, reflected the navigational limitations imposed by the lough's strong tidal currents and its tidal range. The tidal race between Strangford and Portaferry made for a particularly difficult approach, especially under sail, while the lough's shallow intertidal zone limited vessels to those of small draft, generally under 120 tons burden.[20]

To the south of Strangford Lough, the fortunes of Ardglass, which had been in the doldrums since the seventeenth century, also revived during the Napoleonic boom, thanks largely to the efforts of William Ogilvie, who came into possession of the town in 1806. He made many civic improvements and, in 1813, secured parliamentary finance to construct a pier and lighthouse.[21] The government was particularly interested in Ardglass as a port of refuge during poor weather, as it was the only place between Belfast and Dublin which was accessible without a pilot at all states of the tide. John Rennie was engaged to direct this work which was completed after several years. However, it was found that the new pier did not give sufficient shelter to boats, so a second one was erected in the inner bay and a dock was excavated, by Rennie's son John, between 1829 and 1832. By the mid 1830s, Ardglass was described as a 'safe and commodious' port, engaged in fishing, the importation of coal, and the export of grain and potatoes.[22]

Similar economic objectives prompted Michael Ward's son, the first Lord Bangor, to undertake further extensive harbour improvements at Killough during this period (1821-24). Alexander Nimmo, engineer to the commissioners of Irish fisheries, was engaged to direct the erection of two piers, one 600 feet long, at a cost of £17,000.[23] Nimmo also identified the need for a lighthouse at St. John's Point, just south of Killough, in view of the many shipwrecks which occurred in and around Dundrum Bay.[24] However, it was not until 1839 that work on this began, following lobbying by the marquis of Downshire and various ship owners. The light finally became operational in 1844.[25]

Returns of the tonnage and estimated value of exports and imports from Irish ports for 1835 demonstrate Belfast and Newry's dominance of the region's trade.[26] In that year, the combined value of the imports and exports traded through the county's ports totalled £9.3 million, of which Belfast accounted for £8.15 million or 88 per cent and Newry £960,000 or 10.3 per cent. The value of the trade carried on by the county's other ports was thus relatively minor. Linen, grain, meal and flour were the principal exports, along with livestock in the case of Donaghadee. Although coal was the biggest import in terms of weight, other high-value items such as textiles figured prominently in the case of Belfast and Newry. Some idea of the great variety of goods which were traded through local ports at this time may be seen in the customs records of Ardglass and Killough for 1827-34.[27] Potatoes and grain were the principal exports, along with butter, books, brushes, bricks, barrels, cows, candles, fish, flour, flax, goats, glue, horses, hair, herrings, hides, iron, kelp, linen, leather, oatmeal, potatoes, pigs, ploughs, quills, rennet, rabbit skins, rags, salt, soap, sheep, starch, wool, whips and tanner's waste. The main import was coal, but cows, earthenware, flax, hemp, herrings, horses, iron, lime, limestone, maize, marble, potatoes, paper, pigs, roman cement, salt, slates and tar also figured. The scope and scale of this trade provided numerous opportunities for local entrepreneurs. In 1836, for example, the County Down and Liverpool Steam Packet Company was formed, with the intention of providing a trading link between Strangford, Lecale and Liverpool.[28] To facilitate berthing at Downpatrick, David Ker, the local landlord, built Steamboat Quay a mile downstream from the early eighteenth-century quay. However, the venture failed after three years.

From the early-nineteenth century onwards, the government made grants specifically to encourage sea fishing in Ireland. In 1822 Alexander Nimmo reported to the commissioners of Irish fisheries on the state of the Irish ports, with recommendations for their improvement.[29] Newcastle was the first port in the county to benefit from these measures, when money was granted towards the construction of a pier in the 1820s. This stimulated what was to become a thriving stone industry in the Mournes: a short line of railway connected the pier to a quarry on the adjacent Thomas Mountain, from where the architect John Lynn exported granite to Downpatrick, Belfast and Liverpool.[30]

The passing of the 1846 Fisheries (Ireland) Act and the 1883 Sea Fisheries (Ireland) Act empowered the government, through the board of works, to make further grants towards harbour improvements.[31] Again Newcastle benefited, as did Annalong, six miles down the coast and 'considered by sailors a capital port to put into, should a storm come on while making from Carlingford to Belfast'.[32] Nimmo had recommended that Annalong's early-nineteenth-century pier be upgraded, but it was not until 1848 that this was done.[33] Thereafter the port became one of Ulster's principal herring fisheries and the main exporter of Mourne granite, but from 1868 it faced increasing competition from Kilkeel. In that year the gravel bar at the mouth of the Kilkeel River was dredged, enabling extensive development of the town's harbour,[34] and by the end of the century, Kilkeel had supplanted Annalong as Mourne's chief fishing port (plate 22.3). Under the above Acts, piers were also constructed at Ballywalter (1851), Ballyhalbert (1886) and Portavogie (early 1900s).[35]

Plate 22.3   Trading boats and fishing schooners in Kilkeel harbour in the early 1900s (Source: Green collection, Ulster Folk and Transport Museum).

Newry, Warrenpoint, and the Newry Canal

Newry became the principal port of Carlingford Lough when the customs house was transferred there from Carlingford in 1726. Four years later, the commissioners of inland navigation for Ireland began the construction of a canal between Newry and Lough Neagh. Its purpose was to facilitate the carriage of coal to Dublin from collieries near Dungannon. The exploitation of the Tyrone coalfields had begun in the 1720s, when they were seen as a cheap source of indigenous fuel which would lessen the capital's dependence on expensive English coal. The canal followed the Down/Armagh border and joined the River Bann at Whitecoat Point, just south of Portadown. From here, lighters could navigate into Lough Neagh, and then up the Blackwater River towards Coalisland, from where the coal was dispatched.[36] This eighteen mile canal was opened in 1742 and has the distinction of being the earliest summit-level canal in the British Isles.[37] In 1800 responsibility for it was transferred to the directors general of inland navigation. By then, many of the locks were in a poor condition and John Brownrigg was engaged to carry out extensive repairs between 1801 and 1822. A basin and landing stage were also constructed at Scarva at this time.

The canal operated from the 1740s, and its only link with the open sea was along a six mile stretch of the Newry River which, being narrow, shallow and tidal, was difficult to navigate. In 1765 a new canal was opened on the county Armagh side of the river, entering it at Lower Fathom, two miles downstream from the town. However, its relatively shallow depth and the restricted size of the sea lock limited vessels to under 150 tons. Accordingly, two years after its completion, the Irish parliament financed the construction of a quay on the county Down side of the river, just below Narrow Water, where larger vessels could berth.[38] The settlement which grew up adjacent to it formed the nucleus of the town of Warrenpoint.[39]

In terms of its original function – the carriage of coals from Tyrone – the canal was a failure; indeed, considerably more British coal went up the canal than Irish coal came down. However, it did provide a useful conduit for the movement of goods and agricultural produce to and from Newry, and as such acted as a catalyst to the town's demographic, commercial and industrial expansion in the middle decades of the eighteenth century.[40] In 1777 Arthur Young noted that:

> The town appears exceedingly flourishing, and is very well built;
> yet forty years ago, I was told, there was nothing but mud cabins
> in it. This great rise had been much owing to the canal to Loch
> Neagh. ... There is considerable trade.[41]

By 1780, Newry had become Ireland's fourth largest port, with butter and linen being among its principal exports.[42]

During the refurbishment of the inland section of the canal in the early 1800s, the sea lock was widened and lined with stone. In 1803 a lighthouse was erected at Cranfield Point to enable mariners to steer a safe passage through the shallow bar at the mouth of the lough.[43] However, silting of the approach channel to the sea lock posed a continuing problem, which was exacerbated by the progressive increase in the draft of vessels using the port. In 1830, the Newry Navigation Company (a private concern which had taken over the canal the previous year), engaged Sir John Rennie to deepen and widen the approaches to the ship canal. With the completion of this work in 1842, Rennie began upgrading the canal itself. The existing channel was dredged and extended 1½ miles to a deeper section of the tidal river at Upper Fathom. Here the new Victoria sea lock was constructed. Measuring 220 feet by 50 feet, it was (and remains) the largest canal lock in Ireland. At the Newry end of the canal, the Albert Basin was dug out providing much improved berthing facilities. The scheme was finished in 1850 and enabled vessels of up to 500 tons to reach the town rather than having to off-load at Warrenpoint (plate 22.4).[44]

These improvements did not signal the end of Warrenpoint's role as Newry's outport. A regular steamer service was established from Warrenpoint to Liverpool in 1823, and to Glasgow in 1829.[45] In the 1830s, Warrenpoint dock was extended into the river channel, thereby enabling vessels to dock at half tide (rather than only at full tide as before). In 1849, a year before the new ship canal opened, a rail link was established between Warrenpoint and Newry by the Newry, Warrenpoint and Rostrevor railway.[46] The time-saving convenience of the train enabled Warrenpoint to continue as the terminus for the cross-channel ferries even after the opening of the Victoria lock.[47] Parallel with these developments, the town also flourished as a seaside resort.

It was the opening of the Portadown to Newry section of the Belfast to Dublin railway in 1852 which heralded the demise of Newry's inland canal trade.[48] The routes of the canal and railway were virtually identical (with halts on the latter at Poyntz Pass and Scarva), and the fast and efficient trains easily outpaced the horse-drawn barges. However, because of the relatively steep hills around Newry, the main line could not come any closer than one mile to the west, necessitating transhipment by horse and cart. This inconvenience was rectified in 1854 when a branch line was taken off at Goraghwood, 3½ miles north of Newry.[49]

Although the new ship canal facilitated Newry's maritime trade, the

Plate 22.4   View of the Albert basin, Newry, *ca.* 1930 (Source: Green collection, Ulster Folk and Transport Museum).

Lagan canal and Ulster railway had already given Belfast a decisive lead as the main conduit for goods and materials to and from central Ulster.[50] Moreover, the original canal between Newry and Lower Fathom continued to restrict traffic because of its significantly narrower width when compared with the new section. Furthermore, while Newry benefited to some degree from the opening of a direct rail link to Armagh in 1865, the railway also diverted some traffic away from the town to competing ports in county Louth. For example, Dundalk had been a regionally-important port since the building of the town's first quay by Lord Limerick in 1743. Latterly it also became a major nodal point in the Irish railway system when it was linked to Dublin in 1849, Belfast in 1852, and Londonderry and Enniskillen in 1858.

In 1873, the London and North Western Railway Company initiated a cross-channel ferry service between Holyhead and the purpose-built county Louth port of Greenore. This crossing is only seventy-nine miles, compared with 145 miles to Liverpool, and 193 miles to Glasgow.[51] The Greenore route had the further advantage of having, from its inception, direct rail connections between Greenore and Dundalk, and from Holyhead to London. It thus gave much quicker access between the north of Ireland and southern England than any other route.[52]

Donaghadee and the cross-channel mailpacket service

The shortest practical sea crossing between Britain and Ireland is from Donaghadee to Portpatrick on the Galloway coast, a distance of twenty-one miles.[53] Given the vagaries of wind and tide, such a route was decidedly advantageous in the era of sail. Not surprisingly, it was used during the sixteenth century for ferrying military personnel to and from Ireland. In the early seventeenth century, the crown granted Sir Hugh Montgomery exclusive rights to this crossing, and in 1662 a weekly mail service was begun. In 1778 a pier was also erected at Portpatrick to the designs of John Smeaton.[54] At much the same time, Daniel Delacherois, a local landlord, undertook improvements at Donaghadee, again with government assistance. In 1790, a private company headed by the marquis of Downshire was contracted by the recently-formed Irish post office to operate the mailpacket service, which was supplemented by the existing considerable export trade in cattle to Scotland.[55]

In 1814, recognising the importance of this route for the mailpacket, the government commissioned John Rennie to make detailed surveys of both sides of the North Channel with a view to improving the harbour facilities there.[56] Although Portpatrick is the only port between north Wales and the Clyde which can be used at any state of the tide, an exposed rocky shoreline and frequent heavy swells make it difficult to approach. However, the government decided to upgrade the existing facilities rather than develop new ones elsewhere and so, in 1820, work began on new harbours at Donaghadee and Portpatrick under Rennie's direction. On Rennie's death the following year, his son (Sir John) took over and by 1825 work was sufficiently well advanced at Donaghadee for the post office to commence a daily steampacket service, with a journey time of between two and three hours.[57] However, the works at Portpatrick were not completed until 1836.

Although the packetboat also carried passengers, goods and livestock, it quickly proved to be a loss-making venture, and responsibility for both it and the maintenance of Portpatrick harbour was handed over to the admiralty in 1837. They persevered with the packet service, but the mail contract was awarded to a private contractor on the Belfast to Glasgow route, and the Donaghadee service was finally withdrawn in 1849. Thus, despite the expenditure of upwards of one-third of a million pounds on both harbours, steampacket services between them lasted less than twenty-five years.

In 1856, following an approach by the Belfast & County Down Railway (B.C.D.R.), the government agreed in principle to readopt the Donaghadee to Portpatrick route as the official packetboat crossing and to improve the harbour facilities, providing both terminals were connected up to the local rail networks. The following year, the Portpatrick Railway Company (P.R.) was incorporated for the purpose of building a line between Portpatrick and Castle Douglas, from where an existing railway ran onwards to Carlisle.[58] The Lancaster & Carlisle and Glasgow & South Western Railways held a total of £200,000 in shares in this company, and the B.C.D.R. a further £15,000.

Meanwhile, the B.C.D.R. extended their Belfast to Newtownards line (opened in 1850) some ten miles to Donaghadee. This terminated at a station beside the pier and opened in 1861. In the same year, the Portpatrick and Wigtown railway (as it was then known) reached Stranraer, and arrived in Portpatrick the following year. Here a steep branch line connected the main station with the harbour. For its part, the government spent five years prior to 1863 excavating rock from the bottom of Donaghadee harbour. However, it was to be another two years before they completed the construction of a new inner basin at Portpatrick, the work having been delayed by flooding.

Given that the railway was ready to run from 1862, and with no end to the Portpatrick works in sight, the P.R. lost patience and began negotiations with the Belfast and Northern Counties railway (B.N.C.R.) regarding a boat service between Stranraer and Larne. The B.N.C.R. had opened their railway between Belfast and Larne in the same year, and it made little difference to the majority Scottish shareholders in the P.R. whether the ferry operated out of Portpatrick or Stranraer. Although almost twice as long as the established route, both Larne and Stranraer had better approaches and were therefore more accessible during poor weather. Thus, by the time the Donaghadee to Portpatrick boat service got underway, in 1865, the rival route had been operating for three years, an advantage which it subsequently maintained

The government continued to procrastinate over the adoption of the Portpatrick route for the mailpacket, and in 1867 finally decided to withdraw support. All attempts to reinstate the service failed, and six later, in 1873, the government also abandoned the upkeep of Portpatrick harbour which thereafter was allowed to fall into disrepair. So ended some three centuries of mailpacket services. Paradoxically, it was the railways which enabled both Donaghadee and Portpatrick to enjoy a modicum of success as seaside resorts during the present century.

Railways

The opening of Ulster's first railway, between Belfast and Lisburn, in 1839 was quickly followed by its extension to Portadown (in 1842) and Armagh (in 1848).[59] In 1852, the Dublin & Belfast Junction Railway (D.B.J.R.) linked Portadown with Newry, and in so doing connected Belfast with Dublin.[60] The early success of these ventures stimulated considerable interest in the construction of further railways in county Down, but as was so frequently the case in other parts of Ireland, by no means all of the schemes which were proposed saw the light of day (fig. 22.3).

The Belfast & County Down Railway

The B.C.D.R. proposed to construct two lines from Belfast: one to Holywood, by then a select residential and seaside town, and another to Newtownards, a flourishing market and industrial town. Neither route presented any serious engineering problems, and both were deemed cost effective in terms of capital outlay, running costs, and anticipated receipts. In 1846, the company received parliamentary sanction for its proposals, thus enabling finance to be raised.[61] Both works were executed by William Dargan under the direction of John Godwin, the B.C.D.R.'s chief engineer.[62]

The 4½ mile Holywood line opened in August 1848. The *Belfast News Letter* noted that 'the carriages are fitted up very elegantly and with every regard for comfort. The arrangements for the transfer of traffic are carried out with the utmost satisfaction and punctuality'. The line was successful from the outset and in its first six months made a £700 profit on receipts of £1,800. The twelve mile Newtownards line,

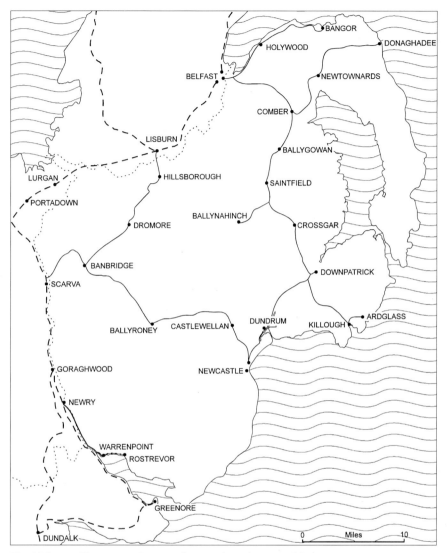

Fig. 22.3   The county Down rail network and principal halts.

which diverged from the Holywood line at Ballymacarrett Junction, opened in 1850. An imposing terminus was also erected at Queen's Quay, Belfast, north-west of the newly opened Queen's Bridge.

Early on during the B.C.D.R.'s deliberations over the choice of route, it was decided that the line would eventually be extended from Comber to Downpatrick. However, due to the then-current economic depression, this work did not start until 1853. Originally it had been proposed to follow the shore of Strangford Lough, but in the expectation of generating a greater volume of agricultural traffic, an inland route via Ballygowan, Saintfield and Crossgar was adopted, with a short branch line to Ballynahinch. Under the direction of a new consultant engineer, Sir John McNeill, a railhead was established at Downpatrick in 1859, Ballynahinch having been reached the previous year. Two years later, in 1861, the B.C.D.R. opened its line between Newtownards and Donaghadee. Although a boat service to Portpatrick was instigated in 1865, it was abandoned within two years. Subsequently, the B.C.D.R. was reliant on summer excursionists to Donaghadee and nearby Millisle, there being no major industries in or near these towns, apart from a few grain mills.

Planning the B.C.D.R. line to Bangor was equally problematic. Originally it was envisaged that the town would be reached by a route around the coast, but this plan was thwarted by a number of foreshore owners, anxious to preserve their access to, and view of, Belfast Lough. With the completion of the Donaghadee link, the B.C.D.R. therefore proposed a three mile branch from it to Bangor. However, in 1860, the Belfast, Holywood and Bangor railway (B.H.B.R.) obtained parliamentary sanction to construct a more direct line to Bangor, thus forcing the B.C.D.R. to abandon their scheme.

Work on the B.H.B.R. line began in 1862, but although less than eight miles long, its construction was not straightforward. On leaving Holywood, the line was forced half a mile inland by the same obstructionist attitudes among local landowners which had forced the changes in the original B.C.D.R. scheme. Hemmed in by the Holywood hills, extensive rock cuttings were necessary at Cultra in order to achieve suitable running gradients over the ensuing 170 foot climb to Craigavad. These cuttings were slow and expensive to excavate and also required numerous road bridges. Closer to Bangor, the deep glen over Crawford's Burn had to be spanned by a substantial five-arch viaduct, while at Helen's Bay an ornate station was built for the marquis of Dufferin and Ava in the Scottish baronial style. It was 1865 before the line finally opened.

In the same year, the B.H.B.R. also purchased the working rights to the B.C.D.R.'s Belfast to Holywood line, thereby giving them control over the entire Belfast to Bangor route. The company erected their own terminus at Queen's Quay, but this proved premature, for in 1873 they were forced by financial difficulties to lease the line back to the B.C.D.R., and were finally absorbed in their entirety by that company in 1884.

From this point on the B.C.D.R. had no competition, but it nevertheless continued to endeavour to increase passenger traffic. Villa tickets, which entitled holders to seven years' free travel, were offered to anyone who built a house within twenty miles of Belfast. Season tickets and cheap day returns were also available, and the company's excursion steamer plied between Belfast and Bangor during the summer months. Easier connections with the county Down lines were facilitated by the opening of the Belfast Central railway in 1875, which linked the B.C.D.R.'s terminus with that of the Ulster railway at Great Victoria Street.

The arrival of the railway in Bangor in 1875 gave new impetus to the town as a seaside resort, and it rapidly surpassed Holywood in this role.[63] As a result, the B.C.D.R. turned their attention to Newcastle, which, under Lord Annesley's patronage, had become a popular, if select, resort. In 1866 the Downpatrick, Dundrum and Newcastle railway (D.D.N.R.) was formed to establish a link between these three towns, and both the B.H.B.R. and B.C.D.R. had substantial share holdings in the new company. The 11½ mile route – over which the B.C.D.R. had exclusive running powers – opened in 1869, and twelve years later the B.C.D.R. bought over the D.D.N.R..

The B.C.D.R. invested considerably in Newcastle in order to develop its potential as a resort for Belfast excursionists. In 1897 the company part-financed the new headquarters for the County Down golf club, while a year later it opened the magnificent red-brick Slieve Donard hotel. Set within landscaped grounds adjoining the beach, the hotel contained 120 bedrooms, therapeutic baths and recreation rooms, not to mention electric lights and telephones. Costing almost £100,000, it was promoted as the largest and finest hotel in the whole of Ireland. Inclusive rail-hotel packages were offered, as were tickets which enabled Belfast office workers to commute whilst their families enjoyed a holiday. A new terminus, with a distinctive clock tower and canopied entrance, opened in 1905.

The Mountains of Mourne, which formed the backdrop to the resort, were also promoted, notably by Robert Praeger in his *Official guide to county Down and the Mourne Mountains*, published in 1898. Norton's horse-drawn car service plied between Newcastle and Rostrevor, enabling visitors to view the mountains and dramatic coastline in the vicinity of Bloody Bridge.[64]

The final section of the B.C.D.R. network connected Downpatrick with Ardglass in 1906. Ardglass was one of the east coast's premier fishing ports, and to boost its industry, the government granted the B.C.D.R. £30,000 to construct a seven mile railway extension to the town. However, with growing competition from road transport, this venture proved unsuccessful, although the village did enjoy modest popularity as a holiday resort.

Railways in south and west Down

The B.C.D.R. was not the only rail operator in county Down. As noted earlier, the Newry, Warrenpoint and Rostrevor railway opened a line between Newry and Warrenpoint in 1849, and this was extended by a horse tram service to Rostrevor in 1878. The line was absorbed by the Great Northern Railway (G.N.R.) in 1886.[65] To promote the merits of south Down as a holiday area, the G.N.R. opened a hotel in Warrenpoint, and also bought the Mourne Hotel at Rostrevor in 1898, renaming it the Great Northern.

By the mid-nineteenth century, the Upper Bann, along with the River Lagan, was the focus of Ulster's linen industry. Banbridge was an important linen centre and market town, and lay on the Belfast to Dublin turnpike. In its vicinity were many large textile mills and associated housing. It was logical therefore, that once the D.B.J.R. had established a main line between Newry and Portadown in 1852, they should build a connection to Banbridge. Accordingly, a spur was constructed off the main line at Scarva by the Banbridge Junction railway between 1852 and 1859, and thereafter worked by the D.B.J.R.. It was of particular benefit to the mills, facilitating the import of coal, flax and yarn, and the export of cloth. In 1863, Banbridge was also connected directly to Lisburn by the Banbridge, Lisburn & Belfast Railway, the line being worked by the Ulster Railway. Its fifteen mile route ran via Hillsborough and necessitated the spanning of the Lagan by a seven-arch viaduct at Dromore. Both it and the Scarva branch were absorbed by the G.N.R. in 1877.

Following the formation of the G.N.R. in 1876, there were only two railway companies in the county – the G.N.R. in the west, and the B.C.D.R. in the east. Seeing the success with which the B.C.D.R. was working the Belfast to Newcastle line, the G.N.R. attempted to forge its own link with this resort via Banbridge. Although Ballyroney, ten miles west of Newcastle, was reached in 1880, it was another two decades before terms were agreed with the B.C.D.R. regarding the operation of the intended link.[66] Following arbitration, the G.N.R. extended their line to Castlewellan, whilst the B.C.D.R. laid the remainder to Newcastle. The through line finally opened in 1906, and was the last to be constructed in the county.

The impact of the railways

Between 1848 and 1906, some 124 miles of railway were built in county Down, of which seventy-nine were worked by the B.C.D.R. and forty-five by the G.N.R.. During this period, three phases of railway construction may be identified: an initial burst of activity up to 1850, when short connections were made from Belfast and Newry; a period

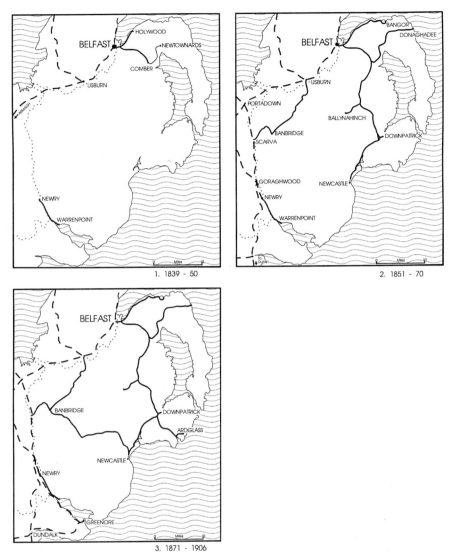

Fig. 22.4   Evolution of the county Down rail network.

of steady expansion between 1851 and 1870, when just over half the total mileage was laid and all the main towns were connected to the network; and a drawn-out phase of 'infill' up to 1906, by which time every part of the county, with the exception of the Upper Ards, was within ten miles of a station (fig. 22.4).

The impact of the railways is difficult to overestimate. To the travelling public, they offered a new level of comfort, reliability and punctuality which was superior to everything that had gone before. Moreover, with the progressive lowering of fares (in real terms), the

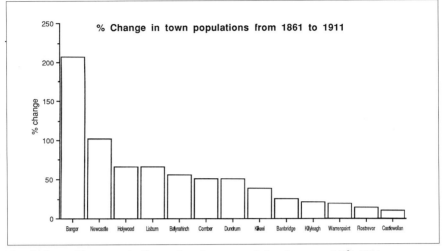

Fig. 22.5   Towns and villages showing a population increase, 1861-1911.
              (Source: *Censuses*).

railways were increasingly accessible to virtually all social classes. It
was also an economical and practical means of moving bulky or low-
value items such as coal, stone, timber, grain, meal, potatoes and
livestock, irrespective of road conditions and weather. For the best-run
railway companies, the potential profits were equally considerable. In
the period immediately preceding 1914, for example, the B.C.D.R.
enjoyed the highest income per mile in Ireland, while its passengers
benefited from what were possibly the lowest fares per mile.[67]

Perhaps the railways' most significant long-term effect was on the
county's demography and settlement. Between 1861 and 1911, Belfast's
population more than tripled, reflecting its development as a major
industrial centre of Britain and the Empire. The trains were instrumental
in this, encouraging the growth of commuter traffic, and directing east
Belfast's expansion towards Holywood and Dundonald. In contrast, the
county's population outside the city declined by almost one-third
during this period, reflecting the nation-wide depopulation of the
countryside after the Famine. Only in thirteen settlements did the
population increase, and of these, all but three (Kilkeel, Killyleagh and
Rostrevor) were directly served by trains (fig. 22.5). The biggest growth
was experienced by the resorts of Bangor and Newcastle (and to a
lesser extent Warrenpoint), followed by Lisburn and Holywood, both of
which were developing as dormitory towns for Belfast.

Late nineteenth and twentieth century developments
The changing economic conditions of the post-Famine years affected

county Down's ports and harbours as much as its railways, but in different ways. Many of the county's smaller ports experienced recession and decline as, with the shift from arable to pastoral farming, cereal exports declined, and it was the coal trade that sustained most of the non-fishing ports. Increasingly, cross-channel trade concentrated on Belfast and Newry, both of which were well connected by rail to much of the county and beyond by the 1860s. Moreover, as vessels increased in size, so those able to negotiate the smaller ports' often shallow approaches became fewer in number. Delays occasioned while waiting for the tide proved a particular handicap to the increasing numbers of steam-powered vessels, many of which had to operate to a tight schedule in order to maintain profitability. However, the relative isolation of the Mourne coast enabled the coastal and cross-channel schooner trade to persist up to the First World War.[68] Paradoxically, it was the coming of the railway to Dundrum in 1869 which encouraged the formation of the East Downshire Steam Ship Company by the marquis of Downshire in 1871, which in turn provided the conduit for the distribution of imported English coal and timber in the area into the present century.[69] Only at Kilkeel and Portavogie has there been any significant investment by the government, and both continue to flourish as the province's principal fisheries.[70]

Despite the expenditure on the Newry ship canal in the mid-nineteenth century, its traffic did not increase significantly in the post-Famine period. Indeed, even while it was being upgraded, vessels of up to ten times its capacity were regularly visiting Belfast. Nevertheless, the canal continued to serve as a conduit for the importation of coal (notably by Fishers), timber and grain, and for the export of livestock. Between 1931 and 1935, under the Newry Port and Harbour Trust (which took over in 1901), the original section of the ship canal was widened and deepened, and watertight metal gates fitted to the Victoria lock.[71] The inland section of the canal, long starved of investment and under maintained, witnessed its last commercial traffic the following year, although it was not officially abandoned until 1949. The ship canal eventually closed to commercial traffic in 1974.

Just as the waterways declined, so too, eventually, did the railways. After the First World War the increasing availability of petrol driven vehicles gave people the choice of more flexible means of transport. In fact, the B.C.D.R. had instigated road freight services as early as 1902, with a steam-traction freight service between Newcastle and Kilkeel, followed by one from Newtownards to Portaferry a year later.[72] Not only did buses, cars and lorries offer a more flexible service to the county's dispersed farming communities, but they also provided competition over established rail routes. Between Belfast and

Ballynahinch, for example, a succession of private bus companies consistently offered a faster and cheaper service. Places like Donaghadee, which could only be reached by train via Newtownards, could now be accessed through Bangor by bus. In 1927 alone, there were no less that twenty-seven independent bus companies in competition with the B.C.D.R. In that year, the company was empowered to set up its own bus services, but it was sometimes forced to compete against itself, as on the Belfast to Holywood route.

Both road and rail transport enjoyed a revival during the Second World War. Recession inevitably followed and, in 1948, the B.C.D.R. was acquired by the government-created Ulster Transport Authority (U.T.A.). As trains could only compete effectively against road vehicles on the main Belfast to Dublin and commuter lines, a rationalisation programme ensued. In 1950, services were withdrawn from the entire B.C.D.R. network with the exception of the Belfast to Bangor line. In 1953, the U.T.A. also took over the Northern Ireland section of the G.N.R.. The Scarva to Newcastle line was axed in 1955, and that between Lisburn and Banbridge the following year. The Newry to Warrenpoint line closed in 1965, and in the same year the Queen's Quay terminal was isolated from the county Antrim lines.

In the space of fifty years, therefore, competition from the roads had led to the closure of almost 90 per cent of the county's railways. With the run-down of the network, roads have re-emerged as the key element in the county's transport system. This is particularly evident in the upgrading of the Belfast to Bangor road to dual carriageway status, the opening of the M1 motor way between Belfast and Dungannon in the 1960s, and the recent opening of the cross-harbour bridge in Belfast. However, railways have lately enjoyed a new lease of life under Northern Ireland railways, with the re-establishment of the Antrim-Down link across the Lagan in 1976, the opening of the Central Station at Maysfield, and the re-opening of Great Victoria Street Station. A substantial investment has also been made at Warrenpoint which has re-emerged as south-east Ulster's main cross-channel port, with a dual carriageway link to Newry along the line of the former railway.

The industrial legacy

Remains abound throughout Down of the county's industrial heritage. The road system is essentially the same as that established in the eighteenth century, and examples of bridges of this period can be seen at Belfast (Shaw's bridge, Drum bridge), Downpatrick (Quoile bridge) and Newry (Old Crown bridge). The section of the Lagan Navigation between Belfast and Lisburn now forms part of the Lagan Valley Country Park; at Lisburn, the Union locks, the largest flight on the system, have recently been landscaped as an amenity area. The Newry ship canal is now used for rowing, fishing and canoeing, and Newry & Mourne District Council have recently refurbished the Victoria lock. Following the success of the recently reopened Erne-Shannon waterway, the feasibility of reopening the entire inland section of the Newry canal as far as Lough Neagh is currently(1996) being investigated. Elsewhere, many small piers and quays are still used for recreational purposes, and some (notably Bangor) have been transformed into yacht marinas. The Rennies' harbour at Donaghadee remains in its original state and is arguably the finest in the whole of Ireland in terms of its architecture and scale. As regards railways, the viaducts at Crawfordsburn and Dromore are perhaps the most impressive remains. Moira station, just outside the county boundary, is now the oldest survivor in the province, having been built in 1840; it is now in the guardianship of the Environment Service. Other stations have also been refurbished for private or commercial use, for example Dromore, Saintfield, Ballyward, Cultra, and Helen's Bay. The Downpatrick and Ardglass Railway Preservation Society regularly run trains on a restored section of line at Downpatrick and have plans to extend it towards Dundrum. Proposals have also been made to reopen the old Comber line from Belfast to Dundonald in order to relieve rush hour traffic. The wheel may be turning full circle.

References

1. For a review of the development of Belfast port, see R. Sweetnam and C. Nimmons, *Port of Belfast, 1785-1985* (Belfast, 1985).
2. For an overview of the Lagan navigation and canal, see E. R. R. Green, *The industrial archaeology of county Down* (Belfast, 1963), pp 70-5 [hereafter *I.A.C.D.*.]; W. A. McCutcheon, *The industrial archaeology of Northern Ireland* (Belfast, 1980) [hereafter *I.A.N.I.*.], pp 55-8, and R. Delany, *Ireland's inland waterways* (Belfast, 1986), p. 32. For the Ulster railway, see *I.A.N.I.*, pp 101-8.
3. Sweetnam and Nimmons, *Port of Belfast*, app. 1.
4. 11-13 Jas. I, c.7. For an overview of the Irish road system, see *I.A.N.I.*, pp 1-28. For details of the county Down network, see J. T. Fulton, The roads of county Down 1600-1900 unpub. Ph.D. thesis, Q.U.B., 1972.
5. 10 Chas. I c.26.
6. *Down*, p. 129. For further details, see P. O'Keeffe and T. Simington, *Irish stone bridges* (Blackrock, 1991), p. 221.
7. Other trusts were responsible for sections between Dublin, Drogheda and Dundalk. In the 1760s, the two county Down trusts were subdivided into the following sections: Dundalk to Newry, Newry to Banbridge, Banbridge to Lisburn, Lisburn to Belfast (via county Antrim), and Lisburn to Belfast (via county Down).
8. 13 Geo. II c.10.
9. 5 Geo. III c.14. This system was already in use for the erection and maintenance

of bridges. In 1772, the parishes were empowered to levy a cess for the upkeep of minor roads.

10. This growth in traffic is reflected in the appearance of purpose-made maps such as A. Taylor and G. Skinner's *Maps of the roads of Ireland* (Dublin, 1777).

11. Fulton, 'Roads', p. 285. The doubling of the mileage between 1767 and 1810 is largely due to the transfer of responsibility for minor roads from the parishes to the grand juries in 1796.

12. J. Dubourdieu, *Statistical survey of the county of Down* (Dublin, 1802), p. 218.

13. *Second report of the commissioners appointed to consider and recommend a general system of railways for Ireland*, H.C. 1837-8, xxxv.

14. *Report of the commissioners appointed to revise the grand jury laws Ireland*, H.C. 1842, xxiv, p. 18.

15. *A.S.C.D.*, p. 391 *et seq.* There had also been a quay and customs house at Bangor since the early 1600s (Ibid., p. 395).

16. *I.A.C.D.*, p. 75 *et seq.*, F. H. Bell, *Newry, Warrenpoint and Rostrevor* (Belfast, 1989), p. 66; A. M. Wilson, *St Patrick's town* (Belfast, 1995), p. 114. Although there was a quay at Downpatrick, Strangford remained its outport for large ships which could not negotiate the shallow River Quoile.

17. Killough was then known as Port St. Anne, after Ward's wife. He did not use Strangford (only 1½ miles from Castleward) because it was owned by a different landlord, to whom harbour dues would have been payable. Ward's activities at Killough are documented in the Castleward letter books, P. R. O. N. I., Ward Mss, D.2092/1.

18. A. Young, *A tour in Ireland, 1776-1779* (Dublin, 1780), i, p. 191; *A.S.C.D.*, p. 433.

19. Ibid., p. 417.

20. At places such as Greyabbey, where there was no quay, boats were loaded on the beach as the tide ebbed.

21. *I.A.C.D.*, p. 79.

22. Ordnance survey memoirs for county Down (Dublin, 1836), [hereafter *O.S.M.*], Ardglass Parish. The outer pier and lighthouse were severely damaged by a storm soon afterwards, but it was not until 1885 that they were finally rebuilt by the Board of Works.

23. *I.A.C.D.*, p. 79.

24. *Fourth report of the commissioners of the Irish fisheries*, H.C. 1823, x, p. 408.

25. Unfortunately, this did not prevent the SS Great Britain from running aground on Tyrella beach in 1846; it was refloated the following year. The light was raised to its present height in 1893.

26. *Second report of the railway commissioners*, p. 813 *et seq.*

27. *O.S.M.*, Ardglass Parish.

28. Wilson, *St. Patrick's town*, p. 163. The company was chaired by Lord Bangor (Edward Southwell Ward).

29. *Fourth report of the commissioners of the Irish fisheries*, app. 2.

30. *The parliamentary gazetteer of Ireland, 1847-48* (Dublin, 1850), iii, p. 17. The harbour also served as a base for HM. Coast guard, smuggling then being rife along the south Down coast.

31. 9 & 10 Vict. c.3 and 46 & 47 Vict.. c.26, respectively. The Board of Works was established by Act of Parliament in 1831, and took over the responsibilities of the commissioners of Irish fisheries. For details of the grants made to various harbours in county Down, see *Second report of the royal commission on Irish public works*, H.C. 1888, xlviii, p. 143 *et seq.*

32. *O.S.M.*, Kilkeel Parish (1836).

33. *Fourth report of the commissioners of the Irish fisheries*, p. 410. For details of subsequent improvements, see M. McCaughan, 'Nineteenth century accounts of maritime activity at Annalong' in T. Steele and P. Robinson (ed.), *Field excursions in Ulster, 3: the Annalong district of the Mournes, county Down* (Cultra, 1985), pp 24-35.

34. M. McCaughan, *Sailing the seaways* (Belfast, 1991), p. 8.

35. J. E. M. Crosbie, *A tour of the Ards* (Belfast, 1990), p. 5; G. H. Bassett, *County Down guide and directory* (Belfast, 1886; reprinted 1988), p. 358; A. Steele, 'Improvements at Portavogie harbour, 1952-55' in *Trans. Institution Civil Engineers N. Ireland* (1956), p. 2.

36. Although work started on a 4½ mile canal between Coalisland and the Blackwater in 1733, it was not completed until 1787.

37. For details of the canal, see *I.A.C.D.*, pp 64-70; *I.A.N.I.*, pp 52-5; and Delany, *Inland waterways*, p. 19 *et seq*.

38. Bell, *Newry*, p. 30.

39. *I.A.C.D.*, p. 80. Convenient access to the quay was probably a decisive factor in the decision to build a large flour-grinding windmill adjacent to it in 1802.

40. T. Canavan, *Frontier town: an illustrated history of Newry* (Belfast, 1989), p. 76.

41. Young, *Tour*, i, p. 155.

42. *I.A.N.I.*, p. 55.

43. *I.A.C.D.*, p. 62. The light was relocated to Haulbowline Rock, further out in the channel, in 1824. A second lighthouse was also erected at Greenore Point, on the opposite side of the channel about 1827. A deeper channel was excavated through the bar in the 1860s.

44. J. Rennie, 'On the improvement of the navigation of the River Newry' in *Proc. Institution Civil Engineers*, x (1851), pp 277-93. Green states that the ship canal and lock were the second largest in the world at that time (*I.A.C.D.*, p. 61).

45. D. B. McNeill, *Irish steamship passenger services* (Newton Abbot, 1971), ii, p. 73.

46. Rostrevor was linked to Warrenpoint by a horse-drawn tram in 1878; this operated until 1915.

47. In the 1850s there were also short-lived connections to Ardrossan and Preston, and in the 1870s to Swansea (McNeill, *Irish steamship services*, p. 78).

48. In 1831, Newry handled 103,560 tons of goods, of which 68 percent was carried by the inland canal. By 1888, however, although the Newry traffic had increased to 363,558 tons, only 9 per cent of it was now carried on the inland section (*I.A.N.I.*, p. 78).

49. This line was constructed by the Newry & Enniskillen railway company as part of a scheme to run a line between the two towns. In the end, it got as far as Armagh.

50. This linkage was strengthened by the extension of the railway from Portadown to Armagh in 1848, and to Monaghan in 1858.

51. *Shaw's tourist's picturesque guide to Carlingford Bay and the county Down* (London, 1877).

52. From 1873 to 1876, the railway company ran a passenger ferry between Greenore and Warrenpoint. From 1880, there was also a feeder to and from Greencastle; this operated until passenger services between Greenore and Holyhead ceased in 1926 (freight services continued until 1951).

53. Although Torr Head to the Mull of Kintyre is the shortest distance (13 miles), their rocky coastlines preclude harbours and the tidal flows make navigation difficult.

54. IA.C.D., p. 76. For details of the port's development see *Report upon the harbour*

of Portpatrick made to the board of trade, H.C. 1884, lxxi, pp 441-59.

55. De Latocnaye, writing in 1797, reported that almost 30,000 cattle had been shipped in a six week period prior to his crossing (J. Stevenson (ed.), *A Frenchman's walk through Ireland 1796-7* (Belfast, 1917), p. 225).

56. *Reports by John Rennie ... relative to the improvement of the communications between Ireland and Scotland by the north*, H.C. 1820, ix, pp 469-77.

57. *O.S.M.*, Donaghadee Parish (1837). It was to be another nine years before the lighthouse at the end of the pier was illuminated, and not until the 1840s that the detached north pier (which acted as a breakwater) was finished.

58. For details of the railway company's development, see the annual reports in *Bradshaw's railway manual, shareholders guide and directory*.

59. This was only five years after the opening of Ireland's first railway between Dublin and Kingstown (now Dún Laoghaire).

60. By 1853, Dublin had rail connections with Cork, Galway, Limerick and Waterford. Shortly after the completion of this link, Belfast was thus connected to all of Ireland's principal towns.

61. Fuller details of the B.C.D.R. are to be found in E. M. Patterson, *The Belfast & county Down railway* (Newton Abbot, 1982), and *I.A.N.I.*, pp 138-57.

62. Both Dargan and Godwin had already been involved with the Ulster railway. Dargan was subsequently to construct so many other lines that he became known as the 'father' of Irish railways.

63. Two large cotton mills, erected in the early nineteenth century, burnt down in 1856.

64. Plans to extend the railway to Greencastle, via Kilkeel, as a feeder to the Greenore ferry never came to fruition.

65. The G.N.R. came into being in 1876 as a result of the amalgamation of the Ulster railway, Northern railway (itself an amalgamation of the Dublin & Drogheda railway and Dublin & Belfast Junction railway), and the Irish North Western railway.

66. Part of this line had already been constructed some years earlier by the Banbridge extension railway, an undertaking formed in 1861. The scheme was halted for about five years and the company went bankrupt in 1868.

67. *I.A.N.I.*, p. 154.

68. For examples of these operations, see H. Irvine, 'Mourne sailing coaster operation in 1900-01' in *12 Miles of Mourne*, i (1987), pp 62-74. Annalong was the last schooner port in Ulster (McCaughan, *Sailing the seaways*, p. 116).

69. J. Magee, *A journey through Lecale* (Belfast, 1991), p. 82.

70. For details of recent work at these harbours, see J. S. Moore, 'The design and construction of the new breakwater extension at Kilkeel harbour' in *Trans. Institution Civil Engineers Northern Ireland* (1955); P. A. Doyle, 'Extension and modernisation of Kilkeel harbour, county Down' in *Trans. Institution Civil Engineers Northern Ireland* (1973); A. Steele, 'Improvements at Portavogie harbour, Northern Ireland, 1952-55' in *Trans. Institution Civil Engineers Northern Ireland* (1956).

71. R. Ferguson, 'Newry ship canal improvement scheme' in *Trans. Institution Civil Engineers Northern Ireland* (1937), pp 51-78.

72 For a fuller discussion of freight and bus services, see *I.A.N.I.*, p. 154; and Patterson, *B.C.D.R.*, p. 30.

Chapter 23

EAST BELFAST AND THE SUBURBANIZATION OF NORTH-WEST COUNTY DOWN IN THE NINETEENTH CENTURY

R. TIMOTHY CAMPBELL AND STEPHEN A. ROYLE

During the course of the nineteenth century, Belfast changed from being a market town with a social, technological and physical structure that was recognisably pre-industrial to a Victorian industrial city. Its population growth, from 53,287 in 1831 to 349,180 in 1901, meant that for every person in the town at the earlier period there were almost seven by 1901, while the town's economy, society and socio-spatial structure changed beyond recognition. Many among the growing population in this 'city devoted to making money'[1] were involved in industry and commerce. Tens of thousands were manual workers in factories, mills and shipyards. Initially, such people were accommodated close to their employment, although later, after the development of reasonably cheap, intra-urban transportation, some lived further from their work. A more pronounced centrifugal movement affected the smaller numbers of industrialists, professional and commercial people. In the 1820s and 1830s many of this group resided in terraced townhouses to the south of the town centre, around Donegall Square. Their removal from these large terraces to the suburbs was a significant factor in the transformation of Belfast's socio-spatial structure, and it had considerable impact on surrounding rural areas, including county Down. In Belfast as elsewhere, the middling groups aped the rich and followed them to the suburbs. This chapter will trace this process of suburbanization as it affected the north-west corner of county Down.

Belfast in the early-nineteenth century
In the early-nineteenth century, Belfast covered approximately 2.5 square kilometres, and within this area, rich and poor lived in close proximity to one another.[2] The town had a need for both cholera carts and sedan chairs. The wealthiest citizens resided in or near Donegall

Square, which in 1837 still contained 'the best situations in town as private residences. Very commodious and handsomely fitted out in every way'.[3] However, nearby were the slums and courts of the Smithfield area. These included Kennedy's Entry near Barrack Street, described in the same year as 'a nasty, dirty, unhealthy entry [with] a very poor set of tenants'.[4]

In these years most of the gentry in the Belfast area – 64 per cent according to Pigot's directory[5] – chose to live in the town itself, alongside the prosperous merchant classes. Other gentry families such as the Montgomerys of Benvarden, the Douglas family from Mount Ida, and the Sinclairs from Brookvale were seasonal occupants, spending the winter 'season' in the town, promenading, throwing parties and going to the theatre.[6] Town living, even on a part-time basis, allowed the rich and powerful to monitor and influence decision-making within what was becoming a key regional centre. Additionally, townhouse acquisition provided a common outlet for local investment before the establishment of banking and trade forums.[7] The wealthy owned numerous properties in the town in the nineteenth century, and these were often leased within their own families or to professional people.

This urban environment was divided into micro-social arenas by major social gulfs which existed over surprisingly short physical distances. The smallest were between different floors in the townhouse terraces, where servants in attic quarters were only a few metres away from 'the quality'. The furthest distance was just the few score metres from the townhouses to the cabins and courts which were found on the western edge of the small town. Other poor people occupied more central property in alleyways and lanes to the rear of the main thoroughfares. Heatley has described Belfast's socio-spatial structure at this time with admirable succinctness. 'The lower classes had their dwellings in the back streets or lived in the cellars or garrets of their employers; the middle or business classes resided in or above their shops on the main thoroughfares'.[8] Such proximity could prove unsettling for the wealthy. Narcissus Batt, a resident of Donegall Place, recalled that the riots between Orangemen from Sandy Row and the Hercules Street butchers often occurred in front of his house, and that on Sundays ladies had to band together for protection to go to church. Writing in 1873 to George Benn, Leonard Dobbin recalled his earliest memory – Lord Castlereagh's lodging house being stoned. Moreover, 'His Lordship had on the previous Sunday been mobbed by the Hercules Street people on his way from St Anne's Church in Donegall Street and escaped more serious consequences by being with a lady at the time'.[9] Even the town's landlord was not safe – on one occasion Lord Arthur Chichester was mobbed and his hansom chair ripped to pieces, whilst during the 1837 elections he was verbally abused by a mob, who showed their contempt for his fashionable beard by taunting him with 'Beardie'.

Wealthy inhabitants also had to endure the spectre of disease which knew no social barriers, even the best houses had inadequate water supplies with cesspools as the main sanitary arrangements. Between 1830 and 1850 numerous epidemics ravaged the town, many being brought in by vessels at the docks. The small Blackstaff river became an open sewer with the filth from numerous factories, institutions and over eight hundred homes flowing into it. The town also became crowded by poor country folk who sought work in the mills, thus avoiding the inherent insecurities of rural Irish life such as harvest failure. O'Hanlon and Malcolm have presented the best-known accounts of Belfast's poverty in the mid-nineteenth century.[10] The field books of the 1837 poor law valuation provide another source of contemporary comment: 'filthy, dirty and unwholesome, has always been infected by the worst of characters' being a typical description, in this case of Fulton's Entry near Hercules Street.[11]

Movement out

In a move made possible by Belfast's growing industrial economy and new transport technology, and made desirable by the deterioration in the urban environment, the wealthy urbanites living in the town centre followed the example of the landed gentry, who had traditionally been seated in the country, and moved out. Collins describes the pattern of housing that had resulted by the Edwardian period, noting that

> its roots were in the early industrial development of the city and the subsequent exodus of the middle and professional classes from their Donegall Square townhouses, whose grandeur had declined as the smokey industrial chimneys increased, to the more spacious and airy suburbs.[12]

By 1860 only ten of the twenty-eight houses in Donegall Place remained as private residences, and by 1884 Donegall Square had become a commercial rather than a residential area. In contrast, the gentrification of Belfast's rural fringe had its beginnings in the mid-eighteenth century, when leases taken by gentlemen began to replace those of farmers.[13] The movement to the countryside became increasingly significant from the early-nineteenth century, when a plethora of minor seats developed on the fringes of the town.

As on the fringes of north and south Belfast, the germ of upper and middle-class suburbia in north-west county Down was the gentry's demesne or park. The well-drained sands and gravels of the county Down side of the Lagan valley influenced the siting of demesnes, while topography, as at Strandtown or Knocknagoney, could also have an effect. Developers certainly tried to avoid low-lying land which might be subject to flooding. This is nowhere clearer than on the Malone Road, in south Belfast, where high class development occupied a ridge of glacial deposits, 'a remarkable case of valuation isopleths [being] concurrent with contours'.[14] Once in place, the larger estates attracted smaller ones and formed semi-rural landscapes and the cores for future suburbs. These owed 'their character more to the immediately preceding landscape of parks than they [did] to the so-called natural landscape'.[15]

Some of these estates were funded from the profits arising from the increased banking turnover in the first half of the nineteenth century. Thus the Herons built Maryfield; the Batts, Purdysburn; the Crawfords, Crawfordsburn; and the Houstons, Orangefield, all largely from banking fortunes. Alcohol production financed Strandtown for the Craigs, Redburn for the Dunvilles and Richmond for the Turnleys, while cotton and linen manufacture built Ballywalter for the Mulhollands, Glenmachan for the Ewarts and Holywood House for the Harrisons. Not surprisingly, shipbuilding also contributed a number of houses, including the Martins' Connsbrook, the Harrisons' Mertoun Hall and the Harlands' (later the Pirries') Ormiston.

In 1833, 117 of these named 'seats' surrounded Belfast and occupied some 4,412 acres (1,787 hectares [ha.]), averaging just under 40 acres (16.2 ha.) per demesne. Fifty-eight were in county Down. By 1901 the overall total had risen to 164 demesnes totalling 5,568 acres (2,255 ha., a third of which was woodland), of which eighty-seven were located in county Down – roughly the same proportion as seventy years previously (fig. 23.1). In the early decades of the nineteenth century, with some notable exceptions, these houses were usually no more than large gentlemen's farmsteads, set between two and five kilometres from the town and with a sizeable amount of land given over to woodland, ornamental gardens and often some type of agrarian industry such as corn milling. Others retained a semi-agricultural base, giving a few fields over to ornamental, kitchen or walled gardens and/or orchards, but with most of the land planted and drained, and used for grazing or arable crops as a picturesque though profitable backdrop. The county Down demesnes included Belvoir, the largest in the region, which at one period incorporated over 706 acres (286 ha.) of pleasure grounds and woodland, three times larger than its close rival and neighbour, Purdysburn.

By the 1830s these developments had created five distinct house-building areas to the east of the Lagan in county Down (fig. 23.2). The most conspicuous was a continuous band of nine demesnes which ran

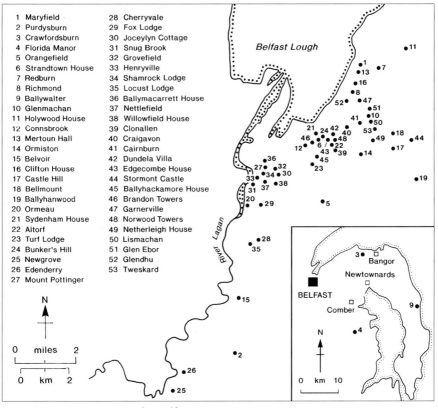

1 Maryfield	28 Cherryvale
2 Purdysburn	29 Fox Lodge
3 Crawfordsburn	30 Joceylyn Cottage
4 Florida Manor	31 Snug Brook
5 Orangefield	32 Grovefield
6 Strandtown House	33 Henryville
7 Redburn	34 Shamrock Lodge
8 Richmond	35 Locust Lodge
9 Ballywalter	36 Ballymacarrett House
10 Glenmachan	37 Nettlefield
11 Holywood House	38 Willowfield House
12 Connsbrook	39 Clonallen
13 Mertoun Hall	40 Craigavon
14 Ormiston	41 Cairnburn
15 Belvoir	42 Dundela Villa
16 Clifton House	43 Edgecombe House
17 Castle Hill	44 Stormont Castle
18 Bellmount	45 Ballyhackamore House
19 Ballyhanwood	46 Brandon Towers
20 Ormeau	47 Garnerville
21 Sydenham House	48 Norwood Towers
22 Altorf	49 Netherleigh House
23 Turf Lodge	50 Lismachan
24 Bunker's Hill	51 Glen Ebor
25 Newgrove	52 Glendhu
26 Edenderry	53 Tweskard
27 Mount Pottinger	

Fig. 23.1   Demesnes in the Belfast area in 1901.

from Knocknagoney to Holywood and overlooked Belfast Lough. This included Maryfield and Clifton House. To the south of this lay a cluster of demesnes sharing the same elevation and prospect of Dundonald, and these had been built around eighteenth-century cores such as Castle Hill and Bellmount, or gentrified farmhouses such as Ballyhanwood. Running parallel to the River Lagan was the smallest set of houses, satellites of the marquis of Donegall's Ormeau. These were owned by Belfast traders. Stretching beyond them towards the slopes of Kocknagoney was another set of houses and demesnes, based around Orangefield and Bloomfield, while at Ballyhackamore an outer fringe of smaller merchant dwellings included Turf Lodge, Conn's Brook and Bunker Hill. Lastly there were the enormous demesnes of Belvoir and Purdysburn near Knockbreda, around which smaller demesnes like Newgrove and Edenderry hugged the Lagan plains to the south of the town. Later these areas would be submerged in the process of suburbanization.

During the nineteenth century, another class of smaller villas began

633

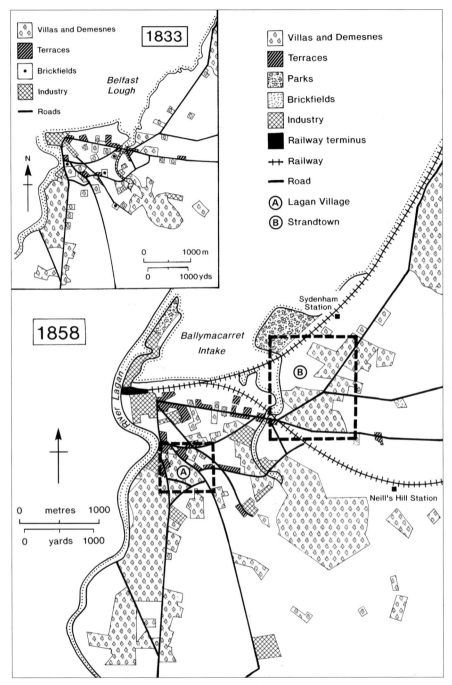

Fig. 23.2 Land-use in east Belfast in 1833 and 1858.

to be built in ever greater numbers. These were constructed for the multiplying middle classes in emulation of the landed aristocracy, and generally stood within two kilometres of the town boundaries – to facilitate commuting. These villas were usually set within nothing grander than a large garden, in contrast to the older and larger houses which ringed them. Doubtlessly, however, as in all cities where this process was taking place, their owners imagined they were living in 'a mini-estate [where] the shrubbery was the woodland [and] the dogs were the livestock'.[16] Their pretensions, rural setting and convenience to the town made these villas popular with the growing commercial class, and they constituted a key element in the nineteenth-century suburban development of Belfast.

This imitation of older and generally larger 'country seats' by smaller farmsteads and villas – average demesne sizes fell to 26 acres (10.7 ha.) in 1901 – met with sharp criticism from the owners of the established properties, who considered themselves to be superior in every way to their unwelcome *nouveau riche* neighbours. Letitia Maria Charley wrote in 1841: 'You little Londoners, who live in suburban villas and see tall dreary brick houses labelled 'Woodlands', 'Glenmore' [and] 'Sunnyside' can scarcely understand the delights of a country home like ours'.[17] Such fulminations were not new to Charley's period. In the late-eighteenth century, at an earlier stage in the cyclical process of suburbanization, Martha McTear had written:

> In Belfast we nor indeed anyone can't now live on a small fortune but in an obscure and what is worse, a vulgar manner, for a small genteel house in a tolerable situation is not to be got at any moderate rent and it is crowded with rich upstarts skipping from the counter to their carriage.[18]

The most important of these proto-urban districts in relation to the development of east Belfast in the early nineteenth century was the inner area, especially the low-lying alluvial townland of Ballymacarrett. Not only was this proximate to the existing town, but it also possessed considerable manufacturing potential close to the port and, later, shipyards, and was to benefit from the release of advantageous leases by its landowner, Lord Templemore. It is useful therefore to examine the evidence from this area to show the processes through which east Belfast developed.

The development of inner east Belfast from the late-eighteenth century to the 1860s

Ballymacarrett had developed as a road junction on the edge of the

Belfast Lough slobland prior to the development of the Long Bridge in 1682. In 1672 it was transferred by the 1st earl of Clanbrassil to Thomas Pottinger, the first sovereign of Belfast for £300 and an annual rent of £30.

The Pottingers were one of the earliest Belfast families to be mentioned by name (in 1662),[19] and gave their name to Pottinger's Entry and other places. They built Mount Pottinger (later called 'The Mount'). This was a large house which was described in the 1837 valuation as being 78 feet (*ca.* 24 metres) tall, suggesting three storeys over a basement. The family had been noted by Harris[20] in 1744 as the only residents of consequence in the district, but had removed from the area in the late-eighteenth century.[21] Their decision to move might have been influenced by the increasing number of disturbances in rumbustious Belfast, just over the bridge; while the possibility of a new road to Newtownards, in 1771, undoubtedly offered the prospect of more traffic in the area. However, the family had also experienced financial problems associated to a great extent with the extravagant spending of a Pottinger widow.[22] It was perhaps this as much as anything which forced the Pottingers to sell Ballymacarrett to Barry Yelverton, lord chief baron, subsequently Viscount Avonmore, for £18,133 5s 0d. Although the house was not involved in this first transaction, they were subsequently obliged to advertise the sale of this, too, in 1787.[23] The Pottinger name, however, continued in the area into the early-nineteenth century: a family member was born there in 1811, but The Mount had certainly been sold by 1823 when James Ferguson lived there.[24] Some of the Pottingers moved to Craigavad, others to the United States, and still others to Mount Pottinger, county Leitrim and other seats.[25]

Following his purchase, Yelverton set about building a number of streets in Ballymacarrett, and

> seeing the advantage which must arise from building a town opposite Belfast, formed an embankment of 300 yards in length, and marked out the places so enclosed into streets, which he let to tenants in perpetuity, in opposition to the custom of Lord Donegall, who set up his leases for sale.[26]

This breakup of the Pottinger leasehold created the first round of significant urban development in the area, as the following advertisement in the *Belfast News Letter* from the late 1780s indicates: 'five acres of land near Mount Pottinger, in Ballymacarrett, for three lives and 41 years from May 1786 at a yearly rent of 45s. per acre. The situation is particularly well adapted for a country seat and excellent brick may be made on the premises'.[27] Another advert offered: 'A Very Good Meadow situated on the third Loaning on the south side of the New road leading from Belfast to the New Bridge, [this site] being the most beautiful on the estate for a Dwelling-House'.[28] However, across the river in Belfast, the 1st marquis of Donegall was not keen to see the development of a rival town outside his control and he bought the entire estate from Yelverton for £20,000. This was not part of the property he was obliged to leave to his eldest son, the notorious 2nd marquis. It was inherited instead by his second son, Lord Spencer Chichester, in 1799.

Prior to Donegall's purchase of Ballymacarrett, the townland of Ballynafeigh was the only toehold the family had in county Down. It was in this district that the Donegalls settled in the early-nineteenth century, at Ormeau, a move which enhanced the residential prestige of that part of the east bank. Ormeau, with its unusual French name meaning 'young elm', had been leased by the Donegalls to Edward Kingsmill (née Brice), an agent for Lord Dungannon and collector of customs for the port of Belfast. When Kingsmill died in 1796[29] its house had been occupied by his son-in-law, Captain Cortland Skinner, until around 1803 when the lease was relinquished. The Donegalls kept possession of the property from this time, favouring it as a country retreat in addition to Parkmount on the Shore Road and their town-house close to the White Linen Hall.[30] When they were obliged to sell perpetuity leases in Belfast in an attempt to clear the massive personal debts incurred by the 2nd marquis, some of the money was spent instead on the development of Ormeau. The house was 'Tudorised' to designs supplied by William Morrison and the work supervised by local architects Michael McGaffigan and Thomas Price at a cost of around £6,000.[31] The first valuation reveals that this work greatly enhanced Ormeau 'Castle' which was then (in 1838) worth £142.

The rural nature of the county Down side of the Lagan, highlighted by the numerous piggeries, cattle sheds and potato houses associated with Ormeau and other demesnes, was in stark contrast to the increasingly crowded, ill-drained and disease-laden Cromac district just across the river. In particular, Ormeau, with its landscaped demesne, pheasantry and racing stud added social prestige to the Ballynafeigh area. It acted as a magnet for the aspiring middle-classes who wanted to live in an elite neighbourhood, convenient to the town centre but not surrounded by rows of labourers' cabins. Houses near Ormeau included Cherryvale, built after 1827, for James Stewart, a businessman, and Fox Lodge, a very substantial house built on 12.2 hectares in 1817, named after William Fox,[32] the first and only town mayor of Belfast (1797-1818). Another advantage offered by this district was the fact that it lay outside the town boundary and thus was subject to fewer building and leasing restrictions, a consideration which also encouraged the development of Strandtown prior to the extension of Belfast's boundary in 1896.

To the north, Ballymacarrett was affected less by the proximity of the Donegalls than by the growth of industrialization. Several industries had developed from the late-eighteenth century including glass houses, a pottery and vitriol works.[33] One of the most important industries as far as residential development was concerned was Edward Stainton's and Victor Coates' Lagan Foundry. Several rows of houses were provided by the foundry to accommodate its workers and these provided the nucleus for the development of Lagan Village. Coates, who had numerous other trading interests, inherited the foundry on Stainton's death in 1802.[34] Prior to his own death in 1822, Coates had expanded its range of products to include mill machinery and marine engines, including those for the first Irish steam ship, *Belfast*, launched in 1820. Later the foundry also made the 240 horse power engines for the *Aurora* launched from Connell's yard on the Antrim shore in 1838.

The *Ordnance survey memoirs* record that by the 1830s, 959 families comprising 3,000 people lived in Ballymacarrett in some 791 houses. Most were Protestant. The Church of Ireland built St Patrick's on the Newtownards Road in 1827 for £1,500, a 'small building, but large enough (560 seats) for the locality'.[35] The First Ballymacarrett Presbyterian Church, also on the Newtownards Road, was erected in 1837. Roman Catholics were catered for by St Matthew's, originally built in 1831 as a temporary chapel, again on the Newtownards Road but with an entrance from Seaforde Street. During the same period over half of the families were engaged in manufacturing whilst only a minority remained in agriculture. As the area industrialized further, so the population rose even more. The *Parliamentary gazetteer* recorded a 17 per cent increase in population between 1831 and 1841 alone with a 27 per cent rise in the number of houses, describing Ballymacarret as becoming 'strictly suburban'.[36] On the ground these statistics were realised in the development of numerous sets of whitewashed 'villages'. They included Lagan Village, Short Strand, Gooseberry Corner, Lennon's Row and Bridge End, the last three 'as a rule almost always bordering on poverty'.[37]

Between these clusters of smaller houses lay the large demesnes, described in the Ballymacarrett tithe applotment books of 1833 as being situated on 'first quality' land. They were owned or leased by local professionals and merchants, many of whom worked in Belfast. In the Lagan Village area for example, several demesnes existed, the most prominent of which was Snug Brook, the residence of Victor

Coates. This had been built on part of the Ormeau demesne as a square Georgian block *ca.* 1800. In 1837, however, the house was modernized and enlarged, a re-edification made possible by the success of the foundry. Nearby Grovefield was leased by a teacher at Belfast Academy before being occupied in the 1830s by Conway Blizzard who had run a damask manufactory in Lurgan.[38] With the exception of Snug Brook, most of these residences, including Wallace's Henryville, John Young's Shamrock Lodge and Blizzard's Grovefield, were of a similar large size. House prices were extravagant. Jocelyn Cottage, for example, was leased to Alexander Finley by the Hon. J. Jocelyn for £36 per year. Such rates were sometimes hard to extract, however, as the Templemore rentals reveal in numerous notes about tenants. John Montgomery of Locust Lodge, for example, was 'a solicitor in Belfast. I have great trouble in getting rent from him'.[39] As well as having trouble paying for their lifestyle, some gentlemen were not, it seems, that genteel. In 1833, for example, Fortescue Gregg, a partner in the Gregg and Boyd Vitriol Works, of Ballymacarrett House and Knockcairn, and his friend, C. M. Skinner, were fined £5 for their assault on a man on the Long Bridge.[40] Gregg was a J.P. and the Dutch Consul; the money went to the Ballymacarrett poor.

Information explaining the distribution of property can be obtained by comparing the returns of the first valuation with the Templemore estate map of 1847 which shows the types of tenure available in Ballymacarrett. From the tenants' point of view, tenancies-at-will were the least secure, as their terms could be altered independently by the ground landlord. As figure 21.2 shows, this type of leasehold generally dissuaded urban investment, although there were some exceptions, such as the Lagan Village school house, which had a rateable value of £4 16s 0d. More typical of a tenancy at will was Bridge End. This was first used as a brickfield and then was subsequently developed in the 1830s with poor quality houses, worth mainly between £3 and £4 a year.

By contrast, the industrial core of Lagan Village was built on the security of perpetuity leases, as were the major dwellings of the period such as Henryville, Grovefield and Snug Brook. Mount Pottinger, just outside Lagan Village, was also built on land held in perpetuity. Such leases provided a safer investment for those wishing to build on a larger scale and they provide the key to understanding the distribution of later proto-urban development. Carleton[41] notes the scarcity and modesty of gentlemen's dwellings in neighbouring Malone in the eighteenth century before longer leases, and perpetuity interests in particular, were made available on the Donegall estate after 1822. Nevertheless, despite giving rise to large urban investments, these secure leases were in themselves no guarantee of the quality of the resulting townscape; money could be made from crowding plots with the small houses for which there was a growing demand. Both Woodstock Road and My Lady's Road, for example, were lined with houses which were so poor that they were exempt from rateable valuation. Typically, their occupants were described in the Templemore papers as 'industrious' but 'poor'.[42] In his autobiography,[43] Samuel Elliott of Gooseberry Corner noted that these poorer houses were supplying the needs of the growing numbers of workers in the factories of Ballymacarrett and in Belfast's booming cotton industry. By 1819, practically every dwelling in Lagan Village housed people spinning for one of the four local cotton manufacturers. These houses, often whitewashed stone cabins of one storey, had in many cases just a single room, with an earthen floor sometimes damp enough to promote rheumatism, fever or ague. Their doors and windows were seldom effective in keeping out the rain. Accommodation of this type rented at around 1s 6d per week. The few two-storey dwellings were more expensive and contained three bedrooms and a front kitchen. Despite its growth, in the first part of the nineteenth century Ballymacarrett was still fairly rural and Belfast continued to be supplied by vegetables grown there, some of them from the front gardens of the small cottages.

By the mid-nineteenth century the Donegall connection with east Belfast was in decline. The 2nd marquis died at Ormeau in October 1844, after which the house was inhabited by Thomas Verner, the acting agent for his cousin and heir, the 3rd marquis. The Donegalls built their last Belfast home, Belfast Castle, back on the Antrim side on the slopes of Cave Hill. Partly auctioned in 1857,[44] the house at Ormeau was largely demolished and empty – save for a caretaker – by the time of Griffith's valuation in the 1860s. In 1865 Edward Kemp put forward plans to develop Ormeau with forty-two substantial villas,[45] but Belfast Corporation acquired the demesne in 1869. Although some housing, a golf course and, in modern times, other leisure facilities have been sited on it, most of the land remains open space as Ormeau Park. The house itself was demolished and its bricks used to build Robb's warehouse in Castle Place.

The Griffith's valuation shows the emerging pattern of leasehold ownership and the distribution and quality of housing in the Lagan Village area in the 1860s. By this stage the area was effectively split in three (fig. 23.3). In the north-west sector the Coates family continued to develop the land they held in perpetuity, having acquired further property at Bridge End. To the east, The Mount, also on a perpetuity lease, was being further developed by Francis Ritchie. To the south and south-east, Lord Templemore continued to hold his own land. In

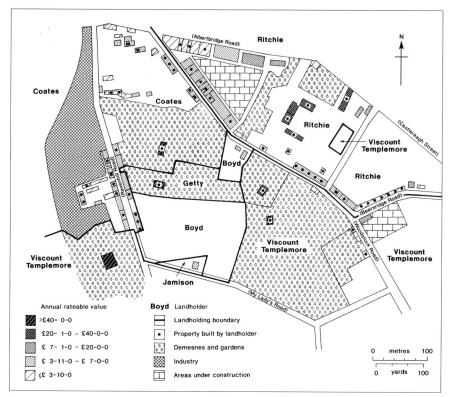

Fig. 23.3   Leaseholding, land-use and rateable value of housing in Lagan Village in the 1860s.

addition there were three other important leaseholders occupying previously less secure parcels of land. In the central area these included Samuel Getty, of Shamrock Lodge, who was the only owner-occupier; Hugh Jamison and the manufacturers, Boyds. Much of this central part of the area between the Woodstock Road and Lagan Village was given over to demesnes at this time.

By 1854 Snug Brook had been renamed Glentoran but remained the residence of the Coates family. By then, their foundry had grown with several outlets in the town, in Castle Street and Fountain Street. Their business success led to there being 'hardly a manufacturing concern ... in [the] district with whom the firm Coates & Son have not agreeable commercial relations'.[46] Glentoran reflected this wealth and the status of the then family head, William Coates, who was chairman of the Belfast Water Trust. It was the largest and most ornamental house in the area, with a demesne boasting both gatelodge and lake. Ironically, despite their wealth and their ownership of most of the leases for Lagan Village, the family remained as tenants of Glentoran.

The newest villa was Nettlefield, built off My Lady's Road probably in the 1850s by Frederick Harold Lewis, a prosperous timber merchant based in Great George's Street. Adjoining this was Grovefield, occupied by Andrew Clarke who had replaced Blizzard by 1854. Clarke was a grocer in Anne Street who saw the advantage of taking his trade to the developing county Down side of the town: he opened a store on the Woodstock Road by 1858. Backing onto Grovefield was Shamrock Lodge which was leased to James Wright, a commercial agent, after John Young died. It was subsequently sold to Francis Devlin who lived there in 1863. At Henryville in Lagan Village, Mr Wallace had been replaced by Herbert Smith, the owner of Hargrave's Commercial Hotel in Victoria Street, by 1858. When he died his wife continued in the house until it was sold in 1878 to W. E. Jamison, a tea merchant from Skipper Street. By the 1860s, Francis Ritchie had built numerous dwellings on the north side of the Woodstock Road of varying quality. Those at Gooseberry Corner were among the worst. Sir Henry's Buildings, built on his leasehold near Mount Pottinger and occupied by skilled and semi-skilled workers, were larger, as were the houses on Castlereagh Street. Between 1838 and 1849, the old Mount Pottinger demesne had been remodelled as a square of substantial gentlemen's houses, complete with spacious gardens. Here the social division split equally between gentry and captains of industry, the professional classes and those with a well-paid skilled occupation.

The social segregation identified by Griffith in Lagan Village was startling. Financially, the gulf between rich and poor was great, but the physical distance between them was small. Inferior cottages and houses, many of less than £3 annual rateable value lined the roads to the very gates of houses with a valuation ten times as large. Often, as at Glentoran, this pattern indicated an industrialist's need to be close to his business – and the fact that those who lived in the larger houses had themselves built the smaller ones. Ritchie built to house the workforce for his factories, while Coates built both for this reason – Lagan Village was inhabited mostly by his employees – and as a speculative venture.

In many cases, Ballymacarrett provided no improvement on the poor housing infrastructure and inadequate sanitary conditions associated with the slum neighbourhoods across the Lagan. In 1849 the sanitary committee's report described the scene:

> A more neglected portion of the town cannot be well conceived. An almost complete want of drainage, extensive accumulations of liquid manure here and there immediately in the rere of dwelling-houses, and a general absence of house accommodations, are its chief characteristics.[47]

Malcolm added that 'the rain from the clouds and the sewage from the dwellings are at liberty to make their own intersections and channels, without any interference on the part of man'.[48] Smaller dwellings were simple two-storey affairs with two rooms on each floor, but many would have accommodated two families, a practice which could still be identified in some courts in Lagan Village as late as 1901.

This poor standard of working-class accommodation helps to explain why the Templemores wished to improve conditions in Ballymacarrett. Henry Spencer Chichester, Baron Templemore, had inherited the area in 1837. In 1849 he had his property surveyed and fours years later had a development plan drawn up by John Fraser, one time surveyor for county Down. Ballymacarrett was to be completely remodelled with a new street pattern and extensive areas set aside for villa development and sites for manufactories. Areas of wet land such as the Connswater estuary were to be drained. Had the plan been acted upon, Ballymacarrett would have developed in an entirely different, more extensive and more ordered fashion. However, the plan was almost completely abandoned, probably because of the cost of buying back land already leased out in perpetuity or on long leases. Of the proposed streets, the only one which was certainly built was Templemore Avenue, named after the landowner. Generous in length and width, the avenue stands out from the other residential and industrial streets in Ballymacarrett. After abandoning his plan, Lord Templemore focused his attention on his other property, particularly in county Donegal, and let the plots in Ballymacarrett out for development by leaseholders, evidently being content with the modest but secure income from leasehold fines and ground rents.[49] Thus in 1843 he received a total of £2,062 from the leases, an average of around £18 per lease. By 1876, Templemore, who was by then living in London, held only 26 acres (10.5 ha.) directly. Worth some £1,405 a year this was less than the sums earned by both Ritchie and Coates. Twenty-five years later, in 1901, the number of income-generating leases on the Templemore's Ballymacarrett estate had fallen by 18 per cent, although the total sum they produced had increased to £6,130.[50]

East Belfast from the 1860s to 1901

The sale of the Templemore property in Ballymacarrett meant that there was now no overall estate control on residential or industrial development in east Belfast. Whereas the Donegalls had been prepared to buy out Yelverton to discourage leasing in perpetuity and maintain overall control, the estate now fell into the hands of a number of Belfast businessmen, many of whom were industrialists. This alone was enough to help dramatically change the semi-rural, socially-mixed villa suburb of Ballymacarrett during the last few decades of the nineteenth century. The expansion of numerous extensive industrial concerns during this period together with the construction of the housing needed for their workforces, which in some cases ran into thousands, transformed the landscape entirely. The semi-rural scene gave way to rows of working class terraced houses, while the leisure facilities which had earlier been sited here, Queen's Park and the Crystal Palace, were transferred to new sites as the area industrialised. These included Victoria Park beyond the Connswater.

The most important of these new industries was shipbuilding, once a fairly minor concern in Belfast involving a number of small yards on the Antrim lough shore. However, shipbuilding became a major industry on the county Down shore, principally as a result of harbour improvements. Access to the port at Belfast was improved in 1839 by dredging deep water channels into the harbour area. The spoil this produced was used to reclaim large areas on the county Down shore, including Queen's Island. Although initially used for leisure purposes, this area with its flat, easily-worked land and direct access to deep water, had considerable industrial potential. In 1854, Robert Hickson of the Belfast iron works established a shipbuilding yard here, and employed Edward Harland as manager. In 1858 Harland bought the yard and in 1861 took on his assistant, Gustav Wolff, as partner. Wolff's acumen and family business connections helped secure orders, while Harland's technical skills made for competitive and reliable designs. Thus, with the growth in world trade, Harland and Wolff rose to be one of the world's premier shipbuilders by 1901.[51] In the late 1860s former employees of Harland and Wolff founded the shipbuilding concern of Workman Clark and company. Although known in Belfast as the 'wee yard', its small size was only in comparison with mighty Harland and Wolff and this firm, too, became a major shipbuilder on a world scale.

Shipbuilding also encouraged the development of numerous ancillary industries, generating business for foundries, engineering works and rope manufactories. For example, the Belfast ropeworks was founded on a four acre site in 1876, and by 1901 was the largest in the world, covering a forty acre site at Connswater which incorporated an enclosed ropewalk approximately 400 metres long.[52] Industrialization drew an unskilled and semi-skilled local workforce to Belfast, although the design and management staff, particularly in the shipyards, was recruited throughout Great Britain. The consequent in-migration resulted in a comparatively young population in the town. For example, in 1901 almost one-third of the population was under fifteen years of age while less than 20 per cent were over forty-five.

This increasing population had to be housed. The rows of terraces which were built in Ballymacarrett during this period were erected with money invested by a wide variety of individuals, many of whom lived in east Belfast. In addition, various building societies and investment companies were also active. Moreover, large contractors such as McLaughlin and Harvey or H. and J. Martin, as well as estate agents like R. J. McConnell were also sometimes involved in projects themselves, particularly during the building boom of 1895 to 1901 (fig. 23.4). By then, landlords and the larger leaseholders played a relatively minor role, a reversal of their position in the 1860s which probably resulted from government regulations of 1864 and 1878. The 1864 Act made landlords responsible for the cost of rates and repairs of all houses with a poor law valuation of less than £8, while the 1878 Act laid down even more rigorous building regulations.[53] Nevertheless landowners as a group did not cease their activity altogether, either in Ballymacarrett or in other districts in county Down. For example, in 1888 the Downshires were directly involved in the development of villa sites on 999 year leases at Cregagh and Castlereagh, while the Batesons of Belvoir built in nearby Galwally and the Strains of Galwally House built in Rosetta, Shandon Park (as the Shandon Estates Company Ltd.) and in Galwally Park.[54] Similarly in the 1890s, Sir Daniel Dixon owned many houses in east Belfast, including some in Glentoran Street, although he was more noted for his parlour and kitchen houses on swampy land-infill sites closer to Belfast Lough.[55]

The mass development of working-class housing and the associated industrialization changed the socio-economic structure of east Belfast completely. Helped by improving transportation, the professional classes and merchant gentry moved out from among the rows of terraces growing up around their demesnes and villas to the distant, but increasingly accessible, rural-urban periphery 'as soon as the brass handle was tarnished', as the old saying has it. Their movement was normally to beyond the Connswater, to Bloomfield, Strandtown and Sydenham, all of which lay outside the town boundary and thus had the advantage of lower rates. The fate of the properties they left behind is exemplified from a 1954 newspaper article on Prospect House in Ormeau, which had been sold to enable the builders H. and J. Martin to make bricks in the demesne. Entitled 'The end of an historic Belfast house', the article concluded that:

The turn of the century and the demands of a rapidly growing city for housing ... saw the lands about the house become smaller and smaller until all that remains is a little patch of ground distinguished only by a single weathered copper beach; the last of a line still standing in its own right.[56]

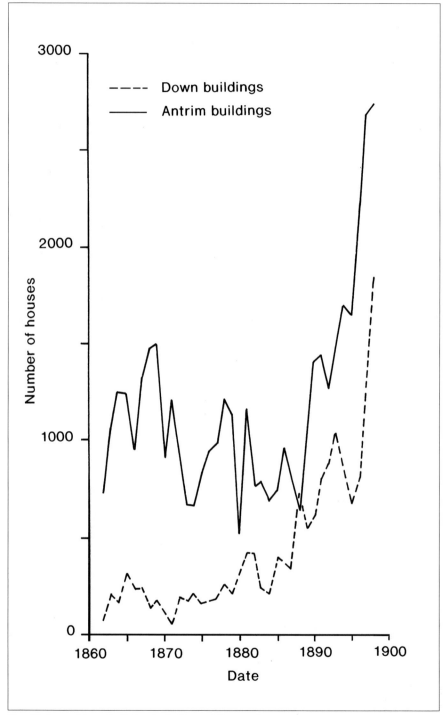

Fig. 23.4   Housebuilding in Belfast, 1860 to 1890.
Source: Belfast Street Directories: 1870-1901.

The processes involved in this late-nineteenth century socio-spatial movement and the consequent urban development of the county Down side of Belfast may be exemplified from two areas—Lagan Village, from where some of the wealthy left, and Strandtown on the urban periphery to which some of them removed. Using the 1901 Belfast revaluation, the 1901 census returns and planning proposals held in Belfast City Hall, it is possible to recreate aspects of the social and urban environment in both of these areas at the turn of the century. The 1901 revaluation is particularly informative, although as yet little used by researchers. It lists the names of occupants, age of house, number of rooms, rateable value, the dimensions of each cubic section of the dwelling, materials used in construction and an estimation of how much it would cost to rebuild. The rebuilding cost has been analyzed to provide the picture of the housing structure of east Belfast in figures 23.5 and 23.8.

The Lagan Village district in 1901

By 1901 inner-east Belfast had become almost solidly working class (fig. 23.5). Only The Mount remained to indicate the district's former prosperity. The approach to The Mount along the Albertbridge Road, with its larger and more expensive houses, prepared visitors for the

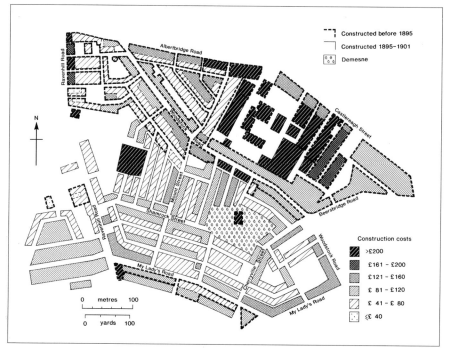

Fig. 23.5   House construction costs in Lagan Village in 1901.

area's comparative opulence. Houses at The Mount were typically ten room three or four storey affairs, costing up to £655 to replace at 1901 prices. Even so, when Francis Ritchie and Sons took over The Mount in 1894 from William B. Ritchie,[57] it had already begun to lose prestige. By then, many of the gentry and industrialists who had formed around a third of total residents in the 1860s had gone, and those who were left formed no more than 4 per cent of its population. Contemporary advertisements in local newspapers hint at this decline. When number twelve was advertised for sale in 1897, its rent was described as 'very moderate'; another advert in 1901 preferred to emphasize The Mount's suitability for stabling rather than its residential prestige.[58] The gentry and captains of industry had largely been replaced by the professional classes and the self-employed, who between the 1860s and 1901 grew from about one third of the residents to 85 per cent. They included bank managers, builders, estate agents, chemists and jewellers.

The Mount may have declined in status but it remained higher class than the surrounding areas. In contrast to other houses in the Lagan Village district, many of its properties (thirty out of forty-seven) recorded at least one servant in the 1901 census. Elsewhere, the socio-spatial transformation of inner-east Belfast was almost complete. By 1901 very bad housing was rare in Lagan Village, but it did occur where the old stone walled cottages remained. Examples included Moore Street and entries off Wallace's Row, where rebuilding costs were only £40 and many houses had only one room other than their kitchen. In Dann's Row, some of the houses would have cost only £38 to rebuild; in Coates Row, £32; one, in Paisley Court, only £26. Elsewhere, most of the working class lived in relatively new, speculatively built houses, many of which had been erected on the sites of the by-now demolished industrialists' villas. Only two of these villas survived to 1901 in the Lagan Village. One, Henryville, a seven roomed two storey villa worth £602, was occupied from 1884 to 1892 by the builder William Kerr, who had used its front lawn as a yard for an iron foundry. In 1901 it was a building yard. The other, Nettlefield, was a larger twelve-roomed villa which would have cost £1,401 to rebuild. It was leased by Lord Templemore to the widow of Frederick Lewis. Another nearby exception was Willowfield House, leased by the Vint family, who were wine merchants. A clause in a family will delayed development of their large (8 acre) garden until 1905, by which time speculative building pressures in the area had greatly declined. Conceivably this is why, of all the villas in the Woodstock Road area, only this one survives to the present day.

Shamrock Lodge, whose gate piers had long been wedged between two terraces on the Ravenhill Road, was demolished in the late 1880s.

Glenwherry Street was built over its garden between 1894 and 1895, while Victoria Street was built on the site of the house by 1901. To the south, Grovefield, where the demesne had already been encroached upon by terraces prior to 1882, was destroyed to make way for Halcomb Street, the project of the estate agent, Thomas McConnell. He gained approval for thirty-four two-storey parlour houses here in 1894. A note in the plans remarks, 'Grovefield House to be removed before these houses are built'.[59] Glentoran, the long-standing seat of the Coates family, was also demolished by 1901 although the gatehouse, lake and parts of the ornamental gardens and woodland remained. William Coates had occupied it until his death in 1871 and his son, also William, continued to live there until the late 1880s. The family then abandoned Glentoran for Clonallen in Strandtown, which David Coates had owned since 1876. The family also owned Glynn Park in Carrickfergus, from where William Frederick Coates, of W. F. Coates, stockbrokers, became the family's first baronet and lord mayor of Belfast in 1906. Glentoran was replaced by kitchen and parlour houses laid out on Dunvegan Street, Ballarat Street and Bendigo Street. Typically, these houses contained five rooms in two storeys, and were built for about £100 for the parlour houses or around £60 for the smaller kitchen houses. They were erected by numerous developers, most of those on the Glentoran site being built by McCracken and Ward of Roden Street. They had gained planning approval for the site in May 1898.[60] The Coates family continued to be involved in urban development in this area, however. They remained the leasehold owners of various streets in Lagan Village, including Wallace's Row, and had themselves built Rathmore Street.

These new developments were not simply rows of uniform houses. They displayed limited but significant variation in their size and rent, and this was reflected in the social and occupational class of the occupants. Generally, houses built to higher standards lined the main roads, save for the Ravenhill Road, where older housing was still standing. For example, the Woodstock Road was flanked by houses costing over £80, whilst the Albertbridge Road had impressive terraces, some worth up to £440, marching towards The Mount. At the intersection between these roads stood Malcome Lane, developed by Ritchie in the 1860s. This housed not the skilled workers of Woodstock Road but general labourers, carters and washer women in more modest terraces worth as little as £49. My Lady's Road recorded an average reconstruction cost of £112 and housed constables, tailors, shoemakers and clergymen, more prestigious occupants in the main than those in the lower value streets to the north. In sum, the smallest variation either within or between terraced streets affected the rents and thus the social status of the occupants, imposing thereby a micro-scale social hierarchy within what was overall an overwhelmingly working-class district.

The new developments were mainly speculative ventures erected by one or other of a series of small to middling-sized building firms. For example, William Kerr built and owned Barrossa Terrace at The Mount as well as Hamilton Place and part of Shamrock Street. William McGowan built part of Empress Street, as did Robert Holmes, while R. J. Dawson built another part of Shamrock Street and forty-one houses in Glentoran Street in 1891. Thomas McConnell, probably the biggest of the twenty-three estate agents in Belfast in 1898, operated from Mount Pottinger to build more than any other developer in Halcomb Street, Maymount Street and Radnor Street. Elsewhere, his activities included the construction of villas at Rosetta for £700 and kitchen houses in the Shankill at five for £345.[61] There was little owner-occupation. Investments in property were widely advertised in the *Northern Whig* in the 1890s, reflecting the increase in multiple-property ownership as letting to tenants became a common source of invest-ment income. After 1899 speculative builders rapidly disappeared as a glut on the market developed. By 1901, many houses were available at knock-down prices in Glentoran Street and elsewhere.[62]

Further from the city the developments were of higher standard. Later suburban houses surrounded those which had previously occupied entirely rural sites. They were built for the entrepreneurial classes who had profited from the growth in Belfast's population and the expansion in its economy. With only a few exceptions, for example, Craigavon, Cairnburn and Ormiston in the Belmont area, these new houses and their demesnes were smaller in scale than their older neighbours, although larger than the 1830s villas in Ballymacarrett. Let us look now at Strandtown as one example of these new suburban areas in north-west county Down.

The Strandtown area from the 1860s to 1901

In the 1860s the Strandtown area had twelve major demesnes stretching in an almost continuous band along the length of the Holywood Road (fig. 23.6). Over half of these, including Turf Lodge, Strandtown Cottage and Conn's Brook House were enlarged early nineteenth century properties. Turf Lodge belonged to John Kane, who was listed in 1822 as the owner of premises in Winecellar Street and who by mid-century owned spirit stores, a glass warehouse and brewery as well as the North Street glass works. Conn's Brook House had been occupied by 'Honest John' Martin (so-called because of his repayment of creditors after an early business failure) who was a wholesale general merchant and, later, shipowner. He had moved here by 1814 from his

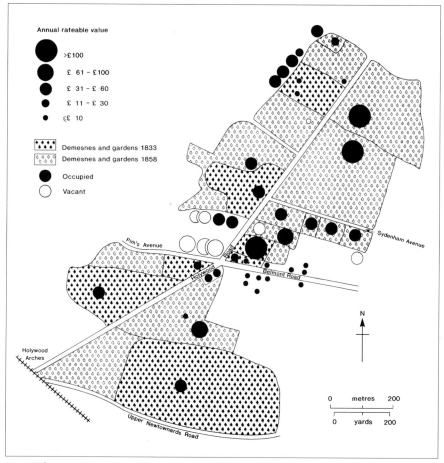

Fig. 23.6   Demesnes in Strandtown in 1833 and 1858.

business in Anne Street. By 1858 the house was owned by John Cleland and leased to William Bathhurst, the owner of a coach factory in Chichester Street. William Harlin, the owner of Strandtown House, had his property surveyed in 1836 when it was typical of the area. It included 12 acres (4.9 ha.) of agricultural land arranged in a number of fields encompassing the orchard, ornamental gardens and lawns of the house. Such Strandtown houses were 'some of the most magnificent structures in villa and mansion architecture that the United Kingdom contains'.[63] Their appearance and extent can be judged from the view of the Strandtown area taken from Belfast Lough by Connop in the 1860s (plate 23.1). Furthermore, the region around Ballyhackamore was 'an immensely large tract of ground well studded with villas, churches, cottages, omnibus and railway stations, as well as the magnificent country seats of some of Belfast's merchant princes'.[64] In the 1860s the

651

large properties here were valued by Griffith at over £100-£175 in the case of the recently-built Edgecumbe House, which was occupied by the shipbuilding Workman family. They had originally lived at York Street and then in Donegall Square, until they moved out to the suburban fringe. Edgecumbe House was sold to the Lemon family after the death of John Workman's widow in 1871, and they occupied it until 1901. The Lemon family had an interesting pattern of residential mobility. James Lemon had been the proprietor of a single ship and a small business at Hanover Quay in the docks area of Belfast and lived nearby. Later, when he had achieved greater commercial success, he moved out to Ardville in Holywood. By 1871 Strandtown had developed into a suitably prestigious location for this merchant family, now consisting of James and his son Archibald, with interests in shipping, chandling and canvas making, and they took Edgecumbe House.

One of the largest properties in this area was Stormont, owned by the Cleland family. They also had 4,385 acres (1,776 ha.) of land at Orangefield, Greenville and Bloomfield, which was worth £6,174 in 1867.[65] Their house, Stormont Castle, contained thirty rooms and had been designed in 1858 in a Scottish baronial style by Thomas Turner. At this stage it was occupied by Samuel Cleland, eldest son of the unpopular John Cleland, whose equally unpopular father had made their fortune when he was Lord Castlereagh's agent by swindling tenants. Samuel succeeded to the estate in 1842 when he was aged six and was only thirty when he became high sheriff for county Down. He died when a wall fell on him whilst he was attempting to demolish the house of his head groom whom he had dismissed.[66] In the decades that followed, Charles Allen, a director of shipbuilders Workman Clark, leased the castle and lived in some style with a housekeeper and eleven servants in 1901. Allen was the castle's last resident prior to its use in the Stormont parliament. Frank Workman and George Clark, the shipyard's founders, lived at Malone in south Belfast and Fortwilliam in north Belfast, and it is a mark of the social prestige of outer east Belfast that their fellow director, Charles Allen, should choose neither of these areas for his house, but Strandtown instead.

Another important property was Bunker Hill, exotically named after the American battle of 1775. It was occupied in 1850 by Chevalier Gustavus Heyn, owner of the Ulster steamship company. He had moved out from Henry Street in the centre of Belfast to Strandtown House and then Bunker Hill. After Heyn the house had a quick succession of tenants, each of whom was an entrepreneur also moving out from central Belfast. In 1858 it was taken by Joseph Farren, of the Eliza Street flax spinning mill. In 1863 the property was bought by

Plate 23.1 View of Sydenham, Belmont and Glenmachan in 1864, by J. H. Connop (Source: Belfast Harbour Commission).

Richard Allen who released three quarters of its 8 acres for building, presumably for new housing, but leased Bunker Hill and the remaining grounds to David Corbett, who was moving out from Henry Street. In 1873 it was taken by Alexander Forrester, a spirit merchant of Arthur Street, who had previously lived above his shop.

Another of the 'merchant princes' in the immediate area was Sir Edward Harland, the shipbuilder, who lived at Ormiston House. He left Belfast to live in London in 1887 but the red brick, Scottish style mansion remained in the firm, having been acquired by another of the partners, William Pirrie. Pirrie extended and improved Ormiston on a scale that can be best gauged by the fact that he put a nine-hole golf course in the grounds.[67] Pirrie's wealth and the status he brought to Strandtown, can be appreciated from the fact that he also owned a house in prestigious Belgrave Square in London and the palatial suburban property of Witley Court in Surrey.

Leading off the main road, new routeways were being created on which were located smaller villas, 'cottages' and 'lodges'. In the 1860s their rateable value varied from £22 per year for some at the rear of Bunker Hill on the way to Sydenham station, to over £64 per year for houses like Brandon Towers at the junction of the Belmont and Holywood Roads. More commonly, villas were valued at between £33 and £50. A great number of new villa properties were being built at this time, but many were as yet without occupants. Thus by the 1860s there were signs of change coming to Strandtown, but as late as 1886 it was still 'a beautiful suburb occupied about entirely by residences of business and professional men belonging to Belfast. Many of the houses ... are surrounded by grounds in which the highest effects of landscape gardening are produced'.[68]

Onto this landscape full suburbanization was about to be imposed. The key process was improved transportation. The earliest form of intra-urban transport in Belfast was the horse omnibus. Until around 1860 this was merely a sideline to the hotel trade, but after this it became an enterprise in itself, ferrying passengers from Belfast to the growing suburbs and acting as an adjunct to the scanty rail service. The Empress and Gowan omnibus companies, for example, linked Strandtown with the Queen's Quay railway terminus. In 1871 a horse tram system was set up by London-based investors and this provided a more efficient, if slightly more expensive service to the eastern suburbs. Between 1884 and 1889 it served first Ballynafeigh and Newtownbreda, then the Woodstock Road, and finally Strandtown with the arrival of the Sydenham service.[69] By the 1890s tramcars had largely replaced omnibuses in Belfast. At first horse trams were unable to go beyond the Connswater bridge, but after its widening in 1890 they went to the

Holywood Arches at the bottom of the Holywood Road. In 1900 the service was extended to the Upper Newtownards Road. The importance of access to these tram services can be seen from contemporary house advertisements which pointed out that the 'tram passes' or that the house was 'near tram and train'.[70] Certainly, ease of access to the city was a factor in the development of housing near the Newtownards Road. The Belfast Street Tramways Company, dating from the 1870s, was taken over by the corporation in 1904, after which its services were electrified, putting more of the outlying areas within reach of the city (after 1888) and the shipyards alike. The corporation even issued cheap workmen's tickets for use at specified times of the day. However, many of the manual workers continued to live within walking distance of their employment in inner Belfast, few of them were moving out to Strandtown and beyond.

In addition to the trams, east Belfast also had railway services. Sydenham had its own halt which was opened in 1848 at the behest of John Entwhistle of Strandtown, a notable suburban estate developer, but this did not provide shelter for passengers until it was enlarged in 1888. Moreover, the station was sufficiently remote to require Strandtown inhabitants to continue to use the omnibus service. In 1850 the Belfast and County Down Railway began services to Newtownards, Dundonald and Comber. There was a stop at Ballycloughan Halt (later Knock Station) and this stimulated the expansion of Ballyhackamore. However, Cleary[71] suggests that stations were not necessarily nodes of suburbanization in themselves. For example, despite the early provision of a railway station (at Bloomfield from 1879) and the offer of free travel for eight years, the Bloomfield land, building and investment company's 84 acre site around Cyprus Avenue near the Upper Newtownards Road was slow to develop. Some of the attractive sandstone cottages built by the company on the Beersbridge Road, remained vacant from 1878 to 1886.

Generally, however, the increasing accessibility of the outer areas of east Belfast and the worsening environment in the inner areas stimulated those who could to move further out. Even the Welsh Unitarian minister for Mount Pottinger, William Jenkin Davis, preferred to live at Strandtown rather than close to his flock in Ballymacarrett. Similarly, the rector of Ballymacarrett Presbyterian church lived along the Holywood Road. Continued growth, both of the urban population as a whole and in the numbers of those with middle-class occupations, led to increasing numbers of new households being formed on the fringes of the city.

By the end of the nineteenth century another change which was beginning to take place was the adoption of some of the houses and grounds for institutional use. One important example of this process, which was to become quite common in the following decades, was the new use for Purdysburn. This Tudor revival mansion was originally the seat of the Wilsons and then subsequently of the Batts, but it was given to Belfast General Hospital in 1895 under the will of Robert Narcissus Batt who had died in 1891. Purdysburn was developed as a mental institution, and replaced an earlier facility on the Falls Road. In a similar fashion many schools in east Belfast were to be sited within demesnes.

The Strandtown area in 1901

By 1901 Strandtown was marked by a social divide that ran along the Holywood Road (fig. 23.7). Where the Holywood Road met the Newtownards Road lay an extension of the working class housing zone of Ballymacarrett, and here a great number of the 2,000 employees of the nearby ropeworks lived in terraced houses with a rebuilding cost of

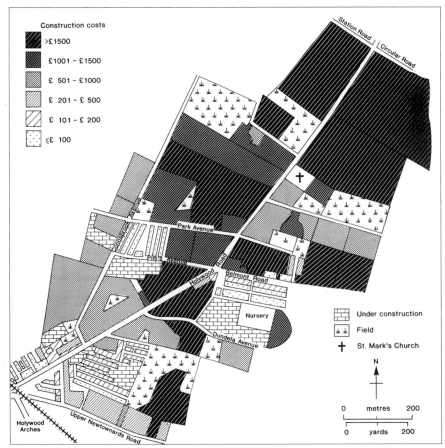

Fig. 23.7   House construction costs in Strandtown in 1901.

about £100. These houses lined streets such as Madison Avenue, and they displayed significant socio-economic differentiation between their skilled and semi-skilled inhabitants. Generally, they were a later addition to the similar developments in or off East Bread Street, Bloomfield Avenue and Factory Street on the other, south, side of the Newtownards Road. However, this area, too, had a pocket of better housing in and off tree-lined Cyprus Avenue. For example, Sandford Avenue was built over a number of years around the turn of the century and contained substantial red brick semi-detached houses. According to the 1901 census they were occupied by draughtsmen, cashiers, insurance agents, commercial travellers and the like.

A little further up the Holywood Road were better quality two-storey terraces typically valued between £130 and £180. These streets, which included Cheviot Street and Lomond Avenue, were developed on the demesne of Turf Lodge. Aimed at professionals and skilled workers, some of the houses were proving difficult to let, and the developer in Lomond Avenue, H. and J. Martin, reduced prices to try and attract customers.[72] Beyond this area a zone of more substantial detached and semi-detached housing with rebuilding costs between £500 and £1,000 had been built on the Conn's Brook and Ballyhackamore House demesnes. Built and owned largely by William Kerr (on the west side), these houses were occupied by small manufacturers like William Kyle, the owner of a hardware concern in Belfast, and Robert Thompson, builder and contractor. Others housed a pawnbroker, surveyors, various business managers and several ministers. Typically the owners advertised their social pretensions by the names they gave to their houses: 'Inglewood', 'Lindesfarne' and 'Glenavon' being examples.

To the north lay what was perhaps socially the most volatile area by 1901. The Belmont Road/Holywood Road crossroads, which had previously been bordered on three sides by demesnes and on the other by cottages and small houses, was undergoing rapid terrace development in the late 1890s. Terraces such as those on Dundela and Wilgar Streets first appeared on the site of the older, poorer houses to the east of this junction, but by 1901 had also developed to the south. To the west, six terraces had been erected so quickly by William Hill that they had not yet been named and were referred to in the valuation simply by numbers. The rapidity of this development brought its own problems, as one valuer remarked about a shop in one of these terraces (in what become Colvil Street): 'This shop would be worth £18 plus in a thriving district but there seems to be difficulty in letting the small houses lately built and very little demand for shops. Two tenants here already tried this shop and left in a short time. District overbuilt'.[73] These new houses, costing, for example, £97 in

Pimm's Avenue, would have been respectable enough in Lagan Village, but were remarkably out of place in the heart of Strandtown, where they were surrounded by detached houses worth up to ten times as much. Nevertheless, they provided a good return for their builders – income from the sale of many inexpensive houses each on a small plot might add up to more than a detached villa with large grounds. Occupants here tended to be skilled members of the working class. To the east of the crossroads, respectable two storey terraced housing (costing between £143 and £162 to rebuild) hid two streets of smaller terraces worth half that amount. These small terraces were occupied by semi-skilled workers and servants, many of whom were unemployed. Development was gradually extending southwards onto land which had been released from the Strandtown House demesne, and into the rural-urban fringe on land which had formerly been occupied by a nursery.

Many of the older, larger houses in the area survived the urban infilling process until the late-nineteenth century, by which time they were still occupied by leading merchants. These included James Heyn of the Ulster steam ship company, who lived at Strandtown House, John Magee, a major stationery retailer in Castle Lane, at Altorf, and Henry Craig, a distiller, at Sydenham House. However, in 1897, Altorf, Strandtown Lodge, Brandon Towers and Dundela Villa were all advertised for sale.[74]

At the end of the century it was only the most remote houses that remained unaffected by east Belfast's suburbanization. Well into the rural part of north-west county Down, however, an area still entirely in demesnes and villas survived. Houses here were worth upwards of £1,100 for villa sites and much more for the older, country seats which tended to occupy the highest ground. Netherleigh, William Robertson's rambling two-storey house, would have cost £9,646 to rebuild and was the most expensive in the neighbourhood. These large houses retained their expansive grounds as yet untouched by new buildings: John Greeves's Lismachan had 18 acres (7.3 ha.), as did James Malcolmson's Cairnburn; Sir Samuel Black's Glen Ebor (leased from Sir Thomas McClure) was surrounded by 22 acres (9 ha.), and James Craig's Craigavon (leased from W. B. Kerr) by 27 acres (11 ha.). The scale and style of these estates can be seen by the 1901 revaluation's note that Sir William. Ewart's twenty-seven roomed Glenmachan (rebuilding cost £6,657) sat within an estate where the glasshouses alone were worth £584. The Hamiltons' Garnerville, a much older, more modest six roomed house (rebuilding cost £1,408) included in its grounds 24 acres of glasshouses worth £420; at the Hendersons' Norwood Towers, (fifteen rooms, rebuilding cost £5,778) they were

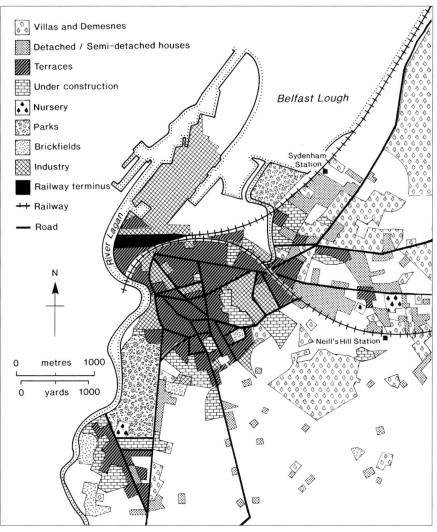

Fig. 23.8   Land-use in east Belfast in 1901.

worth £333. Such sums were the equivalent to the value of entire rows of terraced houses.

Conclusion

This chapter has identified successive waves of suburbanization on Belfast's county Down fringe during the nineteenth century. Wealthy people colonized the area when they moved out of central Belfast. Newly created households of similar rank also took root in the peripheral areas. Then industrialization and associated low and middling status housing crowded the earlier wealthy inhabitants and prompted them to move further out. The houses they left behind were usually demolished and the land re-used, generally for industrial and associated residential development. Further growth in population and industry in tandem with transport developments then placed further pressure on the outer areas to which the wealthy had escaped and the cycle began again.

The spatial results of this process explain both the pattern of land-use in the area in 1901 (fig. 23.8) and the tendency for the socio-spatial structure of east Belfast to display improved housing quality and social status with increasing distance from the inner area.[75] The key element in the development of east Belfast was the presence of demesnes. They created foci for upper, middle and, eventually, working-class housing and, from the end of the nineteenth century, institutions. They formed a point of origin, often structuring the layout, plan and even nomenclature of streets, many of which are named after the old house on whose grounds they stand. Their presence does not, however, explain the mechanisms of suburbanization which included industrialization, transport developments and the activities of builders, speculators and estate agents.

East Belfast was completely transformed in the nineteenth century from its largely rural state to a centre of industry employing thousands of workers, but still with some pleasant areas of good property, particularly on the periphery. Perhaps we should leave the last word to one of the 'merchant princes' who were responsible for this transformation, Gustav Wolff. In 1911, on being made an honorary burgess of the city, he gave the first public airing of a ditty, since famous the length and breadth of east Belfast:

> You may talk of your Edinburgh and the beauties of Perth,
> And all the large cities famed on the earth,
> But give me my house, though it be but a garret,
> In the pleasant surroundings of Ballymacarrett.[76]

Wolff, himself, however, seemed to have been able to resist the charms of Ballymacarrett garrets and lived in rather more spacious accommodation at The Den in Strandtown.

\References

1. B. Collins, 'The Edwardian city', in J.C. Beckett *et al, Belfast: the making of the city* (Belfast, 1983), p. 179.
2. S. A. Royle, 'The socio-spatial structure of Belfast in 1837: evidence from the first valuation' in *Irish Geography*, xxiv (1991), pp 1-9.
3. P. R. O. N. I., Val. 1B/74A.

4.   P. R. O. N. I., Val. 1B/76B.

5.   Pigot and Company, *The commercial directory of Scotland, Ireland and the northern counties of England for 1820-21* (London, 1824).

6.   N. Batt, 'Belfast sixty years ago: recollections of a septuagenarian' in *U. J. A.*, second series, ii.ii (1896), pp 92-5.

7.   P. Ollerenshaw, *Banking in nineteenth century Ireland: the Belfast banks, 1825-1914* (Manchester, 1987).

8.   F. Heatley, 'Community relations and the religious geography 1800-86' in Beckett, *Belfast*, p. 130.

9.   P. R. O. N. I., D. 3113/7/17.

10.   W. M. O'Hanlon, Walks *among the poor of Belfast* (Belfast, 1853); A. G. Malcolm, *The history of the general hospital, Belfast, and the other medical institutions of the town* (Belfast, 1851), reprinted in H.G. Calwell, *Andrew Malcolm of Belfast 1818-1856, physician and historian* (Belfast, 1977); A. G. Malcolm, *The sanitary state of Belfast with suggestions for its improvement,* (British Association, Belfast meeting, 1852), reprinted in P. R. O. N. I., *Problems of a growing city: Belfast 1780-1870* (Belfast, 1973), pp 156-63.

11.   P. R. O. N. I., Val. 1B/77B.

12.   Collins, 'Edwardian city', p. 169.

13.   T. Carleton, 'Malone, Belfast: the early history of a suburb' in *U. J. A.*, third series, xli (1978), pp 94-101.

14.   Ibid., p. 99.

15.   E. Jones, *The social geography of Belfast* (London, 1960), p. 255.

16.   H. Carter, *An introduction to urban historical geography* (London, 1983), p. 187.

17.   P. R. O. N. I., T. 1677/2.

18.   P. R. O. N. I., T. 765/2/2, ii, p. 390.

19.   G. Benn, *A history of the town of Belfast from the earliest times to the close of the eighteenth century* (Belfast, 1887), p. 264.

20.   Harris, *Down.*

21.   G. Benn, *Belfast*, ii, p. 171.

22.   P. R. O. N. I., D. 39213/7/1186.

23.   *Belfast News Letter,* 28 December 1787.

24.   A. Atkinson, *Ireland exhibited to England* (London, 1823).

25.   *Philadelphia Inquirer,* 23 May 1897.

26.   *Gentleman's Magazine,* December 1786.

27.   *Belfast News Letter,* 11 October 1788.

28.   Ibid., 13 October 1788.

29.   P. R. O. N. I., T. 1514/50.

30.   W.A. Maguire, 'Ormeau House' in *U. J. A.*, third series, xlii (1979), pp 66-71; P. R. O. N. I., D. 3113/7/3.

31.   Irish Architectural Archive, *The architecture of Richard and William Morrison* (Dublin, 1989).

32.   P. R. O. N. I., T. 755/5; pp 23, 61.

33.   T. Carleton, and V. Kelly, 'Ballymacarrett: a short history' in *Journal of the East Belfast Historical Society,* ii (1987), pp 24-31.

34.   W. E. Coe, *The engineering industry in Northern Ireland* (Newton Abbot, 1969).

35.   J. F. MacNeice, *The Church of Ireland in Belfast* (Belfast, 1931); p. 37.

36.   A. Fullarton & Co., *The parliamentary gazetteer of Ireland* (Dublin, 1846), p. 178.

37.   S. M. Elliott, *The world as I found it* (Belfast, 1877), p. 53.

38.   *Belfast News Letter,* 8 January 1811.

39.   P. R. O. N. I., T. 3303/5 1: 2.

40. *Belfast News Letter*, 27 August 1833.
41. Carleton, 'Malone'.
42. P. R. O. N. I., T. 3303/5 1: 2.
43. Elliott, *The world as I found it*.
44. Maguire, 'Ormeau House'; P. R. O. N. I., D. 385/13/3.
45. P. R. O. N. I., D. 971/MI/3.
46. *Industries of Ireland, part i: Belfast and the north* (London, 1891), p. 84.
47. Linen Hall Library, BPP 73.
48. Malcolm, *Sanitary state*, p. 159.
49. S. A. Royle, M. E. Pringle and F. W. Boal, 'New information on the development of Ballymacarrett: Lord Templemore's plan of 1853' in *U. J. A.*, third series, xlvi (1983), pp 137-41.
50. P. R. O. N. I., mic 334/2B/22 and T. 3303/5 1/2/67.
51. M. Moss and J. R. Hume, *Shipbuilders to the world: 125 years of Harland and Wolff, Belfast, 1861-1986* (Belfast, 1986).
52. P. Ollerenshaw, 'Industry 1820-1914' in L. Kennedy and P. Ollerenshaw (ed.), *An economic history of Ulster 1820-1940* (Manchester, 1985), pp 62-108.
53. P. G. Cleary, Spatial expansion and urban ecological change in Belfast with special reference to the role of local transportation, 1861-1917, Unpub. Ph. D. thesis, Q.U.B., 1979.
54. *Belfast News Letter*, 28 July 1896.
55. W. A. Maguire, *Belfast* (Keele, 1993).
56. *Belfast Telegraph*, 1 March 1954.
57. P. R. O. N. I., Val. 12B/43A/15.
58. *Northern Whig*, 17 April 1897, 15 January 1901.
59. Belfast City Council, Building Plan 10185.
60. Belfast City Council, Building Plan 13073.
61. J. Bardon, *Belfast: an illustrated history* (Belfast, 1982).
62. *Northern Whig*, 18 January 1901.
63. Elliott, *The world as I found it*, p. 50.
64. Ibid., p. 49.
65. P. R. O. N. I., D. 2929/7/7.
66. P. Carr, *'The most unpretending of places'. A history of Dundonald, county Down* (Dundonald, 1990).
67. Moss and Hume, *Harland and Wolff*, pp 63-4.
68. G. H. Bassett, *County Down: guide and directory* (Dublin, 1886), p. 321.
69. Cleary, 'Spatial expansion'.
70. *Northern Whig*, 1 April 1897, 17 April 1897.
71. Cleary, 'Spatial expansion'.
72. *Northern Whig*, 15 January 1901.
73. P. R. O. N. I., Val. 7B/13/13, p. 25.
74. *Northern Whig*, 17 April 1897.
75. Jones, *Social geography*.
76. Bardon, *Belfast*, p. 130.

Chapter 24

A SELECT HISTORICAL BIBLIOGRAPHY OF COUNTY DOWN

CAROLINE WINDRUM

County Down has a rich history of immigration, conquest and settlement. In turn, it is well served with publications covering life, history and society throughout its various districts. The following list gives an indication of the substantial number of books, monographs, guides and reports which deal exclusively or extensively with the county. Academic journal articles are excluded since these have been extensively referenced in the relevant chapters in this book. For these articles, readers should consult specialist publications such as *Irish Economic and Social History*, *Irish Geography* and, particularly for excavation reports of local archaeological sites, *The Ulster Journal of Archaeology*. The select list presented here points to the breadth of research and commentary by both amateur and professional writers but should be treated as a thematic survey rather than a comprehensive listing. For convenience, the entries are listed alphabetically under the subheadings of architecture, archaeology, biography and family history, Church history and affairs, economic, social and political history, local history and topography, and natural history.

Archaeology

Collins, A. E. P. and Waterman, D. M., *Millin Bay: a late neolithic cairn in county Down: with an account of the human skeletal materials by W. R. M. Morton and J. H. Scott* (Belfast, 1955).

Jope, E. M. et al, *An archaeological survey of county Down* (H.M.S.O., Belfast, 1966).

Mallory, J. P. and McNeill, T. E., *The archaeology of Ulster. From colonisation to plantation* (Institute of Irish Studies, Belfast, 1991).

Architecture

Bell, P., Brett, C. E. B. and Matthews, P., *Portaferry and Strangford* (U. A. H. S., Belfast, 1985).

Bigger, F. J., *The Ancient churches of Raholp and Ardtole* (Belfast, 1917).

Brett, C. E. B. and Dunleath, Lady, *Historic buildings, groups of buildings, areas of architectural importance in the borough of Banbridge* (U. A. H. S., Belfast, 1969).

Brett, C. E. B., *Historic buildings, groups of buildings, areas of architectural importance in the towns and villages of east Down* (U. H. A. S., Belfast, 1973).

Brett, C. E. B., *Historic buildings, groups of buildings, areas of architectural importance in the towns and villages of mid Down* (U. A. H. S., Belfast, 1974).

Department of the Environment., *Historic monuments of Northern Ireland* (H. M. S. O., Belfast, 1983).

Dixon, H., *Historic buildings, groups of buildings, areas of architectural importance in Donaghadee and Portpatrick*

(U. A. H. S., Belfast, 1977).

Dunleath, R. & R., Rankin, P. J. and Rowan, A.J., *Historic buildings, groups of buildings, areas of architectural importance in Downpatrick* (U. A. H. S., Belfast, 1970).

Hamlin, Ann Elizabeth, *Dundrum castle, county Down* (Belfast, Historic Monuments and Buildings Branch, 1977).

Houston, Charles B., *Guide to the ruins of Nendrum monastery Mahee island, Strangford Lough, county Down founded by Saint Mochaoi circa 440 AD* (Belfast, 1925).

Merrick, Tony, *Buildings of Holywood* (Holywood, 1986).

Rankin, P. J., *Historic buildings, groups of buildings, areas of architectural importance in the Mourne area of south Down* (U. A. H. S., Belfast, 1975).

Rankin, P. J., *Historic buildings, groups of buildings, areas of architectural importance in Rathfriland and Hilltown* (U. A. H. S., Belfast, 1979).

Wallace, Richard T., *Castlewellan castle, a short history* (Castlewellan, 1986).

Waterman, D. M., *A guide to Narrow Water castle, county Down* (Belfast, H. M. S. O., 1959).

Biography and family history

Black, Charles E. Drummond, *The marquess of Dufferin and Ava – diplomatist, viceroy, statesman.* (London, 1907, 2nd edition).

Blackwood, R. W. H., *Some biographical notices of the rectors of Loughinisland, 1609-1911* (Downpatrick, 1911)

Burls, John (ed.) *Nine generations, a history of the Andrews family, millers of Comber: from the manuscript of S. Andrews* (Belfast, 1958)

Clarke, R. J. S., *Old families of Downpatrick and district from graveyard inscriptions, wills and biographical notes* (Belfast, nd).

Crowe, W. Haughton, *Mourne View farm, experiences of an Ulster part-time farmer* (Dundalk, 1977).

Davidson, E. F., *Edward Hincks* (London, 1933).

Fitzpatrick, W.J., *A Mourne man's memories* (Newcastle, 1980).

Hamilton, W., *The Hamilton manuscripts* (ed. T.K. Lowry) (Belfast, 1867).

Hayes, Maurice, *Black puddings with slim: a Downpatrick childhood* (Belfast, 1996).

Hill, Rev. George, *Montgomery manuscripts, 1603-1706* (Belfast, 1869).

Hunter, Grace, *Witnessing and working: memoir of Grace Hunter, Downpatrick (with) brief notes on methodism in the locality* (1896).

Malcomson, A. P. W., 'The gentle leviathan: Arthur Hill. 2nd marquess of Downshire, 1753 – 1801' in Roebuck, P. (ed.), *Plantation to partition: essays in Ulster history in honour of J. L. McCracken* (Belfast, 1981).

McClelland, A., *William Johnston of Ballykilty* (Lurgan, Ulster Society, 1990).

Montgomery Hyde, H., *The Londonderrys. A family portrait* (London, 1979).

O'Donoghue, Denis, *Warrenpoint* (Syracuse, 1994).

Rutherford, James, C., *An Ards farmer; or, an account of the life of James Shanks* (Belfast, 1913).

Savage-Armstrong, G. F., *A genealogical history of the Savage family in Ulster, ...with illustrations of arms, mansions, ruins of castles, and ancient sites and monuments connected with the family* (London, 1906).

Smyth, Molly, *Mourne memories, 1940-1950* (Audlem, 1987).

Stewart, A. T. Q., *The Pagoda war. Lord Dufferin and the fall of the kingdom of Ava, 1885-6* (London, 1972).

Woods, C. J. (ed.), *Journals and memoirs of Thomas Russell, 1791-95* (Dublin, 1991).

Church history and affairs

Atkinson, Edward Dupre, *Dromore, an Ulster diocese* (Dundalk, 1925).

Atkinson, Edward D., *An Ulster parish: being a history of Donaghcloney* (Waringstown, Co. Down, 1898).

Carey, J. A., *Historical notes on the abbey and parish of Bangor* (Newtownards, 1979).

Cowan, J. Davison, *An ancient parish, past and present; being the parish of Donaghmore, county Down* (London, 1914).

Donnelly, Maureen, *Inch abbey and parish* (Downpatrick, 1979).

Ewart, L. M., *Handbook to the dioceses of Down, Connor and Dromore* (nd).

Haddock, Josiah, *A parish miscellany, Donaghcloney* (nd).

Hamilton, James, *Bangor abbey through fourteen centuries* (Bangor, 1958).

Keenan, Padraic, *Historical sketch of the parish of Clonduff* (Newry, 1941).

Kennedy, W. E., *An historical sketch of the parish of Ballyculter* (Strangford, 1980).

Lawlor, H. C., *The monastery of St. Mochaoi of Nendrum* (Belfast, 1925).

Long, S. E., *A history of the parish of Dromara, Ireland* (Newcastle, 1979).

Lyttle, W. G., *The Bangor session* (2nd ed., Bangor, 1976).

Macourt, William A., *Forty years on. Diocese of Down and Dromore, Diocese of Connor, 1945-1985* (Newtownabbey, 1985).

McKeown, L., *St Patrick and the parish of Saul* (Belfast, 1932).

Mercer, J. C. G., *Forward march: a short history of the Church of Ireland in Ballyholme* (Bangor, 1961).

O'Laverty, Rev. James, *An historical account of the dioceses of Down and Connor* (Dublin, 4 vols., 1878-89).

Parkinson, R. E., *Historical sketch of the cathedral of the Holy Trinity* (Downpatrick, 1904).

Perceval-Price, Michael Charles, *Saintfield parish under the microscope* (Ballynahinch, 1976).

Pilson, Aynesworth, *Downpatrick and its parish church* (Downpatrick, 1852).

Pooler, L. A., *Down and its parish church* (1907).

Pooler, L. A., *Down and its parishes* (Downpatrick, 1907).

Reeves, Rev. W., *Ecclesiastical antiquities of Down, Connor and Dromore* (Dublin, 1847, reprinted Belfast, 1992).

Reid, William W., *A short history of the Presbyterian congregation at Crossgar* (Coleraine, 1987).

Reside, S. W., *St. Mary's church, Newry: its history* (1933).

Stephenson, S. M., *An historical essay on the parish and congregation of Grey-Abbey: compiled in the year 1827* (Belfast, 1828).

Economic, social and political history

Arnold, R. M., *Steam over Belfast Lough: a look at the railways to Bangor and Larne and especially the work of the locomotives* (London, 1969).

Bardon, J., *A history of Ulster* (Belfast, 1992).

Connellan, Joseph, *The Rathfryland conspiracy of 1820, a vindication of the condemned* (Newry, 1920).

Crawford, W. H. (ed.), *Letters from an Ulster land agent 1774-85* (Belfast, 1976).

Dickson, Charles, *Revolt in the north: Antrim and Down in 1798* (Dublin, 1960).

Dubourdieu, John, *Statistical survey of the county of Down, with observations on the means of improvement: drawn up for the consideration, and by order of the Dublin Society* (Dublin, 1802).

Gillespie, R., *Colonial Ulster. The settlement of east Ulster 1600-1641* (Cork, 1985).

Green, E. R. R., *The industrial archaeology of county Down* (H.M.S.O., Belfast, 1963).

Harris, Walter, *The ancient and present state of the county of Down* (Dublin, 1744).

Kennedy, L. and Ollerenshaw, P., *An economic history of Ulster 1820-1939* (Manchester, 1985).

Knox, Alexander, *History of the county Down* (Dublin, 1875).

Macneice, D. S., 'Industrial villages in Ulster, 1800-1900' in Roebuck, P. (ed.), *Plantation to partition. Essays in Ulster history in honour of J. L. McCracken* (Belfast, 1981).

Maguire, W. A., *The Downshire estates in Ireland, 1801-1845: the management of Irish landed estates in the early nineteenth century* (Oxford, Clarendon Press, 1972).

McCutcheon, W. A., *The canals of the north of Ireland* (London, 1965).

McCutcheon, W. A., *The industrial archaeology of Northern Ireland* (H. M. S. O., Belfast, 1980).

Mourne Observer, *Sailing ships of Mourne, the county Down fishing fleet and Newcastle lifeboat* (Newcastle, 1971).

Newham, A. T., *The Bessbrook and Newry tramway* (Dorset, 1979).

Patterson, Edward M., *The Belfast and County Down railway* (Newabbot, Devon, 1984).

Poe, R. J. A., *Twenty-five years gone* (Belfast and County Down Railway Museum Trust, Belfast, 1975).

Pollock, V., 'Change in the county Down fisheries in the twentieth century' in McCaughan, M. and Appleby, J. (ed.), *The Irish Sea. Aspects of maritime history* (Institute of Irish Studies, Belfast, 1989).

Pollock, V., 'The Seafishing Industry in county Down and its Scottish Connections' in Mitchison, R. and Roebuck, P. (ed.), *Economy and society in Scotland and Ireland 1500-1939* (Edinburgh, 1988).

Robinson, P., *The plantation of Ulster* (Dublin, 1984).

Stevenson, John, *Two centuries of life in Down, 1600-1800* (Belfast, 1920).

Stewart, A. T. Q., *The summer soldiers. The 1798 rebellion in Antrim and Down* (Belfast, 1995).

Ultaigh, Sighle Nic an, *An Dún-óshíol go bláth: the GAA story.*

Wilson, C. A., *A new lease on life. Landlords, tenants and immigrants in Ireland and Canada* (London, 1994).

Local history and topography

Barry, J., *Hillsborough: a parish in the Ulster plantation* (Belfast, 1962).

Bassett, G. H., *County Down guide and directory* (Dublin, 1886).

Biggar, F. J., *Four shots from Down, the tale of the beetle, Rab Russel, the stone cutter, the Buck's Head, and the builder of Stormont* (Ballynahinch, 1982).

Bradshaw, Thomas, *General directory of Newry, Armagh, Dungannon, Portadown, Tandragee, Lurgan, Waringstown, Banbridge, Warrenpoint, Rostrevor, Kilkeel and Rathfryland* (1819).

Buchanan, R. H., 'Downpatrick' in A. Simms and J. H. Andrews (ed.), *Irish country towns* (Dublin, 1994).

Campbell, M. H., *As luck would have it* (Dundalk, 1948).

Blackwood, R. W. H., *Loughinisland: its legends and history* (Belfast, 1923).

Canavan, Tony, *Frontier town, an illustrated history of Newry* (Belfast, 1989).

Carson, William, *The dam builders, the story of the men who built the Silent Valley reservoir* (Newcastle, 1991).

Carson, W. H., *Historic clocks of county Down* (Newcastle, 1980).

Committee of the Downe Hunt, *The Downe hunt* (Belfast, 1959).

Corr, B., *From the mountains to the sea: photographs of the people of Mourne 1955-75* (Belfast, 1989).

Crosbie, J. E. (ed.), *A tour through the Ardes, 1910-1935* (Belfast, 1990).

Crossle, Francis C., *A history of Nelson masonic lodge No. xviii, Newry* (Newry, 1909).

Crossle, Francis, *Local jottings of Newry collected and transcribed* (Vols. 1-34), (Newry, 1890-1910).

Crowe, W. H., *The Ring of Mourne* (Dundalk, 1968).

Crowe, W. H., *Village on seven hills* (Dundalk, 1972).

Day, A. & McWilliams, P. (eds), *Ordnance Survey memoirs of Ireland: parishes of county Down, I – IV* (Institute of Irish Studies, Queen's University, Belfast, 1990 -1992).

Doran, J. S., *Wayfarer in the Mournes* (Rathfryland, 1980).

Doran, J. S., *My Mourne* (Newcastle, 1975).

Downpatrick Hospital Memorial Committee, *The bi-centenary of the Down county infirmary (new Downe hospital): History thro' 200 years, 1767-1967* (Whitehead, 1967).

Evans, E. Estyn., *Mourne country: landscape and life in south Down* (3rd ed., Dundalk, 1978).

Gildea, A. L., *Guide to north Down, Ards and district* (Belfast, 1979).

Grenfell, M., *Victorian and Edwardian Newcastle* (Belfast, 1988).

Hayes, M., *Sweet Killough, let go your anchor* (Belfast, 1994).

Hughes, A. J. and Hannan, R. J., *Place-names of Northern Ireland: the Ards* (Belfast, 1992).

Johnston, John Moore, *Heterogenea: or, medley for the benefit of the poor* (Downpatrick, 1803).

Keightley, Samuel, R., *The pikemen. A romance of the Ards of Down* (London, 1905).

Kirkpatrick, N., *Take a second look (around county Down)* (Newtownards, 1993).

Linn, Capt. Richard, *A history of Banbridge* (ed. W.S. Kerr) (Belfast, 1935).

Lowry, D. E., *Norsemen and Danes of Strangford Lough 790-1103* (Belfast, 1926).

Magee, J., *A journey through Lecale, historic photographs of county Down from the W.A. Green Collection in the Ulster Folk Park and Transport Museum* (Belfast, 1991).

McCavery, Trevor, *Newtown, a history of Newtownards* (Belfast, 1994).

McGrath, Thomas, *Newry by gaslight: a history of the gasworks* (Newry, 1987).

McKay, Louise, *The mountains of Mourne, their charm and their people* (London, nd).

Montgomery, J. W., *Round Mourne* (Bangor, 1900).

Neilson, W., *An introduction to the Irish language* (1808 reprinted Belfast, 1990).

Newriensis (J. F. Small), *An historical sketch of Newry* (Newry, 1876).

Ó Casaide, S., *The Irish language in Belfast and county Down* (Skerries, 1979).

O'Donovan, John, *Letters containing information relative to the (history and) antiquities of the county of Down, collected during the progress of the Ordnance survey in 1834: including interviews with various persons, and bibliographical references* (Dublin, 1909).

Ó 'Duibhinn, Ciarán, *Irish in county Down since 1750* (Lecale, 1991).

O'Laverty, Rev. James, *The history of Holywood* (nd).

O'Mainnin, M. B., *Place-names of Northern Ireland: Newry and south-west Down* (Belfast, 1992).

O'Mainnin, M. B., *Place-names of Northern Ireland: the Mournes* (Belfast, 1993).

Parkinson, R. Edward, *The City of Down from its earliest days* (Belfast, 1968).

Parkinson, R. Edward, *Centenary of the Downshire hospital 1869-1969* (Belfast, 1969).

Patton, M. J. and Shaw, M., *Castle gardens school centenary, 1882-1992* (Newtownards, 1982).

Praeger, Robert Lloyd, *Official guide to county Down and the Mourne mountains* (1898).

Rankin, J. F., *The heritage of Drumbo* (Ballylesson, 1981).

Richardson, James Nicholson, *The ballad of the Camlough River* (Dundalk, 1931).

Robinson, P., 'Bangor' in A. Simms and J. H. Andrews (ed.) *More Irish country towns* (Dublin, 1995).

Rowan-Hamilton, Gawin William, *Annals of the Downe hunt* (Belfast, 1903).

Simpson, W. G., *The history and antiquities of freemasonry in Saintfield, county Down* (Downpatrick, 1924).

Simpson, W. G., *Masonry of the olden time in the Comber district, county Down* (Lisburn, 1926).

Tate, T. M., *Tales and legends of Lecale, county Down* (Downpatrick, nd).

Walsh, C. and Manley, M., *The church on the lough: the story of a village – Killough* (Killough, 1990).

Ward, D., *Newtownards: an illustrated history and companion* (Donaghadee, 1993).

Wilson, B., Buchanan, R. and Magee, J., *Lecale – a study of local history* (Belfast, 1970 & 1977).

Natural history
Belfast Naturalists' Field Club, *A guide to Belfast and the counties of Down and Antrim prepared for a meeting of the British Association* (Belfast, 1902).

Belfast Naturalists' Field Club, *Guide to Belfast and the adjacent counties* (Belfast, 1874).

British Association, *Belfast in its regional setting* (Belfast, 1952).

Brown, R., *Strangford Lough, the wildlife of an Irish sea lough* (Belfast, 1990).

Buchanan, R. H. and Walker, B. M., *Province, city and people. Belfast and its region* (Belfast, 1987).

Cruickshank, J. G. and Wilcock, D. N., *Northern Ireland. environment and natural resources* (Belfast, 1982).

Praeger, Robert Lloyd, *The Mourne mountains* (London, 1895).

Further Reading
A number of organisations based in Down provide facilities for further reading on the county and its history. The South Eastern Education and Library Board based at Ballynahinch, possesses an extensive range of services, geared variously to the needs of different user groups and is a reflection and tribute to the sterling work of the late Jack McCoy. Newspapers are particularly well represented in the Irish and Local History section. It possesses full runs on microfilm of the *Banbridge Chronicle, County Down Spectator, Down Recorder, Dromore Weekly Times, Mourne Observer* among other county papers, all of which have been indexed from 1970. Published indexes are also available for the *County Down Spectator* (1904-1964), the *Downpatrick Recorder* (1836-1886), the *Mourne Observer* (1949-1980*)*, *Newtownards Chronicle & Newtownards Independent* (1871-1900), *Newtownards Chronicle* (1901-1939), *Northern Herald* (1833-1836) and the *Northern Star* (1792-1797). Local history packs on a wide range of topics have been prepared by staff and provide a suitable introduction to source materials. Bibliographical finding aids are available for various regions within the county.

Down County Museum located in Downpatrick is another repository of local information. It also houses a large number of artefacts and photographic collections relating to the people, history and tradition of the county and provides a series of information leaflets and guides. The Institute of Irish Studies at Queen's University of Belfast has produced a bibliography covering a range of source materials for the barony of Lecale (compiled by Jane Leonard), which is available for consultation. Finally, the wealth of interest in local history is further demonstrated by the network of local and family history societies. Many of these groups produce journals, including the following:

Down and Connor Historical Society Magazine
East Belfast Historical Society Journal
Journal of the Bangor Historical Society
Lecale Miscellany
Old Newry Journal
Saintfield Heritage
Seanchas Dhroim Mor (Journal of the Dromore Diocesan Historical Society)
Twelve Miles of Mourne
Upper Ards Historical Society Journal

Plate 24.1   The Hill, Groomsport (Ulster Folk and Transport Museum, WAG 1295).

General Index

McGuire, Michael, 537
McGuirin, 127
McKee family, 414, 416
McKenna, John, 529
McKimins, James, 334
McKinnevin family, 127
McKisack family, 437
McLaughlin and Harvey, 645
McLaughlin, Felix, 530
McMahon family, 162
McMahon, Hugh, 180
McManus, Murtagh, 170
McMaster, John Walsh, 581, 583, 592
McNeill, John, 618
McNeill, T.E., 37
McQuonan, Knoghe, 174
McQuonan, Neil, 174
McShane family, 454
McTear, Martha, 635
McTier, Samuel, 271
McVeagh, Jeremiah, 321
McVeigh, Fergus, 440
Meade family, 210
Meade, John, 303
Meade, Robert, 219
Mellán, British saint, 56
Mensa mistica, 145
Mesca Ulad, 53
Michael, St. (archangel), 50
Milligan, Peter, 461
Miskelly, Patrick, 334-5
Mitchell family, 242
Mo-Choe, 89
Mo-Cholmóc, 59, 64, 86, 89
Mochaoi, naomh, 48
Mochoe = Mochaoi,54
Moira, lord 227, 260
Molyneux, William,143
Montgomery, Arthur, 306
Montgomery, bishop, 125, 131-2
Montgomery family, 142, 147-8, 153, 174, 179, 191, 267, 630
Montgomery, Hugh, 142, 146, 148-52, 155, 173, 205-6, 244, 435, 614
Montgomery, James, 183-4,

188, 190
Montgomery, John, 639
Montgomery, lord, 180, 187-8
Montgomery, viscount 244-5
Montgomery, William, 142, 144
Moore, Judge, 335
Morgan, Austin, 461
Morrison, William, 637
Moryson, Fynes, 166
Moryson, Richard, 166
Mountjoy, lord deputy, 166, 167, 173, 182, 435
Mugdorna tribe, 105, 434
Muirchú, 48
Mulholland, Andrew, 259, 300
Mulholland family, 210, 219, 229, 300, 632
Mulholland, Harry, 323
Mulholland, John, 209, 310
Munro, Daniel, 189
Munro, general, 184, 186, 188
Munro, Henry, 289-90
Murphy, James, 409
Murphy, Michael J., 456
Murray, Daniel, 531
Murray, Danny, 461
Murray, John, 534
Mussen, Fintan, 461

Nassan, British saint, 56
Nath Í, 89, 92
Nathus, 92
National League, 302, 313, 317
Ned Gréasaí, 456
Needham family, 304-5, 310
Needham, Francis, 305
Neilson, James, 533
Neilson, Moses, 438, 443
Neilson, Samuel, 271-2, 283-4
Neilson, William, 438, 443-5, 454-5, 458
Nennius, 89, 91

Nevin, Dr, 333
Newry Commercial Telegraph, 539
Ní Cheallaigh, Máire, 455
Nic a' Liondáin, Máire inghean Phádraig, 440
Nicholson, John, 570, 585
Nimmo, Alexander, 408, 608-9
Ninnian, St, 89
Ninnio, St, 74
Nolan, Finbar, 563-4
Norden, 244
Normans, 58, 433-4
Norris family, 219
Northern Star, 268, 271, 283-5
Northern Whig, 308, 529, 650
Norton, horse-drawn car service, 619
Nova Legenda Anglie, 87-8, 90
Nugent family, 222, 607
Nugent, general, 289-90

Ó Baoill, Cathal, 460
Ó Baoill, Colm, 454
O'Boyle, J.P., 302
O'Cahan, Carroll, 135
Ó Casaide, Séamus, 441-2
Ó Ceallaigh, Séamus, 459
O'Connell, Daniel, 298, 540
Ó Doirnín, Peadar, 440
O'Donovan, John, 444, 452
O'Donovan Rossa, Jeremiah, 536
O'Doran, Patrick, 178
Ó Domhnaill family, 434
O'Donnell family, 179, 434
O'Donnell, Niall Garbh, 166
O'Farrell, lieutenant-general, 188
O'Flynn family, 433
Ó Floinn family, 434
Ó Gealacháin, Peadar, 458
Ó Gnímh, Fear Flatha, 439
O'Gownley, Dónal Óg, 174

Index of Places

Gillhall, 189, 216-7
Girvan, 437
Glascoe, 177, 182
Glasgow, 144, 410, 443,
    612, 615
Glaskermore, 192, 362
Glasquirrin, 172, 175
Glassdrummond, 191, 458
Gleann, an G..., 456
Glen Ebor, 658
Glenapp, 437
Glenavon, 657
Glenavy, 108
Glendhu, 3
Glenmachan, 632
Glenn, 456
Glennawe, 173
Glens of Antrim, 454
Glenshane, 454
Glenties, 377
Glentoran, 641-2, 645, 649-
    50
Glenwherry Street, 649
Gloucester, 188
Glynn Park, 649
Gooseberry Corner, 638,
    640, 642
Goraghwood, 612
Gortnery, 194
Gransha, 27
Great Britain, 644
Great George's Street, 642
Great Grimsby, 305
Great Kerrocks, 162
Great Langdale, 7
Greenan, 163, 177
Greencastle, 38, 42, 109,
    192
Greenock, 150
Greenore, 614
Greenville, 652
Greyabbey, 62, 109, 245,
    259, 433, 435, 498-9
Grimston, 5
Groomsport, 209, 230, 506
Grovefield, 639, 642, 649
Growle, 190
Gulf Stream, 406

Hadrian's Wall, 115
Halcomb Street, 650

Hamburg, 419
Hamilton Place, 650
Hamilton's Bawn, 189
Hanover Quay, 652
Hayes' Mill, 588
Hazelbank, 580
Helen's Bay, 618, 625
Henry's Pass, 161
Henryville, 639, 642, 648
Hercules Street 630-1
Hertfordshire 87, 209
Heynestown, 128
Hillhall, 505
Hillsborough, 108, 173-4,
    189-90, 207, 216, 219,
    222, 227, 231-3, 239,
    259-60, 262, 273-4,
    288, 323, 499, 505-6,
    508, 519, 568, 601,
    603, 620
Hilltown, 207, 224, 230,
    361-2, 528, 555, 601,
    603
Hollymount, 262, 362, 506
Holyhead, 410-1
Holywood, 88, 250, 361-2,
    435, 459, 504, 506,
    526, 604, 614, 617-9,
    622, 624, 633, 652
Holywood Arches, 655
Holywood House, 632
Holywood Road 655-7
Howth 147, 409, 411, 417

Iberia, 23
Inber Sláine, 48
Inch, 56, 58, 64-5, 105,
    109, 118, 161, 369,
    435
Inglewood, 657
Inis-Cumhscraigh, 58
Inisfallen, 72
Inishargey, 434
Inishowen, 453
Insulamreaghe, 163
Iona, 51, 74-5, 78
Ireland, 2-7, 9-10, 12, 14,
    17, 23, 26, 27-8, 33-4,
    41, 43, 47-8, 50-2, 59,
    63, 65, 71, 81, 89, 92,
    103-5, 108-9, 111-4,

    118-9, 121, 123-5, 128,
    129, 136, 142-3, 145,
    154 159, 161, 164,
    167, 169, 173, 177-8,
    180-1, 184, 187-8, 190,
    203-4, 208, 212, 214,
    216-17, 219-20, 226,
    232, 239, 242-3, 247,
    260, 263, 268-70, 272,
    277, 280-1, 287-8,
    298-9, 301-2, 304, 307,
    310-4, 317, 323, 328,
    330, 338, 345, 353-4,
    369, 377, 384, 386-7,
    389-93, 406-9, 411,
    413-4, 416, 418, 421,
    432-4, 439, 442, 444-5,
    448, 453-4, 459-60,
    490-1, 497, 501-5,
    508-9, 513, 518, 524-5,
    528-9, 534-6, 549, 563,
    570, 572, 575, 577,
    581, 588, 591, 599-
    600, 603, 605-6, 609,
    612, 616, 619, 622,
    625
Irish Sea, 6, 33, 409, 411,
    418, 420
Irish Street, 330
Island Magee, 183
Islandmoyle, 161, 174-5,
    191
Islay, 438, 454
Isle of Man, 34, 78, 410-1
    418, 421, 431-2, 437,
    439, 453-5
Italy, 51, 87, 92, 144, 534
Iveagh, 104, 105, 107, 108,
    113, 115, 160-1, 163,
    166-72, 174, 176-80,
    182, 183-4, 186, 188,
    190-94, 224, 355, 357-
    8, 384, 434, 450-2, 579

Jocelyn Cottage, 639

Keady, 408
Kearney, 551, 554, 559
Kells, 166
Kennedy's Entry, 630
Kerry, 187